Introduction to Film Studies

Fifth edition

Edited by Jill Nelmes

Foreword by Bill Nichols

 Routledge
Taylor & Francis Group

LONDON AND NEW YORK

First published 1996 by Routledge
This edition published 2012
by Routledge
2 Park Square, Milton Park, Abingdon, Oxon OX14 4RN

Simultaneously published in the USA and Canada
by Routledge
711 Third Avenue, New York, NY 10017

Routledge is an imprint of the Taylor & Francis Group, an informa business

British Library Cataloguing in Publication Data
A catalogue record for this book is available from the British Library

Library of Congress Cataloging in Publication Data
Introduction to film studies/ edited by Jill Nelmes ; [foreword, Bill Nicholls]. -- 5th ed.
p. cm.
Includes bibliographical references and index.
1. Motion pictures. I. Nelmes, Jill, 1954-
PN1994.I537 2011
791.43--dc22
2011013133

ISBN: 978-0-415-58257-5 (hbk)
ISBN: 978-0-415-58259-9 (pbk)

Typeset in 8.5/11pt Helvetica
by Fakenham Prepress Solutions, Fakenham, Norfolk NR21 8NN
Printed in Great Britain by Ashford Colour Press Ltd., Gosport, Hampshire

Contents

Illustrations

Contributors

Linda Craig is Senior Lecturer in Film and Literature at the University of East London, specialising in Latin America. Her monograph, *Marginality and Gender in the works of Juan Carlos Onetti, Manuel Puig and Luisa Valenzuela* was published in 2005 by Boydell and Brewer, and she has published numerous articles on Latin American and Spanish literature and film, the most recent of these being 'Transnationalism in Pedro Almodóvar's *All About My Mother*', *Transnational Cinemas*, volume 1, no. 2, 2010.

Terri Francis is Assistant Professor of Film Studies and African American Studies at Yale University. Her current research interests focus on Josephine Baker's stardom. Her work on Baker, 'Embodied Fictions, Melancholy Migrations: Josephine Baker's Cinematic Celebrity', has been published in *Modern Fiction Studies*. Her next project will concern Jamaican film history.

Lalitha Gopalan is an Associate Professor and teaches film studies at Georgetown University in Washington, DC. She is the author of *Cinema of Interruptions: Action Genres in Contemporary Indian Cinema* (2002) and *Bombay* (1995).

Chris Jones has taught literature, theatre and film studies for a number of years. He has participated in gay-related theatre and video work. He wrote about Derek Jarman for his film MA. He has taught film theory and creative writing at the University of Greenwich.

Mark Joyce is Senior Lecturer in Communication and Cultural Studies at Southampton Solent University. He is also course leader of the recently validated BA degree programme in Media Communication. He has co-authored *Advanced Level Media* (2001) and is currently writing a chapter on 'Consumer Identities for Key Themes in Interpersonal Communication' (2007).

Searle Kochberg is Senior Lecturer in Film Studies and Video Production at the University of Portsmouth. He also works as a film critic and as a consultant to various media/arts organisations.

Lawrence Napper gained his PhD from the University of East Anglia in 2001. He taught at UEA for a number of years, and has also taught at the University of Warwick and at Kings College, London. He has written variously on British cinema, including articles on Quota Quickies in Robert Murphy (ed.), *The British Cinema Book* (1999) and 'British Cinema and the Middlebrow' in Justine Ashby and Andrew Higson (eds), *British Cinema: Past and Present* (Routledge, 2000). His book on *British Cinema and Middlebrow Culture* is due to be published by the University of Exeter Press in 2007. He currently lives and works in London.

Jill Nelmes is Senior Lecturer in Film Studies at the University of East London. Her research interests include gender and film, and screenwriting. She is editor of *The*

Journal of Screenwriting and *Analysing the Screenplay* (2010) and is currently writing a book on the screenwriter in British Cinema for BFI/Palgrave, while working on her own script projects.

Bill Nichols is Professor of Cinema and Director of the Graduate Program in Cinema Studies at San Francisco State University and a historian and theoretician of documentary film. He edited the two-volume anthology *Movies and Methods* which helped to define film studies. He is the author of *Newsreel: Documentary Filmmaking on the American Left* (1980), *Ideology and the Image* (1981), *Maya Deren and the American Avant-Garde* (2001) and *Introduction to Documentary* (2001).

Patrick Phillips is Principal Lecturer in Film Studies at Middlesex University and heads up its Media Studies Department. He wrote the national syllabus for A level Film Studies initiated in the year 2000 and is Chief Examiner in A level Film Studies. He is the author of *Understanding Film Texts* (2000).

Suzanne Speidel is Senior Lecturer in Film Studies and Course Leader for the BA in Film and Literature at Sheffield Hallam University. She is currently working on a book of film adaptations of the works of E.M. Forster (2008), and has published articles in books and journals on Joseph Conrad and cinema, and TV drama and narrative theory.

Paul Ward is Senior Lecturer in Animation Theory and History at the Arts Institute at Bournemouth. He is the author of *Documentary: The Margins of Reality* (2005), and numerous journal and anthology articles on documentary and animation. His work has appeared in *Animation: An Interdisciplinary Journal*, *Scope: An Online Journal of Film Studies* and the *Historical Journal of Film, Radio and Television*. He is Reviews Editor for *Animation: An Interdisciplinary Journal* and a board member of the Society for Animation Studies.

Paul Watson is a Senior Lecturer in Film and Media Studies at the University of Teesside, UK. He is the co-author of *Three-Minute Wonders: Music Video and the Politics of Representation* (forthcoming) and has written numerous other articles on aspects of film, media and the politics of representation.

Paul Wells is Director of Animation in the Animation Academy at Loughborough University. He has published widely in the field, including *Understanding Animation* (Routledge, 1998), *Animation and America* (Rutgers University Press, 2002) and *Animation: Genre and Authorship* (2002). He has also made a Channel 4 documentary called *Cartoons Kick Ass*, three BBC programmes on British animation and an educational video on special effects for the British Film Institute.

William Whittington is the Assistant Chair of Critical Studies in the School of Cinematic Arts at the University of Southern California, where he teaches and conducts research. He is the author of *Sound Design and Science Fiction* (2007), and is currently working on a new book entitled *Sound Design and Horror* (forthcoming). He has also published articles, chapters and reviews on film technology, theory and industrial practices.

Foreword

Bill Nichols

How to tell the story of a discipline and a medium? This question stands as the challenge that *Introduction to Film Studies* confronts and solves through a series of individually authored but conceptually integrated essays. Each essay reminds us of the power and fascination of the movies as a medium through detailed analyses that are offered of a wide range of film, old and new, local and global, widely popular and sometimes unknown. Each essay also introduces us to the conceptual tools and critical questions that film scholars have asked and are now asking about the nature, function and value of film. Both film studies as a discipline and filmmaking as a practice possess a history that represents diverse attempts to create and understand a range of imaginative worlds that could not exist in any other form in quite the same way as they do in film. Attention to form is necessary so that the distinctiveness of cinematic expression may be fully appreciated, but attention to content is also needed if this distinctiveness is to be under-stood in the wider historical context to which it contributes. *Introduction to Film Studies* marries the two in a seamless blend of astute critical essays that survey the breadth and depth of film as an object of study today.

Apart from a common object, what do the essays in this volume have in common? A commonsensical answer to this question might be that the book provides a map to the most important theoretical tools and critical methodologies currently in use within film studies, and that it surveys the films and types of films, old and new, that loom as works of seminal importance. *Introduction to Film Studies* does offer this sort of answer, but it does so obliquely. Rather than explaining a standardised critical methodology, this book introduces a range of critical approaches and conceptual tools that become more or less valuable as the specific topic of inquiry shifts, and rather than simply pointing out what some of the greatest films have been, this book also introduces a much wider range of films that challenge, complicate and broaden our understanding of what film is and can be. There is a refreshingly broad, complementary array of approaches and commentaries offered here, facilitating for the reader an engagement with the cinema that is distinctive and rewarding in its particularities.

This diversity of critical approaches and rich range of cinematic examples does not prevent a certain sense of commonality from emerge in the essays all the same. Rather than a dominant theory, method or canon of films, this commonality, it would seem, resides in the ways in which each essay undercuts a commonsensical understanding of the cinema. Common-sense ideas are the most typical and unreflective ideas. Not necessarily wrong, they are, most often, limited to the knowledge needed to handle the most common situations. Common sense tells us that most movies are entertaining and disposable but the form of judgement brought to bear in this book tells us that this may well be true in many cases but that memorable works also exist that may support or confound our customary ideas of entertainment and disposability.

These essays go beyond common-sense understandings of movies to help readers see film with an expanded sense of the possible. They help us to see cinema anew, with fresh eyes and refreshing questions that move beyond the impressions and judgements that common sense would have us believe mark the limits of subjective, affective or critical engagement. Common sense tells us that 'Hollywood' is a monolith of immense power that sets the terms and conditions for filmmaking and reception worldwide. True, to an extent, several essays here complicate this truism by examining how British cinema, or documentary film, for example, not only exist but sometimes thrive in the context of a dominant Hollywood model. Other essays question the monolithic quality of Hollywood cinema itself. Film critics have long appreciated the subtle distinctions different directors bring to similar subject matter, especially in genre films. Hollywood films can be understood within the context of individual creativity as well as within an historical frame that must account for massive changes in how dominant, mainstream films have been produced and marketed for well over half a century.

Similarly, common sense tells us that important films for film history must have also been important films for their original audiences. This is not necessarily so, as the essay on 'The Soviet montage cinema of the 1920s' makes clear: the most popular films were the least innovative films and the most innovative films, such as those by Sergei Eisenstein, Dziga Vertov or Alexander Dovzhenko, were seldom popular. This disparity has also been true of the vast majority of documentary and avant-garde films despite their enormous significance to an understanding of the formal and social importance of film. It is also true of the Italian neo-realist films that did not win popular acceptance despite the global impact of the neo-realist style, and also true of the French New Wave, despite its enormous influence on other filmmakers and the continuing productivity of many of its most important figures.

Common sense tells us that movement and waves have their moment; they come and go. The essays assembled here suggest otherwise: important works may or may not find popular acceptance, at first or later, but their impact ripples outward in discernible patterns that can be traced and understood. So, too, the 'settled', common-sense idea that 'of course' a national cinema is a separate and distinct entity can be complicated to understand; how a national cinema often begs the question of a national identity and displays, in its complex weave of stories and styles, influences that are anything but purely national in origin. The monolithic idea of the audience that responds in a uniform way to a film, measured by box office receipts, for example, is also shown to be a common-sensical understanding that neglects to account for the divergent responses of different subcultures, ethnicities and, more obviously still, men and women. Hollywood cinema has historically presented itself as a cinema for all, but as the chapter on 'Spectacle, stereotypes and films of the African diaspora' argues, this commonsense impression has excluded recognition of a long history of filmmaking by and for African-American audiences. Not only did African American performers provide a, usually, stereotypical form of 'entertainment' in front of the Hollywood camera, they also contributed to a parallel stream of largely lost, forgotten or suppressed alternative films whose re-examination broadens our sense of the cinematically possible and of the actual history of film itself.

These are significant achievements, and the *Introduction to Film Studies* deftly guides the reader through the advances in understanding that characterise film studies today. What questions will vex the discipline in the future? These essays suggest some of the directions in which this question might lead, but it will also be the readers of this book who will give the most comprehensive and decisive answer to this question through the patient pursuit of their own desire to know more and understand better.

Acknowledgements

I would like to thank the team at Routledge who have been involved in producing this edition, particularly Natalie Foster, Ruth Moody and Andrew Watts. This book would have been impossible without the generosity and hard work of the authors whose chapters make such interesting and thought-provoking reading. My thanks also go to Robert Murphy, my colleagues at UEL for their patience and understanding, and all those who have been part of the journey of the fifth edition of the book.

Introduction to the fifth edition

Jill Nelmes

Introduction to Film Studies is more than a guide to studying film, it is a celebration of the medium and our desire to understand this complex form. How film is interpreted and perceived and, indeed, how films are constructed are aspects which many find fascinating.

The revised and updated fifth edition is testament to the continued interest in the study of film. *Introduction to Film Studies* was first published in 1996, when it was apparent to many lecturers and students that there was a shortage of film studies texts which explained the subject in a straightforward and approachable way, while still offering a degree of complex analysis. It was not then especially surprising that the first edition was extremely popular with students at FE and HE level and became recommended reading on many film and media courses in the UK. Perhaps more surprising was its burgeoning popularity in various parts of the globe, from the US to countries with very different cultures and very different film industries such as Taiwan, Hong Kong and India. The study of film has become such an integral part of higher education teaching in so many countries that *Introduction to Film* has now been translated into Chinese. The study of film clearly has no national boundaries, as long as there is somewhere to show a film or read a book.

Cinema has now spanned three centuries and, despite new and competing media technologies, the cinema experience is still an extremely popular one. Cinema audiences are at their highest since the 1970s, and DVD sales have encouraged film attendance, propping up the sales of less successful films at the box office. Access to films via the internet is increasing rapidly and the success of YouTube, even though still limited to short film and clips, is unstoppable, with many millions watching the most popular examples. The popularity of film shorts has increased as technology makes it easy to download and view clips on YouTube. Hopefully new media, as was the case with video, will become aids in promoting film and an additional means of viewing the medium. The rise of the internet, pocket-sized computers and mobile phones means that films can be viewed anywhere, on a bus or train or in the park, yet surrendering oneself to the pleasures of the big screen, while watching a film narrative unfold, is still an unmatchable experience.

Each edition of *Introduction to Film Studies* has reflected changing theoretical viewpoints and new concerns regarding the study of film, while continuing to engage with the key concepts that have emerged in the last century. The new edition includes revised and updated chapters, with additional case studies and two new chapters titled 'Contemporary film and technology' and 'Latin American cinema', providing perspectives that are particularly useful for the student of film.

The number of colleges and universities offering film studies at undergraduate and post-graduate level is still growing internationally: film is not just an integral part of Western society but also of many other cultures such as India and China. What is it about this medium, invented over a century ago, that fascinates us? Why do we enjoy watching films so much? Why indeed should we study film? *Introduction to Film Studies* aims to at least partly answer these questions, not only discussing how films are constructed and how they affect us, but also what they tell us about a society, how this differs from nation to nation and how film can challenge our understanding of the world around us.

Film theory has been influenced by many different philosophies, political theorists, cultural theorists and, indeed, film theorists. For film studies to remain 'alive' it must respond to new ways of thinking and react to films which are produced both inside and outside the mainstream and by other cultures. Film theory has, to some extent, moved away from the 'grand theory' that so influenced psychology, literature and philosophy in the 1970s and which focused on the overarching psychoanalytic theories of Freud and Lacan, the political theories of Marx and Althussar and the semiotic theories of Saussure. That is not to say that these theories have no value but they have been re-evaluated rather than completely discarded. Postmodernism has encouraged a critiquing of the grand narrative approach; affect theory, for instance, discussed by Patrick Phillips in Chapter 5 is a less political and more reactive way of analysing our response to film.

HOW TO USE THIS BOOK

Introduction to Film Studies is designed as a resource which can be used either as part of a course or for general interest. It is hoped that the reader will be inspired to read further and extensive cross-referencing to other chapters and the website suggests where to look for related topics and concepts.

Useful features
- Coverage of a wide range of concepts, theories and opinions about film studies. The authors, from both the US and the UK, are subject specialists in their field.
- Detailed discussion of the film industry in Hollywood and Britain, with reference to other cinemas, such as India, and their conditions of production.
- Reference to a wide range of films from different periods and different countries.
- Case studies which include discussion of classical and contemporary film.
- Generous use of film stills.
- Self-contained chapters which introduce the subject area.

New features of the fifth edition
- All chapters have been revised and updated, most including new case studies. The chapters on 'Cinematic authorship and the film auteur' and 'Star studies', both written by Paul Watson, have been substantially modified and extended while Patrick Phillips's chapter 'Before getting to the bigger picture' is a completely revised version of 'Rediscovering film studies' from the previous edition.
- Two new chapters have been included in the fifth edition: 'Contemporary film technology' by William Whittington and 'Latin American cinema' by Linda Craig .
- The chapter 'The French New Wave' written by Chris Darke is now available on the website.
- Many case studies from the 4th edition have been added to the website.
- Linking and cross-referencing to the website.
- An updated foreword by Bill Nicholls, one of the most prominent and respected film theorists in the US.

PART ONE: CINEMA AS INSTITUTION – TECHNOLOGY, INDUSTRY AND AUDIENCE

This part explores the relationship between cinema as a cultural product and as a complex and ever-changing industry, dependent on technology, with its own rules and institutional methods of working. In Chapter 1, 'The industrial contexts of film production', Searle Kochberg first outlines the development of the Hollywood studio system which dominated film style and production in the twentieth century, then discusses the film industry in the UK which has so often been eclipsed by Hollywood. The author explains how the film industry has had to respond to competition, initially from television, then video and most recently the internet, while the power of the Hollywood studios has been dissipated by the rise of the multimedia empires and conglomerates. New case studies are included on *Avatar*, *Paranormal Activity* and *Slumdog Millionaire*. Chapter 2, 'Contemporary film technology', a new chapter written by William Whittington, discusses the role of technology in film, explaining theories of technology and how technology has changed from early cinema to the computer-generated images we see in contemporary film. The chapter includes case studies of *District 9*, *Star Trek* and *Avatar*.

PART TWO: APPROACHES TO STUDYING FILM – FORM AND TEXT

This part addresses methods of interpreting and analysing film, examining the different ways a text may be understood. Patrick Phillips's revised and newly titled Chapter 3, 'Getting to the bigger picture', looks at the development of film as a form, the effect of digital media on how we perceive film and how new media such as YouTube can aid our experience of film and our understanding of film history. The author includes a new case study of a short film made in 1944, *Springtime in an English Village*. Chapter 4, written by Suzanne Speidel, 'Film form and narrative', discusses not only how film is constructed, shaped and formed but also how films tell stories. The chapter refers to a wide range of films, from the classical narrative to the experimental, using examples from films such as *Gladiator*, *Run Lola Run* and *Wild Strawberries*; a new case study is also included: *Loves of a Blonde*, directed by Milos Forman. Chapter 5, 'Spectator, audience and response', authored by Patrick Phillips, explores how the audience makes sense of film and studies the relationship between the film and the audience. The chapter also discusses the spectator in early and contemporary cinema and asks why the cinematic experience is so pleasurable. Chapter 6, 'Cinematic authorship and the film auteur' by Paul Watson, focuses on Hollywood cinema, discussing the role of the director, who has often been viewed as the sole creator and artist of a film, though more recently used as a commodity and marketing tool for promotion. The revised chapter includes a case study of Quentin Tarantino discussing his contribution to film as a postmodern director. The following Chapter 7, 'Star studies: text, pleasure, identity', also written by Paul Watson, examines the notion of the star and how our understanding of the term has changed since the fall of the studio system. A new case study on Tom Cruise is included which discusses the star as celebrity and Cruise's portrayal by the media.

PART THREE: STUDYING GENRE

This part examines genre theory and genre as a form, firstly looking at genre in Hollywood. Chapter 8, 'Approaches to film genre', discusses the legacy left by the studio system and explains that genre works by both difference and repetition. The author argues that genre can still be challenging and surprising and uses *Moulin Rouge* as an example of a postmodern, intertextual film. The following two chapters examine very different genres, the documentary and animation forms, both of which have enjoyed something of a resurgence in popularity in the last decade. A number of documentaries have gained cinema release and surprisingly good box-office takings. Paul Ward's Chapter 9, 'The documentary form', traces the history of the documentary, asking what we mean by the term and how the form can be defined, discussing the boundaries of documentary and docu-drama. Case studies include a discussion of the films of Mitchell and Kenyon, produced in the early twentieth century and *Grizzly Man*, Werner Herzog's exploration of the time Timothy Treadwell spent with grizzly bears before he was killed by them. Chapter 10, 'The language of animation', written by Paul Wells, also gives a historical perspective to the animation form, examining experimental as well as mainstream animation, which has been revitalised by the use of computer software that has allowed the making of films such as *Avatar* and *The Incredibles*. A new case study is included of *Breakfast in the Grass* by Estonian animator Priit Pärn, whose work is much darker than most conventional Western animation.

PART FOUR: CINEMA, IDENTITY AND THE POLITICS OF REPRESENTATION

This part discusses how the different identities of sexuality, gender and ethnicity are represented in film. Chapter 11,'Gender and film', by Jill Nelmes, looks at representations of masculinity and femininity and how these representations may be interpreted by the audience. The author discusses feminist film theory and how theories about masculinity in film grew out of this. A new case study is included on the US independent writer and director, Nicole Holofcener, one of the few women directors to make films that have attracted critical acclaim. In Chapter 12, 'Lesbian and gay cinema', Chris Jones explains the notion of the homosexual 'look' in film and 'queer theory'. The author also discusses the stereotypes used in films which depict homosexual characters and the change from negative stereotypes, in the past, to more recent positive representations. Chapter 12, by Terri Francis, 'Spectacle, stereotypes and films of the African diaspora', explores the history of African American film from 1900 to blaxploitation films of the 1960s to an extended case study of the films of Spike Lee. The author discusses stereotyping and racism in cinema and films of the African diaspora, pointing out that this is a broad field, covering Europe, Africa and the Americas.

PART FIVE: CINEMA, NATION AND IDENTITY

In Western society we tend to think of Hollywood as the dominant form of cinema, yet other national cinemas, past and present, have made their presence felt for a variety of reasons, ranging from their productivity and popularity, as in the case of Bollywood cinema, to their aesthetic or social value. This part focuses on four very different types of cinema; the chapters on British cinema and Indian cinema offer an overview from a historical perspective while the chapter on Soviet montage cinema discusses a particular period in Russian history and the new chapter on Latin American film focuses on the rise of cinema in Argentina, Brazil and Mexico.

Chapter 14, 'British cinema', by Lawrence Napper, asks how we can define a British film. The author discusses how the British film industry has developed, referring to a wide range of films from early British silent film to the present day, looking at films produced in particular periods such as the Second World War and the British New Wave of the 1960s. A new case study is included of *Made in Dagenham*, a film about a group of women factory workers who went on strike for equal pay in the 1960s. Chapter 15, 'Indian cinema'. written by Lalitha Gopalan, studies the development of film in India, exploring narrative and genre in popular Indian film, referring to song and dance sequences, the gangster film and the woman's film. Chapter 16, entitled 'Latin American cinema', by Linda Craig, is a welcome addition to the fifth edition. The chapter provides a history of the development of film in Latin America, discussing the influence of neo-colonialism on cinema, first from Europe and then, when the First World War ended film production, from the United States. The arrival in the 1950s of the 'New Latin American Cinema' is discussed and the influence of the French New wave and political filmmaking movements is explained. Case studies in this chapter include *Lucia*, *Madame Satã* and *Amores Perros.* Soviet montage cinema emerged out of the Russian Revolution in 1917; Mark Joyce in Chapter 17 argues that this cinema has had a lasting effect and the theories developed in the period by filmmakers such as Eisenstein and Pudovkin are still influential today. The chapter includes detailed case studies of films by key directors of that period.

Chapter 1

The industrial contexts of film production

Searle Kochberg

■ The industrial contexts of film production

INTRODUCTION

Films do not exist in a vacuum. Marxist theory of history postulates that the material, economic and social relations of society are the true basis of society, and that to a great degree they determine the way a society thinks. We can apply this theory on a micro-level to film and say that it is the socio-economic organisation of the film industry – its labour relations, its apparatuses, its resources – that largely determines the films that are made, their values, and their aesthetics.

The chapter that follows is a journey through the mainstream institutional frameworks of US and UK film. The American film industry has dominated all others for the last 100 years and for this reason the section largely centres around it. I do not claim the itinerary to be definitive, but I have sought to cite some key issues in the socio-economic infra-structure of American and British film.

The origins and consolidation of the American industry are traced from 1895 to 1930, a period which saw a fledgling industry harness new industrial practices and quickly grow into an important popular medium, organised into highly defined exhibition, production and distribution components.

The Hollywood studio era (1930 to 1949) is the next stop on the tour. Monopolistic practice and the finely tuned industrial organisation of the Hollywood 'factories' are discussed at some length. This section looks specifically at Warner Brothers as an example of a vertically integrated film company during the studio era.

There then follows an exploration of the contemporary institutional framework of US (global) and UK commercial film, starting with a review of the position of the 'Majors' in the light of multi-media empires, new media technologies and (mainstream) independent production. *Avatar* (2009) and *Paranormal Activity* (2007) are reviewed in the light of new media technologies appropriated by the Majors to make money. At the end of this section the production/distribution histories of *Gladiator* (2000) and *Slumdog Millionaire* (2008) are taken as case studies.

For discussion of Gladiator *and classical cinema see pp. 102–4.*

The chapter ends with a review of building audiences for film – the context of viewing – from the 1940s onwards. *The Blair Witch Project* (1999) is taken as a case study.

THE ORIGINS OF THE AMERICAN FILM INDUSTRY (1900 TO 1915)

For an account of the invention of film see Chapter 2.

The American film industry has been in existence as long as there has been American film. This section looks at how the film industry organised itself into three main divisions in the early years of this century, divisions that exist to this day – **exhibition**, **distribution** and **production**.

exhibition
Division of the film industry concentrating on the public screening of film.

Exhibition until 1907

By 1894, the exhibition of moving pictures had been established in New York City with the introduction of the box-like kinetoscope. This allowed an individual customer to watch a 50-foot strip of film through a slit at the top of the machine. In 1895, a projector called the Pantopticon was demonstrated, again in NYC, and for the first time more than one person could watch the same moving images simultaneously.

distribution
Division concentrating on the marketing of film, connecting the producer with the exhibitor by leasing films from the former and renting them to the latter.

Once projectors were available, single-reel films started to be shown in vaudeville theatres as novelties. Exhibition outlets began to multiply and by the first years of the last century small high street stores and restaurants were being converted into small-scale cinemas or nickelodeons. As the name suggests, the cost of entry to these cinemas was 5 cents – an amount affordable to the (predominantly) working-class audiences of

production
Division concentrating on the making of film.

• **Plate 1.1**
A nickolodeon (5 cents entry fee) in New York City in the first decade of the twentieth century. Converted high street stores like this one were typical of the first cinemas

nickelodeons. By the end of 1905 there were an estimated 1,000 of these theatres in America and by 1908 there were 6,000.

Distribution until 1907

As the film industry expanded, exhibitors had a growing commercial need for an unbroken supply of films to show. To meet this need, the first film exchange was in operation by 1902 and acted as a go-between for the producers and exhibitors (Balio 1976: 14). The exchanges purchased (later leased) films from producers and distributed films to exhibitors by renting to them. By 1907 there were between 125 and 150 film exchanges covering the whole of the USA.

Production until 1907

Until 1900 the average length of films was around 50 feet. Three major companies dominated production in the US: Edison, Biograph and Vitagraph. Although filming on location was very common at this stage, as early as 1893 the world's first '**kinetographic** theatre' or film studio was in operation. This was built by the Edison Company and called the 'Black Maria'.

kinetograph
Edison's first movie camera

After 1900, films started to get longer, and by 1903, films of 300 to 600 feet were fairly common. The Edison Company's *The Great Train Robbery* (1903) was over 1,000 feet long (ibid.: 7–9) and is an example of early cinema utilising increased running time and primitive continuity editing to tell, for then, a fairly ambitious story. By this time there were several major film producers in the USA, including (as well as the companies mentioned above) Selig, Kalem, Essanay and Lubin. These companies ensured their dominant position in the industry by holding patents in camera and projection equipment.

The industrial organisation of film production until 1907 has been referred to as the 'cameraman' system of production (Bordwell *et al.* 1985: 116–17). As the name suggests, films were largely the creation of one individual, the cameraman, who would be responsible for planning, writing, filming and editing. Edwin Porter, working for the Edison Company, is a good example of such a craftsman.

Thus, by 1907, the American film industry was already organised into three main divisions: exhibition, distribution and production. The creation of these separate commercial divisions demonstrates pragmatic, commercial streamlining by a very young industry, which was designed to maximise profits in an expanding market.

The Motion Picture Patents Company and industry monopolies (1908 to 1915)

In 1908, the Edison and Biograph companies attempted to control the fledgling film industry through the key patents they held in camera and projection technology. They set up the Motion Picture Patents Company, a **patent pool**, which issued licences for a fee to companies on a discretionary basis. Only licensed firms could legally utilise technology patented by or contracted to the MPPC without fear of litigation. The MPPC was soon collecting royalties from all sectors of the industry, including manufacturers of equipment, film producers and exhibitors. The MPPC's ultimate ambition was to monopolise the film industry in the US. Its goal was a situation in which films would be shot on patented cameras, distributed through its General Film Company and screened on its patented projectors.

patent pool
An association of companies, operating collectively in the marketplace by pooling the patents held by each individual company.

Exhibition and audience during the MPPC era

An important contribution to the profits of the MPPC was from the licensing of projection equipment to exhibitors. In 1908 the most important exhibition outlet was the nickelodeon.

The year 1910 marked the peak of the nickelodeon theatre, with an estimated 26,000,000 people attending the 10,000 'nickels' in the continental US every week (Balio 1976: 63). The meteoric rise of the nickel theatres was remarkable and reflected the general expansion of popular entertainment during America's prosperous start to the twentieth century. Enormous expansion in film exhibition occurred throughout the USA and inner-city locations were particularly important due to their concentrated populations. The growth of the nickelodeon in large American cities has been well documented and may in part be attributable to mass working-class immigration to the US at the time (Allen and Gomery 1985: 202–5).

The exhibition industry understood that its successful future lay in securing a wide audience-base. It appears to have accomplished this even in its nickelodeon years, by successfully positioning nickels in middle-class as well as working-class districts. Exhibitors realised, however, that even greater profit lay in larger theatres and more ambitious narratives. As early as 1909, large movie theatres were being constructed. Film producers were also being encouraged by exhibitors to provide films that would appeal to middle- as well as working-class audiences, including 'women's' stories and one-reel adaptations of literary classics. This process continued to gather momentum in the final years of the MPPC era, when large luxurious theatres began to supplant the nickels in movie exhibition, and audiences reached 49,000,000 per week (Balio 1976: 75). Feature-length films at an average length of four to six reels also became established.

vertical integration
Where a company is organised so that it oversees a product from the planning/ development stage, through production, through market distribution, through to the end-user – the retail consumer. In the case of the film industry, this translates to a company controlling production, marketing and exhibition of its films.

Distribution in the MPPC era

Soon after its inception, the MPPC turned its attention to film distribution and licensed 70 per cent of the film exchanges operating in the US By 1910, the MPPC had set up its own distribution company – the General Film Company – which soon had nationwide cover through the purchase of forty-eight key exchanges in the US (Elsaesser 1990: 192–3). By 1911, the MPPC had constructed the first effective example of **vertical integration** in the film industry through a combination of takeovers and patent rights.

Changing conditions were soon to challenge the MPPC's supreme position in the industry. First, independent distributors, exhibitors and producers quickly and successfully organised themselves in response to the MPPC's attempted monopoly.[1] Then, a charge of anti-**trust** violation was filed against the MPPC by the Department of Justice in 1912. The outcome of the case (announced in 1915) was that the MPPC was ordered to break up. Ironically, by this time, other vertically integrated companies were being organised within the industry (see next section).

trust
A group of companies operating together to control the market for a commodity. This is illegal practice in the USA.

Production during the MPPC era

The years 1908 to 1915 were not only marked by the rise and fall of the industrial giant – the Motion Picture Patents Company – but also by the rise of the multi-reel feature film and the relative demise of the single-reel film. Greater length and greater narrative complexity coincided with the application of scientific management principles to the industrial organisation of film production.

By 1908, the 'cameraman' system of production had already been discarded and replaced by the 'director system' (1907–1909) (Bordwell et al. 1985: 113–20). For the first time a director was responsible for overseeing a group of operative workers, including the cameraman. The director was central to the planning, filming and editing stages of filmmaking. Production was centralised in a studio/factory, permitting greater control of production, thus keeping costs down. Around 1909, this system was in turn discarded in favour of the 'director–unit' system (ibid.: 121–7). Directors were now in charge of autonomous production units within companies, each with a separate group of workers. Companies were subdivided into various departments, for ever greater productivity and efficiency, informed no doubt by the then current 'scientific management' model of labour and workshop organisation popularised by F.W. Taylor.

By the end of the MPPC era, the 'central producer' system (ibid.: 128–41) had been introduced, which was to dominate as a model in production management until the start of the studio era around 1930. This was a fully structured hierarchical system, with a strict 'scientific' division of labour. Production-line filmmaking was now the order of the day, all under the central control of a producer who used very detailed shooting scripts to plan budgets before giving the go-ahead to studio projects.

Summary

During the first twenty years of its life, the film industry increased in scale from a cottage-scale enterprise to an established mass popular medium. Its rapid and enormous growth was largely driven by the explosion in exhibition, which in turn triggered a streamlining in distribution methods and the industrialisation of production. The predominant position of exhibition within the industry was also to be a hallmark of the studio era of American film.

Question
What do you see as the disadvantages to early 'independent' film makers of the MPPC's vertical integration?

THE STUDIO ERA OF AMERICAN FILM (1930 TO 1949)

This section looks at the studio era of film production. By 1930 the film industry in America was dominated by five companies – all vertically integrated – known as the 'Majors' or the 'Big Five': Warner Brothers, Loew's–MGM, Fox, Paramount and Radio-Keith-Orpheum (RKO). Three smaller companies, the 'Little Three', were also part of the **oligopoly**: Columbia, Universal (both with production and distribution facilities) and United Artists (a distribution company for independent producers).

oligopoly
Where a state of limited competition exists between a small group of producers or sellers.

The origins of the studio-era oligopoly (1914–1930)

Vertical integration made sense to the power brokers of the film industry: companies with the financial resources to organise themselves in this way stood to dominate the market-place through their all-pervasive influence and their ability to block out competition.

Despite the alarm bells of the MPPC anti-trust case in 1915, film companies continued to seek out legal ways to construct vertically integrated companies through mergers and acquisitions. In December 1916 an industry merger occurred which became the corner-stone of the future Hollywood studio era. This involved the Famous Players and Jesse L. Lasky production companies and Paramount, a distribution company. By 1920 Famous Players–Lasky (as the new company was called) had established a pre-eminent position in the American film industry with the purchase of theatre chains throughout the US and Canada (Gomery 1986: 26–8).

The trend set by Famous Players–Lasky was soon copied elsewhere in the industry. In 1922 the distribution–exhibition giant First National became vertically integrated with the construction of a large production facility in Burbank, California (Balio 1976: 114).[2] By 1924 Loew's Incorporated, the major exhibition firm, had acquired both Metro Pictures (producer–distributor) and Goldwyn Pictures (producer–exhibitor). Henceforth, Loew's production subsidiary would be known as Metro–Goldwyn–Mayer (MGM).

Exhibition during the studio era

Exhibition continued to be the most powerful and influential branch of the American film industry during the studio era. The reason for this was simple: it was where the money was made. Reflecting this, the Majors channelled most of their investment into exhibition, which accounted for 90 per cent of the Majors' total asset value during the years 1930 to 1949.

In spite of the fact that the Majors owned only 15 per cent of the movie theatres in the US, they collected approximately 75 per cent of exhibition revenues in the US during the studio era. This was possible because the Big Five film companies owned 70 per cent of the **first-run** movie houses in the US during this period. Their numbers were relatively small, but the first-run theatres accounted for most of the exhibition revenue because of their very large seating capacity (on average over 1,200 seats), prime locations (in key urban sites) and higher price of admission. The Majors further strengthened their grip on exhibition by 'encouraging' the (30 per cent) independent first-run theatres to book their films, sight unseen, to the exclusion of competitors (see below). By bowing to the wishes of the Majors, the independents safeguarded their access to the Majors' popular films. All in all, it was the Majors' control of cinemas during the years of vertical integration that ensured their profits.

first-run
Important movie theatres would show films immediately upon their theatrical release (or their 'first-run'). Smaller, local theatres would show films on subsequent runs, hence the terms second-run, third-run, etc.

The successful theatre chains

By the 1920s, American innovations in national wholesaling and chain-store retailing had been absorbed into cinema exhibition methods. The introduction of scientific management methods and economies of scale led to the building up of chains of theatres, lower per-unit costs and faster, more efficient operations.

By far the most financially successful and innovative of the exhibition companies in the lead-up to the studio era was Balaban and Katz, with corporate headquarters in Chicago (until taken over by Paramount in 1925). Its success influenced the whole exhibition industry, especially at the top end of the market. Key innovations of Balaban and Katz included locating cinemas in outlying business and residential areas as well as downtown, building large, ornate, air-conditioned movie palaces (trips to which were 'events' in themselves for movie-goers), and accompanying screen presentations with quality vaudeville acts (Gomery 1992: 40–56).

The 1930s and 1940s saw a continuation of the scientific management practices inaugurated by innovators like Balaban and Katz. Changes were made in exhibition during the studio era, some a direct result of the fall in attendance brought about by the Great Depression which followed the Wall Street Crash of 1929. Vaudeville acts were eliminated in all but the grandest of movie houses and replaced by talkie shorts, new movie theatres were less elaborate, double bills were introduced, air-conditioning was more universally adopted, and food and drink stands – in the form of popcorn (pre-Second World War onwards) and Coke/Pepsi (post-Second World War) – were introduced into foyers. These concession stands became, and were to remain, major profit earners for exhibitors right up until the present day.

The war years (1941 to 1945) and the immediate postwar period were to mark the heyday of studio-era exhibition in the US; 1946 was the year of greatest profits for the Big Five.

Distribution during the studio era

The distribution of films in America was effectively controlled by the Big Five during the studio era, even though the Little Three were also heavily engaged in the distribution business. The reason for this lay in the Majors' complete domination of exhibition. To ensure access for their films to the nationwide cinema network controlled by the Majors, the Little Three went along with the distribution system of the Big Five. Areas were zoned by the Majors, and theatres designated first-run, second-run and so on. The average period between runs, or clearance, was thirty days or more.

When booking films into their own theatres, each of the Majors ensured that precedence was given to their own product, followed by films of the other Majors. Any exhibition slots still available would be allocated to the Little Three. Finally, in distributing films to independent theatres, the Big Five and Little Three utilised a system of advance block-booking (films booked en masse and in advance).[3] Under this system, independent exhibitors were forced to book a full year's feature-film output of an individual film company, sight unseen, in order to secure likely box-office hits (Gomery 1992: 67–9).

For further discussion of genre, stars and marketing, see Chapter 7.

It is worth noting that genre films and star vehicles of the studio era owed their popularity with distributors and exhibitors to the fact that they were useful marketing tools for distributors – providing marketing 'hooks' on which to hang a campaign – and at the same time helped provide box-office insurance for exhibitors, providing product recognition and differentiation for audiences.

Production during the studio era

By the onset of the studio era, the major movie factories were each producing an average of fifty features per year to satisfy the voracious demands of the highly profitable exhibition end of the business. As in other areas of the film industry, production management was 'scientific': film studios were organised as assembly-line plants with strict divisions of labour and hierarchies of authority.

As early as 1931, Hollywood Majors had begun to move away from the central-producer system which had dominated production since 1915. Columbia Pictures was the first company to announce the adoption of a producer–unit system in October 1931. Under the new organisational framework, the company appointed a head of production to oversee the running of the studio. Several producers were then appointed under the head, and each had the job of supervising the production of a group of films and of delivering the films on completion to the head of production (Bordwell et al. 1985: 321).

Those firms that adopted the new system (not all did)[4] were convinced that it was an advance in scientific management for several reasons. First, it was felt that the system saved money, since it allowed each producer to keep a closer control of individual budgets (overseeing far fewer films than a central producer). Second, the system was felt to foster 'better quality' films, and encourage specialisms in individual units, by investing in the creativity of the delegated producers.

Certain production units were associated with particular genres: Jerry Wald's unit at Warner Brothers specialised in noir-melodrama, e.g. *Mildred Pierce* (1945); Arthur Freed's unit at Metro–Goldwyn–Mayer specialised in the integrated musical, e.g. *Meet Me in St. Louis* (1944).

Contracts and unions

It was standard studio practice during the 1930s and 1940s to employ personnel on long-term or permanent contracts. Workers' unions had firmly established themselves in American film production by the early years of the Roosevelt administration (in the mid-1930s) under the auspices of the **National Recovery Administration (NRA)** and the Wagner Act. Ironically, by defining and enforcing rigidly delineated areas of responsibility for specific jobs to protect their members' jobs, the unions were directly instrumental in reinforcing the hierarchical structure of film production practice.

Stars

Long before the 1930s, a whole subsidiary industry of fan magazines and gossip columns in popular newspapers had grown up, promoting the Hollywood 'dream factory', its films

NRA
National Recovery Administration) programme – 1930s' government programme designed to rescue the American economy from the Great Depression (commonly known as the 'New Deal').

For further discussion of the star see Chapter 7.

• **Plate 1.2**
An aerial view of Paramount's production facility in Hollywood in the 1930s. This studio was one of the most modern talking-picture production plants in the world. It covered an area of 26 acres, had fourteen sound stages on the grounds, and had a working population of 2,000 people

and its stars. This continued throughout the studio era, fuelled by the publicity machines of the film companies themselves.

Long-term contracts (normally seven years in duration) secured the ongoing services of stars for the film companies. This was key to the financial security of the corporations since the acting ability and the personality of the stars provided added value to the films in which they appeared. Why? Because stars helped differentiate films that otherwise were very standard in content and format. Their popularity reinforced consumer brand loyalty for the films of individual film companies, and provided the Majors with the necessary 'carrot' with which to entice independent exhibitors into booking blocks of films sight unseen (or 'blind').

Summary

During the Hollywood studio era, a small group of manufacturers-cum-distributors-cum-retailers controlled the film market between them. Smaller US producers were forced to make do with subsequent-run cinemas in which to show their films or to arrange distribution deals with the Big Five and Little Three. Likewise, foreign films could not get a foothold in the US unless they too had arrangements with one of the eight US film companies comprising the oligopoly. Examples of UK production companies that had US distribution through the studio era were London Films (distributing through UA), Imperator Films (distributing through RKO) and the Rank Organisation (distributing through Universal).

It wasn't until after 1948 that the Majors were forced to divest themselves of their cinema chains, as a result of the Supreme Court's decision in the Paramount anti-trust case (see next section).

☐ CASE STUDY 1: WARNER BROTHERS

From its origins as a small production company in the mid-1920s, Warner Brothers rose to become one of the five major vertically integrated film companies by the end of the decade. This was largely achieved through debt-financing – expansion financed through loans. Key to Warner's exponential growth were the following financial deals: its takeover of Vitagraph Corporation (with distribution and production facilities) in 1925, its exclusive licensing of Western Electric sound equipment for 'talking pictures' in 1926, and its purchase of the Stanley Company cinema chain with its associated film company First National in 1928.

Warner Brothers was the first of the Majors to establish the commercial viability of sound in film, and until the onset of the Depression (late 1929) its huge corporate debt (due to corporate expansion) was more than held in check by the enormous profits generated by its first 'talkies'. Starting in 1926, its corporate subsidiary for sound productions, Vitaphone Corporation, premiered Vitaphone 'shorts' and the first Hollywood 'feature' with recorded musical accompaniment, *Don Juan*. This was followed in 1927 by the release of Warner's first feature-length part-talkie, *The Jazz Singer*, and in 1928 by the release of its first all-talkie feature, *The Lights of New York*.

The Great Depression seriously weakened Warner's financial base. While big profits were being generated at the box office, the company could carry its enormous debt-load. However, after 1930 box-office takings fell off so sharply that the company began to lose money and had difficulty meeting its loan commitments. Warner was not to show a profit again until 1935.

Its response to the financial crisis was to sell off assets (e.g. cinemas), introduce production units (to help control film budgets) and to make feature films as cheaply as possible.[5] Its series of studio-bound, fast-paced, topical films in the early 1930s were the direct result of this corporate policy.

By 1935, the fortunes of the company had improved sufficiently for it to return to profit again. As profits increased, so did film budgets. Studio genres changed too, with the entrenchment of the melodrama, biopic, Merrie England and film noir genres in the late 1930s and early 1940s. As with the other Majors, profits reached record levels for Warner during and immediately after the Second World War.

Warner as auteur during the studio era (its authorial style)

As discussed already, film production during the studio era was all about standardised assembly-line manufacturing practice. This is why there is such impressive consistency in the physical make-up of the classic Hollywood film of the period. However, individual film companies also needed to differentiate their products if they were to develop brand loyalty in their customers. Differentiation was partly a reflection of financial profiles of individual companies and partly a reflection of corporate worldview/ideology.

Throughout the studio era, Warner established and consolidated a house style based on casting, subject, treatment and technical standards: all evident across the work of different (contract) directors and across genres. Senior management control was very strong. Staff workers were assigned projects by management, they did not choose them. Indeed, management retained ultimate authority on all matters concerning productions, including control over the final cut, much to the chagrin of directors and stars.

Yet despite the authoritarian management style, ironically Warner's films of the studio era articulate a populist, liberal ethos. Several productions of the early 1930s were hard-hitting social critiques of the then Republican administration. The tone changes, however, from 1933 onwards, as Warner discards its anti-government position in favour of support for the new Roosevelt (Democratic) administration and its NRA programme (popularly known as the 'New Deal'). The ultimate endorsement of the NRA and Roosevelt must be *Footlight Parade* (1933), with its 'Shanghai Lil' dance routine incorporating images of the

• **Plate 1.3**
Still from *Footlight Parade* (Lloyd Bacon, 1933). James Cagney's character at the helm in this NRA-inspired musical

• **Plate 1.4**
Still from *Mildred Pierce* (Michael Curtiz, 1945). This shot typifies the studio-bound cinematographic style and art direction of Warner during the studio era. The scene, photographed by Ernest Haller, is shot with low-key lighting; the art direction by Anton Grot conveys an impression of a quayside through its use of space, shadow, silhouette and perspective.

NRA eagle and Roosevelt, and its leading protagonist (played by James Cagney) apparently inspired by Roosevelt himself![6]

From the mid-1930s onwards, the radical streak in Warner's films is somewhat muted, no doubt reflective of the ideological change in America, changing from a climate of confrontation in the early to mid-1930s, to one of conciliation by the end of the decade. And profits were up again: the company was back 'in the black' by 1935, leading perhaps to greater conservatism in the boardroom, less risk-taking, and a desire for middle-brow respectability. Certainly the shift to costume drama (in the mid- to late 1930s) would suggest this. Whatever, Warner's liberal voice did continue throughout the 1930s and into the War Years (1941 to 1945), its support of the Roosevelt administration unabated. Seen today, the company's films of the studio era retain an 'edge' not really apparent in the films of any of the other Majors, except perhaps RKO in the 1940s.

Warner Brothers (like most of the major film companies of the studio era) specialised in particular genres. Up till the mid-1930s, the company concentrated on low-budget contemporary urban genres such as the gangster cycle, the social conscience film and the fast-talking comedy/drama. The one costly genre that Warner specialised in during this period was the musical. Later, from the mid-1930s onwards, new genres began to dominate: the swashbuckler cycle, the biopic, the melodrama and (later still) the film noir.

As one might expect, Warner's roster of players during the studio era reflected to a large extent the studio's reputation for straightforwardness and toughness. It is worth noting that Warner's stars tended to be very genre-specific; e.g. Bette Davis = melodrama, James Cagney = gangster film/musical, Humphrey Bogart = gangster film/ film noir.

Costume design at Warner was to a large degree in keeping with the contemporary stories of many of its films. The studio's principal designers, Orry-Kelly for instance, designed modern clothes for ordinary people, in keeping with Warner's edgy urban image.

The factory-like regimentation of Warner's production methods meant that its studio style inevitably overwhelmed the individual creative talents of its contract directors. Pressure of work and division of labour meant that there was little active collaboration on projects between director and editor, or director and writer (Campbell 1971: 2). Directors were assigned projects and as soon as their task was done (sometimes directing only part of a film) they were moved on to others. It is thus rather problematic to assign to Warner's contract directors such as Michael Curtiz, William Keighley, Mervyn Le Roy and Raoul Walsh[7] individual authorship of their films.

Warner's films were known for their 'fast' editing style, particularly evident in the early to mid-1930s. Narratives were developed in a rapid succession of scenes, with extensive use of classic Hollywood montage sequences. The overall effect was one of dynamism and compression of time (a good example of this can be seen in *Confessions of a Nazi Spy* (1939)).

Warner's art direction again reflected a low-cost policy: location work was avoided, films were designed around a studio-bound look and sets were regularly reused. The work of Anton Grot, a major art director at Warner during the studio era, typifies the studio style. His sets were designed to convey a mood. To this end his storyboards suggested camera and lighting strategies. The sets were not literal reproductions of life, but instead used shadow, silhouette and angular perspective.[8] He is quoted as saying, 'I for one do not like extremely realistic sets. I am for simplicity and beauty and you can achieve that only by creating an impression' (Deschner 1975: 22). The end result was art direction that was both economic and atmospheric, and in total sympathy with the studio's cinematography. Here, studio cameramen such as Tony Gaudio (see e.g. *The Adventures of Robin Hood* (1938)), Sol Polito (see e.g. *Now Voyager* (1942)), and Ernest Haller (see e.g. *Mildred Pierce* (1945)) reinforced the art direction of people like Grot, utilising a visual style based on low-key lighting, with a propensity for night scenes. Necessity is the mother of invention, and this corporate strategy for economic but effective mise-en-scène soon set the standard for generic conventions across the industry (particularly in film noir, the gangster film and in the swashbuckler).

Finally, most people could recognise Warner's films even with their eyes shut! If in other areas of production the byword was economy, here grandeur was the order of the day. Warner's composers of incidental music were among the most celebrated of the studio era. From the mid-1930s to the end of the studio era, studio composers Max Steiner (*Now Voyager* (1942) and *Mildred Pierce* (1945)) and Erich Wolfgang Korngold (*The Adventures of Robin Hood* (1938) and *King's Row* (1942)) created many scores in the Middle-European tradition of romantic composition, using Wagner-like leitmotifs (recurring melodic phrases used to suggest characters or ideas) throughout.

In summary, Warner's style of the 1930s and 1940s can thus be identified as a composite one, the product of its creative personnel working under the control and direction of corporate management. The various signifying elements that made up this style were reinforced film after film, year after year, producing what one now identifies as the studio-era Warner Brothers film.

Question
How and why did the Warner Brothers film company differentiate its films from the other 'Majors' during the studio era?

THE CONTEMPORARY FILM INDUSTRY (1949 ONWARDS)

The early twenty-first-century film industry is a very different affair from the system in operation during the studio era. This section looks at the contemporary institutional framework of film, first by examining the specifics within the film industry itself, and then by looking at the wider media context within which film exists today.

1949 to the present: a brief review

The Majors were finally forced to divest themselves of their theatres at the end of the 1940s as a result of the 'Paramount' anti-**trust** suit filed against them by the Justice Department of the US government.

The suit had been in the pipeline since the late 1930s, only the War had intervened. Paramount and RKO were the first of the Majors to agree with the US government as to the terms of their **consent decrees** in 1949 (Balio 1976: 317), putting to rest the government's charge against them of monopolistic practice in exhibition. The terms agreed were the divorcement of cinemas from the parent corporations. This effectively marked the end of the studio era.

The next few years saw a retrenchment of the Majors. Shorn of their cinemas, they no longer had a guaranteed market for their films and had to compete with independent producers for exhibition slots. Under the circumstances, they found their old studio infrastructure too expensive in the face of new market competition from the independents.

Meanwhile, for independents, things had never been better, with the Majors only too willing to rent them studio space and distribute their (better) films, and exhibitors eager to show them. The 1950s was to see an enormous explosion in independent production in the US. By 1957, 58 per cent of the films distributed by the erstwhile Big Five and Little Three were independent productions that they financed and/or distributed (ibid.: 353). United Artists led the industry in the distribution of independent films. With no studios to restructure and no long-term contract players, UA was able to respond very quickly to the post-1949 reality. In the year 1957, only Columbia Pictures distributed more films than UA.[9]

trust
A group of companies operating together to control the market for a commodity. This is illegal practice in the US.

consent decree
A court order made with the consent of both parties – the defendant and the plaintiff – which puts to rest the lawsuit brought against the former by the latter.

• Plate 1.5
Early 1950s advertisement for the (then) new Twentieth Century Fox widescreen Cinemascope system. The ad is intended to give consumers an idea of how the Cinemascope image (married with stereophonic sound) vastly improves the experience of cinema-going

Another shock to the film industry around the early 1950s was the postwar focus on the home and on consumer durables, evidenced in the exponential growth of television. People simply didn't go to the cinema in the same numbers any more (see next section). Between 1947 and 1950, the number of TV sets in the US rose from 14,000 to 4 million (see section below on film audiences). The film industry's response was twofold: differentiation from and collaboration with TV.

In the 1950s, various film presentation strategies were introduced to emphasise the difference between the film-going experience and TV viewing in a bid to stave off the harmful competition from film's 'at home' rival. Widescreen, colour, 3-D and stereophonic sound were all introduced in the period 1952 to 1954. However, at the end of the day it proved expedient for the industry to collaborate with 'the enemy'. Film companies began to sell (and later lease) their films to TV,[10] to make films for TV,[11] and to merge with TV companies.[12] By the late 1960s, the futures of the two media industries were inextricably linked. The situation by the mid-1980s was more complicated. The two industries had become integrated into multi-media conglomerates where they represented just two of the many associated interests of their parent corporations.

Cinema exhibition today

Throughout the studio era and before, the most powerful sector of the film industry was exhibition. In today's film economy, however, distribution is the dominant sector (see below). The centrality of marketing (i.e. distribution), allied with the growth of home entertainment, means that profit today is not just a matter of bums on seats. Nevertheless, the profits of Majors *still* depend on product recognition and visibility, and here cinemas continue to be fundamental to the financial well-being of the Industry as a whole.

Theatrical presentation is no longer dominated by large, select, first-run movie theatres as in the studio era. Individual theatres are now usually small mini-theatres (average seating capacity 200 to 300 seats), and mainstream commercial films distributed by the Majors generally open simultaneously at a large number of these 'screens'.[13] Several screens are commonly housed under one roof – in multiplex theatres – where economies of scale (several screens sharing overheads) allow for low per-unit costs. These cinemas are often purpose-built, located on key artery roads outside of town centres (where land is cheaper and more readily available), and associated with shopping-mall developments. Since the mid-1990s there has been a large investment in new screens in the US (and elsewhere): in 1996 there were 26,500 screens in the US sector, and by 2000 the figure was 38,000 screens.[14] As a consequence, cinema attendance has increased, but the construction boom has also led to over-capacity in the marketplace, to bankruptcies and mergers. Now the top five US chains are Regal Entertainment (6,777 screens), AMC Theaters (5,336 screens), Cinemark (3,825 screens), Carmike (2,268 screens) and Cineplex (1,347 screens).[15] If they account for only 52 per cent of the screens in the US sector, they still collect 80 per cent of the American box office revenues. Why? Because the myriad of small theatre owners that make up the rest of the sector cannot compete with them in terms of industry profile and location.

A history of multiplex theatres

The first company to realise the potential of the purpose-built, multi-screen theatre was American Multi-Cinema (AMC) in the 1960s. Its success with the multi-screen formula was so great that by the 1980s AMC was one of the five largest cinema chains in the US. Based on the statements of AMC's senior management in 1983, exhibitor aspirations appear to be the same as those way back in the days of the nickelodeon theatres: 'we prefer to locate theatres in middle-class areas inhabited by college-educated families .... These groups are the backbone of the existing motion picture audience and of our future audience' (Squire 1986: 329–30).

Another company notable for its development of the multi-screen concept is the Canadian company Cineplex. It opened its eighteen-screen Cineplex in Toronto's Eaton Centre in 1979, followed by a complex in the Beverly Centre, Los Angeles in 1982. After its purchase of the Odeon chain in Canada in the mid-1980s, it began its US acquisitions in earnest, so that by 1988 it was the largest theatre-chain in North America (Jowett and Linton 1989: 47). Cineplex–Odeon's UK acquisitions began in May 1988 with the purchase of the ten-screen Maybox Theatre in Slough. Within a year its Gallery Cinema chain in the UK consisted of eleven multiplexes.[16]

From the mid-1980s, Cineplex–Odeon led the exhibition industry in its construction of several mini-picture palaces and the introduction of cafés and kiosks selling film-related materials. The company did find itself in a fragile financial position in 1989: its debt-financing left it over-extended in a major recession (much like Warner in 1931). But by then the company's style and innovation had set the tone for contemporary mainstream exhibition practice.

E-cinema and implications for exhibition

By 2007, around 4,000 of the world's estimated 100,000 screens were equipped with digital projectors (Greenwald and Landry 2009: 119). By 2020 the transition will be complete according to many media analysts. The changeover offers many advantages to the Industry: no more expensive prints to manufacture (currently 35mm prints for a feature are approximately US$1,500); relative ease and flexibility of delivery to theatres (by DVD, IP networks, cable or satellite); and the chance to expand into theatrical pay-per-view non-film content (e.g. football, pop concerts, etc.). And for independent distributors and producers in particular, the move to digital should prove a boon in bringing down their costs. However, there are disadvantages as well, the leading one being the cost and shelf life of the digital projector ($100,000 each, and lasting on average five years) as opposed to an analogue film projector ($50,000, and lasting twenty-plus years). Exhibitors are keen to know who is going to pick up the tab for the conversion, and given the huge financial savings for financiers-cum-distributors, exhibitors are naturally seeking financial support from them. As I write, it appears that installation and conversion costs in mainstream cinemas are now being met largely by the Majors (ibid.: 119). Other challenges to overcome include the assurance that movies will arrive at theatres without being degraded, altered or stolen.

Runs

It is worth noting that there are a variety of different types of cinema-run in operation today. A run can be **exclusive**, **multiple** or **saturation**. Combinations of runs are selected (largely at the discretion of distributors) on the basis of a film's likely performance. For instance, the exhibition of a word-of-mouth 'sleeper' – a small-budget film that does unexpectedly well at the box office – will usually begin with a semi-exclusive run, until it has built up enough of a reputation to warrant a wider run.

A typical example of a saturation run is the release pattern of *Harry Potter and the Sorcerer's Stone* in 2001 (UK title *Harry Potter and the Philosopher's Stone*). It set a record in US exhibition history on Friday 16 November 2001, by opening 'superwide' in a record number of cinemas – 3,672 – and on around 8,000 screens (then approximately 21 per cent of the nation's total). In the UK the number was around 500 cinemas and 1,140 screens (then approximately 38 per cent of the nation's total). In both cases, openings were accompanied by huge marketing campaigns around the time of release (see the end of this section on AOL Time Warner synergy).

The UK scenario

Britain is the third largest cinema market in the developed world, with 3,665 screens. As is the case elsewhere, digitalisation has 'coincided' with the international Majors divesting themselves of cinema chains. Why? Because they control exhibition/distribution money

exclusive run
Where a film is only screened in one cinema.

multiple run
Where a film is shown simultaneously at a number of cinemas. 'Platforming' a movie in a few cities, in up to 200 screens, can help build up word-of-mouth enthusiasm for 'off-centre' (mainstream but not blockbuster) films.

saturation run
Where a film opens 'wide' and is shown simultaneously at an enormous number of cinemas, accompanied by heavy media promotion. Increasingly, 'superwide' openings are becoming an entrenched strategy for 'event' films such as the big summer releases where a film can open in 3,000-plus US and Canadian screens simultaneously. 'Superwide' openings help ensure that big films reap big returns at the box office, particularly on the opening weekend, before the reviews come out.

deals anyway (see below), and big profits up until very recently have been made elsewhere, in the digital home-entertainment sector. In fact, Paramount remains the only Hollywood major to have a presence in UK exhibition (in the form of National Amusements, a shareholder of Viacom – owner of Paramount).

According to industry estimates, the UK's five largest exhibition companies account for 75 per cent of the UK screens and 80 per cent of the box-office returns. These companies are Odeon, Cineworld, Vue, National Amusements Showcase and Empire. Odeon is the biggest of the exhibitors with 840 'screens', followed by Cineworld (773 screens), Vue (655 screens), National Amusements (274 screens) and Empire (213 screens).[17]

Independent cinemas account for only 20 per cent of the box-office revenue in the UK. Under the label 'independent' are many different types of cinema organisation. Some independents are simply smaller chains showing mainstream fare. Others show a mixture of blockbuster, 'off-centre' (mainstream but not blockbuster) and 'art' films. Other cinemas specialise in the screening of minority interest/alternative films.

Schemes to offset the dominance of the blockbuster in UK cinemas include the Europa Cinemas scheme (administered by EU Media Programme) which makes available to UK exhibitors public monies to assist in the showing of European film. However, cinemas must meet a minimum target of 15 to 25 per cent non-national EU/Norway/Iceland/Liechtenstein/Switzerland/Bulgaria films to qualify.

For further discussion of British cinema see Chapter 14.

Power and control are two hotly disputed areas in the film industry in the UK today. Some parties argue that despite the renaissance in cinema-going in the UK, structural domination by the Majors in distribution means that non-Hollywood product (including UK film) does not get a fair crack of the whip in UK cinemas. This is due to the Majors' influence over exhibitors, who will not endanger the main source of their revenue. Others dismiss the conspiracy theories and point out the obvious – that the Hollywood product has the advantage of high production costs, high marketing budgets and film stars, and that these are the films that the public want to see and exhibitors want to show.

Mindful of the problem, in the recent past the (soon to be disbanded) UK Film Council has nudged big cinema chains to widen their exhibition base and show a greater variety of fare. One of the ways it is doing so is through the 'Digital Screen Network', which was set up at the end of 2005. Exhibitors that qualify for the National Lottery-funded scheme have their projectors paid for by the Film Council. The bidding process requires that cinemas identify which screens will be given over to cultural/minority interest film. To date 240 screens have been fitted out digitally under this scheme, all part of a greater Industry programme to full digital conversion of UK cinemas. Currently there are an estimated 550 digital screens in the UK (15 per cent of total UK screens).

Whether considering large chains or small, most UK cinemas are multiscreens today. The turning point in UK exhibition is usually taken as November 1985 when the purpose-built multiplex, the Point, first opened its doors in Milton Keynes. However, it should be noted that the company Screen 4 had been building four-screens in the north since the mid-1960s, and ones that were effectively purpose-built. Nevertheless, the success of the Point and other early multiplexes, such as the Maybox in Slough, triggered a new investment in British exhibition and a resurgence in the cinema-going habit in the UK. A year prior to the opening of the Point, cinema attendance was down to 52 million admissions per year. By 1996, that figure had risen to 123.5 million admissions, by 2005 to 166 million and by 2009 to 173.5 million. The multiplex has played a crucial role in this renaissance of cinema-going by offering the punter a choice of viewing in a modern, comfortable environment. (See section on 'Film audiences' for more information on contemporary UK cinema-going.)

Distribution today

Since the late 1940s' consent decrees, the power base in the industry has shifted from exhibition to production finance and distribution, i.e. from the power base of the pre-1949 Majors to the power base of the post-1949 Majors (Balio 1976: 458–67). This shift reflects the fact that film revenue is no longer purely a function of cinema receipts. With the financial dominance of other distribution 'windows' (especially DVD and VOD – see below) and merchandising spin-offs, access to a major's worldwide distribution/marketing network has become the determining factor in a film's financial success.

The names of the Majors are all very familiar from the studio era: Paramount, Warner Brothers, Sony Pictures, Universal, Disney and 20th Century Fox. Through their domination of marketing and promotion, the Majors ensure that it is their films that the public wants to see and that cinema owners want to secure for their cinemas. Witness the reaction of the public and the exhibitors to the beat of the distributors' tom-tom with blockbuster releases such as *Jurassic Park* (Universal, summer 1993) and *Harry Potter and the Sorcerer's Stone* (Warner Brothers, autumn 2001).

Today, a major financier–distributor stands between the producer (if not directly producing the film itself) and the exhibitor. It will largely dictate the business terms which shape a film's finance and exploitation.

As noted by the ex-chairman of Cineplex-Odeon Garth Drabinsky in 1976:

> If, but only if, a distributor . . . decides that the picture merits release and the kind of expenditures necessary to get it off the ground, the distributor will enter into a distribution agreement with the producer to govern their relationship.[18]

For the most part, the distributor dictates the terms of its deal with the exhibitor as well: the nature of the run, the length of the engagement, the advertising to be employed and the financial split of box-office receipts between the various parties. It has also been reported that it is common practice for distributors to exploit their upper hand with exhibitors and insist on blind-bidding and block-booking.

Distribution windows

Up until the mid-1970s, apart from the theatrical release, the only distribution windows were network and syndicated TV. The new age of film distribution began in 1975 with the introduction of Time Inc.'s Home Box Office cable pay-TV (HBO) and Sony's domestic Betamax videocassette recorder (VCR). The following year, Matsushita introduced the VHS format for domestic VCRs. This format soon overtook Betamax and became the industry standard.

For further discussion on multimedia empires, see end of this section (pp. 30–31).

Roll on two decades, and the first commercial Digital Versatile Disc (DVD) players appeared in Japan in 1996. Early manufacturers were Toshiba, Pioneer and Matsushita. DVDs were designed to compete with VHS, which they have completely superseded. As early as 2001 the DVD market was growing at ten times the VHS market, with Blockbuster Video estimating that 30 per cent of its US rental business was DVD.[19]

For a discussion on DVDs and audiences, see Case study on Gladiator *(pp. 23), and section on 'Film audiences', pp. 31.*

The phenomenal success of DVD lay in the high quality of the image and sound, the increased storage capacity compared to video (up to eight hours of high-quality video, up to eight tracks of digital audio and interactive features) and DVD as a cross-platform. And just like the VHS/Betamax trade war of the 1970s, in 2005/6 manufacturers vied with each other for control of the marketplace. This time around, however, it was Sony who was declared the winner, with its 'Blu-ray' format. Five out of six Majors backed it, in preference to Toshiba's HD DVD.[20] Clearly Sony had learned its lesson well since the Betamax debacle when it had no films to support the launch of the format. Now Sony's holdings in film libraries alone were huge: it owned the rights to the movies/TV of Columbia/Sony Pictures and MGM (its library acquired as part of a consortium purchase in 2005 to add weight to the Blu-ray trade war – Sony owns 20 per cent of MGM). Overall, Sony's pre-eminence in the film business as hardware/software provider made its success in the battle with Toshiba almost inevitable.

The economic importance of DVD has led to a closing of the gap between the cinema release and the DVD release dates. A typical distribution cycle for a Studio film in the US will now be an initial theatrical release of around four months, followed by a DVD window (which remains open for an indefinite period). Usually there is a 30-day period from DVD release to online availability – video-on-demand (VOD) and pay-per-view. This is followed by a premium cable movie channel window (for approximately one year), a free-to-air television window plus other sources of income.

Yet despite the economic importance of DVD and other windows in recent years, the *theatrical window* remains the most important window in film distribution. Without it, the film is a far less valuable commodity. It garners no publicity and is perceived as having no 'value' by punters.

So what of the future? Recent sales of DVDs have fallen since the golden age between 1999 and 2004, seriously affecting Industry profits. Now the DVD is seen as old technology. Industry pundits predict that soon we'll be back to two main windows: the theatrical window and an online, domestic, video-on-demand window, replacing the DVD completely. The home entertainment market will be transformed by a system of 'time critical' downloads whereby customers are charged different prices depending on how long the VOD download is good for on their computers – whether it is permanent or for just a few days.

A little indication of the importance of new media distribution is indicated by the success of web companies like ifilm and atomfilms, who more than five years ago revolutionised distribution of short films by releasing them on their websites. A notable early 'short' to be distributed this way was *405* (2000), put out on ifilm.com. Flash forward a few years, to 2006, and another multimedia company, 2929 Entertainment, announced a 'universal release' (simultaneously on video-on-demand and in cinemas) of their film *Bubble*, directed by Steven Soderbergh. So will the gap between theatrical and VOD eventually disappear altogether, as in this particular case? Not for the time being, but possibly in the future. Ultimately, pressure from consumers will likely decide the outcome (see below).

Marketing

One of the key roles of a financier–distributor is to successfully orchestrate the marketing of a film. The three main types of advertising used in film marketing are: **free publicity**, **paid advertising** and **tie-ins/merchandising**.

free publicity
Free coverage of subjects the media feel are newsworthy.

paid advertising
Promotion on TV, radio, billboards, printed media and the internet (see 'Multi-media empires' below).

tie-ins
Mutually beneficial promotional liaisons between films and other consumer products and/ or personalities.

merchandising
Where manufacturers pay a film company to use a film title or image on their products.

☐ **CASE STUDY 2: MARKETING A BLOCKBUSTER IN THE PRE-INTERNET ERA: *JURASSIC PARK* (1993)**

Below is a summary of Universal's UK marketing campaign for *Jurassic Park* at the time of its cinema release in 1993: [21]

Free media publicity included reports on:

- Spielberg
- the making of the film and the special effects
- the premiere
- genetic engineering
- dinomania

Paid advertising included:

- TV, radio, billboards, newspapers, magazines (today this would foreground the internet)
- A TV blitz the week before and the week of the film's opening

Tie-ins included:

- multi-million-dollar tie-ins with McDonald's and selected hotels

Merchandising included:

For a discussion of Jurassic Park (1993) and computer animation, see Chapter 10.

- JP holographic watches
- JP vinyl model dinosaur kits
- JP pinball machines
- JP socks
- JP briefs
- JP Christmas cards!

☐ CASE STUDY 3: MARKETING IN THE INTERNET ERA. PARAMOUNT'S ONLINE MARKETING CAMPAIGN FOR *PARANORMAL ACTIVITY* (2007) PRIOR TO GENERAL RELEASE

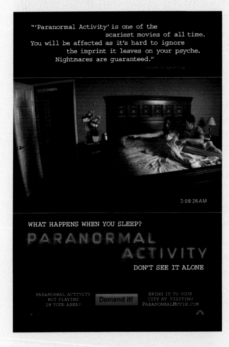

• Plate 1.6
Poster from *Paranormal Activity* (Oren Peli, 2007). In the age of the internet '[the web] spreads the word, it generates loyalty, and it pinpoints the fanbase...' (quoting Stuart Ford)

In the age of the internet, film marketing has been transformed. The story of 'no-budget' *Paranormal Activity* exemplifies the new powers of internet marketing.

In October 2007, there was a sneak preview of the film at 'Screamfest', the LA horror festival. A year later, in November 2008, the film had its first public screening in Santa Monica.

In 2009, Paramount started building a campaign online for this 'pick-up' (a film it distributed but didn't produce/finance). Punters could 'demand' that the movie be screened at a cinema local to them with a click on the computer. Enough clicks and the movie would play there. Quoting Stuart Ford, the film's sales agent, Paramount's cheeky campaign could be neatly summarised as, 'You like it so much? You want it? Then demand it! Tell us where you want it to play and we'll play it there!'[22]

The gambit paid off. Handsomely! On 25 September 2009 the film had a very limited release in the US on twelve screens in 'college towns' across the country (including Boston, Chicago and San Francisco). Only a few weeks later, on 16 October 2009, the film went on national release (763 screens) and straight to the top at the box office. By

23 October, the film was showing at 2,000 screens, and by 29 December 2009, the DVD had been released. The film went on to gross US$194 million at the cinema, with DVD sales at US$14 million.

Again quoting Stuart Ford, '[the web] spreads the word, it generate loyalty, and it pinpoints the fanbase ... It showed us that, for marketing, it can be so much more potent than traditional media.'[23]

For a discussion on building an audience today, see next section on 'Film Audiences'.

The UK scenario

The international Majors dominate UK distribution, and each of them has a UK subsidiary to handle its distribution (namely UIP, Buena Vista International, Columbia/Tristar, Fox International and Warner Brothers International). However, there are also public mechanisms available to assist smaller, independent European distributors with the marketing and distribution of their films. The Media Programme, for instance, is an EU initiative whereby European distributors of films and DVD receive loans to help with distribution and promotion costs within European markets (70 per cent of the Programme's main budget is devoted to the distribution of new films).[24] As welcome as the Programme is, inevitably it is a 'drop in the ocean' when set against the power of the Majors. It is not surprising, then, that the future trends in UK distribution patterns are expected to mirror those in the US.

I have mentioned already the predicted shift to two distribution windows: cinema and VOD. This is because many in the industry see DVD as old technology. The UK market moved a little closer to this in March 2006 when Universal announced a deal with lovefilm.com – an online DVD rental firm – whereby costumers would be able to download the latest Universal releases on to their laptops, either for a few days or for keeps.

Production today

Before examining the key players that dominate mainstream film production today – the Majors, independent producers, agents/management groups and stars (see below) – it is useful to review the current industrial organisation of film production.

The industrial system in operation today is called the 'package-unit' system (Bordwell et al. 1985: 330–7). Under this system, the self-contained studio and long-term contract studio employee of the studio era have been replaced by rented studio space and short-term contract employment.

The shift to the package-unit system from the mid-1950s onwards was a direct response to the combined effects of the 1949 consent decrees: in other words, the rise of independent production, cost-cutting and rationalisation at the Majors' studios, and the Majors leasing studio space to independent producers.

Today, individual producers are responsible for bringing together all the components of a film's production – finance, personnel, the 'property', equipment, studio space – on a short-term, film-by-film basis.

Budget has always been the principal preoccupation of the producer, but today, under the package-unit system, this is true more than ever. So called 'above-the-line' budget costs are those that are up-front (such as book rights, fees for producers, directors, stars), whereas 'below-the-line' costs refer to the day-to-day expenses incurred on a production (such as crew fees, post-production costs).

Majors v. independents

Despite the growth of **independent** production after the consent decrees, the Majors had reclaimed their dominance in production by the early 1970s. Between the years 1970 and 1987, films directly produced by the Majors collected on average 84 per cent of the total US/Canadian box-office returns (Jowett and Linton 1989: 38).

independent
A highly problematic term, meaning different things in different situations. Here, the term simply implies a production realised outside one of the Majors. Here, the term does not imply a production context outside the mainstream institutional framework altogether, nor does it imply a film produced in an alternative aesthetic format to 'Classic Hollywood'.

Today the six Majors typically account for 90–95 per cent of the total box office revenue in the US/Canada sector. Why the increase in their share? Because since the 1980s there has been an increase in corporate consolidation across the media sector by parent companies who own the Majors (see 'synergy' below). These multimedia empires exert a stranglehold on the global marketplace through mergers and acquisitions, e.g. National Amusements (parent company and exhibitor) owns Paramount Pictures (distributor and production company).

New media and production

Launched by Artisan Films at the 1999 Sundance Film Festival (a showcase for independent film), *The Blair Witch Project* (1999) was perhaps the first big box-office film (albeit a 'sleeper' hit) to use extensive digital camera footage. Since then, the industry interest in digital video-making has skyrocketed, due partly to the flexibility of the technology, and to the lower costs of production. So much so that by 2001, more than 40 per cent of the projects submitted to the Sundance Festival were shot on digital formats.[25] In the intervening years Hollywood has also jumped on the digital bandwagon, so that hi-definition cameras on blockbuster productions are now the order of the day in films such as *Superman Returns* (2006), with a reported budget of $225 million.[26]

☐ **CASE STUDY 4: THE ASCENDANCY OF 3D ANIMATED DIGITAL PRODUCTION: *AVATAR* (2009)**

2009 marked a watershed year for digital 3D technology in the film industry, with more than a dozen films released in the new format. In that year, the Industry stopped considering 3D merely as a (profitable) carrot, to enhance the appeal of animated features for young audiences. It was now also seen as a means of offering a new cinematic experience to adult filmgoers around the globe. The breakthrough film was *Avatar*. James Cameron's film raised the bar for 3D cinema by blending seamlessly live action footage with computer-generated images through the use of new technologies. These included new generation motion-capture computer graphics (CG), a 'virtual' camera system (allowing the production team to see in real time how the CG characters would interact with their virtual worlds), and a specially developed 'fusion' 3D camera – a digital system with adjustable lenses functioning like two eyes connected to a single 'brain' (rather than the old 3D camera where the action was filmed by two separate, leaden cameras).

Production costs for Avatar were put at between US$280 million and US$310 million, with US$150 million for marketing. To date the worldwide box office gross has been US$2.75 billion, three-quarters of which has been outside the US/Canada sector.

Agents, stars and Oscars

The ending of long-term studio contracts for creative personnel in the early 1950s (a consequence of the rationalisation of studios by the majors after the consent decrees) meant that important stars, directors, writers and other talent could now negotiate very lucrative freelance deals with film companies.[27] Their increased negotiating power also strengthened the hand of their agents who negotiated their deals with the film companies. The most powerful agency at the time was MCA, controlled by Jules Stein and Lew Wasserman.

So successful was MCA during the 1950s that it purchased Universal in 1959. (The agency's dominance ended in 1962, when MCA closed down its talent agency to concentrate on film and TV production.)

Today there are four big talent agencies in Hollywood: Creative Artists Agency (CAA), William Morris Endeavor Entertainment, International Creative Management (ICM) and

United Talent Agency (UTA). Apart from these four, there are many smaller 'boutique' agencies who handle a select number of important clients.

If it is their clients' faces that appear on magazine covers, it is the agencies that oil the Hollywood film machine. Agencies identify scripts, put them in the hands of their clients – directors, producers as well as actors – and strike the deals with the film companies. Occasionally the big agencies even offer groups of creative personnel (with possibly a literary property as well) as a joint package to a production company for a single film or TV production. A recent example of this was the 'package' UTA put together for the film *Dear John* (2009), utilising clients Lasse Hallström (director), Channing Tatum (actor) and Nicholas Sparks (writer).[28]

In the 2010 Oscar nominations, CAA clients secured thirty-five nominations, those of William Morris Endeavor fourteen nominations, those of UTA nine nominations and those of ICM eight nominations. Is it any wonder, that CAA – with the biggest roster of names (Steven Spielberg, James Cameron, Will Smith, George Clooney, Brad Pitt, Tom Cruise, Oprah Winfrey), should have secured the most nominations? Not really: Oscars are awarded by Industry members of the (US) Academy of Arts and Sciences, and often reflect corporate standing and financial power in the Industry. In Hollywood, artistry, finance and power go hand in hand.

Future trends

At present a star's association with a film project clearly affects the ease with which the film can be financed and marketed, for a star's presence in a film is held to be an important factor in a film's box-office performance. These factors explain the huge salaries agents negotiate today. However, some statistics suggest that stars are less a factor in a film's box-office success than was once the case.[29] And if, as Industry analysts are predicting, film moves away from an exclusive, front-loaded, marketing-led, theatrical window to a concurrent VOD window, then perhaps film companies will no longer be slaves to the 'excessive' demands of agents and their star clients, because marquee value isn't as necessary with VOD.

For further discussion of the star in film, see Chapter 7.

The 2006 departure of Tom Cruise from Paramount is perhaps a note of warning to agents, and – pardon the pun – a 'window' into the future. In that year CAA's deal for his services – in place for years with Paramount – of 20 per cent of the gross and US$20 million up front, *plus* studio expenses for the Cruise team (estimated at US$5 million per year), was abruptly cancelled by Paramount. Industry commentators made the obvious point that despite recent box-office hits like *Mission Impossible III* (2006) – with a theatrical gross of US$400 million – Paramount was not making enough money, given the cost of Cruise and his entourage.[30]

☐ CASE STUDY 5: A US 'BLOCKBUSTER' PRODUCTION, *GLADIATOR* (2000)

Script development and pre-production

In 1996 David Franzoni (producer–writer) approached Dreamworks SKG with a story about gladiators in ancient Rome. The story was then developed by him in collaboration with head of Dreamworks Pictures Walter Parkes and producer Douglas Wick.

The producers felt that their planned film needed a director who could manage the cinematic spectacle that would feature in it. Hence, they approached Ridley Scott who relished the prospect of recreating a detailed historical environment that would be realistic. The creation of detailed worlds that were believable on their own terms, irrespective of genre, had been a hallmark of earlier Scott productions such as *Alien* (1979), *Blade Runner* (1982) and *Someone to Watch Over Me* (1987). Once the great metteur-en-scène agreed to direct, script development began in earnest.

Franzoni produced the first draft of the screenplay, with John Logan and William Nicholson working as collaborators later on. In the process, the games in the Roman

• **Plate 1.7**
Still from *Gladiator* (Ridley Scott, 2000). Maximus (Russell Crowe) and his fellow gladiators – tensile, hard-muscled and armoured – salute the roaring crowds in the Colosseum as they and their Dreamworks/Universal picture enjoy the sweet smell of success

arena came to occupy the central focus of the narrative. And for many months before production began, Scott worked on sketches of the key scenes and on storyboards with Sylvain Despretz. This production was to reflect Scott's long-held notion that direction is akin to orchestration, with incident, sound, movement, colour, sets and computer graphics all knitted together under his watchful eye.[31]

The film would be jointly produced, financed and distributed by DreamWorks and Universal – the former having had a long-standing distribution arrangement with the latter.[32]

It was decided that location shooting would bring down the cost of the production, rather than trying to construct everything in Hollywood. However, filming on the site of historical monuments was impossible because of the likely damage incurred during filming, and because of the often poor condition of the sites to begin with. Therefore scouting commenced in Europe and North Africa for locations that could accommodate new sets. Such was the scale of the production that individual design departments were assigned to each of the major locations (UK, Morocco and Malta) by Arthur Max, the film's overall production designer. In each location, 'sets, props and costumes were custom-made for the film', or sets were added to existing buildings (Landau 2000: 66).

The biggest set, that of 'ancient Rome', was built at Port Mifisalfi, Malta, over nineteen weeks in the winter of 1998–99, just prior to filming. The set included a full-scale section of the Roman Colosseum (the rest would be filled in using computer graphics), as well as sets for the emperor's palace, the Forum and the Roman marketplace. This huge complex of sets was built on to disused nineteenth-century barracks on the site to add an air of authenticity to the look of the production. This is a favoured technique of Scott's to add verisimilitude to the world he is creating, as per the sets of *Blade Runner* which were built on to old Warner Brothers' city sets to legitimise the film's noir mise-en-scène.

Production and post-production

From the beginning, the shoot was a very complex affair. The scale of the production – with a mammoth budget of over US$100 million, scenes involving thousands of extras and a four-month shoot in four countries – necessitated the use of four different crews.

Principal photography commenced at the beginning of February 1999 in Bourne Woods, Farnham, Surrey, after the construction of a Roman encampment, a stake barricade and a forest dwelling. The opening battle scene – set in Germania in the film – was a hugely involved affair incorporating replicas of Roman war machines and an army of 1,000 extras. Shooting was finally wrapped up in the UK on 24 February 1999[33] from where the production moved to Morocco.

Morocco was the setting in the movie for the gladiator school. In preparation for filming, the local production crew had been busy for nine weeks, since December, 1998.[34] In all, the shoot took three weeks here, after which the production moved to Malta for the 'Rome' scenes.

Again, preparation of the sets had begun long before shooting: because of the scale of the set, construction had begun nineteen weeks earlier. And despite bad storms damaging the set,[35] filming commenced around mid-March and was completed by the end of May 1999.[36] This part of the shoot involved the large-scale Colosseum scenes incorporating 2,000 extras.

Finally, there followed a two-day shoot in Tuscany, which was the chosen location for the home of Maximus in the film. This work – involving Ridley Scott, the main crew (which travelled from location to location), doubles and stunt doubles – marked the end of the long location schedule.[37]

The film was then completed at Shepperton studios, but not before the extraordinary computer visual effects work of Mill Film (London) was incorporated into the film to create the composite shots of the Colosseum. Computer-graphic imaging (CGI) was used to complete the circumference of the first tier of the stadium and to create the second and third tiers. CGI was also used to increase the number of spectators in the Colosseum from 2,000 to 35,000, and to extend other vistas on the Rome set.[38]

The film was edited by Ridley Scott and Pietro Scalia, and scored by Hans Zimmer (head of DreamWorks' film music division) and Lisa Gerrard. With the completion of post-production, Scott delivered the picture to DreamWorks on time and on budget (US$106 million).[39]

Distribution and exhibition

For the film's marketing poster, DreamWorks SKG (responsible for marketing the film in the US/Canada territory) and United International Pictures (Universal's marketing arm and responsible for international distribution) promoted a low-angled, medium-long shot of the film's star, Russell Crowe, in costume as Maximus. Here for all to see was the towering presence of a rectilinear, hard, tough male action star with classical adornments of armour and phallic sword. At his feet, literally, lay the Colosseum, across the base of the poster. The powerhouse epic, *Gladiator*, had been launched!

The movie's marketing campaign was the standard one for a blockbuster: saturation booking technique with simultaneous media promotion on a massive scale. The film opened superwide in the US/Canada market on 5 May 2000 in approximately 3,000 screens. With such a big opening, the film caught the imagination of the punters even before the reviews came out – which is of course the purpose of a big opening. But the makers needn't have worried, for the reviews were very favourable. In its opening weekend the film grossed around US$35 million and went straight to number one at the box office. This success was repeated the following weekend in the UK, where the film opened in around 400 screens and grossed approximately £3.5 million.[40]

Merchandising was kept to a minimum so as not to undermine the 'quality' message of the marketing campaign. Available to buy were the soundtrack, books on the film's production and the movie poster – which was soon becoming an iconic image. Tie-ins included Sega games and offers of holidays to Rome.

By the end of the film's box-office run, *Gladiator* had grossed around US$452 million worldwide, with takings of $188 million in the US market alone.[41] But the story didn't end there. On 21 November 2000, the DVD and video were released in the US/Canada market. The DVD two-disc set included the following extras: audio commentary by Ridley Scott, eleven deleted scenes from the movie, a behind-the-scenes documentary, a history of gladiatorial games and a theatre trailer, among others.

Evidently, large sales of the DVD were anticipated for the forthcoming holiday season because prior to the release date 2.6 million copies of the DVD were shipped to retail outlets. *Gladiator* sales more than met expectations, for it went on to become the biggest selling DVD in the US. Sales everywhere were remarkable: in the UK too it became the biggest selling DVD. Eventually, worldwide sales clocked in at around 4.5 million units – the biggest selling DVD up until that time.

And so, with the financial and critical momentum afforded the film, nothing could prevent it from being nominated for twelve Oscars or from winning five in March 2001: for best film, best actor (Russell Crowe), best costume design (Janty Yates), best sound and best visual effects.

The film was, of course, distributed to pay-per-view channels, and subsequently to premium cable/satellite movie channels. In the UK, the film debuted on Sky Premier movie channel in October 2001, and announcements were made in 2001 of a deal having been struck for its terrestrial TV debut in 2003. The keenly contested battle among UK broadcasters for the first-run terrestrial rights was further evidence – if indeed further evidence was necessary – of the global distribution phenomenon that *Gladiator* had become.

In summary, the UK distribution windows for *Gladiator* are to date as follows:
1st commercial theatrical release
12 May 2000

DVD/video release date
20 November 2000

Premium satellite movie channel premiere
Sky Premier
27 October 2001

For further discussion of the funding and finance of British film see Chapter 14, pp. 395–96. For further reference to and analysis of contemporary British film see Chapter 14, pp. 380–96.

The UK scenario

British feature films today are generally made on low to medium budgets, and are usually co-productions where film finance comes from a range of sources. Dominant players are UK and foreign terrestrial TV companies, film companies and cable/satellite companies.

By nature the UK industry is fiscally conservative, and therefore its producers are, by experience, usually short of money. 'Pack-of-cards' financing is usually the order of the day, where each source of funding is dependent on the participation of the other co-producers.

For most low to medium budget productions, a typical sequence of events for developing and producing a feature film is as follows. Applications are first made by the creative team[42] for development money to produce a preliminary script and project budget. Funding sources include the commissioning groups themselves and the European Media programme (19 per cent of whose main budget is allocated for development money).

Having produced its preliminary script and budget, the creative team then seeks sources to fund the production proper. As each source of finance comes on board, the script is changed to fit in with the requirements of the specific investor. The backers are inevitably financiers-cum-distributors, and monies from the distribution deals made for each 'territory' – i.e. US, UK and the rest of the world – are used to fund the production. Once the budget is fixed, pre-production in earnest begins with the preparation of the final script and budget.

TV money for UK film production

For twenty years Channel 4 was the British channel most actively engaged in film production. From its launch in 1982, it participated in well over 300 films including *My Beautiful Launderette* (1986), *The Crying Game* (1992), *Four Weddings and a Funeral* (1994), *Trainspotting* (1996) and *Secrets & Lies* (1996). And like the BBC – its terrestrial rival in film production – it favoured co-productions. But in 2002 C4 announced a huge cutback in film finance, partly as a consequence of the failure of its big budget films at the box office: films such as *Charlotte Gray* (co-produced with Warners, 2001). In the last few years, its old rival, BBC Films, has enjoyed a moderate success, with films such as *Match Point* (2006), directed by Woody Allen. And the Corporation looks like 'upping the ante' with the announcement, in 2006, of a minimum investment of £150 million in domestic film production over ten years (up from £10 million/year). Many in the UK industry are banking on this, and in the words of BBC creative director, Alan Yentob, 'the relationship between TV and film [in the UK] is a very potent one'.[43]

As I write, Film4 (C4's film production arm) has found itself in very financially strained circumstances, despite recent successes like *Slumdog Millionaire* ((2008) – see below). Wherever the future money comes from for UK production, many commentators agree that what is needed are more films like *Slumdog* – popular films that are also distinctive and personal. To these commentators, British filmmaking policy can often appear stuck in an entrenched position of pigeon-holing film as either 'cultural' or 'genre'. Sad as it is, the announcement by Jeremy Hunt, the Culture Secretary, in July 2010, of the abolition of the publicly funded UK Film Council might be reflective of the failure of such a position.

☐ CASE STUDY 6: A MEDIUM-BUDGET UK PRODUCTION: SLUMDOG MILLIONAIRE (2008)

Slumdog Millionaire is a 2008 British film directed by Danny Boyle. It is an adaptation of the novel *Q & A* (2005) by the Indian author Vikas Swarup, and has been chosen as a case study because it typifies the model of film finance most common in the UK today. TV co-productions, with perhaps smaller budgets than *Slumdog*, have dominated UK film production since the late 1980s.

The film was co-produced by Film4 (the movie division of C4 in the UK) and Celador Productions. In 2006, when the co-production deal was signed, Celador was a TV production company and owner of the rights to *Who Wants to be a Millionaire* (1998–present) – the most successful TV franchise in history, and a key part of the future film's storyline.

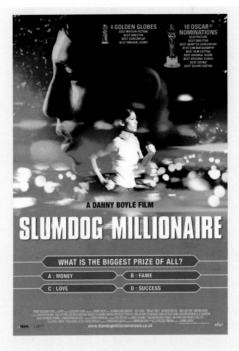

Script research and development

The project began life in 2005 when Head of Film and Drama at C4, Tessa Ross, optioned the book. Simon Beaufoy, the screenwriter of *The Full Monty* (1997) was hired very soon after, with Film4 funding the script development. In preparing the script, Beaufoy made three research trips to India, and interviewed street children.

In early 2006, a co-production deal was signed with Celador Productions, and in summer 2006, after reading Beaufoy's script, Danny Boyle agreed to direct the film.

Distribution deal 1

At this point, the project was greenlit, but still needed extra funds to meet the US$15 million budget. This was provided eventually in August 2007, when Warner Independent Pictures acquired the North American distribution rights to the film for US$5 million. Monies from this deal were used to fund production costs (a standard arrangement).

Pre-production

Casting was difficult and 'took forever' (quoting Boyle) because the three main characters in the film needed to age from seven to eighteen years. Three lots of actors were needed for each character, to play 7-, 13- and 18-year-olds respectively. Dev Patel, who plays the principal protagonist, Jamal (aged eighteen), was cast early on in London. He was an established young actor from the hit series *Skins* (2007–present), produced by E4 – a digital division of C4. The rest of the cast were Indian nationals. Much was made in the press later of the fact that two of the '7-year-olds' were local 'slumdogs'. Anil Kapoor, a big star in India, was also cast in the film as the nasty host of the (Indian) version of *Who Wants to be a Millionaire*.

One of the Indian casting directors – Loveleen Tandan – penned the Hindi dialogue for the script, and stepped in as co-director just before shooting to help with the local cast.

The UK production team travelled to Mumbai in September 2007. A 'pre-shoot' strategy was put in place – filming around Mumbai in advance of the agreed start-up date – ostensibly to try out equipment, test the locations, etc. In the end some of this material appeared in the final film.

Production

'Officially' shooting began on 5 November 2007. The cameraman, Anthony Dod Mantle, shot the film on small digital SI-2K cameras with gyro stabilisers, incorporating a lot of hand-held shots. Why? Because these small cameras made filming on location, in the tight, crowded areas of Mumbai (the slums, the Victoria Terminus) infinitely easier than the bigger film cameras typically used by Bollywood and Hollywood companies – who of course mainly shoot in studios. Also used in the production was the digital CanonCam stills camera, which can shoot at 12 frames per second. These images were imported into the film to give it a definite 'new media' look. The overall digital strategy resulted in a film with an immediacy, an energy, that simply couldn't have been matched with larger 'professional' film cameras.

Distribution deal 2

In August 2008, Warner Brothers, doubting the commercial potential of the (by then) completed film, sold off half its interest in the film to Fox Searchlight (a division of 20th Century Fox), with Fox now handling US/Canada distribution. International distribution was to be handled by Pathe.

Exhibition/distribution

The exhibition formula used to launch this film was a classic strategy for a no-star, moderate budget, 'off-centre' film. The film had its world premiere at the Telluride Film festival on 30 August 2008, where it was positively received, and in September 2008, it won the 'People's Choice' award at the Toronto International Film Festival. The decision to premiere this way was based on a need to build an audience for the film, and is a typical strategy for UK off-centre films being launched in the US (see the case study of *Crying Game* (1993) on the website).

For further discussion of building audiences, see the next section on 'Film audiences'.

The film opened commercially with a very limited run, in ten theatres in the US, on 12 November 2008. This was extended to thirty-two theatres the week after. The film went 'wide' on 25 December 2008, when it opened in 614 screens. The big lead-up to the Oscars had begun. By 23 January 2009, the film was on nationwide release.

In the UK, the release of the film had been delayed, presumably to maximise the build-up of interest (and publicity) from the US. It opened 'wide' in the UK on 9 January 2009, going straight to number two at the UK box office. The film grossed £6.1 million in the first eleven days of its release in the UK, at the end of which it was number one at the UK box office.

In mid February 2009, *Slumdog Millionaire* was nominated for ten Oscars. In March 2009, it won in eight of the categories, including Best Picture, Best Director, Best Adapted Screenplay, Best Cinematography. It also won seven UK BAFTAs into the bargain.

After the Oscars were announced, the film went 'super wide', showing on 3,000 screens. The box-office takings in the US/Canada sector increased correspondingly by 43 per cent. The film became the 'sleeper' of the year: quite a fairy tale, both on and off screen!

In summary, the distribution windows and figures for *Slumdog Millionaire* are to date as follows:

Festival premiere, Telluride FF
30 August 2008

Commercial theatrical release
12 November 2008 (US)
9 January 2009 (UK)
World-wide gross US$377 million

DVD/Blu-ray release date
31 March 2009 (US)
1 June 2009 (UK)
World-wide sales (NB excluding rentals) US$31 million

UK TV network premiere, C4
13 January 2010
(In the UK, TV co-productions generally have an earlier network
premiere than other films.)

Multi-media empires

horizontal integration
Where a parent company acquires several businesses with the same business profile, e.g. the acquisition of several cinema circuits.

lateral integration
Where a parent company acquires a vast empire of different (in our case, media and entertainment) properties, the aim of which is to command a global production/ marketing/sales/ distribution system.

synergy strategy
Combined or related action by a group of individuals or corporations towards a common goal, the combined effect of which exceeds the sum of the individual efforts.

Today, it is not adequate to consider the film industry in isolation, for it is only one part of a network of media, entertainment and communications industries controlled by vertically, **horizontally** and **laterally integrated** multimedia conglomerates.

Examples of such organisations are Time Warner, Viacom (owner of Paramount), Sony Corporation of Japan (owner of Columbia Pictures) and News Corporation (owner of 20th Century Fox).

The underlying philosophy behind corporate mergers and acquisitions is to work across the whole of the corporation's holdings to create new business opportunities/ associations; in other words to affect a **synergy strategy**. A good example of this was the Time Warner 'marketing council' set up with AOL in 2001.

After its merger with AOL, Time Warner set up a 'marketing council' to optimise marketing opportunities across the whole corporation. *Harry Potter and the Sorcerer's Stone* (US title, 2001) was the first substantive evidence of this new synergy strategy in operation. Marketing was planned carefully across all media to take into account the fact that a series of films was planned for 'Harry Potter' (anywhere from three to seven films in the series),[44] and the Corporation didn't want the series to suffer from overkill in the early stages.

As was noted in the *Financial Times* on the film's opening weekend (16–18 November, 2001),[45] the film was being promoted on the HBO and Warners networks in the USA, the music was being issued on Warner Music's Atlantic Records label, and a series of articles was appearing across the Corporation's print media empire. Of particular note, however, was the promotional activity of AOL itself. The online service was offering merchandising (with ninety licensing partners and 700 products), ticket promotions and giveaways tied in with subscriptions to AOL services.

In this instance, the coordinated activities of the marketing council paid off, for on the opening weekend the film took approximately $90 million in the US territory and approximately £16 million in the UK.[46] Alas, in the long run the merger became known as the worst in corporate history. The central failure of the merger's business model seems to have been a flawed AOL Time Warner cable package. By December 2009, AOL had been spun off as a separate company.

A happier, more successful synergy story is that of Sony Corporation of Japan. It purchased Columbia Pictures entertainment in 1989 (for $5 billion)[47] to boost sales of its home electronics hardware and to achieve synergy between its software and hardware enterprises. Since Sony acquired the film company, it has used the studio to showcase its electronic high-definition technology such as high-definition TV, 'Blu-ray' DVDs and interactive multimedia video games. Its holdings in film libraries too are huge, comprising the movies/TV of Columbia/Sony Pictures and MGM (since 2005 Sony owns 20 per cent of MGM). Clearly focused strategic planning – rather than ill-thought-out mergers and acquisitions – lies at the heart of Sony's hardware/software corporate synergy.

The UK scenario

Rupert Murdoch's News Corporation is the media conglomerate with the highest visibility in the UK. As an example of its synergy strategy we need only look at its UK Sky (satellite) digital service comprising hundreds of TV, CD quality radio and pay-per-view channels, interactive services, e-mail and so on. This service uses press media and film and TV production companies owned by News Corporation across Europe, Asia and America (such as the film company, 20th Century Fox and the US terrestrial TV Fox Network) to help promote it and provide programmes for it.

For further discussion of new technology and film see Chapter 2.

Summary

The communications revolution is being orchestrated by only a handful of global players. Although in the recent past some of these multimedia conglomerates, such as AOL Time Warner, have decided to break themselves up, the fact remains that most of them have not. Unless these firms are properly regulated by the international community – an unlikely event given the corporate and political power behind global market liberalisation – they stand to enjoy an oligopolistic power not dreamed of in the far-off days of the MPPC and the studio era.

Question
Why does the distribution sector of the film industry dominate the contemporary film business?

Question
What are the fundamental differences in the marketing of a Hollywood 'blockbuster' versus a 'sleeper'?

Question
In your opinion, which form of corporate integration is the most controlling of the marketplace: vertical, horizontal or lateral integration? Why?

FILM AUDIENCES

Fundamental to the study of cinema as institution is a study of cinema audience. This section reviews the changes in cinema audience patterns/profiles from the end of the

Second World War to the present day, and considers their likely causes. The section ends with a review of how film companies attempt to build audiences for their films.

From the late 1940s onwards

Before the 1950s, cinema-going was a very significant recreational activity. According to one official report,[48] it was the number one recreational activity for most people in wartime America. 1946 marked the peak in cinema-going in the USA, unsurpassed to this day. In that year, the average weekly attendance in the US was 95 million.[49]

Studies of the composition of audiences in the 1940s identify certain key trends. Although men and women registered the same average monthly picture attendance,[50] a greater percentage of men were very high-frequency cinema-goers.[51]

Age was the major determinant in the frequency of attendance. All surveys of the 1940s point to the fact that young people attended much more frequently than older people.[52]

Statistics from the 1940s also indicate that expenditure on motion pictures increased with annual income and that those with higher levels of education (i.e. high school and/or college) were more frequent cinema-goers than those with only a grade school education.[53]

By the 1950s, cinema attendance was in rapid decline. Average weekly attendance figures had dropped in 1950 to 60 million (from their 95 million peak four years earlier), and by 1956 the number had slipped to 46.5 million.[54] What happened to bring about this sudden decline? Two reasons are most often cited: the first is the change in living patterns of Americans following the Second World War, and the second is the establishment of TV.

'Being at home' explains the drop in cinema attendance after the peak of the mid- to late 1940s. There was a radical change in social trends in the US after the war:

home ownership, suburbanization of metropolitan areas, traffic difficulties, large families, family-centred leisure time activities, and the do-it-yourself movement.

(Bernstein 1957: 74)

These new trends put the focus firmly on domestic lifestyle, to the detriment of 'outside-the-home' film entertainment. From the outset, TV was at the centre of this new social phenomenon: the number of TV sets in America grew from 250,000 in 1947, to 8,000,000 by 1950 and to 42.2 million by 1956. TV's rise was directly proportional to falls in cinema attendance, particularly in residential neighbourhoods. It is thus logical to assume that the audiences who previously frequented local theatres were now (in part at least) at home watching TV instead (Bernstein 1957: 73).

A branch of cinema-going that bucked the trend of 'being at home' in the early 1950s was the outdoor drive-in theatre, its rise in popularity clearly a consequence of postwar suburbanisation. Now parents could choose to have a night out at the movies in the comfort of their own car, with the kids in the back of the vehicle. By 1954, there were 3,800 drive-ins in America, whose box-office grosses accounted for 16 per cent of the total US box-office receipts.[55]

The 1960s and 1970s saw an enormous growth in the leisure industry in the US. Yet, despite this, film-going continued to decline: in 1960, the weekly attendance figure had been 40 million; by 1980, the average weekly attendance was down to 19.7 million (Austin 1989: 36, 40–1). A Gallup poll taken in 1977 underlined the dominance of home-based leisure pursuits as a 'favourite way to spend an evening'.[56] The survey also confirmed the long-standing trends of movie-going being more popular with younger persons,[57] those with higher incomes and those who were college educated.

The 1970s and 1980s saw the expansion of home-based, 'TV-related' media entertainment in the form of VCRs, subscription cable and satellite services and video games, all of which weakened cinema-going as a commercial leisure activity.

• **Plate 1.9**
Still from *No Down Payment* (Martin Ritt, 1957). The film industry in the 1950s would certainly have wished this fate on all domestic TV sets!

The UK scenario

The history of cinema attendance in the UK since the Second World War mirrors US statistics to a large degree. As in the US, 1946 marked the peak in UK cinema-going. That year, the average weekly cinema attendance was 31.5 million (Docherty et al. 1987: 14–15), and as in the US, high-frequency cinema-going in the 1940s was predominantly the habit of the young.[58] However, breaking with the trend in the US, cinema-going appears to have been more popular with the working classes than other classes.[59]

Attendance figures fell dramatically in the 1950s: by 1956 weekly attendance was down to 21.1 million and by 1960 to 9.6 million (ibid.: 14–15). As in the US, the precipitous drop correlated with the dramatic rise in the number of TV sets in circulation.[60] This phenomenon was symptomatic of a much larger social change of the 1950s: the growth of outlying residential areas[61] and the subsequent establishment of a home-based consumer culture. The decline in attendance among the frequent cinema-going age group (16–24 years) might also be attributable to the sudden appearance of a distinct youth culture in the 1950s, which led to new forms of recreation for teenagers (ibid.: 26–7).

By the early 1970s, cinema-going was just one of many options in the expanding leisure industry. The long decline continued through the 1970s, so that by the mid-1980s weekly attendance had plummeted to just over one million (ibid.: 29). Other changes were apparent too: by the early 1980s the percentage of working-class people attending cinemas had declined significantly for the first time.[62]

Recent and future trends

Attendance figures have markedly improved in recent decades. By 2005,[63] the figure in the US sector stood at around 27 million tickets sold per week. This increase in attendance (though levelled off since 2000) is partly a product of the growth in multiplexes and the number of 'screens' since the 1990s. Between 1996 and 2009, the number of screens rose from 30,000 to 39,000.[64]

Two factors that continue to be a focus of interest for film industry analysts are age and education level of audiences. In the past, it was the 16- to 24-year-old demographic group that predominated among customers, but today frequent cinema-goers are a more diverse bunch. For starters, there is a *new*, enlarged (and male-dominated) frequent cinema-goer group, the 12- to 24-year-olds: an expansion of the original 16- to 24-year-old group. This group is, at once, the most likely group to attend the opening weekends of blockbusters, and (conveniently for the Majors!), the important target consumer group for the synergetic computer games distributed by the Majors to accompany their blockbusters.[65]

However, if the under-thirties still account for the largest number of yearly admissions at cinemas, in recent years the percentage of the movie audience over the age of 30 has climbed significantly. Now the 30+ individual without kids, and the still older 'empty nester', are identified as important demographic groups in movie attendance figures.

There has also long been evidence to support the claim that increased education levels translate to increased frequency of cinema-going. If, and it is a big if, the number of college-educated individuals continues to rise, as it has in recent years, we can suppose that movie attendance may also go up.

DVDs, PCs and audiences as 'viewsers'

The number of DVD players in the US grew from around 350,000 in 1997 to approximately 1.4 million in 1998, 5.5 million in 1999, 14 million in 2000 and 30 million by the end of 2001.[66] This exponential growth mirrored the growth in numbers of TV sets in the late 1940s, with DVD now replacing video as the latest home-based entertainment phenomenon. Thus by the turn of the new century DVDs' interactive features – multiple story-lines, games, instant search controls, different camera angles for the same action[67] – heralded the new digital home viewer, the viewer-cum-user or **'viewser'**. But this viewer – most likely the 12- to 24-year-old, frequent cinema-goer – had bigger fish to fry, in the form of PC downloads. With DVD sales in decline from 2004, the industry got the message, and now the Majors, such as Universal, offer blockbuster movies as temporary or permanent downloads. Some industry pundits feel that the move to online distribution 'windows' signals the beginning of the end of DVDs.

For a discussion of DVDs see the earlier section on the 'Contemporary film industry'.

For discussion of contemporary British film see Chapter 14, p. 360.

The UK Scenario

In recent years, multiplexes have also been at the centre of a renaissance in cinema-going in the UK. Attendance rose from a derisory 1 million per week in 1984 to 2.7 million per week by 1997 (Buncombe 1998: 9), and levelling off somewhat after that at 2.8 million in 2000[68] and 3.34 million per week in 2009.[69] Similar trends in audience profiles to the US have also been noticed, since if the 30+ individual without kids and the 'empty nester' are both making impacts as 'frequent audience' categories, it is the 12- to 24-year-old group that is, without doubt, the most important demographic group in the UK. Statistics show that among this newly expanded frequent cinema-goer group, A, B and C1 class/education categories are over-represented (in relation to their percentage in the general population), whereas C2 and D groups are under-represented.

The shift towards better-off and better educated young audiences is, in part at least, a consequence of the growth of purpose-built, suburban or out-of-town multiplexes which invariably need to be reached by car. However, new planning guidelines will see cinemas built in city centres and on 'brown-field' sites in a policy of urban revitalisation. This may reverse the demographic trend somewhat.

Equally important, and rarely commented upon in relation to audience demographics, is the price of admission. There is no doubt that the relative rise of A, B and C1s has also been exacerbated by cost, where the price of admission to a multiplex cinema in London now stands at a level 30 per cent higher than in New York.

Building an audience

Since the earliest days of the film industry, there have been attempts by makers, distributors and exhibitors to build audiences for their films. In today's film industry, building an audience is a sophisticated business: audience profiling and advertising (see section on contemporary film industry) are both incorporated to help 'deliver' an audience for a film.

Audience profiling

Audience-profile data – age, sex, income level, education, etc. – is influential in determining the kinds of films that receive finance and the shape the projects take.

Demographic trends – such as the recent rise in the 30+ audience – really do feed back into the films financed and those distributed by the industry. A recent example is the support the Majors gave to 'adult' fare during the 2005–6 winter cinema season. They put their weight behind some of the season's top critical and financial hits: films such as *Walk the Line* (Twentieth Century Fox), *Capote* (Sony Pictures Classics), *Syriana* (Warner Brothers) and *Munich* (DreamWorks SKG–Universal Pictures). Having said all that, the *big* money that season was still on what Edward Jay Epstein has called the **'Midas formula' films**. These are films that are (generally) based on children's stories, feature a child or adolescent protagonist, have a fairy-tale (Proppian) plot, use 3D animation, and have ratings no more restrictive than PG–13 (Epstein 2005: 236–8). Why? The reason is simple enough: because blockbuster films target the most frequent film-goer – the 12- to 24-year-old. The specific films that season were *The Chronicles of Narnia: The Lion, the Witch and the Wardrobe* (Buena Vista Pictures Distribution), *Harry Potter and the Goblet of Fire* (Warner Brothers) and *King Kong* (Universal Pictures Distribution), but the titles are mere detail, because each year the story is the same. The Majors' 'Midas formula' blockbuster films dominate in the multiplex cinemas because these films, and their associated merchandising and tie-ins, reflect the huge consumer power of their adolescent audiences.

'Midas formula' films (coined by E. J. Epstein) Aka 'Blockbuster' films, which are inevitably Proppian fairy tales in cinematic form, often shot in 3D, and targeting 12–24-year-olds.

TV and other advertising

This topic has already been covered in the previous section on the contemporary film industry. However, it is important to restate that TV advertising is an essential tool in building audience interest for big-budget films. And because it is expensive, advertising budgets tend to be very high for such films: in recent years it has been noted that the total marketing costs of a US mainstream film can 'devour' up to 25 per cent of a film's total revenue.

Since the release of *Jaws* (in 1975), concentrated national TV promotion – allied with saturation booking strategies – has proven to be a most effective way to exploit big-budget films. To that we can add the recent focus on online, new media advertising (see the case study of 'AOL Time Warner synergy and marketing' in the previous section), and to a lesser extent the efficacy of the print media.

Blockbusters need to show big returns at the box office in the first week of release, before potentially bad reviews and word-of-mouth reduce the returns. *Jurassic Park* (1993) is a case in point: 'after taking $50 million in its first American weekend in June, [it] took half of that in weekend three.'[70] Thus, to maximise early box-office takings, TV advertising is at saturation level in the immediate weeks preceding and following a theatrical release.

Building audiences is obviously of crucial importance in the exploitation of low-budget films as well. Given the meagre advertising budgets for such films, the techniques involved can be different and highly innovative, invariably incorporating low-cost new media at their heart, as evidenced below.

☐ CASE STUDY 7: BUILDING AN AUDIENCE ON THE
WEB: *THE BLAIR WITCH PROJECT* (1999)

This film earns its place in film history as the first internet-driven theatrical release, although the marketing potential of the web for film had begun to be exploited from the mid-1990s onwards, particularly in the independent sector.

This low-budget video–16mm work cost only $35,000 to make, and was shot and edited by Eduardo Sanchez and Daniel Myrick from late 1997 through 1998. A screening at the Sundance Film Festival in early 1999 resulted in a distribution deal with Artisan Entertainment, who decided to build on the air of 'authenticity' of the handheld footage in the film as a promotional tool.

A pre-existing website for the film had been set up by the makers in June 1998, but Artisan added fake documentary evidence – police records, histories of the Blair Witch, journals, etc. – all to create the film's official site. Www.blairwitch.com posed an enigma around the events depicted in the film: 'Did they happen or is the whole thing invented?'

By April 1999, a trailer for the film had appeared on the aint-it-cool-news.com website, and unofficial sites were debating the authenticity of the story's events. By the time of the film's US release on 16 July 1999, a marketing phenomenon had occurred with the official website having been visited 22 million times.[71] This promotion went a long way to explain the film's eventual box-office take of over $240 million worldwide.[72]

This cross-media phenomenon of film and web has, since its first appearance, reinvented film marketing. 'Word-of-internet' is now an integral strategy of film promotion. And fortunately for the industry, the predominant online users correspond conveniently to the frequent film-goers, the 12- to 24-age group. A marketing strategy such as this makes especially good sense since it is cheap to run and targets the 'lean-forward' young PC viewser/film-goer – the target audience for films like *The Blair Witch Project* – rather than the stay-at-home 'lean-back' TV viewer.

More recently, the cross-media campaign for the blockbuster *Harry Potter and the Sorcerer's Stone* (2001) bears witness to the lessons learned by the industry from the 'no-budget' *The Blair Witch Project*. The campaign used to great effect the web, TV and the press to promote and publicise the movie.

• **Plate 1.10**
Production still from
The Blair Witch Project
(Daniel Myrick and
Eduardo Sanchez,
1999). How to build
an audience: pose an
enigma around the
authenticity of your
footage and mount a
very clever campaign
on the internet to entice
punters to see the film

SUMMARY

Film as communication is not unidirectional, with the producer presenting the consumer with a set diet of consumables. Quite the contrary. Increasingly, ICT allows market analysts to access accurate information from and about movie-goers – information which is then used to determine production decisions.

CONCLUSION

This chapter has centred on the institutional framework of mainstream film, and the historical relationship between text and context. Any change in production, exhibition or distribution practice, in communication technology (both hardware and software), or in audience demographics, will have repercussions for the films we see and how we see them.

Films and their socio-economic contexts are part of a much broader history, that of the cultural history of the last 100 years. That history is a dialectical history – where forces of social, economic and technological change are in a constant dialogue with themselves and the cultural expressions that they give rise to. The purpose of this overview has been to go some way towards illuminating that point.

- The socio-economic organisation of the film industry – its labour relations, its apparatuses, its resources – largely determining the films that are made, their values, their aesthetics, etc.
- The three divisions of the film industry: exhibition, distribution and production
- The historical importance of vertical integration in the film industry
- The control of the Majors, their oligopoly during the studio era. Warner Brothers in the 1930s and 1940s as an example of studio 'authorship'
- Distribution as *central* in the modern era: Majors as financiers-cum-distributors, dictating the business terms which shape a film's finance and exploitation. Marketing a blockbuster in the pre-internet era: *Jurassic Park* (1993). Marketing in the internet era: Paramount's online marketing campaign for *Paranormal Activity* (2007) prior to general release
- Exhibition in the modern era: history of multiplex theatres, the implications of e-cinema
- Production in the modern era: 'package-units'. The ascendancy of 3D animated digital production: *Avatar* (2009). A US 'blockbuster' production: *Gladiator* (2000). A medium-budget UK production: *Slumdog Millionaire* (2008)
- Multimedia conglomerates in the modern era: vertically, horizontally and laterally integrated
- Audiences in the modern era. The economic effects of 'being at home', explaining the drop in cinema attendance after the peak of the mid to late 1940s. A *new*, enlarged (and male dominated) frequent cinemagoer group, the 12-to-24-year-olds: an expansion of the original 16-to-24-year-old group. DVDs, PC-s and audiences as 'viewers'. Building audiences on the web: *The Blair Witch Project* (1999)

QUESTION FOR DISCUSSION

In the modern era, what attracts the frequent filmgoer to the cinema? Why?

NOTES

1 Immediately after the formation of the General Film Company, independents began operating their own distribution company – the Motion Picture Distributing and Sales Company (May 1910). This was superseded by the Film Supply Company of America, the Universal Film Manufacturing Company and Mutual Films in 1912. Later, the introduction of feature-length films further weakened the MPPC, when many of its own members began dissociating themselves from the GFC and distributed their features through alternative distribution organisations (Elsaesser 1990: 194–6, 201).

2 In 1928, First National was purchased by Warner Brothers Film Company.

3 An early form of block-booking had existed during the days of the MPPC called standing-orders (Elsaesser 1990: 193).

4 This system was not universally adopted nor did companies refrain from changing production systems periodically. Taking 1941 as an example, it is interesting to note that the three most financially successful companies, in terms of box-office receipts, were all operating different production systems:
   • United Artists had a system of director units and producer units
   • MGM operated a producer–unit system
   • Twentieth Century Fox used a central-producer system. (Bordwell et al. 1985: 320–9)

5 In 1932, the average production cost per feature was US $200,000, whereas at MGM it was $450,000. See R. Campbell, 'Warner Bros in the 1930s' (1971: 2).

6 See M. Roth's essay, 'Some Warners Musicals and the Spirit of the New Deal', in Altman (1981: 41–56).

7 For a discussion on the relationship of this director to Warner's studio style see E. Buscombe's essay, 'Walsh and Warner Brothers', in Hardy (1974).

8 See drawings for Mildred Pierce sets in Deschner (1975, p. 20).

9 And 30 per cent of Columbia's releases were also produced by them (Balio 1976: 353).

10 The first major film company to sell its film library to TV was RKO, in December 1955 (Balio 1976: 322).

11 From the late 1940s onwards, film companies began producing programmes for TV (e.g. Warner's weekly series for ABC-TV, Warner Bros. Presents (1955)). By the early 1960s, producing TV shows was standard film industry practice and a major source of its revenue. Shortly afterwards (from the mid-1960s onwards), TV networks began commissioning made-for-TV films from major studios and independent producers (Balio 1976: 322–4).

12 For example, in 1956, United Paramount Theatres (ex-exhibition arm of Paramount) merged with ABC-TV (Balio 1976: 324).

13 The pattern of exclusive first-run releases having been broken with The Godfather in 1972 (Jowett and Linton 1989: 59).

14 C. Parkes, 'Everyone Goes to Hollywood', Financial Times, 13 March 2001, p. 10.

15 Source: http://www.natoonline.org, data as at 24 June 2010.

16 Screen International, No. 750, 31 March 1990.

17 Source: Dodona Research.

18 G. Drabinsky, Motion Pictures and the Arts in Canada: The Business and the Law (McGraw-Hill Ryerson, Toronto, 1976), quoted in Jowett and Linton (1989: 56).

19 'DVD Rising', Chicago Tribune, 14 October 2001.

20 The Times, 22 March 2006, p. 56.

21 'The Sunday Review', Independent on Sunday, 11 July 1993, p.15.

22 See K. Maher, 'A Scream Made for a Song', in 'Times 2' section of The Times, 6 November 2009, p. 3.

23 Ibid.

24 See www.ukfilmcouncil.org.uk.

25 See Scott Smith's online article, 'Byte Me ...', dated 24 January 2001, at www.atomfilms.com.

26 Reported in N. Christie, 'A Defining Moment', in 'FT Magazine', Financial Times, 16 October 2005, p. 52.

27 In 1950 James Stewart's agent MCA (Music Corp. of America), arranged for him to be paid 50 per cent of the net profits of the Universal film Winchester '73, in lieu of his normal salary of $250,000. This arrangement would not have been possible under the terms of his MGM contract during the studio era (Kent 1991: 86).

28 Reported by M. Garrahan in 'Show Them the Money', 'Life and Art' section of Financial Times, 20/21 February 2010, pp. 1–2.

29 A 1989 audience survey reported that the presence of stars was not an important factor in movie attendance decisions, but only important as a means of publicising a film (Jowett and Linton 1989: 39).

30 See J. Chaffin and M. Garrahan, 'Hollywood's Ultimatum', in Financial Times, 26/27 August 2006, p. 19.

31 See S. Bukatman's BFI modern classic on Blade Runner (BFI, London, 1997).

32 See www.hollywoodreporter.com/hollywoodreporter/.wrap/wrap00/dreamworks.jsp dated 24 October 2001.

33 See www.upcomingmovies.com/gladiator.html.

34 Source: Ali Cherkaoui, Second Assistant Director.

35 Reported in an interview with Ridley Scott in the 'Magazine' section of The Times, Saturday 25 November 2000, p. 39.

36 See wwww.upcomingmovies.com/gladiator.html.

37 Source: Enrico Ballarin, Mestiere Cinema Productions.

38 See Gladiator UK press release produced by Media Enterprises, 2000, pp.15–16.

39 See the 'Magazine' section of The Times, 11 November 2000, p.39.

40 See http://us.imdb.com/charts.

41 See http://www.the-movie-times.com/thrsdir/top100world.html.

42 In the form of writer/producer teams, writer/producer/director teams, and unattached writers.

43 Source: Guardian, 23 February 2006, p. 7.

44 Warner owns the film rights to J.K. Rowling's first three books and has options on the next four. Reported in an article by T. Reid and L. Peek entitled, 'Potter Playtime ...', The Times, 6 November 2001, p. 11.

45 See C. Grimes's article, 'Harry Potter and the Sales Team', Financial Times, 16 November 2001, p. 17.

46 See Guardian, 23 November 2001, p. 27.

47 See 'Will Sony Make it in Hollywood?', Fortune, 9 September 1991.

48 Report by the US Department of Labour entitled Family Spending and Saving in Wartime, Bulletin No. 822. Quoted in Handel (1950: 104).

49 Film Daily Year Book, and quoted in Handel (1950: 96). As a comparison, attendance figures for 1940 (pre-Second World War) were 80 million/week, and around 85 million/week for 1945 (end of the Second World War) (Austin 1989: 36).

50 Women: 3.75 times per month; Men: 3.7 times per month. See: L. Handel, Studies of the Motion Picture Audience (New York), December 1941. Cited in Handel (1950: 100).

51 Defined as attending ten times a month or more: figures for men were 11.8 per cent, as opposed to only 7.5 per cent for women; see Handel (1950: 100).

52 For example, in a state-wide survey conducted in Iowa in 1942, 31 per cent of men and 24.9 per cent of women aged 15 to 20 attended cinemas over five times a month, as opposed to only 11.4 per cent and 7.6 per cent respectively of those aged 21 to 35 years; see F. Whan and H. Summers, The 1942 Iowa Radio Audience Survey (Des Moines, 1942) cited in Handel (1950: 103).

53 In actual numbers, persons with higher levels of education were a minority among cinema-goers in the 1940s (Handel 1950: 104–8).

54 See *Film Daily Year Book*, quoted in Bernstein (1957: 2).

55 Department of Commerce's census of business for 1954. Cited in Bernstein (1957: 5).

56 Thirty per cent of those surveyed cited watching TV as their favourite way to spend an evening. Only 6 per cent of those surveyed cited going to the movies (*The Gallup Opinion Index*, Report 146, pp. 14–15, September 1977, quoted in Austin (1989: 40)).

57 Defined in this survey as persons under the age of 30.

58 In a 1948 Gallup poll, 79 per cent of people surveyed between the ages of 18 and 20, and 76 per cent of those between the ages of 21 and 29 had been to the cinema within the past three weeks; this declined to 57 per cent for those aged 30–49 (Gallup, cited in Docherty et al. (1987: 17)).

59 In a survey in 1949, 19 per cent of the working-class people surveyed (i.e. those with low levels of income and education) went to the cinema (at least) twice a week, as opposed to 13 per cent of middle-class people interviewed, and 8 per cent of upper-class people surveyed (Hulton research, Cited in Docherty et al. (1987: 16)).

60 'There was an increase in TV licences from 343k in 1950 to 10 million in 1960' (Docherty et al. 1987: 23).

61 Partly a product of 1950s prosperity and a move towards greater owner-occupation, and partly the result of the Town and Country Planning Act of 1947 which 'led to the clearing of slums, the growth of new towns . . . and, crucially, the resiting of large sections of the working class . . . around the edges of cities' (Docherty et al. 1987: 25–6).

62 Dropping from half the total audience to one-third between 1977 and 1983 (Docherty et al. 1987: 30–1).

63 See the MPAA (Motion Picture Association of America) report, *Annual Theatrical Market Statistics* (2005).

64 Source: the National Association of Theatre Owners.

65 Males of this age are the most likely audience for a block-buster movie in its opening two weekends. See D. Denby, 'Aiming Low', *New Yorker*, 13 and 20 June 2005, p. 187.

66 'DVD Shipments Seen Reaching Lofty Heights', Reuters, 24 October 2001.

67 See www.dvddemistified.com.

68 British Film Institute.

69 Dodona Research.

70 Quoted from 'The Sunday Review', *Independent on Sunday*, 11 July 1993.

71 See B. Farrow's article dated 8 October 1999, 'Hollywood Runs Scared', on *The Times* website.

72 See http://us.imdb.com/charts/worldtopmovies.

FURTHER READING

Austin, B., *Immediate Seating: A Look at Movie Audiences*, Wadsworth Publishing Company, Belmont, CA, 1989.

Balio, T. (ed.), *The American Film Industry*, University of Wisconsin Press, Madison, 1976.

Balio, T. (ed.), *Hollywood in the Age of Television*, Unwin Hyman, Boston, MA, 1990.

Bernstein, I. *Hollywood at the Crossroads: An Economic Study of the Motion Picture Industry*, Hollywood Film Council, LA, 1957.

Bordwell, D., Staiger, J. and Thompson, K., *The Classical Hollywood Cinema*, Routledge & Kegan Paul, London, 1985.

Docherty, D., Morrison, D. and Tracey, M., *The Last Picture Show?*, British Film Institute, London, 1987.

Epstein, E.J., *The Big Picture*, Random House, New York, 2005.

Giles, J., *The Crying Game*, BFI Publishing, London, 1997.

Gomery, D., *The Hollywood Studio System: A History*, London, 2005.

Gomery, D., *Shared Pleasures*, British Film Institute, London, 1992.

Greenwald, S. and Landry, P., *This Business of Film*, Lone Eagle, New York, 2009.

Handel, L., *Hollywood Looks at its Audience,* University of Illinois Press, Urbana, 1950.

Jowett, G. and Linton, J., *Movies as Mass Communication*, Sage, Newbury Park, CA, 1989.

Kent, N., *Naked Hollywood*, BBC Books, London, 1991.

Landau, D. (ed.), *Gladiator: The Making of the Ridley Scott Epic*, Boxtree, London, 2000.

Merritt, G., *Celluloid Mavericks*, Thunder's Mouth Press, NY, 2000.

Roddick, N., *A New Deal in Entertainment*, British Film Institute, London, 1983.

http://www.lastbroadcast.co.uk/movies/v/7466-slumdog-millionaire-adapting-the-book.html

http://www.blairwitch.com

FURTHER VIEWING

Key Warner Brothers (genre) films
The gangster film
Little Caesar (1930)
The Public Enemy (1931)
Bullets or Ballots (1935)
Marked Woman (1937)
The Roaring 'Twenties (1939)

The social conscience film
I Am A Fugitive From A Chain Gang (1932)
Wild Boys of The Road (1933)

The fast-talking comedy/drama
Five-star Final (1931)
Lady Killer (1933)
Hard To Handle (1933)

The musical
42nd Street (1933)
Gold Diggers of 1933 (1933)
Dames (1934)

The biopic
The Story of Louis Pasteur (1936)
The Life of Emile Zola (1937)
Juarez (1939)

The swashbuckler
Captain Blood (1935)
The Adventures of Robin Hood (1938)
The Sea Hawk (1940)

The melodrama
Jezebel (1938)
The Letter (1940)
Now Voyager (1942)
Mildred Pierce (1945)

The film noir
The Maltese Falcon (1941)
The Big Sleep (1946)
Dark Passage (1947)

Resource addresses
British Film Institute Library
21 Stephen Street
London W1P 1PL
tel 020 7255 1444

The Cinema Exhibitors' Association
22 Golden Square
London W1R 3PA
tel 020 7734 9551

Dodona Research
12 The Crescent, King Street
Leicester LE2 2YE
tel 0116 285 4550

National Association of Theatre Owners (of America)
750 First Street NE
Washington, DC 20002
tel 1 202 962 0054

Chapter 2

Contemporary Film Technology

William Whittington

■ Contemporary Film Technology

INTRODUCTION

Film technology has never been fixed within the mode of movie production. The development of cinema has seen the shift from silent to sound film, black and white to colour, and the move from 35mm film stock to recent formats such as High Definition (or HD) that capture and project images in digital form. Recent cinematic history includes advances in computer graphics and editing, stereoscopic imaging or 3D, motion capture, and sound recording, mixing and design. This chapter will demonstrate that film technology has developed based on a complex intersection of industrial and aesthetic factors, which include global and industrial economics, advances in other fields such as electronics and computing, shifts in audience expectations, and the needs of specific film productions as well as the preferences of filmmakers.

The first section of the chapter will present an overview of the phases of development for recent technology in cinema, and how these have been critically framed by theories of economics and culture. Subsequently, the focus will shift to a close analysis of three specific technological advances that influence film production and distribution today:

- The first technology to be considered will be computer graphic imaging systems, which have been used to create innovative special effects sequences and computer animation, and which have influenced all aspects of the visual field from set design to colour. The science fiction film *District 9* (2009), which explores issues of audio-visual as well as human-alien hybridism, serves as the case study for this section.
- Second, the chapter will unravel the complexities of multichannel sound formats, which record and encode multiple tracks of audio elements then deploy them within the theatre environment through an array of speakers surrounding the audience. This immersive sound technology has led, in part, to the rise of 'sound design', and in the accompanying case study of *Star Trek* (2009) issues of sound and space are explored in relation to both the technology and the themes of the film.
- Finally, the chapter will examine 3D technology, which currently mimics depth perception in movie theatres with the aid of special glasses. The film *Avatar* (2009), which serves as the case study in this section, has revitalised interest in 3D and pointed contemporary film in a new direction of imagining cinematic worlds in both depth and dimension.

These technologies have changed how filmgoers experience cinema by shifting expectations related to the variety of blockbuster genres, audio and visual design, spectacle and storytelling. As a result, previous distinctions between live action and animation have begun to erode; sound design has become less 'realistic' and more immersive and the notion of storytelling has begun to emphasise spectacle over causality. These innovations have also contributed to current trends related to global production and distribution. It seems the term 'Hollywood' no longer refers to a place, but rather to a process that is shared by many nations. Even the term 'film' does not seem to fit within the borders of the frame as some 'films' never make it to celluloid.

Using a range of theoretical approaches from traditional film studies to scholarship in new media and technology, this chapter aims to provide a technologically informed context for the various critical perspectives presented throughout *Introduction to Film Studies*.

TECHNOLOGY IN MOTION: FROM INVENTION TO AGENCY

Film historian Douglas Gomery has categorised technological development within cinema into three overlapping phases: the first is 'invention', which refers to the conceptualisation and development phase of a technology; the second is 'innovation,' which encompasses the manufacturing and marketing of a technology; and the final phase is the 'diffusion' of a technology or 'the widespread use' within the industry (Allen and Gomery 1985: 114–15). Given the integration of computers and new digital technology into nearly every aspect of cinematic production, I would like to add another phase – the 'update', which can be defined as the ongoing and, often, unscheduled 'fixes' or 'patches' to software and hardware disseminated to users to address quality control concerns and system upgrades. Anyone with a computer should be familiar with this process. In the digital age, technology companies have begun to respond quickly to user complaints and concerns with updates and redesigned versions of software (often numbered 2.0 and so on), not simply to address quality control issues, but often to protect intellectual property rights. Within these broad phases, the path of development for a technology is never uniform. According to film historian John Belton, 'No one technology takes quite the same path to full diffusion as another' (Belton 2004: 901). By contrast, in the classical Hollywood period, the film studios were vertically integrated with control of film production, distribution and exhibition. This control allowed techno-logical advances such as sound, for instance, to be implemented on the set with the assurance that re-recording and playback accommodations would be made through the process of printing the sound on the film reel exhibiting it in the motion picture theatre. The path of implementation assured a sense of quality control within the studio system.

Following the breakup of the studio system, however, the chain of technological invention, innovation and diffusion within the film industry broke down.[1] Significant quality control issues related to sound and picture plagued the US markets throughout the decades that followed, and at the same time, social upheaval, the rise of television and changing economics related to leisure activities all contributed to the decline in box-office receipts. According to film historian Thomas Schatz, 'Studio profits fell from an average of $64 million in the five-year span from 1964 to 1968, to $13 million from 1969 to 1973' (Schatz 1993: 15). By the mid-1970s, however, the film industry shifted strategies in relation to marketing, production and financing, and profits soared with the introduction of the 'blockbuster' film, exemplified by releases such as *The Godfather* (1972), *The Exorcist* (1973), *Jaws* (1975), *Star Wars* (1977) and *Raiders of the Lost Ark* (1981). Technological innovation became part of the strategy for the design and marketing of these 'event' films. 'Behind the scenes' television specials and print-based media revealed the 'secrets' of the audio and visual effects in these films, while new technologies and their inventors received special Oscars for their contributions. Theatre poster art began to include references to the newest innovations, such as 'Presented in Dolby Stereo'. So for filmgoers, new technology became one of the expectations for the blockbuster film, and these expectations then forced filmmakers to 'update' and innovate technology at a much more rapid pace.

Currently, new film technology makes its way into film production and exhibition through a variety of paths, from tradeshows to corporate collaborations. Large trade shows such as ShoWest, Cinema Expo International, and CineAsia often feature educa-tional workshops and demonstrations of new products marketed specifically to the film theatre industry. It is at these trade shows that demonstrations of new digital and 3D exhibition technologies made their debut, as well as at film markets such as the Cannes Film Festival. But these are not simply consumer technologies that can be pulled off the shelf and sold; rather, they often involve customised installation and specialised training for filmmakers and operators.

With the development and integration of any technology, economic risks are inherent in the process, which has sometimes slowed the diffusion of new technologies. When theatre owners balked at the price tag of the first digital projectors, which at the time cost more than $150,000 dollars, some of the early manufacturers such as Technicolor Digital Cinema and Boeing Digital Systems installed their systems at no cost to theatres in major US cities in order to conduct test marketing and to collect data relating to audience

For further discussion on film production, film audiences and the studio system, see Chapter 1.

preferences and box-office receipts (Taub 2003: 1). Over the next several years, when economic trends indicated higher grosses from digital screens, theatres began to convert, though not without substantial underwriting from the studios, which realised substantial cost savings because they no longer had to strike or ship celluloid prints. Currently, three companies – BARCO, Christies Digital Systems and NEC – manufacture the majority of the Digital Light Processing (DLP) projectors used in the ongoing conversion of motion picture theatres today. These projectors offer high contrast ratios, precise delivery resolution and ease of use and maintenance, and fit within the footprint of older film projectors, thus making conversion easier.

It should be noted that such technological development is never conducted in isolation. Behind the scenes, the major studios, theatre chains and global manufacturers work together to make their innovation and integration possible. This collaboration helps to avoid a chaotic marketplace filled with multiple technologies that cannot communicate with one another. Through forums, summits and meeting of professional groups like the Society of Motion Picture and Television Engineers, various standards and practices have been established in all areas of film technology. For example, the Digital Cinema Initiatives (DCI) – a joint venture between Disney, Fox, Paramount, Sony Pictures Entertainment, Universal and Warner Bros – published various position papers and best practices to establish standards for audio and image encoding that addressed not only issues in the theatre, but also those related to broadcast technologies. These specifications, however, are by no means mandatory, and their integration into the system of exhibition is dependent on manufacturers, marketers and even audiences, who have been drawn into the process through communication forums such as surveys and mobile posts. With the increasing prices of movie tickets and downloadable media content, today's audiences have increasingly high expectations for picture and sound quality in theatres as well as on the screens of their mobile devices, computers and televisions. Media technophiles have also driven greater demand for new technology that interlinks voice and data, while providing access to media content and services. This process of synergy has become known as *convergence*, and continues to reshape media creation and delivery beyond the theatrical environment.

Technological development for motion pictures is also fostered by competitive collaborations between studios and high-tech labs and manufacturers, such as Dolby Laboratories, Sony and others. The transition to digital sound saw the development of

• **Plate 2.1**
NEC Projector. An image of one of the popular brands of digital projectors (NEC) used in the ongoing conversion of theatres today.

multiple audio formats including SDDS® (Sony Dynamic Digital Sound), DTS® (Digital Theatre Systems) and Dolby Digital, each of which is aligned with a particular studio or studios that had a stake in the product development and use. For example, the film *Jurassic Park* (1993) was released in the DTS® sound format (6.1 channels), which was produced by collaborative efforts between Universal Studios, Steven Spielberg's Amblin Entertainment and a technology company specialising in immersive surround sound. DTS® was innovative in that it did not deliver the sound on the film print, but on a CD-ROM, linking it to the image by time code (an electronic synchronisation system). The technique harkens back to the first Vitaphone sound-on-disc systems of the 1920s, presenting an excellent example of the cyclical nature of developments in film technology. In 1993, Sony and its subsidiary Columbia Pictures (with an outside company Semetex Corp.) also developed their competing format SDDS® (a variable 5 or 7.1 channel format), while Dolby Laboratories worked with many of the remaining studios to develop its 5.1 channel system, which debuted with the release of the Warner Bros film *Batman Returns* (1992). Ultimately, the Dolby system, with its superior market share and the ability rapidly to integrate its processes into consumer technologies, became the dominant sound encoding and decoding system in the field and its influence will be examined more fully in the section on multichannel sound.

Aside from industry-wide economic factors, perhaps one of the most fundamental drives in the development of new film technology can be found in the proverb: 'Necessity is the mother of invention.' In contemporary cinema, filmmakers and production units often develop new and innovative technologies for the needs of particular production circumstances. In the early 1940s, Disney invented the multi-plane camera, which utilised staggered platens for cel animation, to create the illusion of depth in animated films like *Pinocchio* (1940). In the 1990s, George Lucas encouraged his special effects company Industrial Light and Magic (ILM) to develop computer software that allowed the creation of digital characters for the *Star Wars* prequels (1999–2005), while filmmaker James Cameron, director of *Terminator 2: Judgment Day* (1991), *Titanic* (1997) and *Avatar* (2009), has been personally instrumental in the development of underwater remote filming technologies for both 2D and 3D imaging. These technologies were first developed to capture the documentary footage used in *Titanic* and later fostered the production of several IMAX films based on undersea topics, specifically *Bismark* (2002) and *Ghosts of the Abyss* (2003). More recently, computer technology has made its way onto the sets of many films, in part driven by economic factors to lower production costs. Paradoxically, with the integration of more computer technology into the filmmaking process, the cost of film production has grown greater and greater, in part due to expanding global markets, but also as a result of audience demands and expectations.

If the phases of technological development and integration are never uniform, they are also not bound by predetermined rules of use. Manufacturers and studios have been unable to dictate or limit the specific uses of new technology. For this reason, it is important to complicate the model by examining the unintended consequences of a technology's widespread diffusion and use. For example, the same computer technologies that have made it easier to record, edit and distribute digital films have also made these films more vulnerable to pirating, sampling and remediation. Everyone it seems can be a filmmaker or distributor, if they have the latest consumer editing software on their personal computer. Despite complex encryption protocols during postproduction, pirated digital versions of films often show up on peer-to-peer networks nearly to the day they are released in theatres, and sometimes well before their premiers as was the case with *X-Men Origins: Wolverine* (2009). In addition, fans engage in mash-ups, parodies and slash versions of their favourite films and post them on YouTube. The consequences of remediation are by no means entirely negative in economic terms. Remediated content often expands the mythologies and cultural significance of the original property, and provides fans with a sense of agency or control over the story worlds they have come to love.

THEORIES OF TECHNOLOGY

In film studies, various theories of technology emerge which present both unique perspectives on advancements as well as critical pitfalls. There are three primary theories that are often engaged in the analysis of film technology: the *'great man theory'*, *technological determinism* and *economics*. The 'great man theory' cuts across many disciplines; however, in regard to film, it focuses on the lone inventor, working in a secluded workshop until a 'eureka' moment of discovery (Allen and Gomery 1985: 110). The familiar names that arise in relation to the invention of cinema are Louis Lumière, Eadweard Muybridge and Thomas Edison, and their mythologies are often framed in heroic terms. The notion of the singular inventor, however, is challenged by the fact that each was working in a time period that was steeped in developments from other fields, such as chemistry, engineering and physics, all of which contributed to the invention of cinema. These inventors were therefore not alone. A host of artists, scientists, engineers and craftspeople assisted in the process of creating cameras, film stock, sound and projection systems, and cinema as a mode of production was dependent on producers, directors, writers, technicians and the many individuals listed on film credits. The 'great men' of cinema are perhaps 'great' not because of a 'eureka' moment, but rather because of their ability to frame an understanding of the technology and the direction of its use.

Technological determinism presents a much broader theoretical question: Does the technology itself drive the aesthetic output of a particular period in history and by extension the expectations of society and culture? This critical approach suggests that technology determines what is possible within an art form and that in some measure personal agency and freedom of the artist is lost in the process of use. Science fiction films such as *THX 1138* (1971), *Terminator 2: Judgment Day* (1991) and *I, Robot* (2004) present this approach in the extreme as humanity embraces robotic technology as a kind of saviour, only to become enslaved by these mechanised creations. Popular media outlets, from news programmes to magazines, have co-opted the vocabulary of techno-logical determinism without examining the underlying limitations of the approach. It is highly problematic to draw direct lines between the use of a technology and its social effect because this would ignore the web of interrelated influences, from economics to cultural context, involved in a technologies use. It also fails to address the fact that just because a technology exists this does not mean that a filmmaker or consumer will use it. Currently, we see a trend in which some film artists are reverting to older techniques of mechanical special effects, sound recording formats and make-up as a kind of backlash to the use of computer generated images and sounds. For example, filmmaker Christopher Nolan and his crew limited the use of computer generated effects in his film *Inception* (2010), and instead engaged the use of wiring rigs, rotating sets and slow motion photography for the action set pieces in the film. A similar backlash is forming around 3D releases as well, particularly around films that are converted to 3D after being conceived and shot for a 2D release.

Finally, technology in cinema can also be considered in terms of economics. Within these models, technology is understood and evaluated in relation to market needs and values. But in many ways, like the notions of determinism, this scope of inquiry can be limiting if not contextualised within cultural and creative contexts. To their detriment, these approaches often proceed with the underlying assumption that industries and markets move in ways that are self-sustaining and perpetually seeking advancement in regard to their market share. The history of the film industry (like many industries), however, is replete with examples of poor business decisions, the embrace of inferior technologies, and simple human self-interest and greed over the basic needs of a company or the marketplace. For example, economics does not always account for the rejection of superior technology in the marketplace. The VHS versus Beta (Betamax) formats for videotape were an example of this incongruity. Beta tapes and technology were superior in recording and playback quality and were in fact embraced by many media production outlets, yet VHS format prevailed in part due to marketing, reviews and availability and preferences of consumers. Unexpected adoption patterns plagued the introduction of DVDs and Blu-ray formats as well. Ultimately, when considering technology within a critical framework, it is perhaps best to consider a multifaceted approach, which reflects a balance of theories of technology, economics and social considerations, as outlined above.

COMPUTER GRAPHIC IMAGING SYSTEMS

One of the most transformative technologies to be introduced to contemporary cinema is not a single technology at all, but rather a host of convergent technologies related to computer imaging systems. These emerge in the form of computer hardware, software applications and input devices such as touchpads and pens. Computer graphic imaging systems come in a multiplicity of configurations and platforms, and are often tailored to support the particular needs of a production. Over the past two decades, these systems have transformed the visual field of films, television programmes, commercials and video games through the creation of computer generated images or CGI. Using these workstations, graphic artists control data to design images and forms in 2D and 3D and to establish simulated environments. For example, Image Engine, a special effects company based in British Columbia, used various computer programs to create the 3D wireframe models of the aliens in *District 9* (2009). These digital creatures were covered with various textured surfaces based on insects and bugs, and then placed within the context of the live-action footage that was shot on location in South Africa, creating a realistic composite that evokes the futuristic and the uncanny effects of the film. According to theorist Michele Pierson, 'Computer generated imagery has emerged as a new kind of visual spectacle on the postmodern mediascape' and it offers a 'techno-scientific tour-de-force for the special effects industry and a new kind of aesthetic object' (Pierson 1998: 3). With pixels and programs that simulate physical phenomena, a dead moon became a planet in *Star Trek II: The Wrath of Khan* (1982), and dinosaurs came to life in *Jurassic Park* (1993). These spectacles provide filmgoers with new pleasures that evoke a sense of 'grandeur', 'awe' and 'the sublime' by providing an experience that is outside 'the typical reality of everyday life' (King 2003: 118).

Within the past twenty years, computer generated images have supplanted many of the traditional visual effects techniques and have established a new mode of production within the special effects industry; while at the same time blurring the distinction between 'live action' and animation. Traditional visual effects production involves a host of techniques and technologies to create cinematic trickery. Some of the most common techniques are the use of small and large-scale models, matt paintings, stop-motion modelling, fire and explosive effects, and make-up and prosthetic appliances for creature effects. Examples can be found in the earliest Méliès shorts to the epics of Ray Harryhausen like *Jason and the Argonauts* (1963) and *Clash of the Titans* (1981). The processes to create these effects, however, are often labour intensive – involving long hours of design and manufacture before going in front of the camera. In addition, numerous duplicates must be created for repeated takes, especially when dealing with disaster sequences like those found in *Earthquake* (1974) or *Towering Inferno* (1974). As early as the 1970s, film producers sought to find low cost alternatives to special effects 'tricks', while also providing filmgoers with the newest cinematic spectacles that could then be featured in marketing campaigns. Over the past three decades, special effects houses such as Pacific Data Images, Industrial Light and Magic, Weta and Pixar began to experiment with computer technology as a means of creating effects within virtual environments. Hardware and software, such as the Pixar Image Computer and, later, RenderMan and Maya software, were developed to create digital models and characters,

render colours and surface textures, and create simulated landscapes and environmental effects. This technology is by no means limited to special effects, but extends
to virtual lighting, camera motion effects and even set design and digital make-up. Early
examples produced from the technology can be seen in such films as *Tron* (1982), *The
Abyss* (1989), *Terminator 2: Judgment Day* (1991) and *Forrest Gump* (1994) as well as
more recent film such as the *Lord of the Ring* series (2001–3), the *Star Wars* prequels
(1999–2005) and *Avatar* (2009).

*For further discussion on
computer animation, see
Chapter 10.*

CGI technology has had a profound impact on our understanding of film form.
The visual spectacles created with this technology have become part of the narrative
dynamics of the blockbuster. One particularly interesting aspect of this shift can
be found in the blurring of our understanding of 'live action' versus animation. It is
important to first remember that this technology also fostered a new cinematic form –
computer animation. Pixar is perhaps the most familiar studio in this regard, producing
feature-length animated films such as *Toy Story* (1995), *Monsters Inc.* (2001), *Finding
Nemo* (2003), *The Incredibles* (2004), *Cars* (2006), *Ratatouille* (2007) and, most recently,
Up (2009), *Toy Story 3* (2010) and *Cars 2* (2011). The same technologies that create
computer generated animated worlds have also been used to manipulate images of
the 'real world'. Initially, when computer generated images were introduced into films,
they often stood out because of their crude design or limited ability to integrate with
the live-action footage. In a film like *The Last Starfighter* (1984), the digitally rendered
spacecraft were boxy and geometric, and because of the screen capture methods,
they were steeped in a bluish hue that caused them to separate from their backdrops
when combined with live-action shots. The initial integration did not quite fit in the
context of the story world. As a result, filmgoers and critics often limited their critical
consideration of the 'work' of computer generated images by asking the question:
'Does it look like an effect?' However, this question lost its authority as the integration
of live-action footage and computer images become more refined and seamless.
Michele Pierson argues:

If an effect is only *special* in relation to something else – something that it isn't – how do viewers
decide what is a special effect in this context? Does the scope for the kind of transmutation of the
visual field that might make an effect special even *exist* once a film begins to be made over in the
mode of an animated feature?

(Pierson 2002: 152–3)

The following case study of *District 9* (2009) gives an example of this re-imagining of the
visual field and the resultant shifts in critical reception.

• **Plate 2.2**
District 9 (Neill Blomkamp, 2009). On-set image of actor with
reference marks on his costume to be used in the process of
computer generated image (CGI) insert.

• **Plate 2.3**
District 9 (Neill Blomkamp, 2009). Final image with the CGI alien
inserted.

☐ CASE STUDY 1: *DISTRICT 9* (2009)

District 9 (2009), directed by Neill Blomkamp, follows the story of a bureaucrat named Wikus van de Merwe (Sharlto Copley), who has been assigned to lead a relocation effort of a stranded group of insect-like aliens that have been interned in a slum in Johannesburg, South Africa. Social unrest, xenophobia and violence mar the process of moving the 'prawns' away from the city into segregated camps. The style of the film embraces the inherent capabilities and strengths of digital technology in a kind of Next Wave Vérité style, and the computer graphics exemplifies the blurring of animation and 'live action' in the digital age. The film's Vérité style engages mock-documentary techniques, such as interviews, handheld news footage and overhead surveillance images from inside stores and helicopters to establish a sense of cinematic verisimilitude or truth. Culturally, we as filmgoers are acutely aware of these stylistic uses from modern media, and the filmmakers engaged them to foster a suspension of disbelief within the context of a genre blockbuster. Thematically, the film is about fusion or more specifically the reprogramming of human flesh with alien DNA, but it is equally about the repro-gramming of media images and forms. Within the narrative, Wikus is exposed to alien DNA, which rapidly begins to transform his body into an alien-human hybrid. Government officials and criminal mercenaries grasp the importance of this fusion and seek to kidnap Wikus in order to exploit the weaponry brought by the aliens, which only they can use. Through the use of computers, the film style picks up these themes of hybridism and reprogramming in its visual lexicon. The alien creatures were based on the textures and structures of real bugs, crabs, grasshoppers and spiders and modelled in the 3D virtual environment using CGI technology. On set, actors provided reference positioning for the creature effects by wearing special suits with data markings that the computers would recognise and record. From this set of data, the creatures were created and seamlessly inserted into the documentary style footage with matching lighting and colour gradients. The footage itself then reprograms the tropes of the documentary style, evoking a new era in civil rights media, which also makes reference to the civil rights issues of South Africa. This approach to CGI goes beyond the manipulation of historical footage used to rewrite the past that we have seen in films like *JFK* (1991) and *Forrest Gump* (1994); rather, it present a 'live' cinematic moment that we might see on the news or in a documentary. The computer technology is used to create evidence of what science fiction is fond of calling 'the near future'. Through CGI, the character of Wikus is trans-formed into an alien 'prawn', recognisable only by his longing for what he has lost at the hands of men – his humanity.

• **Plate 2.4**
District 9 (Neill Blomkamp, 2009). CGI technology evokes a News program stylistic, through the use of onscreen graphics and remapping of the visual field.

Multichannel sound

Early experiments in multichannel sound sought to expand the spatial qualities of the cinematic experience, and as with computer imaging technologies, this new audio technology fostered an expansion of our understanding of cinematic form, particularly in regard to immersion and spectacle. In the 1940s, Disney developed 'Fantasound' for the animated feature *Fantasia* (1940), and this is widely considered the precursor to the multichannel sound formats we hear in theatres today. This early multichannel technology featured two synchronised soundtracks that delivered music and effects to fifty-four speakers in specially equipped theatres in the major film markets of New York and Los Angeles (Blake 1984: 20). The system failed to take hold due to synchronisation difficulties associated with interlinking the sound tracks with the 35mm print. The 1950s provided another opportunity for multichannel development with widescreen formats such as CinemaScope and Todd-AO releases. As a result of the introduction of magnetic audiotape, various studios began to experiment with new sound processes on the surface of film prints, stereophonic recording on set and designs for speaker arrays within theatrical venues.[2] With the advent of competition from television, Hollywood studios introduced this new technology in conjunction with various spectacles such as *This is Cinerama* (1952), epics like *Around the World in 80 Days* (1956) and musical extravaganzas like *Oklahoma* (1955) in order to draw filmgoers into theatres. The advantages of the new technology were clear: 'Magnetic sound provided unprecedented fidelity, a dramatically expanded frequency range, and significantly improved signal-to-noise ratio, and a larger dynamic volume range' (Belton 1992: 155). Despite the superiority of the technology and the support of the studios for these systems, though, theatre owners rejected the advance due the costs of conversion, and the 'revolution' stalled.

In the 1960s, however, Ray Dolby of Dolby Labs began experiments in audio noise reduction techniques and sound 'matrixing' or routing that led to an integrated and cost effective system for sound encoding and decoding, specifically tied to multichannel film sound. Filmmakers such as Francis Ford Coppola, George Lucas and Steven Spielberg also played a major role in the renewal of sound presentation in the 1970s and 1980s, demanding greater quality control and presentation of film sound for their films such as *Apocalypse Now* (1979) and *Close Encounters of the Third Kind* (1977). The producers of *Star Wars* (1977) are often credited with ushering Dolby Stereo into widespread use in the domestic US theatre circuit by requiring that prints of the film be Dolby Stereo encoded.

The Dolby Stereo format was introduced in 1974, and reconsidered how the traditional optical track was being utilised. The system divided the allotted space on the celluloid near the sprocket holes into two optical soundtracks, and sent the signals through an electronic matrix. This matrix divided the audio streams into the left, right, centre and surround channels, producing what we have come to know as multichannel *surround sound*. The format provided superior fidelity with the added benefit of new audio streams that could fill up the theatre space, immersing filmgoers in sound and music. The box office success of *Star Wars*, as well as other films such as *Close Encounters of the Third Kind* (1977) and *Superman* (1979), meant theatre owners began converting to accommodate the new sound formats.

As digital technologies developed, sound moved completely into the digital realm, becoming integrated into the various processes from recording to exhibition, and by the 1990s, Dolby and other companies were creating digital sound formats that featured multichannel systems to deliver 'discrete' sound signals to the various speakers throughout the theatre. These new formats provided unprecedented dynamic range and sound fidelity. The Dolby Digital sound track, which runs between the sprocket holes along the edge of the film, provides 5.1 channels of sound. This encoding allows discrete sound channels to be directed to an array of speakers, consisting of left, right, centre, left surround, right surround and low frequency channels (Holman 2000: 42–3).

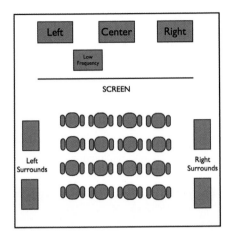

• Plate 2.5
Theatre design. Drawing of 5.1 multichannel speaker array in a motion picture theatre.

From a cultural perspective, multichannel sound has become an integral part of the cinematic spectacle of the blockbuster. In particular, 'tent pole' films or films designed to draw huge audiences such as science fiction, comic book or fantasy films are highly dependent on multichannel sound. These films attempt to create not just a narrative experience, but a cinematic experience that feels like an amusement park 'ride' with immersive images and sounds. For this type of genre cinema, multichannel sound technology has expanded cinematic form in three ways: it has provided greater localisation of sound effects and music, eliminated masking posed by different sounds, and provided sonic enhancement in regard to space. As an example of localisation, the image of a car moving from stage right to stage left and driven by the young James Kirk in *Star Trek* (2009) tracks precisely with the sound effects of the revving engine moving through the right, centre and left speakers, then off into the surrounds. Masking issues (or the condition of sounds lying on top of one another) are also eliminated with this technology. The separate speakers allow complex sound designs that span the dynamic range but do not to interfere with one another because they are separated in space. Low-frequency explosions aboard the Starship Kelvin are set well below the chatter of mid-range frequency dialogue and communications because they are presented in a separate speaker array. Finally, multichannel sound allows filmmakers to plot out sound use in different sound fields within the theatre space, expanding the diegesis of a film well beyond the borders of the screen image into the surrounds, as we will explore in the case study of *Star Trek* (2009).

☐ CASE STUDY 2: *STAR TREK* (2009)

In 2009, producer and director J.J. Abrams took on the ambitious task of 'rebooting' the popular television and film franchise *Star Trek*. The original television show from the 1960s spawned several films with the original crew and a number of spin-off television shows and film series. In the opening sequence, Abrams altered the canonical timeline of the original series, collapsing the past and future to rewrite the origin story of the main characters. The first television series was known for its spare yet unique use of sound, inventing effects for hydraulic doors, phasers and scanning devices. The reboot revives all of these effects in the opening shots of the film to offer intertextual references to the earlier series, but then reshapes the overall sound design into a multichannel assault on the senses as a federation ship is attacked by a hostile Romulan ship and its captain bent on revenge.

Sound designer Ben Burtt, best known for his work on the *Star Wars* series, re-conceptualised many of the sounds for the new *Star Trek* feature. For example, he notes, 'In the original series, the steady blast of the phasers was derived from the [musical] wave with pink noise. The phasers in the new movie are more like the blasters in *Star Wars* in the sense that they are flying bolts ... shorter and sharper', yet these effects 'recall' the originals in tonal design (Kunkes 2009: 1). Through multichannel sound design, Burtt engineered the opening sequence to function as an operatic and heroic overture, while preparing filmgoers with a preview of the overall sound design and themes that would pervade the film.

The attack on the federation vessel USS Kelvin is replete with the sounds of alarms, frantic voices over the communication systems, and explosions moving on and off the

• **Plate 2.6**
Star Trek (J.J. Abrams, 2009). Multichannel sound with action presents a sense of audio-visual chaos aboard U.S.S. Kelvin.

• **Plate 2.7**
Star Trek (J.J. Abrams, 2009). A multichannel blast creates an immersive cacophony as the hull breaches on the ship.

• **Plate 2.8**
Star Trek (J.J. Abrams, 2009). The point of audition shifts as the soundtrack falls silent to reveal the void of space.

screen into the surrounds, creating an immersive effect which is disorientating. But when a missile hits the ship, the sound perspective shifts and all sound ceases as a crew member, whose point of audition we are suddenly hearing, is pulled out into the void of space. The multichannel format allows for not only a rich tapestry of sounds from the highest frequency to the lowest, but also the removal of all sound. The spectacle of silence in space is overwhelming, and underscores the dangers of space travel and exploration through a metaphor of absence. The operatic elements overtake the sound design as a child (the future James T. Kirk) is born during the attack, and the filmmakers drop all sound effects to emphasise the orchestral score during the birth.

The original series' timeline is reclaimed somewhat through sound as well. Surround sound effects are used to explore outer space as well as the inner space of the mind. During the 'mind meld' between Kirk (Chris Pine) and the older Spock Prime (Leonard Nimoy), Spock's words fragment and echo into the surround speakers in order to evoke the sensation of inner thought and memory. In this way, we are allowed to see and hear the timeline that has been lost, while being presented with the sounds of the future that is to come.

• Plate 2.9
Star Trek (J.J. Abrams, 2009). Multichannel sound allows Spock Prime (Leonard Nimoy) to reveal his "thoughts" to the young Kirk (Chris Pine), revealing the sonic dimensions of the mindscape

3D EXHIBITION TECHNOLOGY

In the 1950s, Hollywood studios embraced 3D technology as a means of drawing filmgoers back into the theatre, but like the multichannel sound of the 1950s, the technology failed to take hold. Currently, there has been a revival of interest in stereoscopic imaging, which not surprisingly intersects with the advances in CGI and sound to create new and innovative ways of experiencing cinema. The 3D technique in cinema is a trick of perception. Humans perceive depth as a result of the separation of the eyes, which results in a slightly different view of an object. Three-dimensional cinema mimics this approach by projecting two images onto the screen, which are either differentiated by a two-colour system (most commonly red and green) or by the other commonly used technique that alternately blocks light to the left and right eye in a pattern of opposite polarisation. The filmgoer then views the images through glasses or polarised filters so the right eye sees one image and the left the other. The result mimics three-dimensional perception. Despite a wave of interest in 3D in the 1950s, the technology proved problematic for filmmakers, exhibitors and filmgoers. Filmmakers were unsure of how to best use the technique, raising questions about how often the technique should be used and to what end. The propensity of use fell into the category of 3D objects being thrust outward toward the audience, which often interrupted the narrative flow of a film. The visual poetic of 3D was given only a short time to develop in the 1950s, until filmgoers grew tired of the cluster of similar uses, and became even more frustrated by the lingering headaches that occurred after viewing films in 3D. While some historians argue that the quality of the films alone stifled the diffusion of the technology, this line of criticism is perhaps overstated. A number of high-profile films were released in the format including *House of Wax* (1953), *Kiss Me Kate* (1953) and Hitchcock's *Dial M for Murder* (1954). More likely, complaints by filmmakers, exhibitors and filmgoers together doomed the technology. Exhibitors, in particular, found the images too dark, the glasses too expensive, and sightlines for optimal viewing too limited within the theatrical spaces.

In the current era of digital projection, 3D has experienced a significant revival, though some of the concerns about the technology still linger. The renewed interest in 3D began at amusement parks and in IMAX venues. *Captain EO* (1986), starring Michael Jackson, premiered at Disney theme parks in the mid-1980s, while *Terminator 2 3-D: Battle Across Time* (1996) debuted at Universal Studies a decade later, combining a live-action stage show with 3D projected images. The success of these 3D presentations led to its migration into IMAX theatres with short documentary films such as *Ghosts of the Abyss 3D* (2003), *Deep Sea 3D* (2006) and *Under the Sea 3D* (2009). The technique made the leap into mainstream filmmaking in conjunction with the IMAX format. In November 2004, approximately 25 per cent of the overall box-office receipts for the film *Polar Express* (2004) came from these mixed-format venues. As exhibitors began to refit theatres with digital projection systems, 3D systems were easily integrated into the technology chain, and with the 3D format came the potential for theatre owners to assess surcharges to filmgoers for this 'added value'. Currently, there are a number of competing 3D systems in the marketplace, including Dolby 3D, IMAX 3D, MasterImage 3D, Real D 3D, as well as a host of other systems in development, some of which do not require the use of special glasses.

The integration of 3D exhibition into contemporary cinema is by no means assured. Critics have noted continued problems with line of sight, murky and dark images, and simulation sickness, a kind of motion sickness that plagues some filmgoers. Also, some studios are converting films that were not shot or conceived in 3D and rushing them into the marketplace in order to gather the lucrative surcharges. *Clash of the Titans* (2010) was one such 3D film that suffered from murky images and unreadable action sequences due to the effects of conversion. Countering these criticisms, however, is that fact that new generations of filmgoers, under the age of eighteen, are learning to read the 3D visual poetic not just in the theatre spaces, but also on the screens of their gaming systems. It is perhaps these filmgoers who will set the new expectations for 3D technology, which may only be an intermediate step toward virtual environments and interactive narratives. The film *Avatar* (2009), which is the subject of the case study for this section, is perhaps a glimpse of the stereoscopic future that cinema has to offer.

☐ CASE STUDY 3: *AVATAR* (2009)

'I see you', Neytiri (Zoë Saldana) tells Jake Sully (Sam Worthington) in the science fiction epic *Avatar*, which is set on the lush planet of Pandora. During the course of the film, Sully, a young disabled marine, inhabits an avatar body in the form of an indigenous Na'Vi with the mission to infiltrate and seek the relocation of a Na'Vi tribe from their 'home tree'. A mining company seeking precious minerals beneath the surface of the planet drives this goal. The story becomes one of invasion, occupation and genocide; but the balance of power shifts when Sully begins to 'see' his mistake. In terms of narrative and design, then, the film is about seeing. It is about seeing these landscapes for their beauty, and the inner landscapes of body and soul for their interconnection to each other. Through the use of CGI and 3D technology, the film presents simulated locations such as floating mountains, thick forests and saturated horizons that embrace photorealism in their design and execution. Filmmaker James

• **Plate 2.10**
Avatar (James Cameron, 2009). In a film about perception, Neytiri (Zoë Saldana) tells Jake Sully (Sam Worthington): 'I see you.'

• **Plate 2.11**
Avatar (James Cameron, 2009). Jake Sully in his 'avatar' body in the science fiction epic Avatar.

Cameron and his team developed a web of interrelated technologies to make the 3D filming possible. Using over 140 digital cameras, including head-mounted cameras, the performances of the actors were 'captured' in various networked computers. These digitised performances provided the emotive and physical scaffolding for the virtual characters of the Na'Vi. The filmmakers used an integrated computer and monitoring system that allowed them to review the virtual characters within the context of the background designs. Using various tricks of perception, Cameron adjusted the scale of images in the foreground, middle ground and background to accentuate the dimensions of the locales, and to focus the filmgoers' eyes on specific planes of action. In this way, the eye tracks the image according to these compositions in depth, into the screen rather than outward. The real power of 3D in this instance is its ability to provide a window into the world of Pandora. This process is aided by the multi-channel sound design, particularly the mix of sound levels and localised placement of sound, which draw attention to specific actions in and around the visual field. The success of the system is measured not only in the visual design of the film, but also in the economics of the box-office returns. At this time *Avatar* is the highest grossing blockbuster film to date.

• **Plate 2.12**
Avatar (James Cameron, 2009). 3D imaging maps the planes of action in the foreground, mid-ground, and background.

• **Plate 2.13**
Avatar (James Cameron, 2009). 3D accentuates movements from right to left across the visual field.

CONCLUSION

Cinema technology continues to change with new developments in the fields of engineering, computing, audio, optics and architecture. When thinking about new technology and the subsequent changes to film form, it is important to consider the complex convergence of factors such as economics, industrial practices, history, patterns of adoption and cultural reception that shape the cinematic experience in and outside the theatre.

SUMMARY

- The phases of invention, innovation, diffusion and update.
- Theories of technology and how they overlap and potentially contradict one another.
- The interplay of graphic technologies and how they transform the visual field.
- The continued development of audio technologies from recording devices to repro-duction devices and formats, and how they create new immersive qualities.

■   The dimensions of the screen space and how new technologies continue to pull our eyes and ears from the 2D plane into a 3D experience that mimics our perceptions in everyday life and directs us towards new understandings of cinematic form.

QUESTIONS FOR DISCUSSION

1   How have computer generated images shaped our expectations for the blockbuster?
2   In what ways does *District 9* affirm these expectations and challenge them?
3   What role does computer graphics technology play in this process?
4   Some historians argue that sound and music are simply married to the image to create a 'realistic' effect. How does multichannel technology challenge this assumption?
5   In what ways does sound design in conjunction with sound technology create cinematic spectacle?
6   In what other ways do sound and sound technology create inner and outer space in *Star Trek* (2009)?
7   How does the immersive quality of 3D in *Avatar* change storytelling?
8   Will immersive technologies like 3D and multichannel sound become the new standard for all science fiction blockbusters? Why or why not?
9   How does the film challenge the idea of technological determinism? What are the contradictions that film presents in regard to technology?

NOTES

1   In May 1948, the US Supreme Court handed down its decision in the antitrust lawsuit against the major Hollywood studios. The resolution of the case ended distribution practices of 'blind' and 'block' booking, which had forced exhibitors to take blocks of films, often without viewing them. As a result, studios divested theatres over the next decade.
2   Magnetic tape became the standard for on-set recording and postproduction mixing during this period in part because the medium was reusable. The technology also led to a host of portable recording devices, which further advanced the gathering of raw effects that could be combined later in the editing room. Magnetic tape was one of the foundational technologies that led to the rise of the sound design movement.

FURTHER READING

Allen, R. and Gomery, D., *Film History: Theory and Practice*, Alfred A. Knopf, New York, 1985. This text presents a foundational overview of historical and critical approaches to cinema.

Belton, J., '1950s Magnetic Sound: The Frozen Revolution', in Rick Altman (ed.), *Sound Theory Sound Practice*, Routledge, New York, 1992. A key article on the rise and *stall* of magnetic sound.

Belton, J., *Widescreen Cinema*, Harvard University Press, Cambridge, MA, 1992.

Belton, J., 'Digital Cinema: A False Revolution', in Leo Braudy and Marshall Cohen (eds), *Film Theory and Criticism*, Oxford University Press, New York, 2004. A critical consideration of the often over-used term 'revolution' in relation to new technology.

Blake, L. (ed.), *Film Sound Today*, Reveille Press, Hollywood, 1984. Historical overview of sound processes.

Holman, T., *5.1 Surround Sound: Up and Running*, Focal Press, Los Angeles, 2000. Written by *the* scientist of film sound.

Jenkins, H., *Convergence Culture: Where Old and New Media Collide*, New York University Press, New York, 2006.

King, G., 'Spectacle, Narrative and the Spectacular Hollywood Blockbuster', in Julian Stringer (ed.), *Movie Blockbuster*, Routledge, London, 2003. Critical review of major considerations of film in the blockbuster era.

Kunkes, M., 'Sound Trek: The Audio Explorations of Ben Burtt', *Editors Guild Magazine*, 30, 3, 2009, http://www.editorsguild.com/Magazine.cfm?ArticleID=721 (accessed 3 September 2010). Interview with the sound designer of *Star Wars*, and now the new *Star Trek* film.

Pierson, M., 'Welcome to Basementwood: Computer Generated Special Effects and *Wired* Magazine', *Postmodern Culture*, 8, 3, 1998, http://muse.jhu.edu/journals/postmodern_culture/v008/8.3pierson.html (accessed 4 March 2009).

Pierson, M., *Special Effects: Still in Search of Wonder*, Columbia University Press, New York, 2002. A critical analysis of how popular science magazines have defined our understanding of film technology.

Schatz, T., 'The New Hollywood', in Jim Collins, Hilary Radner and Ava Preacher Collins (eds), *Film Theory Goes to the Movies*, Routledge, New York, 1993.

Taub, Eric, 'Digital Projection of Films is Coming. Now, Who Pays?', *The New York Times*, Media and Advertising, 13 October 2003, http://www.nytimes.com/10/13/business/media/13projector.html?pagewanted=1 (accessed 28 August 2010).

Whittington, W., *Sound Design and Science Fiction*, University of Texas Press, Austin, 2007. An overview of the rise of sound design in the era of multichannel technology.

Zone, Ray, *Stereoscopic Cinema & the Origins of 3-D Film*, University Press of Kentucky, Lexington, 2007.

FURTHER VIEWING

Computer graphics

300 (2006) (Dir.: Zack Snyder)
The Abyss (1989) (Dir.: James Cameron)
Jurassic Park (1993) (Dir.: Steven Spielberg)
The Matrix (1999) (Dirs: Andy Wachowski and Larry Wachowski)
Terminator 2: Judgment Day (1991) (Dir.: James Cameron)
Toy Story (1995) (Dir.: John Lasseter)
Watchman (2009) (Dir.: Zack Snyder)

Multichannel sound

Amélie (2001) (Dir.: Jean-Pierre Jeunet)
Apocalypse Now (1979) (Dir.: Francis Ford Coppola)
The Dark Knight (2008) (Dir.: Christopher Nolan)
Exorcist (1973) (Dir.: William Friedkin)
Fight Club (1999) (Dir.: David Fincher)
Master and Commander: The Far Side of the World (2003) (Dir.: Peter Weir)
Saving Private Ryan (1998) (Dir.: Steven Spielberg)
Star Wars: A New Hope (1977) (Dir.: George Lucas)
Terminator 2: Judgment Day (1991) (Dir.: James Cameron)

3D

Cave of Forgotten Dreams (2010) (Dir.: Werner Herzog)

Clash of the Titans (2010) (Dir.: Louis Leterrier)
Creature from the Black Lagoon (1954) (Dir.: Jack Arnold)
Dial M for Murder (1954) (Dir.: Alfred Hitchcock)
Harry Potter and the Deathly Hallows Part 1, Part 2 (2010–11) (Dir.: David Yates)
Piranha 3D (2010) (Dir.: Alexandre Aja)
Superman Returns (2008) (Dir.: Bryan Singer)
Toy Story 3 (2010) (Dir.: Lee Unkrich)
Under the Sea 3D (2009) (Dir.: Howard Hall)

Resource centres

http://www.theasc.com/ac_magazine/podcasts.php
American Cinematographer Podcasts.

http://www.filmsound.org
Comprehensive site devoted to sound and sound design.

http://www.dolby.com
Corporate website.

http://www.cinefex.com
Premier effects publication with historical and practical entries.

■ Before getting to the bigger picture

INTRODUCTION: CHANGING APPROACHES TO FILM

Film studies finds itself at a crossroads. A future film studies may necessarily be very different as it comes to terms with challenges presented by new modes of production, distribution and exhibition and by new forms of audience behaviour in an increasingly interactive, highly unpredictable cultural space. This is not to say that film studies as now constituted is yet quite redundant. The many forms of textual analysis that film studies uses in order to describe how a film works and what it might mean, together with the significance of that meaning, remain robust – and examples of these will follow later in this book. The aesthetic and philosophical preoccupations of the subject continue to give distinctiveness while film history is flourishing, especially as a 'canonical' version of film history is challenged by scholars not content with the way that a certain narrative of key dates, key people, key films and key film movements has become fixed. One of the principal drives behind this refreshing of film history is the amount of historical film material that has become available through archives and restoration work.

Indeed, one of the very great advances for film studies, coinciding with the internet, is the increasing availability of film material held in archives. Not only has this rich mine of material helped to challenge a more traditional film history, but it has also allowed film studies to ask some of its oldest questions all over again, like: what is a film, what is distinctive about our relationship to film material, how do we use it both in our mental and emotional lives? Archives around the world are seeking funding to digitise their collections, both for preservation purposes and in order to make the material more accessible. A number of important archives have made available online a proportion of their digitised holdings.[1] These have proved enormously popular.[2] Some film archives have created YouTube channels, including the British Film Institute which has responsibility for the UK's National Film Archive. It is on a short film from the National Film Archive found on YouTube that this chapter will focus much attention.

This film, *Springtime in an English Village* (1944), is likely to be accessed on a small screen, possibly the very small screen of a mobile device. This immediately raises a question about what we mean today when we use the term 'film studies'. Distinctions between film studies and media studies, between film studies and television studies are sometimes difficult to make, as all are forms of a broader category: moving image work. 'Screen studies' may seem more appropriate.

At the time of writing (early 2011) much of our casual viewing is on the video-sharing website YouTube. YouTube exceeds two billion views per day and 24 hours of video material is uploaded every minute. This viewing may occur within what we call communities of interest, people connecting with one another because of shared interests and tastes. For example, 46.2 years of video are accessed each day just on the social network site Facebook.[3] This is a site that offers a totally serendipitous, very personal approach to finding, viewing and responding to this material. We can bring into association the most unusual combinations of ideas, forms and experiences – collapsing distinctions between genres, between factual and fictional, between historical and contemporary material and between 'film' and 'television'. Of course, you could describe YouTube, in its own crazily proliferating way, as a film archive, though it would be reasonable to expect an archive to enjoy some scholarly intervention to give shape and order to the material.

The great melting pot of digital moving images, represented not just by YouTube but by many other online sites, cannot be ignored by film studies – it is too rich a resource. Yet in order to retain distinctiveness it could be argued that film studies should retreat to the cinema[4] and the cinema experience: when we enter a communal space and sit in darkness intently watching a narrative fictional feature-length film, exhibited to very high technical standards in terms of both image and sound quality. It is also tempting to confirm the normative understanding of 'film' as a feature-length narrative-based moving image work which is distinguished usually by its production values, budget, level of ambition, by its cultural status as an object that receives significant critical and popular attention, and by assumptions as to its optimum mode of presentation: in a cinema where we gather collectively as an audience but engage with the individual intensity of the film spectator. Some argue that the popularity of blockbuster 'event' cinema in particular will continue as audiences seek out an increasingly distinct experience from our consumption of moving images in the home and on portable devices. But this argument in itself is driven by an awareness of how the moving image landscape has changed and is continuing to change out of all recognition to what it was when film studies established itself as an academic discipline between the 1970s and the 1990s.

A 'film' is not something of any definable length and is unlikely to have been made on film stock if made in the last ten years. It is, as we have already established, likely to be seen in any one of a wide variety of viewing situations. A new kind of cinephilia (love of films) is developing, one that is based precisely on the interaction of big screen and small screen behaviours and pleasures. For example, in developing a community of interest, a group of like-minded people meeting online can explore and add to a collection of moving image work, using that work to trigger both idiosyncratic personal programming and to upload their own material, possibly video production work of their own or remixing found material. This audience-led, interactive, promiscuous and creative approach to film material is the very opposite of the model we associate with traditional film/cinema in which the industry dominates and the audience function as consumers in relation to a controlled and institutionalised experience. Film studies will follow the interesting material wherever it is exhibited – and in so doing will have to take on board the 'contamination' that is inevitable as films are touched by the vast array of cyber-activity that goes on around them. For example, a short film uploaded on YouTube may generate a very large number of comments, some of which may significantly alter the perception of the film. The film may be appropriated, placed in a very different context or, more radically, the images may be re-cut, the sound re-mixed.

This chapter explores some of the possibilities for film studies opened up by the opportunities for accessing material through advances in digital media. It also considers some of the limits of film studies and how we might explore beyond these limits. For example, after we have conducted a study using critical procedures and formulated a series of statements about a film, we may yet feel a frustration, a sense that there is more to be said. The chapter turns to look at specific qualities of film that are hard to pin down. It does so by reference to the photographic image and the relationship between the still image and the moving image. The idea is raised of a certain quality of film, a strangeness and a beauty in moving images that seems in excess of the film's apparent meaning, purpose and effect.

The way an image links past and present time is emphasised throughout the chapter and leads to some specific reflections on time and the different experiences of time that film can highlight. Finally, the chapter touches on some ideas about cinematic memory, particularly the way we recall and value these qualities and moments in a film that escape easy discussion and explanation.

A SHORT FILM ON YOUTUBE

I first saw the six-and-a-half-minute 1944 film *Springtime in an English Village* while visiting the mediatheque at the British Film Institute's Southbank Centre in London.[5] This mediatheque makes available nearly 2,000 films and TV programmes from the National Film Archive which are accessed via computer and headphones in a specialist viewing area. In addition, since 2007 the BFI has had a YouTube channel which makes available a proportion of the material from the mediatheque. The film student's access to this and equivalent resources from other archives, either in drop-in or remote-access form, is a very significant development in the subject area.

Springtime in an English Village is now no longer to be found on the BFI YouTube channel but it remains on YouTube at http://www.youtube.com/watch?v=6QbHhm4620I[6] and it would be most useful to watch the film before continuing with this chapter.

Springtime in an English Village is not a complex film. It has a three-part structure: just over a minute of shots establishing a rural location; over three-and-a-half minutes of shots relating to a village school and the children lining up in the playground while one child appears to be selected for a special honour; and finally just less than two minutes presenting the May Queen, the child selected in the playground, leaving the village church and being crowned. Cinematography and editing are unfussy, the result of a professional practice common to so many short documentary films made during the Second World War by the Ministry of Information. The primary objective is to provide a clear visual presentation of its subject rather than to aspire to some artistic quality. There is no dialogue; the film is shot silent, with a soundtrack of orchestral music including variations on popular English tunes.[7] There are forty-five shots over 6 minutes and 22 seconds of material (excluding opening titles and close). There is a rather leisurely average shot length of 8.5 seconds. This further highlights the extent to which the momentum of the film is in the soundtrack, together with shot composition and movement within the image.

The visual content of the film is, however, in some ways very surprising. The logo at the beginning is that of the 'Colonial Film Unit' with the added initials 'MoI' (Ministry of Information).[8] This alerts us to the purpose of this film – as propaganda, specifically for screening around the British Empire in, for example, Africa, South Asia and the West Indies. This propaganda may have several objectives and we will come back to these later.

However, having been alerted to this propagandist intent, we then are presented with a montage of shots of rural England – shots that may not have been filmed specifically for this film but have been taken from a library of stock material. The image presented of rural England is of a place that is fertile, secure, well ordered – and remember that these images are assembled in the context of the Second World War raging.[9] With shots 9 to 11 there is an increasing sense of activity, as ducks move rapidly from left to right across the farmyard to a pond. This is an England which is both solid, and a delight, a perfect balance of harmony and energy. Shot 12 offers a continuation of this idea as two lively young calves buck their way across a field.

And then quite unexpectedly shot 13 is of two girls running – the shot is an approximate match on action with shot 12 as they, like the two calves, run with a youthful energy across the screen. They are running towards a village school with the church immediately behind and a Union flag flying prominently. This cut is itself a little startling as it breaks the rural montage, but what is very surprising is that, even in long shot and running away from the camera position, it is clear that these two girls are black.

In what follows it is tempting to think that the director is deliberately teasing the audience. For over a minute of screen time we do not catch another glimpse of the two girls who opened this second section of the film. The playground is occupied by white children and their teacher. Then in long shot we spot both of them getting into line, not differentiated by the camera from the other children. After another close up on the teacher, we see one of the two girls, the one standing towards the front of the line, in a closer shot.

As this is a film without dialogue the audience is required to guess what the teacher is saying to the children as they are lined up in front of her. The teacher starts clapping and in the next shot we see the children clapping, including the black girl near the front of the line. In a wider shot we see all the children and at 03.20 the black girl at the back of the line steps forward and walks toward the teacher. It is clearly she who has been presented with some award or honour. In the next shot she is the unambiguous subject of the camera: occupying the whole frame, she smiles and curtsies.

After an establishing shot of school, church and flag, the final part of the film begins with a 27-second shot of a procession leaving the church. The children walk towards the camera and then move off right. The black girl selected in the playground now appears as the May Queen, regaled in white. The other black girl is towards the rear of the procession, again not obviously differentiated from the other children, except that as she passes the camera she seems rather self-consciously aware of it. They procession moves toward a group of adults with children sitting on the grass in front of them. The May Queen is crowned and she takes up her throne in front of the assembly of adults and children. Others in the procession flank her including the other black girl. Then we are presented with a medium close-up of the May Queen with her crown and bouquet, followed by a wider shot in which she and the girls around her appear to be singing. At this point the film ends.

Two related questions require answering: what does this film mean and what is it for? The Colonial Film Unit had as a general objective to communicate a positive vision of the United Kingdom as the 'motherland' and to do so by providing images that reinforced a broader set of ideological messages communicated throughout the empire about the primacy of the UK's political, religious, educational and civic institutions. Beyond this there was the need to give colonial subjects the opportunity to imagine this motherland – to see it in the mind's eye as wholly admirable. By 1944 there was a more particular need: the motherland required labour to help with the war effort and possibly in anticipation of shortages in the post war reconstruction economy. To present an idyllic image of rural England, together with the village school and village church, was standard fare, but to present this rural world as one where black children could live harmoniously, totally integrated into the local community and with equal opportunity to be selected for a quintessentially English role (as May Queen) was clearly to go much further.

The journal *Colonial Cinema* included in its June 1944 edition an article called 'African Girl as May Queen'. It stated that 'Among the children sent to Stanion, a small village in Northamptonshire were the two daughters of an African seaman in the Merchant Navy. The foster parents of these two children sent them to attend the village school.'[10] The same article says that 'a story like this was too good for the unit to miss' and 'The result is an extremely pretty little film which we think will have an appeal, not only in Africa, but also in the whole Colonial Empire.'

Research in Stanion revealed that the two girls – twins – Stephanie and Connie Antia had been evacuated from London when they were four. They continued to live in the village till they were teenagers. Stephanie's friend recalled years later that 'We didn't know what propaganda was but they told us the film was made to be shown in African countries to show that we British were not a dreadful race of people.'[11]

Inevitably the appearance of the film on YouTube increased considerably the amount of information about the film. For example, the daughter of Stephanie (the May Queen) came across the film at home in the USA and this prompted her to visit England and find out more about her mother's childhood. Here is a contribution from one of the girls in the film who still lives in the village of Stanion:

MsJoy15 I am in this film, the fidgety one with a bow in her hair, standing behind the black twin called Connie, Stephanie the Mayqueen was my best friend at school, we were reunited 3 yrs ago by her daughter, lots of our memories have been published, and yes we all voted for her to be the Mayqueen, the school children still hold this festival in the village, its a wonderful place to live and I for one are thankful to enjoy it.[12]

This kind of direct participation by ordinary people in the creation of knowledge is now very familiar to us – but we should remember how very recently this practice has become established. Critical comments on the film show a wide variety of responses, including some that are highly engaged with ongoing debates about race and representation, suggesting that this film is seen as some quaint old curiosity and no more. Indeed, some of these comments, stated very frankly and crudely, highlight how understated *Springtime in an English Village* is as propaganda, delighting and surprising the audience rather than conveying a heavy-handed message. And the film is not so unsophisticated, especially in the way its surprises are created – from the first appearance of the twins through to the full pomp of the May Queen procession.

For further discussion of race and representation, see Chapter 13.

The above analysis and discussion illustrate some of the variety of tools that film studies brings to the table, enabling us better to understand and appreciate even a very short and simple film such as *Springtime in an English Village*. In summary, the above has applied, however briefly, the following procedures of film studies:

- A study of the film's provenance (its original production context and its present site of exhibition).
- A study of the film's form, structure and style.
- A study of the film's meaning and significance by means of: (1) textual study and (2) contextual study, the latter the result of research.
- A study of contemporary responses, in this case made possible through the large number of YouTube and other online comments.

If we stop at this point, we may feel that a lot has been said. Yet there may be a lingering thought that something fundamental in the film or in our response to the film has been left untouched by our analysis. This has to do with a particular kind of impact the film has as a set of moving images of the past, and a certain strangeness and beauty contained in these images. In order to take this further, it is necessary to move from something small (a six-and-a-half-minute film) to something smaller (the film sequence) by way of something smaller still (the single image).

THE STILL AND THE MOVING IMAGE

When we pull an old photograph out of a box we are aware of a number of things. In front of us is an image from the past. The people in it will have grown older; they may have died. The landscape or cityscape may have changed out of all recognition. The photograph provides a document, a visual representation. As such it is interesting, like written documents from the past, for the information it contains. As we look at this photo-graph, this document from the past, we may begin to realise that it offers us much more than information: it provides us with an imaginative connection between ourselves in the present and the past time of the photo, a bridge between then and now which makes the past present. There is something amazing about this 'presence' of an image, something that goes beyond description and analysis of form, meaning and significance. On the one hand we are aware of the interconnection of image and its vast array of contexts. On the other we become increasingly aware of the photo as having its own independent existence. The photo exists as itself, in its own right.

The process of photography has long been associated with a ghostly quality, especially in the pre-digital age. The result of a timed exposure, light reflected from an object forms an image on film. Through the chemical developing process this image emerges from negative to positive print.[13] The ghostly reality of the photographic image is something we will return to.

Another commonly referred to quality of the photo is its ability not only to capture the real (again the idea that photographic process includes the 'ghostly' imprint) but to present the real in such a way that we see things differently, often with increased perception of the qualities possessed by the object photographed. In this respect the photograph shares a quality with other visual forms of representation that artistically revisualise the object, often an object that is very familiar and commonplace. For example, we may pass a street corner with shop and post box and bus stop every day of our lives. We then see a beautifully composed photographic image of that street corner, let's say with the added quality of it being presented in a picture frame and hanging on a wall in the local library. A form of transformation has taken place in which the familiar becomes defamiliarised[14] – and the result is that we may see with fresh eyes and new insight. Indeed, it can be said that we make images in order to enable us to see things in the real world more fully.[15]

Exercise

1   From a collection of old photographs select one that catches your interest. Reflect on the different ideas and emotions you experience when you look at the photo.

2   Select a contemporary image that has some significance for you. In what ways does this image allow you to see more and think more fully about the 'real' person or place represented?

These two characteristics of the photograph – its ghostliness and its capacity to defamiliarise – are ones that we will return to. Perhaps what needs to be acknowledged at this stage is that to study a photo, a still image, is something we can do at our leisure and at length. The moving image of film (most commonly 24/25 still images per second – in contemporary projection) prevents us from enjoying the same contemplative viewing opportunity provided by the still image. There is an old joke about how a teacher of art history spends an hour with her class looking at the slide projection of a single painting while the film teacher comes by and quips that in her class they deal with 24 of those images every second. In fact there is much more to be said about the difference between still and moving image than its availability for close scrutiny.

The moving image is different in that there are other images either side which locate it within time, within a before and after.[16] For example, a popular mainstream narrative film is based on movement in time, sometimes presented quite literally with a clock ticking down as a deadline approaches and suspense intensifies. When we pause a film, we break the causal link between the previous and the following image. At this point the image is freed from its containment within time and becomes a still image, a moment that can exist out of time.[17]

While the film student may find it useful to pause a film and take stock by close scrutiny of a particular and perhaps significant image, the transformation of a moving image into a still image may seem an odd thing to do. However, as well as being better able to put aspects of cinematography and mise-en-scène under the microscope, our ability to pause a film allows us to enter into a different relationship to the film, one in which we shift our attention from narrative, movement and time to presence.

It is useful at this point to think more about the relationship between still images and moving images and the particular qualities of each. Let is consider briefly three different film examples:

The American filmmaker Ken Burns has produced several highly successful documentaries on historical subjects, including *The American Civil War* (1991) and *The West* (1996). Central to his work is the simple and common technique of zooming in, out and panning across photographs, thus giving the impression of a certain kind of movement. These 'animated' photographs provide us with a strange hybrid experience. As still images they provide powerful visual documentation; as moving images heavily mediated by voice-over commentary, they support the historical narrative drive of the work as a whole. Repeatedly Burns offers the viewer the apparent opportunity to engage in the (ghostly) presence of these images that exist in an in-between state: they are still but moving and their impact comes from a sense of dramatic life being breathed into them which only increases the melancholy and sense of loss they contain. Elements within the still images begin to form new relationships with one another and with the wider narrative to which they bear witness and support. The word 'animate' may seem appropriate – but so does the word 'animism',[18] the idea that these objects have some essence, some inner quality magically brought to life.

In 1940 John Ford made a film version of John Steinbeck's novel *The Grapes of Wrath*. This film tells the story of poor farmers ('Oakies') migrating in the mid-1930s from the Oklahoma Dust Bowl to California in search of the promised land. The film visualises the novel by constructing moving images that are based on the now famous still photographs taken as part of the Farm Security Administration (FSA) project begun in 1935 and documenting the lives of the rural poor.[19] *The Grapes of Wrath* invokes these images in order to give the film a high degree of historical accuracy (verisimilitude). In addition, the film's cinematography,[20] created by the great Gregg Toland, transformed the work of the FSA photographers by producing moving image equivalents, moments of heightened intensity and beauty within the film. Like the work of Ken Burns, we here have a dramatising process which brings a sense not just of external physical movement but of a kind of inner movement too.

In 2003 Lars Von Trier made a film set in the same period as *The Grapes of Wrath* about a poor white community. Von Trier's three-hour *Dogville* is filmed entirely on a sound stage in which there is no attempt to create a realistic set. In fact there is no conventional scenery with walls of buildings indicated by masking tape as in a rehearsal studio. The brilliant move by Von Trier is to show the audience how much they contribute to the realism of the film by projecting their own imagination. In the final credit sequence we experience what may seem like the reverse of the experience presented by *The Grapes of Wrath*. After the work of imagining and projecting on to the film much of the mise-en-scène, the audience is presented with a long sequence of very vivid still photos documenting the poor, mainly taken in the 1930s and including some by the FSA photographers who inspired Ford's imagery in *The Grapes of Wrath*.[21] Accompanied by David Bowie's song 'Young Americans', each photo emphasises a strong sense of its own, often confrontational, presence. These images are animated by the energy that the audience has brought to the previous three hours and which continues to flow in and through these photos out of the cinema.

The French film critic and theorist Jacques Rancière distinguishes in his *Film Fables* between two kinds of art experience. One he calls the 'poetics of action and repre-sentation', which is, for example, the basis of film storytelling. The other he calls the 'poetics of presence' and it refers to the possibility of the whole of some phenomenon or experience being contained in a single image 'statement'. In each of the above examples

• Plate 3.1
The Grapes of Wrath (John Ford, 1940)

• Plate 3.2
Once a Missouri farmer, now a migratory farm labourer on the Pacific Coast, California

there is a very interesting interplay between action/representation on the one hand and presence on the other. Rancière writes:

Cinema, the predominantly modern art, experiences more than any other art the conflict of these two poetics, though it is, by the same token, the art that most attempts to combine them. Cinema is the combination of the gaze of the artist who decides and the mechanical gaze that records, of constructed images and chance images.

(Rancière 2006: 74)

Film studies often seems very much led by Rancière's poetics of action/representation, perhaps because there are many more agreed things that can be said about a film at this level. We are also much more comfortable with the idea of intentionality, of a filmmaker and collaborators working consciously and deliberately to construct narrative and manage the film's meaning and emotional impact. By contrast film studies can shirk away from what Rancière calls the poetics of presence – the way the image impacts on us in multiple and often very personal ways. So the meaning and purpose of a film can often dominate discussion and analysis in film studies, but the consequences of 'chance' produced by the 'mechanical gaze' may be left untouched.

A well-known example of the fascination with 'chance' movement from very early cinema is the 40-second Lumière Brothers' film of 1895, *Le Repas de Bébé* (http://www.youtube.com/watch?v=s8nZesAxyeA). As parents feed their baby in the garden, the interest may appear to be focused on the three human figures. However, reports suggest that the first audiences for this were most taken by the bushes rustling in the background in a strong breeze. While audiences were well used to watching human figures perform roles in a theatre space, they were unused to the background moving. Odd as it may seem to us, this was the great confirmation that the new invention of film had something going for it. The mechanical gaze captures movement unintentionally, as if by chance, and as a result the medium of film is alive with the promise of allowing us to see with fresh eyes, to see differently and to see what might otherwise have remained invisible.

For a further discussion of Mitchell and Kenyon films, see Chapter 14.

Exercise

Let us go back to the BFI channel on YouTube. A number of short films from the vast Mitchell and Kenyon collection are included. Mitchell and Kenyon travelled around the cities and towns of Northern England in the early 1900s, filming scenes of everyday life. They screened the films that very evening or the next in a cinema of attractions[22] where people could see themselves on screen. The camera mounted on a tripod does not move. Like the earliest moving images of the Lumière Brothers in France, movement is within the static frame, usually right and left but sometimes towards the camera and out of the bottom of the frame. This is very simple material, but as well as having proved extraordinarily rich as a resource for social historians, these films have been recognised for other qualities.

A typical example is *Preston Egg Rolling* from 1901, a 2-minute, 42-second film. It can be found at http://www.youtube.com/user/BFIfilms#p/search/23/n0tOv47Iyic. These events filmed on Easter Monday in a public park have an element of orchestration about them, but what strikes us most strongly is the 'chance' image captured by the mechanical apparatus of the camera. The fixed camera records movement but many of the people filmed stand still, pose looking straight at the camera and respond to the new technology as if having their still photographs taken.

What is your response to these images? You may wish to reflect on the idea of cinematic 'presence'. You may wish to think about the power old moving images have to communicate with us in the present.

Or let us take a second example: *Miners Leaving Pendlebury Colliery* from 1901. It can be found at http://www.youtube.com/user/BFIfilms#p/c/F3E52E5E9162CCE1/2/FFKyrUXmCMk. This is a stock subject of very early cinema: workers leaving their place of employment and passing in front of the camera.[23]

Exercise

Create a series of still images from the film using the pause facility and reflect on their qualities both as social documents and as images of presence. (Thinking historically, there is a particular and striking face in the crowd – which links this film to *Springtime in an English Village*.) Contrast the experience of looking at these still images and looking at the film as a whole as a continuous moving image.

In the discussion of *Springtime in an English Village* it was suggested that there may be a lingering sense that all had not been said about the film and its impact. Wherever we pause the film, we reconstruct a still image that makes up one of the twenty-four passing through a film projector each second. This may seem to be a very artificial and unrealistic thing to do, but it allows us to reflect on the power the film gains from its photography. However, the fundamental unit of the film is not the still image but the shot, including its duration: that is, movement in time. So a 10-second shot, made up of over 200 still images in traditional film terms allows us the opportunity to observe movement, even if it is just a leaf swaying in a breeze. It can be said that there is something fascinating and something melancholic about the pastness of photographs that we look at in the present. Fascinating in that we have vividly presented to us a world that no longer exists in quite the same way. Melancholic because, in being aware of time past, we are confronted with mortality, the passing, death of those represented. This is even more true of the shot, especially as we consider those elements that are not a conscious part of the representation, the chance elements caught by the camera but only 'seen' in later projection, aspects of material reality only the camera was able to see. Again we are reminded of the ghostliness of the image.[24]

Now it may be argued that this kind of argument may be relevant to the study of 'actuality', documentary material, but is surely less relevant to fictional film. But are the two forms so different? Jean-Luc Godard remarked that all films are documentaries and a fiction film is a documentary of actors in performance (and to some degree a documentary of the places and cultures within which the narrative is located). To extend this we might say that every film is a tension between its premeditated and contrived aspects and its chance encounters with the real.[25] *Springtime in an English Village* is a documentary and it is a fiction, perhaps one can say it is a documentary of a fiction. It is safe to say that the world it documents is not indicative of England in 1944.

Gilberto Perez writes eloquently about the tensions between the apparently different forms:

Every film is in some way poised between the documentary and fictional aspects of its medium, between the documentary image the camera captures and the fiction projected on screen. The films that stress their documentary aspect are especially called upon to deal with the problem of fiction, of negotiating the uncertain frontier where documentary and fiction meet. Between documentary and fiction, camera and projector, index and icon, absence and presence, past and present, narrative and drama, material and ghost, the film medium seeks its poise.

(Perez 1998: 49)[26]

Exercise

Take three shots from *Springtime in an English Village* and reflect on each in relation to the quotation from Perez above:

Shot 13   01.47–01.57
Shot 23   03.25–03.33
Shot 31   04.56–05.07
Shot 45   06.25–06.40

Use these shots – and others of your choice – to explore any qualities of the moving image which may help to explain the way this short film 'exceeds' its subject – offers us something more and different from what we might reasonably assume was intended.

TRYING TO NAME A CERTAIN QUALITY IN FILM

A number of filmmakers, theorists and philosophers besides Rancière have at different points in film history tried to account for qualities within the film image that exceed their practical narrative and representational functions. Some, like Rancière, tend to put a particular emphasis on 'presence' and qualities of the photographic image. Terms like 'ghostliness' and 'defamiliarisation' have already been used in the previous section and can be found to recur directly or indirectly in the writings of those who have tried to account for the 'excess' contained within film. Paul Coughlin defines these as 'sublime moments' which he describes as:

that indefinable moment in modern life or art when sensation consumes the spectator with an overwhelming and indescribably profound intensity. The overriding effect of this experience is the inability to verbalise or rationalise the encounter with any certitude. The sublime moment is individual, personal, and subjective, suggesting that it cannot be defined absolutely or resolved conclusively.[27]

One of many ways of trying to put into words this idea of the sublime moment in film was by reference to the concept of photogénie which began to be used in France in the mid-1920s and is a term particularly associated with the avant-garde filmmaker and theorist Jean Epstein. It is sometimes thought that the term refers to some magical transference, a literal adaptation of the idea of the 'ghostly' medium in which material not visible to the naked eye makes an imprint on exposed film stock. Neither here nor elsewhere should we consider the use of 'ghostly' or 'uncanny' as more than a metaphorical way of speaking about film – it is not being proposed here that film is a mechanically mediated séance experience!

What Epstein and others were actually referring to was a broadly based attitude toward the medium, one that rejected narrative as the central function of film.[28] As Robert Farmer says, photogénie is best understood as 'either an approach to filmmaking, or it is a way of thinking about film. It is perceptible in the filmmaker's attitude towards the medium, and our understanding of the medium.'[29] That attitude, that understanding, is one based on the idea of the film medium as strange, as capable of the extraordinary – and it is an approach that encourages experimentation with the technologies of film to discover more of the possibilities of a medium, which already by the mid-1920s was locked into a particular conception of the 'movie' by commercial film practice, especially that developed in Hollywood. Epstein was fascinated with movement within the shot, especially in the close-up, where small details become visible creating a particular kind of visual drama. For example, in the close-up of a human face the smallest details of movement may be caught on camera. These capture not just aspects of body language which may be reducible to meaning, but aspects of energy and the movement of light, of qualities that require some kind of 'enhancement' through the transformative gaze of the camera. In the process they become more beautiful, more fascinating and, in Epstein's terms, more 'moral'. He wrote the following:

What is photogénie? I would describe as photogenic any aspect of things, beings or souls whose moral character is enhanced by filmic reproduction. And any aspect not enhanced by filmic reproduction is not photogenic, plays no part in the art of cinema.[30]

In some respects these ideas are carried forward, though within a very different context by Walter Benjamin, the German theorist writing in the 1930s. He talked about all those things the human senses are somehow aware of but which only a camera 'sees'. He writes in his famous essay, 'The Work of Art in the Age of Mechanical Reproduction':[31]

Our bars and city streets, our offices and furnished rooms, our railway stations and our factories seemed to close relentlessly about us. Then came film and exploded this prison-world with the dynamite of the split seconds so that now we can set off calmly on journeys of adventure among its far-flung debris.

Then, like Epstein, he puts particular emphasis on the close-up and other 'resources' of the moving image camera:

With the close-up space expands, with slow motion, movement is extended. And just as enlargement not merely clarifies what we see indistinctly … but brings to light entirely new structures of matter … We are familiar with the movement of picking up a cigarette lighter or a spoon, but know almost nothing of what really goes on between hand and metal, and still less how this varies with moods. This is where the camera comes in with all its resources for swooping and rising, disrupting and isolating, stretching or compressing a sequence, enlarging or reducing an object.[32]

Benjamin talks about 'another nature which speaks to the camera compared to the eye'. He makes an analogy between the unconscious mind and what he calls our 'optical unconscious': 'It is through the camera that we first discover the optical unconscious, just as we discover the instinctual unconscious through psychoanalysis.'[33]

    Epstein and Benjamin both indirectly reinforce the central distinction running through this chapter: Rancière's distinction between film working in the service of action/representation on the one hand and film as presence on the other. This idea of presence is further amplified by the French theorist André Bazin writing in the late 1940s and early 1950s. In his essay 'The Ontology of the Photographic Image' he famously wrote:

Only the impassive lens stripping its object of all those ways of seeing, those piled-up preconceptions, that spiritual dust and grime with which my eyes have covered it, is able to present it in all its virginal purity to my attention and consequently to my love. By the power of photography, the natural image of a world that we neither know nor can see, nature at last does more than imitate art: she imitates the artist.

(Bazin 1971, vol. 1: 15)

Bazin has been derided for many years by those who accuse him of a naive belief in some unmediated cinematic process in which reality is made present as if without any element of intervention by the filmmaker. In fact Bazin wrote at length about the very opposite. He was well aware of the commercial and ideological motivations of those responsible for the finished film and of how the tried and tested professional practices of filmmaking were used to create a visual 'language' that would work. Bazin writes:

As for the film maker, the moment he has secured this unwitting complicity of the public, he is increasingly tempted to ignore reality. From habit and laziness he reaches the point when he himself is no longer able to tell where lies begin or end. There could never be any question of calling him a liar because his art consists in lying. He is just no longer in control of his art. He is its dupe, and hence he is held back from any further conquest of reality.[34]

Bazin here identifies the filmmaker who works within formulae: narrative forms and generic structures at the macro level; conventional ways of framing, cutting, etc. at the micro level. Bazin is saying that such a filmmaker does not look, does not see, does not engage with his or her world.

Exercise

The above outline of ideas developed by Jean Epstein, Walter Benjamin and André Bazin all suggest a particular capacity of the camera to record reality in a way that enhances our way of seeing, our sense of 'presence'. In your view is it possible to draw an opposition between filmmakers who strive to do this and those who are only concerned to make films that are driven by commercial considerations, using commercial techniques? Is it possible to argue that any film can contain what we have described here as 'sublime moments'?

You may wish to think about a mainstream commercial film you have recently seen or, at the other end of the spectrum, return yet again to *Springtime in an English Village*.

TIME AND MEMORY

The qualities of the moving image have concerned us in the last two sections. It is important now to turn, however briefly, to a consideration of the time in which moving images are experienced. In part this includes quite literally the duration of a moving image – the length of a shot. More broadly, it requires some thinking about the different ways in which we experience time, maybe even some thinking about different kinds of time.

Film studies has been very strongly influenced over the past ten years by the writings of the French philosopher, Gilles Deleuze, and specifically the two books, *Cinema 1: The Movement Image* (1983) and *Cinema 2: The Time Image* (1985). You will recognise just from the titles that these two books pick up on the contrast that has been made throughout this chapter between the emphasis on action/representation (movement) and the emphasis on presence (time).

Deleuze's cinema of the movement image embraces most of what we might loosely call mainstream popular narrative film. Here the image serves the purpose of narrative and is based on a mechanical concept of time. Deleuze proposes that the movement image addresses a particular capacity within the spectator which he calls the sensory motor mechanism. This 'mechanism' is the means by which we recognise familiar patterns and systems and fit the material of a particular film into these in order to make sense of what we are watching. This 'mechanism' is therefore a structure of thought and one that tends to fold experiences back into conventional ways of making sense of our world. The images that make up a film are likely to be accessed very much in relation to their 'before' and 'after' – images as the interlocking pieces of a chain of meaning with an inevitable forward direction towards narrative completion and the film's end. An image becomes a function of a certain conception of (chronological) time.

Deleuze is interested in those filmmakers who at different points in film history have tried to break with what he calls the movement image, to break the grip of the sensory motor mechanism. A particular place is given in Deleuze's argument to a group of Italian filmmakers working at the end of the Second World War who collectively produced a body of work that is now referred to as neo-realism. (This same film movement was the centre of focus for André Bazin writing thirty years earlier.) A key emphasis within neo-realism was the primacy of the image and a different approach to cinematic time in order to allow the image to be 'present'. Roberto Rossellini, the key figure of the movement with his films *Paisa, Rome Open City* and *Germany Year Zero*, had begun his career working in the mainstream fascist-controlled cinema and wanted a clear break in Italian cinema after the fall of that regime. The Rossellini films, together with others made between 1944 and 1950, perhaps most notably Visconti's *La Terra Trema*, put an emphasis on the iconic, the image in time, yet taken out of time or existing in its own time, not necessarily subordinate to narrative.

Deleuze goes on to argue for this as perhaps the fundamental distinction within film and filmmakers – between those who conform to action and the time of action – and those who seek to create different kinds of temporal systems within which the image can function quite differently, challenging rather than reinforcing the audience's 'mechanism' for engaging with the film and, at one remove, with the world. Rossellini's *Journey to Italy* (1952) has been described as the first modern film because it lets go of narrative priorities. Instead it creates a series of encounters between the central female character (Ingrid Bergman) and objects and places. In doing so, the film captures a sense of how the past invades the present, putting a 'normal' relationship with the world into crisis and requiring a deeply reflective response to the nature of the self in time.

One of the more obvious ways of looking at different ideas of time and of how time can be represented is in the contrast between our narrative selves and what we might call our memory selves. Our narrative selves construct and develop stories, including our own life stories, based on chronological time and a cause–effect set of relations between different things that happen to us. This approach helps us literally to make sense of things. Our memory selves experience different planes of time simultaneously: for example, my memory may bring to mind things from different points in my life. As memories these experiences are not 'past' – they exist only in the present moment of their recollection. Again, we encounter this sense of the bridging of past and present, of the impossibility of separating past and present except by imposing a narrative structure; in effect, we manage time as movement rather than experience time as presence, time as before/after rather than time as now.

The development of cinematic modernism in the late 1950s and early 1960s becomes another key moment in Deleuze's re-mapping of film history. During this period an increasing number of directors began to consider how else to represent human experience, including time and memory. For example, Alain Resnais's 1959 film *Hiroshima mon amour* works between the present of Hiroshima, fourteen years after the dropping of an atomic bomb on the city, and a town in France, Nevers, where in the same war a young French woman had a relationship with a German soldier. A Japanese man who lost his family in 1945 and this French woman, now an actress working on a film in the city, have a brief affair in which the present of their past is beautifully presented in an exploration of history, memory and subjective experience.

Some postmodernist films take this montage of past and present further, scrambling the chronological order of events, creating an obsessive relationship to time as something that is continually either running away or slowing down or speeding up or that seems to fold into or emerge out of other time zones. (Digital technologies allow an apparently limitless range of possibilities that we are only at the beginning of exploring.) In films that capture something of the flow (rather than the tick) of time, there is often a compulsive need to register 'clock time' – if only to demonstrate how time is actually experienced: how time slows down, speeds up, days drag, years fly. This is well illustrated in most of Wong Kar Wai's films from *Days of Being Wild* to *2046*. Fixing time is a way of trying to hold on to an experience, so Yuddy, near the beginning of *Days of Being Wild*, meets Su Lizhen and the following conversation takes place:

Yuddy: What's today's date?
Su Lizhen: 16th

Yuddy: April 16th … April 16th, 1960, one minute before 3 o'clock. We were here together. I'll always remember that minute because of you. From now on we're one-minute friends. It's a fact. You can't deny it. It's already happened.

By isolating moments, extracting from time the flow of time, we try to create memorials to them. Memories need fixing or they flow, merge, overlap, disintegrate one into another. You could say that we all try to maintain a working belief in the sensory motor mechanism as it allows us not just the illusion of fixing points in time but thereby the possibility of creating narratives that structure and make sense of these flows of time. Wong Kar Wai's films are often about the impossibility of two people being able to 'connect', suggesting that love is impossible. But perhaps it is time that is impossible. Even as characters measure change in their material and physical lives by reference to conventional measures of time, memories sweep in, feeding nostalgia and melancholy and collapsing the good order of historical time.

Springtime in an English Village might appear the most modest of films to refer back to in the context of this discussion. However, as a final thought in this section, it is interesting to speculate on how digital moving image archive material may be used in the present. We have already noted the availability of this (and many thousands of other similar films) for re-editing, mixing with new material or other archive material, for 'framing' the film in different ways that offer up the images for different interpretation and open the possibility of their different impact. Online contributions to the meaning, significance and value of *Springtime* will also continue to grow as a live discourse around the film. In these ways, interaction with a complete film from the past has the possibility of freeing that film from the past in different and challenging ways.

Exercise

Find a short film from the BFI archive – or from another online archive – and consider how you might work creatively with the film, applying technological means, in order to increase the sense of time or presence.

In doing this, you may also wish to reflect on any ethical issues relating to interacting with existing film material.

CONCLUSION: FILM FRAGMENTS

This chapter began by suggesting particular challenges that film studies faces with the proliferation of moving image material available to us in some many different forms and has proceeded to explore some of the ways in which distinctive qualities of film that are not easily identified or talked about may provide a focus for new kinds of work within the subject. Central to this exploration have been ideas such as 'presence' and the 'sublime'. In more straightforward terms, the emphasis has been on the image, on time and on memory – the linking of past and present.

The Japanese film *Afterlife* (Kore-eda, 1998) offers a useful illustration of how memory is unpredictable and unruly. The film's fantasy location is a transit camp between death and the afterlife, in which those who have just died are asked to nominate one memory to take with them into eternity. This memory is reconstructed and filmed. As soon as the film representation of the memory has been screened, its subject disappears forever. At the beginning of the process, the newly dead believe they should nominate the significant events in their lives, the big narrative moments like the day of their marriage or a day of particular professional success. However, after reflection they most often end choosing some apparently trivial incident or experience – but marked strongly in the memory, perhaps by a distinctive sound or smell. Kore-eda makes a deliberate connection between memory and cinema, suggesting that film has the capacity both to provoke our memory and to present audiovisual equivalents of these memories.

Film, of course, not only connects with memories from our personal lives, it also generates its own memories. We recall particular moments from a wide variety of films we have seen – and not just our favourites. When we recollect a film it is surprising how often it comes to consciousness as a particular image – and possibly a line of dialogue or a few bars of music. Indeed, this may be all we can recollect! Like the personal lives of the subjects in Kore-eda's film, the memories they throw up are surprising. For example, a film may have been more or less gripping at the time of viewing but story, theme, character may all have subsequently become a blur. Sometimes we cannot even remember the name of the film – though an image is clear in our mind. These images, scattered fragments, can be replayed, outside of narrative time, possibly with one fragment triggering a second, though it may apparently be quite unrelated. These scattered fragments constitute a kind of personal history of the movies existing in the present of their recollection.

Much has been written about cinephilia – the love of cinema – and about different ways in which cinephilia expresses itself: perhaps in a vast DVD collection, perhaps in a huge library of film books, perhaps in keen attendance at a repertory cinema and at film festivals. In their different ways the fan and the cultist are perhaps less sophisticated, more selective cinephiliacs. They are likely to have an encyclopaedic knowledge of a favourite genre, an ability to quote extracts of script and describe in precise detail key sequences in much-loved films. All are likely to find websites that support their passion and which link them with many others with similar tastes and interests. Perhaps the most interesting aspect of cinephilia is its dependence on memory as described above.

In the late 1980s Jean-Luc Godard set about producing an audiovisual history of cinema, or rather histories of cinema, in his *Histoire(s) du cinéma*. It is very demanding to watch as the film fragments not only seem to have little connection with one another at first viewing but are often overlapping with others, while the soundtrack may be from an entirely different film again. The complexity is made greater by the director's own poetic and gnomic voice-over utterances and by words that appear on screen as additional commentary. As a piece of installation art, it is very beautiful to watch and to listen to – as history, it seems to lack any narrative coherence.[35] Godard presents us with history as present memories competing with one another, influencing one another and producing meaning through their apparent chance intersection.[36]

What is being illustrated here yet again is the tension between action/representation and presence.[37] The cinephiliac knows the annoying tendency of film fragments to assert

• **Plate 3.3**
Marilyn collage from essay
by Jean-Luc Godard,
Histoire(s) du cinéma (1998)

their presence. As digital film archives become increasingly available to us online we are likely to work with an even more vast patchwork of material. These archives are not only a huge treasure of historical material for scholarly research and dissection, they offer us an enormous playground for creating all sorts of audiovisual mischief as we celebrate the presence of the past, the ghostly lure of the image and, in a more melancholic frame of mind, a sense of mortality.

Let us imagine a viewer on YouTube who comes across *Springtime in an English Village*. Like me, she is surprised, delighted, concerned, confused by the moment when two black girls appear running left across the frame towards the entrance to a village primary school. Long after she may have forgotten the film's title or the circumstances in which she viewed the film, this image remains present, remains resonant. It is not an image recollected from a feature-length film, or a film seen in the cinema but from a short propaganda piece made in 1944 and accessed on YouTube. But it is an image which has imposed a particular presence – 'individual, personal, and subjective'.[38] Such a memory is worth acknowledging, worth exploring. And beyond the particular example, the nature of film itself as a medium is worth further reflection. We are forced to think about whether our present ways of working with film are sufficient if these moments that impact so strongly are left unspoken.

Exercise

Think about how true it is for you that your recollection of much film material comes in the form of fragments. What do you do with these fragments?

SUMMARY

- There is a rich and vast amount of material available in online film archives in relation to the feature-length film and the cinema experience.
- The practice of film studies can be applied productively in studying archive film material.
- Questions raised by how some qualities of even a short and very modest film remain untouched by our standard film studies work, and wondering about this 'excess' and what we may do with it.
- Some theoretical ideas to help identify and discuss more clearly this idea of 'excess' within film.
- Much of our cinephilia (love of cinema) is connected with this 'excess' material and the way we recall it in memory.

NOTES

1   The Moving History archive at http://www.movinghistory. ac.uk/archives/ offers the best overview of UK film and television archives held in the public sector. It is worth following links to the different regional archives. Outside of the UK, the Prelinger Archive offers over US 2,000 films online: http://www.archive.org/details/prelinger. The National Film Board of Canada offers the NFB Screening Room: http://www.nfb.ca/.

2   An online report identified the huge growth in visitors to the National Film Board of Canada site in its first year:
Total Film Views on NFB.ca (Jan. 2009–Jan. 2010)
- 3.7 million total online film views since we launched a year ago

- 2.2 million online film views in Canada (59% of views)
- 1.5 million views International (not including Canada) on the web
- Total international views: 1.45 million views
- Total views: 3,768,628
- Film Views on iPhone App (October 21 2009–January 21 2010)
- 396,190 views on iPhone in Canada
- 131,332 views on iPhone outside Canada
- 527,522 Total film views on iPhone
- Total number of apps downloaded: 171,271
(Matthew Forsythe, 21 January 2010: http://blog.nfb.ca/ 2010/01/21/online-video-stats/

3 http://www.viralblog.com/research/youtube-statistics/.

4 'Cinema' is sometimes used to describe a building or an auditorium within a building. But 'cinema' is also a collective noun for films, all films. A history of cinema is not likely to be a history of buildings, but rather of films and their contexts of production. For example, a book on British cinema will look at a variety of factors – political, economic, industrial, cultural – in examining a body of films. It is likely that the greatest emphasis will be on the close study of individual films to establish connections between them that may allow for a term like 'British cinema' to have some justification (see Chapter 14).

5 It is to be noted that the BFI chose to use the term 'media-theque' rather than 'cinematheque', indicating the inclusion of both film and television material (see n. 1 above). At the time of writing there are four additional mediatheques around the UK. These are at Derby: the QUAD Centre for Art and Film; Cambridge: Central Library; Newcastle-upon-Tyne: Discovery Museum; Wrexham Library.

6 The BFI appears to have uploaded the film on 9 January 2009.

7 The film has no credits.

8 The Ministry of Information was established on 4 September 1939, the day after Britain declared war against Hitler's Germany. The MoI was responsible for managing infor-mation and creating propaganda for the population of the United Kingdom and also for keeping loyal and committed its allies and for its vast colonial Empire.

9 For a very famous example of a wartime propaganda film that evokes the sturdy traditional attitudes and national values, see Humphrey Jennings' *Listen to Britain* (1942), http://www.youtube.com/watch?v=6h8pHumy7NE. British film propaganda in the Second World War focused very much on the national culture and everyday life as a way of reminding people what they were fighting for.

10 *Colonial Cinema*, July 1944, p. 27. Also see http://www.colonialfilm.org.uk/node/1923.

11 *Propaganda Coup Of England's First Black May Queen*, Vanessa Thorpe, *The Observer*, 21 June 2009, http://www.guardian.co.uk/world/2009/jun/21/black-may-queen-youtube.

12 Posted 2 April 2010.

13 The digital process is quite different with light picked up by pixel array sensor. Each pixel is then given an electronic charge for the purpose or electronic processing and storing in a computer image file. There is a view that the digital image has neither the 'existence in itself' nor the ghostliness of 'presence' that are often associated with photos produced using the older chemical process. This view can be challenged.

14 Defamiliarisation is an important concept in art. Some art very consciously distorts familiar objects, presenting them in new and surprising ways. This kind of defamiliarisation is easier to recognise than that contained in a realistic image produced by a mechanical instrument (a camera). It may be argued that all acts of representation have the capacity to defamiliarise us to their object, even when the apparent aim of the representation is documentary accuracy.

15 This process of artistic transformation has often been misunderstood. For example, the French philosopher Pascal, writing in the seventeenth century, said: 'How vain is painting, which attracts admiration by the resemblance of things, the originals of which we do not admire!'

16 See Perez (1998), chapter 1, 'The Documentary Image'.

17 See n. 26 below.

18 Animism is commonly used as a term to talk about how apparently inanimate objects possess an inner life, a soul.

19 See James Agee and Walker Evans's *Let Us Now Praise Famous Men* (Penguin, London, 2006) – the book that made these images famous. In 1933 the new president, Franklin D. Roosevelt, passed legislation to deal with unemployment in the wake of the Depression. It was the foundation for Roosevelt's 'New Deal'. Among the measures taken was the setting up of the Farm Security Administration (FSA) in 1935 to support small farmers. Roy Stryker was appointed to organise a photographic collection of the FSA's work. To carry this out he employed a small group of photographers that included, among others, Russell Lee, Dorothea Lange, Arthur Rothstein, Walker Evans, John Vachon, Carl Mydans and Ben Shahn (see references to Lars Von Trier's *Dogville* below).

20 Photography derives from the Greek words for light and making representations through drawing; cinematography relaces the word 'light' with the word 'movement'.

21 The photographs used are credited to Russell Lee, Dorothea Lange, Jack Collier, A. Siegel, Ben Shahn, Carl Mydans, John Vachon and Arthur Rothstein.

22 Tom Gunning's famous article 'The Cinema of Attraction: Early Film, Its Spectator, and the Avant-Garde' can be found in *Film and Theory: An Anthology*, ed. Robert Stam and Toby Miller, Blackwell, Malden, 2000, pp. 229–35. Gunning argues that early cinema viewers were primarily interested in the image itself – rather than in, for example, narrative. In other words, the first audiences were primarily interested in 'presence'.

23 Often claimed as the very first film is the Lumière Brothers' *Workers Leaving a Factory* (1895) which can be found at http://www.youtube.com/watch?v=HI63PUXnVMw.

24 Laura Mulvey's *Death 24x a Second* (2006) is a useful book for expanding many of the ideas touched upon here. One particularly interesting insight is Mulvey's reference to the 'pensive spectator':

> The new technologies work on the body of film as mecha-nisms of delay, delaying the forward movement of the medium itself, fragmenting the forward movement of narrative and taking the spectator into the past. Whatever its drive or desire, this look transforms perception of cinema just as the camera had transformed the human eye's perception of the world. In the first instance, this is literal delay to the cinema flow, holding back its temporal sequence, through repetition and return. But this act of delay reveals the relation between movement and stillness as a point at which cinema's variable temporality becomes visible.
>
> (Mulvey 2006: 181–2)

25 We are reminded of John Grierson's famous definition of documentary as 'the creative treatment of actuality' (see Chapter 9).

26 As used in this quotation, 'index' refers to the (as it were) direct imprint through exposure of the real on to film stock while 'icon' refers to the significance this image gains, as in the earlier example of the familiar street corner made less familiar by its representation as an image.

27 Paul Coughlin in *Sublime Moments* at the 'Senses of Cinema' website: http://archive.sensesofcinema.com/contents/00/11/sublime.html.

28 René Clair, the great French filmmaker and a contemporary of Epstein, said 'all we ask of a plot is to supply us with subjects for visual emotion, and to hold our attention'. This was a very common attitude towards the end of the silent era. Stories could be very simple, only needing to provide a sufficient plot to allow the film to do other things, specifically to exploit its aesthetic potential. See, for example, F.W. Murnau's ravishingly beautiful and wholly simple 1928 film *City Girl*, made at the very end of the silent era.

29 Robert Farmer's essay on Epstein and photogénie can be found on the Senses of Cinema website at http://www.sensesofcinema.com/2010/great-directors/jean-epstein/.

30 From 'On Certain Characteristics of Photogenie', again quoted from Farmer.

31 Walter Benjamin, *Selected Writings Volume 3, 1935–1938*, Harvard University Press, Cambridge, MA, 2002, p. 117.

32 Ibid.

33 Ibid.

34 André Bazin, 'An Aesthetic of Reality: Neo-Realism', in Bazin (1971, vol. 2). In examining Bazin's legacy, Peter Matthews writes:

> On his death an obituary notice in *Esprit* cited Bazin as predicting that: 'The year 2000 will salute the advent of a cinema free of the artificialities of montage, renouncing the role of an "art of reality" so that it may climb to its final level on which it will become once and for all "reality made art".' In this as in so much else, Bazin the jubilant millenarian has been proved exactly wrong. At no other period in its history has cinema been so enslaved by escapist fantasy – and never have we been less certain of the

status of the real. (http://www.bfi.org.uk/sightandsound/feature/176)

35 In fact there is an argument running through the work – an attempt to come to terms with cinema's relationship to the horrors of the Second World War.

36 It is very interesting to compare an extract from Godard's *Histoire(s) du cinéma* with Martin Scorcese's film history, *A Personal Journey with Martin Scorsese through American Movies* (1995).

37 Rancière (2006: 186) claims that 'In *Histoire(s) du cinéma*, Godard announces a poetics – of pure presence.' He argues that Godard accuses the cinema of having betrayed its specific role as a medium of poetic presence through its preoccupation with narrative, with the 'movement image' of mainstream cinema. Godard's work becomes an embodiment of Deleuze's cinema of the time image.

38 See n. 27.

FURTHER READING

The following are the books that have most directly informed this chapter. None of them give up their ideas easily and you may well find that thinking through the ideas raised in this chapter by reference to films that you know and are fascinated by is the best way of developing your understanding, before turning to these books at a later stage.

Bazin, André, *What is Cinema?*, vols 1 and 2 (ed. Hugh Grey), Berkeley, University of California, 1971.

Deleuze, Gilles, *Cinema 1: The Movement-Image*, Athlone Press, London, 1992.

Deleuze, Gilles, *Cinema 2: The Time-Image*, Athlone Press, London, 1989.

Mulvey, Laura, *Death 24x a Second*, Reaktion, London, 2006.

Perez, Gilberto, *The Material Ghost*, Johns Hopkins University Press, Baltimore, MD, 1998.

Rancière, Jacques, *Film Fables*, Berg, Oxford, 2006.

FURTHER VIEWING

Films referred to in this chapter:
Days of Being Wild (Wong Kar Wai, Hong Kong, 1991)
Dogville (Von Trier, US, 2003)
The Grapes of Wrath (Ford, US, 1940)
Hiroshima mon amour (Resnais, France, 1959)
Histoire(s) du Cinema (Godard, France, 1998)
Springtime in an English Village (UK, 1944)
The West (Burns, US, 1996)

Resource centres
Websites that you may find useful include:
http://www.film-philosophy.com
Film philosophy.

http://www.sensesofcinema.com
Senses of cinema.

Online archives
http://www.movinghistory.ac.uk/archives/
The Moving History archive offers the best overview of UK film and television archives held in the public sector. It is worth following links to the different regional archives.

http://www.archive.org/details/prelinger
Outside of the UK, the Prelinger Archive offers over 2,000 US films online.

http://www.nfb.ca/
The National Film Board of Canada offers the NFB Screening Room.

Chapter 4

Film form and narrative

Suzanne Speidel

form and narrative

INTRODUCING FORM AND NARRATIVE

Films tell stories. Of course, this is not true of all films: documentaries, abstract animations, and early film genres such as 'cinema of attractions' (see Tom Gunning in Elsaesser 1990: 57) are all types of film which exploit other properties of cinema besides its narrative capabilities. Yet for most of us, our principal experience of cinema is the experience of narrative film. This chapter seeks to analyse how films tell stories, and what kinds of stories films tell.

For a film to be a 'narrative' it must present us with a series of events in ways that imply connections between one event and the next. Narratives must, therefore, have constituent parts, which are also discernibly related (though the type of relationship may vary greatly). Most commonly we expect a 'cause-and-effect' relationship: one event has the effect of causing another event, which causes another, and so on. Narratives also require 'narration', or communication. Cinematic narration is arguably the most sophisticated of all narrative media, because it is 'multi-track', both visual and audio. This enables films to co-opt the communicative capabilities of a whole host of other media and forms.

Since moving images also record the three-dimensional physical world, film can incorporate other visual arts, such as painting, still photography, theatre and architecture. Thus the tomb of 'El Khasne' in Petra, Jordan, features in *Indiana Jones and the Last Crusade* (Steven Spielberg, 1989), Richard Neutra's modernist Lovell House is used as a location for *LA Confidential* (Curtis Hanson, 1997), while Alberto Libera's Casa Malaparte is the Capri setting of *Le Mépris* (Jean-Luc Godard, 1963). In Grigori Kozintsev's *Hamlet* (1964), meanwhile, pictures and tapestries that resemble the film itself decorate the walls within the castle of Elsinore. Films not only have the potential to photograph the other visual arts, they may also copy their techniques. The techniques developed in theatre, painting and photography in staging, framing and image composition have been highly influential in shaping cinema.

In its narration and its narrative structures cinema has also been heavily influenced by the novel. The conventions of Classical Hollywood, in particular, owe much to the traditions developed in the nineteenth century classic novel, which, like Hollywood cinema, was a popular, commercial narrative form. Film is a linguistic as well as a visual medium, a fact that film scholars, in their efforts to establish film and film studies as areas of scholarship that are distinct from literature, have tended to downplay (see Elliott 2003: 77–112). Films have linguistic communication through the presence of dialogue or voice-over on the soundtrack, as well as the inclusion of printed text within the image (such as intertitles, shots of newspapers, books, letters).

The advent of sound and the introduction of dialogue transformed the narrative capabilities of the film medium as a whole, enabling it to draw much more closely on linguistic narrative conventions developed for theatre. Spoken and written language are integral elements of cinematic narration, with voice-overs and intertitles able to offer exposition both elaborate (as in the 'literary' voice-over narrator of *The Age of Innocence* (Martin Scorsese, 1993)) and economic (as in the opening 'crawls' of George Lucas's *Star Wars* films, which provide substantial narrative background in very little screen time). Cinematic expression owes much of its richness to the interplay between the visual and the audio, and between the word and the image: in *Das Leben der Anderen/ The Lives of Others* (Florian Henckel von Donnersmarck, 2006), for example, the control the East German secret police (or Stasi) exercises over its people is demonstrated through repeated visual emphasis on speech and language (as when close-ups of headphones and tape recorders accompany conversations on the soundtrack or typed surveillance reports are superimposed over the actions described). Thus whilst it is undoubtedly the case that many significant aesthetic movements during film's history have been predicated on notions of 'pure cinema' – that is a cinema whose codes and conventions are specifically, exclusively, 'cinematic' – the true range of what cinema can achieve can only be understood through an appreciation of the medium's vast mimetic capabilities. We should understand (and value) filmic expression as combining practices which are unique to narrative cinema with those it has borrowed and developed from other media.

This chapter will examine both the techniques which make up cinematic narration and the structures which combine to make a narrative. It is concerned with rules (or 'codes') which shape the production of images and sounds on the small scale and with rules (or 'conventions') which shape the depiction of scenes, events and characters on a large scale. The visual codes of cinema may be broadly divided into **mise-en-scène** and **editing**. The audio codes may be divided into speech, music and noise.

CONVENTIONS, HOLLYWOOD, ART AND AVANT-GARDE CINEMA

The notion of 'rules', albeit ones that are fluid and adaptable, is crucial to the study of form and narrative. As with other narrative media, such as novels, theatre, comic books and epic poems, films organise stories according to sets of conventions, which are understood by filmmakers and recognized by film viewers. Thus we respond to films based not only on our experience of the 'real world', but also the expectations we have formed through watching other films. Film narratives only gain meaning through these expectations, which may be met, or else thwarted in ways that reference and influence such expectations.

The history and evolution of cinematic narrative conventions allows us to distinguish between, on one hand, '**classical Hollywood**' or mainstream cinema, and on the other, art cinema, which has traditionally been the province of Europe. In other words, it is possible to identify a series of narrative conventions which emerged out of the imperatives of commercial cinema, in which the project of entertainment for the purpose of profit is paramount, and a series of narrative conventions which emerged in industries where state subsidies, and a tendency towards small-scale independent production, facilitated an emphasis on aesthetic innovation and personal expression.

Obviously such generalisations require qualification. For example, in contemporary Hollywood horizontal integration and increasing conglomeration have brought about the emergence of large independent producers and specialised production and distribution wings within the major companies. This environment has resulted in films such as *The Usual Suspects* (Bryan Singer, 1995), *Memento* (Christopher Nolan, 2000) and *Crash* (Paul Haggis, 2004) which arguably use a number of art cinema characteristics. Conversely European film industries have consistently produced films, such as comedies and musicals, belonging to genres popularised by Hollywood, while the European propensity for art cinema may also be understood in commercial terms, with aesthetic and national specificity proving a profitable means of product differentiation in a global market. As narrative categories, classical and art cinema are linked, each responding to the methods, creativity and competitive presence of the other. Thus French New Wave cinema pays homage to and parodies film noir (itself indebted to German Expressionism). Hollywood cinema, always particularly adept at cinematic 'borrowing', has tended to adopt art cinema aesthetics and conventions as a means of refreshing its own genres, and the inventiveness of the films listed above may be understood in these terms.

Art cinema is also closely related to a further category, the **avant-garde**. The avant-garde is most readily distinguishable from art cinema in economic and institutional, rather than aesthetic, terms, in that avant-garde films are distributed outside the structures of the film industry (in film clubs, galleries or academic institutions). Art films, though frequently subsidised, are exhibited in commercially run cinemas and their larger

mise-en-scène
Meaning, literally, 'putting into the scene', this term originated in the theatre. Precise critical definitions differ, but it is most simply understood as everything which appears within the frame, including setting, props, costume and make-up, lighting, the behaviour of performers, cinematography and special effects.

editing
Sometimes also referred to as 'montage' (from the French 'monter', meaning 'to assemble'), this refers to the joining together of different pieces of film stock in post-production.

classical Hollywood
This term refers both to an historical period within Hollywood cinema (which ended with the decline of the vertically integrated studio system in the 1950s), and to the narrative and formal conventions established and promoted during this time; the terms 'classical narrative' and 'Hollywood narrative' are frequently used interchangeably with the term 'mainstream narrative,' since this constitutes cinema's dominant mode of story-telling.

avant-garde
Meaning literally 'advanced guard' (those who 'march ahead' of the troops in a military campaign), 'avant-garde' has been taken up as an aesthetic term for art (and artists) seeking to challenge, subvert or reinvent artistic tenets and conventions.

Modernism
This refers to
a dramatically
experimental trend
within the arts (painting,
sculpture, architecture,
literature, music and
film) which emerged at
the start of the twentieth
century, encompassing a
wide array of movements
(Expressionism,
Vorticism, Symbolism,
Imagism, Surrealism)
along with the
innovations of individual
artists not directly
affiliated with a
particular movement.
Modernism involved a
rejection of nineteenth-
century styles,
traditions and ideas,
and a self-conscious
(or 'self-reflexive')
approach to aesthetic
forms, in which artistic
expression was itself
explored, questioned and
reinvented.

Russian formalism
A literary theory which
developed in Russia in
the early 1920s, which
sought to establish a
scientific basis for the
study of literature and
literary effects.

dissolve
A dissolve is an
editing technique
using superimposition,
which produces a
gradual transition
between one image
and the next, during
which the two shots
for a time occupy the
frame simultaneously,
appearing merged
together.

production scales demand greater financial success than do avant-garde films. In terms of content and form the two categories are overlapping, and both may be related to the rise of **Modernism**.

Both art cinema and avant-garde cinema may be understood in terms of responses to – and *reactions against* – mainstream cinema. Indeed many critical accounts of art cinema define its conventions as being opposite to Hollywood's, describing it explicitly in terms of what Hollywood is not. As a means of getting to grips with art cinema's conventions this is a useful approach, but it is important to bear in mind that art cinema is not only this. In its relation to Modernism, and in its existence within different national cinemas, art cinema is varied, and has conventions of its own that are not simply 'other' than what Hollywood does.

The above definitions of both 'mainstream' and 'art' in cinema are admittedly Western and 'first-world centric', since the former is conceived in terms of Hollywood and the latter in terms of Europe. This reflects Hollywood's global domination of the film industry, and the powerful influence American and European cinematic traditions have had worldwide. However, there are a number of other powerfully influential national and transcontinental cinemas which offer their own art and commercially orientated conventions (the cinemas of India and Japan most obviously come to mind).

Story and plot

In order to understand the fundamental components of any narrative it is first necessary to make a distinction between a narrative's 'story' and its 'plot'. 'Story' (labelled 'fabula' by **Russian formalist** literary theorists) refers to the events of the narrative, and the actions and responses of characters. 'Plot' (or 'syuzhet') refers to the ways in which the story is presented to us in terms of its order, emphases and logic. A succinct distinction between these two ideas has been provided by Seymour Chatman, who suggests that 'the story is the *what* in a narrative that is depicted', and plot 'the *how*' (Chatman 1980: 19).

The most conspicuous way that the plot shapes how the story is told is in terms of its chronology. One way in which a plot may present a story is the order in which we presume events take place and the characters experience them. Thus the film *Bambi* (David Hand, 1942), which is essentially the story of the central character's life from birth to parenthood, has a narrative in which the story and plot order are the same. By contrast, Marcel Carné's *Le Jour se lève* (1939) has a plot which begins close to the end of the story (and the hero's life), with François (Jean Gabin) committing a murder. There then follow three separate flashbacks, which show us the events that led to the murder. This plot structure clearly has the effect of creating intrigue by raising the question of how François could have descended to such desperate measures. It also imbues the film with a pervasive air of pessimism, since even as flashbacks show us a burgeoning romance, we know that the liaison must be ill-fated.

Thus our responses to the story are shaped by the manipulations of the plot. Plot strategies which play with the story's chronology demand that we piece together the order in which we presume the events take place. The ease with which this can be done depends on the method and degree of connection between one story-moment and the next. *Le Jour se lève*, for example, employs cinematic codes (such as the **dissolve)** to make such links clear. (Of course, these only work because there is a shared under-standing between filmmakers and viewers that dissolves frequently introduce characters' memories.) The plot can also emphasise or de-emphasise moments of the story through other types of temporal manipulation. The least important moments of story are liable to be missed out of the plot altogether (as when, for example, a character travels from one story-location to another). The omission (or ellipsis) of a portion of the story from the plot may have a number of other effects, such as the evocation of mystery. In *Bambi* the plot does not dramatise the period of Bambi's life immediately after the death of his mother, a gap which eases our shock and allows us to assume, without having to witness it, that Bambi has recovered from his grief. The film's tone is immediately lifted with the lively, comical 'Let's Sing a Gay Little Spring Song' number; thus the plot manipulates our emotional responses to the story, providing a musical interlude as recovery-time and as a means of cheering us up.

Film plots also operate in conjunction with film running times; where an ellipsis occurs the portion of the film's running time assigned to the incident in question is none; however, a story-incident can be emphasised if a large portion of the film's running time is devoted to it. Thus, Robert Mulligan's *To Kill a Mockingbird* (1962) devotes thirty-five minutes of its 129-minute running time to the trial of Tom Robinson. The plot's uneven distribution of the story across the running time of the film gives us time to appreciate Atticus's (Gregory Peck) defence tactics, the injustice of the racially motivated conviction, and the profound effect the trial has on Atticus's children. The relationship between the three temporal categories of story, plot and running time can be further manipulated by such cinematic codes as editing and fast- or slow-motion photography.

The plot also stages the story across space as well as across time. In *Bambi* the story takes place in the two distinct spaces of the forest and the meadow, and we are guided as to the type of story-incident liable to occur in the meadow on Bambi's first visit there, when his mother warns him that 'Out there we are unprotected'. When the plot next dramatises a scene in the meadow Bambi is stranded while gunfire sounds off-screen, and in the third meadow scene Bambi's mother is shot. The plot therefore uses the spaces of the story to alternate between periods of safety (represented by the forest) and danger (represented by the meadow). The climax of the narrative is signalled by a breaking of this pattern, and we are alarmed by the threat of the hunt and the fire precisely because they invade the safe spaces of the forest.

The plot's staging of the action in space is also crucial to our grasp of narrative point of view. The presentation of point of view takes place at the level of cinematic codes, where editing and camera movement may be used to posit certain shots as representing (or approximating) what it is a particular character sees. However, a broader notion of point of view – or what Gerard Genette (Genette 1980: 189) has termed 'focalisation' – also exists at the level of narrative conventions, in that we often infer that a particular story 'belongs to' someone. Where the plot remains always, or for the most part, in the same space as a particular character, then the film will seem entirely, or principally, 'focalised' through that character (as in *The Big Sleep* (Howard Hawks, 1946) where Philip Marlowe (Humphrey Bogart) is shown in almost every scene, so that we know and understand as much as he does). Curtis Hanson's *LA Confidential* (1997) uses multiple focalisation, with the three opening scenes introducing our three police-officer, central characters in turn. Our understanding of the ensuing narrative is dictated by the way the plot switches between the investigative activities of the three men so that we know more than any one of them.

The operations of focalisation are crucial to the emotional investment most Hollywood films ask us to make in the fate of central characters. Often focalisation through a particular character invites us to like that character, since we understand what causes them to act as they do. *LA Confidential* engages our interest by guiding us to understand why two focalising characters, Bud (Russell Crowe) and Ed (Guy Pearce), conceive a violent dislike for each other. We like and understand both men, though they do not like or understand each other, and this heightens our expectations of the moment when they realise that they are in fact on the same side. However, focalisation through a particular character need not necessarily result in our feeling empathy for them: Thompson is the 'focaliser' of *Citizen Kane* (Orson Welles, 1941) but remains little more than a narrative device, since he only sees the story rather than acts in it. A number of Hollywood films in recent years, such as *The Shawshank Redemption* (Frank Darabont, 1994), *The Sixth Sense* (M. Night Shyamalan, 1999), *Fight Club* (David Fincher, 1999) and *Memento*, have played with the conventions of focalisation, providing focalisers whose understanding is partial or deluded. Such strategies influence our response to characters, either through provoking distrust of the characters' unreliability or pleasure at the plot's ingenuity.

Hollywood and mainstream narratives

Many of the examples given above shed light on the key characteristics of classical film narratives. Because entertainment is the principal priority, the operations and conventions of mainstream films are dictated by the need to arouse and sustain our interest. This has led to a particular stress on character – on active characters, whose exploits reveal motives we can readily appreciate – and on what may be termed 'benevolence' and 'transparency'.

Hollywood narratives and codes are dictated by a desire to make the story readily comprehensible to the audience. This does not mean that techniques and structures are themselves simplistic; rather it means that a sophisticated set of conventions has evolved which aims to guide viewers through the story (in this sense they are 'benevolent'). The techniques are 'transparent' because they seek to keep viewers focused on the story; they are therefore unobtrusive, so that audiences remain absorbed in *what* is happening, rather than become distracted by *how* the story is told. Part of the sophistication of Hollywood narratives and techniques lies in their invisibility, in the effort involved in appearing effortless.

It is in Hollywood narratives where the principle of cause and effect is adhered to most rigidly, since it is this which produces story clarity. It is usually character which provides the causal elements, driving the story forward and providing connections between the elements which the plot places side by side. For this reason most Hollywood films feature heroes who have definite goals: the central character desires something, seeks to achieve something, and the story consists of the actions the character undertakes to fulfil such aims. In most cases the story is 'closed'; that is, the ending offers a complete conclusion to the character's goal (obvious exceptions to this include where a film is part of a franchise, so that the ending sets up the scenario for a sequel). The narrative will end with the character's goal having been met, or the attempt having failed – although the industry's aim of giving pleasure has led to the predominance of the former outcome.

Sometimes heroes have more than one goal, although usually such multiple goals will coincide and reinforce each other. In *His Girl Friday* (Howard Hawks, 1939), for example, Walter (Cary Grant) seeks to prevent Hildy (Rosalind Russell) from marrying Bruce (Ralph Bellamy), because he wants regain his star 'newspaper "man"' at the *Washington Post*, and because he wants to marry her for a second time himself. Thus his professional goal and his romantic goal result in his pursuing a single course of action. In *Grosse Pointe Blank* (George Armitage, 1997), meanwhile, contract killer Martin Blank (John Cusack) pursues two different courses of action when he is forced into taking on one last 'hit', while trying to win back the love of his former girlfriend Debi (Minnie Driver). However these two goals intersect when Martin discovers that the man he is supposed to kill is Debi's father, and he is able to gain her love by changing his approach to his professional goal, killing his employers instead. Most mainstream movies contain a romantic story-line of some kind, and the interweaving of romance with another story-line represents a common type of multiple-goal narrative. In mainstream narratives characters' methods of achieving goals are shaped by personality 'traits' which are clearly identified: in *LA Confidential*, for example, Bud is motivated by a need to protect women from violent men. Characters provide direction for the story, and the narrative provides clear delineation of what characters are like, and what they want.

For an illustration of classical narrative see Case study 1.

Of course, not all narrative goals are conspicuously aligned to characters and their psychology. In *Avatar* (James Cameron, 2009) ex-marine Jake Sully (Sam Worthington) is positioned as an outsider amongst his fellow 'avatar drivers', since he is not a scientist and is only sent to the planet Pandora because he is genetically identical to his dead twin brother. The early goals Jake embraces are directly opposed to those of his colleagues

• **Plate 4.1**
The goal-oriented hero
of *Gladiator* (Ridley
Scott, 2000)

as well as the 'humanoid' Pandora natives, the 'Na'vi', since he agrees to spy for
the commercial company which is mining the planet for its minerals, and is impatient
with the scientists' diplomatic project of peaceful negotiation through the medium of
genetically engineered Na'vi-human 'avatar' bodies. The narrative's cause-and-effect
structure serves to guide Jake towards more noble goals, as he becomes increasingly
fascinated by the Na'vi, their symbiotic relationship with their forest habitat and Neytiri,
the daughter of their tribal leader. Jake's initial ignorance and hostility renders his journey
more complete, whilst simultaneously making his focalisation the most useful to the
viewer who must also be initiated into the Na'vis' enchanting, alien world. The narrative
also signals that Jake's conversion is its goal through the fact that his acknowledged
desires are actually in keeping with the story's outcome: he is a paraplegic to whom
the company has promised a restorative operation, but his cure is in fact gifted to
him at the outset in the form of his brilliantly agile, avatar body (which he will embrace
permanently, rejecting his damaged human body and way of life). Whilst Jake's personal
motives sometimes cause story action, they do not directly signpost narrative trajectory;
in fact, our understanding of the narrative is shaped by an expectation that he will learn
and change. Ultimately Jake chooses love over memory, insurgency over imperialism,
and ecology over relentless industrialisation. Thus the narrative conforms to mainstream
Hollywood conventions in that its conclusion is rendered clear to us on a thematic level
by virtue of its overwhelming desirability.

Art cinema narratives

Because art films are not governed to the same degree by a commercial imperative
to provide entertainment and pleasure, their narrative conventions differ from those of

mainstream films. Art films are not shaped by the formulaic approach to story-telling described above, although in their oppositional position to mainstream cinema they offer recurring characteristics that suggest broad guidelines in terms of conventions.

Art films are not governed by the narrative strategy of cause and effect: coincidence, chance and random sequences of events are common in their narratives. Frequently the story connections offered by the plot are jarring and confusing rather than elucidatory: thus Bernardo Bertolucci's *The Conformist* (1969) does not make clear for some time that early scenes in a radio station are a flashback in relation to the plot's opening car journey, and our sense of dislocation is furthered by the presence of flashforwards within the flashback sequence. The film's structure is highly fragmented, with individual story moments repeatedly interrupted by other moments in a disorientating fashion. Similarly the motivations of characters are also not readily discernible, and they cannot be relied on to explain the logic and direction of the story. In *Le Mépris* (1963), for example, Camille (Brigitte Bardot) vacillates between reassuring her husband Paul (Michel Piccoli) that she still loves him, and angrily voicing her contempt for him. Art films do not necessarily invite us to like their heroes and heroines: Godard's *A bout de souffle* (1959) presents us with an arrogant central protagonist (played by Jean Paul Belmondo) who repeatedly insults his girlfriend; *The Conformist*, more radically, depicts a character who spies for the fascists, and passively colludes in murder.

In many art films characters are not particularly active, and typically the story moves more slowly than in Hollywood films, with plots assigning long portions of running time to scenes showing little story progress. In *Le Mépris* much of the film's first seventy-two minutes are taken up with little more than Paul's indecision about whether he will accept film producer Prokosch's (Jack Palance) offer of a job, and Camille's indecision about whether she will accompany him. François Truffaut's *Baisers volés* (1968) contains a scene in which Antoine Doinel (Jean-Pierre Léaud) sends a love letter, and there follows a series of shots of the letter as it is sucked down the vacuum-tubes of the postal system and delivered to its destination. This sequence constitutes a plot dramatisation in which no significant action takes place, and is pointedly superfluous to the unfolding of the story.

Art cinema also tends to avoid closed endings, favouring instead a sense of irresolution and indecision. Many art films give the impression that they have 'stopped' rather than 'ended' – that the plot has ceased to dramatise rather than resolved the story's dilemmas. Famously, François Truffaut's first Antoine Doinel film, *Les Quatre cents coups* (1959), ends with a freeze frame as Antoine is in the process of running away, while *Le Mépris* cuts short the marital conflicts of its protagonists with a shocking car crash.

For further discussion of the French New Wave see the website www.routledge.com/cw/nelmes

All these properties may be related to a number of broad preoccupations which art cinema explores. While in mainstream narratives the characters and their traits are put in service of telling the story, in art cinema the logic, progress and resolution of the story are often subordinate to the exploration of character. Characters' subjectivity and mental states become a key focus, and it is not uncommon to find characters who are emotionally unbalanced – or even psychotic – acting as the principal focalisers of the narrative (as in, for example, Robert Wiene's *The Cabinet of Dr Caligari* (1919) or Roman Polanski's *Repulsion* (1965)). The subjectivity of characters is one way that we may account for the films' fragmented structures and dramatic ambiguities, although such readings are not usually confirmed for us by the narrative.

Implicit in these uncertainties is the idea that human behaviour and human stories cannot be as readily resolved in life as they are in mainstream narratives: our experience of the world is not one of neat cause and effect, nor do we necessarily approach our lives with clear-cut goals in mind and an understanding of our motives. Art films suggest that characters cannot control events, and that the action will not necessarily reward us with satisfying answers. *The Conformist* constitutes an exploration of the idea that people and causes can never be understood, in that initially it seems to suggest that it will uncover why people become fascists; however, its fragmented structure seems to bury rather than reveal explanations, implying that the causes of history and human behaviour can never be fully comprehended.

Just as story is put in service of character, it is also subordinate to plot. Art cinema prioritises the question of *how* narrative is presented rather than *what* is told. Despite the fact that many of its archetypal films were released decades after the era of Modernism, art cinema is Modernist in that it takes up a self-conscious position in relation to its own aesthetic forms, seeking to explore the properties of cinematic expression itself. This may take the form of jarring, fragmented or superfluous narrative devices, which make the operations of the plot conspicuous as opposed to transparent; it may also take the form of experimental cinematic codes, such as the **jump-cuts** of Godard's *A bout de souffle*, which again force us to notice, rather than enjoy, cinematic technique. A number of art films, such as *Le Mépris* and Federico Fellini's *8½* (1963), are also more blatantly self-referential in that their stories are themselves concerned with filmmaking. In such instances it is often the limitations of the medium which are explored, as the frustrations of undertaking fictional film projects serve as metaphors for the fractured narratives of the films themselves – and perhaps also for the impossibilities of achieving any satisfactory communication.

Art cinema is sometimes – problematically – associated with the personal expression of the director in ways that Hollywood cinema is not. This is in part because the production contexts of art films mean that the director's role is likely to be more prominent than it is in larger, commercial ventures. In addition, the self-consciousness of art cinema encourages us to associate the films with a particular artist, since the invitation to notice techniques draws our attention to the possible creative presence behind them. The figure of the auteur originated in European cinematic discourses and has been central to much critical writing on European cinema, although more recent interest in European popular genres has eroded this dominance (see Dyer and Vincendeau 1992). However, since auteurism has also featured prominently in critical approaches to Hollywood, and has been subject to considerable revision and critique, it is an approach towards art cinema which should perhaps be treated with caution.

Some critics also define art cinema in terms of a tendency to engage in political and/or social commentary (see Street 1997: 47). This does not typify all art cinema but there are certain national movements (such as Italian Neo-realism or the British New Wave) where this criterion does apply. It is also the case that the art cinema of certain countries displays a preoccupation with questions of national politics and history. This is particularly apparent where countries have turbulent national histories, as in the case of new German cinema which seeks to explore Germany's Nazi past and legacy. The New Waves of Poland, Hungary and Czechoslovakia, meanwhile, are distinct from the French New Wave which inspired them by virtue of their (often critical) political engagement with the socialist systems in which they flourished.

jump-cut
An elliptical cut, where the transition between one image and the next is disruptive because it is in some way spatially or temporally inconsistent, or because the two images involved are very similar.

For further discussion of auteurism see Chapter 6, pp. 142/164.

For further discussion of British New Wave, see Chapter 13.

CINEMATIC CODES

Critical accounts of cinematic codes have tended to differ in the ways they have broken down, or categorised for analysis, cinema's key communicative procedures. This chapter considers three basic areas – two visual codes (mise-en-scène and editing) and one audio code (soundtrack).

Mise-en-scène

The term 'mise-en-scène' originated in the theatre. Meaning literally 'putting into the scene', it referred to the staging of a drama within theatrical space. The term as it has been applied to cinema may be understood in two ways. For some critics it has retained its theatrical connotations, and is used only to refer to those elements of the shot which are staged in front of the camera at the time of filming. These elements comprise setting, props, costume and make-up, lighting and performance. For others the term has broader significance, and is used to refer to everything which appears within the frame of the finished film. According to this definition cinematography and special effects are both aspects of mise-en-scène, even though the former is performed by, rather than placed in front of, the camera, and the latter are often added to the image during post-production. For the purposes of this study I will adopt this second definition, but will maintain the distinction between the different 'phases' of mise-en-scène by dealing first with what takes place in front of camera at the time of shooting, then with what the camera does, and finally with what is added to the image afterwards.

Setting

Setting is a crucial part of film's expressive capabilities, and because it is subject to the techniques of other aspects of mise-en-scène (it may be lit strikingly, or elements may be shown in close-up) it constitutes much more than simply a backdrop for the action of a story.

A filmmaker may select a setting from a pre-existing environment, or may construct a set within a studio lot or sound stage. Films may also use a combination of construction and pre-existing environments: the Roman scenes of *Gladiator* (Ridley Scott, 2000), for example, were shot in a Napoleonic barracks in Malta to which new structures were added.

In many instances the primary aim of the setting is to suggest authenticity, and the content and style of the set are dictated by what is appropriate to the story's time and place. Period dramas are often marketed on the basis of the setting's visual pleasure, and also on the efforts undertaken to provide accurate re-creations of the past. Setting is central to bringing plausibility and clarity to the narrative **diegesis**: in *Bladerunner* (Ridley Scott, 1984) the film's elaborate futuristic skylines with its postmodern architecture and flying 'cars' combine with rainy, chaotic, street-level marketplaces and squalor to suggest a fictional world which is at once startling and convincing in its scope and coherence.

Setting may also be used to imbue the image with graphic properties which comment on story and characters: in *The Conformist*'s fascist ministry, for example, the patterns of straight lines provided by windows, pillars and staircases are strongly suggestive of prison bars. Setting, particularly in art films, may also create a sense of alienation from the story, or draw attention to the narrative's artificiality: in *Le Mépris*, bold, vibrant colours recur in ways that make the narrative and its environment feel staged even where real exterior locations are used. Clearly for films shot on colour film stock, colour shades and contrasts are important ingredients of the mise-en-scène; the film *Pleasantville* (Gary Ross, 1998) bases its narrative premise around the effects of colour, using **CGI** to turn a black and white world into a colour one as the knowledge and freedom of the central characters grow.

The German Expressionist movement of the 1920s took the metaphoric possibilities of setting to their furthest extreme, making sets representative of the psychological disturbances of characters. Thus in *The Cabinet of Dr Caligari* the exaggeratedly canted, angular backdrops are conspicuously artificial in that they are painted sets (even 'light' and 'shadow' are painted on), and are ultimately revealed to exist only inside the mind of one of the characters. In other Expressionist films, such as *Destiny* (Fritz Lang, 1921), the setting, though not the product of a character's imagination, nevertheless takes on non-naturalistic, often nightmarish appearances, which reflect characters' experiences or inner torment. With the financial take-over of the German studio UFA in 1927 and the rise of Nazism in 1933, key Expressionist directors such as Lang and F.W. Murnau, along with many members of their creative teams, left Germany for Hollywood; this assisted in the spread of Expressionist tendencies in mainstream cinema – most obviously in Universal Studio's horror cycle of the 1930s and in the film noir cycle of the 1940s and early 1950s.

diegesis
The fictional world in which we presume the story takes place.

CGI
An acronym for 'computer-generated imagery', meaning the use of digital software to create, change or enhance aspects of mise-en-scène.

Props

The term 'props', short for 'property', refers to movable objects within the set, specifically those which take on a significant function within the story. Thus props are more than simply 'things' which are used to dress the set: they may serve as iconographic demonstrations of genre (we associate stakes, crosses, coffins and silver bullets with horror films, guns with westerns and so on); they may also be used to drive the narrative forward, and, crucially, may also take on metaphoric significance.

Props can provide narrative drive in a number of ways. Most obviously they may contribute to character motivation: in *Pirates of the Carribean: Dead Man's Chest* (Gore Verbinski, 2006), the story is structured around competing characters' desires to possess four related artefacts – the magic compass which may point the way to the 'dead man's chest', the key which opens the chest, the chest itself, and the still-beating heart which is the chest's contents; the possession of these four props is what motivates all the leading characters (though each character has a different reason for this need), and each prop is in turn (often comically) abandoned as the importance of the next prop is revealed. Props may also contribute to the unfolding narrative by shaping the staging of action across time and space: in *His Girl Friday*, for example, the constantly ringing telephones of the newsroom contribute to our sense of the environment's frenetic pace, but they also contribute the pace of the plot itself, continually interrupting one event with news of action taking place off-screen, and providing reasons for characters to enter and depart, often at high speed.

Props may also take on metaphoric significance, depending on how attention is drawn to them through cinematography or dialogue. In *Rebecca* (Alfred Hitchcock, 1940) our unnamed heroine (Joan Fontaine) and her husband (Laurence Olivier) forget to take their wedding licence with them after they are married; it is dropped down to them from the registry office staircase, and is shown floating downwards in a way that suggests a downward spiral in the couple's future marriage. This example provides a clear illustration of why props are highly significant to film's ability to signal metaphor and connotation, since one of the most common, and expressive, forms of cinematic metaphor is metonymy (see Metz 1983). Metonymy refers to a figure of speech whereby an object or detail associated with an idea is substituted for the idea itself (thus, in *Rebecca*, the marriage licence stands in for the entire conjugal relationship). In cinematic metonymy, therefore, props play a key role in suggesting a whole array of meanings beyond what is shown; they are a rich, and extremely economic, source of connotative expression.

Crucially, the prop as metaphor may also draw on metaphorical associations which exist outside the film itself: when, in *Pleasantville*, a black and white Margaret (Marley Shelton) plucks a bright red apple from a tree and gives it to David (Tobey Maguire), the moment takes on significance because it references, and renders positive, the biblical connotations of picking forbidden fruit. Props are more likely to imply metaphorical significance if they are shot in ways which draw attention to both the prop and the cinematic techniques used to shoot it: in *Pleasantville* the shot of the apple stands out as unique, and therefore symbolic, because once the apple is picked it reveals the moon through the branches behind it (the camera refocuses quickly so that we see first a blurred orb, then a clear, glowing, full moon). Similarly props tend to take on symbolic meanings when they are repeated in the narrative and mise-en-scène: in *The Draughtsman's Contract* (Peter Greenaway, 1982), for example, fruit is a recurring motif, and is piled high in opulent displays and frequently eaten by the characters. The visual properties of the fruit suggest multiple metaphoric possibilities (which we draw from both specific narrative contexts and wider cultural connotations), such as sexual pleasure, the luxuries of aristocratic life, and the urgent need for wealthy women to 'bear fruit' in the form of male heirs.

Costume

Costume and make-up have similar expressive and symbolic capabilities to the other graphic properties of mise-en-scène, but are also explicitly connected to characterisation.

• Plate 4.2
Fast talking in *His Girl Friday* (Howard Hawks, 1939)

Costumes may be used to indicate to us information about the personality or status of the character. In *His Girl Friday*, for example, Hildy Johnson's pin-striped suit and jaunty hat (which resembles the trilbies worn by the film's male journalists) indicate that she is better suited to the cut-throat environment of the *Washington Post* than to child-rearing in Albany, despite her own protestations to the contrary.

As with props, costumes may draw on existing cultural connotations: thus in *William Shakespeare's Romeo and Juliet* (Baz Luhrmann, 1996) our hero and heroine first meet at a fancy-dress ball at which Romeo (Leonardo DiCaprio) is dressed as a knight and Juliet (Claire Danes) as an angel. Here the inclusion of a story occasion involving dressing up is used to establish clear associations of goodness and innocence which stand out in an otherwise corrupt world. At the same time, the bold symbolism of the costumes also subtly suggests that the characters' sudden, extreme infatuation with each other may be attributed in part to a teenage propensity to 'play-act' certain roles.

Costume can function to signal a change in a character's status, as in *Trading Places* (John Landis, 1983) where Winthrop Winkle's (Dan Ackroyd) privileged life is indicated by his elegant suit and tie, and his change in fortune is accompanied by comical, humiliating changes in clothing – culminating in a filthy, soaking-wet Santa outfit. Changes in costume may equally reflect alterations in a character's psychology: in *The Madness of King George* (Nicholas Hytner, 1994), the king's mental disintegration, as well as his medical torture, are emphasised by his ragged appearance in undergarments and straitjacket. In *Metropolis* (Fritz Lang, 1926), meanwhile, although the evil Robot Maria frequently wears the same costume as her virtuous human counterpart, their differences in morality are connoted by the heavier, darker, eye make-up worn by the robot. Costume may also take on significance in its relationship to other elements of mise-en-scène: in German Expressionist cinema costume and setting as well as lighting and performance are complementary, creating the impression of a single, coherent visual design in which people and environment merge together. Similarly in *The Draughtsman's Contract* the characters' elaborate wigs often seem to complement the displays of fruit in ways suggestive of ludicrous extravagance and vanity.

Performance

Performance is an extremely rich area of cinematic expression. As with narrative itself, many elements of cinematic performance have their origins in conventions imported from the theatre. Thus the vaudeville tradition informs the types of performance often found in musicals and comedies, where physical dexterity – in the form of dancing, acrobatics, slapstick or mime – may be required. The more high-brow theatrical traditions of repertory theatre inform many performances which seem more naturalistic (that is, closer to the way we feel people behave in 'real' life), particularly those where emphasis is placed on the actor's voice – as in Philip Seymour Hoffman's performance in *Capote* (Bennett Miller, 2005). In the 1950s Lee Strasberg's 'Actor's Studio' had an important influence on Hollywood cinema through its promotion of 'method acting', in which actors were encouraged to explore their own psychology and personal history as a means of producing performances. In practice 'the method' often produced highly mannered, 'visible' acting styles, such as Marlon Brando's in *A Streetcar Named Desire* (Elia Kazan, 1951).

However, it is important to note that notions such as 'naturalism' and 'visibility' are relative terms, in that they operate in relation to existing conventions and audience expectations. Thus what may, to one generation of movie-goers, seem like a highly naturalistic performance, might, to their children, seem overtly stylised and exaggerated, because these judgements are based not so much on how people actually behave in life, but on what audiences are used to seeing on stage and screen. Having said this, it is clear that certain performance styles do seek to draw attention to their own artificiality. German Expressionism falls into this category, with actors – many of them trained by theatre director Max Reinhardt – adopting highly exaggerated gestures derived from theatrical melodrama (as when, in *Metropolis*, Maria clutches her hands over her heart to signify anguish).

Any analysis of performance involves breaking down what it is an actor does into constituent elements. This can be difficult, since we are accustomed to decoding performances in terms of the motivations and emotions of characters, rather than the techniques of the actor. Richard Dyer, however, has identified the following performance 'signs': 'facial expression; voice; gestures (principally of hands and arms, but also of any limb, e.g. neck, leg); body posture (how someone is standing or sitting); body movement (movement of the whole body, including how someone stands up or sits down, how they walk, run, etc.)' (Dyer 1979: 134). These categories allow us to make distinctions between how characters behave and what actors do. Thus, for example, in *Rebecca*, when our heroine encounters the housekeeper Mrs Danvers (Judith Anderson) on her first morning in her husband's stately home, we see that she feels out of place – that she is lonely, inexperienced and extremely nervous. The actress, Joan Fontaine, meanwhile, conveys this through the following performance signs: she wraps her arms around her body and turns her head jerkily as she walks; she slumps into a chair, and jumps and recoils when she is interrupted; her hands shake when she answers the telephone and she stammers and swallows as she speaks; she gives short, twitching half-smiles and she licks and bites her lip. As this list suggests, actors' performances and our decoding of them are shaped by our everyday shared understanding of human body language, which alerts us to the possibility that the act of chewing a lip, for example, may signify anxiety.

Lighting

Lighting is clearly crucial in that it shapes how we respond to all of mise-en-scène's other properties, providing compositional emphasis through illumination and shadow. Lighting may come from sources that we see on screen (lamps, torches, candles and so on which are part of the setting or props), but more typically they come from off-screen sources. Conventionally in mainstream cinema lighting set-ups are designed to be consistent with the light sources we see on-screen, so that we are not distracted from the action of the story by shafts of light which seem to come from nowhere (again, therefore, our attention is directed towards story rather than techniques). However, inconsistencies between on- and off-screen light sources are sometimes used to disturbing effect (for example, in horror films). Colour also provides an important stylistic variant within lighting set-ups: in Wong Kar-wai's *Chungking Express* (1994), for example, scenes are frequently illuminated by blue, yellow and green tinges of light.

Classical Hollywood lighting traditionally involves either a two- or a three-point system, in which a key light is the primary light source, and normally corresponds to visible light sources on-screen. A fill-light, frequently placed just over 90 degrees from the key light, serves to soften the effect by cancelling out some of the shadows cast by the key light. In some cases a back light is also used; normally this is placed behind actors to highlight their shape and make them stand out against the setting. Thus lighting set-ups are usually dictated by the position of actors in relation to the camera; where more than one actor is in shot, one actor's key light may serve as another's fill, and vice versa; each new camera position, however, demands a rearrangement of the lighting. The precise nature and arrangement of the lights determine whether or not the overall lighting effect of an image is **high-key** or **low-key**.

Lighting is also important to characterisation: backlighting, frontlighting, toplighting or underlighting may influence the light (in the metaphorical sense) in which we view characters. In Carl Dreyer's *La Passion de Jeanne d'Arc* (1928), for example, toplighting shines down on the face of Joan of Arc (Renée Jeanne Falconetti), intensifying our impression of her holiness. By contrast, in *The Draughtsman's Contract*, underlighting serves to exaggerate protagonists' facial features, so that our sense of their debauchery is heightened. (Underlighting is also a staple technique in horror films, giving an otherworldly air to monstrous or psychotic villains.)

Crucially, lighting also creates shadows, and these play an important part in the expressive properties of mise-en-scène. Setting and props may be transformed by shadows cast by, and on to, them: in the ministry scenes of *The Conformist* it is not only the structural elements of the setting which suggest prison bars, but also the long shadows cast on the floor. Several genres, most noticeably German Expressionism and film noir, owe much of their stylistic properties to the effects of light and shadow, and the use of low-key lighting. Film noir is a cycle of thrillers and detective films of the 1940s and 1950s, adapted from hard-boiled fiction of the the 1930s. The lighting in film noir is low-key and evokes a dangerous world, in which characters (especially

high-key lighting
This term refers to a lighting design (normally using a three-point system) where there is little contrast between the light and shadowed areas of the frame.

low-key lighting
This term refers to a lighting design where there is a stark contrast between the light and shadowed areas of the frame. Frequently it is produced using only one light source.

femmes fatales) are not what they seem. In *Out of the Past* (Jacques Tourneur, 1947), for example, the character of Kathy (Jane Greer) is frequently shrouded in shadows, and when she and Jeff (Robert Mitchum) first kiss, we scarcely see her face at all, which sets an ominous tone for their relationship. Later, when Jeff and his business partner fight, their movements throw a series of shadows over Kathy, so that we see her watching (and enjoying) the violence in a pool of erratically flickering light. This serves at once to illuminate her true character while also implying her continued threat. The device of minimising fill lighting, so that a character's eyes remain in shadow, is frequently used to alert us to a character's untrustworthiness – as in Hitchcock's *Sabotage* (1936), where the saboteur's hat casts a shadow across his face when we first see him. Film noir, in particular, has had a lasting impact on cinema as a whole in terms of lighting techniques, and lighting as a tool in shaping characterisation and tone.

Cinematography

The precise parameters of what 'cinematography' refers to have been defined differently by different critics. It is used here to refer to all those elements of cinematic expression which are performed or controlled by the camera. These include framing and shot scale, camera angle and movement, and depth of field and focus. Clearly the presentation of all elements of mise-en-scène are shaped by the way they are treated and recorded using camera and film stock; thus, although it is important to be aware of the distinction between what the camera photographs and what it does, in the processes of film analysis these elements are often considered in terms of their relationship to one another.

The basic component of film is the **shot,** or take, which may constitute a static **framing** or a mobile one. In a mobile framing the image within a single shot may change radically as the camera moves. The frame itself is crucial to the presentation of the image, since all aspects of mise-en-scène are subject to their placement within the rectangular space of the flat screen. The composition of an image may be balanced or unbalanced, depending on whether the right and left, and top and bottom of the frame offer matching, harmonious, or mismatched, uneven patterns. A shot may also appear 'shallow' or 'deep' depending on whether the mise-en-scène is framed in a way that suggests few or many **depth cues**. *The Draughtsman's Contract*, which features an elaborately landscaped, seventeenth-century garden, is an exercise in such aspects of framing: shots of the garden emphasise deep space, with lines of trees, shrubs, ornaments and pathways receding backwards, or else crossing the screen horizontally to suggest planes, or layers, to the space. We also see the garden shot through the grid which the draughtsman uses to compose his drawings, so that the frame itself is divided into sixteen rectangles. This helps us to recognise the compositional balance created by elements of the mise-en-scène, which are distributed in precise geometric patterns within the cinematic frame. The film provides a Modernist demonstration of the picturesque possibilities of cinematic space.

Shot scale is another crucial element of cinematography, and is measured according the following categories: the **close-up**, the **extreme close-up**, the **long shot, the extreme long shot**, the **medium long shot**, and the **medium shot**. These framings are crucial in depicting characters and their interactions: the medium long shot is the scale frequently adopted in Hollywood films for **two-** or **three-shots**, while the close-up affords the opportunity for intimate scrutiny of characters, and has facilitated approaches to screen performance not possible on stage, since the smallest changes in expression (such as eye movements and flinches) may be witnessed by viewers. A predominance of certain shot scales may serve to convey particular aspects of character or situation: the accumulation of close-ups in *La Passion de Jeanne d'Arc* creates a proximity between viewers and Joan of Arc which heightens our sense of her suffering. In *North by Northwest* (Alfred Hitchcock, 1959), meanwhile, when Roger Thorwald (Cary Grant) is under attack from the crop-duster aeroplane, his vulnerability is stressed through a number of extreme long shots conveying his remote location; in particular, the opening

femme fatale
A term which originated in critical discourses on film noir; it refers to dangerous, seductive female characters who are normally literally 'fatal', in that they cause the death of the hero.

shot/take
One uninterrupted (uncut) image on-screen whether it is shot with a mobile or a stationary camera. During shooting, a 'take' refers to a single, uninterrupted recording of the camera before the director calls 'cut'.

framing
The choices made about what to include within the frame and what to exclude.

depth cues
These are provided by the arrangement of setting, lighting and props within the frame, which determines the degree to which the space depicted in the cinematic image appears to recede backwards and to take on three-dimensionality. Converging lines, size diminution, and the suggestion of different 'planes' in the fore-, middle- and background of the shot all accentuate the sense that there is a lot of space between the camera and the farthest visible object in the frame.

shot scale
This refers to the range of shots which suggest the apparent distance of an object from the camera; it is conventionally defined according to the framing of the human form.

close-up
A framing in which the object shown takes up most of the screen (as in a shot where a person's face is shown from the neck up).

extreme close-up
A framing in which the object shown takes up virtually the whole screen (as in a shot of a body part, such as a leg or an eye).

long shot
A framing in which the object shown (typically a human body shown from head to toe) fills around three-quarters of the height of the screen.

extreme long shot
A framing in which the object shown (typically a human body shown from head to toe) fills a small fraction of the screen.

medium long shot
Also known as the 'plan Américain' because of its frequency in classical Hollywood, this is a framing in which the human body is shown from mid-calf or knees upwards.

medium shot
A framing in which the human body is shown from the waste upwards.

two-shot/three-shot
A framing containing two or three people.

high-angle shot
A framing where the camera looks down from above on to the objects or scene filmed.

low-angle shot
A framing where the camera looks up from below at the objects or scene filmed.

straight-on shot
A framing where the camera is at the same level as the objects or scene filmed.

canted framing
A framing where the camera is not level, causing the mise-en-scène to appear slanted within the frame.

pan/whip-pan
A 'pan' is a camera movement in which the camera itself remains in the same place but swivels round horizontally; a 'whip-pan' is a very fast pan.

track/tracking shot/dolly shot
A camera movement in which the camera moves horizontally by travelling along the ground (originally on 'tracks' on which a wheeled support – or 'dolly' – for the camera could be mounted).

• **Plate 4.4**
Jane Greer looks on as the men fight in *Out of the Past* (Jacques Tourneur), 1947

shot of the scene is a **high-angle shot**, in which the vastness of the landscape is accentuated by the converging lines of the road, crops, fences and telegraph poles.

Camera angle is another key element of framing, and the crop-duster sequence in *North by Northwest* also contains a number of **low-angle shots**, in which we see the plane from below as it swoops down to attack, as well as **straight-on shots** as we watch Thorwald scanning the horizon or taking cover. Camera angle can also be instrumental in conveying character and establishing (literal and figurative) point of view: thus in *Oliver Twist* (David Lean, 1948) we frequently either look up at adults from Oliver's eye-level, or we look down at Oliver from the perspective of adults; both angles enhance our sense of Oliver's helpless, disempowered position in a dangerous world. **Canted framing** is also important in conveying mood and point of view: thus in *The Third Man* (Carol Reed, 1949), repeated canted framings suggest Holly Martin's (Joseph Cotton) fear and confusion, as well as the structural disintegration of post-war Vienna, and sometimes also Martin's literal view as he hides amidst the rubble.

The camera also has four basic types of mobility – the **pan**, the **track**, the **tilt** and the **crane shot**. The latter, especially in conjunction with distant framing, is particularly useful for the narrative convention of the **establishing shot**. Camera movement can again be used to suggest character point of view, as in *North by Northwest*'s crop-duster sequence, when Thorwald hesitatingly approaches a man at the bus-stop, and the camera produces his viewpoint by tracking in on the man. This cinematic code makes the moving camera a powerful tool for the horror genre: in *Halloween* (John Carpenter, 1978) the camera's pans and tracks follow Laurie (Jamie Lee Curtis) as she walks to school, creating the uneasy impression that someone is stalking her. Camera movement, since it results in a continuous change in the space occupying the frame, can make us powerfully aware of the area outside the frame, a property again exploited in horror films, where characters may seem continually under threat from things we cannot see. A number of art films also use camera movement to draw our attention to cinematic space: *Jules et Jim* (François Truffaut, 1961), for example, employs **whip-pans** and fast tracks to jarring effect in the scene where the two friends visit a statue; both *Le Mèpris* and *The Draughtsman's Contract*, meanwhile, stage conversations with the camera tracking slowly between speakers in ways that emphasise the distance (literally and emotionally) between characters, and the dimensions of the space they occupy.

Depth of field is another key aspect of cinematography. This is the distance between the farthest and nearest point from the camera at which subject details will be recorded in sharp focus. Depth of field is determined by the **aperture** and **focal length** of the camera lens: in order to obtain a wide depth of field a shorter focal length lens is used, and/or a smaller aperture; in order to use a smaller aperture, either more light is required in the mise-en-scène, or a **faster speed film stock** may be used (or a combination of the two). *Citizen Kane* (Orson Welles, 1941) was highly influential in its use of large depth of field (or 'deep focus'), achieved by the use of fast film stock, short focal-length lenses and powerful lighting set-ups. The effect in Welles's film was to create extremely rich images in which cavernous spaces are clearly defined in sharp focus and contrasting tones of light and dark. Another important function of the camera lens is its capacity to **zoom**. The abrupt change in framing brought about by the zoom tends to make its effect jarring (as in the end of *North by Northwest*'s crop-duster sequence where Thorwald is nearly hit by a truck, and his alarm, as well as the vehicle's speed, is signified by a sudden zoom in on Grant).

Special effects

'Special effects' is a broad term referring to image manipulations that change the appearance of other aspects of mise-en-scène: it includes **superimposition**, **matte shots** and CGI (computer generated imagery). While digital technology has seen radical

• Plate 4.5
The crop-dusting sequence of *North by Northwest* (Alfred Hitchcock, 1959)

tilt
A camera movement in which the camera remains in one place but swivels up or down.

crane shot
A camera movement in which the camera moves above the ground in any direction (for which it is mounted on the arm of a special 'camera crane').

establishing shot
A shot at the start of a film or scene which establishes spatial relationships within the mise-en-scène and locates the story within the diegesis.

aperture
The opening within a lens controlling the amount of light that passes through the lens to the film; the smaller the aperture, the less light will hit the film.

focal length
This refers to the ability of a lens to bend the incoming light on to the film plane; a shorter focal length will provide a wider angle of view (which dictates what appears within the frame); a longer focal length will provide a narrower field of view but greater magnification of what is shown; for any given set of conditions a shorter focal length will provide a larger depth of field.

faster speed film speed/speed of film stock
Sensitivity of the photographic emulsion of the film to light; a higher speed of film will require less light (i.e. a smaller aperture may be used) in order to produce a properly exposed image; faster speed film stock tends to provide greater contrast in tone than a slower film stock.

zoom
A shot in which the lens alters the angle of view (either from narrow to wide or wide or narrow); the effect is a sudden change in shot scale within one take.

superimposition
The process by which more than one image is exposed on the same frames of the film stock.

matte shot
A type of shot in which aspects of mise-en-scène are photographed separately and then combined into one image in post-production. Opaque images mask out certain areas of the film negative, and subsequent passes through the camera allow the initially matted-out space to be exposed with another image. Nowadays, matting is often achieved using 'blue screen', a process where action is filmed in front of a blue screen; this footage is then used to create an image of the performers in front of a dark background, and a silhouette of the performer against a clear background, which is used to 'cut out' space for the performer in the scene on to which the action is to be matted.

For further discussion of film and technology, see Chapter 2.

advances in the possibilities of such manipulations, special effects are not in themselves new to cinema: at the turn of the twentieth century, for example, George Meliés used such techniques as hand-tinted film stock in his fantasy films. Nowadays most special effects are achieved by 'laboratory' work which takes place in post-production.

Among the effects which the advent of CGI has heralded, two important techniques are digital matting and motion capture. Digital matting enables shots to be stitched together out of a series of other images, some of which may be photographed, some of which may be designed and animated using computer software. In *Gladiator*, aerial shots of Rome were created by matting computer-drawn buildings on to a helicopter shot of the production's Malta location; the stone and brick textures of these 'virtual' structures were then matted on to the image using photographs of existing buildings.

Motion capture is a technique which combines live-action performances with computer-generated animation: in *The Lord of the Rings: The Two Towers* (Peter Jackson, 2002) and *The Lord of the Rings: The Return of the King* (Jackson, 2003) the character of Gollum was created by recording the performance of actor Andy Serkis while he wore a suit with nodes identifying key parts of the body. The movements of these nodes were scanned into a computer, and used to define the movement and posture of the wholly computer-generated Gollum. This enabled the expressiveness of the individual actor's physical performance to be replicated by the virtual character. The case of Gollum is interesting, in that it suggests that advances in CGI utilise, rather than usurp, the craft that actors bring to films.

One of the great strengths of CGI is the imaginative scope and versatility it brings to mise-en-scène. In *Avatar* the otherworldly landscapes of Pandora, with its luminous vegetation, vividly coloured creatures, and mountains that float in the clouds, were all rendered digitally. CGI was of course used to generate the stereoscopic perspectives necessary for the 3D presentation of these spectacles.

Because of such technology it is becoming increasingly difficult to distinguish between effects achieved during shooting and those of post-production: in *Gladiator*, for example, there is a sweeping pan across a battlefield; however, the shot was achieved

• **Plate 4.6**
CGI-generated mise-en-scène in *Avatar* (James Cameron, 2009)

using three 'locked off' (stationary) cameras, whose images were scanned into a computer and joined together digitally. The panning motion was then performed during post-production in the computer rather than on location using a camera. This enables the film to show in one fluid, mobile shot, a battle featuring many more times the number of soldiers than there were extras employed on the production.

Editing

The actual process of editing involves the joining together of separate pieces of film. Each take consists of one or more exposed frames on a length of film stock, and it is the task of film editors to review all recorded footage, 'cutting' unwanted material, and joining the wanted strips of film in the desired order. Formerly, editing took place in the laboratory, the join being achieved with either a dry splice, using tape, or a wet splice, using liquid cement. Nowadays editing is undertaken digitally, using specialist hardware and software, such as those developed by Avid Technology, Inc during the 1990s. Digital editing involves the importing of a film's rushes on to hard disk, after which the material may be edited in a non-linear fashion, with each cut saved on an 'edit decision list', so that no alteration is irreversible and no material is destroyed in the process.

Unlike mise-en-scène, which inherited and developed its codes from other art forms, the practices of film editing are unique to cinema. Without editing, the expressive and narrative capabilities of the moving image would not be anything like as rich as they are. The power of editing lies in its ability to create juxtapositions, which in turn may change the impact and meaning of each individual shot. Soviet filmmakers of the 1920s sought to explore the possibilities of such juxtapositions (in the movement known as Soviet Montage cinema), and in a now famous experiment filmmaker Lev Kuleshov cut together shots of actor Ivan Mosjoukine's face with three other images – a bowl of soup, a child at play and a body in a coffin. Kuleshov claimed that audiences 'read' the actor's performance as being different in each case, their responses shaped by the shot with which the face was juxtaposed. Kuleshov probably overstated his case: the experiment undervalues the role of performance, the footage has not survived, and several attempts to re-create it have not produced the decisive results to which Kuleshov laid claim (although a reconstruction using shots of actor Bruno Ganz, posted on the University of Alabama website by the Department of Telecommunication and Film, is not unconvincing). Regardless of its precise veracity, the story remains suggestive of editing's potential to shape and override the content of a single shot.

The juxtaposition between one shot and the next may be presented in a number of ways: a **cut** provides an immediate change from one image to the next, while a dissolve offers a more gradual transition, as does the **fade**. Early filmmakers made use of other types of transition, such as the wipe (offering a similar change-over to 'magic-lantern' slide shows), and the **iris-in** and **iris-out**. These were intended as additional attractions to the phenomenon of the moving image (see Salt 1992: 53 and 84), and are nowadays used most often for comic effect, or as the type of self-conscious device found in Modernist narratives: Tony Richardson's *Tom Jones* (1963), for example, uses its wipes and iris shots to add to the ironic playfulness of its tone. In narrative cinema different transitions have come to signify particular types of plot organisation; thus fades in and out often signal breaks between scenes. Dissolves sometimes suggest story ellipses: in *Stand by Me* (Rob Reiner, 1986), for example, the night the boys spend out in the forest is rendered using dissolves to show snippets of their aimless, comical, camp-fire conversation. The scene is a variant of the montage sequence, in which segments of story are summarised through the editing together of images which 'typify', or symbolise, events: thus in *Jules et Jim* a montage of shots of the two men (and various women) in cafés, forests and river boats sums up their early romantic relationships. Dissolves and fades are useful for rendering ellipses in that their slow transitions provide visual metaphors for missed out portions of story-time; however, it

For further discussion of Kuleshov and montage editing see Chapter 17.

cut
The joining of two strips of film in the editing room, and the resulting immediate change from one image to another on-screen.

fade
An editing technique in which one of the juxtaposed images is a black screen. With a 'fade-out' the image slowly darkens; with a 'fade-in' the image slowly emerges out of darkness.

iris-in/iris-out
Editing techniques in which the transition from one image to another is marked by the closing and reopening of an 'iris' or circular hole in the centre of the frame.

• **Plate 4.7**
Jules et Jim (François
Truffaut, 1962)

should be noted that such techniques do not automatically signal specific plot devices, the narrative function of editing being shaped by the content of the shots involved and the context in which they are placed.

In that editing itself involves the cutting together of images filmed at different times and of different spaces, it is clearly instrumental to how films plot stories in time and across space. The development of **cross-cutting,** for example, pioneered by D.W. Griffith, enables films to imply that two different actions, dramatised alternately on screen, take place simultaneously in the story. Because editing imbues sequences and scenes with particular rhythms in cutting, it can also be highly influential in generating mood: the shower scene in *Psycho* (Alfred Hitchcock, 1960), for instance, contains seventy-eight separate shots (see Maltby 1995: 218), with aggressively rapid cutting that emulates the slashes of the knife; in this scene the editing forms a kind of visual assault on the viewer, chopping up the time and space of the film with a violence of its own. By contrast, Hitchcock's *Rope* (1948) was shot entirely in ten-minute takes that were edited together to disguise the joins so that the film appears to have no cuts at all. This, combined with very mobile framing, produces tension in that the camera seems to probe unremittingly the space of the story. Long takes may suggest tranquillity, however: the beginning of *Pride and Prejudice* (Joe Wright, 2005) features a one-and-a-half-minute take which follows Elizabeth (Keira Knightley) as she walks home, tracks through the house, out of a window, then back into the house. The effect is a serene opening, allowing viewers time to observe the dilapidated charm of the Bennets' home, and the pastoral aimlessness of the girls' lives.

Editing also creates juxtapositions between all the aspects of the mise-en-scène, and may be used to suggest matches, or contrasts, between setting, costumes, props and performances. Soviet montage director Sergei Eisenstein used montage's potential for spatial juxtaposition to maximum metaphoric effect in his use of 'non-diegetic inserts' – that is, shots which do not belong to the narrative context, but serve to commentate on (or symbolise) narrative content: *October* (1927), for example, features cuts between Kerenksy and images of Napoleon and of a peacock, which imply the tyranny and vanity of the leader of the Provisional Government. Eisenstein wrote extensively on editing, and his films abound with striking montage innovations, from jump-cuts, fast, rhythmic

cross-cutting
Editing that alternates shots occurring in different story locations to imply that the events shown are occurring simultaneously.

editing (most famously in the Odessa steps sequence of *Battleship Potemkin* (1925), **impact editing** and **overlapping editing**. His films are powerful demonstrations of the potential of editing as a tool of expression and persuasion.

Continuity editing

The conventions which govern editing in classical Hollywood cinema, and which have come to dominate much filmmaking outside Hollywood, are known as 'continuity editing'. Continuity editing developed early in cinema's history, and most of its key features were in place by around 1919. The purpose of continuity editing is to maintain the viewer's understanding of, and engagement with, the story. As with Hollywood's treatment of plot, the guiding principle is transparency – that is, the rendering of techniques unobtrusively so that audiences retain their focus on what is happening, and not on how things are shown.

This means that shots are generally juxtaposed in ways that minimise the disruption inherent in editing. Cuts are designed to avoid confusing ellipses, or disorientating changes in screen space. The convention of the establishing shot assists this in making clear the layout and parameters of a scene; the closer shots which follow may then be understood as framings within this larger space. Another frequently employed technique is the **180° rule,** which ensures spatial consistency across successive shots, preventing aspects of mise-en-scène which appear on one side of the frame in one shot from appearing on the other side of the frame (as if in mirror image) in the next. The **30° rule** operates in a similar way in that it ensures sufficient change in framing from one shot to the next so that jump-cuts are avoided. Also central to achieving smooth, coherent spatial juxtapositions are techniques which 'match' successive shots – such as the **eyeline match** and the **match on action**. These map out for us the spatial position of one framing in relation to the next, using the story itself – its characters and actions – to link shots together.

As is implied by eyeline matching, editing is central to the cinematic construction of characters' point of view (meaning, literally, what they see, as opposed to the metaphorical connotations implicit in the term 'focalisation'). Conversely the phenomenon of on-screen characters who look at things is also extremely valuable in conveying intelligible links between shots. This may be seen in another recurring technique of continuity editing, namely **shot–reverse shot** constructions. These are used most frequently for the staging of conversations between two characters, in which the camera looks at each character in turn over the shoulder of the other character. The technique offers us a clear understanding of where each speaker stands and what each sees, while also affording intimacy in the staging of character interactions.

The opening of *His Girl Friday* provides a demonstration of the operations of continuity editing: the film's establishing shot is a track through the newsroom of the *Washington Post*, which makes clear both the bustle of this environment and the relative locations of the editor's office (on the right of the set), the journalist and typist pool (in the middle) and the elevators (on the left). Following a dissolve to bring us to a closer shot, Hildy and Ralph exit an elevator; their subsequent exchange is depicted in an over-the-shoulder, shot–reverse shot sequence, which contrasts the previous mobile framings and seems to place the two in a world of their own amidst the newsroom commotion. A series of tracking shots then follows Hildy, and a match on action is used as she leaves the pool and enters Walter's office. Hildy at first stands in the doorway looking slightly to the right of camera, and there follows a shot of Walter and Louie, whom we identify as the object of her gaze. Hildy announces herself, and a cut introduces a medium long shot showing all three characters, which in turn establishes the layout of this new room.

Following initial greetings and an interruption by Duffy, a medium long two-shot introduces a prolonged exchange between Hildy and Walter, during which Hildy crosses to sit behind Walter: she is now to the right of the frame with Walter on the

impact editing
Editing that produces violent contrast between images, most often by switching between close and long shot scales.

overlapping editing
Editing where shots repeat part or all of the action shown in the previous shot.

180° rule
An editing technique which dictates that the camera should remain on one side of an imaginary line drawn through a scene.

30° rule
An editing technique which dictates that the camera should be stationed at an angle of at least 30° from its location in the previous shot.

eyeline match
A cut in which one shot shows a person looking at something off-screen, and the other shot is thereby posited as the object of that person's gaze. More usually the shot showing the gazing person comes first, although cuts which show the gazer second are by no means uncommon.

match on action
A cut which joins two spaces together by virtue of the fact that an action shown in the first shot is then completed in the second.

shot–reverse shot
A cut which switches between complementary spaces, sometimes with the camera stationed in almost opposing/ facing positions within the confines of the 180° rule.

left. Walter responds by swivelling his chair so that he sits facing her with his back to the camera; there follows a cut so that Walter is now facing us. Although this cut involves a transition from Walter with his back to us to Walter facing us, the camera has moved less than 180°, as is made clear by the fact that the first shot has Walter slightly to the left of camera, while the second has him slightly to the right; there follows a point-of-view shot of Hildy, in which the spatial relations of the earlier medium long shot are retained, with Hildy still on the right and Walter's shoulder on the left.

This scene adheres to continuity editing and shows how variety is available within continuity rules. We might also note that Hildy's move to sit behind Walter serves to alter the position of the imaginary line governing the 180° rule: while the scene contains four people, three of whom enter or leave, the line runs from the door to the window; once the scene involves only Walter and Hildy, Hildy effectively realigns the scene along an axis which runs straight through the characters, thus expanding the number of camera positions possible overall. This also subtly uses editing to signal a shift in the character interaction as Walter and Hildy embark on a bantering, bickering reminiscence. Throughout the scene the editing is unobtrusive, serving and enhancing our appreciation of story in ways that, normally, we scarcely notice.

While continuity editing remains central to film 'language' in mainstream and art cinema, it is also the case that audiences' increasing film literacy has enabled such rules to be broken with greater frequency. The 180° rule, in particular, is frequently discarded in action sequences, for example, where camera mobility and variety in framing complement dynamic mise-en-scène. Art films also frequently disrupt editing continuity (as in Godard's use of jump-cuts) as part of their self-conscious exploration of film technique.

For further discussion of Godard's filming technique see the chapter on French New Wave at the website www.routledge.com/cw/nelmes

Sound

Sound was introduced to cinema in 1927, and is now an extremely rich element of cinematic expression. Its properties and possibilities extend beyond the scope of this chapter, but some key considerations are noted here.

Although sound played an important role in cinema exhibition before 1927, in the form of live musical accompaniment and sometimes commentating 'showmen', the advent of the recorded soundtrack had a profound effect on the stories films told and the possibilities of cinematic narration. Synchronised sound, of course, brought speech to cinema, and this allied cinema more closely with theatre than previously. New cinematic genres arose, such as the musical and the screwball comedy, which had their roots in theatrical traditions, and which offered sound as a key attraction. While recorded speech is clearly crucial to screenplays, it is not the only element of sound to have significantly shaped cinema's development, and we might divide film sound into three basic areas – speech, music and sound effects.

Sound in film narrative may be identified as either diegetic or non-diegetic – in other words, it either belongs within the story 'universe', or we attribute it as originating from outside the fictional world inhabited by characters. The film's musical score is the most common form of non-diegetic sound, although it is not the only one: we might distinguish, for example, between diegetic voice-overs spoken by characters – as in *The Big Sleep* or Amy Heckerling's *Clueless* (1995) – and non-diegetic voice-overs, which originate from seemingly omniscient 'narrators' – as in *Jules et Jim*. Films may blur the distinction between diegetic and non-diegetic sound, sometimes for comic effect and sometimes as an element of aesthetic innovation. Early sound films frequently introduced non-diegetic score unobtrusively by including melodies diegetically first. This occurs in Jean Vigo's *L'Atalante* (1934), where the melody played by Père Jules (Michel Simon) suddenly becomes a non-diegetic accompaniment to two singing voices as we see the honeymoon couple embrace. Diegetic and non-diegetic sound should not be confused with on- and off-screen sound: a sound may originate off-screen (as when a person not in shot speaks or cries out) but still belong within the diegesis. Off-screen sound has the effect of changing our relationship with the image, drawing our attention specifically to the space outside the frame (making it another staple technique of horror films).

The presence of sound alongside the image creates a whole series of possible relationships between sound and editing, and sound and mise-en-scène: the rhythms of noise and music, for example, may seem to match the rhythm of editing or of movements within the mise-en-scène, or they may seem at odds with them; sound-effects may appear faithful to the sources we assume produced them, or may seem incongruous with them. In *The 39 Steps* sound and editing are used to create a striking scenic transition, in which there is a cut from a woman who is about to scream to a train exiting a tunnel; the train's screeching whistle is substituted for the woman's cry, making the human reaction to the story's murder scenario seem piercingly acute. Sound, in the form of **sound-bridges**, may also be used as a means of smoothing over divisions between scenes.

The distinction between sound which seems faithful to image and sound which does not may be extremely subtle: in *The English Patient* (Anthony Minghella, 1996) the sound-track of the desert scenes includes a whole series of effects – clicks suggesting insects, rubbing noises representing grains of sand – many of which would not, realistically, be picked up by the human ear. However, these noises evoke the desert terrain, and paradoxically give us an eerie sense of 'a space that is silent' (Ondaatje 2002: 118). Thus the sounds, though not precisely true to what we might hear in this location, do not strike us as out of place, since they enhance both the mood of the setting and the metaphors of emotional isolation within the narrative. As with performance, therefore, our assessment of the verisimilitude of noise is as much shaped by cinematic conventions as it is by our experiences of real life. In terms of sound volume in relation to image, we conventionally expect some degree of 'sound perspective', so that loud sounds represent actions depicted in close-up or near depth planes, while quieter sounds represent actions depicted in longer shot scales or distant depth planes. However, films may subvert this rule, as Godard does in *Weekend* (1967), where the characters' indoor conversations are sometimes drowned out by the outdoor noise.

The selection, generation, recording, distortion, amplification and mixing of film sounds create an array of possibilities for films' audio tracks, which means that we may consider them as 'soundscapes' – as a sophisticated orchestration of multi-faceted techniques comparable to the production of the film's visual elements. Technological advances that originated in the music industry have led to the advent of soundtracks where speech, music and noise may overlap and fluctuate in highly complex ways: in *Apocalypse Now* (Francis Coppola, 1979), for which the chief sound editor was, as with *The English Patient*, Walter Murch, sounds of war, jungle, speech, diegetic and non-diegetic music are mixed in a disorientating, multi-layered fashion which evokes the (drug-enhanced) terrors of the soldiers in Vietnam. The degree of multiplicity within the audio track is aptly demonstrated by the trouble Murch and his team went to in producing the sound of crickets: one cricket was recorded close to a microphone, the sound was electronically multiplied and all the resulting noises were then all overlaid on top of each other; this mix was then itself mixed with other elements of the soundtrack. The effect is to produce a cricket noise which is not so much a lifelike version of how many crickets sound as it is a nightmare rendition of a jungle cacophony.

Sound in cinema fluctuates not only in volume and rhythm, but also in **pitch** and **timbre**. These properties are particularly important to music, although they also charac-terize vocal performance and sound-effects: in *His Girl Friday*, for example, Cary Grant's voice frequently veers to a high pitch suggestive of urgency (or even megalomania), while in *L'Atalante* Père Jules entertains Juliette (Dita Parlo) with series of toys that produce noises and notes of contrasting timbre (ranging from tinkling glockenspiel to a

sound-bridge
An audio connection between scenes, where sound from one scene continues into the beginning of the scene which follows, or where sound belonging to the opening of a scene begins during the close of the scene which precedes it.

pitch
The height or depth of a musical sound as it is determined by its frequency relative to other notes.

timbre
The tonal quality of a musical sound; timbre is what makes a saxophone sound different from a clarinet, for example.

hollow rattle). A film's non-diegetic music conventionally matches timbre, pitch, volume and rhythm to the action depicted on screen – so, for example, Alfred Newman's score for *Wuthering Heights* (William Wyler, 1939) has soaring strings accompanying its love scenes. Thus music guides and enhances our responses to the story. In *Jaws*, for example, John Williams's rhythmically monotonous score, with its modulation between only two notes, alerts us in advance of imminent danger, heightening our fear of the seemingly relentless predator.

In his economy of melody, Williams was heavily influenced by film composer Bernard Herrmann, whose work with Alfred Hitchcock has been particularly influential in shaping and advancing approaches to film music. In Herrmann's score for *Psycho,* for example, three notes recur and form the basis of the violent chords of both the opening theme and the shower scene's screeching violins. Timbre, as well as pitch, play a role in the score's insistent menace, in that Herrmann omitted both the woodwind and brass sections from his orchestra, limiting the tonal 'colour' of the music only to strings. Herrmann, throughout his career, made innovative, unexpected choices in his allocation of musical instruments to particular visual motifs, as, for example, in Hitchcock's *Vertigo* (1958), where the 'vertigo effect', achieved by the camera's simultaneous track in and zoom out, is accompanied in Herrmann's score by harps. Herrmann demonstrated that considerable expressive possibilities are opened up through the selection or composition of seemingly incongruous non-diegetic music: thus *2001: A Space Odyssey* (Stanley Kubrick, 1969) transforms our impression of space flight into something balletic and peaceful through its appropriation of Johann Strauss's *The Blue Danube*.

☐ CASE STUDY 1: CLASSICAL CONVENTIONS IN *GLADIATOR* (RIDLEY SCOTT, 2000)

For a case study on the production process of Gladiator *see pp. 23–26.*

At first sight Ridley Scott's *Gladiator* (scripted by David Franzoni, John Logan and William Nicholson) may not seem to conform to mainstream conventions, in that our hero, Maximus (Russell Crowe), dies at the end. However, the film constitutes a persuasive demonstration of the dominance of classical story-telling, in that its norms persist even in this tale: all the hero's goals are met, and the film is so ingeniously plotted that death itself is presented to us as a 'happy ending'.

The film opens with intertitles that set the scene as AD 180 during the reign of Roman Emperor Marcus Aurelius; the plot begins prior to the last battle between the Roman Empire and Germania; however, the battle is preceded by a fleeting moment of tranquillity achieved by shots of golden cornfields, which are then posited as Maximus's imaginings. With the battle won, the significance of this becomes clear: Maximus, the great Roman general, wants to go home. This is the character's primary, overarching goal, but almost as soon as it is established a second goal is presented which must delay the achievement of the first: Marcus Aurelius charges Maximus to 'give Rome back to the people', a task he will undertake as 'Protector of Rome' after the emperor's death. Marcus Aurelius gives Maximus until sunset to decide his course of action, but before then the emperor is murdered by his son, Commodus. Commodus orders Maximus to be murdered also, but Maximus escapes and returns to his farm in Spain. At this point the narrative seems to thwart, permanently and horrifically, Maximus's goal of returning home, because his wife and son have been crucified and his farm ransacked and burnt. It seems therefore that this goal, motivated by love, will be replaced by one motivated by hate, namely revenge against Commodus. However, even this goal is thwarted, because at the end of the first act, an injured, distraught Maximus is captured by slave-traders.

In this opening, the motivations for characters' actions are made clear: Marcus Aurelius wants to rid Rome of corruption and leave behind a noble legacy; he chooses Maximus because he loves him as a son and because he is untainted by politics;

Maximus, because he is uncorrupted, wants only to return to his family and a quiet, country life; however, he is also motivated by his sense of duty towards Rome and by his love for the emperor. Commodus's motives, meanwhile, are at once psychologically complex and childishly simple: he is ambitious, but this in itself is rooted in a desire to be loved; we see his desperate longing for his father's approval, and his hatred of Maximus is a product of both political rivalry and 'fraternal' jealousy; Commodus wants to be emperor because he seeks to substitute the love of the people for the father's love he cannot win, and because his love for his father makes him want to live up to him.

At the start of the next act Maximus is sold to Proximo, a gladiator 'impresario', and so becomes a gladiator. All the goals of the previous act are therefore left hanging, and are replaced by new ones necessitated by his changed circumstances: he needs to stay alive in the arena, and he also seeks to avoid the humiliation of becoming an 'entertainer', of turning the fighting skills which once brought glory to Rome into a public spectacle. Maximus's reluctance to win over the crowd posits his character as the exact opposite of Commodus's, and the plot now switches between Maximus in Zucchabar, and Commodus in Rome, who conceives the idea of 150 days of gladiatorial games as a means of winning the people's love. An ironic cause-and-effect pattern is therefore set in motion, in that Commodus's desire to be loved leads directly to the arrival in Rome of Maximus, Commodus's former rival for his father's affection. Maximus learns that Proximo used to be a gladiator, and that he was granted his freedom by Marcus Aurelius; this conversation changes Maximus's goals, because he realises that by winning over the crowd as a gladiator 'entertainer' he may meet Commodus again. Thus Maximus and Commodus are again rivals (this time for the love of the Roman people) and Maximus's goal of killing Commodus is made clear.

We are now presented with the first spectacular fight at the Colosseum, and the plot turns this into a high point in character interaction too, because Commodus realises that Maximus is alive. Maximus postpones killing Commodus because Lucius, the son of Commodus's sister Lucilla, is present, but the scene marks a turning point in the narrative, in that Maximus's popularity blatantly renews his status as Commodus's rival: the two men now pursue parallel goals of murdering each other. Lucilla visits Maximus, and a third source of rivalry is now spelled out, in that Lucilla, for whom Commodus has an incestuous love, was once romantically involved with Maximus. Motivated by grief for her father, attachment to Maximus, duty towards Rome and, above all, fear for her son's life, Lucilla urges Maximus to meet with Senator Gracchus and plot the overthrow of Commodus. Maximus refuses, saying that he is a slave, and not the man he used to be. This establishes a path for Maximus which he himself does not acknowledge – namely to rise to be again the man he once was. From now on the narrative charts the recovery of his former goals, a process initiated by Maximus's reunion with Cicero, a friend whose loyalty convinces Maximus that his former regiment will fight for him. Cicero's absence from, and return to, the story is explained by the fact that Maximus was previously assumed dead; his return reminds us of Maximus's former, foremost goal – to return home – in that he restores to Maximus keepsakes of his wife and son that he used to carry. Maximus now agrees to Lucilla's scheme, but Gracchus is subsequently arrested. Commodus threatens Lucius, thereby forcing Lucilla to confess their plans, but a cause is now picked up from much earlier in the plot, in that Proximo frees Maximus, motivated by loyalty towards Marcus Aurelius, the man who freed Proximo himself. Maximus is captured, however, owing to Lucilla's confession, and the scene is now set for a final showdown between Maximus and Commodus; as Commodus says: 'People want to know how the story ends.'

Although Maximus still wishes to kill Commodus, his motives have been transformed in the second half of the film: he is no longer driven primarily by revenge, but is now fulfilling the goal of 'giving Rome back to the people' set for him by Marcus Aurelius. He retains our sympathy through his restoration to a man fulfilling a duty out of love, as opposed to a man bent on murder as vengeance. Commodus, of course, still wishes to kill Maximus, but his difficulty is that if he kills such a popular man, he will fail in his other goal of securing the people's love. This dilemma motivates Commodus to fight Maximus himself in the Colosseum, since he is seeking precisely the adulation accorded to gladiator 'entertainers'; the plot therefore utilises Commodus's weaknesses as a means of accommodating its implausible dramatic climax. Commodus's willingness to battle a champion in public is further explained when he stabs Maximus in secret before the fight. In the Colosseum a dying Maximus kills Commodus with the concealed dagger Commodus used to stab him, and asks Lucilla to free Gracchus and honour her father's wish of re-establishing a republic. The film's recurring motif of the golden cornfields which are Maximus's farm accompany his death, and kneeling by Maximus's body, Lucilla whispers, 'You are home.'

Thus the film offers Maximus's death as his longed-for reunion with his lost wife and son. The plot signals this trajectory right at the start, when Maximus, briefing his soldiers before battle, tells them, 'If you should find yourself alone, riding in green fields with the sun on your face, do not be troubled, for you are in Elysium and you are already dead.' The story's end is also anticipated through the scenes Maximus shares with fellow gladiator Juba, with whom he discusses the wife and son who are 'waiting for him'. The evocation of Maximus's family as at once dead but waiting is both moving and convenient, since it offers a romantic story of marital fidelity which does not conflict with the more intriguing unfulfilled romance with Lucilla. The plot's ingenuity rests in the way it manages to pull off the story it promises at first but then seems irretrievably to subvert: Maximus does exactly what Marcus Aurelius says he will do – he performs one last task for his emperor and Rome, and then he goes home.

The above analysis demonstrates the film's goal-oriented, cause-and-effect plot structure. It seeks, not to tell the story, but to show the logic by which the story is told. However, we may also use it to draw out other aspects of the film, namely its meaning, or 'themes'. These operate on several levels: most simply, the narrative promotes love over hatred in its depiction of a man who rises above revenge to do his duty and is rewarded with eternal happiness; the narrative also promotes democracy over tyranny, and its repetition of Marcus Aurelius's lament that 'there once was a dream that was Rome' aligns Maximus with an American 'dream', and Rome's projected republican future with contemporary Western conceptions of 'democratic freedom'. Moreover, the film demonstrates a preoccupation with 'entertainment', and since the gladiators fight for their lives for spectacle and profit they provide an obvious metaphor for both contemporary sports industries and the film industry, where 'players' are 'owned' by huge corporations. We might conclude that the film critiques such dehumanisation, but this message is subtly undermined by the way that the gladiatorial arena increasingly becomes the political arena: Commodus and Maximus fight there over the future of Rome, and the gladiators who formerly fought for sport are transformed into Maximus's 'real', loyal army. Thus the film offers us a celebration of Commodus's games and of itself, where 'truth' and true heroism are represented by 'the entertainers'.

☐ **CASE STUDY 2: ARTISTRY, COMEDY AND AMBIGUITY IN *LOVES OF A BLONDE/LÁSKY JEDNÉ PLAVOVLÁSKY* (MILOS FORMAN, 1965)**

Before his Hollywood career, and critically acclaimed films such as *One Flew Over the Cuckoos Nest* (1975), *Amadeus* (1984) and *The People vs. Larry Flynt* (1996), Milos Forman was a leading exponent of the Czech New Wave, a movement which flourished during a period of artistic and expressive freedom in socialist Czechoslovakia (prior to the 1968 invasion by the Warsaw Pact powers) and drew inspiration from other influential

European art cinemas, such as Italian neo-realism and the French New Wave. *Loves of a Blonde* was co-written by Forman with his recurring creative collaborators, Jaroslav Papousek and Ivan Passer, and was shot using mostly non-professional performers.

The central character of *Loves of a Blonde* is Andula (Hanu Brejchová), the blonde of the title, who is a worker in a shoe factory in Zruc, a small, isolated town in Czechoslovakia. The film is frequently very funny, but its humour both masks and enables the narrative's critique of the Czechoslovak Socialist Republic's labour movement, in which the enforced mobilisation of young people to work in factories was undertaken at the expense of personal lives and protective family environments.

The film opens with Andula in bed in the dormitory she shares with hundreds of other girls, confiding in whispers to a friend that her boyfriend Tonda has given her a 'real diamond' ring. Before we see the girls (who are curled up in bed together in a manner suggestive of childhood innocence) we are first shown a close-up of their hands as they play with the ring, and the camera also pans and cuts across the room, so that we see both the crowded conditions and the ringless hand of another girl which hangs over the side of a bed. The two girls then switch their attention to a photograph of Tonda, and following the friend's suggestion that Andula should also give Tonda a gift, there is an abrupt cut to a snow-covered wood, where a tracking shot brings us, not to Tonda, but to a tree sporting a tie. In the woods a forest ranger first reprimands Andula for 'dressing up' the tree, but then asks her out. The scene then cuts back to Andula and her friend in bed, where Andula confides that the forest ranger is married.

This opening is disorientating and elliptical, in that the two incidents of the girls in bed are not visually marked as taking place at different times, nor is the woods scene given any detailed explanation. The viewer is therefore tempted to read it is as flashback which interrupts, and is framed by, the girls' intimate conversation. It is only by paying careful attention to the dialogue that we realise that the two bedtime sequences take place at different times, and that Tonda, who does not show up for the date where she plans to give him the tie, has been substituted in the narrative by another man (just as he is substituted in the mise-en-scène by his ring, his photogragh and a tree). The opening is characteristic of art cinema in the conspicuousness of its cinematic codes (the striking close-up of hands, the abrupt cut and slow track to the tie in the forest), which draw our attention to the film's techniques. It is also modernist in its fragmented, elliptcal story-telling, which is confusing whilst simultaneously establishing a pattern for the story to come – in which young men prove unreliable, older men seek to seduce pitifully hopeful young girls, and prospective lovers of both sexes appear to be readily, repeatedly replaceable by other, more immediately available partners. In these scenes, as in the film as a whole, the charm of performances and aesthetics are contrasted and at play with the loneliness of characters, and the impersonal, oppressive nature of their situations.

In the scenes that follow we are given a clarification of Andula's predicament, with the factory's paternalistic foreman appealing to army officials to station a regiment nearby, in order to provide company for the many young women whom the state has conscripted to Zruc in order to meet quotas for the manufacture of shoes. Soldiers are duly posted to the town, but they are not athletic young heroes serving their country, but rather a regiment of mostly middle-aged reservists. Andula and two friends attend a dance celebrating the regiment's arrival, and in a protracted scene are approached by three soldiers (all of whom, it is implied, are married). In this scene comedy is derived from elements of physical performance and slapstick (as when one of the soldiers crawls between the legs of three girls he has just rejected in order to retrieve his lost wedding ring).

The dance scene also demonstrates the film's indebtedness to cinema vérité in that its cinematic codes are reminiscent of documentary cinema. Shots of the principal characters are intercut with those of extras, so that, except for Andula, we do not at

• Plate 4.8
The playful aftermath of Andula and Milda's encounter in *Loves of a Blonde* (1965)

first distinguish between those who will play a part in the drama and those who are 'background'. Much of the interaction between soldiers and factory girls takes place without dialogue, increasing the impression of a haphazardly roving camera simply capturing what it encounters (in interviews Forman has explained that he shot the scene using two cameras, one devoted entirely to filming the extras, who were not always aware when their performances were being recorded). In addition, the camera is hand-held and its movements are sometimes erratic, as when the camera's pursuit of the soldier's rolling wedding ring is sometimes obscured by moving feet on the dance floor.

These techniques contribute to the narrative's social critique, since they evoke the idea that what the camera captures is 'truthful'. *Loves of a Blonde* features the real workers and factory of Zruc, and was also allegedly based on a real-life encounter Forman had with a factory girl. Such facts (available to us through auteurist discourses such as director interviews and film-festival publicity) feed into our viewing practice and reinforce the film's impression of the 'ordinariness' of its faces and voices. In both its style and its production, the film is thus linked to other European art cinema movements renowned for the apparent pursuit of verisimiltude, most obviously Italian neo-realism and the French New Wave. In fact the Czech New Wave is now credited with having utilised more widely than either of these movements, a number of production strategies (such as the casting of non-professionals and a reliance on dialogue improvisation) with which Italian neo-realism and the French New Wave are particularly associated. Its connection with these movements, and its development of them, clearly places the Czech New Wave within European art cinema traditions, particularly one in which auteurist intent and aesthetic experimentation are marked by a paradoxically stylised realism.

The evening at the dance ends with the girls rejecting the three soldiers, but Andula is accosted by the dance band's young, good-looking piano player, Milda (Vladimíra Pucholta). Once again the narrative is simultaneously playful and disquieting, for our enjoyment of the couple's flirtation is undercut by Milda's ruthlessly persistent seduction; our sense that Andula has been saved from an undesirable sexual encounter (because her suitor was balding, middle-aged, overweight and married) is contradicted by the egotistical immaturity of the handsome, young substitute. Afterwards charm predomi-nates in both the mise-en-scène and dialogue, which are at once memorable and eccentric: a high-angle shot shows Milda and Andula lying naked at ninety degrees to one another, his head in her lap, whilst on the sound track he tells her that she is shaped 'like a guitar … but one made by Picasso'.

In the final portion of the film, Andula rejects Tonda and goes in search of Milda in Prague, causing consternation in his mother (Milada Jezková) when she arrives at his family home in the night with a suitcase. The mother's relentless interrogation of Andula (whom she initially assumes is pregnant) arouses our sympathy by emphasising the young girl's friendless state, but also echoes the audience's sense that Andula's actions are impractical (as well as only partially accounted for within the narrative). More comedy ensues when Tonda returns home from another evening of music and attempted seduction: he is dragged by his mother into his parents' room, and forced to spend the night sharing their bed (separated from Andula, who is on the living-room sofa). The incident is farcical, as well as apposite in demonstrating the childishness of Andula's supposedly sophisticated big-city lover, and the film devotes a full five minutes to a one-take scene in which the family bicker over who has the most covers and who is to blame for Milda's failings. This humour is abruptly contrasted with a shot of Andula kneeling on the floor outside the bedroom, crying. The film finishes as it starts, with Andula in bed in the dormitory in Zruc, confiding to her friend. This time the pitiful nature of Andula's fantasies of escape from factory life through romance are very clear, as she whispers to the vicariously hopeful friend how nice Milda's family are and that she plans to visit them often.

The narrative of *Loves of a Blonde* is modernist in the way it eschews story closure and offers only a 'snapshot' of a few days in the heroine's life. The characterisation of Andula is economical and ambiguous, with significant details about her history (her parents' divorce, her troubled relationship with her mother, her attemped suicide) signalled but never explicated. In this the narrative strategy mirrors Andula's psychology and her situation, for Andula seems almost obdurately innocent in her romantic delusions, whilst both her family and the state which has ostensibly taken on her guardianship are indifferent to her individuality and her emotional needs.

The film is also consistent with art cinema in its own inconsistent tone, with whimsicality and cruelty often juxtaposed and even interdependent in the dialogue and story. There is similar ambivalence in the film's style, and its referencing of seemingly oppositional cinematic practices: observational, documentary-style filmic codes are combined with elements of self-conscious artistry, so that both authenticity in subject matter and auteurist intervention are strongly signalled. Such ambiguity enables the film to offer a compelling social critique in a country where outspoken criticism could (even amidst the freedoms permitted in Czechoslovakia at the time) incur censorship and censure: modernist irresolution and auteurist idiosyncracy serve to camouflage political content and legitimise a narrative strategy where much is left unsaid. At the same time, the film's open ending is also one of its most powerful political comments (paradoxically revealing the freedoms within the Czechoslovak, nationalised film industry), in that it seems to imprison Andula inescapably in her homeless, lonely existence.

☐ CASE STUDY 3: POSTMODERNISM AND PLAYING GAMES IN *RUN LOLA RUN/LOLA RENNT* (TOM TYKWER, 1998)

Director and script-writer Tom Tykwer has described *Run Lola Run* as 'an experimental film for a mass audience' (Halle and McCarthy 2003: 401), which suggests that it seeks to break down some of the conventional distinctions between mainstream and art cinema. Its two opening-intertitle quotations – one by T.S. Eliot, the other by the former coach of former West Germany's national football team Sepp Herberger – reinforces this

pastiche
From the Italian verb 'to paste', this refers to a patchwork of references from, or imitations of, other works of art.

blurring of boundaries. In its mixing together of styles and forms from high and popular culture, and its frequent use of **pastiche**, *Run Lola Run* constitutes a 'postmodern' narrative.

The film tells three stories, or rather it provides three alternative sets of outcomes all proceeding from the same opening. The narrative premise makes use of a plot technique known as a 'time lock' (Hunter 1994: 51), or story deadline; this is a common means of generating suspense in mainstream film narratives which makes use of the audience's experience of cinematic running time. In *Run Lola Run*, Lola's (Franka Potente) boyfriend Manni has lost DM100,000 (the proceeds of a stolen car deal with which a gangster, Ronnie, has entrusted him) on the Berlin underground, and Lola has twenty minutes to replace the money and deliver it to him. Over the phone, Manni tells her that Ronnie will kill him, and that if she does not deliver the money by noon he will commit robbery to obtain it. The film plays out the story three times. Lola always chooses the same solution (to ask her bank-manager father) but for each version a different cause-and-effect chain is set in motion and so the outcome changes: first she dies, then Manni dies, then she obtains the money legally while Manni recovers the lost funds. The final version is the happy ending on which the film finishes.

The film does not explain the links between the stories, and its ambiguity, coupled with the themes of fate and all-conquering love which are suggested, seem to align it with art cinema. However, the narrative also offers us the possibility of another explanation which draws on contemporary popular culture, namely that this constitutes a live-action enactment of a computer game: thus Lola keeps playing until she overcomes all obstacles and 'wins'. Several aspects of the film point to this: when Lola runs down the stairs the camera zooms in on a television set on which an animated Lola is seen; Lola also sometimes seems to learn from one story to the next as if through trial and error (as when she releases the safety catch of the gun in the second story, or when the cartoon Lola takes a huge leap over the dog in the third). The narrative is also free of any ethical consideration of Manni's actions, as if the story exists in the 'virtual moral vacuum' of, for example, *Grand Theft Auto*: as the film's opening football metaphors attest, this is all a game.

Run Lola Run is one of a number of recent films, such as *eXistenZ* (David Cronenberg, 1999) and *The Matrix* trilogy (Andy and Larry Wachowski, 1999, 2003, 2003), which draw on the phenomenon of computer games to construct narratives where 'reality' and illusion are blurred, or where 'the real' emerges as a type of fictional construct. These films draw on the work of postmodern theorists such as Fredric Jameson and Jean Baudrillard, for whom the pervasiveness of contemporary mass media and popular culture has led to an obliteration of 'reality' and history, in favour of an endless production and recycling of images (of 'reality' and history). Tykwer's film invites us to invest in the urgency of Lola's story without identifying which outcome is 'real', or if the stories themselves are a story (or game) within a story. This suggests the absence of 'truth' which is again central to postmodern thought, whereby there are no overarching 'grand narratives' (such as religion, patriarchy, Marxism, science), only different ways of telling stories. Thus the narrative's imitation of a computer game becomes a metaphor which expounds postmodern philosophy.

Run Lola Run, with its frenetic plot, dizzying camera mobility, split-second montages, split-screen framings and pounding soundtrack, also draws on the style of the music video, a postmodern pastiche which functions simultaneously as a Modernist critique of the benevolent, transparent codes of classical cinema. Finally, the film offers us a self-reflexive exploration of mainstream narratives. The operations of cause and effect are demonstrated, so that, for example, when Lola runs more slowly in the second story than she does in the first, because she trips down the stairs, her slightly later arrival at each subsequent encounter shapes the different events shown. Similarly the film draws our attention to classical narrative's focus on central characters, through its 'snapshot'

• **Plate 4.9**
'Pop culture' imagery in *Run Lola Run* (Tom Tykwer, 1998)

montages of what happens next to three people whom Lola encounters (these stories too are different each time, suggesting an endless web of possible outcomes). However, the film eschews 'grand narratives' and single answers, and this extends to its self-reflexivity, since it does not always demonstrate cause-and-effect logic: in the third story Lola jumps over the dog, does not hesitate on the stairs, and so, we assume, is slightly ahead of 'schedule' this time; nevertheless, she appears to arrive in front of Herr Meyer's car slightly later than she does in the first story, and what follows is shaped by this unexplained variation. Thus, as with Modernist narratives, a 'single' reading of this narrative of multiplicity is not possible. The film incorporates popular culture into a European tradition of innovation and ambiguity. It blurs the categories of mainstream and art cinema and at the same time affirms their cultural distinction and importance, since we can only appreciate what *Run Lola Run* does through our familiarity with film's form and its various narrative traditions.

CONCLUSION

This chapter outlines the narrative conventions and the cinematic codes which govern the telling of stories in cinema. It details the 'transparent' approach to form and narrative which dominates mainstream, Hollywood cinema and the self-conscious artistry favoured by art cinema. The final case study suggests how these practices may be referenced and blurred in a postmodern film.

Students of film should adopt a two-part approach to formal and narrative analysis. In the first place, codes and conventions need to be accurately identified and detailed. Second, you should also seek to explain the significance of the techniques you describe, in terms of how codes and conventions have shaped your viewing, and your interpretation of story, characters, meanings and themes. Just as Hollywood narratives operate through clear cause-and-effect logic, techniques and their significance should also be clearly linked; a good way to ensure this is to check that what you say in terms of sigificance cannot equally be said about other moments within the film, but is specific and exclusive to the narrative instance under discussion.

Because film is entertainment, there is often an assumption that its analysis will spoil it and take the fun out of going to the movies. This chapter proceeds from the opposite premise: a thoughtful, perceptive analysis of a film enhances our understanding of it, and of how cinema works to engross, influence and communicate with us. This may change our viewing experience, but in doing so, it also brings us great viewing pleasure of its own.

SUMMARY

- For a film to be a narrative it must present us with a series of events in ways that imply connections between one event and the next. Most commonly we expect a 'cause-and-effect' relationship: one event has the effect of causing another, which causes another, and so on.
- When studying form and narrative it is useful to make the distinction between the 'codes' which shape the production of images and sounds, and the 'conventions' which shape the depiction of the scenes, events, and characters of the story.
- Story ('fabula') refers to the events of a narrative, whilst plot ('syuzhet') refers to the ways in which the story is presented in terms of its order, emphasis and logic.
- Hollywood narratives and codes are dictated by a desire to make the story readily comprehensible to the audience. They are often termed 'benevolent' and 'transparent,' because they seek to keep the viewer absorbed in the story – on *what* is happening, rather than on *how* this is presented to us.
- Art films are not as governed by cause and effect as mainstream narratives: coincidence, chance and random events are common in art-cinema narratives. Art films often feature fragmented narrative structures, open endings, as well as characters who are inactive, contradictory and even not likeable or unbalanced.
- In its broadest sense, mise-en-scène refers to everything that appears in the frame of the finished film. It includes everything that takes place in front of the camera at the time of shooting, as well as what the camera does (cinematography) and all that is added to the image afterwards (special effects).
- Cinematography refers to all aspects of cinematic expression that are controlled by operating the camera, including framing, shot scale, camera angle and movement, and depth of field and focus.
- Editing, or montage, involves the joining together of separate pieces of film stock to create expressive juxtapositions on screen. Unlike mise-en-scène, which inherited and developed practices from other art forms, the practices of film editing were developed specifically within the cinema, and they are crucial to film's capacity for rich, narrative expression.
- The purpose of continuity editing is to maintain the viewer's understanding of, and engagement with, the story. Its guiding principle is transparency, so that its practices seek to minimise the disruption inherent in editing.
- Film sound may be broken down into its constituent elements of speech, music and noise, and is either diegetic (that is, it belongs within the story 'universe') or non-diegetic (in that we understand it as originating from outside the fictional world inhabited by the characters).
- The selection, generation, recording, distortion, amplification and mixing of film sounds create an array of possibilities for film audio tracks, which means that we may consider them as 'soundscapes' – as a sophisticated orchestration of multi-faceted techniques comparable to the production of the film's visual elements.
- The analysis of film form and narrative involves not a retelling of a story, but a demonstration of the structures through which a story is told. It is important in film analysis to identify accurately and in detail cinematic codes and conventions. It is

equally important to explain their significance in terms of how codes and conventions shape our viewing experience and also our interpretations of story, characters, meanings and themes.

QUESTIONS FOR DISCUSSION

1 Analyse the use of sound in the opening twelve minutes of *Gladiator* in the scene of Rome's last battle against Germania. How does the layering of diegetic and non-diegetic sound, as well as on- and off-screen sound (comprising speech, music and sound effects) contribute to the film's presentation of warfare?
2 Identify further elements of the cinematography, editing, soundtrack and performances of in *Loves of a Blonde* which resemble the codes and conventions of cinema vérité and documentary filmmaking.
3 Analyse the stories contained in the 'snapshot' montages in *Run Lola Run*. How do these stories-within-the-story achieve cause-and-effect structures and characterisation in their seconds-long running times?

FURTHER READING

Bordwell, David, *Narration in the Fiction Film*, Routledge, London, 1997; originally published Methuen, London, 1985.

Bordwell, David and Thompson, Kristin, *Film Art: An Introduction* (7th edn), McGraw-Hill, Boston and London, 2004.

Bordwell, David, Staiger, Jenet and Thompson, Kristin, *The Classical Hollywood Cinema*, Routledge, London, 1985; reprinted 1994.

Chatman, Seymour, *Story and Discourse: Narrative Structure in Fiction and Film*, Cornell University Press, Ithica, NY, 1980.

Dyer, Richard, *Heavenly Bodies* (2nd edn), Routledge, London, 2004.

Maltby, Richard, *Hollywood Cinema*, Blackwell, London, 1995.

Monaco, James, *How To Read a Film* (3rd edn), Oxford University Press, Oxford, 2000.

Neupert, Richard, *The End: Narration and Closure in the Cinema*, Wayne State University Press, Detroit, 1995.

Smith, Murray, *Engaging Characters: Fiction, Emotion and the Cinema*, Oxford University Press, Oxford, 1995.

FURTHER VIEWING

All film viewing constitutes appropriate study activity for the subject of this chapter. In order to understand further the differences and relationships between mainstream and art cinema, careful viewing of the examples cited in the chapter – such as *His Girl Friday*, *Bambi*, *Le Mépris* and *The Conformist* – is recommended. You will also find the films cited in the sections on film form useful. Some further examples – chosen for the conspicuous and/or unusual use they make of particular techniques – are listed below.

Setting, props, costume and make-up
Black Narcissus (Michael Powell and Emeric Pressburger, 1947)
The Fifth Element (Luc Besson, 1997)
Orlando (Sally Potter, 1992)
Ying xiong/Hero (Yimou Zhang, 2002)

Performance
All About Eve (Joseph L. Mankiewicz, 1950)
Rebel Without a Cause (Nicholas Ray, 1955)

Lighting
Double Indemnity (Billy Wilder, 1944)
The Man Who Wasn't There (Joel Coen, 2001)
Nosferatu (F.W. Murnau, 1922)

Cinematography and special effects
Citizen Kane (Orson Welles, 1941)
Heavenly Creatures (Peter Jackson, 1994)
The *Matrix* trilogy (Andy and Larry Wachowski, 1999, 2003, 2003)
Vertigo (Alfred Hitchcock, 1958)

Editing
JFK (Oliver Stone, 1991)
The Man with Movie Camera (Dziga Vertov, 1929)

Sound
Blackmail (Alfred Hitchcock, 1928)
The Conversation (Francis Ford Coppola, 1974)
Singin' in the Rain (Stanley Donen and Gene Kelly, 1952)

RESOURCE CENTRES

http://www.filmeducation.org
http://www.bfi.org.uk
http://www.screensite.org
http://www.ukfilmcouncil.org.uk

Chapter 5

Spectator, audience and response

Patrick Phillips

■ Spectator, audience and response

INTRODUCTION

A central reason for studying film is to better describe and explain our response to the film experience. In a response study, we ask how and why we react as we do – both emotionally and intellectually. We may extend this to consider reasons for the uniformity or diversity of reactions among a group of people.

Chapter 3 explored some of the many and diverse ways in which moving images are now consumed away from the traditional cinema and indeed even away from home cinema's attempts to replicate the cinema experience in the family living room. The distribution and exhibition of moving images on the web and delivery through a whole variety of new technologies will become an increasingly important area of Film Studies. However, this chapter attempts to explain some of the characteristics of the traditional cinema experience, including the very distinctive hold that a film has over us when we sit in front of the big screen in a darkened auditorium. In doing so, it is important to acknowledge how much of Film Studies from the 1970s has been preoccupied with this topic.

Film studies has distinguished between the response of social groups, collectives of people – an *audience* – and the response of the individual – a *spectator*. This chapter will consider some of the ideas that have informed thinking about the film spectator and the cinema audience and it will use these as a springboard for an introductory examination of *response*.

THE CINEMA SPECTATOR

Film studies has assigned great importance to spectatorship. The following are some of the working assumptions that have underpinned this work since the 1960s. Here are three, each of which may be considered open to dispute or be in need of considerable qualification:

- ■ spectatorship is primarily concerned with the way the individual is positioned between projector and screen in a darkened space
- ■ the audience ceases to exist for the individual spectator for the duration of the film
- ■ although the spectator is singular, a figure alone before the screen, spectatorship studies tries to generalise about how *all* spectators behave

Let us consider each of the above.

Spectatorship is primarily concerned with the way the individual is positioned between projector and screen in a darkened space

You or I are referred to as spectators when we position ourselves in front of a screen to watch a film. It has been argued that the cinema experience is much more completely separated from the rest of our lives than the act of watching a film on a television screen. We enter a public space having paid an admission charge. We are predisposed to a certain level of investment of ourselves in the film screening – if only because we have paid for it. The fact that we have paid also indicates that we have certain expectations which will further increase our willingness to concentrate. The cinema is, in a peculiar way, both more public and more private than our own homes. As a public place it offers us the chance to enjoy a different set of comforts and facilities from those at home. While the lights are up and the advertisements or trailers are playing, we are aware of the other members of the audience. The popcorn being crunched and the drinks being slurped don't annoy us particularly. When the lights go down and the film credits appear we are suddenly alone. Now the crunchers and the slurpers run the risk of seriously annoying us – we realise we have come here to lose ourselves in the images and sounds of the film.

The technology of cinema exhibition holds us much more powerfully than does television. The size (and shape) of the screen, the quality of the images, the clarity of the sound all invite much more attention – indeed they demand it. We are held in our comfortable seats; all around us is near-darkness except for exit signs. We have no control over the film. If we go to the toilet we can't put the film on 'pause'. Not only that; we can only engage in the briefest of whispers about what has happened in our absence.

It is important to consider the upturn in cinema visits at a time when DVD systems, multi-channel satellite/cable TV and online entertainment dominate the domestic space. The cinema 'experience' is acknowledged as special and different – and is considered as worth taking seriously as a topic of study. Of course, much of the above begs the question whether we therefore need to develop quite different approaches to spectatorship when we watch a film on television or on a computer screen where the scale is so much smaller and where, most often, we cannot lose ourselves in the dark (see Ellis 1992); and more than this, whether we need to revise our ideas of spectatorship in relation to digital projection as part of a 'home cinema' system. Certainly other explanations seem to be required for the viewing of a film or video work as an installation within a gallery space.

The audience ceases to exist for the individual spectator for the duration of the film

Do we lose ourselves in the dark? It could be argued that the public and social nature of cinema-going works against this experience. After all, we enter the auditorium as a member of the audience, our expectations possibly enhanced by the chat around us. Many people go to the cinema with one or more other people and their physical proximity is something that cannot easily be put out of our mind. Even if alone, we are conscious of shared reactions during a screening; sometimes this takes audible form – laughter, groans, screams – any of which can be infectious, altering the individual spectator's response (see Hill 1997).

On a broader front we may say that we exist as audiences for a movie well away from the cinema. We are constructed as members of a 'potential' audience in at least two ways. We become exposed to the promotional and marketing hype designed to create expectations. We are also drawn into conversation about issues relating to a movie which may be circulating within our culture, resulting particularly from the profile the film enjoys in other media. In moving from 'potential' to 'actual' audience member, we have both an individual and a collective sense of what we are doing – we are self-aware.

After the screening we may well engage in yet another expression of audience membership as we discuss our reactions in a variety of contexts – on the bus, in the pub, online – maybe for days afterwards. Nevertheless, for better or for worse, theories of spectatorship have tended to isolate the self that exists more or less alone with the film for the duration of its screening. We will have more to say about this later.

Although the spectator is singular, a figure alone before the screen, spectatorship studies tries to generalise about how *all* spectators behave

Even though theories of spectatorship isolate the self, this self is an abstract concept, rather than a self with individuality and differences from other spectators. In other words, interest is not in observing and explaining the response of actual people but rather in the attempt to generalise about a 'state of being' common to all people when they position themselves before a screen and watch a film. Generalisations about this theoretical

ideological effects
have political
significance,
manipulating the
spectator into specific
ways of thinking about
and relating to the world.

spectator show some very interesting shifts. In the 1960s and 1970s the dominant model was of a 'passive' spectator controlled by the overwhelming mechanisms and physical presence of the film screening, so that they were made vulnerable to the assumed **ideological effects** of the film experience. The emphasis more recently has been much more on an 'active' spectator who makes meaning and 'negotiates' with the film in the act of consuming it. Either in conceiving of a 'passive' or an 'active' spectator, what we find are attempts to generalise about the complexity and significance of the film – spectator interaction.

THE FILM AUDIENCE

*For further discussion
of the film audience in
US and UK cinema see
Chapter 1.*

The study of film audiences has emerged from a quite different academic base to that for spectatorship. Audiences exist in the culture, as social phenomena, and it is through media sociology and cultural studies that much of the work on audiences has developed. Here are three characteristics of film audience studies which, like those outlined above in relation to spectatorship studies, are open to question and debate:

■   the audience is primarily of interest as an object of study *before* and *after* the film
■   audiences are seen as constructed by mass-media institutions and exist in a dependent relationship with these institutions
■   audience study, even though concerned with large collections of people, is now less likely to generalise than is spectator studies; it is concerned rather with local and specific factors that may explain audience behaviour

Let us consider each of the above.

The audience is primarily of interest as an object of study *before* and *after* the film

The audience disappears when the lights go out. Spectatorship theories, as we have already seen, kick in at this point, with the audience de-aggregated into individuals alone before the screen. This may seem odd – audiences certainly remain 'whole' at other spectator events such as music concerts and football matches. In film studies it seems that, on the one hand, the audience is the 'immanent' audience, the one forming for the event, constructed by a range of factors ranging from the influence of advertising to fan obsession. On the other hand, the audience is the 'virtual' audience, existing after the film, a group which remain a collective because of what they do in their wider cultural lives with the film experience they have shared. What audiences 'do' with a film is often expressed in terms of *uses and gratifications* – which is another way of talking about what needs in the audience are met by the film experience.

One concept that holds on to the audience as a collective during the film screening is that of the 'film event'. The film as an 'event' has been developed from a variety of contrasting perspectives. At one end of this spectrum we find political activist cinema, such as that of Latin America in the 1960s, where the film is something that can be stopped and argued over, where active participation in debate is the very purpose of the event. At the other end of the spectrum we have what might be called the 'carnival' film event, such as when an audience dresses up and sings along, as to *The Rocky Horror Show* or *The Sound of Music*.

The very exceptional nature of these 'events' relative to the standard movie-going experience reminds us of how oddly obedient the audience are within the standard film screening. The audience remain more or less silent, more or less unmoving in the seat they have chosen or been allocated. The experience remains remarkably similar to that of going to the theatre. In light of this it is perhaps not surprising that studies have focused on the *before* and *after* of this act of social conformity.

Audiences are seen as constructed by mass-media institutions and exist in a dependent relationship with these institutions

Audiences, especially fans-as-audience, may be seen to be very dependent on the media institutions that produce, promote and sell the product they consume. Just as the spectator may be seen as engaged in a symbiotic (and dependent) relationship with the film text and cinema apparatus, so the audience may be seen as engaged in a similar kind of relationship with the cinema institution. The demands of the audience are met (sometimes? always? hardly ever?) by corporations who supply the films that occupy the multiplex screens and meet the 'home cinema' market in video and DVD formats.

One interesting debate here is the extent to which audience demand for films, particu–larly as expressed through fan behaviour, determines supply, that is, the actual films produced by the industry. Certainly as an industry dependent on consumer choice, it might be expected that extreme sensitivity is required in interpreting indicators of audience preference. In practice, the audience is potentially so vast and diverse in its preferences that responding to audiences often means responding to a 'core' audience – the so-called 'avids' who go to the cinema most often. Of course, the more a market strategy is designed around these 'avids' the more they will dominate the audience in a closed circle of mutual interest to the exclusion of other audiences and their film prefer-ences (see Dale 1997).

What we find here is indeed a parallel between the way spectatorship is managed by forces outside the control of the spectator and the way audience is managed by the power brokers of production, distribution and exhibition, operating within an international commercial market.

Audience study, even though concerned with large collections of people, is now less likely to generalise than is spectator studies; it is concerned rather with local and specific factors that may explain audience behaviour

From the earliest studies of film audiences it is clear that the routine methods of social science research could tell us a great deal. In these audience studies and in many others like them since the 1910s, what we have are deductions made from the collection of quantifiable information – information about, for example, frequency of visits to the cinema and genre preferences. (This contrasts with the inductive approach of specta-torship, which starts with a theory and then projects it on to the object of study – the person in front of the movie screen.)

The purpose of audience studies has usually been to identify – and then interpret – broad tendencies. So although information comes from actual individuals who describe their real behaviour, the interest in collecting this data has been in order to see larger patterns of behaviour. More recently, under the influence of cultural studies, there has developed an increased sensitivity to local conditions and circumstances; a move towards what are sometimes referred to as 'thicker' studies. A 'thick' approach to audience study respects the diverse backgrounds and motivations of subgroups who constitute the larger audience.

RESPONSE STUDIES

Who is it that we should talk about as responding to a film – the spectator or the audience?

Perhaps neither, so much as you or me as an individual, not quite contained within theories of the spectator or general sets of observations about the audience (both of which we will look at further in this chapter). Film studies, influenced by Cultural Studies,

Bill Nichols writes:

The goal of providing explanations for cultural forms and social practices loses its appeal in favour of an emphasis on the (preferably 'thick') interpretation of specific forms, practices and effects. It is in particulars rather than abstractions that larger generalities take on forms that have emotional impact, social effect and ideological import.

(Gledhill and Williams 2000: 38)

• **Plate 5.1**
Land Girls (David Leland, 1998). What is the audience's starting point: romance, nostalgia or history? A simple film may produce wildly varied responses

is increasingly likely to centre on local, small-scale and precise groups of people who share, perhaps, some social or political 'formation'. Their behaviour both as individuated spectators and as a collective of people forming an audience is likely to be better understood if we respect and try to understand the importance of the particular life experiences and social attitudes they bring with them to the viewing situation.

Here is a very literal example. We could carry out a study of former members of the Women's Land Army, 'land girls', women who were sent to work on farms in Britain during the Second World War to make up for the labour shortage. These women who would now be in their eighties are invited to a screening of David Leland's *Land Girls* (UK, 1998). They form a 'community of interest', that is, a group of people who though not living in physical proximity to one another are identifiable as a community due to a shared interest. In fact we would discover many individual differences, as well as collective similarities in their response. For example, they may all experience to some degree a nostalgic glow for the period of their youth and for the romance of their contribution to the war effort – even if in reality they had very varied experiences as land girls from that represented in the film. On the other hand, their sophistication as film-goers may vary enormously, with some more able to see how the film is constructed at least as much around other films of a similar kind as it is constructed around any attempt at historical accuracy. As a result, tolerance levels for what is perceived as not very 'realistic' in the film may prove very varied.

It may soon become clear that even this approach, involving an apparently homogeneous group of women watching a film that locks into a key moment in their personal histories, is too big, too likely to produce fairly crude generalisations. We quickly become aware that the 'formation' of each person is only partly the result of their public and social selves. Each of us brings to the film event an interior self, a self of countless memories and desires, some scarcely acknowledged let alone understood. Major themes in *Land Girls*, for example, revolve around female friendship, sexuality and personal relationships. We can well imagine how, for each woman in our study, very specific memories and associations may be stimulated by these themes.

In this light we may have to consider that not only does every individual have a unique relationship with the film he or she is watching, but that this relationship is likely to change in subtle ways from one viewing of the film to the next. Response draws in the whole of the self, a self that includes:

- a social self who can make meaning in ways not very different from others with a similar ideological 'formation'
- a cultural self who makes particular intertextual references (to other films, other kinds of images and sounds) based on the bank of material she possesses
- a private self who carries the memories of her own experiences and who may find personal significance in a film in ways very different from others in her community of interest
- a desiring self who brings conscious and unconscious energies and intensities to the film event that have little to do with the film's 'surface' content

The land girls of history came from different class backgrounds, enjoyed different educational opportunities and would subsequently have lived very different lives from one another (indeed, this is captured in Leland's film). Each of them would watch a fiction film loosely based on their experiences of the 1940s with different needs and thus different levels of personal investment in the viewing experience.

My example is a simple one – but it raises a problem of response study that is more or less the equal and opposite one to that raised in spectator study. If spectatorship study risks losing itself in the 'master narrative' of a generalising and theoretical account of how we watch films, response study can lose itself in the very particularity of each interaction between film and spectator.

WHAT WE CAN LEARN FROM EARLY CINEMA

We tend to take film viewing and our behaviour as consumers for granted, and so theories of spectatorship and studies in audiences can alert us to the complexities of our own response to film and the cinema experience. Very often the best way of trying to understand something we are so familiar with that we take it for granted is to take an historical perspective. Certainly one of the most fruitful ways of understanding the relationship between mainstream commercial film, spectatorship and audience construction is to study how they evolved in the period referred to as 'Early Cinema', dating from around 1895 to 1915. Here we may ask not only how spectatorship and audience developed but reflect on how they could have developed differently.

For further discussion of early Hollywood cinema see pp. 3–8 and early British cinema see pp. 363–370.

Film historians tend to agree that by about 1917 nearly all the fundamental features of what we now consider mainstream film 'language' were in place. Film had, in just twenty years, evolved ways of managing time and space, particularly through editing, and of managing the distance between object and audience, particularly through camera movement, which made the experience of cinema very different from that of the theatre. We must remember however that films still very clearly showed their relationship to popular forms of theatre such as melodrama and vaudeville, especially in their story-lines and character types.

The evolution of film form in Early Cinema

In very early films the camera is static before action and character. This can be accounted for purely by reference to the technical limitations of the equipment. However, there is also an assumption being made about spectator viewing position – the camera 'eye' assumes the position of a member of the audience sitting in the middle of the stalls of a proscenium arch theatre. The theatre spectator cannot move closer to a key character or observe a key event in more detail. Early films seem particularly clumsy to

For discussion of film form in classical Hollywood and contemporary cinema see Chapter 4.

• Plate 5.2
The Birth of a Nation
(D.W. Griffith, 1915).

our eyes in that they often include shots full of people and a variety of action without any guidance as to which action or indeed which character is particularly significant for the development of the plot.

Not only do early films not offer us close-ups but they fail to offer any guidance as to what we should give our attention to within the mise-en-scène. Also undeveloped is any systematic organisation of point-of-view shots which just a little later became so important as a means of drawing us into the action and emotion of an event.

It is useful to list some of the ways in which the spectator began to be drawn into a particular relationship with the screen through control exercised by camera movement, mise-en-scène and editing:

- camera movement towards and away from an object – usually the camera fixed to a train or a car – in order to give the spectator a greater sense of physical involvement
- camera position nearer or further from an object – long, medium and close shots motivated by a concern to 'direct' the spectator's attention and increase engagement with the emotions of characters
- mise-en-scène organised to enhance the meaning and emphasise the significance of particular actors or objects through positioning, set design and lighting
- the frame of the mise-en-scène exploited to create interest and desire in what cannot be seen beyond the edges of the frame
- editing used as the means by which shots can be organised and, thereby, the means by which the spectators' seeing is 'managed', for example:
  - parallel editing so that two events can be followed simultaneously encouraging the spectator to make and respond to assumed dramatic and thematic connections
  - editing used as montage – to encourage a particular interpretation of one shot by the influence exercised on the spectator's mind by the shots on either side of it
  - editing used particularly to move the spectator between different points of view within the mise-en-scène

the look
Developed as a central concept in relation to the control of the spectator. Cinematic looking has also been associated with theories of desire and pleasure, theories often founded in psychoanalysis.

A way of pulling much of the above together is by reference to the concept of **the look**.

The evolution of film spectatorship in Early Cinema

Early Cinema needed to find ways of controlling the look of the spectator as part of a move towards producing a more appealing and standardised 'product' for commercial exploitation. For example, it became essential to try to:

- ensure that the meanings intended by the film's makers were those taken by the members of the audience
- replicate for realism of effect the ways in which we engage in the act of looking outside the cinema
- provide greater pleasure in the act of looking

It is possible to talk about developments in the use of the camera, mise-en-scène and editing as ways of *controlling the look*. The camera offers a particular 'eye' on the world of the film. This 'eye' may be the camera as the impersonal storytelling device or it may be the 'eye' of a character within the film as represented by the camera. These are literally 'points-of-view'. Even when the camera is not aligned with the viewing position of a particular character but is 'objectively' pointing at a mise-en-scène, the spectator look could be directed by the looks and glances exchanged by the on-screen characters in order to draw attention to a significant plot detail. Editing allows the spectator to adopt different viewing positions; to share in an exchange of looks, most commonly in a shot-reverse-shot dialogue sequence.

One spectator 'effect' of the development of film form is particularly important. It is the way in which the spectator is drawn into the world of the film, caught inside and between characters. This is achieved through editing and point-of-view and results in the **interpellation** of the spectator who is drawn inside the psychic, and physical life of the fiction. This 'effect' is at the heart of so many debates around spectatorship and manipulation in popular cinema.

Of all the ideological aspects of spectatorship, none have received as much attention as those around notions of voyeurism – the look of the peeping tom, able to see without being seen. Early Cinema very frequently represents the female, dissected by the close-up into a fetishised object of the male look. It is certainly interesting in relation to ongoing debates around the proposition that overwhelmingly in mainstream cinema the 'camera is male', that the evolution of this out of crude peepshow technology should be so evident from the beginning of popular cinema. Two of the most famous films exploring voyeurism are Hitchcock's *Rear Window* (1954) and Powell's *Peeping Tom* (1960).

Practical solutions, common sense or ideology?

It is fascinating to study these developing strategies in Early Cinema, especially as they do not appear to have been systematic. Some are used, then discarded, then used again. Through trial and error, filmmakers found a set of procedures that worked – aesthetically, emotionally, intellectually and, most of all, commercially. There are different ways to account for how mainstream commercial film form developed the way it did by 1917.

It may be interpreted as entirely 'natural':

- a set of practical solutions to the problem of making the film more intelligible to an audience, motivated by commercial considerations
- a common-sense set of solutions to problems of replicating how the spectator engages with the real world through the act of looking

Alternatively, it may be interpreted as ideological:

- a reflection of the ways of seeing of Western culture and particularly of the male within Western culture
- a recognition of the medium, if only for commercial reasons, as a powerful manipulative medium, capable of controlling representation and response

In fact these two positions are not opposed: what appears 'natural' and 'common sense' is rooted in a set of **hegemonic** choices and constructions. The very naturalness of these

See Chapter 11 for more on the idea that the look is male. The idea was proposed by Laura Mulvey (see Mulvey 1975, 1981).

interpellation
Refers to the distinctive way the film spectator is, as it were, placed inside the fiction world of the film, placed by the apparatus and by the conventions of film form (such as in shot–reverse shot dialogue editing). Literally we are 'hailed' or called into a place we have no control over.

hegemony
Captures the idea that a set of ideas, attitudes, practices become so dominant that we forget that they are rooted in the exercise of power – and that we could choose differently. Hegemonic ideas, attitudes, practices appear as 'common sense' and any alternatives appear odd or potentially threatening by comparison. Hegemony is the ideological rendered invisible.

choices simultaneously provides spectator/audience pleasure and a largely invisible and, therefore, particularly effective form of spectator/audience control.

A study of Early Cinema forces us to ask questions, the most fundamental of which is this: Could film have been different from what it is and still have attracted a mass audience? Those frustrated by the way a particular conception of cinema came to dominate (the mainstream Hollywood-type film) sometimes look to the period of Early Cinema which may be seen as a kind of Garden of Eden – a period of innocence and infinite possibility. Studies in Early Cinema often encourage us to think what other ways film form – and, therefore, spectatorship – could have developed from the way in which they did. For example, a model for a radical alternative form of cinema might be conceived as one which does not guide us every step of the way through close-up, shot–reverse shot and so on. In a static camera long shot, for example, we are given freedom to choose for ourselves what we wish to focus upon. In not being interpellated, we are free to engage more objectively and thoughtfully with what we see and hear. There is not the space here to explore these arguments. However, it is necessary to recognise that much of the interest in Early Cinema is motivated precisely by a desire to reflect on other kinds of spectatorship possibilities than that established by the kind of cinema which Hollywood (and not just Hollywood) had evolved into by around 1917.

The evolution of the film audience in Early Cinema

In the introduction to this chapter, the interrelationship of spectator and audience studies was pointed out. With regard to Early Cinema, just as interesting as the study of the development of film form as it relates to spectatorship is the development of film exhibition as it relates to audiences.

Film gradually emerged from a fairground attraction of 1895 to the nickleodeons of the early 1900s. Audiences were overwhelmingly working and lower-working class. The medium of cinema had a very low cultural status. In the USA the move from nickelodeons, usually just small dark rooms with benches, to movie theatres, which accelerated in the early 1910s, was both cause and result of the move to make cinema-going more 'respectable' and controllable.

The commercial concern was to raise the social image of movies and this had to involve both making them into more sophisticated products and placing them within more 'theatrical' auditoria. A key objective was, as the founder of Paramount, Adolphe Zucker, said, 'to kill the slum tradition in the movies'. An anarchy in film response had to be contained if film-going were to be more appealing to the middle classes. This anarchy derived in part from the fact that the films were silent. This gave them a wonderful 'universality' on the one hand, but also offered them as particular to different audiences – for example, to the vast diversity of immigrant groups arriving on the East Coast of the USA. More specifically this anarchy derived from two factors. First, the lack of a controlled viewing position prior to the development of a standardised film form, as described in outline above, meant that the spectator was much freer to make meaning from the images presented on the screen. Second, the 'untrained' behaviour of the audience who used the cinema space as a noisy, interactive meeting place meant that the movie-going experience was held in very low regard by those sections of the middle classes that took it upon themselves to 'police' social behaviour. Neither the film's textual operations nor cinema's organisation of the viewing event was able to isolate and control the spectator. The peculiar nature of the film experience as both isolated (in spectatorship) and collective (in audience membership) was itself evolving – or rather, being constructed – towards greater uniformity.

The fact that film audiences were socialised into a particular cinema practice (e.g. sitting quietly) at the same time that film form had been evolved to manage the act of spectatorship (e.g. control over the look) is highly significant. The standardisation of both film form and of cinema exhibition from very early in the history of cinema has encouraged film theorists to develop ideas based on:

- a normative spectator unified as the 'subject' addressed by the film
- the viewing situation as a constant (rather than as variable according to who is the spectator, when and where they are and what they are watching)

The strengths and shortcomings of this approach to spectatorship, already highlighted above, are further considered in the two sections that follow our first case study, which focuses on the early cinema audience and response to a particularly controversial film.

☐ CASE STUDY 1: THE RESPONSE TO *THE BIRTH OF A NATION* (D.W. GRIFFITH, 1915)

The purpose of this case study is to reflect on the most spectacular early experience of film – the discovery of the power of the medium to generate intense response both inside and outside the cinema auditorium. D.W. Griffith's film of 1915, *The Birth of a Nation*, is of great significance in the history of cinema. It brought together most of the developments of the previous years in film form in order to cement them in place in what we now sometimes call the **Institutional Mode of Representation (IMR)**. At the same time it offered the kind of film spectacle that accelerated the move of cinema into 'picture palaces'. The fact that the film remains one of the most racist films ever made offers a third key area of interest. In what follows, the emphasis is on the evolution of audiences and the idea of the film event, and on the increasing cultural (and political) significance of cinema within a developing industrial-commercial 'public sphere'.

Griffith was a perfect figure for social reformers of early cinema to have as an ally because of his commitment to what may loosely be described as Victorian, conservative values combined with his brilliant understanding of the potential of the medium. He carried forward a complex project intended to advance cinema as an art form to be respected by the arbiters of culture and simultaneously to rein it in so that it might be experienced as a more standardised commodity. Perhaps a little harshly, Larry May describes Griffith's achievement as not one of aesthetics 'but simply size, scale, prestige'. In other words, Griffith's achievement was to synthesise developments over

Institutional Mode of Representation (IMR)
Captures the concept that a normative set of ideas about what constitutes a 'mainstream' film became established around 1915 to 1917. The IMR may be seen as an example of hegemony – establishing an apparently 'common-sense' notion of how a film should be constructed and how it should communicate with an audience.

• **Plate 5.3**
The Great Train Robbery (Edwin S. Porter, 1903). This still illustrates the static camera of Early Silent Cinema. For a spectator accustomed to the 'standard' film language established twelve to fourteen years after this film, Early Cinema provides major problems. For example, the static camera does not create the expected involvement or draw attention to significant objects in the frame which might help create narrative clarity

the previous years and turn this into a more spectacular product. The complication to this neat narrative is that the most historically significant of Griffith's films, while certainly conservative in ideology and while certainly laying down a benchmark for the standard narrative realist film form, produced a disruptive social effect on a national scale far beyond anything in the short history of cinema up until that point – or arguably since then (May 1980: ch. 4). In fact Griffith may appear as a very contradictory individual. His conservative values centred on ideas of the home, the family and on an essentially patriarchal sense of leadership by wise, enlightened men. At the same time, his defence of the freedom of speech (especially in defending his own work!) seems to put him in a much more liberal camp. His eye for sensational images of sex and violence certainly seems to fly in the face of any sense of him as a Victorian prude.

The Clansman, as the film was first known after the title of Thomas Dixon's novel, started production on 4 July 1914 and was completed at the end of October. The initial $40,000 budget was spent on just the battle scenes – the film finally cost an unbelievable $115,000 – a scale of production which tells us much about the 'invention' of cinema as fantastic spectacle. The film was previewed on 8 February 1915 at Clunes Theatre, Los Angeles. The event was unprecedented as the entire Los Angeles Philharmonic took up their places to accompany the film. Here, Karl Brown, assistant to Griffith's great cameraman Billy Bitzer, describes in a 1976 interview the moment the film began:

This and the other testimony quotes in this case study come from *D.W. Griffith – the Father of Film*. This is a three-part documentary produced by Keith Brownlow and David Gill in 1983.

[A]nd when [the conductor] raised his baton and held it for a moment – down it came and everything blew just straight out of the can – oh it was the most tremendous gust of sound I'd ever heard.

It was renamed *The Birth of a Nation* before formally opening on 3 March 1915 at the Liberty Theatre, New York with usherettes dressed as southern belles. What it meant to go to the cinema was redefined by the scale of the film both as a film and as a cultural event – it changed people's idea of what cinema was, how it could be experienced, what effects, visceral, intellectual, moral, it could have on a society. The film had a lot of firsts – the first to run for three hours, the first to have a musical score played by a seventy-piece symphony orchestra, the first to have scheduled performances, the first to have an intermission, the first to charge $2 for reserved seats. It has also been described – flying in the face of what we might think of as 'silent cinema' – as one of the noisiest films ever made. A small army of people was employed backstage in the big city screenings to produce a complete range of sound effects.

The audience was constructed by national advertising and promotional campaigns. It was the first film to use large billboards, the first to take full-page ad space in newspapers. It was the first full-length film to be screened at the White House. No one could fail to know about it as an 'event'. It made huge profits – most famously making the future founder of MGM, Louis B. Mayer, his first fortune – simply by owning the distribution rights to *The Birth of a Nation* in the New England area.

This commercial hype was, of course, compounded by the controversy the film created. Many people were outraged by the film's racism and yet caught in a double bind – as liberals, many of these people were also against censorship. So *The Birth of a Nation* may also be regarded as the earliest example of a film demanding a collective response and yet dividing people as to what that response should be. Karl Brown, in his 1976 interview, recounts how when told that showing the film in Atlanta would cause race riots, Griffith replied, 'I hope to God they do'. Brown continues:

It wasn't that he was particularly anxious for a riot or people to be hurt or anything of the sort. But it's the old story that if someone gives you a tremendous pat hand, you're going to play it.

This confirms a view that Griffith was engaged in an act of provocation. Apologists for Griffith would argue that his main motive was not to promote racism but to prove and promote the idea that cinema was a new cultural form of great significance. However naive or calculating, what is clear is that Griffith was locked into a social formation in white, male, southern states culture that made it almost inevitable that the hegemonic form of representation of African Americans – a racist representation – would manifest itself in his film.

The National Association for the Advancement of Colored People (NAACP) organised nationwide protests against the film, starting immediately after the Los Angeles preview one month before the New York premiere – even though members were in principle against censorship. There was plenty to be upset about – from the intertitle in Griffith's 'Prologue' which stated that 'The Bringing of the African to America planted the first seed of disunion' to the crudely racist representation of black men, especially in the post-Civil War second half of the film. Several screenings of the film were delayed and the Film Boards in some US cities required changes to the film in response to the protests. An Epilogue, paid for by the Hampton Institute, was made to show the positive contribution of African-Americans and this was first tagged on to the film at Boston's Tremont Cinema in 1916. A near riot broke out when a larger number of black people arrived to a screening to establish how useful the Epilogue was in correcting the damaging effects of the film – and were refused admission.

The effect of the film on black audiences, still at this time subject to segregation in cinemas, cannot be understated. Here is William Walker speaking in the early 1980s about his experience of having seen *The Birth of a Nation* in a blacks-only movie theatre in 1916:

[S]ome people were crying. You could hear people say, 'Oh, god' and some 'damn'.... You had the worst feeling in the world. You just felt like you were not counted, out of existence. But I tell you, I just felt like there could have been some way so they couldn't see me so I could kill some of them. I just felt like going out to kill every white person I saw in the world.

Between 1915 and 1973, the right to screen *The Birth of a Nation* was challenged in the US courts at least 120 times. However, the very controversy surrounding the film was a key incentive for those wishing to develop the full-length motion picture as a powerful and significant form of mass entertainment. The film showed that cinema could produce 'effects' for both individual spectator and collective audience on such a scale that there was no turning back. The commercial and cultural significance of cinema was proven to a very large degree by this one film.

This brief case study (much more could be said if space were available) demonstrates that a focus on audiences and the film 'event' draws together key areas of film studies. *The Birth of a Nation* is uniquely able to force the following questions: What kind of experience does cinema offer, and what kinds of social and cultural effects can a film have? What competing ideological forces are put into circulation by a film which dares to offer such amazing spectacle on the one hand and such pernicious messages and values on the other? *The Birth of a Nation* established that cinema matters. It demonstrated that some films at least enter into the public sphere, are experienced by audiences coming to the event with their different personal and community formations in ways that tell us not just about the movies but about the force-fields at work within the society.

In looking at issues of film reception, it shows us how issues of spectatorship and audience are difficult to untangle. Here is Karl Brown talking about the Ku-Klux-Klan rescue sequence with Wagner's 'Dance of the Valkyries' as accompaniment. Brown's construction by the film text as spectator is clear – but so, also, by implication at least, is his predisposition to a certain response determined by his own ideological formation and his construction as a member of an enthusiastic audience, expectant of the kind of thrills provided:

It was like a call to arms – you just couldn't let go. You weren't watching people ride, you were riding with them and you weren't riding with them to rescue somebody but you were riding on a stern determination for vengeance, vengeance for the death of that little girl you'd learnt to love so much.... And the fact that the showing of 'The Clansman' started riots and put blood on the streets was proof beyond proof that this was a great picture – regardless of what critics might have to say about it. The proof was there.

The Birth of a Nation was hugely significant in the evolution of both film spectatorship and the audience experience. However, like all historical case studies it needs to be considered in its specificity – as a unique case – as well as in its function as establishing a precedent which changed people's perceptions of what a movie was and what an evening at the cinema could offer.

This case study of audience responses to *The Birth of a Nation* suggests a very active audience. A film is resistible – both its content and its effects. The mechanisms of spectatorship are not all determining. *The Birth of a Nation*, even today, provides an excellent example of the peculiar tension between the power of spectatorship and the power of audience solidarity. These mixed messages about 'active' and 'passive' are the subjects of the next two sections.

THE SPECTATOR OF THEORY

What mental and emotional activity goes on in a spectator during the watching of a film? So much has been written on this – indeed, it has probably been the single most recurring area of investigation for film theory – that it is impossible to do more than summarise some of the main lines of thought.

The fact that spectatorship has been a subject of theory is itself an issue. There is a significant difference between a theoretical and an empirical scientific approach. After the dominance of theory in the 1970s and 1980s, in which hypothetical 'models' of spectatorship were built, based on then fashionable ideas emerging from linguistics and psychoanalysis, the period from the mid-1990s has tended to be dominated by 'post-theory'. This latter approach has attempted to undermine the spectator of theory, arguing that we should seek explanations much more in scientific theories of how the brain functions in response to stimuli and in processing information. In practice post-theory approaches to film spectatorship have not been very much more empirically based than what went before, although they are based on a science – cognitivism – which does make use of 'hard' empirical observation and testing. It is interesting that the battleground over different ways of trying to make sense of spectatorship has been broadly divided between academics from Western Europe, particularly France, and academics from the United States.

Structuralist and post-structuralist theory

The acronym SLAB has been created around the names of these four theorists. This rather derogatory term suggests how the theory that defined film studies in the 1970s and 1980s is now open to serious attack. For a sense of the arguments against SLAB theory, see Bordwell and Carroll 1996).

What derived from France (and the UK) was a combination of Saussurean linguistics, Lacanian psychoanalysis, Althussarian neo-Marxism and Bartheian semiotics which produced a very powerful intellectual framework that dominated film studies when it was first establishing itself as a serious academic subject in universities. What resulted was a model of spectatorship and the effect of films, especially mainstream films, that was very deterministic. From linguistics came the idea that language did our thinking for us – so that as we enter into a language system (and film was seen as language-like), we can only operate on its terms. From psychoanalysis was developed the idea that as we sit in front of the screen we regress to the narcissistic 'mirror phase' of very early childhood. The spectator was seen as locked into the 'cinema apparatus', somewhere between projector and screen. At the same time he or she was interpellated into the world of the film according to the controlling operations of the film's formal systems of editing, point of view and so on. From neo-Marxism came the idea that surrender to the apparatus and to the formal mechanisms of cinema also had powerful political effects. The spectator was tied into the invisible relationships of power and control that replicated the deepest levels of Western ideology. In brief, the spectator was vulnerable to a kind of waking dream experience that was stupefying. The pleasure was in the surrender, in the comfort the cinematic experience offered in playing out our fantasies and at the same time controlling them.

This first phase of structuralist theory gradually became modified as it was clear that the results of applying it were too deterministic – both in explaining films and spectator behaviour. There was the need to produce a lighter touch model that allowed for greater complexity, greater variation. Often it seemed that this model of the spectator was produced by cinephobes, that is, people with a hatred of cinema, in order to demonstrate how dangerous cinema is, politically and psychically! In its post-structural phase, theory became more open to variation. Psychoanalysis remained central, but instead of the spectator being seen as fixed in place by an (imaginary) unified self-image projected on to the screen, he or she was now considered capable of 'playing' or 'struggling' with different positions. He or she could occupy different and contradictory roles – male/female, hero/villain/protagonist/victim – and thus was able to exercise conflicting fantasies within the self. In addition, semiotics increasingly emphasised different kinds of response within an audience, as individuals decoded audio-visual material according to their own situation and needs. The political dimension of theory became more flexible too, especially through adopting the concept of hegemony, emphasising how in society (as in a film) we can adopt one of several positions that are available to us within a social order that seems to evolve through consensus rather than through stark exercises of power and control.

Cognitivism

In opposition to explanations of spectator activity deriving from structuralist and post-structuralist theory, approaches to spectatorship, especially in the United States, have tended to prefer a much more pragmatic view of how, moment-by-moment, the brain works with the stimulus it is bombarded with by the film in order to make sense and gain emotional experience. This can be described, in broad terms, as a cognitivist approach. Rather than focusing on unconscious activity and the 'subjectification' of the spectator by the 'apparatus' of cinema, this approach takes as its starting point the idea that response can largely be tracked and explained by reference to conscious and routine activity. The brain works to recognise, process and 'place' the stimulus in such a way that it becomes possible to 'read' the film's meaning and manage its effects. This emphasis on cognition certainly supports the idea of an 'active' spectator, even if much of the mental processing seems entirely automatic. For example, we learn to read a film in all kinds of ways – through recognition of the familiar aspects of narrative, genre conventions and the common audio-visual techniques of film's communication system (such as continuity editing and synchronised sound). We do this by bringing our knowledge and experience of previous films to bear in responding to a new film experience.

One way to explain how spectators make meaning is by reference to **schemas**, a concept used in studies of the human thinking process. When we are confronted by a new experience, we look for familiar patterns that allow us to orient ourselves and make sense of what is in front of us. In the experience of watching a film we automatically look for the schemas we have become accustomed to from our previous experience of film. As well as narrative and genre mentioned in the previous paragraph, we may find, for example, that an auteur schema or a star schema is useful in mentally processing what we are being presented with by a film.

schema
Refers to a familiar pattern recognised by the mind that allows us to orient ourselves and make sense of what is in front of us. In the experience of watching a film we automatically look for the schemas we have become accustomed to from our previous experience of film. By extension we can talk about auteur, genre and star schemas.

Cognitivism may be seen as an instrument of hegemony by providing 'normal' explanations for phenomena and experiences that might otherwise seem to lie outside and challenge the way we think and see. Again I quote Bill Nichols:

Analytical philosophy and cognitive psychology cling to the same assumptions of abstract rationality and democratic equality that led to a politics of consensus (based on the denial of bodily, material difference) and the repression of a politics of identity.
(Gledhill and Williams 2000: 42)

This may suggest that competence in carrying out these cognitive procedures takes many years to learn – well, some may – such as learning to recognise an auteur structure/schema. However, the fundamental schemas relating to, for example, narrative and genre, do not – and certainly learning to 'read' the basic communication system of film does not. One explanation for this ease with which we 'read' a film was provided as early as 1916 by a psychologist, Hugo Munsterburg (see Langdale 2002). He pointed out that what was remarkable about film was that it seemed to be organised to allow us to respond using the kinds of cognitive processes we bring to our everyday lives. Indeed, going back to the evolution of narrative film in Early Cinema, it may be argued that filmmakers were evolving by trial and error a form of cinema that made mental processing as 'natural' as possible. If cinema can be described as 'realist', then it is most profoundly so in the way it replicates mental activity rather than physical reality. Our brains effortlessly (but not passively!) function to make meaning from and manage response to the kind of stimulus the film throws at us second by second. Cognitivism could therefore be described as a 'realist' approach to spectatorship and response.

However, a major criticism of cognitivist approaches is that in relating the film experience to everyday routines of mental processing, it can only emphasise the similarities rather than the differences between the film experience and other kinds of 'everyday' activity. What, for example, of the very particular ways in which films provide us with moments of intensity, mobilising our desires, triggering memory in the dark of the movie auditorium? The activity of the 'active' spectator of cognitivism involves working to make safe the film experience, repeating conventional ways of thinking and processing stimulus material – in this case stimulus produced by a film. It would appear to elaborate on what in Chapter 1 was referred to as a 'sensory motor mechanism' (see p. 12). The real challenge for the filmmaker is to create a different kind of film experience, encouraging or even forcing the spectator to look and think differently; to celebrate difference.

Affect and excess

The different approaches to spectatorship outlined thus far all appear to derive from a strong need to explain how the potential waywardness of seeing and listening and responding in multiply different ways is managed – whether by the cinema apparatus, the formal features of the film itself or by the normative procedures of the mind. A very different approach to spectatorship is one that confronts this waywardness – where cinematic effects produce complex and diverse affects.

The theory deriving from Lacanian psychoanalysis emphasises 'lack'. It proposes that from early childhood we are aware of incompleteness, and our fantasy lives are driven by the need to complete this lack. Cinema may, in this context, be seen as a perfect machine for doing so. And for doing it endlessly, since desire can never be fulfilled by a film, as it is just a film – it can only enact our desire, encouraging us to come back for more. This theory suggests that as desiring subjects driven by lack, we fit into the regimes of seeing and hearing that are provided for us. The film experience is too little, indeed almost nothing at all at the material level – just the play of light on a screen. Even in relation to the imagination, we are placed within one or more systems that contain our fantasy lives within its structures.

Arguably, the experience of cinema is not lack, despite the undeniable fact that we never leave the cinema with anything other than memories of projected images. Perhaps it may be said that far from giving us too little, film gives us a huge excess of stimulus – more than we can manage, more than we want to manage. Steven Shaviro writes:

But is it really lack that makes images so dangerous and disturbing? What these theorists fear is not the emptiness of the image, but its weird fullness; not its impotence so much as its power. Images have an excessive capacity to seduce and mislead, to affect the spectator unwarrantedly. What is the source of this mysterious power?

(Shaviro 1993: 17)

Shaviro answers his own question by saying that an image is like a 'residue' of something that existed – and what disturbs is not its absence but the fact that it just won't go away! It exists not as a lack, but as something too much.

> The fleeting insistence of weightless images, of reflections and projections, of light and shadow, threaten to corrupt all standards, to exceed all limits, and to transgress every law
>
> (ibid.).

Is our desire for the visual, indeed for the audio-visual, actually excessive, always overflowing the controls and containments described above? Perhaps rather than focusing on how the cinematic apparatus is contributing to the endless reproduction of 'given' ways of experiencing our world, ways that fold us back into mechanisms of control, we could run with a very different kind of theory which is entirely affirmative of cinema as an imaginative medium in which an image, a sound, is always more than what it represents, what its narrative function might be. This is not to suggest that we have any control over this experience, but that we can rethink what we do with it. Shaviro writes: 'My own masochistic inclination is to revel in my bondage to images … rather than try to rectify it.'

A shift in emphasis away from the concept (meaning, system of representation) to the affect (feeling, emotion) becomes important. An affect is what lingers, what was described earlier as a 'residue', something we feel which is in excess of the representational system that produced it. So, for example, a film which at a 'conceptual' level appears rather conventional, even simple-minded, may leave me with a profound sense of loss or sadness. Thinking about affect forces us to question what we think of as knowledge. As Claire Colebroke writes:

> What we can acknowledge is that art is not about knowledge, conveying 'meanings' or providing information. Art is not just an ornament or style used to make data more consumable. Art may well have meanings but what makes it art is not its content but its affect, the sensible force or style through which it produces content. Why, for example, would we spend two hours in the cinema watching a film if all we wanted were the story or the moral message?
>
> (Colebroke 2002: 24–5)

Much of film studies has been dominated by representation, by concepts. In fact a film has the capacity endlessly to free sounds and images from their referents (their 'thing' – in the world), they become not something less (a lack, an absence) but something more. Shaviro argues that what in fact the apparatus of cinema does is 'deterritiorialize' the image, that is, remove it from its routine, conventionalised place in the world, in the order of things, and this 'leads directly to the visceral immediacy of the cinematic experience' (Shaviro 1993: 36).

This may appear as a retreat from the political priorities of theory, towards some kind of decadent surrender to pleasure. Perhaps it would be more accurate to say that it is a different kind of politics. Rather than one based on diagnosing 'symptoms' and ascribing negative effects for the purpose of increasing our wariness of the film experience, Shaviro's approach, which derives from the writings of Deleuze, is about foregrounding the imagination and its 'lines of flight'. Certainly this is a more liberating approach and more congenial to a cinephiliac – someone who loves cinema and who wants to share that love with others.

Melodrama is a good example of a genre where the gap between the conceptual and the affective is very pronounced. An ideological analysis of a 1950s, American melodrama may reveal all the ways in which it promotes a particular value system, one that is highly conventional and working to support ideas of social stability and coherence. However, at the level of affect, the experience may be very different, especially for the target audience – women. Here is what Jeanine Basinger writes about her own experience of growing up with 'the Woman's Film':

We grew to understand and accept the great secret of the Hollywood film: its ambivalence, its knowing pretence. You were a fool to believe any of it, but you were a fool if you didn't. You could have it both ways, neither way, one way or the other. It didn't matter, because movies were really only about one thing: a kind of yearning. A desire to know what you didn't know, have what you didn't have, and feel what you were afraid to feel. They were a door to the Other, to the Something Else.

(Basinger 1993: 4–5)

The following section is primarily an exploration of possible 'lines of flight' in our response to a particular film sequence.

RESPONSE

How we respond to a film is very complex. film studies has long moved away from a 'transmission' model based on the idea that meaning and emotion is all bottled up in the film itself. We bring so much to the interactive experience of film-watching, both as spectators, defined in our isolated relationship to the film, and as audience members, enjoying a shared experience.

One influential idea that emerged from post-structuralism, particularly from the work of Roland Barthes, was that of the 'death of the author'. Rather than hold to the view that the reader/spectator is entirely at the service of the producer of the work, the opposite was argued. A text (a book, a film, a painting) only comes into existence in the act of 'reading' it. In this way the reader of the text is, in a way, simultaneously its creator. The actual author (writer, filmmaker, painter) is 'dead'. Each of us comes to a film with our own personal 'formation' – the result of all our life experiences. These will predispose us to certain interpretations of character, certain attitudes towards moral and political issues and certain emotional responses to events. In its most dramatic form this suggests that there are in fact as many 'readings' of a film as there are spectators – and that an audience will typically be made up of people reacting in very different ways.

With mainstream commercial cinema, three factors work against this diversity of response. First, the audience will have been attracted to the film for broadly similar reasons to do with narrative, genre and star expectations – they will already be in some ways a collective defined by the 'promise' of the film. Second, the film most usually reflects ideological values that are generally accepted as 'common sense' by the majority of the audience. Within a given society people share a very similar constructed sense of social reality, what is sometimes described as a shared social imaginary. Third, the operations of the film will tend towards triggering a processing system that is common to all members of the audience – whether we call this the operations of cognitive processing or the sensory motor mechanism (see p. 12).

This idea of 'openness of meaning yet determinacy of effect' is a useful compromise in explaining how individual spectators form a collective called an audience. What needs to be added to the mix is what has been said in the last section about affect. Cognitive responses – making meaning – may be broadly similar but affective response may vary considerably. In addition, less conventional films, films that break with some of the features of the typical mainstream commercial film, are likely to produce greater diversity of response. First, expectations will be more varied, with the audience less singular in its make-up. Second, aspects of the taken-for-fragmented social imaginary are likely to be disturbed, leaving individual members of the audience to make what they can of the experience. Third, the film may deliberately deny the easy mental processing, as it breaks with the mechanisms of conventional representation and narrative development.

See Lapsley and Westlake 1988. This book gives a good overview of SLAB theory.

• **Plate 5.4**
Jungle Fever (Spike Lee, 1991). Spike Lee directs provocative films that produce a range of responses. Lee seems to be teasing out the ways in which different spectators within an audience go with the apparent messages of the film, adopting the 'preferred' response or whether they oppose that meaning – or whether they find themselves negotiating between these two positions in some way

Towards 'thicker' approaches to response

Another useful idea to emerge from semiotics is the distinction between four different kinds of response.

A '*preferred* reading' of a film is one in which the spectator takes up the intended meaning, finding it relatively easy to align with the messages and attitudes of those who have created the text. An '*oppositional* reading' is one that rejects this intended response. Generally, a 'preferred' response will be associated with the pleasure of reassurance that comes from the comfortable and familiar. Most often an oppositional response refuses some aspects of what the film has to offer. This can lead not simply to a lack of pleasure, but possibly to a different kind of pleasure – one that is based on using the film to reinforce the spectator's sense of independence. More crudely, there may be the temptation to associate a 'preferred' reading with the 'passive' spectator and an 'oppositional' reading with an active spectator.

Generally, the spectator attempts to work with those who have produced the work, best-guessing what they were intending, and sometimes compensating for perceived deficiencies. This *negotiated* response is the result of a particular kind of interaction between the spectator and the film, possibly motivated by a genuine sense that there is a mixture of appealing and unappealing elements. Perhaps a negotiated response arises from an over-compensation by the spectator in a situation in which the film is unappealing but where some justification is needed for having bought a ticket!

If we take early Spike Lee films such as *Do the Right Thing* (1989) or *Jungle Fever* (1990), we can identify strong differences in response which may be described in relation to 'preferred', 'oppositional' and 'negotiated' readings.

Lee's films are clear in the positions they adopt. Some films, especially those which use irony, are much more difficult to define in terms of their 'preferred' reading. Coppola's *Apocalypse Now* (1979) was intended by its director to be an anti-war movie. However, its spectacular battle sequences could be seen as celebrating war – if the irony is missed. Is 'I love the smell of napalm in the morning' spoken by a character called Kilgore really meant to be taken at face value? Films which are ambiguous or subtle or plain confusing are likely to lead to a fourth kind of response, the *aberrant*. While it may be said that there is no single 'right way' to respond to a film – an aberrant response is so far off track that it may simply be described as 'wrong'.

Looking at particular films and the range of responses possible allows a move away from theoretical generalisations about the spectator, towards an approach which takes account of diversity – both among different spectators within a single audience and between different audiences in different locations or in different historical moments. This 'thick' study is increasingly informing film studies from the broader discipline of Cultural Studies.

The words used here – recognition, alignment and allegiance – are taken from Murray Smith's *Engaging Characters – Fiction, Emotion and the Cinema* (Oxford: Clarendon Press, 1995).

In a three-part process we 'recognise' a character quite literally – that is, we know how to place him or her from experience as a particular type, maybe with a particular narrative function – and this is usually an automatic process.

Second we become 'aligned' with a particular character in that we experience some of the story through this figure. Film theory would say that this alignment is involuntary, as we are placed by the complex and powerful technical and textual mechanisms.

'Allegiance' describes how we choose to associate imaginatively with a character based on our assessment of their worth and appeal. As with alignment, film theory would tell us that allegiance is constructed by forces outside our control and that we

☐ CASE STUDY 2: PLEASURE AND EVALUATION – *PULP FICTION* (QUENTIN TARANTINO, 1994)

In this two-part case study we will consider the moment-by-moment response to a well-known sequence from Tarantino's *Pulp Fiction*. In the first part Vincent (John Travolta) picks up Mia (Uma Thurman) on the instructions of his gangster boss, Mia's husband, and takes her out to a diner. In the second part he has to cope with her overdosing, resorting to some rather shocking emergency treatment.

In exploring the first part of the sequence, the emphasis will be on responding to character and situation. In the second part, my emphasis will be on cinematic shock. In both parts, there is the opportunity to reflect on how we make meaning and obtain pleasure from the details of a film as we engage both intellectually and affectively in the act of spectatorship. What will also become clear is that central to response are judgements that we must make constantly – judgements that express favour or disfavour, and which may be deeply rooted in our personality, in our formation as a human being.

Thirty minutes into *Pulp Fiction* we have established that Vincent is a ruthless hitman but also a rather ordinary guy, appealing, even slightly vulnerable, in whom the audience can take an interest. (He is also John Travolta – a fact that significantly colours our sympathies.) Immediately before his arrival at Mia's house he has taken drugs. We have no significant knowledge of Mia, although our expectations based on the gangster genre (what cognitivists in particular refer to as the schema we rely upon to 'navigate' through fictional films) may lead us to expect a typical 'moll' or 'femme fatale'. So, in different ways, we are already working as spectators, either in placing and coming to terms with a character we have some knowledge of or in anticipating one we have yet to get to know.

Part one: Picking up Mia and Jack Rabbit Slim's

Vincent approaches the house of his employer Marsellus Wallace. The spectator follows him from behind, first in long and then in medium shot. As he takes a message from the door, there is a cut to close-up and we hear what we assume (from our familiarity with film conventions) is the voice of the person who has written the note, Mia. The voice invites Vincent to enter. There is a cut to the interior as Vincent feels his way gingerly – he's on unknown territory; he's high on heroin. The spectator is then presented with a shot of Mia from behind as she sits in front of four televisions relaying close-circuit surveillance pictures of Vincent. During the rest of the two-minute sequence, until Mia's fingers pick up the stylus, Dusty Springfield's version of 'Preacher Man' provides an accompaniment to what we see, generating a distinctive feel to the sequence and also opening up the affective dimension of our response. There is next a big close-up of Mia's lips at a microphone. Her call 'Vincent' startles him. All his movements seem to require additional thought. The spectator processes a range of information contained in the mise-en-scène: soundtrack, dialogue and performances. The information is controlled by the film's maker. To this extent the spectator is in a dependent situation. However, it is precisely because of this limited access to information that the spectator becomes active.

In the twenty-two shots before the couple leave the house, we do not see Mia's full face. The spectator's curiosity is increased, partly for this general reason, partly for the specific reason that she has been in control throughout. She is in a position of power because: (1) she is the boss's wife; (2) she controls camera and sound technology; and (3) Vincent's condition is not likely to produce assertiveness! Our alignment is increasingly with Mia, all the key point-of-view shots are hers, including ones where she prepares and then snorts cocaine. Our allegiance, however, is with Vincent. He is the object of the camera's look – which becomes the object of the female look. Our recognition is based on what we know of him from the first thirty minutes of the film. If an allegiance has formed, it is based in part on the attributes of the Vincent character as already established, in part on the attributes of the Travolta star persona. We quite literally do not recognise Mia yet (although it is almost certain that we will have an image already in our minds from publicity material in circulation outside the space of the cinema auditorium) and must move towards forming an allegiance based only on her behaviour, voice (and lips).

An evaluation of the two characters will, for experienced film spectators, depend less on judging them against a set of moral criteria from the real world than from those that are operative within the world of Tarantino's film. The recognition given by someone with no awareness of Travolta and with little ability or willingness to engage imaginatively within the terms of the film's genre and form may well be very different. In other words, we can anticipate the spectrum of 'preferred', 'negotiated' and 'oppositional' responses. Another way of discussing this is in terms of the competence of the individual spectator. This refers to the skills possessed by the spectator, most obviously their 'cine-literateness'. One could imagine a spectator who is either too inexperienced in

are manipulated into these allegiances. However, this seems to sell short the spectator's ability (indeed opportunity) to align with different characters within a fiction film, to 'try out' identities.

• Plate 5.5
Pulp Fiction (Quentin Tarantino, 1994). Uma Thurman in medium close-up

• **Plate 5.6**
Pulp Fiction (Tarantino, 1994). Travolta and Thurman in two-shot. The diner scene between Mia (Uma Thurman) and Vincent (John Travolta) is made up in large part of a classic shot-reverse-shot rhythm which 'sutures' (stitches) the spectator into the space between the characters producing intense involvement. Plate 5.5 is a typical Vincent point-of-view shot of Mia. However, Tarantino can surprise us as in the side-on two-shot (Plate 5.6). Suddenly the spectator is on the outside in much more of an observer role

• **Plate 5.7**
Pulp Fiction (Tarantino, 1994) Travolta and Thurman re-enter the apartment after Vincent returns Mia to her home. The spectator has been drawn into alignment and allegiance with these two characters. As a consequence of our involvement further anticipation and tension is created. After their very flirtatious night out, will Vincent risk taking things further with the boss's wife? Our privileged information on Mia's condition leads us to consider a different scenario. We care because we have been drawn into the situation by the calculated use of film techniques in the previous scenes. An unusual feature of *Pulp Fiction* is that our caring, our allegiance, is sometimes set up only to be wiped out by some turn in the plotting or structure of the film

contemporary popular cinema or too unsophisticated to pick up Tarantino's tone and his attitude towards his characters.

There is a cut from the Wallace residence to a red Chevrolet. The camera pulls out and pans left to establish that Vincent and Mia have arrived in the diner car-park. We see Mia full face for the first time. Tarantino has used one minute seventeen seconds of screen time to establish the world of Jack Rabbit Slim's diner and get the two characters to their seats.

In looking at the sequence from Mia's 'What do you think?' to when she goes to 'powder her nose', we are presented with a very familiar shot–reverse shot dialogue sequence. As is typical of such a sequence, there are a large number of edits: seventy-five in five minutes thirty seconds of screen time with an average shot length of 4.4 seconds. The spectator is very much drawn into ('stitched' into) the space between the two characters. However, there is no obvious sense in which this involves spectator passivity. In terms of processing the visual and verbal information with which we are provided, very considerable 'active' processing is taking place. This is in part a consequence of the specific nature of this shot-reverse-shot dialogue: the characters are themselves objectifying the person opposite them, weighing them up. It is intended that the spectator becomes fascinated by the complex forces put into play: Mia's power over Vincent; Vincent's odd mix of coolness and vulnerability; the separate knowledge we have of the state of mind of each of them. This becomes particularly apparent during the 'comfortable silence' when the spectator is shifted from point-of-view shots to side-on 'observer' views of each character separately. The sequence, and its continuation after Mia returns from the ladies, requires the spectator to be both caught up within the exchange of looks and yet remain observant, responsive to the character information being revealed.

The spectator is very often both 'privileged' in possessing information which an on-screen character lacks and 'restricted' in that key information is withheld. Both are ways in which our interest is created and maintained. We may feel we have limited access to information at various points in this episode but in one important way we are in a position of superior knowledge: we know that *both* of them are high on drugs. Relative to Vincent, the spectator is 'privileged' on three separate occasions: before, during and after the trip to the diner we see Mia taking cocaine. Not only does this inform our understanding of and positioning with the Mia character, it also significantly shifts the spectator's expectations on what dramatic results are likely to follow. Having returned from Jack Rabbit Slim's, Vincent is observed in a bathroom of the Wallace home telling himself not to become sexually involved with Mia but to go home. This is a darkly comic situation, intensified by the Vincent/Travolta performance and made dramatically ironic by the knowledge given to the spectator that Mia is in the sitting-room with very different preoccupations.

There is then a sudden shift in tone after Vincent's bathroom monologue:

So you're gonna go out there, drink your drink, say 'Goodnight, I've had a lovely evening,' go home and jack off. And that's all you're gonna do.

(Tarantino 1994: 69)

We do not expect a close-up of Mia's face, suddenly deathly white, sick coming from her mouth, blood from her nose.

Part two: OD'ing

After Mia has overdosed, there is a two-minute ten-second sequence involving Vincent driving towards the house of Lance, trying all the while to communicate the desperateness of his situation on his mobile phone (while the Three Stooges play on Lance's TV). There then follows just under two minutes of frantic activity, much of it filmed using a handheld camera. (Tarantino's script offers the following description: 'everything in this scene is frantic, like a documentary in an emergency ward, with the big difference here being nobody knows what the fuck they're doing'.) There is then a quieter but hardly calmer one minute twenty-five seconds spent preparing for and giving the adrenaline shot to the heart that causes Mia's instant recovery.

The entire six minutes ten seconds before we see Mia, ghostly white, being driven home by Vincent is simultaneously suspenseful, shocking and comic. It is a rollercoaster ride of affect. In the act of spectatorship there are undoubtedly some responses which are involuntary just as there are in our responses to shocks and surprises outside the cinema. In this sequence, the most obvious illustration of this involuntary response is when Vincent, after a long pause, takes aim and plunges the syringe into Mia's heart. The shock of an entire audience is audible! However, for most of an action sequence, spectator involvement is far from involuntary. We need to *care* what happens – and this is directly related to the allegiances we have formed with the two central characters, specifically here as a result of our 'participation' in the previous long sequence in the diner. In considering some of the alternative ways of responding to the 'OD'ing sequence', it is first necessary to list some of the alternative ways of responding to the episode as a whole:

A   primarily at the level of character and the emotions generated by their circum-
     stances – a very 'affective' response
B   primarily at the level of genre/form in which characters and situations are under-
     stood in relation to familiarity with the 'schemas' of different kinds of cinema – a
     'cine-literate' if usually quite automatic response
C   primarily at the level of the film as 'construct' in which there is a strong awareness
     of the film's makers – an 'intellectual' response

These can be mapped against pleasure (1) and displeasure (2). In the abstract the alternatives look like this:

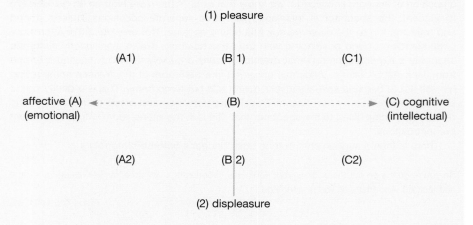

One way of interpreting these divergent responses is by reference to 'preferred', 'oppositional' and 'negotiated' readings.

In relation to the particular sequence, different responses may include the following:

A1   intense concern for Mia (that she recovers) and for Vincent (that he does not suffer
      the consequences of Mia's death)
B1   amusement at the mix of black comedy and farce
C1   delight in the way Tarantino mixes melodramatic intensity (1) with comedy and farce (2)

A2　distaste for Mia and Vincent, their behaviour and the values they represent

B2　disorientation at the mix of black comedy and farce in a situation involving a drug overdose, and possibly outrage as a consequence

C2　irritation at the 'smart' way Tarantino mixes melodramatic intensity (1) with comedy and farce (2)

Of course, these can be mixed: A1 could operate alongside B2 and C2, for example. And, of course, these are not the only responses.

The tone of *Pulp Fiction* needs to be carefully measured. It is most appropriately approached as a black comedy – arguably the 'preferred' response. So, for example, Mia is hardly treated with respect or care after her overdose. She is unceremoniously dropped on the grass outside Lance's house while Vincent begs for help for his *own* survival. 'That was fucking trippy' is the summary offered by Jody, Lance's girlfriend, at the end of the 'emergency', and, in relieving the tension of the situation, is meant to speak on behalf of the spectator. By contrast, one could well imagine a spectator who finds the world of the characters, the attitude towards drugs in particular, so disturbing as to 'oppose' the film. Some fairly hard 'negotiating' would be required by the spectator who is simultaneously delighted and shocked by the characters and events, and the manner in which they are depicted. We could also imagine a different kind of spectator, one who is committed to crime, violence and drugs. In seeing the film as endorsing criminal lifestyles, would they be closer to a 'preferred' reading?

A complementary way of trying to explain different responses is again in relation to the concept of spectator 'competence'. In some respects 'competence' and evaluative judgement are clearly separable from one another. For example, I may be perfectly capable of appreciating artistically and cinematically what Tarantino is doing – while despising it morally and ideologically!

In other respects, however, it is more difficult to disentangle competence from evaluative judgement. For example, the inexperienced spectator may not be able to engage with fictional characters in the kind of playful, imaginative way a film such as *Pulp Fiction* clearly requires. The film invites us to take pleasure in all of A1, B1 and C1 as identified above. It is only possible to do so if the spectator is simultaneously 'inside' and 'outside' the fiction, able to empathise with character, imagine the situation and yet still recognise its fictional nature. The active spectator, like the active reader of literature, is able to use fiction to expand their experience, become capable of new insights, more mature judgements – beyond the limitations of their actual experience in the 'real' world.

The most notorious example in *Pulp Fiction* of the mixing of tones is the accidental shooting of Marvin by Vincent as he sits in the back seat of a car – which then has to be meticulously cleaned!

In a variety of formulations this remains the key debate running through the whole of this chapter:

Films do have 'effects' (otherwise we would not bother to go and see them). These effects are the product of powerful communication processes. These effects will be handled by different spectators differently – on the basis of their 'formation' and their 'competence'. Most spectators, constituted as an audience, behave in more or less the same way because, other than in personal details, their social formations and their mental formations are very similar within a given community. However, film effects create 'affect'. The affective dimension of film response is much more personal, difficult to predict and to account for.

So, is the spectator 'passive' or 'active'; 'worked upon' or 'working'?

• **Plate 5.8**
Arrivée d'un train en gare à la Ciotat (The Lumière Brothers, 1895). Movement towards the camera thrilled and terrified the first cinema audiences. There are a number of examples of the sadistic delight taken in 'running down' the audience; for example, in R.W. Paul's *The Motorist* (*c.* 1902), a car 'hits' the spectator head-on

Imagining

While the last paragraph attempts to summarise much of what has been said thus far, there is the need to say a little more about the imagination. The 'passive' spectator is seen as one who somehow surrenders completely to the film experience in a form of imagining which can only be compared to some sort of infantile regression. The 'active' spectator is seen as one who is able to be simultaneously inside and outside the world of the film. A somewhat different way of expressing this is by considering two different kinds of imagining.

In *The Thread of Life* (1984), Richard Wollheim makes a fundamental distinction, corresponding to a big divide between two modes of imagination: '*central*' imagining and '*a-central*' imagining. A rough guide to the distinction may be found in linguistic clues. While central imagining is often expressed in the form 'I imagine ...', a-central imagining is expressed in the form 'I imagine that ...' (see Smith 1995: 76).

There are certain times when a spectator experiences central imagining, particularly when a film recreates a physical sensation such as falling or walking in a daze. With the move towards ever more spectacular forms of visual and aural cinema – such as with the IMAX technology – we are being offered are forms of cinema providing more opportunities for central imagining: 'I imagine sitting on the rollercoaster ... I imagine the sensation of para-gliding over mountains ...'. What is being created is the effect recorded as early as 1896 of spectators imagining a train coming towards them in the Lumière Brothers' *Arrivée d'un train en gare à la Ciotat* and made fun of as early as 1901 in Paul's *The Countryman and the Cinematograph*.

Most of the time the spectator operates in the 'I imagine that ...' mode. *I imagine that it must be pretty scary to have a gangster's wife overdosing in front of you when you are responsible for her! I imagine that having to plunge a syringe into a woman's heart in order to bring her out of a coma must be, well, quite stressful and I can't imagine that I could ever do such a thing!*

In practice it seems wisest to approach spectatorship as a complex mixture of central and a-central imagining, especially in films that combine narrative with spectacle, using the full powers of digital technology.

Staying with *Pulp Fiction* a little longer, consider two further details in the 'Vincent Vega and Marcellus Wallace's Wife' episode which draw particular attention to the film as a construct rather than as a film trying to disguise its construction so that we may 'suspend our disbelief'.

The first is a brief moment when Vincent and Mia are still in the car having just arrived outside Jack Rabbit Slim's.

Vincent: Come on, Mia, let's go get a steak.
Mia: You can get a steak here, daddy-o. Don't be a . . .
Mia draws a square with her hands. Dotted lines appear on the screen forming a square. The lines disperse.
Vincent: After you, kitty-cat.

(Tarantino 1994: 51–2)

This is a particularly blatant admission to the spectator of the film as a construct. It is a characteristic particularly common in 'postmodern' art. The spectator is invited to take pleasure in a certain complicity with the filmmaker – this is a 'game' made possible due to the coming together of the 'playful' imaginations of both.

The second incident is when Mia demands that Vincent join her to dance the twist. The spectator is confronted with a fine distinction between John Travolta's role and his star identity as the dancing star of *Saturday Night Fever* (1977). The relationship between film and extra-film information is clearly being exploited here in order to acknowledge the star 'myth'. A model of spectatorship which presents the interaction between spectator and film as closed off from wider contexts of audience and culture seems particularly inadequate in explaining what happens at moments such as these. Again, this may be described as a characteristic moment of postmodern cinema, this time involving a 'play' between the role of a character within the fiction and the persona-image of a star who exists outside that fiction. Tarantino mobilises a knowledge and a set of associations held by the spectator, not to enhance the fiction but to intensify a sense of the spectator and director making meaning and generating affective response together.

Maybe we can talk of two tendencies in contemporary cinema. One is the ever more costly attempts to produce the spectacular realist illusion, especially in action movies – moving towards the kind of IMAX experience discussed above. The other is towards an ever more 'playful' kind of cinema – such as that exemplified by *Pulp Fiction*. Maybe we need different conceptions of spectatorship for each. 'I imagine . . .' for the first. I imagine that . . .' for the second. Whichever way one looks at things, the point holds: for the majority of films it seems wisest to approach spectatorship as a complex mixture of central and a-central imagining.

SUMMARY

There has not been space in this chapter to do more than outline a variety of approaches to the study of spectators, audiences and the responses they produce to films.

- The first section outlined some working assumptions about spectator and audience study which you may now wish to revisit and question or add to.
- The second section encouraged a study of Early Cinema in order to gain a better appreciation of the evolution of the spectator and audience.
- The third section looked at the constructed spectator through the application of theory. This theory is in fact a composite of ideas deriving from structuralism and psychoanalysis. In its first phase it tended to emphasise the passivity of the spectator vulnerable to the power of the moving image and soundtrack. In its

second phase it moved toward a more balanced consideration of the interaction between the spectator and the film, an interaction in which the spectator was now conceived as a more active participant in making meaning and managing the affective dimension of the film experience.

■ The distinctions between concept and percept, between meaning and affect are highlighted with a suggestion that a greater attention to the percept and its affective impact is worth much more of our attention as film students.

■ The case study which takes up the final section of this chapter proposes a model which captures something of the variety of responses to the same sequence of film. In so doing it highlights what we bring to the viewing situation: our prior formation as an individual with specific tolerances and intolerances, reacting with pleasure or unpleasure to the moment-by-moment development of the sequence.

QUESTIONS FOR DISCUSSION

■ Is it still useful to explore in detail what is distinctive about the cinema experience, given the many and varied ways in which films are now viewed?

■ Is the distinction between audience and spectator a useful one?

■ What aspects of the evolution of spectator and audience in early cinema have encouraged you to look more closely at the films of this period?

■ Broadly speaking, is it true to describe the cinema spectator as passive – and if so, is that a bad thing?

■ How would you describe the interaction between film and spectator in the cinema?

■ Which theoretical perspectives touched upon in this chapter seem productive and worth finding out more about?

■ What is the value of giving greater emphasis to the affective dimension of the film experience in our studies?

■ Apply the model used to identify and place different responses to a sequence from *Pulp Fiction* to a sequence from a film of your choice. Having done so, evaluate the model and discuss how it could be improved.

■ What is the difference between central and a-central imagining?

■ Which is more dominant in your own film viewing?

 **FURTHER READING**

Overview of shifts in film studies/film theory
To track the shift from 'subject–apparatus' approaches, through American pragmatism/cognitivism, to cultural studies perspectives, these three books provide a chronological map:

Bordwell, David and Carroll, Noel, *Post-theory: Reconstructing Film Studies*, University of Wisconsin, Madison, 1996.

Gledhill, Christine and Williams, Linda (eds), *Reinventing Film Studies*, Arnold, London, 2000.

Lapsley, R. and Westlake, M., *Film Theory: An Introduction*, Manchester University Press, Manchester, 1988.

Spectatorship and film
The following are accessible, with Judith Mayne's the most useful summary of the area:

Ellis, John, *Visible Fictions: Cinema, Television and Video*, Routledge & Kegan Paul, London, 1982; repr. 1992.

Mayne, Judith, *Cinema and Spectatorship*, Routledge, London, 1993.

Phillips, Patrick, *Understanding Film Texts*, British Film Institute, London, 2000.

Stacey, Jackie, *Star Gazing: Hollywood Cinema and Female Spectatorship*, Routledge, London, 1993.

Turner, Graeme, *Film as Social Practice*, Routledge, London, 1988; repr. Routledge, London, 1993.

The following are more demanding:

Shaviro, Steven, *The Cinematic Body*, University of Minnesota Press, Minneapolis, 1993.

Smith, Murray, *Engaging Characters – Fiction, Emotion and the Cinema*, Oxford University Press, Oxford, 1995.

The ideas of Deleuze, particularly important in the shift towards the study of affect, may be found in:

Colebroke, Claire, *Gilles Deleuze*, Routledge, London, 2002.

The following give a sense of a cognitive approach – though both are quite difficult:

Person, Per, *Understanding Cinema: A Psychological Theory of Moving Imagery*, (Cambridge University Press, Cambridge, 2003.

Plantinga, Carl and Smith, Greg, M (eds), *Passionate Views: Film Cognition and Emotion*, Johns Hopkins University Press, Baltimore, MD, 1999.

On Early Cinema and the development of spectatorship

The first two volumes of the University of California History of the American Cinema series are particularly useful:

Bowser, Eileen, *The Transformation of Cinema 1907–1915*, University of California, Berkeley, 1994.

Musser, Charles, *The Emergence of Cinema: The American Screen to 1907*, University of California, Berkeley, 1994.

The following are also very readable:

May, Larry, *Screening Out the Past: The Birth of Mass Culture and the Motion Picture Industry*, Chicago University Press, Chicago, IL, 1980.

Robinson, David, *From Peep Show to Palace – The Birth of American Film*, Columbia, New York, 1996.

The Silents Majority: On-line Journal of Silent Film; online at http://www.silentsmajority.com

Other books referred to in this chapter include:

Basinger, Jeanine, *A Woman's View: How Hollywood Spoke to Women 1930–1960*, Chatto & Windus, London, 1993.

Hill, Annette, *Shocking Entertainment*, John Libby, Luton, 1997.

Wollheim, Richard, *The Thread of Life*, Yale University Press, New Haven, CT, 1999.

Case studies

Birth of a Nation:

The script and a range of essays are contained in: Lang, Robert (ed.), *D.W. Griffith – Birth of a Nation*, Rutgers University Press, New Brunswick, NJ, 1994.

An educational site with useful links may be found at: http://webster.edu/fatc/birth.html

Pulp Fiction:

Polan, Dana, *Pulp Fiction*, British Film Institute, London, 2001.

Tarantino, Quentin, *Pulp Fiction – The Screenplay*, Faber & Faber, London, 1994.

FURTHER VIEWING

Clearly all films raise issues in relation to spectatorship and response. The following twelve films, listed chronologically, are suggested for study purposes, as they raise particular questions or issues:

Early Cinema – Primitives and Pioneers (BFI compilation, DVD, 2005)

The Birth of a Nation (Griffith, US, 1915)

Man with a Movie Camera (Vertov, USSR, 1929)

Rear Window (Hitchcock, US, 1954)

Peeping Tom (Powell, UK, 1960)

Blow Up (Antonioni, UK/Italy, 1966)

Klute (Pakula, US, 1972)

Man Bites Dog (Belvaux and Bonzel, Belgium, 1992)

Natural Born Killers (Stone, US, 1994)

Festen (Vinterberg, Denmark, 1998)

Fight Club (Fincher, US, 1999)

Memento (Nolan, US, 2000)

Timecode (Figgis, US, 2000)

Hidden (Haneke, France, 2005)

RESOURCE CENTRES

http://www.sensesofcinema.com
http://www.film-philosophy.com
Two excellent online film journals. Both include some advanced theoretical and critical debate, but also much that is accessible, especially *Senses of Cinema*.

http://www.geocities.com/Hollywood/7606/pulp.html
A site with most things a fan could wish for.

Chapter 6

Cinematic authorship and the film auteur

Paul Watson

■ Cinematic authorship and the film auteur

INTRODUCTION

This chapter sets itself the task of defining what is at stake when we claim that certain films are authored, that is, the creative expression of an individual artist, in a way more or less analogous to the way we speak of the author of a novel, a letter, a poem or an opera. In other words, we will examine the contentious idea that both a film's meanings and its significance may be attributed to a single creative source who is responsible for bringing together its disparate elements into a coherent thematic and stylistic vision. But already, right here, we confront the theoretical dilemma of cinematic authorship, where traditional and common-sense conceptions of the author fail to describe the inherent complexity of filmmaking, a process which director Peter Bogdanovich describes as involving '300 different opinions and 500 alternative possibilities' (Bogdanovich 2002: 9). So, even if it is possible to make a case for a writer or painter to be the author of a work on the grounds that it might be entirely generated by a single individual, who out of more than 1000 people who contributed to the production of *Avatar* (2010) shall we single out as its author? Because, as we will see, the question of cinematic authorship has routinely been posed as a question of directorial control over visual style and narrative themes, precisely as a question of a director's individual vision, the paradigmatic reading of *Avatar* posits James Cameron as its author just insofar as it is possible to impute to him, as its director, considerable control over textual operation and meaning. Indeed, the dominant view of cinematic authorship has been that, like novels and paintings, films have a single author usually held to be the director. And, of course, when we speak of seeing the latest Quentin Tarantino or Martin Scorsese film we are, at least on a basic level, rehearsing this romantic notion of authorship as origin, a model in which the figure of the film director is stitched together with the notion of free authorial agency.

THE THREE PARADOXES OF CINEMATIC AUTHORSHIP

Boiling down the notion of cinematic authorship to such commonsensical simplicity, however, belies not only the theoretical and methodological complexities which bear on the study of authorship, but also the controversies that have attended the history of the concept in film studies. In other words, while Adrian Martin is right when he says that cinematic authorship is a 'quite a simple principle' with a twofold emphasis on *the art of film production* and a method of *understanding films as legitimate artworks*, this in itself tells us little about the implied relationship between human material activity, creative processes and the critical practices involved in defining and valorising films as art. Nor for that matter does it necessarily shed light on the political economy of filmmaking in terms of either the commercial frameworks in which any putative creativity takes place or the ways in which directors/authors often function as marketable commodities in their own right (see Martin 2001). Indeed, despite numerous attempts to variously overcome, fix or dodge them, and despite a number of changes in critical fashion since its inception, a number of stubborn dilemmas continue to dog the notion of cinematic authorship. This perhaps explains the current situation in which, on the one hand, critics have given up on the whole idea and 'flee in great haste from the mere mention of its name' (Patterson 2007), while on the other hand continuing to claim that 'auteur cinema is alive and well and all over the globe' (James 2010: 24).

Given that the concept of authorship has been consistently defined and redefined in different historical periods and in relation to changes in critical mood, a first question impels us to ask what the term actually refers to. As Tag Gallagher points out, 'even those who admit that some movies have an "author" disagree about what the term means'

(Gallagher 2001). Moreover, how do these various accounts of cinematic authorship sit with accounts derived from other disciplines? What models of authorship most adequately describe creative agency in relation to cinema? Can models be imported from elsewhere, say, literature or architecture, or are we impelled to devise a bespoke theory attuned to the specificities of the cinematic form? On another note, where is the critical efficacy of authorship to be found? Is authorship, as Janet Staiger argues, a question of 'causality for the film', one sensitive to the 'material reality of human actions' (Staiger 2003: 28, 49), or does it, as Jonathan Rosenbaum suggests, 'exist largely for the convenience of critics … [as] a way of reading movies, not explaining how they're made' (Rosenbaum 2000: 84)? Approaching the same issue from the other end, if authorship is no longer the *raison d'être* of film studies then what is the purpose of author/director studies? Is it specific to the disciplinary purview of film studies or should it be hooked up with the political concerns of cultural studies? Moreover, can authorship survive the theoretical challenge brought by developments in post-structuralist and postmodernist thinking, and if so where is the author to be found – still embodied in the figure of the director; in other creative personnel such as producers, screenwriters, actors and so forth; as a distinctive outcome of collaborative working practice; or as markers of institutional or corporate identity? As we proceed, we will, by necessity, begin to unpick this theoretical knot in order to tease out the threads required to plait a model of cinematic authorship which is by turns pragmatic, flexible and, above all, useful, that is to say, one that is attuned to both the authoring practices of real individuals and the various socio-economic contexts which always frame such practices. However, one thing is clear. The notion of cinematic authorship is paradoxical, and paradoxical in three distinct, albeit related, ways. Nevertheless, paradox can be productive insofar as it directs attention towards points of intellectual friction which, if probed with care, can often ignite the critical imagination and generate fresh thinking. As such, before turning to a consideration of the history of cinematic authorship and its subsequent development, it is worth entertaining paradox for the sake of progress.

The paradox of collaboration: 'Get me my agency!'

If on the one hand it is now commonplace to speak of the director as the author of his or her films and those films as the direct expression of individuated agency (the idea that 'a Spielberg film' implies a coherence of expressive techniques and meanings in a way that, say, 'a Dreamworks picture' does not), on the other hand, it is also a given of academic film studies to acknowledge that the overwhelming majority of filmmaking, and Hollywood studio production as a whole, is a fundamentally collaborative practice, and collaborative in crucial ways which affect the textual operation and meanings of a film. This is the first paradox of cinematic authorship: given the fundamentally collaborative working dynamics of industrial filmmaking, is it possible, or indeed plausible, to attribute authorship to a single creative source? Underpinning this problem is the question of the suitability of models of authorship developed in relation to literature and the arts for explaining filmic enunciation. For simply transposing the primary terms of traditional authorial analysis to the study of film may not only belie the intrinsic differences between the traditional arts and film, but more worryingly conceal more complex axes of art-making practice and expressivity that characterise cinema's mode of production. Either way, it is far from clear whether the assumed analogy between the collective and collaborative nature of most filmmaking and the individual novelist or painter is an appropriate one.

This already vexed issue is further complicated when we take into account the various strategies adopted by film scholars to deal with the implications of the first paradox of cinematic authorship. In attempting to fix that paradox by adding progressively finer detail to the concept of the film author, the level of complexity required to sustain the idea becomes incrementally geared up. As Berys Gaut observes:

It has been held that the film author is the director, the screenwriter, the star or the studio; that the film author is an actual individual, or a critical construct; that there is not one film author, but several; the claim of film authorship has been held primarily as an evaluative one, or an interpretive one, or simply as the view that there are authors of films as there are authors of literary works.

(Gaut 1997: 149)

Indeed, Gaut himself argues that while there is 'a core truth' to claims of cinematic authorship and that it 'should not be rejected in the cavalier fashion in which some critics have dealt with it', the fact that commercial films are typically the result of the work of many agents leads him to conclude that the notion of 'multiple-authorship' is a more 'theoretically sound and critically fruitful' model than the dominant view of singular authorship (Gaut 1997: 149, 150). Other critics have addressed this same paradox by uncoupling the agent of enunciation from the flesh-and-bone figure of a biographical self so as to 'squeeze out' the author 'from his position of prominence and transform the notion of him [*sic*] which remains' (Wollen 1973: 84). And what does remain from this process, depending on which critical position one adopts, is a picture of the author as variously: a source/product of discourse; a function of ideology; an unintentional 'signature' traceable across a number of films; a position or voice constructed by/ within the narrative; or a construction produced by the spectator in the act of reading/ comprehending a film or group of films. Either way, it is this degree of elaboration and contradiction which leads Catherine Grant to argue that 'despite the continual attention accorded to film directors during the last four decades, film authorship has rarely been considered a wholly legitimate object of contemplation' (Grant 2000: 101), and David Gerstner to suggest that the 'pleasures and politics associated with authorship studies' must to some degree 'remain suspect' (Gerstner 2003: 21).

The theoretical paradox: the immortal monster

The scepticism directed towards the idea of cinematic authorship prompts the second paradox of authorship. On the one hand, in turning away from authorship and towards such theoretical concepts as semiotics, structuralism and psychoanalysis that are abstracted from the actual practices of filmmaking, film theory either confined the author to the sidelines of its debates, or simply ignored the question of cinematic authorship altogether. On the other hand, however, and in the face of such stubborn indifference, authorship continues to survive as a going academic concern with major academic publishers commissioning series after series of books dedicated to the work of single directors. It is in this respect that John Belton describes cinematic authorship as 'not so much a theory as it is a crime scene to which critics and theorists seem to be drawn again and again. The bodies on the floor change but the scene remains the same' (Belton 2005: 62). He goes on to discuss the notion of the author as a 'monster who will not die, the mesmerizing figure that the field of film studies has been unable and unwilling to exorcise' (Belton 2005: 60). It is this theoretical peccadillo, the seemingly irrepressible urge to scratch the author-itch, which accounts for the fact that the idea of the director-as-author 'remains probably the most widely shared assumption in film studies today' (Bordwell and Thompson 1994: 38). Indeed, not only do writers and publishers continue to organise output around the work of directors/authors, but, as Barry Keith Grant notes, and chapters such as this one attest, the study of authorship remains a 'standard' approach in the academic study of film with courses being taught 'under a variety of auteurist rubrics' at a range of different educational levels (Keith Grant 2008: xi). So while there seems to be a tacit agreement among professional film scholars, even those who have in recent years attempted to resuscitate and reinvigorate authorship approaches, that the work of individual filmmakers is best understood as a thread in a much more complex tapestry of technological, social, historical, institutional, cognitive and cultural practices, this stance accounts for neither the individuated creative crafts involved in film production in the first instance, nor, in the final instance, the continued fascination and identification with the figure of the cinematic author by the film industry, film critics and film audiences.

The cultural paradox: authors, authors everywhere

Claims that the author is somehow dead, or a theoretical irrelevancy, appear out of step not only with our intuitions, but more crucially with contemporary media culture. For instance, it is possible to argue, with Timothy Corrigan, that far from being supplanted by the apparently more rigorous approaches of semiotics, structuralism, psychoanalysis and audience studies, the figure of the cinematic author may in fact be 'more alive now than at any other point in film history' (Corrigan 1991: 135). This irony has been more recently expressed by John Patterson who, after declaring that the idea of auteurism bores him and that he is 'done with it', nevertheless concedes that there are plenty of auteurs about (2007). Indeed, with the growth in digital film technologies and the rapid proliferation of convergent media platforms, it seems that the *visibility* of the author is now more pronounced than ever. Perhaps the two most powerful examples of this re-emergence of the auteur are to be found in possibilities opened up by home cinema technologies for new cultures of spectatorship and the role that the 'director's homepage' can play in the construction of an intentional authorial agency. Let us briefly consider both of these arenas of authorial visibility.

For more detailed discussion of the impact of new media on film see Chapter 2.

Janet Harbord argues that 'a truism of our times is that film is not what it used to be' (2007: 1). Underpinning this claim is the observation that film has become uncoupled from (the) cinema. Not only is film no longer primarily consumed in cinemas, but it has become a destabilised, multiple and heterogeneous object. One way of unpicking this idea is to consider the viewer/consumer experience offered by the notion of home cinema, an experience which, on the one hand, seeks to replicate the conditions of cinematic spectatorship while, on the other hand, providing ancillary experiences which exceed those offered by traditional film-going. For example, the fact that the storage capacity of DVD and Blu-ray discs exceeds the amount required to contain a film has opened up not only new commercial possibilities, but also new modes of consumption based around the addition of 'Special Features'. Indeed, the time it would take to watch the panoply of deleted scenes, exclusive footage and other 'featurettes' contained on the three-disc 'Limited Extended Collector's Edition' of *Avatar* (2010) would far surpass the viewing time of the film itself.

Notwithstanding the significance of the sheer amount of material that is now routinely jam-packed on to DVDs and Blu-rays, both Parker and Parker (2005) and Alex Cox (2001) attach particular salience to the 'director commentary' as a means of both analysing individual authors and making a case for the continuing relevance of authorship studies. The former argue that such commentaries can not only articulate the 'specifics of intention' (that is, the local and specific decision-making processes carried out by a director from scene to scene, and the 'suppressed' or 'residual' intentions of other potential authors such as screenwriters or cinematographers), but also the 'limits of intention', the way contingency, expediency, chance and luck can all bear upon the final film's style and affect (Parker and Parker 2005). The latter agrees that the change in the way movies can be now watched and comprehended on DVD and Blu-ray 'can provide some sort of film literacy, even insight'. More important for Cox, however, is the potential of the director commentary to breathe new life into debates about cinematic authorship insofar as the inscription of the authorial voice into the film text itself can literally be seen as evidence of 'the Return of the Director' (Cox 2001: 10).

If home cinema technologies represent one site where cinematic authorship seems to have re-emerged as a kind of special feature, then Nuria Triana-Toribio suggests that the official homepages of certain directors can be understood as a similar such site. She argues that the 'director's official homepage is a versatile invention that can survive the decline of cinemagoing and accommodate the "afterlife" of film' (2008: 264). Triana-Toribio's analysis explores the way in which Spanish directors such as Pedro Almodóvar, Álex de la Iglesia and Isabel Coixet, use their personal web pages 'to create and perpetuate a cult of personality' based around the presentation of themselves as authentic individual artists (ibid.: 270). The way this is achieved is not only through the complex mix of biographical information, personal diaries/blogs, 'private' images and exclusive news about upcoming projects offered by these sites, but more complexly thorough the construction of a unique public persona through the assertion of individual taste. In other words, the filmmaker's official homepage allows directors to articulate quite precise preferences not only in film culture (though this is important, especially in the way it allows the directors to distance themselves from the putatively crudely commercial imperatives of industrial filmmaking), but in culture and politics more broadly – what food they like, where they like to shop, what leisure activities they enjoy, which authors they read, what music they are listening to, and so on. For Triana-Toribio, the provision of such preferences simultaneously reinforces the sense of direct connection to fans and plays a prominent role in establishing a recognisable 'image' of the director as an inimitable creative agent. Moreover, this kind of 'e-auteurism' now finds enhanced expression through social network sites such as Twitter, Facebook and Myspace. Twitter in particular extends many of the ideas identified by Triana-Toribio inasmuch as the sense of *privileged access* offered by the filmmaker homepage becomes even more immediate and intimate as we access minute-by-minute updates on the thoughts and feelings of the director on our computers and smartphones. The main point here, however, is that the pleasures offered by, or associated with, both the director's commentary and the director's homepage are intimately entwined with, and to a significant extent predicated precisely on, the *presence* of the knowable author.

This, then, is the third paradox of cinematic authorship: that at a time when many critics would like to think that film theory has finally wriggled free from its fascination with the figure of the cinematic author the discourse of authorship seems once more to present itself as a vital node in understanding the relationship between the film industry, the film text and its audience. Indeed, as borne out by the commercial and cultural complexities bound up with the 'director commentary' and 'filmmaker homepage' phenomena, there remains what Dana Polan has called a simultaneous 'desire *of* the director' and 'desire *for* the director' (Polan 2001b). The first of these terms refers to a director's 'recourse to filmmaking as a way to express personal vision', and the subsequent attempts by critics to identify and understand their 'primary obsessions and thematic preoccupations' as the product of individual artistic desire. The second term, the desire *for* the director, directs attention away from what the director wants and instead focuses it on the activities of fans, critics and scholars who continue to want to 'understand films as having an originary instance in the person who signs them' and who arbitrate on the relative worth of a film based on who that signature belongs to (ibid.). It is in these respects, then, that if authorship is a fiction, it is, as Thomas Elsaesser notes, a necessary one insofar as it names a pleasure 'that seems to have no substitute in the sobered-up deconstruction of the authorless voice of ideology' (Elsaesser 1981: 11). This perhaps goes some way towards explaining why, despite the paradoxes it prompts, film authorship remains, as Thomas Schatz puts it, 'the single most challenging issue in film studies and the abiding mystery of cinema' (Schatz 2008). Indeed, these pleasures, challenges and mysteries seem to have regained some academic respectability in recent years with a number of scholars beginning once again to see the task of theorising cinematic authorship as both possible and worthwhile. Much of that work has attempted to reincarnate, recast or rethink what is variously referred to as classical authorship or vulgar **auteurism**. It is to a more detailed examination of those approaches, their origination, development and efficacy, that we now turn.

For further discussion of auteur theory and the French New Wave see the website www.routledge.com/cw/ nelmes.

auteurism
see **auteur**

auteur
A French term that originated in the pages of the film journal *Cahiers du cinéma* in the 1950s to refer to directors who infused their films with their distinctive personal vision through the salient manipulation of film technique. Auteurs, seen as genuine artists, were contrasted with **metteurs-en-scène** who were held to be technically competent directors who merely executed the processes of filmmaking without consistently stamping their 'personality' on the material from one film to the next. To study film as if it were the creative expression of a single individual, usually held to be the director, is often called **auterism**.

WHAT'S THE USE OF AUTHORSHIP?

In spite of its troubled theoretical career, the common-sense position – that a film bears traces of its creator(s) – has proved remarkably durable precisely because it addresses a number of crucial questions, questions that refuse to go away, about the role of cinema as an art form, a commodity and a communicative practice: exactly how are the makers of film and the audience bound together in the activities of creation, communication and comprehension; what kind of communication is this and are there really any grounds for erecting theoretical boundaries between the practices of filmmaking and the experience of watching movies; and why, in the final instance, do audiences and critics continue to hanker for the cinematic author when 'the challenge to the concept of the author as source and centre of the text … has been decisive in contemporary criticism' (Caughie 1981: 1)?

As we shall see, the emergence of authorship offered film critics a set of tools with which to:

- Argue for the artistic and academic legitimacy of cinema by claiming that there are film artists just as there are literary or visual artists and that the work of these artists should be afforded the same intellectual scrutiny as the traditional arts.
- Interpret films as the creative expression of those who made them by shifting the critical focus away from film narrative (what happens) towards film style (mise-en-scène and thematics).
- Evaluate the relative artistic merits of both a film and its maker(s) and make more precise differentiations between individual films and filmmakers.

It is these three principal critical procedures which continue to make cinematic authorship not only a controversial idea, but a useful critical tool as well. There are, however, two important implications that emerge from these various dimensions of authorship. First, we cannot assume that authorship means the same thing in every context. For the question of how authorship relates to a film's meanings and enunciative techniques is not the same as how an author creates value in a film. And second, we may have to look for a more pragmatic definition of film authorship which recognises the importance of the distinct contribution of a broader range of cinematic roles to the meaning and value of film. This would involve, on the one hand, a reconsideration of the *critical function* of authorship theory (what we expect its yield to be in the way of results), and on the other, a reconsideration of *how and where we look for evidence of authorship*, and with it reconsideration of some of those elements that have, up until now, tended to be assigned to the director. Before doing so, however, it is first necessary to review some of the most salient steps in the history and development of authorship theory in order to: (1) locate the above discussion of the paradoxical nature of the authorship debate in its proper historical context; (2) identify the useful aspects arising from the various incarnations of authorship theory; and (3) establish how it may be possible to shape those aspects into a critical method for analysing contemporary cinema that chimes with both current theoretical concerns and our intuitive attraction to the author.

The emergence of the auteur

Today, both filmmakers and critics take for granted cinema's status as an art form. Some sixty or so years ago, however, when not altogether ignored by scholars as beneath serious critical attention, cinema was often vilified along with other forms of mass culture as a blemish on art, or worse, a dehumanising agent of cultural oppression. Despite attempts to designate film as 'the seventh art', and notwithstanding the work of such prototypical auteurists as Parker Tyler and James Agee, cinema's search for artistic legitimation was more of a hope than a prospect. Cinema, and Hollywood cinema

mise-en-scène
Refers both to *what* is filmed (setting, props, costumes, etc.) and to *how* it is filmed (cinematographic properties of the shot such as depth of field, focus and camera movement). In an attempt to counter the imprecision of the term, this latter aspect is sometimes called 'mise-en-shot'.

in particular, was seen first and foremost as a business governed by economic logic and the conventions of product marketability. And, as Gallagher notes, 'conventions have nothing to do with art. Art is original, individual. Conventions are collective – what everyone knows' (Gallagher 2001). As such, the origins of cinematic authorship may be understood as a response to three simultaneous lines of argument which conspired to exile film from artistic and intellectual respectability. First, the idea that cinema's technological means of production precludes individual creativity. Second, the claim that the collaborative nature of industrial filmmaking and the specialised division of labour it entails necessarily forestall self-expression. Third, the notion that commercial filmmaking's need to attract and sustain large audiences necessitates a high degree of standardisation and conventionality which are incompatible with original artistic expression. In all of these propositions the blanket rejection of cinema as artistically illegitimate depends on the idea that art is necessarily the result of the creative activities of an individual, and can be appreciated and understood as such.

Within this context, therefore, authorship offered first and foremost a ready-made strategy for vindicating film as an art form precisely by installing in cinema the figure of the individual artist. Moreover, to a significant extent the infant discipline of film studies was underwritten by the theoretical legitimacy and disciplinary vocabulary associated with the ideas of authorship and individual artistic expression which had already been well rehearsed in literary criticism and art history. Richard Dyer neatly summarises this idea, stating that authorship

made the case for taking film seriously by seeking to show that a film could be just as profound, beautiful and important as any other kind of art, provided, following a dominant model of value in art, it was demonstrably the work of a highly individual artist.... The power of authorship resided in its ability to mobilize a familiar argument about artistic worth and, importantly, to show that this could be used to discriminate between films. Thus, at a stroke, it was proclaimed that film could be art (with all the cultural capital this implies) and that there could be a form of criticism – indeed, study – of it.

(Dyer 1998: 5).

So although film had been discussed as art before the notion of the film author had taken shape, in borrowing some of the academic legitimacy from more established disciplines by making the author-as-artist a necessary sufficient condition of the serious study of cinema, cinematic authorship entwined the notion of the value of film with the person who was deemed aesthetically responsible for it. As such, at the heart of the various complexities associated with authorship lies the idea that films are valued when they are deemed to be the work of an artist, traditionally identified as the director. In other words, the critical strategy on which this move is predicated is to assume the 'director as the creative source of meaning' and their 'output as an oeuvre'; that is to say, 'a repetition and enrichment of characteristic themes and stylistic choices' which bear traces of individual personality (Bordwell 1989: 44).

These ideas were cultivated most notably in the pages of the French journal *Cahiers du cinéma* during the 1950s and were subsequently formulated into what became known as 'auteur theory' by the American critic Andrew Sarris in the 1960s. While the idea that a film's director should be considered its author certainly did not originate in the pages of *Cahiers du cinéma*, the central role which the journal played in propagating and disseminating that thesis cannot be underestimated. Likewise, despite the critical venom subsequently directed towards Sarris's contribution, especially by Pauline Kael in her scathing 1963 essay 'Circles and Squares', it is his work that is chiefly responsible for publicising ideas of cinematic authorship in America and shaping it into a critical method for analysing and evaluating the particular art of Hollywood production.

The *Cahiers* critics, as they became known, writers such as François Truffaut, André Bazin, Jean-Luc Godard, Jacques Rivette, Claude Chabrol and Eric Rohmer, not only formulated the fundamental principles of film authorship which Sarris later recast into auteur theory, but also implicitly and explicitly outfitted the study of cinema with an analytical method and critical vocabulary. In what is often seen as the founding document of cinematic authorship, 'A Certain Tendency of the French Cinema', François Truffaut chides the inclination of the dominant mode of French cinema of the 1940s and 1950s for its bourgeois values and dependency on literary sources for its inspiration. For Truffaut this notion of 'quality cinema', motivated by traditional models of high culture and leaning on 'respectable' literature for its value, offers little in the way of art besides the technical transposition of literary scripts to the screen. Indeed, on this account the merits of a film are relatively unconnected with the practices of filmmaking, but are rather determined by the putative literary pedigree of the script. In contrast, Truffaut argued for the recognition, in terms of both filmmaking and its critical reception, of the 'audacities' specific to the medium of film: an attention to the cinematographic properties of film style, especially the way mise-en-scène was deployed by a filmmaker (see Truffaut 1976). This manifesto for seeing film *qua* film through an attention to the *craft* of filmmaking found perhaps its most well-known expression, somewhat ironically, in the title of Bazin's 1957 article, 'La Politique des auteurs'. It is ironic insofar as Bazin's essay simultaneously provides not only the titular 'policy' that Sarris would later recast as 'theory' and the terms of authorship analysis which would subsequently be used both to teach auteurism and to conduct studies of specific auteurs, but also one of the strongest cautions against the excesses of auteurism. Indeed, after warning against the dangers of, on the one hand, ignoring the work of directors deemed not to be auteurs and, on the other, side-stepping consideration of the material conditions in which directors produce their work, he concludes with the reproof, '*Auteur*, yes, but what of?' (Bazin 1996). Nevertheless, the foundations of 'auteur theory' had been laid and its propositional cornerstone – the recognition of the director as a film's principal creative source – set squarely in place. For, generally speaking, the *Cahiers* critics believed that film ought to bear the personal stylistic signature of its director; that is, to announce what William D. Routt has called the 'auteurprints' of its creator. Indeed, Routt goes so far as to suggest that 'La politique des auteurs' evinces 'perhaps the most radical assertion of the shaping power of one individual in popular art' (Routt 1990). In this way, then, auteurism's first provocative move was to locate the author and creative centre of a film not as its writer but as its director insofar as it is the director who orchestrates the visual aspects of cinema.

Auteurism's second and perhaps most provocative intervention was the championing of certain Hollywood directors as genuine, even exemplary auteurs. Indeed, to a significant extent, the idea that it is possible, even desirable to adopt a serious, critical stance towards Hollywood cinema became knotted together with the auteur approach. For in the work of directors such as Alfred Hitchcock, Howard Hawks, Nicholas Ray, Orson Welles, John Ford and Douglas Sirk the *Cahiers* critics detected a style and purity of technique undiluted by the cultural dead-weight of literary heritage. As Jonathan Romney puts it, the *Cahiers* critics 'wrote as if Alfred Hitchcock, Howard Hawks, Nicholas Ray et al were as sophisticated and as consistent in their styles, worldviews, personal "signatures" as, say, William Faulkner – and thanks to *Cahiers*, few cinephiles would today think of disputing that' (Romney 2010: 30). It is in this sense, then, that auteurism's most profound and influential critical tactic is not the mere attribution of individuated creative agency in what is a collaborative medium, but rather the exaltation of Hollywood directors, hitherto seen as mere cogs in a vulgar commercial machine, as auteurs. Indeed, Bill Nichols argues that 'a frequent tenet of *auteur* criticism is that a tension exists between the artist's vision and the means at his [*sic*] disposal for realizing it: studio pressure, genre conventions, star demands, story requirements. These constraints are also seen as a source of strength, imposing discipline and promoting cunning subversions' (Nichols 1976: 306) As such, it is precisely the industrial restrictions and formal constraints that were previously evoked to define Hollywood studio productions as anonymous genre fodder that, ironically, the *Cahiers* critics valorised as the conventional environment against which the great directors' ingenuity and personal vision take shape. Hitchcock, Hawks and others were championed as auteurs because they realised personal expression in the face of the industrial constraints imposed on them. In other words, their work was valorised not despite the barriers to its expression, but precisely because of them. Moreover, if it could be demonstrated that auteurs exist in the most restrictive filmmaking system in the world, then they can exist anywhere.

Auteurism as method

Auteurism, as it emerged from the pages of *Cahiers du cinéma*, thus not only imbricated cinema with the traditional arts through the ascription of director-as-author, but evolved into a critical strategy for sorting the artistic wheat from the generic chaff of Hollywood cinema. The principal method by which this was achieved was the establishment of the hierarchical distinction between those directors dubbed mere '**metteurs-en-scène**' and genuine auteurs. While metteurs-en-scène were deemed technically competent directors, film-to-film their work nevertheless evinced little or no stylistic coherence or thematic consistency. By contrast, the auteurs infused their work with a personal vision, leaving behind a distinctive signature or worldview across a significant number of films. Unlike the tradition of 'quality' filmmaking in France, for the auteur the script was merely a pretext for engaging in the proper practices of filmmaking – *the intentional and salient manipulation of cinematic techniques for enunciative and/or expressive ends*. Privileged among these stylistic techniques was mise-en-scène. For it is through the specific organisation of mise-en-scène, critics argued, that a director leaves behind the footprints of his or her vision, individual stylistic touches that accrue to resemble the unique personality of the auteur. John Caughie argues that 'it is with the mise-en-scène that the *auteur* transforms the material which has been given to him or her; so it is in the mise-en-scène ... that the auteur writes his or her individuality into the film' (Caughie 1981: 12–13).

metteur-en-scène
See **auteur**

Of course, such a fundamentally evaluative critical method not only enabled cinema's great works and the great film artists to be ranked alongside the great works and artists from the classical arts, but it also presented critics with a methodology and vocabulary for studying cinema. Armed with such a method, it was possible for the critic to contribute to the task of winkling out traces of authorship in a range of filmmakers' work. As Robert Stam notes, 'one of the pleasures of auteurist criticism was discerning style and individuality where it had not been detected before' (Stam 2000b: 2). Thus, the critic skilled in auteur archaeology roves across the surfaces of a director's work brushing away the dust of conventionality until aspects of film style and technique deemed salient are unearthed, aspects which can then be explicated and retroactively strung together into a coherent vision of the director-as-auteur who is positioned behind them as their originator. In other words, the critic's work is that of ferreting out the unique marks, flourishes and touches of a director so that they may be credited back to or projected upon their source: the auteur. As such, figures like Hitchcock and Welles were deemed significant in the first instance not necessarily for advancing cinema technically, but rather for a certain aesthetic consistency and salience.

It is this avowedly evaluative form of cinematic authorship that Andrew Sarris trans-lated into North American film criticism and in so doing added a false veneer of rigour to the approach in modifying 'auteur policy' to 'auteur theory'. In other words, what started out in the pages of *Cahiers du cinéma* as artistic-political polemic that called for the 'true' art of cinema to be recognised and for its artists to use their skills to transform real-world politics became, with Sarris, a prescriptive method for evaluating the worth of directors and championing the putative supremacy of American film. In a much quoted essay, 'Notes on the Auteur Theory in 1962', Sarris sought to shake both art criticism and film criticism out of its blindness towards Hollywood cinema and was willing, in Janet Staiger's phrase, to 'out-auteur' many of the French critics in order to do so (Staiger 2003: 36). In further refining the distinction between metteurs-en-scène and genuine auteurs, he argued that 'the way a film looks and moves should have some relationship to the way a director thinks and feels'. Moreover, he advocated 'wrenching' directors from 'their historical environments' in order to subject them to an aesthetic analysis which could both discern their 'personal signatures' and be used to determine their proper place within his pantheon. Sarris proposed three criteria for establishing the auteurist credentials of a director which correlated with the 'circles' of that pantheon: technical competency; distinguishable personality; and the 'interior meaning' of a film arising from the tension between the director's personality and the material. While the first two of these premises were criterion of value, the latter, for Sarris, 'is the ultimate glory of the cinema as an art' (see Sarris 1963, 1996). On the one hand, the lineage to the *Cahiers* critics is clearly visible in this strategy inasmuch as the worth of a film remains firmly indexed to the director's ability to inscribe his personality across a series of films in spite of the limitations imposed on individual creativity by the industrial and commercial pressures of filmmaking. On the other hand, however, Sarris's legacy to the auteurist debate resides in the slippage from the *evaluative* method established in 'La Politique' into a method explicitly based on *value judgements*. For in *The American Cinema* Sarris not only deployed the principles of auteurism to recast the history of American film as a pantheon – a nine-part hierarchical system which ranked films top to bottom according to his own criteria for determining value – but went further in declaring that, film for film, American cinema was superior to that of 'the rest of the world' (Sarris 1996).

For a discussion of Warner Bros Studio as auteur read pp. 10–13.

Sarris's regressive use of auteur theory to reconstruct film history, however, represents only one snag in the frayed theoretical rug that underlays the idea of cinematic authorship. Indeed, it is not surprising that such an anachronistic move – the installation in the cinema of the romantic figure of the artist – would provide a broad enough, and easy enough, target to attract a range of far-reaching criticisms.

THE PROBLEMS OF AUTEUR THEORY

If, as Dyer suggests, auteurism is film studies' 'greatest hit', then it is also perhaps its most criticised and controversial idea (Dyer 1998: 5). Indeed, as Routt argues, the 'absurd pretences' on which the entire notion of cinematic authorship is founded 'are easy to see, and to reject, as all sober folk of good intentions have rejected and continue to reject them' (Routt 1990). For while the desire to forge a critical method capable of bestowing intellectual and artistic credibility to cinema, that is, to interrogate cinema's distinctive contribution to the arts, does not in itself invoke essentialist or Romantic conceptions of the artist and all the political problems thus entailed, its significance nevertheless does lie in the foregrounding of a specific relationship between filmic enunciation and the creative activities of individuals. And it is here that the difficulty of cinematic authorship continues to replay itself, raising uncomfortable questions about the relationship between the film text and the spectator implied by the model of communication that underpins it. For a number of crucial problems become clear once we view auteurism through the lens of subsequent developments in film theory.

First, and most obviously, auteurism was attacked for belying the collaborative conditions of cinema's mode of production. As discussed above, the analogy between writer or painter and the auteur becomes difficult to sustain when one takes into account the material realities and creative diversity of the filmmaking process in which collaboration is standard and undeniable. A corollary argument to this is the idea that auteurism was insufficiently rigorous or simply whimsical, that at best it depended on the taste of a few specialised critics who pronounced on a film's worth by appealing to the already shop-worn principles of the traditional arts, and, at worse, resembled personalised and impressionistic conjecture. This prompted critics to try to correct some of these charges of imprecision by grafting auteurism on to the quasi-scientific methodology of structuralism. In an effort to counter the individualist paradigm of the Romantic artist axiomatic to its predecessor, auteur-structuralism, as it became known, was an attempt to probe beneath the surfaces of individuated agency into the 'deep' underlying socio-cultural structures which imbued a film with significance and meaning. Its apparent sophistication resided in its conception of the auteur not as the biographical figure who intentionally 'put the meaning into the film' so to speak, but as a structure identifiable in the text. As such, the concept of the auteur was, in the final instance, neither necessarily the director, nor even a person, but an indeterminate structure unearthed in the critical process of reading a film. Peter Wollen's (1972, 1973) work formed a central pillar in this line of thinking inasmuch as he recast the author from an *a priori* figure responsible for putting the meaning into a film to 'an *a posteriori* construction produced by the spectator to identify the particular bundles of oppositions that structured a group of texts associated with the author figure' (Belton 2005: 60). In other words, auteurs no longer produced films intentionally, rather films produced auteurs unintentionally.

Passing through various other theoretical modifications, this line of thinking progressively diluted auteurism's theoretical respectability to the point where Roland Barthes's 1968 article, 'The Death of the Author', seemed to nail the lid shut on the possibility of authorship generally, let alone the film auteur. Underscoring Barthes's argument, as well as most of the above objections, is the suspect notion of 'ideal' comprehension, where the author's/director's intentions coincide with the spectator's/critic's reading of a film. Often referred to as the **intentional fallacy**, the model of communication implied by the classical auteurist approach is one in which spectators are subjected to the vision of the director, a vision they reconstruct more or less faithfully in line with the map provided by the author through the film's stylistic salience. In other words, communication and signification become a closed circuit with authors jam-packing films full of meaning and spectators subsequently unpacking that meaning during the act of viewing. This is a problematical model for a number of reasons. Not only is it at odds with cognitive models of cinematic comprehension which attribute a far more important stake to the spectator in actually creating meaning, but specifically in terms of cinematic authorship it tends to confine the significance of the auteur to the evidence of his or her activities left behind in the film text itself. To put it another way, auteurs now have an increasing cultural visibility which, in the last instance, is not tied to their role as director. Timothy Corrigan calls this extratextual notion of cinematic authorship 'the commerce of auteurism' (Corrigan 1991). For Corrigan, auteurism has become 'a *commercial* strategy for organizing audience reception, as a critical concept bound to distribution and marketing aims' (ibid.: 103).

intentional fallacy
A phrase coined by Monroe Beardsley to describe the difference between a text's meaning(s) and what its author intended. As such, criticism dependent on or directed towards uncovering the intentions of the author/artist falls foul of an 'intentional fallacy' insofar as the meaning of a text is not fixed within it, but created in the historically situated act of reading.

A BIOGRAPHICAL LEGEND: THE COMMERCE OF AUTHORSHIP

Corrigan's intervention in the debate is to locate auteurism's critical and performative impetus not with filmmaking but rather with film consumption. He argues that 'in today's commerce we want to know what our authors or auteurs look like or how they act' and that, accordingly, the concept of auteurism is now defined by institutional and commercial agencies 'almost exclusively as publicity and advertisement' (ibid.: 106). This is the idea of *auteur as star* and, like film stars, auteurs peddle their celebrity currency in the promotion, marketing and publicity of their film to the extent that our primary access to the auteur is not through the film itself but through the numerous interviews, talk shows, reviews, trailers, websites, award ceremonies and guest appearances the auteur undertakes in selling a film to us. In other words, instead of struggling against the system in order to express their personal vision, authors are located as a function of the system, summoned up by the industrial forces and mobilised according to institutional needs. As such, to study an auteur one no longer focuses exclusively on the markers of individual style left behind in the film, but rather their 'biographical legend' – the term

David Bordwell (1988) uses to describe the *image* of a director that one constructs not only from their films, but from the full range of extratexts in which they appear.

Once again, the role of 'director commentaries' and other 'special features' available on DVD and Blu-ray discs, as well as the filmmaker homepage and social networking sites, may be seen as particularly significant in this respect. For the sense of privileged access to the authentic voice of the auteur that we get through these kinds of text functions not simply to mediate her or his intentionality, nor solely as another marketable asset that can be sold to consumers, but rather as a *performance* of authorial agency which implies yet exceeds both. In other words, both on general and specific levels, the director commentary and the filmmaker homepage expose an interesting slippage between textual and extratextual models of cinematic authorship.

For instance, while the director commentary is intimately related to the film it annotates, it nevertheless complicates how we experience it and how we understand it. But it is not just the experience of 'watching' director commentaries that reveals the performative act of the auteur but also the process of producing them, a process described by filmmaker Alex Cox as 'sitting watching a video of a film made, usually, several years previously. As the film plays, [the director] is expected sagely to regale a microphone with anecdotes about the making of the film. It helps if the director has managed to snag someone as "back-up" – the producer, the writer, an actor or the composer. Quite often, their recollections will be completely different' (Cox 2001: 10). Cox's anecdote prompts two observations. First, there is no *a priori* reason to believe that the director is the most knowledgeable, reliable or even honest commentator about either their own role in the filmmaking process or the finished film itself. Indeed, with DVDs which have an audio track with multiple commentators or multiple audio tracks with a single commentator a range of possible descriptions become available of the same events and processes. This has the potential not only to complicate the dynamics of authorial intentionality and possibly unseat the director from the assumed position as the film's controlling centre, but also to prompt consideration of instances where authorship might be more plausibly conceived as collaborative or multiple.

Second, and perhaps more complexly, both the director commentary and the filmmaker homepage deliberately foreground authorial agency through a network of extra textual relationships not only as a method of representing the artistic worth of a film and thus differentiating it within the market, but also as a way of stabilising the possible ways in which it is received. That is to say, if the conception of the auteur developed in the pages of *Cahiers du cinéma* and circulated by Sarris depended on the discernible textual evidence of artistic agency, auteurs are now 'placed before, after and outside a film text … in effect usurping the work of that text and its reception' (Corrigan 1991: 106). Access to a blow-by-blow account of a director's intentions, influences, tastes and ideas – that is to say, evidence of the relationship between individual agency and aesthetics – short-circuits the critical need to unearth those intentions since they are already provided by the auteurs themselves through interviews, commentaries, diaries, blogs, tweets or other kinds of personal cultural enunciation. In this respect, developments such as the directorial commentary and filmmaker homepage as described by Triana-Toribio can be seen as a logical extension or complement to the model of commercial auteurism outlined by Corrigan in which a *refusal of interpretation* becomes tied in with cinematic pleasures. He argues that many of the pleasures of contemporary cinema lie 'in being able to already know, not read, the meaning of the film in a totalising image that precedes the movie in the public images of its creator' (ibid.: 106). In this sense, the notion of authorship functions as a *precept of aesthetic expectation* insofar as the extratextual construction of the auteur implies a particular mode of consumption and endorses a range of possible understandings *in advance* of viewing a film. The logical destination of this line of thought, therefore, is the idea that it is possible to understand and consume the work of an auteur without the requirement to watch the films. Viewed from the other end, this means that *the principle* of authorship in cinema is predicated neither on the vagaries of spectatorship nor even on the 'fact' of the film text itself, but is rather redirected through the institutional circuits of extratextual mediation which surround a film and which act as a pre-condition to its reception.

TOWARDS A PRAGMATIC CONCEPTION OF CINEMATIC AUTHORSHIP

While on the one hand it is undeniable that auteurs are increasingly sustained and understood extra-textually through the journalistic practices of reviewers and critics, as well as through the institutional commodification of the director precisely as a signature, on the other hand *the films* those people make remain irreducible to the commercial process of mediation and branding. In other words, it is one thing to agree that cinematic authorship is a perplexing, far from coherent theory, but it is quite another to deny or unduly discard its usefulness as a critical tool for helping us understand cinema as both an art form and a cultural phenomenon. The persistence of auteurism testifies to that, and although its meaning and function are historically malleable, at times ambiguous, this is no reason to dismiss it *in toto*. Indeed, for every good reason not to pursue authorship studies there is equally good reason to do so. For instance, whatever else it may or may not do, auteurism remains cued into the creative practices and aesthetic achievements of cinema and, as such, 'is a formidable approach for comprehending style, technique and expression' (Gallagher 2001). The question of causality for film, however, is not simply an aesthetic matter but, as Staiger argues, a political one: 'taking studies of the author off the table can eliminate the politically crucial question of causality for texts – something highly undesirable from the point of view of critical theory' (Staiger 2003: 29). For social groups who have historically been denied authorship, those whose voices have been variously ignored, marginalised or silenced, for those people who seem finally to have won a position from which they can speak and be heard, the claim that the author is dead seems to be not only an act of supreme authorial privilege itself, but also political sabotage. In this respect, then, authorship matters greatly to those 'in non-dominant positions in which asserting even a partial agency may seem to be important for day-to-day survival or where locating moments of alternative practice takes away the naturalized privileges of normativity' (ibid.: 27).

For these reasons, then, as well as a host of others, all of the attempts to twiddle and tweak conceptions of cinematic authorship in the wake of the post-structuralist challenge to it never really stuck. Indeed, it seems that the more authorship was recast as a 'sub-code', 'a discourse', 'a signature', 'a reading position' or whatever, the less the figure of the author seemed to matter. And all such machinations tended to dodge the material reality of human actions; that is to say, the activities of real people in real socio-historical situations which affect both the art and politics of cinematic representation. Given this, the notion of cinematic authorship needs to be revived and recast to take account of agency in such a way as to avoid the twin pitfalls of romanticism and erasure. The question, then, is: What model of cinematic authorship is able to account for both the artistic and commercial concerns of filmmaking while simultaneously acknowledging the political dynamics which frame all authorial claims?

The recent renewal of interest in cinematic authorship has produced a number of answers to this question which, albeit in different ways, attempt to negotiate a critical position somewhere between simply resurrecting the tenets of older approaches and total reinvention. For instance, whereas classical auteurism tended to rest on assumptions about the working practices of a director, a number of critics are now focusing squarely on the concrete material conditions which structure creativity. This work tends to privilege the craft of filmmaking, that is to say, the ways in which a director deploys film technique in precise ways within specific conditions to achieve innovation. A second, though related, move has been to direct attention to the business of filmmaking.

This shifts the point of study away from the 'art' of the finished film and locates it in the political economy of film production. Third, as we have already noted, work by Corrrigan and Bordwell suggests that authors/auteurs may be understood as marketable commodities that are produced by, and fulfil the needs of, corporate and commercial institutions. Yet other strategies for rethinking authorship in the current moment have focused on unearthing authorial voices ignored or marginalised by classical auteurism. In some cases this has involved studying directors who have been previously hidden from history and elsewhere it has led to a discussion of sources of creativity other than the director.

The answer to that question I want to pursue here, however, is non-partisan insofar as it does not adhere to any one of these approaches at the expense of the others. It does not think that one approach is necessarily better than another and, more precisely, that the approach one employs should be determined on a case-by-case basis in relation to the specifics of the research question. For example, starting out from the same predetermined theoretical/methodological position is of little use if we want to study, on the one hand, directors/auteurs such as Quentin Tarantino, Darren Aronofsky, Jim Jarmusch, Sofia Coppola, Jane Campion, Paul Thomas Anderson or Ang Lee, or on the other hand, corporate authors such as Disney, Pixar or Industrial Light and Magic. In other words, it accepts that cinematic authorship is an untidy concept but sees that untidiness as grist to its mill. It is an approach I call pragmatic. Like the word 'author' itself, pragmatism is an overworked word which is used to mean any number of different things. I use it here, however, to suggest a model of analysis which stops asking the question 'Do authors exist?' and starts from such questions as 'Is it useful to study this or that film *as if* it were the product of a creative agency?', or 'Might it be useful to study this or that person *as if* they were an author?' In other words, the theoretical question of whether the notion of authorship in cinema is plausible *per se* is different from the piecemeal approach which asks how individual agency relates to film style. The result of such an approach will not settle the debate about whether or not authors exist or whether the concept of authorship is or can be intellectually watertight, but produce a rather more modest and useful *enrichment of our understanding of cinema and our experience of it*. So, what does a pragmatic conception of cinematic authorship look like?

The first move is to shake off some of the unnecessarily convoluted aspects of the critical vocabulary associated with cinematic authorship that have tended to sink auteur analysis even before it has begun. For what is lost at the more dizzying levels of abstraction associated with much theoretical writing on auteurism is precisely the ability to make critically interesting and useful judgements about the relative artistic, political and aesthetic merits of a film and its makers. As such, instead of searching for the intangible evidence of a film's unifying figure, it is perhaps useful to think of *creativity as constitutive at every level of cinematic activity*. To put it another way, the question of cinematic authorship can usefully be posed on a range of labour, creative and commercial levels. In this respect, director Alexander Kluge's observation provides a useful starting point: 'auteur cinema is not a minority phenomenon: all people relate to their experiences as authors – rather than as managers of department stores' (quoted in Corrigan 1991: 118). Kluge's quip alerts us to three important ideas: first, that the people who make films tend to understand their respective roles and practise their individual crafts in ways that can meaningfully be thought of as art-making; second, that the material reality of human actions has genuine consequences for the way a film looks and sounds as well as for how we experience it; and third, that we need a more useful way of engaging with the question of the link between individual agency, self-expression and authorial function in order not only to liberate the notion of cinematic authorship from 'the cult of the director' and thus open up the possibility of finding other, potentially more complex authorial voices, but also to remain sensitive to the politics that determine the limits of self-expression.

A first step, here, is to prune back our vocabulary and focus on the concepts that inhere in the notion of authorship, ideas such as art and artist, aesthetics and style, craft and technique, meaning and enunciation, practice and agency. A second move is to become more modest in ambition in the sense of stopping trying to solve the paradox of auteurism and instead attending to localised descriptions of how specific artistic, creative, and institutional practices relate to both a film's style and affect. In other words, a more plausible method for discussing cinematic authorship entails tracking back and forth between the various practices of film production and the film text to see how these concepts may be deployed to help us describe and better understand those practices and their relationship to how we experience the film.

☐ CASE STUDY 1: STYLE AS SUBSTANCE: QUENTIN TARANTINO AND THE DIRECTOR-AS-AUTEUR

Indeed, it is just such a pared-down approach to film authorship which allows us to explore Quentin Tarantino as a particularly persuasive case for the contemporary director-as-author not only because of the distinctive stylistic and expressive person-ality that his films evince at a textual level, but also for the commercial performance of auteurism he enacts extratextually. Indeed, what is interesting about Tarantino is the complex way in which these two faces of contemporary auteurism coalesce in one figure to produce a fascinating image of the postmodern auteur and postmodern authorship, one that depends on citation for originality, irony for substance, and artifice for authen-ticity. And it is this paradoxical position that Tarantino seems wilfully to flaunt, apparently staking out a future for auteurism while simultaneously nailing its coffin closed, that both excites and frustrates critics. Michael Atkinson captures some of this critical irritation when he says that 'Tarantino might be the most famous' contemporary director, but he is also 'the most guileless'. Articulating his frustration with Tarantino's 'adolescent' media outpourings about his work, he nevertheless concedes that 'no other American film-maker has understood the ardent precepts of Godard so well' (Atkinson 2010: 42).

Clearly then, much turns on how we seek to understand the relationship between what we might call textual-Tarantino, the one we approach through analysis of his films, and extra textual-Tarantino, the one we encounter through interviews, websites, and other official and unofficial publicity materials that promote those films. In this respect, the debates occasioned by the release and critical reception of his 2009 film, *Inglourious Basterds*, offers us an instructive point of access. We might begin, therefore, by amplifying Nick James's remark made in reference to the film that Tarantino 'is what the *politique des auteurs* is all about – a single creative source in control of his medium' (2009b: 5). What James is suggesting here is not simply that *Inglourious Basterds* is a good film, nor that Tarantino is relatively exceptional inasmuch as he is able to write, cast, and direct his films without significant interference, but more importantly that *Inglourious Basterds* can be understood as a significant contribution the Tarantino oeuvre. Atkinson himself concedes this point in claiming that 'if there were doubts about Tarantino's control of his own movie life after [his previous movie] *Grindhouse* (2007), the zest and cinemania of *Inglourious Basterds* vaporised them' (Atkinson 2010: 42). In other words, implicit in both critics' pronouncements is the idea that, following the dominant model of film authorship established by the *Cahiers* critics, the significance and meanings of the film can usefully be explained through an analysis which interrogates the interrelations between its stylistic and expressive salience and Tarantino's individual agency

Critics have identified a number of facets that define Tarantino's cinema – the distinctive blend of ultraviolent set pieces and 'blood-guts-and-brain-style' with 'carefully calibrated irony' (Levy 1999: 144; Willis 2000: 279); the emphasis placed on 'realistic' or phatic language to establish characters and advance the plot (White 2011: 397); the talent for 'fantasy casting' actors which 'bring a celluloid past like a rap sheet' (Bauer

• Plate 6.1
Inglourious Basterds
(Quentin Tarantino,
2009) is the most
complex manifestation
of Tarantino's brand of
postmodern authorship.

2001: 253; White 2011: 393); and the use of complex, non-linear storytelling structures which take the audience on 'a wild narrative ride' (see Polan 2001a; Brode 1995: 239). However, it is Atkinson's reference to 'cinemania' that directs us to the most important and the most interesting aspect, the one that holds these other elements of the Tarantino signature together. This is, of course, the radical intertextuality of Tarantino's films or, more precisely, his use of what Nigel Wheale calls the 'lexicon of postmodern technique' to articulate his vision and inscribe his signature (Wheale 1995: 42). In this regard David Bordwell (2006) has noted that, in the brand of filmmaking that emerged in the post-1960s freewheeling allusions to old or previous Hollywood movies became commonplace inasmuch as the burgeoning media culture 'bred a pop connoisseurship' that demanded 'film references as part of the pleasures of moviegoing' (Bordwell 2006: 25). However, Tarantino's novel intervention is to cast his net further and wider than the Hollywood film for inspiration, particularly in the exaltation of B-movies, exploitation film, pulp fiction and other kinds of 'trash culture', or by turning his gaze to other film cultures, particularly those found in Europe and Asia. It is in this sense that his films' citations and cultural reference points overturn the Hollywood canon by 'replacing the Western with blaxploitation and kung fu, Ford and Hawks with Dario Argenton and Chang Cheh' (Bordwell 2006: 24–5). Indeed, in discussing the two volumes of *Kill Bill* (2003/4), Bordwell argues that Tarantino had constructed 'a hermetically sealed universe out of Asian action pictures, Eurotrash exploitation, and Japanese Anime. Movie references, instead of ornamenting a freestanding storyline, coalesced into a virtual world' (ibid.: 2006: 60).

The eclectic range and sheer number of citations and allusions which characterise Tarantino's films operate in complex, multi-layered fashion. Such references can be internal to Tarantino's own fictions, as when a character from one film reappears in altered form in another (when Tarantino sells a film or script to a studio he nevertheless retains the rights to his own characters so that he can engage in precisely this kind of self-referentiality) or, as in the case of the notorious 'Madonna' scene in *Reservoir Dogs*, they can be references to external icons, objects or texts. More complex still is the use of a certain stylistic device or mise-en-scène to perform a specific narrative function in the particular film in which it appears while simultaneously referencing another film through it in such a way as to retain a vestige of its past significance and

• Plate 6.2
Kill Bill: Vol. 1 (Quentin Tarantino, 1993) presents the viewer with a virtual cinematic universe constructed from Asian action pictures, Eurotrash exploitation, and Japanese Anime.

importing some of that meaning into the new context. Obvious examples of this strategy of double-articulation are the dance sequence at Jack Rabbit Slim's in *Pulp Fiction* which uses John Travolta's performance as Mia Wallace's reluctant dance partner ironically to invoke his role in *Saturday Night Fever* (1978) and the yellow and black catsuit worn by Uma Thurman in *Kill Bill* which recalls the iconic outfit worn by Bruce Lee in *The Game of Death* (1978). However, it is *Inglourious Basterds* that evinces the most complex manifestation of Tarantino's brand of postmodern authorship, one which may well 'evaporate any historical specificity or social referentiality' through its hyperconscious recycling, re-articulation, and reworking of previous films, but does so in such a way as to create a unique assemblage in which it is possible to discern the distinctive thumbprint of its auteur (Willis 2000: 279). Nick James's discussion of the film points us in this direction in distinguishing between the relatively straightforward story of the film and the 'aesthetic indigestion' caused by the 'complex field of references' used to tell that story (James 2009a: 19). For despite ostensibly being a war film about a Jewish-American guerilla unit dispatched to kill Nazis in German occupied France, and despite the narrative's revisionist move to end the war a year early by assassinating the entire Nazi high command in a cinema, it is in the sophistication of its reflexive narration and its sedimented mise-en-scène that we find the impress of Tarantino's style. This is James's attempt to capture some of the aesthetic dynamism at work in *Inglourious Basterds*:

Give me an entreé of Sergio Leone, with a dash of Michael Cimino at his most self-indulgent, lashings of Tinto Brass *mise en scene* (but hold the copulation), and a bit of von Sternberg on the side. Actually no, give me some Renoir romance with a piquant sauce of Nazi UFA films, some Riefenstahl camera angles, but leavened with a one-two punch of Sam Fuller tabloid heart ... Everyone is impersonating actors from the past – Pitt is Clark Gable, Briihl, Audie Murphy and Diane Kruger is any number of UFA stars such as Brigitte Helm ... Indeed, its cultural cramming makes it seem hysterical.
(Nick James 2009a: 18)

This circuit of referentiality isn't simply confined to the film's visual elements. Not only is the film's title itself a modification of Enzo G. Castellari's 1978 *The Inglourious Bastards* (itself heralding the tag line 'Whatever the Dirty Dozen did, they do it dirtier!'), but

Tarantino 'patchworks a bizarre range of film scores, with scant regard for the 1940s setting' (Newman 2009: 73). For example, the film's opening homage to Sergio Leone is signalled by way of Morricone-style music that is in fact scored by Ennio Morricone himself, though not for this film but for Sergio Sollima's 1966 film *The Big Gun Down* (*La resa dei conti*) in which it originally featured. Indeed, it is precisely this kind of authorial method, one we might describe as inscription through re-inscription, that not only defines Tarantino's style as a filmmaker but also allows us to make the case for describing him as a distinctly postmodern auteur. In other words, Tarantino's originality of expression is derived from his insistence of speaking through others, through what has already been said, through allusion, citation and homage. This is no simple process of textual abduction or blatant 'theft', as many of his critics argue. For in transporting his grab bag of textual artefacts from the past and transplanting them into new contexts in the present they are transformed into something original, something the *Cahiers* critics or Sarris might call an inimitable expression of the director's vision. Following this line of thinking, then, one might say that *Inglourious Basterds*, like so many of Tarantino's films, is less another passé instance of style *over* substance than an example of creating substance *as* style.

Of course, none of this is to suggest that Tarantino's name and the biographical legend it invokes are not figured within institutional forces and commercial discourses every bit as much as, say, Spielberg's. Indeed, to a significant extent Tarantino is Corrigan's auteur-as-star writ large, a figure whose function is chiefly commercial and who is rendered meaningful 'primarily as a promotion or recovery of a movie or group of movies, frequently regardless of the filmic text itself' (Corrigan 1991: 105). One example of this can be found in the promotion of *Hostel* (2005). Despite being directed by Eli Roth, the film posters and other publicity material produced to promote the release of the film boldly declared that it was 'presented by Quentin Tarantino'. Even though Tarantino did act as executive producer on the film, it is the celebrity of his agency that was activated to promote the film to the/his audience and establish a specific set of expectations based, not on Roth's authorship, but rather the Tarantino brand. Indeed, the coining of the adjective 'Tarantinoesque' and the noun 'Tarantiness' as shorthand descriptions of a particular style, genre or sensibility bear testament to the marketing potential of the Tarantino name.

• **Plate 6.3**
Pulp Fiction (Quentin Tarantino, 1994)

Perhaps more interesting, however, is Tarantino's construction, promotion, and defence of his own auteurism through the media, a process of performing 'a certain intentional self' deemed to be 'the motivating agent of texuality' (Corrigan 1991: 108). In this respect, Glyn White argues that Tarantino emerges from his frenzied engagement with the press as a 'garrulous autodidact often reckless in his desire to defend an opinion against all comers' (White 2011: 394). While this perhaps oversimplifies some of the sophistication of his encounters with the media, it nevertheless remains the case that Tarantino uses the press, and in particular the director interview format, to dramatise his identity as an auteur. For example, in 2008 he 'felt slighted' by the editor of *Sight & Sound* after it published a negative appraisal of his latest film *Deathproof* (2007). In the interview that was subsequently arranged, Tarantino defends the film against the charge of being 'hokey' or 'trashy' by stating that 'I don't think slasher films are trashy or bad ... [and] if I'm trying to do a remembrance of the films of the past, the slasher film is a legitimate subgenre in horror film' from which to draw (in James 2008). Moreover, in the interview's final coup Tarantino claims that 'one of the biggest inspirations for the film ... was Carol Clover's book *Men, Women and Chainsaws*. I really truly think that her chapter on the "final girl", the role that gender plays in the slasher film, pins down the best piece of film criticism I've ever read' (in James 2008). In a single knight's move, therefore, Tarantino claims legitimacy for both his film and his own status as an auteur by appealing to the authority of academic criticism and film theory.

This event repeated itself more recently with the release of *Inglourious Basterds*. Again taking umbrage with Nick James's account of his film previously published in *Sight & Sound*, Tarantino uses his interview with Ryan Gilbey to reimpose his vision of the film and reassert his authorial agency. Early in the interview Tarantino makes it clear that he 'didn't agree' with where James's critique 'was coming from' insofar as he saw it as another crude attempt to match the critic's cinephiliac wits against his own by engaging in a kind of 'spot-the-reference' game, thus missing the true complexity and meaning of the film (in Gilbey 2009: 18). The remainder of the interview then proceeds to proffer a description of the film as a spaghetti-western set in the 'brual landscapes' of 'Europe during World War II' and an interpretation that sees it as being not about war at all, but 'entirely about language' (in Gilbey 2009: 19–20). Indeed, such is the power of this explanation of intent that the magazine's editorial claims that the interview 'will leave the reader in no doubt that [Tarantino] is the sole author of his work' and that the director's 'very existence disproves the fashionable notion that auteurism is somehow dead' (James 2009b: 5). One implication of this is that both the consumption and analysis of Tarantino invokes the critical tautology identified by Corrigan inasmuch as he is a figure 'capable of being understood and consumed' without the need 'to see the films themselves' (Corrigan 1991: 106). However, perhaps a more interesting implication is that Quentin Tarantino seems to fulfil the twin desires imbricated in the idea of auteurism identified by Dana Polan (2001b): the textual *desire for* access to the personal vision of the auteur through the films he directs; and the *desire of* the director accessed through the extra textual construction of a creative intentional self.

MODES OF AUTEURISM

Despite its value in understanding directors such as Tarantino, we should not expect to be able to deploy this model of analysis with equal success in every case, or that the results will necessarily be comparable. For individual films may be marked by the presence, but also the absence of a coherent authorial voice. Indeed, attention to the pragmatics of film production, to the web of crafts and industrial contingencies that interact in the process of filmmaking, will determine which, if any, notions of authorship are on the table. Such a pared-down and modest theory of cinematic authorship is built from piecemeal accounts of how the images and sounds made by a film hang together in meaningful and expressive patterns, one which can be fitted into or contrasted with other accounts of the technological, institutional and social contingencies which intersect in any film. As Richard Shusterman argues, conceived in this pragmatic fashion, theory is 'understood as critical, imaginative reflection on practice, emerging from practice' and also 'judged pragmatically by its fruits for that practice' (Shusterman 2000: 59–60).

Moreover, if we accept that there are a range of criteria available to us for deploying ideas of authorship in the effort to better understand film, then auteurism is not neutralised but refurbished by the absence of singular and transcendental notions of the artist. For once we let go of such essentialist notions of art-making, a whole host of potential auteurs emerge from the theoretical sidelines: creative personnel, agencies, even corporations whose influence on the art of cinema cannot be recognised by the stifling romanticism of previous conceptions of auteurism. As such, auteurism might profitably be thought to exist in, and operate as, a variety of modes. For instance, Andrew Darley argues that in an age of digital visual culture, creativity and innovation become 'first and foremost a technical problem' in which 'technique, technicians and technology itself take command' (Darley 2000: 141). Within this context, it is significant that a set of company names such as 'Industrial Light and Magic' (ILM) and Pixar now operate as an index of artistic style alongside or in front of individual creative agency. Indeed, one implication of this situation is not only that authorial agency might usefully be located with creative personnel other than the director, but that it becomes possible, even desirable, to locate authorship at an institutional or corporate level. As such, Pixar and ILM may be seen as corporate authors precisely to the extent that their respective company names act as signs which organise and execute highly specialised and distinctive forms of industrial aesthetic practice within cinema, practices which exist beyond the economic or creative scope of any one of the individuals it employs. For example, *Transformers, Transformers: Revenge of the Fallen,* and *Transformers: Dark of the Moon* (2007/9/11) all may well have been directed by Michael Bay, but in this case authorship might be more profitably understood not as a product of individuated human agency but rather as the product of corporate agency. For it is ILM that functions as a precondition to the film's technical realisation in the first instance and, in the final instance, can be understood as the site through which its key enunciative and expressive techniques are executed and cohere.

For further discussion of Disney, ILM, Pixar and computer technology in animation read Chapter 10.

• **Plate 6.4**
In the Mood For Love (Wong Kar Wai, 2000). Chris Doyle's multi-textured cinematography and distinctive framing are key contributors to the look and feel of the film, and may be read as salient markers of his role as an intra-auteur

Paul Wells argues in relation to animation that the notions of the 'supra-auteur' and the 'intra-auteur' throw into relief two further models of cinematic authorship elided by the obsessive focus on directors. In this respect, Walt Disney may be understood as a supra-auteur insofar as even after his death he fundamentally denied authorial inscription to anyone else and created 'an identity and mode of representation which, despite cultural criticism, market variations, and changing social trends, transcends the vicissitudes of contemporary America' (Wells 2002a: 90). By contrast, Ray Harryhausen's stop-motion work in films such as *The 7th Voyage of Sinbad* (1958) and *Jason and the Argonauts* (1963) figures him as an intra-auteur 'by in effect authoring a text from within its ostensible live-action boundaries' (ibid.: 101). This latter concept, the notion of intra-authorship, is a particularly useful one for attending to sources of creativity other than the director. For instance, the densely textured collages so often evident in Chris Doyle's cinematography, or the balletic grace of Yeun Woo-Ping's wire-work fight choreography, or the mixture of formal experimentation and pathos found in Charlie Kaufman's screenplays, not to mention numerous others, may all be usefully seen as specific examples of the work of intra-auteurs. The main point here, however, is that in locating the study of film authorship in a pragmatic framework, one attuned to both the practice and affect of filmmaking, it becomes both possible and desirable to study the work of stunt directors, production designers, visual effects supervisors, concept illustrators, computer animators, costume designers, sound engineers, fight coordinators, composers, specialist post-production houses, studios as well as screenwriters, producers, editors, actors and directors in terms of film aesthetics and comprehension.

CONCLUSION

The model of auteurist analysis which emerges from this pragmatic redescription of cinematic authorship, then, recognises two necessarily simultaneous practices: (1) the particular creative, expressive and artistic activities of the personnel who collaborate in varying degrees to make a film and whose respective individual agencies determine in complex ways film style; and (2) the socio-cultural practices of contemporary media culture which construct the auteur as a commodity, a logo so to speak, which stands not behind the text as in Romantic notions of authorship, but rather in front of it precisely to explicate, expand and legitimise the marks of individuality, expression and style in a film.

In accepting the 'intentional fallacy' as the last word on romantic notions of auteurism, such a pragmatic reconfiguration of cinematic authorship, one attuned to the primacy and complexities of filmmaking *practice* as well as to the *commercial imperatives* of media culture, affords us the opportunity of capturing some of the continued allure of the auteur while locating the focus of our critical gaze back in the art of filmmaking. Indeed, in negotiating the moment between the textual and the extratextual activities of the auteur, a pragmatic approach to the question of authorship confronts itself back where it began: as a tool for helping us look for the art in cinema.

SUMMARY

- The idea of film authorship and the concept of auteurism have been historically contentious.
- Film authorship and the idea of auteurism allowed critics to argue for the cultural legitimacy of cinema by claiming it to be an art form like literature or painting and thus the product of a highly individual artist.
- The idea that a film's author is the director began in the pages of the French journal *Cahiers du cinéma* and persists today.
- Critics now study a broader range of texts, such as filmmaker homepages, interviews,

director commentaries, and not just the films themselves in order to study the work and function of auteurs.

- It is not just directors who are now seen as auteurs. Screenwriters, actors, producers, cinematographers and even companies and corporations have been studied as authors of the products they are involved in producing.
- A pragmatic conception of cinematic authorship is a useful approach because it focuses attention on the material activities of real human agency and the results it produces for the way a film looks and feels.

QUESTIONS FOR DISCUSSION

1　The auteurist method is largely founded on mapping similarities of technique and style across a number of films by the same director. Use a resource such as the Internet Movie Database (http://www.imdb.com) to compile a filmography of a director and then watch a sample of his or her films and note any consistencies of style and/or theme that occur across more than one film. See if it is possible to detect a 'personal statement' or 'worldview' in the films.

2　The method described in question 1 is not limited to directors. Repeat the exercise using a cinematographer, actor, fight choreographer, or even a studio such as Disney or Pixar, to see if other figures/agencies can be usefully analysed 'as if' they are an auteur.

3　Auteurs now exist as much outside the film text as inside it. Try watching a film on DVD or Blu-ray while listening to the director's commentary. How does this effect, delimit or anchor the possible meanings of the film around the director's putative intentions? Moreover, in relation to the release of a new film, track the director's performance of 'being an auteur' across the full range of media – chat show appearances, interviews on radio, in newspapers and on the internet, and public appearances at premieres and other related events.

 **FURTHER READING**

While it is neither possible nor necessary to list them here, there are many books and articles which discuss the work of individual auteurs. As such, most of the works listed below tend to deal with cinematic authorship as a theoretical problem.

Key texts

Caughie, John (ed.) (1981) *Theories of Authorship: A Reader*, Routledge, London. Despite its age, Caughie's book remains a useful resource in terms of both the seminal work it anthologises and his own commentary on that work.

Gerstner, David A. and Staiger, Janet (eds) (2003) *Authorship and Film*, Routledge, London. A very useful collection of essays which both contributes to the recent resurgence of interest in authorship studies but also puts forward a number of ways for thinking about issues of agency, identity and politics within auteur analyses.

Keith Grant, Barry (ed.) (2008), *Auteurs and Authorship: A Film Reader*, Blackwell, Oxford.

A recent collection which combines 'classic' works in the field with more contemporary essays which seek to reinvigorate historical debates about film authorship. Its final section offers eleven close readings of films using a variety of auteurist methodologies.

Wright Wexman, Virginia (ed.) (2003) *Film and Authorship*, Rutgers University Press, New Brunswick, NJ. This collection anthologises a number of influential works produced since the publication of Caughie's book. Indeed, the essays span a number of approaches to authorship including post-structuralism, feminism, post-colonialism and cultural studies.

Useful anthologies

Braddock, Jeremy and Hock, Stephen (eds) (2001) *Directed by Allen Smithee*, Minneapolis: University of Minnesota Press.

Tasker, Yvonne (ed.) (2011) *Fifty Contemporary Filmmakers*, (2nd edn) Routledge, London.

Useful Compendiums

Allon, Yoram, Cullen, Del and Patterson, Hannah (eds) (2002) *Contemporary North American Directors: A Wallflower Critical Guide* (2nd edn), Wallflower Press, London.

Murphy, Robert (ed.) (2006) *Directors in British and Irish Cinema: A Reference Guide*, BFI, London.

Online reading

Film-Philosophy, Vol. 10, no.1 (2006), 'Reanimating the Auteur' [online at], http://www.film-philosophy.com/

Screening The Past, Issue 12 (2001), [online at] http://www.latrobe.edu.au/screeningthepast/current/cc0301.html.

Two online special issues dedicated to rethinking aspects of cinematic authorship.

Chapter 7

Star studies: text, pleasure, identity

Paul Watson

■ Star studies: text, pleasure, identity

INTRODUCTION: SCREEN ICONS TO CULTURAL BYGONES?

In December 2005 readers of the UK film magazine *Empire* voted Tom Cruise the 'biggest film star of all time'. The following year Cruise emerged from *Premiere* magazine's list of the most powerful people in Hollywood as 'the most powerful actor in the world' (*Premiere*, June 2006). This was due in significant part to his role in the box-office success of *War of the Worlds* (2005) which grossed in excess of half a billion dollars and earned Cruise a reported $100,000,000 through his contract's lucrative back-end deal. Moreover, the release of *Mission: Impossible III* (2006) the following year extended to seven Cruise's run of consecutive films which grossed in excess of $100 million in domestic ticket sales, took the franchise's global earnings past the $1.4 billion mark and earned Cruise more than $250 million in the process (see Hansen 2000; Gray 2006). Indeed, to date the films in which Cruise has starred have grossed approaching $7 billion at the box office alone, made Cruise one of the most recognisable people in the world, and led industry analysts to claim that he is 'the most bankable star of the last twenty years', 'the safest bet' in the film industry, and 'one of the most powerful – and richest – forces in Hollywood' (see Shepatin 2008; Epstein 2007).

How, then, do we understand such claims and what models of stardom might they imply? In the case of the *Empire* poll, does the idea of the 'biggest film star' mean the 'best' film star, the most popular star, or that Cruise is the most accomplished actor currently working? Alternatively, does it mean that audiences have consistently enjoyed the films in which Cruise stars, or that the action-adventure genre that he is often associated with is a hit with readers of the magazine? Moreover, are either the billion-dollar profits generated by the films in which Cruise features or the multi-million dollar salaries he commands for appearing in those films any reliable index of his value as a star? In other words, is 'starpower' simply reducible to economic influence, to, say, Cruise's ability to get films 'green-lit' simply by attaching his name to the project? The answers to such questions become further vexed when we take into account the fact that the readers of the same magazine who voted Cruise the 'biggest star of all time' also named him the world's most irritating star (*Empire*, December 2005). Indeed, despite Cruise's evident box-office success since the release of *Top Gun* in 1986, in August 2006 Paramount Pictures decided to end their fourteen-year contract with him, declaring that the negative publicity generated by news of his 'bizarre' offscreen behaviour 'had cost the company between $100m and $150m in lost ticket sales' (Burkeman 2006: 1). In the period since then none of Cruise's movies have managed to break the $100-million mark in domestic receipts, with *Lion for Lambs* (2007) barely returning $15 million, less than half of the film's budget. Cruise's most recent film, *Knight and Day* (2010), in which he stars alongside one of Hollywood's leading female stars, Cameron Diaz, did gross over $76 million at the US box office, but this was not only significantly less than its $117 million budget, but, as Nick Roddick points out, the film took three weeks to reach what the animated film *Despicable Me* (2010) did in a single weekend (see Roddick 2010).

And what of female stars? For if Cruise is the highest ranked actor at number 13 on *Premiere*'s 'power list', then what are we to make of the observation that the highest ranked actress, and for that matter the highest ranked woman, Reese Witherspoon, only manages number 29? Diaz herself is ranked at number 37 on the 2006 list, but makes it to number 12 on *The Numbers*' 2008 'box office power' model and, at number 60, is ranked as the fourth most powerful actress behind Sandra Bullock, Angelina Jolie and Jennifer Anniston on *Forbes*' 2010 'Celebrity 100' list. In discussing this kind of discrepancy, a situation in which female stars such as Diaz dominate magazine covers and publicity circuits but are dominated by men in terms of their influence and status.

Peter Krämer argues that 'Hollywood's female stars do not count a lot at the box office' and that there are numerous other 'indicators showing that ... they usually don't amount to much' and, as a consequence, 'have comparatively little power' (Krämer 2004: 89–90). Are female stars, then, somehow less popular with audiences than male actors, or does the structure of the film industry force them, as Christine Geraghty notes, to 'operate in a different context than their male counterparts' (Geraghty 2000: 196)? Or might the *Forbes* list point us in the direction of a much more general trend: not simply the idea that stars are increasingly subsumed under the much broader category of celebrity, but the question of whether, if only eight actors appear in the top fifty of the most powerful celebrities, stardom itself is in a state of all-purpose decline.

THREE APPROACHES TO CONCEPTUALISING STARDOM

Even if the kinds of issue which emerge from such polls and lists are on one level clearly a product of the terms and conditions which govern the list-making process itself, on another level they do serve to throw into relief a number of important questions and confusions which bear on the study of stardom: When is an actor also a star? What is the relationship between performance and stardom? What stake does the star hold in the processes of film production? Does the idea of a star mean the same thing across different historical moments and production contexts? Is there a difference between stardom and celebrity? Why are film stars so fascinating to us and what are the pleasures we get from them? Do male and female stars operate in the same context and can we understand them in the same way? These are, of course, some of the questions we will ask in this chapter. Yet, while these issues have always proved troubling, in cinema's third century the answers to such questions become even more complex. However, before attempting to unravel some of them we shall begin by surveying the three principal approaches developed for discussing stardom in the cinema.

Star as commodity

studio system
Usually seen to have developed *circa* 1920 and lasting until *circa* 1950, the studio system indicates the period of Hollywood history in which the major studios controlled all aspects of the production, distribution and exhibition of their products.

The first of these approaches locates the star within the economic contexts of film production and film marketing. During the era of the **studio system**, when creative and technical personnel were tied to long-term contracts, stars 'provided one of the principal means by which Hollywood offered audiences guarantees of predictability' by embodying a set of particular expectations and, by extension, particular kinds of pleasure (Maltby 2003: 145). Indeed, the introduction of the star system to Hollywood's mode of production has been seen by many critics as a key way in which actors could create a kind of 'personal monopoly' through the cultivation of a distinctive image (King 1985). And, as Finola Kerrigan notes, such an image was variously 'linked to aesthetic factors, associations with certain types of roles, or as a sort of quality mark for films within an increasingly crowded marketplace' (Kerrigan 2010: 83). Moreover, since the collapse of the studio system in the 1950s, stars have become arguably the key element of the package-unit around which movies are produced. Susan Hayward explains that 'producers will put up money for films that include the latest top star' and 'stars can attract financial backing for a film that otherwise might not get off the ground' (Hayward 2006: 330). Moreover, even a cursory glance at the promotional material surrounding a film's launch – posters, trailers, interviews in print, on TV and online, as well as a host of further publicity and merchandising products – reveals the considerable stake stars hold in announcing the film's presence and generating an audience of sufficient size to recoup costs. On this account, then, the star is understood as a specific form of *industrial commodity* not only insofar as, like genre, stars function to 'differentiate films within the market' (McDonald 2000: 104) but also insofar as they are often the key 'mechanism for selling movie tickets' by guaranteeing certain pleasures and functioning as a commercial strategy for marketing films (Maltby 2003: 142).

However, a star's commercial capacity is inextricably bound up with his or her ability to 'be liked' by large numbers of people from a range of cultural and national contexts. The remaining two approaches to studying stars are sensitive to these more social and psychical aspects of stardom inasmuch as they turn away from industrial questions, focusing instead on the ways in which the figure of the film star generates specific meanings and pleasures.

Star as text

The second approach seeks to understand the star as a sign, that is to say precisely as an *image* constructed through a network of **intertextuality**. This blend of semiotics, sociology and ideological criticism is the most familiar approach to questions of stardom and is associated most strongly with the seminal work of Richard Dyer (1979). Indeed, so influential is Dyer's work that the critical vocabulary it proposes for discussing stars has provided the centre of critical gravity for almost thirty years inasmuch as it is virtually impossible to discuss stardom without nodding in its direction. Central to this approach is the idea that stars are not reducible to flesh-and-blood actors but are conceived of as 'complex personas made up of far more than the texts in which they appear' (Tasker 1993a: 74). There are two important implications of this observation. First, while on the one hand stardom is literally *embodied* in real human beings and is, to a significant extent, therefore anchored by a star's name, physical appearance, voice quality, and specific performance skills, on the other hand 'we never know them as real people, only as they are found in media texts' (Dyer 1979: 2). The second, and related, point is that stardom manifests not only in the films in which a star features, but across all kinds of other 'official' and 'unofficial' media texts in which the star may or may not appear in person: publicity and marketing materials, newspapers, magazines, television, websites, DVD 'special features', biographies and so forth. Indeed, within this web of intertextuality 'the star' itself becomes understood, and thus *understandable*, as a specific form of text only insofar as stardom is accessible to us through texts, and thus only *exists* as a text. The crucial point here, however, is, as Paul McDonald notes, that 'the study of stars as texts ... cannot be limited to the analysis of specific films or star performances' since they are precisely 'the product of intertextuality in which the non-filmic texts of promotion, publicity, and criticism interact with the film text ... In other words, the star's image cannot be known outside this shifting series of texts' (McDonald 1995: 83). On this account, the aim of star studies is not to peel away these layers of textuality in order to reveal the *true* self of the star, but to analyse the explicit and implicit meanings of precisely that mediated image and to read it in the context of wider ideological and social discourses.

Star as object of desire

Whereas the intertextual approach focuses on the ways in which stars are realised in and through texts, the third principal approach addresses the *consumption* of stars. Indeed, if the audience remains *implicit* in the 'star as text' approach as the locus of meaning, the point where the star image is (re)constructed through the act of reading, then the politics of spectatorship and the pleasures of 'star-gazing' form the explicit foci of work which theorises the star–spectator relationship. James Donald argues that while spectatorship 'is the most hotly disputed question in the whole study of stars' there is, nevertheless, 'a good case for starting not with the return on capital invested in film production, but with the unquantifiable returns on our emotional investments in ... those moments of erotic contemplation of the spectacular figure of the star' (Donald 1999: 39). By the same token, in pointing out some of the limitations of ideological approaches to stardom, Alan Lovell argues for a framework of analysis based on aesthetics and performance that 'should be concerned with ... beauty, pleasure and delight' (Lovell 2003: 270). On this account, the star is seen, first and foremost, as an object of desire and is studied in terms of the

intertextuality
This term, strongly linked with **postmodernism**, designates, in its narrow sense, the ways in which a film either explicitly or implicitly refers to other films (through allusion, imitation, parody or pastiche, for example), or in its broader sense, the various relationships one (film) text may have with other texts.

For a more detailed discussion of spectator and audience see Chapter 5.

ways in which spectators identify with, find meaning in, and gain a certain fulfilment from his or her image.

For further discussion of feminist film theory see Chapter 11.

Perhaps the most influential strain of this approach is an offshoot of feminist psychoanalytic work on gender which theorises the orchestration of visual pleasure in cinema. Classically, the female star is held to be a sexualised spectacle that disrupts narrative momentum in moments of erotic exhibitionism which exceed the bounds of the story, while, on the other hand, the male star/hero is located as an ideal ego who controls the narrative and is thus the central mechanism for audience identification (see Mulvey 1975). More recently, work such as Jackie Stacey's *Star Gazing* (1994) and Rachel Moseley's *Growing Up with Audrey Hepburn* (2003) has attempted to ground this attention to pleasure and spectatorship in the study of *actual audiences*, that is to say historically situated moviegoers. For example, in contrast to the general, theoretical explanation of why audiences like stars offered by psychoanalysis, Stacey develops an ethnographic approach to the star–spectator relationship which uses a combination of interviews with, and surveys of, viewers, as well as information drawn from personal letters and diaries. From this primary data, Stacey catalogues the different ways in which female viewers respond to, identify with and use images of stars. As such, unlike the universalising tendencies of psychoanalytic methods, Stacey is able to distinguish between various modes of identification and different types of pleasure.

WHEN IS A STAR NOT A STAR?

The three approaches to stardom sketched above have held sway in film studies since the late 1970s. And as Geraghty (2000) notes, the definition of stardom that has emerged from these approaches has tended to turn on a series of dualities: between a star's onscreen presence and his or her offscreen existence, between actor and character, glamour and ordinariness, and between public and private spheres. As such, she argues that, generally speaking, 'the model for work on stars and their audiences has been that of an unstable and contradictory figure, constructed both intertextually (across different films) and extratextually (across different types of material)' (ibid.: 85). Indeed, it is precisely this putative instability of the film star, that is to say the way a star might mean a number of potentially conflicting things, that has underwritten academic work on stars to the extent that, until recently, hardly anyone has noticed that such work has almost entirely been forged in the shadow cast by the star system and the stars who were deemed to exemplify its operations. So although the practice of tying stars into long-term fixed contracts which ceded overall control over their public and private image to the studio was over by the 1950s, the sub-discipline of star studies remains heavily influenced by the critical vocabulary used to analyse figures such as Marilyn Monroe, James Cagney, Humphrey Bogart, Marlene Dietrich, Greta Garbo and so on.

Today, however, the question of stardom is considerably more vexed than it was in the 1970s when the groundwork for star studies was being laid. In the first instance, the term 'star' itself is now culturally hierarchised alongside the celebrity, the superstar and the megastar. Moreover, the notion of stardom has undergone significant broadening in the sense that we now routinely speak of pop stars, rock stars, soap stars, star footballers and stars of sport generally, star DJs, star artists, star buildings, star fashion designers, star models, star politicians, even star academics. If cinema once provided 'the ultimate confirmation of stardom' (Gledhill 1991: xiii), then the growing number of Hollywood films which co-opt stars from other areas of the entertainment industry (pop princesses Jennifer Lopez, Madonna, Beyoncé Knowles, Whitney Houston, Jessica Simpson and Lindsay Lohan; WWF champion Dwayne Johnson/The Rock; ex-fashion models Cameron Diaz and Charlize Theron; as well as a host of talent drawn from television, George Clooney and Jennifer Aniston being perhaps two the most notable) certainly seems to question cinema's presumed privileged relationship to stardom.

In the second instance, in the information age and in the wake of transformations brought about by digital image-making technologies and computer animation, 'the definition of "film" as an object of study has not only broadened considerably but has also been destabilized as an object and form' (Sobchack 2000: 301). In this way, not only is there now a new breed of **synthespians** or computer-generated stars to contend with (in this respect figures such as Buzz Lightyear and Woody from the *Toy Story* movies (1995, 1999, 2010) and Shrek and Donkey from the four *Shrek* films (2001, 2004, 2007, 2010) are perhaps the apotheosis of the economic logic of the star system – fully contracted, entirely reusable, totally manipulable, and not subject to the ageing process), but increasingly the 'star' of the movie is more plausibly described as a digital entity or special effect (a twister, tsunami, volcano or storm; prehistoric dinosaurs, extraterrestrial invaders or mutant reptiles; a mythical, spiritual or fantastical force; or an earth-threatening or city-destroying catastrophe of either natural or alien doing). Thus, in uncoupling the filmic image and the cinematic process from photographic technology, the notion of the film star is now neither necessarily a flesh-and-blood human, nor for that matter even a character in the traditional sense of the term. Nick Roddick's quip that Hollywood would now 'rather motion-capture Tom Hanks than put him on the screen' suggests that the notion of the traditional film star is becoming ever more redundant in an industry that increasingly relies on technologically engineered spectacles and franchised narratives (Roddick 2010: 13). Indeed, in discussing a range of forthcoming film projects based on the concept of adapting toys and games into movies (e.g. Stretch Armstrong, Battleship, and Monopoly), Universal Pictures chairmen Marc Shmuger and David Linde declared that we are living 'in an era where brands have become the new stars' (in Fleming 2009). It is in this context of technological and commercial convergence that Shrek and Donkey's guest appearance at the 2002 Academy Awards® to collect the Oscar® for best animated feature served to foretell of these more complex articulations of stardom in contemporary popular culture, articulations which cause us not entirely to supplant the dominant models for analysing stars, but to rethink the concepts and descriptions we use to account for these *different modes of stardom*.

synthespians
A recently coined term which describes 'virtual' or non-human actors. The term relates to digitally scanned or motion-captured versions of 'real' actors, as well as entirely computer-generated characters.

MODES OF STARDOM IN CONTEMPORARY CINEMA

Christine Geraghty argues that while the term *star* should not simply be abandoned because of its non-specific, catch-all nature, we do, however, need to examine contemporary configurations of film stardom within the broader contexts of popular entertainment and media culture: 'Film stardom … has to be seen in the context of the drive in the media to create and exploit the status of being famous across the whole range of entertainment formats' (Geraghty 2000: 188). The notion of *being famous* is important here, since it allows us to see the notions of star, superstar, megastar, as well as celebrity and actor, as points on the same fame continuum, a continuum which is itself bound up with, and fuelled by, the operations of mass-mediated culture. In other words, it permits us to speak of different modes, forms or degrees of stardom. On this account, different articulations of 'the star' become differences of kind not circumscribed or delimited by the specificities of different mediums or different forms within individual media. On the contrary, contemporary configurations of film stardom must be seen as inextricably entwined with broader orchestrations of fame across and through all media platforms. It is in this sense that Geraghty attempts to rethink stardom through the categories of 'celebrity', 'professional' and 'performer' inasmuch as 'these distinctions better help us to understand what film stars have in common with and how they differ from other media public figures' (Geraghty 2000: 187).

Star-as-celebrity
Celebrity is a mode of stardom relatively unconnected to the sphere of professional work. In other words, celebrity is sustained not by someone's talent or ability in their chosen

profession, but almost entirely by notoriety, scandal and infamy. In this sense, Geraghty argues that celebrity privileges biographical information about a star to the extent that his or her stardom is almost entirely rooted in, and constructed through, 'gossip, press and television reports, magazine articles and public relations' (Geraghty 2000: 187). As such, rumours about a film star's latest failed relationship, hearsay concerning his or her love of chihuahuas, or paparazzi shots of them falling out of a taxi 'the worse for wear' circulate alongside similar tittle-tattle about musicians, sportsmen and women, royals, soap stars, It-Girls, socialites, designers, TV presenters and so forth. For instance, the cover of the December 2010 edition of *OK!*, a British weekly magazine dedicated to celebrity reporting, announces rumours about a possible New Year wedding between Brad Pitt and Angelina Jolie. Yet 'Brad and Ange's' story is dwarfed by the lead headline about the latest marriage break-up of glamour model and reality TV star Katie Price, and struggles for prominence alongside *X-Factor* contestant Harry Styles 'speaking out' about his rejection of a 'lovesick TV presenter' and Coleen Rooney's announcement that she and her and footballer-husband are 'not ready to have another baby' (*OK!*, December 2010). Indeed, a cursory glance at the covers of any of the plethora of photomagazines dedicated to peddling stories of celebrities' private lives simultaneously reveals how 'knowledge of the star's "real" life is pieced together through gossip columns and celebrity interviews' and how film stars 'literally interact with those from other areas' of the entertainment world (Geraghty 2000: 188). In this respect, it is easy to track, for example, the trajectory of Tom Cruise's romantic relationships – from his divorce from his first wife Mimi Rogers, his role alongside Nicole Kidman as one half of Hollywood's first couple, to the partnership's demise and his subsequent relationship and marriage to Katie Holmes – just by looking at the covers of such magazines. Moreover, this cultural thirst for celebrity now finds heightened expression in websites such as *Perezhilton.com* which serve up a more or less continuous stream of Hollywood news, gossip, rumour and tittle-tattle through our web browsers, smartphones, RSS feeds and social network sites. The main point here, however, is the idea that the discourse of celebrity shifts attention towards the drama of the star's 'private' life, not his or her public work as a professional actor.

Generally, then, we can identify three interrelated aspects to the star-as-celebrity. First, it is the public circulation of information about the putative 'real' private life of the star that sustains the category of celebrity. Second, the notion of intertextuality is not only descriptive of the *form* and *practice* of celebrity culture, but also *analytic* in the sense that, in this mode of stardom, such intertexts provide the primary focus of research precisely insofar as 'it is the audience's access to and celebration of intimate information from a variety of texts and sources which are important' (Geraghty 2000: 189). Third, and perhaps most crucially, whereas traditional models of stardom emphasise the film text as the primary site of stardom, or at least the place where the star image is completed (see Ellis 1982), the celebrity mode forestalls the primacy of the films themselves inasmuch as it constitutes a mode of stardom which does not necessarily involve spectatorship. In other words, it is not just that 'the star can continue to command attention as a celebrity despite failures at the box office' (Geraghty 2000: 189) but rather it is quite possible to be a fan of, to admire, or simply to 'like' a star without watching the films in which he or she appears. In short, it is not simply that the image of the star-as-celebrity exceeds the film text, but instead that it is dislocated from it altogether and dispersed across a range of extra-filmic texts. Indeed, the adaptability and ubiquity, as well as the centrality of 'celebrity culture' to media culture *per se*, make 'celebrity' perhaps the key mode of contemporary stardom.

Star-as-professional

If star-as-celebrity is understood as part of the much broader operations of media consumption which are relatively divorced from the cinematic text, then the star-as-professional is, at least in the first instance, rooted squarely in the film text itself. So while on the one hand it appears increasingly the case that film stars are appreciated independently of their professional work, on the other hand 'it is quite possible to understand and enjoy the meaning of the star without the interdiscursive knowledge which the star-as-celebrity relies on' (ibid.).

Crucial to the star-as-professional mode of stardom is the degree of 'fit' between the specificities of a particular star image and the corpus of professional roles played by the actor. In other words, the star-as-professional makes sense when it *appears* that the actor's 'real' personality corresponds more or less accurately and more or less consistently with his or her performed personas This is the idea that the actor him- or herself is *personified* in their professional roles. Maltby argues that 'classical Hollywood's star system engineered a correspondence between star and role' to the extent that 'scripts were written specifically to exhibit already established traits and mannerisms in their stars' (Maltby 2003: 385). As such, 'the fact that a star's persona circulated in the media as part of the promotion of specific movies allowed for a considerable interaction between the star's performance and offscreen persona, and in many respects substituted for variation in the roles a star undertook' (ibid.). For example, onscreen and offscreen, Marilyn Monroe embodied the persona of a beautiful yet innocent sex goddess, thus dissolving her 'real' personality into her professional performances. Indeed, the idea that we can detect Monroe the star in and through her roles, that her repertoire of gestures, expressions, and movements are her own and not the property of any individual character, is central to the economy of pleasure associated with this mode of stardom.

More recently, in the light of the dissolution of the star system and the change in the distribution of films brought about, in particular, by the DVD/Blu-ray rental markets, the star-as-professional mode has become reconfigured with the star now being associated or identified with a particular genre. In organising the vast number of titles available to audiences in rental outlets, 'video stores tend not to use the more specific genre categorisations of westerns, gangster films and horror genres and employ vaguer descriptions ... such as "action movie", "comedy" and "drama"' (Geraghty 2000: 189). It is within these broader groupings that individual stars delineate more precise sets of expectations and pleasures. For instance, Jackie Chan, Jet Li and Steven Segal are closely linked to specific forms of martial arts/action cinema; Jim Carrey is associated with a certain form of physical comedy while one would expect different comic pleasures from a film featuring Chris Rock, Ben Stiller, Will Ferrell or Eddie Murphy; and despite the glut of male stars of the action film, the star image of figures such as Bruce Willis, Arnold Schwarzenegger, George Clooney, Tom Cruise, John Travolta, Nicolas Cage, Keanu Reeves, Harrison Ford, Jason Statham, Vin Diesel and Gerard Butler arguably indicate relatively precise variations of masculine agency and thus provide a quite distinct set of expectations within the overarching category of action cinema. Indeed, Geraghty suggests that 'a stable star image' is crucial for the star-as-professional insofar as 'too much difference from the established star image may lead to disappointment for the intended audience' (ibid.). This observation offers one explanation for why actors such as Clooney, Willis and Cage, actors whose star image, though related to their physical appearance, is not in the end predicated primarily on the display of muscularity or physical force, have been able to work successfully in a number of genres while similar generic transitions for Schwarzenegger, Stallone, Van Damme and Jet Li have proved less successful. In this way, then, Geraghty suggests that stars who inhabit the star-as-professional mode 'operate for cinema and video in the same way as a character in a television series, providing the pleasures of stability and repetition and the guarantee of consistency in the apparent plethora of choice offered by the expanding media' (Geraghty 2000: 191).

Star-as-performer

In a reversal of the star-as-celebrity mode, Geraghty's final category shifts the emphasis away from biographical aspects of a star's private life towards notions of *performance* in deliberately focusing attention on the job and art of acting. Thus while to some extent stars have always been understood in relation to their acting abilities and style, Geraghty suggests that the discourse of performance 'now takes on particular importance as a way for film stars to claim legitimate space in the overcrowded world of celebrity status' (ibid.: 192). If in hypermediated culture film stars are often levelled down to celebrities and have to struggle for exposure alongside footballers, pop stars and royals, then the concept of star-as-performer may be understood as perhaps the primary mechanism for reinscribing some of the cultural prestige of film stardom precisely by redirecting attention towards the film text as a privileged site for displaying the skill, craft and technique of acting. Indeed, such an emphasis on performance not only serves to distinguish certain film stars such as Marlon Brando, Robert De Niro, Al Pacino, Sean Penn, Johnny Depp, John Malkovich, Jodie Foster, Meryl Streep and Philip Seymour-Hoffman from the celebrity hoi polloi, but also operates as a key way of 'claiming back the cinema for human stars' from special effects and a growing number of non-human or animated stars (ibid.).

It is possible to identify two principal ways in which film stardom is legitimised through this appeal to the craft of performance and the art of acting. The first concerns a particular tradition of acting associated with the Actor's Studio in New York known as the Method, an approach to acting which Maltby argues has become 'the dominant account of how actors create naturalist performances' (Maltby 2003: 394). Method acting, on the one hand, is rooted in the presence of the actor's self as the emotional and psychological basis of *all* performance. As such, in order to be able to 'get inside' the mind of a character, the Method actor must first investigate his or her own anxieties, repressions, motivations and drives 'as the mine from which all psychological truth must be dug' (Vineberg 1991: 6). On the other hand, the authentic performance can only be fully realised and understood when the distinction between actor and character is abolished in the seamless fusion of performer and role. It is in this sense, then, that Method acting reclaims a degree of cultural prestige for the star-as-performer precisely 'by making the celebrity trappings part of the detritus which has to be discarded' if the performance is to be 'real' and thus worthwhile (Geraghty 2000: 192). Accordingly, it is not simply that actors such as Brando, De Niro and Penn often threaten to disappear into their roles, immersing themselves in the complex psyches of their characters, but, moreover, that their cultural status as performers is enhanced in rejecting the 'vulgar commercialism' of Hollywood. Brando was for many years renowned for being a semi-recluse, while James Kaplan writes that Penn 'gives interviews sparingly and reluctantly' while being a performer who 'has consistently taken roles in challenging films, as opposed to films that earn big money' and has 'effectively turned himself into an actor's actor, a remote star with a lingering air of menace and inaccessibility' (Kaplan 2001).

The second way in which film stardom becomes legitimised through a collocation with performance is related to a particular actor's *selection of projects*. This works on two levels, the first reconfirming the primacy of the film text to the star-as-performer noted by Geraghty, the second diluting such a primacy by acknowledging the rhetorical construction of the actor as a serious artist precisely through an extended circuit of mediation. In the case of the former, actors such as Penn, Depp, Pacino and Streep have tended to resist roles which might compromise their pretensions towards serious acting, instead choosing parts which enable them to put on display the highly visible and recognisable mannerisms of the Method. In the latter case, the star-as-performer reclaims cultural value for his or her work through a route of extra-filmic mediation which complements and commentates on both his or her performances and choice of roles. Often through a combination of star interviews, public pronouncements and self-authored articles, the star-as-performer sets him or herself apart from the vacuities of celebrity and the cold commercialism of Hollywood. For instance, Kevin Spacey's much publicised decision to take on the role of artistic director at London's historic Old Vic theatre shifts the emphasis from his star image to his creative talents. In other words, if, as Andrew Higson observes, 'acting and stardom are … by no means necessary to each other' inasmuch as stardom depends 'as much on image as technique', then Spacey's move, at least in part, is one way of rejecting the image and promoting technique (Higson 2001: 71–2). Similarly, the recent glut of Hollywood stars, Julia Roberts being perhaps most notable among them, who have taken up roles in West End or Broadway productions beg to be considered, for better or worse, not in terms of their star persona, but rather in terms of the way they demonstrate the craft of acting.

One final example will serve to highlight the complex ways in which onscreen and offscreen, textual and extra-textual, images of a star can interpenetrate to produce a relatively sophisticated version of stardom. Sean Penn, while perhaps the contemporary epitome of the rhetorical construction of the 'serious actor', also provides us with an example of the way in which the two aspects of the star-as-performer often inform each other. For on the one hand, after declaring that he doesn't like acting and announcing a number of pseudo-retirements, he 'came back' 'determined to attach himself only to projects of impeccable aesthetic integrity' (Pulver 2001). On this level, his performances in such films as *Carlito's Way* (1993), *Dead Man Walking* (1995), *U Turn* (1997), *The Thin Red Line* (1998), *Hurlyburly* (1998), *Sweet and Lowdown* (1999), *Mystic River* (2003), *21 Grams* (2003), *The Assassination of Richard Nixon* (2004), *The Interpreter* (2005), *All The King's Men* (2006) and *Milk* (2008) have earned him the reputation of being 'the most powerful actor of his generation' (Ebert 1996), 'all fireworks and brooding Method' (Pulver 2001). On the other hand, Penn complements the status of his onscreen performances with a series of public tirades against the 'trash ethos' of Hollywood in which 'everything is about entertainment and no politics' (Penn, cited in Gibbons 2001). 'The one thing you can count on in Hollywood – across the board – is cowardice' (Penn, in Kaplan 2001) Penn has said, and if 'you are willing to put two ideas into a picture you are ahead of the game' (Penn, cited in Gibbons 2001). At the 2001 Edinburgh Festival, Penn made perhaps his most controversial public outburst when he accused certain big-name directors of 'raping society' and claimed that they 'should be sent running home screaming with rectal cancer' because

they don't care about the films they make, or about what is going on around them or the effect they are having on their audience … The definition of a good film now is one that makes the bank happy – not one that shines a light on people's lives.

(Penn, cited in ibid.)

As such, Penn's prestige as an actor is not only claimed through his performances in the film text, but through a more or less self-conscious rhetoric of prestige constructed extra-textually. So while 'the claim to stardom as a performer depends on the work of acting being put on display', such a display is not necessarily limited to the films in which an actor appears but can extend, as in the case of Penn, Spacey and others, to a series of extra-filmic performances which serve to reinforce their putative distance from either 'stars-as-celebrities who can become famous for "being themselves" and stars-as-professionals who act as themselves' (Geraghty 2000: 193).

☐ CASE STUDY 1: MASCULINITY ON A KNIFE-EDGE: ANALYSING TOM CRUISE

Geraghty's categories offer a sophisticated model of contemporary stardom and an enrichment of the vocabulary available to us for describing the ways in which stars embody meanings and pleasures. They take us a stage beyond the emphasis on the duality of the film star that defined earlier approaches to stardom and allow us to explore a more complex range of discourses that now frame the production and consumption of film stars and the different concepts that are thus entailed. It is in this context that

Tom Cruise offers a particularly interesting and surprisingly nuanced example of the contemporary film star. In part this is because Cruise is 'indisputably the number-one star of his generation' (Kelly 2004: 50), one of only a handful of people in Hollywood 'who can reliably deliver a billion-dollar franchise' (Epstein 2005). However, the sheer scale of his 'megawattage' stardom, what Matheo calls 'Cruise the phenomenon', tends to belie not only the precarious and contradictory nature of his star image, but also the idea that that image articulates a 'curious spectacle' of masculine identities (Rapold 2010: 64; Matheou 2006: 59; LaSalle, 2006). Indeed, in a career that now encompasses four decades and more than thirty films, Cruise has at some point embodied all three of Geraghty's categories of stardom in ways that have variously *reinforced* and *undercut* the production of a coherent Cruise identity. This perhaps offers some explanation as to why, despite his unrivalled success as a star, Cruise-the-person has, as Pols points out, consistently 'run the gamut of public opinion', from 'brash and irresistible', the 'crush-worthy hunk of *Top Gun*', to 'a robo-dumbass', the 'weirdo who jumped on Oprah's couch' (O'Hehir 2010; Pols 2010).

Manohla Dargis argues that 'at first glance, no star persona comes across as more coherent than that of Tom Cruise' (Dargis 2000: 20). Dana Stevens describes this persona as 'Tom Cuise-ness', an apparently 'natural resource' that remains 'undiminished and virtually unchanged since its discovery in 1983' (Stevens 2010). This 'resource' is usually described as a particular mixture of physical attributes and personality traits, a combination in which his special good looks and athleticism – 'Those teeth! Those abs! That shining, perfectly coiffed helmet' (Holden 2001) – compensate for the fact that, to all intents and purposes, he is a 'bland white guy' with a 'breezily facile macho personality' (Dargis 2000). In terms of his performative style, LaSalle describes it as 'a taut bundle of calculation, eternally boyish, always aware of what his face is doing, always insisting that we like him, prodding us with smiles and frowns and a sincerity that almost looks real' (LaSalle 2006). What emerges from these accounts is a version of the Cruise star persona predicated on us seeing him as a 'consummately ordinary' guy, but one who has 'an indefinable something special' (Dargis 2000: 21). Most often, it is Cruise's smile which is seen as the focus of his specialness, the signal that he really is 'superior to us mere mortals' (Foundas 2006). It is variously described as a 'killer', 'ice-cold', 'maniacal', 'blood freezing', 'shark-white smile', an 'easy-does-it, no-problem grin', or a 'Gervasian Wince'. Dargis argues that no other actor has shown such 'genius for turning a simple human reflex into an epic of conquest and seduction' (Dargis 2000: 21). Indeed, above all else it is his distinctive 'flashing-choppers mode of performance' (Denby 2010), the way that he delivers those 'terrifyingly pearly whites' (Kois 2010), that has become Cruise's signature, a synecdoche for his sex appeal and cocksure physicality.

Following this conventional reading of Cruise, it is possible to construct an analysis of his star image as paradigmatic of Geraghty's star-as-professional category insofar as his public persona appears seamlessly to correspond with his onscreen roles. This is the idea captured by Kois when he says 'there's never been a particularly crisp line between intense, superawesome Tom Cruise and the characters he plays' (Kois 2010). Indeed, Cruise's long-standing identification with the action-adventure genre and the considerable success of films such as *Top Gun* (1986), *Days of Thunder* (1990), *Minority Report* (2002), *Knight and Day* (2010) and in particular the *Mission: Impossible* franchise suggest that his star image does function as a 'reliable indicator' of the meanings and pleasures a film offers, and provides 'a guarantee of predictability' in the marketplace (Geraghty 2000: 189, 191). For some critics, Cruise's success in the over-crowded world of the action-movie star is surprising given that he not only 'lacks the personality and breezy humour of Harrison Ford, the everyman quality of Bruce Willis, [and] even the cartoon appeal of Schwarzenegger and Stallone' but also 'doesn't even look as though he likes a scrap' (Matheou 2006: 59). However, it is his 'toothy good looks, physicality and a desperate desire to be liked' that 'drag the viewer through his adventures with him' (ibid.). In other words, it is the idea that Cruise so often appears to be playing

himself onscreen, that there is little gap between actor and character, that marks out his territory in the genre. Perhaps the most instructive example of this 'stabilising' function of Cruise's stardom is his role as Ethan Hunt in the *Mission: Impossible* films. For to a significant extent Hunt's intense physicality, supreme self-belief and disarming sex appeal are the ideal onscreen personification of Cruise's star image, a situation in which the star's personality seems entirely consonant with the role. Indeed, such is the strength of this conflation that Cruise is often condemned by critics when either his performance does not 'fit' the genre or he attempts to broaden his range and style. For example, Dargis argues that his performance of German army officer Claus von Stauffenberg in *Valkyrie* (2008) 'doesn't work ... because he's too modern, too American and way too Tom Cruise to make sense in the role' (Dargis 2008).

Given that Cruise seems so readable using the star-as-professional category, is there a need to move on to a second-level analysis and invoke the other two categories, star-as-celebrity and star-as-performer? What is it about his star image that demands additional explanation? The answer to such questions returns us to the question of the unusually complex masculinity that attends Cruise's public persona. So while on the one hand, analysis of the films discussed above does tend to lead to a view of Cruise as 'the apotheosis of redblooded American masculinity' (Foundas 2006), a 'high-strung human racehorse oozing ambition like perspiration' (Holden 2001), on the other hand the totality of his star persona has, as Dargis notes, 'failed to cohere' around a single identity, one that is 'either masculine or feminine, gay or straight.' (Dargis 2000: 23). The implication of Dargis's observation, the idea that Cruise's stardom is essentially built on a series of contradictions, impels us to turn to Geraghty's other two categories in order that we might not only explore instances where Cruise's performances appear to work against the putative stability of his star image, but also place our analyses in the context of the celebrity culture in which his stardom is both produced and circulated.

Even though Geraghty notes that the star-as-celebrity category works particularly well for female stars inasmuch as its emphasis on discourses of personal relationships, domesticity, leisure and consumption chimes with longstanding associations between women and the private sphere, Cruise's career has from the first been attended by an intense stream of gossip, rumour, scandal and speculation about his private life. Perhaps the two key strands of this dramatisation of Cruise's identity, strands which are in fact closely intertwined, relate to, on the one hand, the intertextual mediation of Cruise's relationships with a number of high-profile Hollywood actresses and, on the other, fairly consistent conjecture about his sexuality. This latter speculation initially emerged as a reaction to the narcissism associated with the roles he played in his early films, roles which very often required him to pose half-naked and display his body for the visual pleasure of the audience; it gained momentum with the subtextual homoeroticism of *Top Gun* which saw him literally 'playing with the boys', and reached fever pitch in his portrayal of Lestat in *Interview with the Vampire* (1994) when he sunk his teeth into Brad Pitt's neck. Since then there have been a number of pseudo-outings, suggestion that his marriage to Nicole Kidman was a front designed to disguise his homosexuality, rumours of a gay sex tape featuring Cruise, not to mention umpteen legal cases relating to the media's obsession with his sexual identity.

However, notwithstanding the persistence of the public fantasy concerning Cruise's sexuality, perhaps an even more powerful preoccupation of celebrity magazines, gossip columnists and talk show hosts concerns his 'straight' relationships with, and subsequent marriage to, female members of the Hollywood glitterati. Indeed, this is a drama that is quite easy to piece together simply by tracking the covers of a publication such as *Hello!*, a UK photomagazine dedicated to peddling stories of celebrities' private lives. For example, the cover of issue 620 (July 2000) features Tom Cruise with his second wife, Nicole Kidman, talking about how he 'would step on landmines to protect his family'; issue 650 (February 2001) features Kidman and Cruise in one of their final public appearances together before the announcement that their marriage was over; issue 686 (October 2001) leads with 'intimate photos' of Cruise and Penélope Cruz apparently revealing 'the depth of their love' as well as a feature on Kidman talking about 'the truth' of her 'life with Tom'; issue 711 (May 2002) leads with a feature on Penélope Cruz speaking about her relationship with Cruise and the absence of bad feeling between herself and Kidman; and, more recently, issue 947 (December 2006) offers us privileged access 'inside the magical wedding' of Cruise and his third wife, Katie Holmes, while issue 1040 (December 2008) features an article in which Cruise 'talks of his love for his two girls'. This narrative is itself complemented and confused by a simultaneous narrative constructed through other magazines and online gossip blogs which construct Cruise as a 'weirdo', who 'controls every move' of 'Katie's tortured life', and who 'will take her baby away' if she leaves him. Most recently the public perception of Cruise as overly intense and psychologically unhinged has revolved around three events: his longstanding membership of, and public support for, the controversial pseudo-religion of Scientology, a situation which led one biographer to declare that he was the church's 'de-facto second in command' (see Tapper 2008); his 2005 public tirade against psychiatry on the *Today Show*; and, most notorious of all, what has become known as the couch incident, or 'jumping the couch', which saw Cruise jump around the set during an interview on the *Oprah Winfrey Show*, then hop onto the couch before falling to one knee in the repeated profession of his love for his new girlfriend Katie Holmes. The main point here, however, is not simply that the category of star-as-celebrity is every bit as revealing in the analysis of Cruise's star identity as it is for many female stars, nor that in recent times 'Cruise the movie actor has increasingly been held hostage by Cruise the perceived weirdo' (O'Hehir 2010), but that the very fact of his association with the trappings of celebrity in the first place has the effect of undermining any straightforward sense of Cruise's masculine identity through its/his association with traditionally feminine discourses of love, romance, families and gossip.

This complicated reading of Cruise becomes further vexed when we consider his possible relationship to the star-as-performer category. While some critics dismiss Cruise as a 'wooden or blank actor' (James 2002: 13), 'lacking the true actor's readiness to fall on his face, play ugly or foolish' (Kelly 2004: 50), it nevertheless remains the case that a number of his films have required him to 'flex his acting muscles' (Brooks 2002: 64) in a way usually associated with more serious performers. So even though Cruise is not a Method actor in the strict sense of the term, such character-centred roles as

Charlie Babbitt in Barry Levinson's *Rain Man* (1989), Ron Kovic in Oliver Stone's *Born on the Fourth of July* (1989), Frank T.J. Mackey in Paul Thomas Anderson's *Magnolia* (1999) and Dr William Harford in Stanley Kubrick's *Eyes Wide Shut* (1999) have allowed him to engage in performances of 'heightened emotionalism' that manifest as intense expressive outpourings. These outbursts of emotion shift the emphasis from Cruise's physical athleticism to the inner life of the characters he plays and can thus be understood to be generated by 'an underlying vision of the individual as divided between "authentic" inner and a potentially repressed/repressive outer self' (Counsell 1996: 63). And, of course, it is just such markers of realism or naturalness that are regularly viewed as evidence of the authenticity and value of the performance.

However, while it is possible to pursue this line of inquiry further – *Born on the Fourth of July* is particularly fertile in this respect insofar as Cruise's portrayal of Vietnam veteran Ron Kovic combines suffering and impotence, emotion and sentiment in a way that, as Robert Burgoyne argues, marks a shift from 'spectacular images of muscular masculinity ... to a more internal, psychologically-nuanced model of male identity' (Burgoyne 1994: 220) – there is another, potentially more interesting, way in which Cruise operates as a star-as-performer. This is to do with an aspect of his performance style which critics very often read as evidence of his blankness or inauthenticity as an actor, or which is used to position Cruise as simply one amongst many actors who enact 'the role of modern action hero as cipher' (James 2002: 13). In short, unlike the Method-influenced approach of stars such as DeNiro, Pacino and Foster, it is precisely Cruise's intense physicality and the spectacular deployment of his body in hazardous action set pieces that can be seen to reclaim the cinema for human stars.

● **Plate 7.2**
Tom Cruise 'flexing his acting muscles' in *Born on the Fourth of July* (Oliver Stone 1989)

When critic Roger Ebert asks 'why do so many movies find it obligatory to inflict us with CGI overkill?' (Ebert 2010), he speaks for several prominent reviewers who increasingly find Hollywood's reliance on digital visual effects at best unconvincing and unsatisfactory and, at worst, 'clumsy and ugly' (Scott 2003). Lisa Purse has explored this dissatisfaction in specific relation to the 'virtual action body', a computer-animated stand-in or stunt double for the flesh-and-blood body of the star. Her analysis focuses on the question of how the presence of such virtual bodies in films such as the *Spiderman* franchise 'impact on the construction of the hero's physicality' and affect 'the spectator's pleasurable engagement with the spectacles of empowerment and heroic endeavor' the action genre offers (Purse 2007: 7). She argues that the negative critical reception that so often attends accounts of the virtual action body speaks to 'an anxiety around the visual possibilities of the computer-animated body – possibilities that we do not want to *see* visualized' (ibid.: 15). These cultural anxieties centre around the dematerialisation of the human body and the inherent malleability of the virtual body: 'the virtual body's inherent mutability reverberates with unspoken fears of phenomenological instability and potentially monstrous metamorphoses within which state of flux the distinct self is somehow lost' (ibid.: 16). Moreover, in confronting these fears the spectator is snapped out of 'their imaginative immersion in the film world' thus disrupting the generic pleasures associated with the action film and the heroic body (ibid.: 12). Of course, the most effective way to assuage such anxieties and restore pleasure is to 'return to the material physicality of the pro-filmic body' and relocate heroism in the flesh-and-blood of real actors (ibid.: 22). It is in this light, therefore, that it becomes significant that much has been made by of the fact that Cruise performs 'a remarkable number of his own stunts' (LaSalle 2006). Indeed, *LA Weekly* critic, Scott Foundas, argues that Cruise is 'the most graceful physical performer to occupy the screen since Burt Lancaster' and in the role of action hero 'he's just about peerless' (Foundas 2006). Similarly, Mick LaSalle suggests that Cruise 'acts as though performance were a physical act of will' and that in the action genre he is 'the ultimate screen creature' (LaSalle 2006). Nick James captures the flavour of this kind of critical response in his suggestion that Cruise has turned the job of film star and the filmmaking process into 'a risky extreme sport' (James 2002: 15). The important point here, though, is not simply that Cruise performs his own stunts, but that in doing so 'a very different action experience' is created for the audience (LaSalle 2006). In other words, 'the audience's shivery thrill of recognition' at the beginning of *Mission: Impossible II* (2006) that 'it's the star himself' hanging by his fingertips from the edge of a mountain, 'risking death for our delight', cannot be reproduced using virtual actors. And it matters that 'the camera is able to stay on Cruise's face as he jumps off a 60-foot wall and lands inches from the ground' in *Mission: Impossible III* precisely because such scenes 'stay personal' (ibid.). In this context, then, both the presence and performance of Cruise's physical body in the action genre can be read not only as the refusal of the virtual body, but also as a complexification of the star-as-performer category in which the star body and the hyper-visible display of its physical possibilities function as 'the test bed of authenticity, the last stand of the real' (Dargis 2000).

CONCLUSION: STARDOM AND CULTURAL IDENTITY

For further discussion of representations of masculinity and performance see Chapter 11.

Richard Dyer argues that 'being interested in stars is being interested in how we are human now' (Dyer 1987: 17). As we have seen, this is because 'the territory of the star image is also the territory of identity', a space where identity formations, subjectivities, or 'ways of being human' are negotiated and renegotiated through cultural representation (Tasker 1993b: 233). As such, the phenomenon of Tom Cruise's stardom provides an insightful point of access for thinking about the performative construction of masculinity in contemporary cinema, a process described by Tasker as 'the ongoing formulation and reformulation of "ways of being a man"' (ibid.: 233–4). For in applying Geraghty's categories to the study of Cruise, what emerges is a complex image of masculinity, one which oscillates between spectacular images of muscular masculinity and a more internal, psychologically nuanced model of male identity. In part this is because all three modes of stardom reveal different properties of Cruise's star image, properties that can mutually reinforce our understanding of that persona or rub against each other to undermine our sense of who or what he is. This is one explanation for why Cruise's career has seemed 'rife with contradictions from the start' and that 'his on-screen persona depends more on contradiction than coherence' (Dargis 2000: 20). Indeed, the cash value of Geraghty's schema is that it helps us to unpick some of those contradictions a little more precisely. This is especially the case when we consider that one of the most fascinating aspects of Cruise's stardom is a consistent engagement with roles in which these three modes of stardom interpenetrate to produce a kind of meta-commentary on his own star image.

There are a number of facets to this. First, a number of his roles have included a scenario involving the dramatic uglification of Cruise's face. Whether it be the extreme face-peels of *Mission: Impossible* as Hunt removes his latex masks, the characters' physical disfigurements in *Vanilla Sky* (2001) and *Minority Report* (2002) or the prosthetic make up used to turn him into Les Grossman in *Tropic Thunder* (2008), Cruise has indulged in the public fantasy/private anxiety concerning the loss of his signature pretty-boy looks. The fact that these transformations are temporary (either within the narrative itself or because we 'know' that his looks will be restored outside of the film) is less crucial than the masochistic desire it signals to mutilate the emblem of his appeal and the sadistic pleasures it offers viewers as witnesses to that loss. Moreover, in the case of *Vanilla Sky* and *Minority Report*, the fact that these physical disfigurations are tied to narratives of male reconfiguration serves to implicate the audience in their tales of tragic heroic decline and redemption. In this sense, any identification with Cruise in these roles is, on some level at least, an ambiguous identification with the ideas of masculine loss and renewal.

Second, a significant number of Cruise's roles, and his performance in those roles, self-consciously trade on the part of his persona that constructs him as 'the vainest, cockiest master of the universe ever to strut across the screen wearing an obnoxiously triumphant grin' (Holden 2001), the aspect of his image described by David Denby as 'shiny, overwrought [and] deluded about his own charm' (Denby 2010). For instance, as far back as his portrayal of poolroom hustler Vincent Lauria in *The Color of Money* (1986), Cruise has drawn on our memories of him in earlier films, in this case the cocksure Maverick of *Top Gun* and the shy know-all Joel in *Risky Business* (1983), for either comic or cathartic affect. Indeed, the critical reception of *Knight and Day* (2010) was marked by the desire to read the film's super-spy protagonist Roy Miller as a kind of 'meta-Cruise or a Cruise pastiche' insofar as the film 'adopts his damaged public persona as its theme and subject' (O'Hehir 2010). In this respect, Stevens reads the film as 'a kind of treatise on the state of Cruise-itude in our time [inasmuch as] the character of Roy Miller is so quintessentially Cruise-ian that he skirts the edges of self-conscious parody' (Stevens 2010). Perhaps more interesting, however, is when the deliberate confusion between role/character and actor/image forms part of a narrative of masculine redemption. While this process of, so to speak, playing one Cruise off another in order to deconstruct masculine subjectivity characterises a number of Cruise's films – *Rain Man* (1988), *Jerry Maguire* (1996), *Eyes Wide Shut* (1999), *Vanilla Sky* (2001) – it finds its most powerful manifestation in *Magnolia* (1999) in the role of motivational sex guru Frank T.J. Mackey who is forced to confront the hubris of his machismo as he watches his father die.

The kind of re-evaluation of cinematic masculine subjectivity that is played out through Mackey's pain and suffering in *Magnolia* finds a surprising corollary in Cruise's depiction of estranged father Ray Ferrier in Steven Spielberg's *War of the Worlds* (2005). This is not simply because it is another in a long list of films in which Cruise

• **Plate 7.3**
Tom Cruise's portrayal of motivational sex-guru, Frank T.J. Mackey, in Paul Thomas Anderson's *Magnolia* (1999) explores the relationship between the outward physicality of his star persona and the traumatic inner-life of the character. It is in this sense that the film plays one 'Cruise' off of another in order to deconstruct masculine subjectivity

plays a character whose male familial relationships are complex, absent or indeterminate, but rather because of its conception of, and Cruise's embodiment of, male heroism as ineffectual and defunct. After taking custody of his teenage son Robbie and ten-year-old daughter Rachel for the weekend, Ray is forced to flee with his children in order escape the devastation wrought by a hostile alien invasion. And fleeing is all he is able to do. After commandeering the only working car in the neighbourhood, Ray witnesses the awesome destructive power of the invading tripods as they turn people and buildings to dust. However, this is not the action-hero Cruise we find in *Top Gun* or the *Mission: Impossible* films, the character who believes in himself so passionately that he knows, like we do, that he will save the day (and the world) in the end. For this time, in seeing the military's impotence in attempting to combat the attack, Cruise, unlike Robbie, does not rush to join battle with the invaders, but rather grabs his daughter's hand and rushes to hide out in a cellar with another survivalist. Indeed, the substantial part of *War of the Worlds* revolves around the drama of Cruise's/Ray's inability to act, to exert influence on the world around him. For ultimately humanity is not rescued by Cruise's/Ray's actions but rather by something altogether less determinate, an arbitrary twist of fate – the fact that the aliens have no resistance to earthly viruses. In this respect, Cruise's Ray can be seen as an analogue to the role identified by Scott Benjamin King in his discussion of *Miami Vice* insofar as the film's principal male character takes on 'a role usually given to women: the ragged survivor of the narrative' (King 1990: 292).

What emerges from this analysis, then, is an image of Cruise that is defined by contradiction, complexity and incoherence. For in his appeal to traditional masculinist concepts of bellicose physicality, inexorable action and limitless virility, and in his concomitant questioning of those ideals through parody, pastiche and self-mockery, Cruise's star image exhibits a striking combination of certitude and ambiguity. So

• **Plate 7.4**
The limits of the action hero? Tom Cruise as the 'the ragged survivor of the narrative' in *War of the Worlds* (Steven Spielberg, 2005)

although his films are replete with stereotypical images of masculinity, the totality of his star image nevertheless places substantial pressure on those longstanding myths of masculinity that work to construct it as an unproblematic, fixed and immutable category. The gendered and sexual confusions that have percolated through Cruise's career and which now reside at the heart of his star image demonstrate that masculinity is not a universal category, that it is always performed (whether onscreen or offscreen), raising questions concerning what it takes to be a man today, and what the consequences are, and the alternatives might be, of macho male subjectivity. In this way then, analysis of Cruise's stardom can not only shed considerable light on the way masculinity is narrated and performed in contemporary cinema but also contribute to a broader project of understanding how masculine identities are instigated and negotiated through forms of cultural representation more generally. For the fundamental incoherence of Cruise's image demonstrates not only that the business of being a star is now a fraught one, but also that that 'the business of representing men is a precarious one indeed' (Cohan and Rae Hark 1993: 3).

SUMMARY

- Since the establishment of the studio system, film stars have been understood to perform a key economic function in relation to product differentiation and marketing.
- Critics have sought to expand on this view of stardom by offering explanations of how stars seem able to embody specific meanings and offer specific pleasures.
- The most influential approach to stardom conceives the star as an image or persona constructed through a network of intertextuality which includes both the films in which the star performs and the broader web of publicity and marketing materials through which the totality of the 'star text' is constructed.
- Recent developments in Hollywood cinema (the rise of the synthespian, the dominance of CGI spectacles) together with the rise of celebrity culture more generally (the weakening of the definition of stardom) have led some critics to question the efficacy of traditional approaches to star studies.

- The idea that stardom might now exist in a range of 'modes' and can be studied using a series of categories helps us to understand what, if anything, distinguishes film stars from celebrities and other famous people as well as to identify what they have in common.
- The value of engaging in star studies is not simply that it provides an explanation of the role of actors/stars in the film industry, but that it offers us an insight into formations of cultural identity and how these are forged and reforged through cultural representation.

QUESTIONS FOR DISCUSSION

1   Pick one male and one female contemporary film star and consider:
    (a) the frequency with which, and the ways in which they are represented in celebrity magazines and the press;
    (b) the ways in which knowledge of their private lives overlaps with or informs their onscreen roles;
    (c) the ideological meanings associated with their star image.
2   To what extent do pop stars, star footballers or stars from other areas of the media fit or resist the models of film stardom discussed in this chapter?
3   Which categories of stardom do animated stars such as Woody and Buzz Lightyear fit into, or how might we modify those categories in order to describe this phenomenon?
4   In what ways is it possible to analyse and understand a special effect such as a twister, an earthquake, an alien or a computer-generated toy as a star?
5   Discuss the idea that film stars are no longer crucial to an industry that relies on franchises and special effects for selling movie tickets.

FURTHER READING

Introductory texts

McDonald, P. (2000) *The Star System: Hollywood's Production of Popular Identities*, London: Wallflower Press.

This is a relatively short but excellent introduction to the historical emergence and development of the star system in the American film industry.

Selected key works

Dyer, R. (1998) *Stars* (2nd edn), BFI, London. Since its first publication in 1979, Dyer's book has been the key critical work in the field of star studies to the extent that it is virtually impossible to find any subsequent work that hasn't taken S*tars* as its point of departure. The updated edition also features a useful supplementary chapter by Paul McDonald which traces more recent developments in star studies. It is also worthwhile consulting Dyer's later book, *Heavenly Bodies*.

Dyer, R. (1987) *Heavenly Bodies: Film Stars and Society*, BFI, London.

Gledhill, C. (ed.) (1991) *Stardom: Industry of Desire*, Routledge, London. This anthology contains many seminal essays in the field of star studies.

Useful anthologies

Austin, T. and Barker, M. (eds) (2003) *Contemporary Hollywood Stardom*, London: Arnold.

Fischer, L. and Landy, M. (eds) (2004) *Stars: The Film Reader*, London: Routledge.

Marshall, P.D. (ed.) (2006) *The Celebrity Culture Reader*, London: Routledge.

Redmond, S. and Holmes, S. (eds) (2007) *Stardom and Celebrity: A Reader*, London: Sage.

Willis, A. (ed.) (2004) *Film Stars: Hollywood and Beyond*, Manchester: Manchester University Press.

FURTHER VIEWING

This chapter explores the construction of Cruise's star image and its implications for how we understand contemporary masculine agency. As such, the list of films below is instructive viewing inasmuch as it articulates some of the incoherence and ambiguities that define his star image. However, it is quite possible to employ a similar method to the one pursued here to analyse the star image of people such as Brad Pitt, Johnny Depp, Jodie Foster, Julia Roberts and Nicole Kidman.

Collateral (2004)
The Color of Money (1986)
Eyes Wide Shut (1999)
Interview with the Vampire (1993)
Jerry Maguire (1996)
Knight and Day (2010)
Magnolia (1999)
Minority Report (2002)
Mission: Impossible (1996)
Rain Man (1988)
Risky Business (1983)
Top Gun (1986)
Valkyrie (2008)
Vanilla Sky (2001)
War of the Worlds (2005)

RESOURCE CENTRES

Online reading

Feasey, R. (2004) 'Stardom and Distinction: Sharon Stone and the Problem of Legitimacy', *Scope*, http://www.nottinghamac.uk/film/scope archive/articles/stardom-and-distinction.htm. An essay in the online film studies journal *Scope*, which discusses Sharon Stone.

Grieveson, L. (2002) 'Stars and Audiences in Early American Cinema', *Screening the Past*, No. 14, http://www.latrobe.edu.au/screeningthepast/classics/cl0902/lgcl14c.htm.

Perez Hilton, http://perezhilton.com, Perhaps the most famous online source for Hollywood gossip.

Chapter 8

Approaches to film genre – taxonomy/genericty/metaphor

Paul Watson

■ Approaches to film genre – taxonomy/genericity/metaphor

INTRODUCTION

Common questions we ask each other before going to the cinema or renting a movie are: 'What sort of film shall we watch?'; 'What kind of film do you feel like seeing?' Alternatively, in making our selections we might say things such as: 'I don't like horror films'; 'I'm not in the mood for a weepie, let's watch a comedy'. These kinds of questions and statements identify, at least on an informal level, a film's *genre*, a French term imported to film theory from literary studies meaning 'type' or 'class'. The result of such deliberations is, say, the choice of watching a thriller over a western, a comedy over a musical, a science fiction film over a crime movie or, more generally, the idea that we have particular likes or dislikes for certain types of film. Moreover, the issues that underpin such deliberations and discriminations – issues of taste, preference, identity and pleasure associated with particular kinds of film – are, of course, precisely the issues that producers of film need to take into account in the effort to make their product appealing to audiences, and, by implication, a contained economic risk. Likewise, attention to those same issues provides the film reviewer with a tactical means of evaluating a film's relative merits in terms of the way it may be said to be a classic of its genre, or, moreover, if it affords particular pleasures by extending, usurping, challenging or reworking particular generic elements. On this everyday level, genre resembles a golden thread that knits the concerns of the film industry together with the desires of its audiences.

Seizing on this sense of continuity, much genre criticism is underpinned by the assumption that genre is a conceptual prism that allows critics to simultaneously address the activities of industry, audience and culture insofar as it functions as: (1) a financial security blanket for the industry by providing a logic, or framework, for organising its output so as to capitalise on previous models of success and thus minimise financial risk; (2) a set of precepts and expectations for audiences to organise their viewing; and (3) a critical framework for reviewers to arbitrate between the distinctiveness and putative success of the product and the taste of its implied audience. In this way, Peter Hutchings argues that 'part of the appeal of studying genre is that it offers the opportunity to deal with cinema, and Hollywood cinema in particular, as both an industrial and popular medium' (Hutchings 1995: 61).

GENRE THEORY AND HOLLYWOOD CINEMA

Partly because of its promise of theoretical ubiquity, and partly due to its apparent affinity to Hollywood cinema, genre has been a key concept in the development of film theory, and, in return, cinema has provided an important staging ground for the broader discussion of genre in relation to both mass entertainment and the arts. For genre criticism is marked by the possibility it affords critics to analyse the cinema as an *industrial form of aesthetic practice*; that is, precisely as a major form of mass entertainment.

In this respect, it is important to note that genre's more extravert and inherently inclusive critical disposition contrasts sharply with auteurism's introversion and intrinsic exclusivity. Indeed, the emergence of genre criticism in the late 1960s and early 1970s is usually understood as either a development, qualification, corrective or outright rejection of auteurism. Whereas auteurist criticism was overwhelmingly trained upon the work of relatively few directors which could be distilled from the general category of cinema by appealing to Romantic conceptions of the artist, genre, in casting its critical net wider, seemed to offer critics a far more inclusive and democratic method, one which was attuned to the industrial and commercial imperatives of Hollywood. It is in this sense that Gledhill sees genre as a 'conceptual space' in which 'issues of texts and aesthetics ... intersect with those of industry and institution, history and society, culture and audiences' and describes the term as reclaiming the 'commercial products of Hollywood for serious critical appraisal' (Gledhill 2000: 221, 222). Stam talks of genre as the 'crystallization of a negotiated encounter between film-maker and audience, a way of reconciling the stability of an industry with the excitement of an evolving popular art' (Stam 2000a: 127). It is for these reasons that, when used in the context of cinema the term 'genre' itself has, as Barry Keith Grant argues, come to refer simultaneously to a

particular mode of film production ... a convenient consumer index, providing audiences with a sense of the kind of pleasures to be expected from a given film; and a critical concept, a tool for mapping out a taxonomy of popular film and for understanding the complex relationship between popular cinema and popular culture.

(Keith Grant 2007: 2)

It is this holistic approach to studying cinema that seemed to early genre critics capable of extending and advancing critical interest in popular cinema in a way auteurism could not. For in trying to skim the cream off Hollywood's output, auteurism tended to either construct popular cinema as the insignificant counterpoint to genuine art, or worse, to simply ignore it altogether. In short, the logic of much auteurist writing runs that it is not the film but in fact the artist that is important, and by implication that it is a few individual creative geniuses who are the proper focus of film studies rather than the industrial, historical and social nexus that frames the cinematic process. Or, to put it another way, auteurism valued the exception rather than the rule inasmuch as it threshed the artistic wheat from the generic chaff, while genre criticism, on the contrary, set itself the task of understanding precisely the 'rule'-governed practices of cinema as a mass entertainment medium.

In trawling deeper and wider than auteurism, genre criticism may be seen as an attempt to deal with Hollywood cinema as an industrial mode of film production which is itself bound up with, not to mention limited by, a much broader economic system governed by the imperatives of commodification and commercialism. For a generic analysis of cinema offers not only the possibility of describing the systematic nature of Hollywood as an industry in which differentiation between individual films occurs only within an overarching logic of product standardisation, but also prompts consideration of different genres in terms of their collective significance or deeper meanings. In other words, exactly the same value judgement which served to marginalise the *standard* practices of Hollywood in the hands of auteur critics provided genre critics with a critical vocabulary appropriate to the art of those practices.

Genre theory and contemporary cinema

For further discussion of the studio system see Chapter 1.

Ironically, such has been the success of genre criticism in describing popular cinema that Hollywood is now often equated with generic filmmaking. As Keith Grant notes, the notion of genre is now a 'pervasive presence' in contemporary culture with popular cinema being 'organised almost entirely according to genre categories' (Keith Grant 2007: 2, 1). Similarly, Tom Ryall argues, 'whatever else it is, Hollywood is surely a cinema of genres, a cinema of westerns, gangster films, musicals, melodramas and thrillers' (Ryall 1998: 327). However, such an equation tends to hide as much as it reveals. For such claims tend to emerge from analyses of Hollywood's classical period and cannot automatically be transposed to the contemporary situation. Indeed, since the assimilation of Hollywood studios into larger multinational conglomerates and the concomitant shift away from the factory-like manufacture of films towards what has been described as the 'package-unit' model of film production, genres are no longer associated with specific studios in the way they were in the heyday of the

studio system. In addition, cinema-going nowadays is for most people a relatively infrequent event in comparison to the time devoted to other media forms. In fact, the majority of film viewing itself now revolves around our television sets, whether that is tuning into a movie broadcast on terrestrial networks or one of a proliferating number of dedicated satellite and cable channels; hiring a DVD or Blu-ray disc from a rental outlet; or watching a movie from our own personal collection on our home cinema system, Smartphone, or iPad. Indeed, at a time when movies resemble less the self-contained entities often implied by notions of classical Hollywood, and more 'multi-purpose entertainment machines' (Schatz 1993: 9–10) that initiate 'an endless chain of other cultural products' (Wasko 1994: 4), it is perhaps not surprising that the film text itself is only one among many possible sites where genre condenses. Likewise, much contemporary cinema evinces a variety of technological, formal, thematic and stylistic affinities with other media forms as well as itself spawning a host of other media commodities. Indeed, Janet Harbord sees these lines of convergence as evidence of the simultaneous dispersal and translation of film (dispersed into other ancillary objects and translated into new material forms through digital technologies), a series of transformations which 'threaten not only the coherence of Hollywood, but the foundations of the discipline [of film studies]' (Harbord 2007: 62).

Given these cultural changes, some critics have recently become less convinced of the security of genre for describing Hollywood's industrial mode of production. Harbord herself argues that film studies is 'poised to reorganize its field' since the idea of genre is now only capable of describing 'the well-worn categories of large-scale film production' that characterise Hollywood's past (Harbord 2007: 9). Taking a different tack, Steve Neale, maintains that it is not genres that are Hollywood's primary commodity, but rather narratives inasmuch as 'the system of narration adopted by mainstream cinema serves as the very currency of cinema itself' (Neale 1980: 20). On this account, genre is simply a mode, albeit a key one, of Hollywood's narrative system. More recently, Andrew Darley has suggested that in a **postmodern** culture of institutionalised **intertextuality** and radical **eclecticism** brought about by new technological developments, genre, while not entirely disappearing, has 'a far more limited structural role to play', perhaps reliably referring to nothing more than 'the general level of a form itself – narrative cinema' (Darley 2000: 144). Such a move divests genre theory of precisely the critical dexterity that distinguishes it from other critical approaches to studying popular film, while some critics even suggest abandoning the term itself in favour of other terms that more plausibly describe Hollywood's commercial activities within the global mediascape – terms such as repetition, seriality, cycle, trend and mode.

Simply disposing of the term, however, or replacing it with other cognate terms, not only seems counterintuitive on an everyday level but also risks unnecessarily jettisoning some useful conceptual tools for thinking about cinema on a range of theoretical levels. For if on the one hand we do need to rethink and reorganise our conceptions of film genre by looking beyond the film text for our inspiration, to place the question of film genre squarely within broader multi-discursive formations, on the other hand it is precisely the complexity of those formations, the thoroughgoing intertextuality of contemporary media culture, that makes genre not less but more pertinent to understanding contemporary Hollywood. In other words, we need to stop seeing genre as a one-dimensional entity descriptive of Hollywood's historical output and to recast it as a ubiquitous contemporary phenomenon common to all instances of discourse. And, as Steve Neale argues, one implication of this multifaceted (re) conceptualisation of genre is that we must modify both the perception and location of Hollywood genres: 'No longer the sole or even the principal site of genre in the cinema, Hollywood instead becomes just one particular site, its genres specific instances – not necessarily paradigms – of a much more general phenomenon' (Neale 2000: 31). Clearly, then, much turns on how we choose to define genre.

studio system
Usually seen to have developed *circa* 1920 and lasting until *circa* 1950, the studio system indicates the period of Hollywood history in which the major studios controlled all aspects of the production, distribution and exhibition of their products.

postmodern
Used by critics in a number of different ways, it can refer to the contemporary historical moment (the period after modernity); an artistic or aesthetic style which privileges surface appearances over 'deep meaning' or 'truth' (characterised by strategies of irony, **intertextuality**, pastiche, bricolage, **eclecticism**, **self-reflexivity**); and a theoretical position which adopts a sceptical attitude towards totalising notions of truth, reality and progress.

intertextuality
This term, strongly linked with **postmodernism**, designates, in its narrow sense, the ways in which a film either explicitly or implicitly refers to other films (e.g. through allusion, imitation, parody or pastiche), or in its broader sense, the various relationships one (film) text may have with other texts (see also **eclecticism**, **palimpsest**).

eclecticism
An aesthetic style in which a new composition is assembled wholly or in part from elements selected from a range of previous styles, forms, texts, genres drawn form different periods and from both high and popular culture. This is one of the principal aesthetic strategies of **postmodern** art (see also **intertextuality**, **palimpsest** (p. 121), **self-reflexivity**).

DEFINING GENRE(S)

At a general level work on genre seeks to understand film as a *specific form of commodity* and at a more refined level attempts to disentangle *different instances of that commodity*. In other words, genre is addressed as a system for organising production as well as groupings of individual films which have collective and singular significance. It is important to note, however, that a number of approaches have developed that address Hollywood's generic structures, all of which are underpinned by different assumptions about the purpose of genre criticism. It is possible to trace three key lines of theoretical development here: firstly, the **taxonomic** view of genre which attempts to map the boundaries between generic classes; second, the view of genre as an economic strategy for organising film production schedules; and third, the view of genre as a function of cognition, as a contract between producers and consumers which on some level renders films intelligible to their audiences.

Genre as taxonomy

Tom Ryall argues that 'if genre criticism were simply a matter of constructing taxonomies and allocating films to their places in the system, then the intellectual basis of the exercise would certainly be open to doubt' (Ryall 1998: 336). While Ryall is right to caution against viewing genre criticism *merely* as a question of fitting films into their appropriate generic hole, it nevertheless remains the case that the question of genre routinely emerges as a border dispute: defining the boundaries between one genre and another. For whatever else it might be, genre implies a process of categorisation; that is to say, sorting cultural products into discrete groupings based on similarities and common properties. Here, defining genre involves a twofold process: describing the differences between individual genres, that is, between thrillers, westerns, musicals, horror films, gangster films, action movies and so forth, as well as mapping the common elements that members of any one genre share. Indeed, the notions of *difference* and *sameness* that taxonomies imply are, albeit in various ways, central to all generic criticism. As such, Richard Maltby argues that the genre critic seeks to 'place movies into generic categories as a way of dividing up the cinematic map of Hollywood into smaller, more manageable, and relative discrete areas' (Maltby 2003: 75). So despite the paradox implicit in this process noted by Neale – that, on the one hand, genre critics insist on 'the importance of genre as a means of conceptualising links between Hollywood's films and US society' while, on the other hand, using genre as a way of 'avoiding detailed study of anything other than selective samples' of those films – critics have nevertheless devised a number of methods of classification, a range of strategies precisely for producing a typology of cinematic genres and associated typologies of films. Indeed, as I discuss below, while it is neither possible nor desirable to annex genre studies exclusively to the process of classifying cultural texts into their 'proper' corpuses, it remains the case that to engage in the study of genre necessitates on some level or another an engagement with ideas of identification, association, filiation and differentiation. Quite how critics have gone about this sorting process, however, has resulted in the production of typologies of vastly different size, scale and complexity.

Theoretical taxonomies

In *Poetics*, perhaps the *locus classicus* of genre studies, Aristotle sets out to categorise poetry into its 'various kinds' on the basis of the apparently incontrovertible properties of the poetic text. As Rick Altman points out, this move 'set genre theory on to a virtually unbroken course of textual analysis' (Altman 1999: 2–3). Moreover, it is founded on certain problematic assumptions to do not only with the model of genre it implies – that genre is somehow already 'out there' as an essential structure of texts – but also to do with the activity of 'doing genre studies' – the application of theoretical and analytical

---

taxonomic
See **taxonomy**

taxonomy
The practice of classification. In this sense, the practice of classifying films into groups based on similarities of form and/ or content.

rigour in the description and coding of texts in order to uncover their distinct internal characteristics. While the former assumption rests on the ahistorical premise that genre exists in itself and that it inevitably has essential qualities that can be revealed through proper analysis, the latter assumption tends to mask the productive role of critics/scholars in the definition of generic categories and the institutional frameworks within which such practices take place. Nevertheless, despite these problems, problems which Altman argues have had the effect of 'narrowing genre theory ever since', Aristotle's model of genre analysis has proved remarkably influential and durable (Altman 1999: 2). So, in the same way that Aristotle identifies the epic, comedy, tragedy and so forth as essential genres of poetry insofar as they are seen to exist in themselves as 'pure' categories of literature, Alan Williams has identified the principal film genres as the narrative film, experimental/avant-garde film and the documentary (Williams 1984: 121). For Williams, these categories are the conceptual equivalent of, and thus share the same sense of permanence as, those described by Aristotle. He argues that, in reserving this general or theoretical level for the term genre, 'then film genres will by definition have the staying power seen in literary genres' (ibid.: 122). On this account, the labels we ordinarily use to distinguish between films of various kinds – thriller, horror, comedy, romance, and so on – actually refer to sub-genres of the narrative film.

There are, however, a number of problems with imposing theoretical generic categories onto cinema. First, and most obviously, it is counterintuitive in the sense that genre becomes abstracted from both industrial and cultural usages of the term. Second, ascending to this level of theoretical abstraction tends to belie the inherent complexity of cinematic forms. For instance, animation doesn't fit comfortably into any of Williams's categories in the sense that animation's fundamentally graphic economy permits it to straddle those categories which are clearly erected to describe photographic modes of enunciation. One answer would be to put forward animation as a fourth principal genre. Yet this simply compounds the fundamental problem of theoretically instigated cinematic genres insofar as the complex and highly productive relationship between animation and narrative, non-fiction and experimental film, would be further obfuscated behind discrete generic walls. A similar problem arises in the distinction between narrative and documentary film in that narrative is every bit as important and complex in documentary forms as in fictional forms. Indeed, as Alan Renov notes, the distinction between fiction and documentary genres is an unsustainable one given that 'nonfiction contains any number of "fictive" elements' to the extent that 'it might be said that the two domains inhabit one another' (Renov 1993: 2, 3).

Historical taxonomies

Given the problems of defining genre and drawing classificatory boundaries using a set of theoretical principles, most critical writing has adopted a more historical stance to genre in seeking to map more selective 'groupings of actual films inductively linked on the basis of common themes, styles and **iconography**' (Ryall 1998: 329). Instead of asking questions such as 'What markers of cinematographic representation differentiate one genre from the next?', an historical approach to genre asks, 'What distinguishes a western from a gangster film, a thriller from a crime movie?' and so forth, and 'how does an individual western film relate to the broader category of the western?', and 'why are certain genres popular at particular times, but not at others?' In short, unlike the essentialism implied by purely theoretical definitions of genre, this model of genre criticism attempts to cut cinema at its generic joints precisely by acknowledging the historical contingency of generic forms. A variety of tactics have been used to make the dissection ranging from attention to a genre's relation to history; to common subject matter, themes and content; to the presence of certain shared formal elements; to their intended affect on the audience; to looser groupings organised around stylistic or cinematographic properties. Table 8.1 schematises some of the different ways in which genres may be seen to be held together.

iconography
A term used to describe and categorise visual motifs in films. It is usually associated with genre insofar as visual patterns of setting, dress, props and style have been used to classify and analyse films generically, but it also shares similarities with **mise-en-scène**.

Genre	Defining criteria	Differentiating criteria
Western		American West in the second half of the nineteenth century
Gangster film		1920s urban America
Epic	Historical subject	Large-scale productions usually about biblical or ancient history/myths
War film		Specific historical conflicts
Biopic		Story of a historical or significant person's life, or portion of a life
Film noir		Postwar America
Horror		Intended to horrify or scare
Thriller	Intended affect	Intended to thrill and excite
Comedy		Generation of laughter
Musical		Presence of diegetic song and dance performances
Action movie	Formal criteria	Presence of hyperbolic action set pieces and spectacular visual effects
Pornography		Presence of sex acts
Science fiction		Futuristic technologies/future worlds
Fantasy		Impossible worlds/fantastical characters
Disaster		Natural or man-made catastrophe
Crime film	Subject matter	The perpetration and investigation of criminal activities
Melodrama		Domestic drama and heterosexual romance
Road movie		Journey or road-trip, usually across America
Film noir		Crime and institutional corruption
Children's films	Target audience	Stories designed for consumption by children
Family movie		Stories designed for consumption by family groups
Blockbuster	Style	Narrative organised around spectacular events
Film noir		Chiaroscuro lighting/dark mise-en-scène

Table 8.1

However, if such schematisation does demonstrate *possible* criteria for differentiating genres, it also belies the inherent complexity and mutability of generic definitions. For example, as indicated in Table 8.1, film noir could quite easily sit in any one of three groupings, or all three simultaneously depending on which criteria one chooses to privilege. Alternatively, we could make the case, as many critics have done, that film noir is, in fact, not a genre at all but merely a particular stylistic inflection of the crime film. Moreover, and notwithstanding a host of further possible objections one might raise, not only is it possible to relocate, say, the western and gangster film to the category demarcated by formal criteria on the basis of the presence of 'the gun fight' and 'the shoot-out' respectively, but we might also collapse all categories into the one which sees differences exclusively in terms of subject matter. It is also possible, for that matter, to locate all of the above groups as subcategories of the feature film – Hollywood's principal product – and to therefore argue that all films are fundamentally multi-generic.

Part of the problem with this method of genre building, of course, is that genres are defined in a number of different contexts. So while some genres such as the western and the musical are established industrial categories of production readily recognised by both filmmakers and audiences, others, such as the 'gross-out comedy', or 'torture porn' are constructed by critics only after the film has been released. Moreover, generic labels generated by critics are often appropriated into studio production cycles and marketing materials while the most long-standing generic categories continue to act as a key point of reference in the critical evaluation of a film.

By the same token, such highly schematised generic classifications suffer from what Stam calls the problem of extension – the implied scope of a generic category (Stam 2000a: 128). For example, herding films together under the generic banner 'comedy' seems straightforward enough but actually tells us very little about individual films beyond the intention to incite laughter. For if the 'generation of laughter' is the comedy genre's definitive convention then not only does it, by definition, mark all modes of comedy – slapstick, screwball, farce, satire, parody – but also encompasses the comic elements or funny moments that routinely appear in most if not all other genres. Indeed, the co-presence of laughter and fear is common to the horror film, while compound generic categorisations such as romantic comedy, sex comedy and gross-out comedy address at promotional and journalistic levels precisely comedy's nomadic generic existence. Approaching the same problem of extension from the opposite end, if comedy seems too broad as a class, then 'funny films about paranoid retired CIA agents', or 'science fiction films concerning time travel' seem too narrow. Either way, the issue of extension betrays the fundamental difficulty of demarcating generic borders in any empirically reliable or conceptually final way, a problem telescoped by the extreme eclecticism and **self-reflexivity** of much of contemporary Hollywood. To take just one example, *Moulin Rouge* (Baz Luhrmann, 2001) is simultaneously distinguished historically (its depiction of *fin-de-siècle* Paris); formally (the performance of song and dance routines); stylistically (an exemplar of postmodern filmmaking); and in terms of its organisation of subject matter (quasi-melodramatic narrative of heterosexual romance).

Visual taxonomies

From the late 1960s critics attempted to refine the ways of defining the criteria which policed generic boundaries. Derived from art history, and in particular from the work of Erwin Panofsky, the notion of iconography seemed to offer an empirical methodology more suited to the task of classifying cinema's visual terrain. As Ed Buscombe writes, 'since we are dealing with a visual medium we ought surely to look for our defining criteria at what we actually see on the screen' (in Neale 1980: 12). Thus, strictly aesthetic criteria – variously referred to as 'motifs', 'visual conventions', 'patterns of visual imagery' and 'sign-events' – were seen as essential indicators of generic differentiation. Simply stated, an iconographic approach to genre analysis involved the identification, description and interpretation of cinematic objects, events, figures, and so forth in order to see how one type of film was marked off from another on the basis of differences in visual conventions. As such, the western was distinguished by its settings, both specific and general (the West, the frontier, deserts, mountains, Monument Valley, saloons, homesteads); costume (the Stetson, waistcoat, gun belts, boots, chaps and spurs of the cowboy; the facial paint, feathered head-dress of the Indian; the tight-bodiced dress and gartered stockings of the Saloon whore); specificities of props (Colt 45, horses – especially pintos – bows and arrows); even individual actors (John Wayne, Gary Cooper, Clint Eastwood).

However, if an attention to iconography worked well for the western and gangster film, it proved difficult to translate such a visually specific methodology to other kinds of films. For instance, it is difficult to isolate distinct iconographic systems for crime films, thrillers, film noirs and most action films with any clarity. Guns and weaponry are common to each and, unlike the western and gangster film, there is not necessarily any historically specific criteria to regulate aspects of setting and costume. Moreover, consideration of comedy and animation once again tends to blunt the usefulness of iconography as a generic arbitrator. In the case of the former there is no connection between the comic elements of a film and specific iconography beyond the incidental deployment of resources (verbal, physical and material) in gag-specific scenarios, while

self-reflexivity
Used to describe films or texts which self-consciously acknowledge or reflect upon their own status as fictional artefacts and/or the processes involved in their creation. This is one of the principal aesthetic strategies of **postmodern** art (see also **eclecticism**, **intertextuality**, **palimpsest**).

the self-enunciating visual language of animation has an abstract or arbitrary relation to the concept of iconography insofar as the notions of setting, costume and props are always provisional.

Multi-dimensional taxonomies

In criticising tautological approaches to genre devoted to the discovery and analysis of individual genres, Tom Ryall argues that 'by and large genre criticism has confined itself to producing taxonomies on the basis of "family resemblances", allocating films to their position within generic constellations, stopping short of what are the interesting and informative questions about generic groupings' (Ryall 1975–76: 27). A decade later, Rick Altman made a similar complaint in suggesting that, following the logic laid out by Aristotle, genres continue to be 'treated as if they spring full-blown from the head of Zeus' and that even some of the more sophisticated attempts to understand generic texts 'still hold on to a notion of genre that is fundamentally ahistorical in nature' (Altman 1984: 8). Both authors called for a less reductive approach to genre, one which was both theoretically plausible and sensitive to the historical conditions in which genres circulated and were consumed by audiences. Indeed, Ryall himself put forward what he termed a new 'master image for genre criticism' consisting of 'a triangle composed of artist/ structures/audience'. From this basis, he argues, 'genres may be defined as 'patterns/ forms/styles/structures which transcend individual films, and which supervise both their construction by the film maker, and their reading by an audience' (Ryall 1975–76: 28). On this account, each genre is a rule-governed territory, one which shares a conventionality not only of visual imagery, but more complexly of particular expectations of plot and narrative structure, and how these, in turn, motivate and justify the specificities of props, costume, milieux and subject matter within and across the generic spectrum. Thus, guns are common to westerns, thrillers, gangster films, action films, film noirs, war films and science fiction films, but their significance, function and consequences differ depending on a host of other contextualising factors established in the narrative and thematic structures of genre films. For Ryall, therefore, genre is not a transhistorical property of the film text, but rather a complex socio-cultural negotiation between the film industry and film reviewers on the one hand, and audience expectations and competencies on the other.

Despite the more nuanced approaches to genre suggested by Ryall (1975–76) and Altman (1984), as well as Neale (1980, 1990), it nevertheless remained the case that critics tended to mobilise the expanded definitions they put forward for taxonomic ends. There are two complementary and contradictory aspects to this. On the one hand, given that the checklist of generic markers had apparently been broadened, more films could be added to encyclopaedic lists of genre films. On the other hand, however, in the face of such an inexorable growth of generic corpora, critics could once again become preoccupied by the desire to find generic exemplars; that is to say, those films which are deemed to represent a specific genre more completely and more faithfully than others. These responses, of course, are really only two sides of the same taxonomic coin: the first aims to produce an *inclusive* list of all possible instances of a genre while the second concerns itself with an *exclusive* list of classical instances in the hope of discerning the 'true' structure and meaning of a genre.

The limits of generic taxonomies

Even if a taxonomic approach to genre offers a way of managing, organising, and interrogating vast numbers of films and can, as Gledhill argues, operate as a useful 'empirical tool for collating the range of cultural knowledges' which genres assume, this kind of approach inevitably privileges the analysis of the structural components of individual genres, however defined, over the more general theoretical questions relating to the nature and operation as genre (Gledhill 1999: 140). Moreover, in the end, all taxonomic writing on genre suffers from what Andrew Tudor calls the 'empiricist dilemma' – the inescapable circular logic which means that to study, say, a western in order to define its distinctive generic characteristics the critic must *already* know what those characteristics are in order to identify it as a western in the first place, yet such an identification ought surely to be made on the evidence of the film *after* it has been watched. Thus, the genre critic is 'caught in a circle which first requires that the films be isolated, for which purposes a criterion is necessary, but the criterion is, in turn, meant to emerge from the empirically established common characteristics of the films' (Tudor 1974: 137). The result of this logic, for Tudor at least, is that 'genre is what we collectively believe it to be' (ibid.: 139).

GENRE AS ECONOMIC STRATEGY

If taxonomic approaches to genre ask questions such as 'How do we cut cinema at its generic joints?', and 'Have we drawn our lines in the correct places?', then an economic approach to genre asks 'What functions does genre perform?' This refocusing directs attention to the role genre plays within the industrial practices and structures of Hollywood. Indeed, genre criticism is often justified precisely on the grounds that, unlike most other approaches, it is plugged into Hollywood's commercial practices in the first instance and that there is a correspondence between its object of inquiry – genres – and the ways in which Hollywood seeks to organise its output in the last instance. So even if, as Neale points out, film companies rarely planned or plan their production schedules in terms which correspond exactly with traditional critical conceptions of genre, and notwithstanding reductive histories of the studio era which attempt to simply equate specific studios with the production of specific genres, it nevertheless remains the case that genre serves as a useful tool for understanding the capitalist business practices in which films are both produced and consumed (see Neale 2000). Simply put, despite the 'facelessness' of contemporary American genre filmmaking identified by Wheeler Winston Dixon, and the 'more of the same' logic which he suggests now drives Hollywood production schedules, what is incontestable is that every film *is* different (Winston Dixon 2000: 1, 8). As such, production and promotion are governed not simply by the need to employ familiar ingredients and recycle previous products in order to secure maximum capital returns, but also by the need to celebrate and sell difference. Indeed, it is precisely in respect of this tension between the 'tried and tested' and the 'new and unknown', that is to say, between formula and innovation, that Hollywood's generic regime performs two crucial interrelated functions: to guarantee meanings and pleasures for audiences; and to offset the considerable economic risks of industrial film production by providing cognitive collateral against innovation and difference. Let us consider these one at a time.

Generic pleasures

Genre works to stabilise or regulate particular desires, expectations and pleasures offered by the cinema. On this account, while genre is not simply an institutionalised strategy to delimit choice, if we choose to watch, say, a horror film, then we expect certain pleasures in return: that we will encounter, and be scared by, a monster of some description; that some characters will be killed by the monster while one, usually the lead character, will kill it; and so on. By the same token, each genre implies its own set of desires, expectations and pleasures. Indeed, Neale argues that much of the pleasure of popular cinema lies precisely in the process of 'difference *in* repetition', that is, both in the recognition of the familiar elements of a generic framework *and* in the way individual instances of that genre introduce unfamiliar elements or orchestrate familiar elements in more or less original ways. This process perhaps finds its most refined expression in films such as the *Scream* or *Saw* series which transpose certain familiar elements across successive sequels while at the same time incorporating new material into each individual film. Yet the same pull between familiarity and difference is no less crucial to looser generic groupings. For the success of, say, any individual action film, both in terms of the profit it generates and the pleasures it affords audiences, is rooted not simply in its promise to deliver action set-pieces but, more accurately, in the expectation that *the way it delivers its action* will be, at least on some level, notably distinct from other action films.

Genre as insurance policy

The capital-intensive nature of Hollywood film production requires a market of sufficient size to generate surplus revenue in order to both satisfy investors and plough back into future productions. This means that, as far as possible, the economic risk associated with any individual film must be contained insofar as its potential market must be predictable. Genres, on this view, allow the film industry to offset some of its financial investments against the cognitive collateral of presold generic expectations and pleasures. Neale writes that genres are crucial to industrial modes of film production inasmuch as they 'serve as basic and "convenient" units for the calculation of investment and profit, and as basic and "convenient" categories in which to organise capital assets so as to ensure that their capacity will be utilised to the maximum' (Neale 1980: 53). While this economic logic does not account for the existence of mass-produced genres *per se*, nor the emergence and popularity of any one genre at any one time, it nevertheless does, at least in part, explain why Hollywood is a cinema of genres.

However, Darley argues that in an age of visual digital culture characterised by aesthetic and economic synthesis between media formats we cannot regard genre in the same way, that cultural production is now organised around principles other than generic ones. He refers to this shift as a 'poetics of repetition', a situation in which 'old categories and boundaries are breaking down, blurring in the face of self-referential impulses spawned by new technological development' (Darley 2000: 142). Darley argues that, while the modifying variable, or differential element of the 'difference in repetition' model of commodity production, 'is even more vital today, precisely because of the apparent de-differentiation that is under way', at the same time the markers of difference become 'smaller in scale and simpler in operation: a mechanism for miniscule formal or surface distinctions' (ibid.: 143). Within this intensified mode of commodity production, he claims, the idea of genre is merely nominal, and, moreover, that the notion of *seriality* is 'coming to replace or subsume genre in more recent manifestations of mass visual culture':

> Seriality is akin to genre ... and yet it is subtly different from it. The serial mode appears to operate and organise – in the first instance at any rate – at a more general or inclusive level than does genre, whilst at the same time being more precise and prescriptive in terms of the processes it defines. Lacking the more open (and involved) character of genre, it appears to be tied as much to the demarcation and regulation of *forms and modes* within material production processes as to the distinguishing of types or kinds (along with their aesthetic delineation) in aesthetic ones. It seems thereby, to be more intimately bound to the standardisation involved in commodification itself.
>
> (ibid.: 126)

This is instructive for a number or reasons. First, the notion of seriality directs our attention towards Hollywood's predilection for sequels, prequels, series, follow-ups and franchises not in terms of their putative aesthetic paucity, but rather as the most potent distillation, besides rereleases, of the economic imperatives of genre described by Neale. Second, the notion of 'mode' might represent a more persuasive description of contemporary Hollywood production trends. That is, notions of 'the blockbuster', 'special effects movies', 'event cinema', 'summer movie', even 'action cinema' which tend to fall outside of, or in between, traditional generic groupings, are perhaps more plausibly described as *modes* of filmmaking which, in turn, entail particular modes of viewing. Third, subsuming genre within a broader poetics of repetition which frames contemporary cultural practice permits us to see cinema as an *intermedia*, that is, as thoroughly implicated in a bi-directional system of aesthetic commodification exchange which extends far beyond its own textual and formal borders through merchandising, product tie-ins, product placements, franchise deals, branding, sequels, TV spin-offs, video games, novelisations, and other forms of adaptation and appropriation. In this sense, the notion of film genre dissolves into much more multiple and diverse commercial configurations of *themed entertainment*.

It would, however, be premature to entirely abandon the notion of genre to seriality in seeking to understand the economies of contemporary film production. While the term *genre* struggles to cope with much of contemporary Hollywood in terms of both manufacturing principles and aesthetic classification, the prominence of generic motifs within marketing and promotion campaigns seems to be increasing in importance insofar as, today, 'the commercial drama surrounding a movie's promotion can say as much as the fictional drama of the film itself' (Watson 1997: 79). Indeed, the idea of film as merely a pretext or staging ground for a much more extensive commercial venture often goes hand in hand with marketing strategies which foreground generic discourses in a hypervisible display of its attractions. On this view, the modal seriality of contemporary Hollywood production and the primacy of generic imagery in promotional material can be seen as two sides of the same process – the institutionalisation of exploitation cinema: a mode of film production in which textual considerations are subordinate to the considerations of marketing and promotion (see ibid.).

GENRE AS COGNITION

Neale argues that 'genres are not simply bodies of work, however classified, labelled and designed' (Neale 1990: 46). On the contrary, he sees genre as being equally constituted by 'specific systems of expectation and hypothesis which spectators bring with them to the cinema and which interact with the films themselves during the course of the viewing process' (ibid.: 46). The clear implication of this observation is that the question of film genre can be posed not merely along industrial and aesthetic axes of the cinematic process, but as a question of film comprehension insofar as cognitive primacy is afforded to the spectator in the act of reading a film. Another way of making this point is to say that the question of film genre is, in fact, part of much broader questions to do with cultural cognition and structures of visual communication. As such, the purpose of genre criticism may be regarded as an inquiry into how we make meaning from film.

On this cognitive view, textual conventions are important not as a means of dissecting cinema into discrete categories, but instead for the way they activate certain mental processes in what Jonathan Culler calls the 'operations of reading'. He argues that 'the function of genre conventions is essentially to establish a contract between writer and reader so as to make certain relevant expectations operative and thus permit both compliance and deviation from accepted modes of intelligibility' (Culler 1975: 147). As Culler suggests, acts of communication are rendered intelligible only within the context of a shared, conventional framework of expression. Ryall notes that for Hollywood films this communal framework is provided by the generic system which constructs a framework for comprehension, an 'ideal world' or 'fictional reality' through which the individual film 'sustains at least some of its levels of comprehensibility and maybe its dominant level of comprehensibility' (Ryall 1998: 336). Genre, here, becomes understood not as a corpus of comparable films, but as provisional and malleable conceptual environments: a cognitive repository of images, sounds, characters, events, stories, scenarios, expectations and so on. Genre may thus be seen as part of a cognitive process which delimits the number of possible meanings of any individual film by activating certain conceptual constellations while leaving others dormant.

sophisticated hyperconsciousness
A term used by Jim Collins to describe the extreme 'knowingness' and high degree of media literacy evinced by both contemporary cinema and its audience.

Such a cognitive view of film genre not only forestalls the taxonomic impulses of much genre criticism by reformulating genre as fundamentally an intertextual process, but is more sensitive to what Jim Collins calls the '**sophisticated hyperconsciousness**' of contemporary Hollywood cinema (Collins 1995: 133). Collins argues that in the same way that television changed the production, circulation and consumption of popular entertainment during the 1950s and 1960s, contemporary Hollywood cinema marks a 'new form of entertainment', one which is simultaneously a response and a contribution to media-saturated culture (ibid.: 156). 'Genericity' is the term he chooses to deploy in order to describe the shift in production and consumption initiated 'by the ever increasing number of entertainment options and the fragmentation of what was once thought to be a mass audience into a cluster of "target" audiences' (ibid.: 128). Indeed, the eclecticism and appropriationism of popular cinema today involves levels of hybridity and inter-textuality that work 'at cross-purposes with the traditional notion of genre as a stable, integrated set of narrative and stylistic conventions' (ibid.: 126). In short, many contemporary Hollywood films are composed almost entirely of generic elements hijacked from the image banks of both popular and high culture and reassembled in ways that either circumnavigate, short-circuit or contradict singular generic understanding.

□ CASE STUDY 1: FROM TEXT TO INTERTEXT: GENERICITY AND *MOULIN ROUGE*

As a number of critics are now rightly pointing out, it would be a mistake to assume that generic hybridity, intertextuality and allusion are simply products of either the post-studio era or the postmodern film. Indeed, genre mixing is not a recent fad but is both a crucial aspect in the creation and evolution of genres themselves and a long-standing economic and stylistic strategy used by Hollywood to produce and promote new products. However, it is also the case that an increasing number of contemporary films display not only a flagrant disregard for generic boundaries, but also seem to revel in blatant referentiality. For instance, about half-way into *From Dusk Till Dawn* (1996), at the precise moment when Salma Hayek's character transforms from a border-town showgirl into a vampire, the film shifts genres from a thriller to schlock-horror. The robbery–hijack premise which motivates the first half of the narrative is thoroughly recast around different generic conventions: the loot cannot buy them safety, guns are rendered defunct as, in the battle against the undead, impromptu crosses and crucifixes are the order of the day. If *From Dusk Till Dawn* exemplifies the shapeshifting possibilities of the contemporary genre film then, as Anton Bitel (2011) has noted, *Skyline* (2010) signals the extent to which contemporary cinema is 'genre savvy' insofar as it blatantly co-opts and redeploys narrative scenarios and action set pieces culled from films such as *The Brain from Planet Arous* (1957), *Independence Day* (1996), *Signs* (2002), *The War of the Worlds* (2005), *Cloverfield* (2008) and *District 9* (2009). Moreover, the intertextual overload that characterises *The Matrix* trilogy (1999, 2003, 2003) not only defies singular generic description but offers a challenge to the idea of generic law. Indeed, its various generic echoes are not simply *mixed* together, but *remixed* into an eclectic techno-aesthetic comprised from cinema, of course, but also video games, anime, comic books, music videos, cyberpunk novels, and postmodern philosophy, all rendered through a seamless fusion of live action and computer animation.

However, in looking to identify exemplars of the way certain contemporary Hollywood films operate through intertextual aesthetic strategies we could do worse than start with *Moulin Rouge* (2001). Indeed, to ask what genre the film belongs to we have to be ready to say 'feature-length music video' as readily as 'musical', 'blockbuster' as easily as 'a Baz Luhrmann film', 'postmodern film' as quickly as 'American film', and 'romance' as swiftly as 'star vehicle'. For *Moulin Rouge*'s giddy assemblage of cinematic refer-ences, historical intertexts and cultural allusions simultaneously *defies* singular generic categorisation yet *implies* a high degree of prior orientation with precisely those generic formations in order to comprehend their disorientation and rearticulation. So while on one level the film may be described generically, and was promoted generically – as a musical which tells of the tragic love affair between a penniless writer and a starlet showgirl – this actually tells us very little either about the semiotic excess of the film or the cultural literacy it demands of its audience. Likewise, if, as many critics have hinted, *Moulin Rouge* redefines the film musical it does so partly by wrenching itself free of musical conventions and hooking up with a range of other generic formations, most obviously the music video, but also Bollywood, burlesque theatre, television advertisements, and computer animation. Indeed, almost every shot is an ironic collage of popular cultural images and sounds, conjuring up a highly eclectic range of intertexts from the past and the present in a sophisticated **palimpsest** image. The result is a text which is simultaneously *decorative*, demanding to be looked at, and *dense*, demanding to the read *through*.

We can begin to apprehend the film's exhilarating eclecticism through analysis of the way it first introduces us to the Moulin Rouge. Indeed, while on a general stylistic level the sheer excess of the scene not only recalls the set-piece dance extravaganzas of Busby Berkeley's Warner musicals and the graphic energy of many of Toulouse Lautrec's studies of Cancan girls, but at a more specific level the entrance of Satine (Nicole Kidman) begs comparison to Lola-Lola, the Cabaret artist played by Marlene Dietrich in *The Blue Angel* (1930) (see Plates 8.1 and 8.2). Moreover, as Satine begins to sing the opening lines of 'Diamonds Are a Girl's Best Friend', a song made famous by Marilyn Monroe's performance of Lorelei Lee in *Gentlemen Prefer Blondes* (1953), it is not only the song which is 'out of time', but also Kidman's raspy vocal performance. However, when she later shifts style and launches into the chorus of 'Material Girl', it is not simply the image of Madonna which the film inherits, but that of Monroe once again, since in the video for the song Madonna is dressed as Monroe in her pink gown from the 'Diamonds' number (*see Plates 8.3, 8.4 and 8.5*).

Moreover, not only does the scene itself unfold around a melody, or more precisely a remix, of 'classic' popular music, but much of the film's dialogue is a montage of lines hijacked from the lyrics of popular ballads, love songs and well-known literature. 'Love is a many-splendoured thing, love lifts us up where we belong, all you need is love' Christian (Ewan McGregor) waxes lyrical to Satine. Indeed, if on the one hand the film may be seen as a relatively 'old-fashioned' love story then, on the other, the pathos that attends the tale, if in fact there is any at all, is entirely generated through the co-option and rearticulation of romantic sentiments that have *already* been said and which are

palimpsest
Defined literally, a palimpsest is a manuscript written over a previous text that has been entirely or partly erased. In a figurative sense, however, the term is often used to describe a film or text with multiple levels of meaning created through dense layers of **intertextuality**. In this way, the term has become associated with **postmodern** aesthetics.

• **Plate 8.1**
Moulin Rouge (Baz Luhrmann, 2001). As Satine (Nicole Kidman) descends towards the drooling punters on a swing, she is dressed in a manner which closely resembles Marlene Dietrich in *The Blue Angel* (1930)

• **Plate 8.2**
Der Blaue Engel/The Blue Angel (Josef von Sternberg, 1930). Marlene Dietrich plays nightclub songstress Lola-Lola – an image which is appropriated in Luhrmann's *Moulin Rouge* (2001)

• **Plate 8.3**
Moulin Rouge (Baz Luhrmann, 2001). As Satine (Nicole Kidman) begins to sing 'Diamonds Are a Girl's Best Friend' the film recalls the image of Marilyn Monroe performing the same number in *Gentlemen Prefer Blondes* (1953)

• **Plate 8.4**
Gentlemen Prefer Blondes (Howard Hawks, 1953). Lorelei Lee (Marilyn Monroe) performs the famous 'Diamonds Are a Girl's Best Friend' song and dance number. This sequence is summoned up as part of *Moulin Rouge*'s multi-layered intertextuality

• **Plate 8.5**
Material Girl (Mary Lambert, 1985). When
in *Moulin Rouge* Satine segues from
'Diamonds Are a Girl's Best Friend' to
'Material Girl' it is not simply Madonna
who is inscribed but Monroe again, since
Madonna has already hijacked Monroe's
image from *Gentlemen Prefer Blondes* and
reactivated it in this video

already familiar because they are in constant circulation in the imaginative landscape of popular culture. It is in this respect that McGregor's rendition of Elton John's 'Your Song' functions simultaneously as the film's authentic emotional refrain and clearest marker of its thoroughgoing inauthenticity.

In these ways, then, *Moulin Rouge*'s textual articulations are, in fact, always double articulations insofar as its images and sounds relate to both the internal narrative and aesthetic 'life' of the film as well as to their external 'lives' in popular culture. The fact that the film's textual and emotional economies proceed almost entirely through quotation reflects not just the increasing sophistication of the genre text *per se*, but also a change in terms of audience competence and the kinds of pleasures associated with contemporary manifestations of genre cinema. For the co-presence of generic traces from a number of different forms of popular culture, as well as from a number of specific different generic texts assembled from a range of different historical periods, results not in the collapse of genre into an 'anything-goes' version of postmodernism, but more precisely in a kind of meta-genre. In other words, individual generic features are not the property of specific genres but rather mediated *artefacts* which circulate through popular culture, retaining traces of their past articulation but which are reinscribed in the present moment. *Moulin Rouge*, then, may be understood as an extreme version of what Collins calls a 'techno-palimpsest', that is to say, a film in which a whole host of generic traces can be 'immediately called up, back to the surface to be replayed, or more precisely, recirculated' (Collins 1995: 139). And, of course, if judged by the referents of the 'classic film musical', then many of its quotations, allusions and appropriations seem inappropriate. However, the main point is that they are entirely appropriate to a culture in which past and future co-exist in/with the present and in which an increasing amount of popular entertainment is predicated on profound intertextuality and the reactivation of past generic artefacts. In this way, then, *Moulin Rouge*, like so much of contemporary Hollywood, presents us with a generic paradox: simultaneously being *post-generic* in the sense that the hyperconsciousness of its text spills over singular classificatory boundaries yet attaining intelligibility precisely in relation to those generic formations.

RETHINKING GENRE: MULTIPLICITY AND METAPHOR

Most of the more interesting recent work on film genre picks up on this expanded and more complex configuration of textuality, history and economics that bears upon the operation and meanings of both individual films and the concept of genre as such and has sought to situate the study of genre within the broader 'inter-textual relay' in which

extra-textual
In a broad sense,
designates the 'outside'
of the film/text, the range
of cultural texts which
relate in some way to
the film/text, but in a
narrower sense refers to
the non-filmic intertexts
which in varying degrees
relate to the film/text
(such as marketing and
promotional materials,
film reviews, and so on).

cinema is figured (see Neale 2000). In other words, in departing from traditional notions of genre as a stable system for classifying films into their proper grouping, a system untroubled by historical and cultural change, this work has approached genre as a multi-faceted discursive system involving not only the films themselves but also a whole range of other **extra-textual** and cultural phenomena. For some critics this has meant paying much more careful attention to the historical conditions which give rise to a genre in the first place and in which any given instance of 'genre cinema' circulates and is under-stood by its audience. This (re)turn to history no longer prioritises the film itself as reliable evidence for the definition and circulation of genres, but affords primacy to institutional categories, marketing materials and journalistic practices which are seen to provide original and contemporaneous testimony to generic configurations. Indeed, in recog-nising the limitations of his earlier text-centred work, Neale argues that not only do such industrial, cultural and journalistic labels constitute crucial evidence for understanding both the significance of genre to industry and audiences in the present moment, they also offer 'virtually the only available evidence for a historical study of the array of genres in circulation, or of the ways in which individual films have been generically perceived at any one point in time' (Neale 1990: 52). One notable example of this kind of work is Mike Chopra-Gant's (2005) re-evaluation of popular US cinema in the postwar period, specifi-cally those films released in 1946. On the basis of his analysis of the publicity material used by the studios to promote the films released that year, he argues that there is a glaring inconsistency between standard academic accounts of genre cinema during that period and the empirical data. So while critics have tended to focus on film noir as the significant genre of the postwar period inasmuch as it seemed to capture the zeitgeist of an anxious nation as it moved from war to peace, Chopra-Gant suggests that, in fact, 'two generic subsets' of movie predominate in the promotional strategies of the studios, the 'quality narrative film' and the 'sensuous, spectacular film' (ibid.: 131). Importantly, however, he argues that, despite these discrepancies between genre scholarship and genre practice, what this shift in methodology reveals is that 'generic hybridity rather than purity' appears to be the norm (ibid.).

In *Film/Genre* (1999), Rick Altman maps out a similar, yet distinct, model of generic analysis offered by Neale and pursued by Chopra-Gant, one he calls a 'semantic/ syntactic/pragmatic approach'. In refusing the textual determinacy of previous work and basing his own analysis on a general theory of meaning, he argues that 'what we call *genre* is in fact something quite different from what has always been supposed' (Altman 1999: 214). Indeed, his work stresses precisely the multivalence of the term *genre*, a term used differently by different users for different purposes and which can mean multiple and often conflicting things depending on the context in which it is being used. 'While genres may make meaning by regulating and co-ordinating disparate users', he writes, 'they always do so in an arena where users with divergent interests compete to carry out their own programmes' (ibid.: 215).

The expanded, more flexible approach to genre recommended by Altman (ibid.) and Neale (1990, 2000) has many advantages. For example, it recognises that the way in which audiences 'use' genre in the comprehension of a film's textual and extra-textual codes is by no means a stable or uniform process, but one which is capable of embodying significant differences between one historical period and another, or even between one spectator and another. By extension, critics are prompted to interrogate not only those moments of 'user agreement' in which the generic labels of production and promotion unproblematically coincide with their understanding by critics, reviewers and audiences, but also those moments of conflict in which there is a distinct lack of agreement about the attribution and comprehension of generic labels. So even though it is impossible, and for that matter undesirable, to completely extract textual structures from the institutional and cultural discourses that frame them, it nevertheless remains the case that they cannot simply be collapsed into each other: to say that neither can speak independently of the other is not the same as saying that they inevitably say the same thing. One further advantage of this kind of approach is that the notion of generic evolution, so often treated as a natural and inevitable property of genre itself, can be mapped more precisely against both trends in cinema itself and broader social and historical shifts and developments more generally. Either way, the picture of genre which is emerging from work of this kind differs considerably from earlier taxonomic conceptions of the term insofar as it is concerned less with establishing a clear and stable definition of the term than with the attempt to capture and understand its multiplicities in a critical vocabulary that is simultaneously theoretically motivated and historically grounded.

It is at this point that we are able to rethink film genre not as a literal concept – as either inventories of comparable films or as an economic explanation for Hollywood's production trends – but as a *metaphorical process*. Describing film genre as a *web of metaphorical expressions* allows us to capture in our analyses some of the 'liveness', volatility and malleability of contemporary (post)generic configurations by hooking understandings of film cognition up with aesthetic and industrial aspects of the cinematic process. Another way of putting this is to say that it helps us explain *why* genre can only ever be what we collectively believe it to be. For metaphors in themselves do not tell us anything, but rather draw attention to a *relationship* between things and prompt us to start looking for ways of making meaning. Indeed, the basis of metaphor is a process of *transference*: the transference of aspects of one object to another object so that the second object has an *implied resemblance* to the first object, yet is an original expression. It is precisely the ideas of *transference* and *implied resemblance* that help us describe genre as a metaphorical process. Thus film genre becomes understood as a metaphorical redescription, reworking or redeployment of cinematic and cultural vocabularies. Individual films, likewise, become original in precisely the ways they *interfere* with those vocabularies; that is to say, in the ways they deviate from the implied intertexts which form the reservoir of cognitive resemblances that make comprehension possible. Such a metaphoric conception of film genre focuses attention on the *nature* of textual transference and the process of *interference* between intertexts – on the ways in which a film deploys familiar things in unfamiliar ways.

To see the operations of genre not as a literal, circumscribed process but as a metaphorical process is to stop asking questions such as, 'To what genre does *Moulin Rouge* belong?', and to restrict ourselves to more pragmatic questions such as, 'What other cultural objects does *Moulin Rouge* resemble?', and 'How does it cause us to compare it to other experiences?' So while on the one hand we can say that *Moulin Rouge's* opening shot of Montmartre looks *as if* it were shot by the Lumière brothers, and that Kidman sounds *like* Madonna and Monroe, on the other hand these are not literal transferrals – it is not Lumière footage and it is Kidman's voice we hear – but metaphorical expressions that alter the meanings of those extrapolations in the specific relationship of their rearticulation. It is here that a metaphorical conception of genre chimes with cognitive approaches in the sense that the spectator has to *do* something: to explore the nature of the assemblage, transferrals, and interferences in the act of comprehending the film.

Equally crucial, here, is the idea that metaphors are constantly being renewed, with old ones dying off and forming part of the cultural 'memory bank' which itself serves as the foil for the creation of new ones. In other words, *Moulin Rouge's* kaleidoscope of generic metaphors are themselves unrepeatable, but will be assimilated into our shared cognitive frameworks which then serve to throw future metaphors of expression into relief. For instance, the recent advert (2010) for the UK frozen foods supermarket Iceland works as a reprise of the scene in which Christian first visits the Moulin Rouge, only this time ex-soap actor and star of the stage version of *The Adventures of Priscilla Queen of the Desert* (1994) Jason Donovan plays a transvestited Harold Zidler, the Cancan girls are played by a troupe of 'real Iceland mums' and the song they perform to is a mashup of 'The Galop' from Jacques Offenbach's operetta *Orpheus in the Underworld* and the guitar riff from T-Rex's song '20th Century Boy'. Perhaps more noteworthy in this respect, however, is the 2004 mini-movie advert for the perfume Chanel No. 5 insofar as it really only coheres if understood as a post-*Moulin Rouge* film. Directed by Baz Luhrmann and starring Nicole Kidman, the advert works as a generic reprise of *Moulin Rouge*'s narrative and stylistic features, and rearticulates and recirculates many of its generic metaphors which, of course, are themselves already hijacked from elsewhere. So, not only do we get Nicole Kidman playing Satine, playing 'the most famous woman in the world', playing Nicole Kidman all played *by* Nicole Kidman, but in the same way that the Parisian rooftop cityscape becomes both the location and the backdrop for *Moulin Rouge*'s fairy-tale romance then an equally stylised geography frames much of the action of Luhrmann's advertising film.

CONCLUSION

On the account elaborated here genre not only becomes a cognitive mechanism of film comprehension but also one of the most important principles by which cinema advances, changes and develops. Indeed, remaining alert to the multiplicity and multivalence of genre, and adopting an analytic approach directed towards understanding the metaphorical artefacts that circulate in all generic forms, helps us to avoid the narrow reductionism associated with taxonomic approaches to genre studies. Metaphors stretch cultural expression by casting about for unpredictable resemblances, surprising relationships and unexpected associations so that, in the process of watching a film, we have to constantly revise our hypotheses and expectations to fit the new material. And, of course, the notions of 'transference' and 'implied resemblance' are not only useful for explicating the film text but can be mapped in relation to other industrial and commercial practices as well, from the way a producer assembles a production package; to the way a film is promoted to its audience; to the broader commercial ventures it entails. Indeed, rethinking genre as a metaphorical process allows us to situate the textual analysis of film within the context of a hyper-commodity culture of symbolic exchange which sees cinema's product both being derived from, and exploited across, the full range of information and entertainment platforms.

SUMMARY

- The notion of genre is usually invoked to identify, classify and differentiate kinds or types of film.
- Genre has been a particularly useful concept in the study of the commercial practices of Hollywood because it addresses cinema as an industrial form of aesthetic practice and gives critics a vocabulary for discussing and appraising the products of mass culture.
- Even though it is impossible to avoid the taxonomic impulses associated with the act of defining genres and classifying films, it is impossible to design a universal typology of genres that can accommodate and classify all films at all times.
- Recent work has attempted to expand the scope of genre studies to include approaches that address the function genre plays in both the financing and promotion of films, as well as the way they are consumed and comprehended by audiences.
- The result of much recent thinking on genre sees it as a multifarious idea which links cinematic texts to a whole host of other cultural texts and practices.
- The implication of this line of research is that genre as a textual system always operates as an abstract category and that individual instances of genres or generic texts may be best comprehended as characterised by hybridity and fluidity.

QUESTIONS FOR DISCUSSION

1. Categorising films into discrete genres is always a purposeful act. One avenue into genre studies is to try to understand the nature and function of that act. As such, compare the way that genres are defined in different ways in different contexts. Some contexts you might consider looking at are: rental outlets (both physical and online); different kinds of shops where you buy DVDs or Blu-rays (supermarkets, record shops, iTunes and other online stores such as Amazon or Play.com); film guides, reference works or compendia (e.g. *Halliwell's*, *Variety*, *Time Out*, IMDB, etc.); film reviews (compare the reviews of the same film by different critics); and TV listing magazines and niche television channels (e.g. *Radio Times*, Sky Indie, Turner Classic Movies (TCM), Movies4Men). Where are the moments of overlap, and when do categorical discrepancies occur? Can you explain these?

2. In writing about *The Matrix* trilogy of films, David Bordwell has suggested that, in order to 'track the films fully, one would have to enter the Matrix through many media portals' (2006: 59). Try engaging in this tracking activity by exploring the films' generic relationship with Japanese manga and anime, Hong Kong action cinema, cyberpunk novels, music videos and computer games.

3. Try analysing how a computer game such as *Red Dead Redemption* reactivates many of the generic markers and metaphors that circulate in western films in the attempt to offer gamers both an 'authentic' generic narrative experience and a sense of 'realistic' gameplay.

 **FURTHER READING**

Although it is impossible to list them here, there is a multitude of books which address individual genres from a variety of historical and theoretical standpoints. The following works, therefore, represent some of the key attempts to conceptualise genre generally and film genre specifically.

Introductory texts

Frow, John (2005) *Genre*, London: Routledge. Part of Routledge's *New Critical Idiom* series, Frow's book serves as an excellent introduction to the notion of genre generally as well as offering some fresh ideas on the ways in which genres actively generate and shape our knowledge of the world.

Keith Grant, Barry (2007) *Film Genre: From Iconography to Ideology*, London: Wallflower Press. This book forms part of Wallflower Press' *Short Cuts* series and, like many of the books in that series, combines an excellent survey of the field as well as introducing some new ideas.

Moine, Raphaëlle, (2008), trans. Alistair Fox and Hilary Radner, *Cinema Genre*, Oxford: Blackwell. This is a recent theoretical overview of the topic of genre as practiced in British, American, and French film criticism.

Selected key works

Altman, Rick (1999) *Film/Genre*, London: BFI.

Langford, Barry (2005) *Film Genre: Hollywood and Beyond*, Edinburgh: Edinburgh University Press.

Neale, Steve (1990) *Genre*, London: BFI.

Neale, Stephen (2000) *Genre and Hollywood*, London: Routledge.

Useful anthologies

Keith Grant, Barry (ed.) (1986) *Film Genre Reader*, Austin: University of Texas Press.

Keith Grant, Barry (ed.) (1995) *Film Genre Reader II*, Austin: University of Texas Press.

Keith Grant, Barry (ed.) (2003) *Film Genre Reader III*, Austin: University of Texas Press.

Neale, Steve (2002) *Genre and Contemporary Hollywood*, London: BFI.

Winston Dixon, Wheeler (2000) *Film Genre 2000*, Albany, NY: State University Press of New York.

FURTHER VIEWING

One approach to the study of film genre is to track the ways in which any one genre has changed over time. As such, watch a range of films of the same genre from different periods. For example, if you were to investigate the western film then the following would give a good indication of both the continuities and changes that have occurred within the genre.

The Great Train Robbery (Edwin S. Porter, 1903)
Stagecoach (John Ford, 1939)
My Darling Clementine (John Ford, 1946)
Shane (George Stevens,1952)
High Noon (Fred Zinnemann, 1952)
Johnny Guitar (Nicholas Ray, 1954)
The Searchers (John Ford, 1956)
3:10 to Yuma (Delmer Daves, 1957)
A Fistful of Dollars (Sergio Leone, 1964)
Billy the Kid Versus Dracula (William Beaudine, 1966)
Butch Cassidy and the Sundance Kid (George Roy Hill, 1969)
The Wild Bunch (Sam Peckinpah, 1969)

True Grit (Henry Hathaway, 1969)
Little Big Man (Arthur Penn, 1970)
McCabe and Mrs Miller (Robert Altman, 1971)
Blazing Saddles (Mel Brooks, 1974)
The Outlaw Josey Wales (Clint Eastwood, 1976)
Back to the Future III (Robert Zemeckis, 1990)
Dances with Wolves (Kevin Costner, 1990)
Unforgiven (Clint Eastwood, 1992)
Dead Man (Jim Jarmusch, 1995)
The Quick and the Dead (Sam Rami, 1995)
Last Man Standing (Walter Hill, 1996)
Shanghai Noon (Tom Dey, 2000)
Tears of the Black Tiger (Wisit Sasanatieng, 2000)
Open Range (Kevin Costner, 2003)
Brokeback Mountain (Ang Lee, 2005)
The Proposition (John Hillcoat, 2005)
The Three Burials of Melquiades Estrada (Tommy Lee Jones, 2005)
3:10 to Yuma (James Mangold, 2007)
The Assassination of Jesse James by the Coward Robert Ford (Andrew Dominik, 2007)
True Grit (Coen Brothers, 2010)

■ The documentary form

INTRODUCTION

actuality
Derived from the French term *actualité* given to the short nonfictional films made in the early period (1895–1906 or so). These films often consisted simply of people going about their everyday business, or of particular events (sporting contests, visiting dignitaries).

Direct Cinema
A type of documentary filmmaking that emerged in the US in the 1950s, associated with Robert Drew, Richard Leacock, Don Pennebaker, Frederick Wiseman and the Maysles Brothers. Direct Cinema films often have a 'fly on the wall' aesthetic, linked to the strong belief that the filmmakers were mere observers of the reality they were filming. This apparent detachment and neutrality has been as controversial as it is influential.

cinéma vérité
The French term, literally meaning 'cinema truth', is sometimes confused with a US kind of filmmaking which is actually closer to **Direct Cinema**. The confusion stems from the common 'immediacy' that the films have – filming people with handheld cameras and portable sound recording equipment – but cinema verité properly has a foundation of interaction between filmmaker and filmed, rather than the detachment seen in Direct Cinema films. Nevertheless, it is common to see a range of different films referred to as 'cinema verité' (or sometimes just 'verité'), and it is important to distinguish between them.

This chapter offers an overview of one of the most important and enduring forms of cinematic expression – the documentary. The past two decades or so have seen something of a renaissance in terms of documentaries finding an audience in cinemas – big-screen successes such as *Hoop Dreams* (1994), *Touching the Void* (2003), *Supersize Me* (2004), *Fahrenheit 9/11* (2004), *An Inconvenient Truth* (2006), *Man on Wire* (2008) and *The Cove* (2009) attest to the potential popularity of documentary films. At the same time, investigative journalism such as that seen in John Pilger's *The War You Don't See* (2010) – an indictment of the complicity and 'embeddedness' of the mainstream media in the so-called 'War on Terror' – demonstrated that there is still a vital role for documentary to play in educating the public and holding the powerful to account. The film was shown on television but also received a limited theatrical release and is also available to view on YouTube (see: http://www.youtube.com/watch?v=p7wXhN5h_Pg). Indeed, the film's use of footage from WikiLeaks and other forms of 'citizen journalism' show not only how important documentaries can be hewn from such material but also how they can be distributed and exhibited via 'new media' outlets. There has also been a major expansion in critical and scholarly attention to the form particularly concerning how documentary addresses its viewers in this new media landscape, how it makes meaning and the relationship it has to fictional filmmaking. I use a more or less chronological framework to outline some of the key moments in documentary's history and examine the key figures involved. The most important questions addressed are:

■ How do we actually *recognise and define* documentary as a distinct form?
■ What *types* of documentary are there, and how do they overlap and interact with each other?
■ What relationship does documentary have with *fiction*, *drama* and *reconstruction*?
■ In what ways does the notion of *performance* problematise documentary as a form?

I begin by discussing some different definitions of documentary and then move on to examine the documentary status of early nonfictional films (**actualities**). These apparently simple recordings of a slice of life contrast with the more overtly constructed, narrativised films of Robert Flaherty, and the 'creative interpretation of actuality' as espoused by John Grierson, the person at the forefront of the British documentary movement of the 1930s. Central to understanding all of these films as 'documentary', however, is the relative level of intervention by the filmmakers: it has to be stressed at the outset that all documentary – despite its sometimes 'unmediated' appearance, its apparent capturing of life as it happens – is a construction. This needs to be kept in mind when discussing the work of the post-Second World War US filmmakers of the so-called **Direct Cinema** movement, as they are more guilty than most of professing a naïve belief in documentary's ability to simply 'capture' reality. The consideration of this movement is contextualised by comparing it with the more 'interventionist' **cinéma vérité** filmmaking, before moving on to consider the issues raised by overtly 'authored' or 'performative' documentaries. The questions raised by considering performance in documentary lead on to a consideration of drama and documentary, and the sometimes fractious relationship between these two modes.

Before proceeding, I will briefly comment on television. Although there are important debates to be had about the institution of television and the place of documentary within it, especially the role of '**reality TV**' and its impact on documentary as a form, these have been sidelined from the current discussion to a great extent. This is not to deny their importance, but rather to retain more of a focus on what are considered to be the most important issues for film documentary. Some discussion of television's influence is inevitable, but it cannot be the main focus of this chapter.

WHAT IS DOCUMENTARY?

There is much debate over what exactly defines a 'documentary', stemming from the overlaps and hybridity exhibited by different modes. We examine some of the more commonly accepted modes or subtypes of documentary as a form, but first of all we need a working definition of the term 'documentary'. Documentary is, broadly speaking, a subcategory of nonfiction – it is a form that tells stories, makes assertions or observations about the real historical world, rather than the fabricated worlds of fiction. It is often believed that a documentary must use literal 'actuality' footage – images and sounds recorded as they happened – and it is certainly the case that a great many documentaries do rest on this foundation of things observed and recorded. However, it is entirely possible for a text to be considered a documentary, even if it consists predominantly of reconstructed or re-enacted scenes. (Of course, those documentaries that *do* function in this way have been labelled with some other name – e.g. drama–documentary – something we return to below.) Documentary, in this sense, is a very broad church; the key defining factor is that the film or programme in question makes assertions about the real world, and provides audio-visual evidence to back up such assertions. This 'assertive' stance and 'evidential' basis need not necessarily mean that documentaries are explicitly laid out as 'arguments' (as we shall see, this is the preserve of a specific kind of documentary, the expository). Documentaries can and do use a variety of techniques as fits their aims and purpose – explicit argument, more allusive or associative connections between things, dramatic reconstruction, and different levels of filmmaker 'intervention' in the reality they are interpreting.

The most useful delineation of documentary modes has been provided by Bill Nichols (2001). He identifies six modes 'that function something like sub-genres of the documentary film genre itself: poetic, expository, participatory, observational, reflexive, performative' (2001: 99). We briefly consider each of these in turn. The poetic mode will

reality TV
A relatively recent development in television, a form of highly structured programme using observational material of ordinary people. The programmes have a 'documentary' basis in the sense that they use actuality footage, but they are often shaped to fit specific formats (neighbours from hell, the rise of a successful business, a game show involving weekly tasks). In this respect, reality TV is a good example of how documentary can be taken and recontextualised by contemporary television to suit its schedules.

• **Plate 9.1**
Nanook of the North
(Robert Flaherty, 1922).
The film presents man's struggles with nature in a narrativised documentary format

seem more allusive and use 'associative' editing to capture a mood or tone rather than make an explicit argument about a subject. The so-called 'city symphony' films, such as Walter Ruttmann's *Berlin: Symphony of a Great City* (1927), Alberto Cavalcanti's surrealist portrait of Paris, *Rien que les heures* (1926) or Ron Fricke's epic environmental visual poem *Baraka* (1992) may all be seen as 'poetic' documentaries – they evoke a mood rather than stating or asserting things directly.

rhetorical
Designed to persuade. Rhetorical strategies in documentary are those that relate to the film's or programme's argument. This may be explicit (e.g. a voiceover or presenter actually stating what the argued points are), or it may be less immediately obvious (e.g. a filmmaker might cut from an image of a political leader to a library shot of a firing squad; this could be seen as an argument against the politician).

Expository documentaries on the other hand do use explicitly **rhetorical** techniques in order to make points about aspects of actuality. The expository mode often uses voiceover and has a relatively straightforward 'show and tell' structure to guide the viewer through the material. Many television documentaries follow this template, where the voiceover provides the connection, the logic, between what might be disparate shots. Such films and programmes that are labelled 'expository' are often didactic in nature – for example, the *Why We Fight* (1943–45) series of films about the Second World War 'tell the story' of the War (and make a case for US involvement) using voiceover and other expository techniques such as maps and diagrams. The aforementioned *The War You Don't See* is another example of an expository documentary: it has a clear, argued structure, with Pilger's journalistic gravitas guiding the viewer through the footage they are seeing, his eloquent rhetoric a *deliberate corrective* to the mainstream media that is the subject of critique in the film.

Such direct address may be contrasted with the observational mode, where the documentary appears to take a detached and thereby 'neutral' (or 'objective') stance towards its subject matter – overtly 'interpretive' techniques such as editorialising voiceover or music (which are common in other modes of documentary) are eschewed in favour of an apparent capturing of reality as it unfolds. The films of Frederick Wiseman are excellent examples of this mode in that Wiseman presents his material in a detached, observational style with no voiceover, thereby seeming to allow viewers to make up their own mind. The fact that Wiseman's subject matter is generally US institutions – for example, education in *High School* (1968), the military in *Basic Training* (1971) – gives this seeming detachment a cumulative power; rather than offering an obviously didactic viewpoint on what he is representing, Wiseman allows the people and situations shown to apparently 'speak for themselves'. However, it is possible to discern a critical 'voice' running through Wiseman's films; in his editing and shot decisions we can discern that even the seemingly detached observational mode involves choices, juxtapositions and contrasts.

The participatory (sometimes referred to as the 'interactive') is a documentary mode where the filmmaker does *not* remain aloof from the subject matter, but actively engages with it – by openly participating or interacting with the people and institutions on show. Michael Moore's first film for the cinema, *Roger and Me* (1989), exhibits many participatory characteristics: Moore is directly implicated in the subject matter (he is of course the 'me' of the title) and arguably many scenes would not unfold in the way they do without his specific participation. This results in a documentary form which is very far removed from the detached or straightforwardly didactic.

The reflexive mode is a mode that attempts to offer a commentary on the means of representation itself. A reflexive documentary is a film which uses techniques that encourage the viewer to question the very idea of 'documentary' as a category or mode; this questioning can also lead to a critique of larger categories such as cinematic realism. For instance, in Errol Morris's *The Thin Blue Line* (1988), the story of a miscarriage of justice, the highly stylised reconstructions and repetitions of scenes from different viewpoints are reflexive strategies that Morris uses to encourage the viewer to think about relative levels of 'truth' and self-deception.

Finally, the performative is a mode that raises all sorts of questions about filmmaker and subject 'performance' – not simply in the commonsense meaning of 'performing' in front of the camera (which is often referred to in the negative, as if it detracts from the essential truth of what is going on), but the notion of the filmmaker and their subjects *actively creating* the documentary by performing certain social actions. As Stella Bruzzi has noted, there are some documentaries that are 'given meaning by the interaction between performance and reality' (2000: 154); far from berating some documentaries for containing self-conscious performances, it follows here that such performances are actually *central* to this specific mode of documentary filmmaking. The films of Nick Broomfield are central to the performative mode, and are discussed below.

The most important thing to note about this typology of different modes is that it is constantly evolving. In addition, these modes are not mutually exclusive, and they can and do overlap across the history of documentary as a form, and co-exist, sometimes within the same documentary. It is entirely possible for a single documentary to use expository, poetic and observational techniques as suits its purpose at any one time. It is also important to remember that, despite some overviews of documentary (including this one) taking a roughly chronological form, this way of constructing history is precisely that – a construction. The vibrancy of documentary as a type of filmmaking resides in the ways that practitioners and audiences engage with different films about the real world of actuality.

'PROTO-DOCUMENTARY' – THE CASE OF EARLY FILM ACTUALITIES

Arguably, the first 'documentaries' were the actualities of the first filmmakers, such as the Lumière Brothers in France or Sagar Mitchell and James Kenyon in the UK. The camera was used much like a stills camera would have been, to mechanically capture a slice of reality. Such films are of intrinsic interest, not just for film historians but for historians in general: they document the specificities of a particular milieu. There is however a paradox of sorts here, in the sense that the apparently simple and straight-forward representing of actuality was played up as a 'novelty' – come and see the moving pictures! – and even the simplest of these films can show some evidence of directorial intervention. As Bill Nichols points out, it is therefore problematic in one sense to 'trace back' the beginnings of documentary film to its 'mythic origin' in early cinema (2001: 82–7). We need to be careful not to construct a simple 'lineage' from early nonfictional actualities to the later more complexly structured documentaries, as such a 'linear' view of history tends to ignore other potential avenues (e.g. the use of film technology for scientific rather than cinematic purposes). Having said this, a lot can be learned from examining how these proto-documentaries are similar to or differ from other forms of nonfictional output.

For further discussion of early British cinema see pp. 363–370.

Despite the fact that these short actualities may be seen as what Noel Carroll (2003: 231) calls 'paradigmatic documentaries' – i.e. they exist as a model or proto-typical example of the form – their original exhibition context was one of novelty and wonderment. Dai Vaughan notes that the soon-to-be-famous filmmaker Georges Melies, who was present at the first ever Lumière screening in Paris in 1895, drew specific attention to details like rustling leaves in the background of one film (Vaughan 1999: 4–5). In other words, despite the tendency for future commentators to emphasise the naïvety of those first viewers – the oft-repeated tale of people flinching as the train approached in *L'arrivée d'un train en gare de la Ciotat* (1895) – they were fascinated by the ability of the cinema to accurately render (or 'document') an appearance of reality. It is also worth remembering that, although we can now look back on these early cinema films with a sense of their quaintness, their raw and unpolished appearance as 'mere recordings' of a slice of actuality, in their original exhibition context they would doubtless have been accompanied by some contextualising remarks from the exhibitor/showman; the equivalent of a voiceover in a 'proper' modern-day documentary. The point here is not to suggest that these early actualities are the same kind of documentary as later and clearly more complex films, but to draw attention to the fact that seeing them just as simplistic recordings is equally inaccurate. As film scholars such as Tom Gunning (1995) and Dan North (2008) have made clear, even these early documentary-like films need to be read in a context of what Gunning refers to as 'an aesthetic of astonishment', where self-conscious display and connections to the spectacle of the magic theatre are foregrounded despite the often quotidian content of the films themselves.

□ CASE STUDY 1: THE FILMS OF MITCHELL AND KENYON

topicals
The name given to nonfictional 'news' items in the early period. A royal visit, the opening of a factory, a sports event – anything that could be of interest to a local audience – could be labelled 'a topical'. As documentary developed as a form, topicals were subsumed into newsreels and other forms of film reporting.

Mitchell and Kenyon, a pair of entrepreneurs from Blackburn, certainly used the novelty factor of capturing real people and events as the selling point for their films, to increase interest. They filmed everyday events (or '**topicals**') in and around Lancashire and Yorkshire during the 1897 to 1910 period and the 'hook' for getting people to come and see their films was that the viewer might well see themselves on the screen. Their company mottos – 'Local films' and 'We take them and make them' – attest to their desire to capture the specificities of local life, but do so in a way that could be sold to the subjects of the films. As Dan Cruickshank, the presenter of the BBC television series *The Lost World of Mitchell and Kenyon* (2004) says, 'they weren't meant to be documentary records of the time but were made for purely commercial reasons'. He later quotes the tagline of one of the posters of the time advertising such films: 'Nothing is so great a draw as a local subject.'

These original Mitchell and Kenyon films may be termed 'proto-documentaries' or at the very least be referred to as nonfiction films. On the face of it, the films are completely observational in the sense that the camera appears to merely observe events unfold and there is no 'shaping' of the material in the ways we might expect of a 'proper' documentary. To say that there is no shaping at all would be inaccurate, though, as all of these early nonfiction films show some signs of 'authorial' shaping. There is even one point in the series *The Lost World of Mitchell and Kenyon* when we see Kenyon caught on camera actively directing a crowd of workers by hurrying them along a pathway. Even the most naturalistic slice of life required some directing, in the same way as a 'natural' photographic portrait required some posing. Another good example is the scene of some miners, many of them with faces and clothes blackened with coal dust, emerging from work in *Pendlebury Colliery* (1901).[1] As the scene progresses – with the by-then conventional glancing into the camera by many of the passers-by – a black miner wanders past having a good-natured jostle with another miner. The black miner, in pristine white shirt-sleeves, stands out like the proverbial sore thumb. It is hard not to discern some level of directorial shaping of the material here; indeed, Cruickshank speculates that the black man may have been a fairground worker planted in the film, precisely to draw out such visual contrasts.

One fascinating thing about these short actualities is their *changing status*: they have moved from being simple, short actualities, with arguably no pretence at 'documentary' status, to having sociological and historical importance. The way the original films have been mounted and recontextualised within the three-part series *The Lost World of Mitchell and Kenyon* is interesting because the original footage, shot for specific reasons, takes on new meanings and resonances; in short, it takes on a documentary status as opposed to arguably being a 'mere' document. For instance, the moment from *Pendlebury Colliery* is part of a wider commentary in the television series, examining attitudes to black people in Edwardian Britain.

Now, of course, the majority of people who view these films do so in the recontextualised format of the documentary series about the films. In this respect, the 'natural material' of the original films is 'creatively interpreted' by the makers of the documentary series. For example, there is one sequence where a man named Mick Judge views a video copy of one of the Mitchell and Kenyon films, a rugby game from 1901 where

• **Plate 9.2**
Pendlebury Colliery
(Sagar Mitchell and
James Kenyon, *circa*
1901). The capturing
of everyday 'actuality'
footage apparently as
it happened – though
with some signs of
mischievous directorial
shaping in the
positioning of certain
characters

one of the players was Judge's great-grandfather. As he views the footage on his home television set, his own son playing in the background, Judge marvels at being able to see someone from all those years before running around, flesh and blood. The ordinariness, the everydayness is accentuated here, as Judge points out that his relative was not a famous person – underlining the ways in which historical traces of things are usually biased in favour of certain types of people. What is important here though is the fact that the original Mitchell and Kenyon film is placed in a context, a 'frame' that draws out some of the peculiarities of it as a piece of film, and this is done in such a way as to emphasise the contrasts with the modern day. Certain assertions are made by virtue of the clever juxtaposition of historical 'moments'.

It is this 'ethnographic' or 'anthropological' dimension to the footage that is interesting in terms of its status as documentary film. In another sequence, Cruickshank speaks in voiceover while we see the original Mitchell and Kenyon film of Nottingham town centre *circa* 1901. This footage is cross-cut with present-day footage of the same places; the viewer is actively encouraged to see what has changed in the intervening century. What was originally shot as something that was meant to be little more than an ephemeral crowd pleaser, of little or no interest to anyone but those who actually appear in it, has become an important social document. Again, though, it is in the creative juxtaposition of this footage with something else (the modern-day footage) that specific points are made.

THE SHIFT TO NARRATIVE STRUCTURE IN DOCUMENTARY

Despite their historical importance and the possibility that they can be read as 'proto-documentaries', however, such early film actualities lack the decisive creative shaping that distinguishes documentary from other forms of nonfictional filmmaking. It is in the dramatic narrative structures imposed on real material by a filmmaker such as Robert

Flaherty (1884–1951) that we first see the move to a more immediately recognisable type of documentary form. Flaherty's work is often held up to be among the most influential of the early documentary filmmakers. Apart from anything else, films such as *Nanook of the North* (1922), *Moana* (1926) and *Man of Aran* (1934) were a huge influence on John Grierson, who went on to become an important figure in the British documentary movement of the 1930s and 1940s (and, later, founded the National Film Board of Canada). As with many of the most influential documentary filmmakers, Flaherty's work is both important and controversial for its methods.

Flaherty was not interested in merely recording reality – instead, his films were dramatically structured, with clear narrative goals and expectations set up for the viewer. Richard Meran Barsam points out that 'it would be misleading to think of Flaherty as the originator of the documentary film as we know it: the socio-political didactic film ... [instead, his filmmaking] poetically celebrates man and his life; his films are humanistic statements, not political ones' (1974: 124). Time and again in his films, Flaherty focuses on real people in real situations, attempting to draw out some of the mythic resonance of certain lifestyles. This approach has not gone uncriticised however – there are issues relating to Flaherty's methods and the romanticising of his subject matter that raise problems for much contemporary documentary practice.

In *Nanook of the North* (1922), for example, Flaherty immersed himself in the lifestyles of the Inuit people, spending a year living with them. Such a method perhaps implies a **participant observation** approach, where the filmmaker observes unobtrusively and creates as objective a record as possible. However, when it came to the construction of the documentary, Flaherty was not averse to fabricating events. It is often remarked that he constructed a special open-sided igloo to allow filming of interior shots; even more contentious is his filming of Nanook hunting with traditional harpoon rather than the more modern weapons that he actually used. Flaherty's *Moana* (1926) also included scenes of the Polynesian natives performing for the camera rituals they had long-since stopped doing in everyday life.

Such methods are in fact central and arguably unavoidable techniques in documentary production, and most certainly were in the period where filming on location, with handheld cameras and portable sound recording (things that were to become commonplace in the post-Second World War era) was simply not possible. However, the 'justifiable' use of reconstruction has remained as controversial as it is important in the intervening years since Flaherty, and is something that links into debates about drama and re-enactment, discussed below. It also raises the spectre of **ethics**: is it *ever* admissible for a documentary filmmaker to fabricate things in order to achieve the 'higher' aim of revealing the 'inner truth' of the subject matter? Flaherty certainly thought so, as he consistently (re-)constructed things before the camera in order to reach what he saw as the essence of what he was portraying. As Jay Ruby points out, for instance, '"family members" in *Nanook of the North*, *Man of Aran* and *Louisiana Story* (1948) are not related to each other; they were selected because they suited Flaherty's conception of what makes a good Eskimo, Irish or Cajun family' (2005: 215).

JOHN GRIERSON AND THE BRITISH DOCUMENTARY MOVEMENT

As noted above, Flaherty's work was a direct influence on John Grierson. Grierson was born in Scotland in 1898 and went on to have a profound influence on the documentary form, especially those films produced at the Empire Marketing Board and General Post Office in Britain in the 1930s and 1940s. Although Grierson himself directed only two films (1929's *Drifters* and 1934's *Granton Trawler*) he is often credited with bringing together a diverse set of filmmakers to work under the aegis of these governmental organisations as well as industry sponsors. Films such as *Coal*

participant observation
A social science methodology where researchers immerse themselves in the social context/group they are studying, often for years at a time. In documentary terms, such an approach arguably leads to more 'natural' responses, as the subjects have become used to the filmmakers and cameras.

ethics
Concerning morality, or codes of conduct. There is a strong ethical discourse running though the history of documentary, and debates to be had about the ethical dimension of things like reconstruction, filming people without their consent, informing the viewer of the extent of filmmaker intervention, and so on.

• **Plate 9.3**
Housing Problems
(Edgar Anstey and
Arthur Elton, 1935).
Housing Problems
offers insights into a
social problem by using
real people to directly
address the audience –
an innovation for the
time

Face (1935), *Night Mail* (1936), *Housing Problems* (1935), *Spare Time* (1939) and *Song of Ceylon* (1934) used a variety of techniques and modes of address to inform and educate. Grierson's view, influenced by the mass media theories of Walter Lippmann (whose ideas Grierson encountered when he spent some time in the US in the mid-1920s), saw cinema as a potential tool for informing and educating the masses. At the same time, however, Grierson saw filmmaking as an art form – documentary filmmaking especially so. This perhaps explains the sometimes disconcerting combination of techniques within some of these British films. *Coal Face* is at times the expository documentary *par excellence*, with a robotically informative voiceover furnishing the viewer with facts about the coal industry, accompanied by maps and other graphic devices. At other times, though, it is more overtly 'poetic' in its evocation of the spaces, textures and sounds of the industry and the people who work within it. (These people remain little more than ciphers, however.) *Housing Problems*, on the other hand, appears more straightforward in its exposition of slum dwellings, the people who live in them, and the houses' clearance to make way for new homes. The film, directed by Arthur Elton and Edgar Anstey (with some involvement from Ruby Grierson, John's sister – see Macdonald and Cousins 1996: 122) nevertheless also uses what was for the time extremely unusual location shooting of interviews with ordinary people. The film was sponsored by the Gas, Light and Coke Company (i.e. the gas industry), who also funded *Enough to Eat?* (1936), a film about malnutrition in Britain. The potentially radical edge that these films had is somewhat reduced when they are viewed in a wider context, however. Rather than openly questioning the social structures that *caused* slums and unequal food distribution, we instead see the gas industry perhaps unsurprisingly positioned as the height of progress in slum clearance and construction of new dwellings, complete with gas supply. The causes of the problems are not really examined, and the real people involved here are arguably mere fodder for what Brian Winston labels 'the tradition of the victim in Griersonian documentary' (1988: 269–87).

There were, then, strong links between the British documentary filmmakers of this period and industry sponsors or government departments, with the consequence that there is a strand of discourse about documentary that sees it as mere propaganda (though that term should not be seen as simply pejorative; Grierson certainly saw propaganda as potentially positive and educative). This assumption that documentary must rely on sponsorship or governmental support is pervasive; as already noted, Grierson saw the role of documentary as a kind of mass educational tool, and saw the term documentary as one that, while not ideal – he is on the record calling it 'a clumsy description' (1966: 145) – at least had its uses. Alberto Cavalcanti, one of Grierson's colleagues in the 1930s, did not like the term 'documentary' as a description for the kinds of films he made. Grierson's response, Cavalcanti recalled, was: 'I have to deal with the Government, and the word "documentary" impresses them as something serious' (quoted in MacDonald and Cousins 1996: 117). We can also see in a film like *Housing Problems* that the social problem is constructed as something that can be easily 'answered' or remedied by the actions of the film's sponsor.

As already noted, a key conceptual distinction that needs to be made is that between films which simply record, with little or no discernible authorial shaping, and those which intervene, dramatise and editorialise in some way. Such a distinction is one that Grierson was at pains to make when he suggested that there were 'lower categories' of nonfiction film, such as 'lecture' films, which lacked the organisation that characterised documentary proper (1966: 145–6). Grierson famously coined the phrase 'the creative interpretation of actuality' (1932: 8) to emphasise that documentary films should not simply record material. Despite the fact that documentary cinema is 'an art based on photographs, in which one factor is always, or nearly always, a thing observed' (1966: 199), to qualify as a documentary there has to be *more* than mere observation. For Grierson, although documentaries will in all likelihood be based on recorded footage (or 'natural material' as he terms it (1966: 145)), it is in the *creative interventions* made by the filmmaker (specific use of sound, certain edited juxtapositions) that the 'documentariness' resides. The distinction, as Grierson points out, is between 'a method which describes only the surface values of a subject, and a method which more explosively reveals the reality of it' (ibid.: 148). This echoes the point made earlier about Flaherty, who fabricated events (albeit ones that would be perceived as 'probable' or likely to have actually happened) in order to represent what he saw as the essential truth. Grierson's point is similar: it is through creative juxtaposition and interpretation, rather than simply 'capturing' that any truth or meaning will emerge. It is via the filmmaker's *shaping* of the natural material, through whatever means, that the 'reality' of the subject matter is communicated.

However, one of the thorniest issues to trouble documentary since its inception has been the *extent* to which events are shaped or directed by the filmmaker (and/or the participants themselves – something that will be discussed in some detail below). A simplistic, but abiding, school of thought is that documentary footage can *only* have a claim on the real if it is somehow captured 'unawares'. As we shall see, this was never true and is certainly not true now. All documentaries rest on a shaping or creative treatment of the material, though that material may have a direct indexical link to a pro-filmic reality. We are now going to move on to examine some of the post-Second World War developments in documentary – developments that incorporate debates about the objectivity and neutrality of the filmmakers, and the extent to which they creatively interpret their material.

POST-WAR DEVELOPMENTS IN OBSERVATIONAL DOCUMENTARY

Alongside the influential Griersonian idea of documentary and the more narrative-driven films of Flaherty, the most dominant form, especially in the post-Second World War era, has been the observational documentary. This arguably covers a number of styles, but it is easy to see why the notion of a more or less detached observationalism might pervade ideas about what constitutes documentary. There is a sense that it distils all the ideas about the camera (and film) as a recording device that can capture an unmediated slice of actuality, with attendant beliefs in accuracy, objectivity and impartiality. The fact that there are distinct problems with an overly naïve belief in the ability of the camera to objectively record things that happen before it has made the various types of observational film and their proponents hugely controversial. The immediacy and apparently unvarnished nature of the images and sounds produced in such documentaries are emphasised by the technological developments of the era – more portable cameras and (crucially) sound-recording equipment made filming on location more feasible, without recourse to reconstructing scenes or dubbing the sound in post-production.

It is important to make a distinction between different types of filmmaking practice that are often lumped together and referred to as 'cinema verité' (or sometimes just 'verité' or 'fly on the wall'). The original cinema vérité practitioners were the French anthropologist Jean Rouch and sociologist Edgar Morin. Their approach was not one of simple, detached observation, but involved much more interaction between filmmaker and subject. In this respect, a cinema vérité film like Rouch and Morin's *Chronicle of a Summer* (1960) would come under Nichols's category of the 'participatory' rather than 'observational'. The adaptation of the notion of cinema vérité in the US context saw it transformed into so-called 'Direct Cinema', as exemplified by the work of filmmakers such as Richard Leacock, Robert Drew (founder of Drew Associates) and Don Pennebaker. Films such as Leacock's *Primary* (1960), on the campaign trail with John F. Kennedy and Hubert Humphrey, and Pennebaker's *Don't Look Back* (1967), a behind-the-scenes look at Bob Dylan on tour, had an unobtrusive style far removed from that of Rouch and Morin. The direct cinema practitioners believed that the presence of the camera and filmmakers did not have an impact on the subjects – or not much of one, at least. As Leacock said in an interview when asked about the differences between him and his colleagues and Rouch:

We don't think that [the filmmaker's presence] affects people very much, at least I don't. Let me add that, of course, it affects them in Jean Rouch's films, since the only thing that's happening to them is the fact that they're being filmed. There's nothing else to think about. How can they ever forget it?

(quoted in MacDonald and Cousins 1996: 256)

This comment touches on one of the abiding distinctions between different types of documentary – the relative 'obviousness' of the filmmaker's presence and the extent to which they are acknowledged by their subjects. It was noted earlier how in Frederick Wiseman's films, even though the viewer might discern some level of authorial 'voice' or critique stemming from Wiseman's choice of shots and how they are combined, what really comes across is that the subjects of his films do tend to carry on with their business *as if* the camera is not present. This is the key signifier of direct cinema and what marks it out as very different from cinéma vérité.

As with all these categories, though, there are grey areas, overlaps and hybrids – this is what keeps documentary developing as a field. Even with filmmakers such as the Maysles Brothers, often described as proponents of Direct Cinema, we can discern in their work some tensions between different documentary modes, and it is worth exploring these tensions, since they help us to understand the documentary field more fully. The Maysles Brothers, Albert and David, began working with Drew Associates in the late 1950s but formed their own production company in the mid-1960s. They directed some of the most memorable documentaries produced in the US in the 1960s and 1970s, including *Salesman* (1969), which follows a travelling Bible salesman, *Gimme Shelter* (1970), which documents the notorious Rolling Stones concert at Altamont in 1969, and *Grey Gardens* (1975). We are going to focus on the last of these films, as it is an interesting example of what happens when different documentary modes meet.

☐ **CASE STUDY 2:** *GREY GARDENS* **(MAYSLES BROTHERS, 1975)**[2]

Grey Gardens is a very famous 'fly-on-the-wall' documentary about Edith Beale and Edie Beale, Jackie Kennedy's aunt and cousin, who live in the East Hampton mansion of the title. Over the years, their eccentricities and obsessions have led to the house becoming more and more dilapidated, and the film appears to revel in their oddness and squalor. The film begins in a seemingly 'random' fashion, a classic signifier of fly-on-the-wall transparency: over shots of the ramshackle house, and a montage of Hampton locations, two female voices argue about a cat. The title 'Grey Gardens' appears over a shot of the house itself, a shot which then transforms into a newspaper image, leading to an expository/scene-setting sequence where the backstory to the documentary is told via newspaper clippings. We learn that the two women have been told to clean up the mansion or face eviction, and that they resent such interference in their lives. In one shot of a clipping, the Maysles themselves are mentioned, along with the fact that they are making a film about the women.

Despite the fact that the Maysles are often celebrated as one of the main proponents of US Direct Cinema, this film is a far cry from simple, unobtrusive observation. The filmmakers are implicated throughout. After the opening scene-setting, we hear Edie's voice screech 'It's the Maysles!!' and there is a cut to a photograph of the two brothers with camera and sound equipment. We then see Edie chatting to the off-screen filmmakers. She says: 'What do you wanna do now? Where do you wanna go? Upstairs? You wanna go up and photograph it from the top porch?' Later still, there is one very odd sequence where Edie is standing on the porch, in long shot, adjusting her head-dress. Not speaking at this point, she almost seems to be waiting for a signal. Off-screen, Albert Maysles says 'Dressed for battle, Edie?!', and she then starts walking off the porch, talking as she goes. She sashays up to a medium close-up and talks straight into the camera. There is a sense here that the creative shaping, the directing of events for the camera, is being emphasised; the sequence plays out as if an off-screen voice had shouted 'Action!', and Edie's behaviour echoes that of the Gloria Swanson character in *Sunset Boulevard* (Billy Wilder, 1950), melodramatically approaching the camera saying, 'I'm ready for my close up now, Mr De Mille.'

● **Plate 9.4**
Grey Gardens (Maysles Brothers, 1975). A compelling combination of fly-on-the-wall observation and more overt 'participatory' techniques by the Maysles, where they directly interact with the subjects of their film

In other words, far from being a straightforwardly observational record of these two eccentric women, this is a cleverly structured (some might say highly manipulative and ethically suspect) film that engages with notions of performance and (self-)representation. The two women (especially Edie) interact with the Maysles, playing up to the cameras. In one scene they pore over old photographs – some of which are shown to the audience via rostrum camera shots – and reminisce about the old times. As the camera lingers in close-up on some of the photographs, there is a nice disjunction between the images and the bickering women on the soundtrack. At one point they fight over one photograph, Edie grabbing for it and tearing it while shouting, 'I wanna show it to Al!'

Such self-conscious performing for the cameras, in the context of a kind of observational filmmaking, is very interesting. In many ways one can see *Grey Gardens* as a precursor to contemporary 'reality TV' material, where people invite the cameras into their lives and appear to be playing to the filmmakers and the audience. One of the criticisms of a great deal of reality TV output is that the participants are 'not being themselves' or are in some way exaggerating certain characteristics to make the film or programme more entertaining. In the case of *Grey Gardens*, one gets the impression that these women are actually like this (though Edie certainly appears to do some things that she would not otherwise do, for the benefit of the camera). However, it is the case that the film resembles more recent reality TV output in some respects (though it does not have a voiceover, which is standard-issue for most reality TV formats). There is a sense that the women in the film are 'performing' a version of themselves, a variation on what John Corner has described (in a discussion of *Big Brother* and reality TV) as 'selving' (2002: 263). *Grey Gardens* is therefore better understood not as a simple exercise in fly-on-the-wall observational filmmaking, but as a film where the filmmakers are interacting with their subject matter; where *both* filmmakers *and* subjects are revelling in their respective performances.

THE MOVE TO PERFORMATIVE AND REFLEXIVE DOCUMENTARY

There are, then, different degrees to which the subjects of a documentary might be perceived to be performing for the cameras. From the very first actualities, through apparently purely observational films such as *Primary*, to more recent films that foreground the notion of a self-conscious performance, the playing out of social roles has always been central to the documentary project. Likewise, there have been degrees of self-consciousness or recognition by the filmmakers of the role they are performing in the construction of a documentary. The categories of reflexive and performative documentary filmmaking are arguably where the most interesting current work is being produced. The reflexive refers to those documentaries where the actual process of representation and construction is somehow foregrounded. The performative may be seen as a subcategory of the 'reflexive'. Due to the fact that documentaries will always be about the real world, real people and real issues, the notion of performance within them is potentially radical and reflexive, as it seems opposed to notions of authenticity and unvarnished reality. As Stella Bruzzi has pointed out though, it is important to see this in context: there have always been films of this kind, documentaries that foreground those elements of construction (and reflexivity) and draw attention to the varying types of performance going on within them. As she says about the work of Nick Broomfield, he is 'acting out a documentary' (2000: 155). His very presence suggests that the objective, detached observer is a myth and his 'performance' as 'documentarist' implicitly (and sometimes explicitly) draws attention to the performances of his subjects. For example, his interventions in his two films about convicted killer Aileen Wuornos (*Aileen Wuornos: The Selling of a Serial Killer* (1992) and *Aileen: Life and Death of a Serial Killer* (2003)) consistently and self-consciously draw attention to his role as filmmaker and mediator of meaning. This means, ultimately, that his films are as much about him and the process of image-making as they are about Wuornos; this, in fact, works very well, as there is a sense that the 'truth' behind the Wuornos story was never going to be definitively told, and the Broomfield films end up being a savage indictment of the media circus and a legal system gone mad (see Ward 2005: 40–8). Broomfield's films therefore foreground the role of the documentarist, and the ways in which the filmmaker's interaction with the reality they are filming impacts on the resulting footage. In *The Leader, His Driver and the Driver's Wife* (1991), a documentary about the South African white suprem-acist leader Eugene Terreblanche, Broomfield uses (deliberate) miscommunication and foregrounding of 'hitches' in the filming process to draw out and emphasise the ludicrousness of Terreblanche, his beliefs, and his inflated sense of his own importance. This is a technique that results in a strong critique of Terreblanche (as well as being highly amusing) – but would not have been possible without Broomfield's explicitly 'performative' strategies. In many respects it is Broomfield's bumbling attempts to act like a documentarist that so infuriate Terreblanche and lead to most of his outbursts.

☐ CASE STUDY 3: *GRIZZLY MAN* (WERNER HERZOG, 2005)

A very interesting recent example of such 'performative' tendencies in documentary is Werner Herzog's *Grizzly Man* (2005). Rather than the deliberately clumsy, knowing style of Broomfield, however, this film consists of its main character assuming a specific role in front of the camera, and seeming to believe it himself. At the film's heart is a strong belief in the ability of documentary footage to act as evidence; ultimately, however, the footage is recontextualised and made to say something other than its creator intended.

• **Plate 9.5**
Grizzly Man (Werner Herzog, 2005). The film draws attention to the very processes of recording and interpreting reality, as Timothy Treadwell's self-mythologising footage is recontextualised by Herzog's interviews and ironic voiceover

This raises interesting questions about how actuality footage can be (re-)interpreted in different contexts.

Grizzly Man tells the story of Timothy Treadwell, a self-mythologising 'eco-warrior' who took it upon himself to live among the various communities of Alaskan grizzly bears each summer for thirteen years, spending the rest of the year touring and lecturing on the subject. In 2001, Treadwell (and his female companion, who is virtually absent from any of Treadwell's footage) was attacked and eaten by one of the bears. While living in Alaska, Treadwell amassed a vast archive of footage of the bears, and some of this remarkable footage features in the film. However, what is most interesting about this film as a documentary is the way in which Treadwell's original footage of him and the bears is taken and recontextualised by Herzog. There is little doubt that Treadwell was a somewhat delusional, odd character, who saw 'saving' the bears as his vocation. There are countless scenes in *Grizzly Man* where Treadwell appears in front of the camera and speaks at (repetitive) length about how much he 'loves' the bears. As Herzog points out in one of his laconic voiceover moments, Treadwell's view of nature was 'sentimentalised'; he constantly anthropomorphises the animals, in the way that some people talk about their domesticated pets. At one point, for example, after some stunning close-up footage of two male bears fighting, Treadwell surveys the battleground after the two bears have departed and exclaims of one of them: 'Sergeant Brown went to the bathroom, did a number two during his fight' while pointing at a pile of bear dung.

The film is interesting therefore because the vast amounts of footage that Treadwell shot (100-plus hours), with the presumption or knowledge that he would edit this into some sort of documentary shape, actually falls into the hands of someone else. In a sense, then, there are two documentary 'voices' at play in *Grizzly Man* – that of Treadwell, who consistently appears in front of the camera presenting his version of events; and Herzog, whose ironic editorialising voice permeates the film, on the soundtrack and via some of the strange interviews he sets up (e.g. with the coroner, Treadwell's friends). On the one hand, we can see that Treadwell did indeed film some remarkable footage. But he is also shown to be grossly manipulative of the material, often filming and refilming particular speeches to camera to get just the right tone of weepy indignation. On one level this is not a problem – many documentaries will film some shots a number of times, or use some other kinds of 'justifiable' re-enactment or reconstruction. But there is something disconcerting about watching Treadwell (whom we now know to be dead) obsessively re-enact and perform certain scenes. As Herzog opines at one point on the soundtrack, as we move into a sequence which shows Treadwell emoting straight to camera, it was as if the filming process had become a 'confessional' for him. After a tearful moment, where he states, 'I will die for these animals … I had no life. Now I have a life', Treadwell disappears behind the camera, emerging again as he says, 'Now, enough of that!' He then strikes a pose and delivers an exaggeratedly upbeat 'continuity style' line straight to camera ('We've gotta find Banjo! He's missing!') – clearly meant to provide an edit point and link for a completely different section of his film.

These shifts in gear – something that gives a glimpse 'behind the scenes' as it were, and would of course have been excised by Treadwell, or at least recontextualised as he creatively interpreted or shaped his material – are what give the film its tragi-comic or ironic tone. Treadwell, far from the committed and steadfast activist he sees himself as, comes across as a buffoon and a narcissist, with little or no real understanding of the workings of nature. At one point, the film cuts to him sitting next to a dead fox cub. The cub, we learn from Treadwell, was savaged the previous night by some wolves. Instead of recognising that this is part of nature – predators and prey – Treadwell coos in a sentimental manner about the death of the cub: 'I love you … and I don't understand. … Expedition 2001 has taken a sad turn, but it's a real turn, and I mourn the death of this gorgeous baby fox.' As he says this, looking mournfully into the camera, a fly that has been buzzing around the corpse alights on the cub's eye. Treadwell's reaction is indicative of his overall stance: he petulantly waves at the fly, saying, 'Get out of his eye ... frigging fly'. He then stomps off, frame left, with the parting shot: 'Don't do it when I'm around. Have some respect. Fucker!' He is clearly angered by this imposition of nature (a fly feeding on a dead body) as it contradicts his sentimental view of things. The viewer might also speculate that Treadwell is equally annoyed that the fly has ruined the perfect 'spontaneity' of his moment with the dead fox cub.

Clearly, Treadwell comes across in *Grizzly Man* as someone who is actively performing and playing a role. While also coming across as delusional, one suspects Treadwell knew that some of his antics in front of the camera were meant for the cutting-room floor (or for his own personal viewing only). This inflects the finished product in an interesting way, because Herzog is also 'performing' a role, that of the sage and measured documentarist who uncovers the 'truth' of what happened, and places Treadwell the man, and his footage, into some sort of context.

DOCUMENTARY, DRAMA AND PERFORMANCE

The discussion of a self-consciously performed documentary such as *Grizzly Man*, the knowing playing up to the cameras seen in *Grey Gardens*, as well as the questions raised by re-enactment and reconstruction generally, mean that we do need to examine documentary's relationship with drama. There are, of course, strong traditions of drama/documentary hybrids (the best discussion of these is Paget (1998)) and various reasons for filmmakers using these techniques. A recent film such as *United 93* (2006), for example, uses unknown actors and a highly naturalistic style to tell the story of what happened on the United Airlines flight that was hijacked on 11 September 2001; some of the passengers fought back and overpowered the hijackers. The events depicted on the screen are of course 'speculative', though based as much as possible on the available evidence (flight recorders and so on). On the other hand, a documentary such as *One Day in September* (2001) offers an account of the events at the 1972 Munich Olympics, where Israeli athletes were killed by terrorists, but does so using many 'dramatic' conventions. The events depicted in this film are more easily verified and a matter of public record, and the people we see are the actual people involved rather than actors as in *United 93*. Nevertheless, both of these films are in the grey area of the spectrum where documentary and drama meet. (See Ward (2008) for further discussion of *United 93* and performance in drama documentary.)

One of the main reasons for a documentarist to use drama and reconstruction is due to the lack of any original footage of the events being depicted. This then takes us back to the notion of 'sincere and justifiable' reconstruction as arguably seen in the work of Flaherty and the Griersonians. If the events depicted may be said to be typical, probable, and a part of the subject's usual routine, does it matter that we reconstructed (i.e. fabricated) that specific scene? Clearly there is a difference between such scenes and those that have been reconstructed due to lack of any original footage – for example, the scenes we might see in a documentary about the Middle Ages, or the battle scenes in Peter Watkins's *Culloden* (1964) – but it really is one of degree. While dramatised and reconstructed scenes appear to fly in the face of documentary as a mode, it must be remembered that it is only really one type of documentary – the observational, and especially the direct cinema variant of this – that appears to rule them out without reservation. The dramatic rendering of events – even those events that have not happened yet, as seen in *The War Game* (1966), *The Day Britain Stopped* (2003) or the BBC series *If . . .* – can play an important documentary role.

There is also an interesting tendency in recent years for certain films to use documentary techniques but to do so in conjunction with improvised dramatic reconstruction, often using non-professional actors (real people who are more often than not an integral part of the milieu shown in the film). For example, in the made-for-TV film *Twockers* (part of the BBC Storyville strand, directed by Pawel Pawlikowski and Ian Duncan, 1998), Pawlikowski (a renowned documentary filmmaker) uses a cast of unknowns to play out the real drama.

☐ CASE STUDY 4: *TWOCKERS* (PAWEL PAWLIKOWSKI AND IAN DUNCAN, 1998)

In *Twockers*, we see the tale of a gang of feral children living near Halifax, West Yorkshire. They take drugs, engage in petty crime and vandalism, and commit breaking and entering and the 'twocking' of the title – 'twockers' is the acronymically derived name given to those who engage in 'taking without owner's consent', usually referring to car crime. Clearly, this is not a documentary in the accepted sense of the term, quite simply because it consists of 'acted' or 'performed' scenes where the characters engage in criminal activity. The general style of the film is highly naturalistic, observational, though it does have a focalised narrative following Trevor (Trevor Wademan) as he falls for a local pregnant girl, and tries to go straight instead of hanging out with his younger and even more out-of-control friend Steve. The film bears some similarities to *Tina Goes Shopping* and *Tina Takes a Break* (Penny Woolcock, 1999 and 2001), both films that explore the British underclass via improvised, highly naturalistic docudramatic technique. The Woolcock films use direct-to-camera address by some characters which *Twockers* does not, but the same people-playing-themselves points apply. *Twockers* includes some point of view voiceover from Trevor reflecting on his inability to go straight – he does take a job in a chicken-processing factory, but cannot stick with

For further discussion of contemporary British cinema see pp. 381–96.

• Plate 9.6
Twockers (Pawel Pawlikowski and Ian Duncan, 1998). The use of non-actors – real people playing a variation of themselves – and authentic social settings result in a highly convincing documentary-like drama

it – but for the most part the film unfolds in such a way that the characters behave as if the cameras are not present.

These films are in the tradition of Ken Loach and Tony Garnett's TV work such as *The Wednesday Play*. As with much drama-documentary, there are debates to be had about the extent to which these films actually have any documentary worth – that is, aren't they just highly naturalistic fictions? Pawlikowski was commissioned by the BBC to make a documentary, but worked with the young cast to make this improvisational docudrama instead. As Pawlikowski notes, 'the kids we found and improvised with knew what they were doing' (Gibbons 2001). It is evident that Pawlikowski is interested in engaging with social realities in such a way that a more 'conventional' documentary approach, one that merely observed or asserted things about these people in an expository framework, cannot. During the film there are recurring scenes of the town and its 'sink' estates, shot from a hillside where the gang of youths hang out; they have even placed a battered sofa on the top of the hill. These shots are reminiscent of what Terry Lovell, referring to fictional kitchen sink dramas, has called 'that long shot of our town from the hill' (1990: 369) – a particularly resonant image for British social realist films. It is hard not to see some sense of irony in *Twockers*'s recurring use of this shot.

A film such as *Twockers* is in a grey area with regard to documentary status – it cannot be dismissed as an out-and-out fiction, and yet it is clearly approaching its nonfictional/real life locations, events and characters in a very different way to a conventional documentary. There are things which happen in the film that one would never see in a 'proper' documentary – indeed, virtually all of the events depicted would be 'inadmissible' due to their criminal status. For example, what are we to make of a scene where Trevor and Steve break into a supposedly empty house, only to find an old man dead in a chair, and then proceed to burgle the house? The ethical and legal ramifications of course mean that this scene comes clearly 'indexed' as something that is being acted or performed (whereas there are some other scenes – for example, when the youths engage in petty vandalism or raucous behaviour – that could feasibly be viewed as 'actual' rather than 'acted'). The point is that docudramatic films such as this rely on the viewer's interpretive activity, but it is becoming increasingly difficult to distinguish with any certainty between specific modes. The ways in which actuality is mediated by documentary modes, their use of dramatic reconstruction and different types of performance, remains central to an understanding of the field.

CONCLUSION

What we can draw from an examination of documentary in all its manifestations is that it is a highly flexible and discursive category of filmmaking (with very strong connections to television as an institution, and now new media forms). It is important to think about documentary not so much as a discrete and monolithic category, which simply 'captures' reality, but as a diverse set of practices that seeks to critique and – at its best – transform reality.

SUMMARY

- The conceptual and practical issues involved in defining documentary as a form.
- The relationship between documentary and nonfiction as categories.
- The ways in which early cinema 'actualities' may be seen as 'proto-documentaries'.
- The role of performance across a variety of documentary modes.
- The ways in which narrative and dramatisation can lead to a greater understanding of the intersecting range of films and programmes that are termed 'documentary'.

QUESTIONS FOR DISCUSSION

1　In what ways do early cinema actualities behave as documentaries?
2　Why is it important to examine these films in their changing viewing contexts?
3　Does *Grey Gardens* manipulate or exploit its subjects? If so, in what ways?
4　How does *Grizzly Man* mobilise ideas of construction and authorship? Does this make it problematic as a 'documentary'?
5　How do dramatised documentaries such as *Twockers* raise ethical and moral dilemmas? For whom?

1　This film may be viewed online at http://www.movinghistory.ac.uk/archives/bn/films/bn7colliery.html.
The reason he speculates about a 'fairground worker' is that the fair would have been one of the original exhibition sites for Mitchell and Kenyon's films, as there were no cinemas at this point. Indeed, a number of the Mitchell and Kenyon actuality films were commissioned by fairground operators – see http://www.bfi.org.uk/features/mk/about.html

2　*Grey Gardens* is available on DVD from the Criterion Collection. It is also a film that has attracted a cult following – see the 'fan site and homage' at: http://www.greygardens.com/.

Corner, John, *The Art of Record*, Manchester University Press, Manchester, 1996.

Gunning, Tom, 'An Aesthetic of Astonishment: Early Film and the (In)Credulous Spectator', in L. Williams (ed.), *Viewing Positions: Ways of Seeing Film*, Rutgers University Press, New Brunswick, 1995, pp. 114–33.

Nichols, Bill, *Representing Reality*, Indiana University Press, Bloomington, 1991.

Nichols, Bill, *Blurred Boundaries*, Indiana University Press, Bloomington, 1994.

Paget, Derek, *True Stories? Documentary Drama on Radio, Screen and Stage*, Manchester University Press, Manchester, 1990.

Plantinga, Carl, *Rhetoric and Representation in Nonfiction Film*, Cambridge University Press, Cambridge, 1997.

Rosenthal, Alan and Corner, John (eds), *New Challenges for Documentary* (2nd edn), Manchester University Press, Manchester, 2005.

Ward, Paul, 'Drama-documentary, Ethics and Notions of Performance: The "Flight 93" Films', in T. Austin and W. de Jong (eds), *Re-thinking Documentary: New Perspectives, New Practices*, McGraw-Hill/Open University Press, Maidenhead, 2008, pp. 191–203.

Winston, Brian, *Claiming the Real*, BFI, London, 1995.

Baraka (Ron Fricke, 1992)
Basic Training (Frederick Wiseman, 1971)
Berlin: Symphony of a Great City (Walter Ruttmann, 1927)
Biggie and Tupac (Nick Broomfield, 2002)

Bowling for Columbine (Michael Moore, 2002)
Capturing the Friedmans (Andrew Jarecki, 2003)
Cathy Come Home (Ken Loach, 1966)
Chronicle of a Summer (Jean Rouch and Edgar Morin, 1960)

Coal Face (Alberto Cavalcanti, 1935)

The Day Britain Stopped (Gabriel Range, 2003)

Don't Look Back (Don Pennebaker, 1967)

Drifters (John Grierson, 1929)

Early Cinema: Primitives and Pioneers (BFI DVD)

Etre et avoir (Nicolas Philibert, 2002)

Fahrenheit 9/11 (Michael Moore, 2004)

Forgotten Silver (Peter Jackson and Costa Botes, 1995)

Gallivant (Andrew Kotting, 1997)

Gimme Shelter (Albert and David Maysles, Charlotte Zwerin, 1970)

Granton Trawler (John Grierson, 1934)

Grey Gardens (Albert and David Maysles, 1975)

Grizzly Man (Werner Herzog, 2005)

High School (Frederick Wiseman, 1968)

Hoop Dreams (Steve James, 1994)

Housing Problems (Arthur Elton and Edgar Anstey, 1935)

In the Year of the Pig (Emile de Antonio, 1968)

Kino-Pravda (Dziga Vertov, 1925)

Kurt and Courtney (Nick Broomfield, 1998)

The Leader, His Driver and the Driver's Wife (Nick Broomfield, 1991)

Little Dieter Needs to Fly (Werner Herzog, 1997)

London (Patrick Keiller, 1994)

The Lost World of Mitchell and Kenyon (BBC, 2004)

Louisiana Story (Robert Flaherty, 1948)

Man of Aran (Robert Flaherty, 1934)

Man with a Movie Camera (Dziga Vertov, 1929)

Moana (Robert Flaherty, 1926)

Murderball (Henry Alex Rubin and Dana Adam Shapiro, 2005)

Nanook of the North (Robert Flaherty, 1922)

Night Mail (Harry Watt and Basil Wright, 1936)

Primary (Robert Drew, 1960)

Rien que les heures (Alberto Cavalcanti, 1926)

Robinson in Space (Patrick Keiller, 1997)

Roger and Me (Michael Moore, 1989)

Salesman (Albert and David Maysles, Charlotte Zwerin, 1969)

Super Size Me (Morgan Spurlock, 2004)

Tarnation (Jonathan Caouette, 2003)

The Thin Blue Line (Errol Morris, 1988)

Tina Goes Shopping (Penny Woolcock, 1999)

Tina Takes a Break (Penny Woolcock, 2001)

Touching the Void (Kevin MacDonald, 2003)

Twockers (Pawel Pawlikowski and Ian Duncan, 1998)

United 93 (Paul Greengrass, 2006)

Why We Fight (Frank Capra, 1943–45)

RESOURCE CENTRES

http://www.screenonline.org.uk/film/id/1084507/index.html

Screenonline/BFI page listing details of Mitchell and Kenyon films, including playable versions of some.

http://www.dfglondon.com/

The Documentary Filmmakers Group, based in London, but including details of training courses, history of documentary and other material.

http://www.nd.edu/~igodmilo/reality.html

Documentary filmmaker Jill Godmilow in conversation with Ann-Louise Shapiro, a useful and provocative discussion of some important aspects of documentary.

Chapter 10

The language of animation

Paul Wells

■ The language of animation

INTRODUCTION

Obviously, in a chapter of this length, no justice can be done to the many kinds of work in the animation field, nor the gifted animators who make it. While one could mention Svankmajer, Norstein, the Quay Brothers, Pitt, de Vere, Neubauer, Driessen, Rbycynski, Plympton, Park and Dudok de Wit as important names, this already neglects many others, and it is hoped that the chapter raises a general awareness of the field in order that students will seek out new work and cultivate tastes and preferences.

In the contemporary era, animation both constitutes a particular and distinctive form of cinema, and operates as a language of expression in a range of diverse forms on television, on the web, and in other delivery platforms such as computer games, mobile phones and electronic displays. At the very same time that animation has achieved prominence as a filmmaking practice, though, the speed of change in the digital era has once more rendered the form subject to a range of questions and challenges. Such was the nature of animation's neglected status it was once necessary to argue not merely that animation was 'different' from live action as a filmmaking process, but as a 'political' point, to resist those who would always dismiss it, and once more consign it to the margins of cinema history, art and popular culture. In the digital era, 'live action' – the process of photographic recording with a camera – is much more reliant on post-production processes, and arguably, a great deal of contemporary 'cinema' is constructed in the computer. At the very moment when the dominant aesthetic of feature animation is computer-generated imagery, the space between 'animation' and 'live action' is a narrow one, and sometimes indistinguishable.

But in many ways this has always been the case, and requires, as some writers such as Cholodenko and Manovich (see Cholodenko 1991; Manovich 2002) have argued, the acceptance of the view that all cinema has in some way been a variation on 'animation', and not the reverse. While this validates 'animation' as the core language of cinema *per se*, and seems wholly pertinent to the post-photographic digital era, it remains insufficient as a way of viewing animation as a form. The computer is really 'a red herring'. As John Lasseter, the key creative driving force at Pixar Animation has often noted, 'the computer is just a tool', and operates no differently from the range of approaches which have characterised animated shorts and features in the past, by implication suggesting that the 'definition' of animation resides elsewhere.

While we might very well see a great deal of 'animation' in feature films like *Avatar* (2009), and the films of Pixar, Disney, DreamWorks and Blue Sky are self-evidently 'animated', this does not take into account the thousands of animated films made with different styles and techniques throughout the history of animation and in the present day. Further, this merely demonstrates that history repeats itself. 'Animation' was profoundly prominent in film spectaculars like the original *King Kong* (1933), but few thought of it as such, and pioneers such as Willis O'Brien, whose stop-motion animation created the lovelorn gorilla, were not seen as 'animators' or 'auteurs' but as effects artists, their identity and their work made invisible and absorbed within the special effects tradition. This, like many aspects of animated film, is important work to recover because it has also been the case that 'animation' has been viewed merely as 'the cartoon', and for the most part, 'the American cartoon', and furthermore, the 'Disney' cartoon in too many contexts where the form has been scrutinised. For many years, Disney defined the history and identity of animation, and many American pioneers such as Winsor McCay and Otto Mesmer were forgotten, but perhaps even more importantly, work going on in many countries worldwide remained absent from animation history, and the sheer diversity of the form went unrecognised – this is especially significant when it is clear that the West's domination and interpretation of 'animation' has consigned it to secondary status as a film form whereas in the East, for the most part, it has always been viewed as a prominent aspect of the graphic and fine arts.

This chapter will once again seek to provide an analysis of its distinctive vocabulary (looking in the latter part of the discussion at how the computer has become an embedded part of the production process, and technologies such as 'motion capture' have become ready tools in the animation armoury), and aspects of animation history, noting that with the increasing impact of animation from across the world comes more information about alternative animation histories and traditions; and different models of animation which reveal the intrinsic versatility and progressiveness of the form. One need only note that with the impact and affect of Marjane Satrapi and Vincent Parannaud's *Persepolis* (2007), Ari Folman's *Waltz with Bashir* (2008), Andrew Stanton's *Wall-E* (2008) Henry Selick's *Coraline* (2009), James Cameron's *Avatar* (2009) and of course, the *Toy Story* trilogy (1995/1999/2010) animation has been able to continually experiment aesthetically and technologically while it has increased its audience and popularity. This in itself makes it unique within entertainment forms.

WHAT IS ANIMATION?

In the post-photographic filmmaking era, the question of 'what is animation?' has taken on new meaning and prompted fresh debate. If 'live action' and 'animation' have in some senses been effaced by digital technologies, it is still the case that animation is somehow recognisable as 'different'. We still know animation when we see it, especially in its form as a cartoon, or a 3D stop-motion film, or even in its specific incarnation as a computer-generated phenomenon, and sometimes, even when it is at its most photo-realistic. So what is it, that still signals this 'difference' and 'particularity'? Animation is still the art of the impossible, and whether it be the fertile imaginings of independent filmmakers represented in vivid symbolic images of inner states, or the seamless interventions of visual effects animators producing spectacle in major movies, animation remains the most versatile and autonomous form of artistic expression. In the pre-digital era, it was comparatively easy to argue that animation was a process art in which pro-filmic materials (drawings, a puppet with malleable limbs, clay, sand or ink on glass) were filmed 'frame-by-frame', and in between each frame an alteration of the materials was made to create the illusion of movement in phases of imagined action, when the film was projected at twenty-four frames per second. For this kind of filmmaking such a definition remains pertinent. The determining aspects of this kind of practice, of course, are the self-conscious pro-filmic construction of 'motion' in figures, objects and so on, and the notion of 'the frame' as the presiding increment by which this illusion is created. In the digital era, it is still the case that animation mostly uses artificially created and previously conceived movement instead of transferring movement from the natural world, but the 'frame' is no longer the determining factor in the measure of the advancement of this movement.

Norman McLaren, one of the medium's acknowledged masters, suggested of traditional animation practices that 'Animation is not the art of drawings that move, but rather the art of movements that are drawn', noting that 'what happens between each frame is more important than what happens on each frame' (Solomon 1987: 11). McLaren is arguing that the true essence of animation is the manipulation of movements between frames, and his observation still provides an insight about how animation is made, even in the digital era. Fundamentally, it has always been a misconception that animators are wholly concerned with 'the frame'. Actually, they are only concerned with 'a space' in which the motion of artificial figures, objects and forms is sequentially constructed over time. The computer interface, while being less concerned with 'the frame', is absolutely concerned with 'the space', and it is in this that traditional and contemporary animation are one and the same (see Telotte 2010). As animator and author Mike Wellins has observed: 'Motion is easy; making something move from one place to the next is as simple as two mouse clicks, but doing true dynamic motion that is sharp, quick, full of energy, responds to physics, and adheres to the rules is never easy. The computer does do a lot; it creates every frame, applies colour and shading, and keeps shapes consistent. However, it does not, for the time being, create animation' (Wellins 2005: 77–8). It is still the animator's pro-filmic investment in the artificially constructed modes of movement that is at the heart of animation.

It is important, too, to recognise that animation is essentially based on stylisation and abstraction to some degree, even in its most apparently photo-realistic form. The animators of the Zagreb School in former Yugoslavia stressed these creative and philosophic aspects of the craft: 'To animate [is to] give life and soul to a design, not through the copying but through the transformation of reality' (quoted in Holloway 1972: 9). The Zagreb School wished to emphasise that literally 'giving life' to the inanimate was to reveal something about the figure or object in the process which could not be privileged or effectively achieved in live action. It was this distinctiveness in the form that John Halas, of the British Halas and Batchelor studio, sought to theorise in the immediate postwar period when he tried to convince industry, business and education of the value of animation as a specific language of expression and communication, and crucially one that could support serious messages. He suggested that animation's key characteristics were:

- symbolisation of objects and human beings
- picturing the invisible
- penetration
- selection, exaggeration and transformation
- showing the past and predicting the future
- controlling speed and time

(cited in Halas and Wells 2006: 160)

This is a very helpful 'check-list' of qualities specific to the animated form. Symbolism can work to clarify and simplify an idea – a flag can represent a nation; a moving arrow, the direction of an invisible force, like the wind; a single iconic soldier, the military ambitions of a whole country. Such devices can 'picture the invisible', too. Sound waves, magnetism, radar and other physical properties characterised by laws not visible to the eye can be rendered clear and apparent. Halas suggests that animation can also 'penetrate' interior workings of the body or a machine, or other kinds of complex inner state (dream, memory, consciousness, fantasy), and provide a literal and conceptual interpretation which enables them to be more readily understood. Further, by 'selecting' an aspect of a scene or scenario to be visualised this can be accentuated or brought into the foreground for effect; thus it may be 'exaggerated' or 'transformed' to better reveal its properties or significance. All of these elements can be contextualised within various time frames – things can be represented from the long past and projected easily into the future, perhaps on the one hand depicting extinct fauna and flora, or on the other, reimagining nature in a thousand years time as a consequence of current ecological issues and effects. The speed and time in which this is presented can also be varied – a split second can be extended while millions of years can be truncated into a minute or two. The animator can intervene in these time frames, also, accelerating or showing in slow motion particular details. Halas's theories reinforce the control the animator has in constructing an artificial world that can be determined on its own terms and conditions, and with varying degrees of 'realism' or to the point of complete abstraction.

Julianne Burton-Carvajal goes so far as to suggest that '[T]he function and essence of cartoons is ... the impression of irreality, of intangible and imaginable worlds in chaotic, disruptive, subversive collision' (Smoodin 1994: 139). Walt Disney himself endorses this point when he says, '[T]he first duty of the cartoon is not to duplicate real action or things as they actually happen – but to give a caricature of life and action ... to bring to life dream fantasies and imaginative fantasies that we have all thought of [based on] a foundation of fact' (Disney, quoted in Barrier 1999: 142). Animation can defy the laws of gravity, contest our perceived view of space and time, and endow lifeless things with dynamic, vibrant properties. In short, animation can change the world and create magical effects, but most importantly it can interrogate previous representations of 'reality' and reinterpret how 'reality' might be viewed – a point well understood by pioneer filmmakers such as Georges Melies, and early animators Melbourne Cooper, Alexander Shiryaev, J. Stuart Blackton, Emile Cohl, Winsor McCay and Ladislaw Starewicz.

EARLY ANIMATION

Animation as a practice did not emerge fully formed and recognisable as a distinctive way of making films, but rather came out of the experimental approaches to making images move from the long distant past, and in the early technological innovations that eventually led to 'cinema'. As early as 70 BC there is evidence of a mechanism that projected hand-drawn moving images on to a screen, described by Lucretius in *De Rerum Natura*.

In the sixteenth century, 'Flipbooks' emerged in Europe, often containing erotic drawings which, when riffled, showed the performance of sexual acts. In 1825, Peter Mark Roget developed what was later to be called the persistence of vision theory, determining why human beings could perceive movement. Basically, the human eye saw one image and carried with it an after-image on to the image that followed it, thus creating an apparent continuity. Though this assumption has now been challenged by neuro-science, offering the alternative point of view that our perception of motion in cinema may operate on the same cognitive terms and conditions as we perceive and understand movement in everyday life, it is nevertheless the case that our engagement with motion in live action still operates as a model of record while motion in animation is a constructed, choreographic principle. It is the intuitive understanding of the breakdown of such movement and its intrinsic meaning that suggest to audiences the essential enunciative commonality and difference between live action and animated forms. This essential difference was made apparent even with the earliest optical toys because the illusion of motion itself could only be achieved through the participation of the viewer in enabling it. In pre-cinematic toys the artifice of how the motion was created was clear because the viewer had to facilitate its mechanism. Only when cinema took these same principles into its own mechanism did the illusion somehow become mystical and invisible. Developments like the **phenakistoscope** in 1831, the **kinematoscope** in 1861 and the **praxinoscope** in 1877 ensured, then, the eventual emergence of the primitive cinematic apparatus. Intrinsic to these diversionary 'toys' was the idea of the moving image as something magical – a colourful, playful, seemingly miraculous practice, and it was this that characterised the early forms of animation itself.

Also in place by the 1890s was the comic strip form in the American print media industries. This is important because the comic strip was to provide some of the initial vocabulary for the cartoon film: characters continuing from episode to episode; speech 'bubbles'; visual jokes; sequential narrative and so on. By 1893, the *New York World* and *New York Journal* were using colour printing in their strips, and these may be seen as prototypes of later animated forms.

At the centre of the development of 'trick effects' in the emergent cinema was Georges Melies. His discovery of the 'dissolve' (that is, when one image cross-fades into another) led him to pioneer a whole number of other cinematic effects that have become intrinsic to the possibilities available to animators. These included stop-motion photography, split-screen techniques, fast and slow motion, and the manipulation of live action within painted backdrops and scenery. Melies was also a 'lightning cartoonist', caricaturing contemporary personalities, speeding up their 'construction' on screen by undercranking the camera.

By 1906, J. Stuart Blackton made *The Enchanted Drawing*. He appeared as a 'lightning cartoonist', drawing a man smoking a cigar and drinking some wine. By the use of stop-motion, one drawing at a time is revealed and the man's face is made to take on various expressions. Various similar films had preceded this, including *The Vanishing Lady* (1898) and *A Visit to the Spiritualist* (1899). These films may be classified as **proto-animation**, as they employ techniques which are used by later animators

For further discussion of the early film industry see Chapter 1

Early developments in the moving image
The **phenakistoscope** was made up of two rotating discs which appeared to make an image move. The **kinematoscope** was more sophisticated, and employed a series of sequential photographs mounted on a wheel and rotated. The **praxinoscope**, pioneered by Emile Reynaud, was a strip of images mounted in a revolving drum and reflected in mirrors; a model later revised and renamed theatre optique, which may claim to be the first proper mechanism to project seemingly animated images on to a screen.

proto-animation
Early live-action cinema demonstrated certain techniques which preceded their conscious use as a method in creating animation. This is largely in regard to stop-motion, mixed media and the use of dissolves to create the illusion of metamorphosis in early 'trick' films.

animated documentary
In recent years, there has been an exponential rise in the production of animated documentary. This has essentially been characterised by the fusion of documentary tropes – non-fiction subject matter, participant interviews and analysis, use of statistical and archival evidence – and animation, resulting in a reclamation of what might be termed 'naive histories' in the spirit of offering alternative perspectives on the dominant grand narratives of contemporary social, cultural and national existence.

incoherent cinema
Influenced by the 'Incoherents', artists working between 1883 and 1891, a movement principally led by Cohl, this kind of animation was often surreal, anarchistic and playful, relating seemingly unrelated forms and events in an often irrational and spontaneous fashion. Lines tumble into shapes and figures in temporary scenarios before evolving into other images.

character animation
Many cartoons and more sophisticated adult animated films, for example, Japanese anime, are still dominated by 'character' or 'personality' animation, which prioritises exaggerated and sometimes caricatured expressions of human traits in order to direct attention to the detail of gesture and the range of human emotion and experience. This kind of animation is related to identifiable aspects of the real world and does not readily correspond with more abstract uses of the animated medium.

but are not strictly or wholly made frame by frame. The 'lightning cartoonist' became particularly established in the music-halls in Britain, and key figures who were to essentially develop the first British animation school, Lancelot Speed, Max Martin and Harry Furniss, all graduated from this performance context, though it should be stressed that each had worked in illustration, theatre design and fine art before undertaking 'lightning cartooning', and all were well versed in the long-established caricatural and satirical traditions in Britain. Against this background they diverged from their American counterparts, and animation in Britain therefore took a different course. This is but one example of the way various indigenous arts contexts and traditions globally informed emergent animation styles and processes, which were ultimately different from the dominant form that was to emerge from the US. In the late 2000s, this perspective has been yet further evidenced by the public emergence of the early films of British stop-motion animator, Arthur Melbourne-Cooper, and the persuasive argument that he was making stop-motion matchstick figure films – *Animated Matches Playing Volleyball* (1899), *Animated Matches Playing Cricket* (1899) and *Matches Appeal* (1899) as early as 1899 (see De Vries and Mul (2010)); and the extraordinary 2D drawn and 3D puppet animations of Russian classical ballet dancer, Alexander Shiryaev, who recorded the nearly lost and forgotten national folk dances of the classical tradition in an animated form between 1904 and 1906 (see Beumers, Bocharov, Robinson (eds) 2010). In some senses, both approaches operated as an early model of **animated documentary**, though both were concerned with aesthetics, performance and technique.

J. Stuart Blackton, himself an émigré Briton, achieved full animation in *Humorous Phases of Funny Faces* (1906). Although using full animation in key sequences, the film was essentially a series of tricks. Primitive notions of narrative animation followed in the early work of famous comic strip artist Winsor McCay, who under Blackton's supervision at the Vitagraph Brooklyn Studio made an animated version of his most celebrated strip, *Little Nemo in Slumberland*, in 1911. Blackton clearly recognised that the animated film could be a viable aesthetic and economic vehicle outside the context of orthodox live-action cinema. His film *The Haunted Hotel* (1907) included impressive supernatural sequences, and convinced audiences and financiers alike that the animated film had an unlimited potential.

In France, caricaturist Emile Cohl's *Fantasmagorie* (1908) created animation as **incoherent cinema**, less predicated on the comic strip and more related to abstract art. In Russia, Ladislaw Starewicz was making extraordinary three-dimensional puppet films. *The Cameraman's Revenge* (1911) features insects in a melodramatic love triangle and self-consciously shows the power of cinema itself to show human life. Both Cohl and Starewicz were preoccupied with using the form to address both personal and practice-orientated issues, looking at the limits and boundaries of narrative, whether drawing upon avant-garde notions of almost Dadaist comic incongruity or the amoral agenda of the Eastern European folk tradition of storytelling.

It is Winsor McCay, however, who must be properly acknowledged for his influence on Disney and American cartoonal tradition. McCay's *The Story of a Mosquito* (1912) is a mock horror story of a mosquito graphically feeding on a man until it is so bloated with blood that it explodes! Such a film anticipates his development of personality or **character animation** through the creation of *Gertie the Dinosaur* (1914). The playful dinosaur, Gertie, gleefully hurls a mammoth into a lake in the film and clearly displays an attitude. McCay included this film as part of his touring revue show debuting at Chicago's Palace Theatre in February 1914, and appeared to be directly talking to and acting upon his character. This **anthropomorphism** is key within animation in general, but most significantly in the films of Walt Disney that were to follow.

While Disney is acknowledged as the main figure in moving animation towards an industrial process, this is to neglect, however, the work of John R. Bray who pioneered the cel animation process using translucent cels in 1913, and made a film called *The Artist's Dream*. The Bray Studios then released a series of cartoons with a continuing character,

Colonel Heeza Liar, and demonstrated the viability of animation as a commercial industry capable of mass production. Cartoons emerged in the marketplace in the US principally from studios in New York, and Earl Hurd's *Bobby Bumps* series and Paul Terry's *Farmer Al Falfa* cartoons were soon very popular. As Felix the Cat, created by Otto Messmer and Max Fleischer's Koko the Clown in the *Out of the Inkwell* series became stars in the US, and Bonzo the Dog, created by George Studdy, became a popular character in Britain, having his own moving icon in Piccadilly Circus, London and a range of merchandising, more experimental abstract animation was beginning to emerge out of European avant-garde cinema practices, particularly through filmmakers such as Walter Ruttmann, Hans Richter, Viking Eggeling, Lotte Reiniger, Fernand Léger and Oskar Fischinger. The work of individual artists like these sought to explore the aesthetic boundaries of filmmaking, largely working out of fine art experimental practices, while rapid advances in filmmaking technologies in America encouraged the emergence of a variety of organisations making films, and the creation of a commercial industry. In Japan, Oten Shimokawa, Seitaro Kitayama and Jun-Ichi Kouchi had made innovative shorts, and the first studio, Kitayama Movie Factory, was established by 1921, mainly producing educational and instructional films for the government. Following the Tokyo earthquake and fire in 1923, the studio recovered to make folk-tales and erotic animation, and though the animation from the United States, was to make a major impact – as it did worldwide for those able to see it – it is useful to remember that models of animation 'production', 'industry' and 'output' did exist elsewhere.

In the US, after initially working at the Bray Studios, the Fleischers established an efficient streamlined animation process, and were one of the first studios to experiment with sound. It is Walt Disney, however, who remains synonymous with animation, through his radical technical and aesthetic innovation between 1928 and 1942, perhaps the 'Golden Era' of cartoon animation.

THE LEGACY OF DISNEY

Walt Disney Productions was founded in 1923. Disney himself was a draughtsman on his first 'Laugh-O-Grams' – fairytales like *Puss in Boots* and *Cinderella* – but soon realised that his greatest flair was as an entrepreneur and artistic director (see Wells 2002a: 77–90). His film *Alice in Cartoonland*, a mix of animation and live action, was successful enough to secure distribution and finance to develop his ideas further. Fundamentally, Disney wanted to move towards the establishment of an industrial process and a studio ethos and identity which was competitive with and comparable to the established Hollywood studios. In 1927, Disney began working on his *Oswald the Rabbit* series of cartoons and during this process he developed 'the pencil test' (i.e. photographing a pencil-drawn sequence to check its quality of movement and authenticity before proceeding to draw it on cels, to paint it and so on). In 1928, Disney premiered *Steamboat Willie* featuring Mickey Mouse, which was the first synchronised sound cartoon. Following continuing experiments in the use of sound effects and music in differing relationships to the visual images, the cartoon began to standardise itself as a form which moved beyond the illustration of different kinds of music into one which accommodated narrative and a series of related jokes. Disney introduced Technicolor, the three-strip colour system, into his silly symphony *Flowers and Trees* in 1932, which later won an Oscar.

All Disney's animators undertook programmes of training in the skills and techniques of fine art in the constant drive towards ever greater notions of **realism** in his cartoons. Even though Disney was dealing with a form that arguably was more suited to abstract, non-realist expression, he insisted on verisimilitude in his characters, contexts and narratives. He wanted animated figures to move like real figures and to be informed by plausible motivation. Former Disney art director and veteran of the 'Golden era' Zack

anthropomorphism
The tendency in animation to endow creatures, objects and environments with human attributes, abilities and qualities. This can redefine or merely draw attention to characteristics which are taken for granted in live-action representations of these things, and literally create original 'worlds', which nevertheless have a high degree of familiarity and identification.

realism
Live-action cinema has inspired numerous debates about what may be recognised as 'realism'. This is really a consideration of what may be recognised as the most accurate representation of what is 'real' in recording the concrete and tangible world. Clearly, the animated form in itself most readily accommodates 'the fantastic', but Disney preferred to create a hyper-realism which located his characters in plausibly 'real' worlds which also included fantasy elements in the narrative. Crucially, Disney's version of 'realism' sought to properly reproduce perspective illusionism in the frame, and not the surreal and 'eccentric mise-en-scène' of the Fleischer Brothers' films. Overall, animated films have a tendency to create their own realms which obey their own 'inner logic', however, and though a film may be fantastical, abstract, non-linear, surreal and so on, it will probably obey its own codes and conventions which establish its own authenticity and plausibility.

Schwartz suggests that even though the figures moved in an anatomically correct way, they still required an element of caricature which ironically appeared to make them 'more real' on screen, and that what Disney really wanted was a state of conviction in the characters that reconciled the realistic with the caricatural (see Wells 1997: 4–9). This level of 'reality' was further enhanced by the development of the multi-plane camera, developed by Disney's first and most influential animator, Ub Iwerks, who remained fascinated by animation technologies throughout his career (see Telotte 2010: 113–30). Traditionally, in the two-dimensional image, the illusion of perspective had to be created by the artist. The multi-plane camera achieves the illusion of perspective in the animated film by having the relevant image painted on a series of moveable panes of glass placed directly behind each other. Elements of the image can be painted in the foreground; other elements in the mid-spaces; other elements in the receding background. In this way the camera can move through the elements, seemingly keeping them in perspective. This directly aped live-action shooting and was successfully demonstrated in another Oscar-winning silly symphony, *The Old Mill* (1937), with its most advanced aesthetic use in the first full-length, Technicolor, sound-synchronised animated cartoon feature, *Snow White and the Seven Dwarfs* (1937).

Animation had reached a position of maturity, acknowledged in this form as 'art'. *Pinocchio* (1940), *Fantasia* (1940) and *Bambi* (1941) only consolidated this prestige, moving the animated film into the contemporary era, effectively reconciling fine art, a sense of Classicism and a model of traditional American folk culture, ironically drawn from many European influences (see Allan 1999). The rise of Disney and the populist utopian ideology which appealed to the American mass audience has resulted in the neglect of other kinds of animation, but perhaps even more significantly, the popular cartoon, as exemplified in the work of Tex Avery, Robert McKimson, Bob Clampett, Frank Tashlin and Chuck Jones at the famous 'Termite Terrace' lot at Warner Brothers' Studios (see Wells 2002b). An analysis of Chuck Jones's classic cartoon *Duck Amuck* (1953) may usefully offer, however, some points which both valorise the art of the cartoon short, offer an oppositional perspective on Disney's dominance within the field, and provide a vocabulary by which 'animation' itself may be studied.

□ CASE STUDY 1: DECONSTRUCTING THE CARTOON: *DUCK AMUCK* (CHUCK JONES, 1953)

Duck Amuck, directed by Chuck Jones, is the perfect example of a cartoon which is wholly self-conscious and reveals all the aspects of its own construction. Consequently, it is possible to recognise the cartoon as a mode of **deconstruction**. As Richard Thompson points out,

It is at once a laff riot and an essay by demonstration on the nature and conditions of the animated film (from the inside) and the mechanics of film in general. (Even a quick checklist of film grammar is tossed in via the 'Gimme a close-up' gag.)

(cited in Peary and Peary 1980: 221)

Daffy begins the cartoon in anticipation that he is in a musketeer picture and swashbuckles with due aplomb until he realises that he is not accompanied by suitable scenery. He immediately recognises that he has been deserted by the context that both he and we as the audience are accustomed to. He drops the character he is playing and becomes Daffy, the betrayed actor who immediately addresses the camera, acknowledging both the animator and the audience. Perceiving himself as an actor he localises himself within the filmmaking process and signals its mechanisms, all of which are about to be revealed to us.

deconstruction
All media 'texts' are constructed. To understand all the components within each construction it is necessary to deconstruct the text and analyse all its elements. For example, the cartoon is made up of a number of specific aspects which define it as a unique cinematic practice (i.e. its frame-by-frame construction; its modes of representation and so on).

Trouper that he is, Daffy carries on, adapting to the new farmyard scenery with a spirited version of 'Old Macdonald Had a Farm', before adjusting once again to the Arctic layout that has replaced the farmyard. The cartoon constantly draws attention to the relationship between foreground and background, and principally to the relationship between the character and the motivating aspects of the environmental context. Daffy's actions are determined by the understanding of the space he inhabits. These tensions inform the basic narrative process of most cartoons: all Daffy wants is for the animator to make up his mind!

Each environment is illustrated by the visual shorthand of dominant cultural images (e.g. the Arctic is signified by an igloo, Hawaii by Daffy's grass skirt and banjo!). The white space, however, becomes the empty context of the cartoon. Daffy is then erased by an animated pencil rubber and essentially only remains as a voice. However, as Chuck Jones has pointed out, 'what I want to say is that Daffy can live and struggle on in an empty screen, without setting and without sound, just as well as with a lot of arbitrary props. He remains Daffy Duck' (Peary and Peary 1980: 233; see also Furniss 2005). This draws attention to the predetermined understanding of Daffy as a character, and to the notion that a whole character can be understood by any one of its parts. Cartoon vocabulary readily employs the **synecdoche**, the part that represents the whole, as a piece of narrative shorthand. Daffy may be understood through his **iconic** elements, both visually and aurally. No visual elements of Daffy need be seen for an audience to know him through his lisping voice, characterised by Mel Blanc. We need only see his manic eyes or particularly upturned beak to distinguish him from Donald Duck and other cartoon characters, who all have similar unique and distinguishing elements in their design.

At the point when Daffy asks 'Where am I?', even in his absence the audience know of his presence. When he is repainted by the anonymous brush as a singing cowboy we anticipate, of course, that Daffy will sing, although the genre probably prohibits him singing 'I'm Just Wild about Harry', which remains one of his favourites! Initially, Daffy finds there is no sound and holds up a small sign requesting 'sound please', thus drawing the audience's attention to the explicit vocabulary of sound necessitated by the cartoon form, and one immediately familiar to the anticipated viewer. When Daffy attempts to play the guitar, it sounds first like a machine-gun, then a horn, then a donkey, thus simultaneously showing the necessity of sound and image synchronisation for narrative orthodoxy, and the creation of comedy through the incongruous mismatching of sound and image. This is developed after Daffy breaks the guitar in frustration – a standard element of the cartoon is the process of destruction – and attempts to complain to the animator about his treatment, especially as he considers himself 'A Star'. He is given the voice of a chicken and a cockatoo, and, just when he is at his most hysterical in his attempt to speak, he is allowed his own voice, but at increased volume. Daffy is visibly humiliated and his attitude once again reveals to an audience his helplessness in the face of the power of the animator. The animator is at liberty to manipulate the image completely, and to create impossible and dynamic relations which need not have any connection with orthodox and anticipated relations.

This manipulation of Daffy's image and identity also tells an audience about his essential character traits – egotism, ambition, frustration, anger and wilfulness – which are constantly challenged in most of the narratives through the resistance offered by the world around him. In *Duck Amuck*, he is also defeated by the animated context within which he exists. He pleads with the animator for orthodoxy and is greeted with a child's pencil drawing for a background, slapdash painting for the scenery and an absurd reconstruction of his own body in wild colours and a flag tied to his newly drawn tail indicating that he is a 'screwball'. Despite protestations that he has fulfilled his contract, Daffy continues to be treated with contempt. Just when he seems to have been granted the legitimacy of 'a sea picture' – an obvious reference to both Donald Duck and Popeye –

synecdoche
The idea that a 'part' of a person, an object, a machine, may be used to represent the 'whole', and work as an emotive or suggestive shorthand to the viewer, who invests the 'part' with symbolic associations.

iconic
The iconic is defined by the dominant signs that signify a particular person or object – Chaplin, for example, would be defined by a bowler hat, a moustache, a cane and some old boots, while Hitler would be defined by a short, parted hairstyle and a small 'postage stamp' moustache.

Daffy is subjected to the standard cartoon gag of recognising that he is temporarily defying gravity by standing in mid-air only to drop into the sea the moment he realises. Seconds later he is on an island, but the image is merely a small frame within the normal frame, this time drawing the audience's attention to the compositional elements of the cartoon and, indeed, of film language itself. We can hardly hear Daffy as he calls for a close-up, and receives one at rapid speed, only showing us his eyes.

Once again calling upon the audience's recognition of the frame as a potentially three-dimensional space, Daffy then tries to cope with the sheer weight of the black background scenery which falls upon him like a heavy awning. He eventually tears up the 'screen' in sheer frustration and demands that the cartoon start, even though it has already been running for several minutes. A screen card with 'The End' comes up, accompanied by the Merrie Melodies theme. Daffy then attempts to take control of the film by returning to the key notion of himself as an entertainer performing a vaudevillian soft-shoe shuffle. He is trying to reclaim the idea of the cartoon as a medium for entertainment rather than deconstruction. His song-and-dance routine is interrupted, however, by the slippage of the frame as it appears to divide the screen in half and expose the frames of celluloid the film is supposedly composed of. The two frames, of course, reveal two Daffys, who immediately start to fight and disappear in a blur of drawn lines – the fight merely becomes a signifier of cartoon movement, a symbol of kineticism unique in embodying character and signifying form.

Narrative life improves for Daffy as 'the picture' casts him as a pilot. This is merely a device, however, to demonstrate a series of conventional cartoon gags, including an off-screen air crash, the appearance of the ubiquitous anvil as a substitute for Daffy's parachute and an explosion as Daffy tests some shells with a mallet – by this time, however, he is a gibbering heap, devoid of dignity or control, the two qualities Daffy most aspires to. As he tries to assert himself one last time, Daffy demands to know 'Who is responsible for this? I demand that you show yourself!' The frame as we understand it is then completely broken as the scene changes and the camera pulls back to reveal the drawing-board and 'the animator' – Bugs Bunny, Daffy's arch-rival. As Thompson remarks, 'Duck Amuck can be seen as Daffy's bad trip; his self-destruction fantasies and delusions, with their rapid, unpredictable, disconcerting changes of scene and orientation, are the final extension of ego-on-the-line dreams' (quoted in Peary and Peary 1980: 233). This is an important point in a number of respects. It locates Daffy as a character firmly in a relationship between form and meaning. Each narrative establishes and develops the vocabulary which defines the underpinning imperatives of both character and the form the character inhabits. This leads to the cartoon animation embodying a number of **ideological** positions. Disney's films, for example, often play out an orthodox narrative form to reinforce an ideological status quo. In other words, Disney's films support and illustrate what Robert Sklar calls 'the spirit of social purpose, the re-enforcing of old values' (quoted in ibid.: 61). This idealised world is often challenged by the anarchic worlds of Tex Avery (see Adamson 1975; Wells 1998) and Chuck Jones, and, indeed, other kinds of animation which send complex and often subversive messages.

The animated film reached maturity in the 'golden era' of the American cartoon, and in doing so had established Disney as synonymous with animation. This has led to animation being understood in a limited way. Disney perfected a certain language for the cartoon and the full-length feature which took its model from live-action filmmaking. This overshadowed other kinds of innovation and styles of animation which have extended the possibilities of the form and enabled other kinds of film to be made. Disney's art remains the dominant language of animation and we can term this 'orthodox animation', using its vocabularies and traditions to useful, sometimes self-reflexive storytelling ends. The cartoon *Feed the Kitty* was used as a key template for the emotional exchanges between Sulley and the little girl Boo in *Monsters Inc*, when Sulley believes Boo has

For further discussion of narrative, film form and meaning see Chapter 4

ideological
Although a complex issue, ideology may be seen as the dominant set of ideas and values which inform any one society or culture, but which are imbued in its social behaviour and representative texts at a level that is not necessarily obvious or conscious. An ideological stance is normally politicised and historically determined. In the first instance, cartoons seem especially 'innocent' in this respect, but they are characterised by implicit and sometimes explicit statements about gender, race, nationality, identity and so on which are the fabric of ideological positions, and require interrogation and inspection.

been crushed into a metal cube. This notion of 'orthodox' animation needs to be addressed in the light of Disney's aesthetic now being overtaken by the prominence of computer-generated animation, and principally the work of Pixar Animation. Many of the Pixar staff are classically trained Disney animators, and are also well versed in animation history. The work of the studio has in essence sought to enhance the classical tradition defined in 'the Golden Era' through conscious use of the aesthetic and technological advances enabled by the computer. Consequently, while the work may have a different aesthetic, and the process by which it was made has significantly changed, the sense of 'orthodoxy' in the Disney style remains fundamentally unaltered. There is still the preoccupation with character animation, narrative cause and effect, aesthetic consistency, 'cartoonal' reference, an apparently non-interventionist authorial voice (though all animation is essentially self-reflexive and self-figurative – see below), and a reliance on dialogue and a traditional musical soundtrack to drive and define the story. This kind of work – also termed by Shilo McLean as 'the new traditionalism' (see McLean 2007) – can still be usefully compared to two other areas of the form, which we may classify as developmental animation and experimental animation, the former demonstrating degrees of divergence from the dominant 'orthodoxy'; the latter, essentially seeking out alternative methods of expression using the versatility of the form, and readily defined by non-representational, non-objective, non-linear, 'visual music' and the stylistic pluralism of more abstract works.

These kinds of animations operate in a way that echoes Maureen Furniss's view that all forms of animated film have varying degrees of reference either to 'mimesis' (literally, like 'realist' representation) or 'abstraction' (which abandons realist referents and signifiers in preference to other models of representation) (Furniss 1998: 6). In despite of such variation, animation remains a singularly enunciative language, literally announcing its intrinsic difference on-screen from live-action work and other modes of artistic expression. More importantly, in announcing itself, it further announces what Donald Crafton has called its 'self-figurative' nature (Crafton 1993: 11); this is the particular aspect of animation which suggests that the 'author' of the film is present on screen or imbued in its text in a self-evidently auteurist way. This may be literally with the presence of the animator seeming to actually draw or create the animation in films like those from the Fleischer Brothers' *Out of the Inkwell* series featuring Koko the Clown, or more complexly, in the way that the self-conscious handling of the distinctive language of the animation text is used by the filmmaker. In embracing **metamorphosis**, for example, the animator is resisting the model of record and edit that is the primacy of live action, and specific to the ways in which image, text and narrative make literal, frame-by-frame, special manipulations of motion construction, or on-screen transitions in animated film. This highly self-reflexive medium enables animators to verify the freedoms of the form, and foreground perspectives which serve as a comment on the act of filmmaking *per se*, but more importantly, as a revision of accepted or naturalised constructions of 'reality', and a reinterpretation of received knowledge. Virgil Widrich's playful narrative, *Fast Film* (2003) serves as a good example of this.

metamorphosis
The ability for a figure, object, shape or form to relinquish its seemingly fixed properties and mutate into an alternative model. This transformation is literally enacted within the animated film and acts as a model by which the process of change becomes part of the narrative of the film. A form starts as one thing and ends up as something different.

□ **CASE STUDY 2: ANIMATION AS A SELF-REFLEXIVE LANGUAGE:** *FAST FILM* **(VIRGIL WIDRICH, 2003)**

Virgil Widrich's extraordinary short *Fast Film* is composed of 65,000 photocopied stills from over 400 notable Hollywood feature films from the silent era to the present day. Widrich and his team viewed over 1,200 films selecting images and sequences, which in their photocopied form were folded into three-dimensional objects, and recomposed and animated into a narrative about the codes and conventions of Hollywood narratives. Simply, the 'story' is one in which a woman is abducted, a man seeks to find and save

For further discussion of Hollywood genre see Chapter 8.

her, and confronts a villainous enemy who seeks to thwart him in a series of spectacular chases. This does not begin to describe the self-reflexive complexity of the piece, however, in which nominal figures of the 'hero', 'played', among others, by Humphrey Bogart, Sean Connery, Cary Grant and Harrison Ford, and a 'heroine', represented by Lauren Bacall, Janet Leigh and Audrey Hepburn among many, engage in typical 'live-action' scenarios of pursuit, threat, suspense, conflict, escape and resolution, but which are self-consciously executed in a deliberately rough-hewn animation style, in which digital still photographs were animated with post-production software. The images appear to 'boil', producing an 'authentic' sense of the frame-by-frame animation, while foregrounding recognisable images from a range of Hollywood genres, including the western, the horror film, the film noir, the spy film and so on. This apparently 'low-rent' style is conducted with state-of-the-art technology, and this points up the significant changes in the production process, while demonstrating the very conventions of the Hollywood classical narrative that animation customarily subverts and reworks. Widrich and his team carefully delineated the formulaic aspects of different kinds of action sequence; for example, a train chase is broken down into four elements: 'crossing a train', 'getting on a train', 'getting under a train' and 'splitting a train'. So, by cross-cutting newly configured elements, in animation, from films as diverse as *Sherlock Jnr* (1927); *The General* (1927); *The Lady Vanishes* (1938); *The Train* (1964); *Butch Cassidy and the Sundance Kid* (1969); *Runaway Train* (1985); *To Live and Die in LA* (1985) and *Broken Arrow* (1996), the construction of narrative events and emotive visual cues could be readily revealed yet reworked.

The film may also be read as an implicit history of Hollywood, and cleverly shows the formulaic aspects of the hero's journey, informed by variations on spectacular action; the role of the heroine as a passive subject; the clichéd aspirations of the 'villain' or 'monster' in their alternative underground worlds; and the sense of resolution played out through chases and conflicts – here, in the images below, in the guise of an aerial 'dogfight' – and principally, in the romantic kiss and embrace shared by the hero and heroine. These conventions are highlighted, but ultimately revised through animation, and their limited resonance and meaning exposed and playfully critiqued. The self-figurative and self-reflexive nature of the piece invites the viewer to see the transparency, yet basic appeal of formula 'live-action' narratives, while acknowledging the self-conscious art, technique and intensity of suggestion in the animated form. Even the title is playful – 'Fast', in English, signals that this is a highly **condensed** version of the Hollywood movie, but 'Fast', in German, means 'almost'. Animation as 'almost film' suggests both its sense of differentiation and its revisionist agenda.

condensation
The compression of a set of narrative or aesthetic agendas within a minimal structural framework. Essentially, achieving the maximum amount of suggested information and implication from the minimum amount of imagery used.

PERPETUAL 'MODERNITY'

Throughout its history, even in its most supposedly conservative and orthodox forms, animation has consistently sought to progress its art, resisting the notion of a dominant form created at the Disney Studios. While even in the contemporary period, Disney still casts a long shadow on the field of animation, it is clear that both in the US, and elsewhere, while there remained an extraordinary degree of respect for the art and culture of the Disney Studios, and recognition of its achievements and influence, there was always the desire to achieve different things in animation. For example, as a consequence of the strike at Disney Studios in 1941, Canadian animator Stephen Busustow left the company and established United Productions of America (UPA). He, along with other talented animators John Hubley, Pete Burness, Bob Cannon and Bill Hurtz, wanted to pursue a more individual style that the Disney 'look' could not accommodate. This led to work that was less specifically 'realist' in its approach, and, as Ralph Stephenson has suggested, 'the cynicism, the sophistication, the depth of adult attitudes are not ruled out' (Stephenson 1969: 48).

• **Plate 10.1**
Individual frames from Hollywood movies are created
as A4 images, which are then folded into particular
shapes to be animated. Here, John Wayne, flying in a
jet fighter, is re-presented as a paper plane

• **Plate 10.2**
Hundreds of 'paper planes' are created featuring the
incremental movements of John Wayne flying his
jet fighter, ready to be 'animated' in a new aerial
sequence

• **Plate 10.3**
Wayne in his 'paper plane' is reconfigured against a
new background featuring other fighter planes. This
image shows how a traditional 'frame-by-frame'
method is being used to create the new 'dogfight'
sequence

• **Plate 10.4**
The playfulness of the sequence is readily signalled
in reconfiguring the spectacle of a live-action
sequence as a seemingly basic animated action
played out through the use of the 'paper plane'.
This simultaneously parodies the excesses and
predictability of Hollywood chase sequences,
and draws attention to the self-figurative and
self-reflexive nature of the animation process

• **Plate 10.5**
An image from the final sequence from *Fast Film*
featuring Wayne in his paper plane aircraft fleeing his
pursuers

squash and stretch
Many cartoon characters
are constructed in a way
that resembles a set of
malleable and attached
circles which may be
elongated or compressed
to achieve an effect of
dynamic movement.
When animators 'squash'
and 'stretch' these
circles they effectively
create the physical
space of the character
and a particular design
structure within the
overall pattern of the
film. Interestingly,
early Disney shorts
had characters based
on 'ropes' rather
than circles and this
significantly changes the
look of the films.

reduced animation
Animation may be
literally the movement
of one line which, in
operating through time
and space, may take on
characteristics which an
audience may perceive
as expressive and
symbolic. This form of
minimalism constitutes
reduced animation which
takes as its premise
'less is more'. Literally
an eye movement or the
shift of a body posture
becomes enough to
connote a particular
feeling or meaning. This
enables the films to work
in a mode which has an
intensity of suggestion.

Ironically, this 'sophistication' was achieved through non-naturalist, fairly unsophisticated technical means. These included minimal backgrounds, 'stick' characters and non-continuous 'jerky' movements. The **squash-and-stretch** conception of movement in conventional cartoon characters, based on a design where the body is thought of as a set of circles, was replaced by the representation of a body as a few sharp lines. Backgrounds, which in Disney animation were positively voluptuous in their colour and detail, were defined by a surrealist minimalism, where stairs led nowhere and lights hung from non-existent ceilings. This kind of development expanded the vocabulary of the animated film and more readily defined animation's relationship to modern art, and the desired 'shock of the new' imbued in its form. More importantly, it challenged the ideological and aesthetic premises by which Disney animation came to define 'American' animation (see Wells 2002b). Crucially, the division that Disney had effected in separating the notion of 'art' from the 'artisanal' by insisting upon all of the essential 'collaborativeness' of a hierarchical production process being absorbed within the authorial 'brand' named as 'Walt Disney', was challenged by a more self-evidently and individually 'authored' model of the cartoon. UPA, though operating a studio system, nevertheless privileged the work of specific directors and artists, once more reuniting the art with the artisanal – those who produced the work were acknowledged as its intrinsic creators. In many senses, this was a more self-conscious model of what actually occurred at the Warner Bros studio, largely because UPA were prepared to name the cartoon as 'art' and not merely comic diversion. It is pertinent to recall, though, that it was the British studios Halas and Batchelor, and W.E. Larkins, who incorporated the idioms of modern art into their work much earlier, during the Second World War, prompted by the émigré sensibilities of their leading figures John Halas and Peter Sacks. Both had been powerfully influenced by the work of the Bauhaus, and principally Laszlo Moholy-Nagy, and though the films made by the studios acknowledged the art of Disney, their work embraced the aesthetic principles of Klee, Kandinsky and others (see Plates 10.6–9).

Halas and Batchelor and the Larkins Studios sought to operate essentially as renaissance studios, and like UPA, sought to resist Disney-style hierarchies of production. In championing a politicised 'auteurism' even within studio confines – in direct opposition to Disney's subjugation of individual styles to the established aesthetic – UPA also echoed a similar vision to that held at the Zagreb Studios in the former Yugoslavia, whose aesthetic was drawn from the same modernist sources as those championed by Halas and Sacks.

Influenced by UPA's *Gerald McBoing Boing* (1951) and *The Four Poster Bed* (1952), designed by John and Faith Hubley, the Zagreb animation industry developed around the two key figures of Dusan Vukotic and Nikola Kostelac. Initially making advertising films, the two progressed to making cartoons deploying **reduced animation**, which is described by Ronald Holloway:

Some films took an unbelievable eight cels to make, without losing any of the expressive movement a large number of cels usually required. Drawings were reduced to the barest minimum, and in many cases the visual effect was stronger than with twice the number of drawings.

(Holloway 1972: 12)

Liberated from the limitations of orthodox animation, these films increased the intensity of suggestion located in the images and moved towards a more avant-garde or experimental sensibility which was able to embrace aesthetic development as a model of ideological progress and political critique. Many developmental and experimental animators saw animation itself as a vehicle by which they could challenge established forms of filmmaking practice, privilege their own vision, and refresh any stagnation in the animated form, too. While Disney's work was undoubtedly a pinnacle in the form, it both marginalised other 'cartoonal' forms and their pioneer creators, and rendered

• Plate 10.6
Balance, made in 1950 by the W.E. Larkins Studio, under the direction of Peter Sacks, was a detailed address of ICI's expenditure and profit, with a commentary by Roger MacDougal and a score by Halas and Batchelor stalwart, Francis Chagrin

• Plate 10.7
Predicated on simple modernist art forms, principally those advocated by Paul Klee, the film uses pertinent symbols, shapes and lines to present direct and accessible information

• Plate 10.8
Sacks's direction proved highly influential, as Steve Bosustow, Head of UPA, saw the film, and echoed its style and approach in *Fudget's Budget* (1952)

• Plate 10.9
The W.E. Larkins Studio, and particularly, the Halas and Batchelor Studio, created important work which represented a distinctively 'British' style that not merely influenced modernist animation in the US, but also provided a platform for the development of an animation industry in Britain, acknowledged by its most important successors, Aardman Animations, even in the contemporary era

more progressive work as somehow unrelated to the dominant aesthetic and cultural identity defined by the cartoon. Although explicit here, the ways in which animated films can simultaneously make statements and advance the self-reflexiveness and modernity of the form itself are many and varied. Crucially, these kinds of works have responded to the changing creative and cultural climate in which they were made, using animation as a vehicle by which both subversive and alternative perspectives may be maintained. Ironically, though, it was economic factors which prompted radical change in the American animation industry. As the major studios closed their animation production units, unable to support the rising costs of producing cartoons, the era of theatrically distributed shorts was at an end. Despite misgivings that this was somehow 'the end' for animation altogether, television became the new exhibition context, and Hanna Barbera perfected a method of reduced animation – not dissimilar to the Zagreb and UPA approach – which was based on a limited number of movement cycles, but enhanced with high-quality vocal performances by, among others, Daws Butler and June Foray, and sharp, gag-laden scripts. From the *The Huckleberry Hound Show* through to *The Flintstones*, Hanna Barbera defined the television cartoon and sustained the animation industry. Unfortunately, the television cartoon in the period between the 1950s, almost through to the emergence of *The Simpsons*, is still often denigrated, but this is to neglect important work, and to once more reduce the animated form to an art with connotations of innocence and undemandingness, but of course, in response, this has been readily exploited by animators knowing that the very 'cuteness' of their expression may be the mechanism by which they can position the viewers' expectations only to challenge them. John Kricfalusi, one of the key directors of the contemporary television era, is a case in point.

One of the most interesting aspects of the way that this has occurred since the fall of the Berlin Wall is in the way that European traditions, and, most notably, the work of artists based in the former Soviet Union and its satellites, has influenced the American cartoon. Creator-driven television work by figures like John Kricfalusi in *The Ren and Stimpy Show* directly references and extends the American cartoons of the 'Golden Era'. Kricfalusi notes Dave Fleischer's 1930s 'Talkertoons', Grim Natwick's 'Betty Boop' designs, movement cycles in the *Popeye* cartoons, Chuck Jones's incongruous comic juxtapositions of classical music and cartoonal slapstick, Bob Clampett's *The Great Piggy Bank Robbery* (1946), and Hanna Barbera's *Tom and Jerry* cartoons as specific influences. But a different graphic styling has increasingly influenced shows like *The Rugrats*, *The Wild Thornberrys*, *AAAHH!!! Real Monsters!* and *Phineus and Ferb*, which has its source in the achievements of master Estonian animator, Priit Pärn.

□ **CASE STUDY 3: RECALLING AND REVISING
   ANIMATION TRADITION:** *BREAKFAST ON THE GRASS*

For many years, the history of animation was essentially defined by the history of the American animated cartoon, but with the increasing development of animation scholarship many additional contributors to animation's rich heritage worldwide have been recognised for their work, and for prompting recognition that there are other tradi-tions of cartoon animation in other countries. One of the key figures to emerge from this necessarily revisionist approach is Estonian, Priit Pärn, whose work before the fall of the 'Iron Curtain' and after has proved equally influential on both independent artists and Hollywood's mainstream. Pärn's distinctive caricatural style is matched with an almost Bunuelian imagination, making his work highly personal and inherently challenging, combining the freedoms of the animated form with an anti-narrative perspective on Western codes and conventions of storytelling. There is sufficient allusion to Western iconography and cultural practices, however, to know how Pärn views the dominant 'grand narratives' (largely the brand identities, political narratives and core influential figures of a late-industrial capitalist economy) in the West, and how he privileges his alternative, idiosyncratic world-view. Pärn points out that even to be working in animation is already to signify that there is a different model of thinking being employed and, conse-quently, an alternative kind of expression. Crucially, this has enabled Parn to express himself in a way that preserves the resistant sensibility that characterises his outlook in the Soviet era, while also encouraging his exploration of symbolic and metaphoric approaches to his own emotional condition in the independent era. This creates a persistent tension between Pärn's implicit commentary on the seemingly absurd preoc-cupations of a free, late capitalist, culture and a set of values and ideologically charged ideas, drawn from his past but defining his contemporary sensibility. This results in an approach which always foregrounds 'interior states' and reinventions of sometimes familiar contexts, conduct and conditions, often in a spirit of black humour and political satire, but equally, in personal images that sometimes refuse a common reading. One of the key tools that Pärn employs, however, is making his imagery operate in a fashion that at one and the same time is provocative but leavened by its very illusionism. This is common in animation and can work as a language of dilution in some circumstances and of amplification in others. Pärn can create a personal and sometimes politically incorrect or subversive narrative because the seemingly unpalatable or challenging aspects of his work are diluted by the assumption that this is 'merely' animation – ink and paint, and no more – and that animation does not carry with it charges of difficulty and unacceptability. Clearly, the worldwide reception and critical response to Pärn's work is testament to the view that animation can be seen as an amplification of challenging perspectives, equally legitimised and sustained by their artifice. His belief that the use of animation overtly signals a different way of thinking about life has enabled Pärn to use his highly distinctive imagery to address the common complexities of existence, while retaining a distinctly personal vision. Pärn is actually dealing with 'reality' but one less known to Western audiences, both in the experience it records and in the way that it is represented. Animation enables him to achieve this.

Steve Lillebuen, writing about Pärn's *Time Out* (1984) in a short catalogue published to support a retrospective of Pärn's work in Canada in 2005, suggests it has a 'Yellow Submarine' world; is reminiscent of a Warner Bros. cartoon with its bookending theatrical curtains; and even works as a 'morbid combination of *Monty Python* and *Ren and Stimpy*', but ultimately concedes that 'this is about as far from the *Bugs Bunny* and *Tweety Show* as you can get'. This perspective is informed by the way Pärn uses the language of animation, in that he is resisting dominant forms of graphic and narrative expression by recalling and revising them. His view of 'caricature' is very important in this respect, since it is not a 'funny drawing' but a metaphor which points to a certain absurdity which may or may not thereafter be amusing. This is why his drawing resists the kind of 'cute', 'big-eyed', 'squash'n'stretch' character animation of the American or Japanese tradition, preferring puppet-styled grotesques which, rather than suggesting 'ugliness', prompt a recognition of the reality of physical ordinariness, the 'warts'n'all' 'unattractiveness' of humankind, rejecting the idyllic construction of innocent and appealing human forms. Thus Pärn uses his perception of the world to focus on his own internal and insular conventions to reclaim the image from exhausted conventions of representation in other kinds of animation. His concern is not mainstream recognition but to reach those who would see the reality he was depicting. At one and the same time he references the cartoon tradition of the US and the graphic idioms of the French, Czech and Polish caricaturists and political cartoonists in animation, but refreshes their aesthetic, metaphorical and ideological assumptions.

This is especially pronounced in his film *Breakfast on the Grass* (1988) which was submitted to the authorities in 1983 but refused production, and it was only the thaw of Perestroika that permitted the film to be made in 1986. The narrative begins with a dedication 'to the artists who did everything that they were permitted to do', a double-edged acknowledgement of the efforts of artists to sustain freedom of expression in the light of the oppressions of totalitarian government, and also the limitations this still imposed. The narrative is divided into five episodes, featuring four characters, Anna, Georg, Berta and Eduard, who unbeknownst to each other share the similar bleak terrain of life determined by an impoverished but authoritarian regime. They are referenced in each other's narrative, with the implication that all are only defined by the moment in which they live, their lack of identity in the midst of the mass, and the minimal achievements in merely surviving. Pärn begins the film with a car accident, an extended scream and a goldfish bowl crashing to the floor in Anna's appartment, as she rushes to get ready when she realises she is late for work. This is not merely anxiety, though, but a genuine fear about engaging with the outside world, as her umbrella blows away in a rain storm, where the grotesque mass of people mock her, people compete aggressively for a place on a bus, and she must defend herself from potential sexual assault. Pärn exposes the irony of a tyrannical regime in which there seems to be the superficial order of oppressive routine, habit and service to the state, but which is actually characterised by a venal culture fighting in whatever way possible for pleasure and resources. A

• Plate 10.10

Breakfast on the Grass (Priit Pärn, 1988): A black marketeer bargains with Anna for sexual favours. Pärn uses the apple as a symbol for commodity, sexuality, and lost paradise

• Plate 10.11

Pärn uses the image of blindmen queuing for the opticians as a metaphor for irrevocabile break down in the political and commodity system under Communist rule

• Plate 10.12

Berta's drawn-on face simultaneously evokes her need to construct an identity in the light of faceless anonymity but also the authorial playfulness of the animator's presence and vision

• Plate 10.13

A one-eyed bureaucrat blinds himself with his tea-spoon – another visual joke to suggest the absurdity of authoritarian government

• Plate 10.14 and 10.15

Pärn presents his four leading characters in a pose which recalls Manet's 'Déjeuner sur l'herbe', demonstrating that life is but surfaces, and underneath there are many complex and contradictory aspects, which have all been illustrated in the earlier parts of the film

shopping trip is a competitive trauma, for example, where Anna loses apples to opportunist children, and is tricked by a black marketeer into getting an apple in return for sexual favours.

Pärn felt he had explored the formal principles of metamorphosis and the mutability of form in his early film *And Plays Tricks* (1978), deploying a sense of physical and material dissolution in the service of making the characters' world have a sense of inexplicable temporariness and passing ephemera. This is especially the case in Georg's episode, which begins with Georg's fantasy of himself as a bourgeois intellectual, versed in the fine arts and in possession of material wealth. This fantasy literally dissolves into a context in which everything is black, rotting and broken, and with it there is the realisation that it is his ambition to embrace quasi-Western values and culture. Ironically, the fantasy lifestyle he dreams of has already been appropriated by a corrupt government, and he understands that to achieve this he must become a successful senior bureaucrat. His pursuit of an appropriate jacket projects him into an absurdist farce in which he is persecuted into facilitating ways in which those people who can help him get the jacket are themselves in some way helped in their own pursuits. Georg must get a pair of glasses for the tailor, for example, but is confronted by a queue of blind men blocking his way to the optician's. He becomes party to the fact that Soviet life is actually an oppressive mechanism, where power resides with those who manipulate others and kill those who do not conform. Once he finally puts on the jacket, however, he is content to accept the implicit status quo.

There has now been a generation born since the Berlin Wall came down, and some contemplation on the part of Eastern Europeans about their experience. While many have seen benefits, and there have been many changes, any number of people feel disadvantaged by the fact that their work is now not state-supported and their endeavours have been subject to the most exploitative aspects of Western capitalism, while there has been no preparation for a market-led culture, and a lack of investment in a competitive infrastructure. Fundamentally, many believe that their efforts to live under Soviet law left them better placed and happier than under the vestiges of a market economy. Essentially, much to the incomprehension of some Western ideologues, many people were content in the Soviet system simply because they had learned to live within it. This is Berta's story; the third episode in Pärn's narrative. Even though Berta is faceless and feels she has literally to construct her identity by drawing on her face – another aspect referential to animation itself – she reconciles herself with her domestic life by caring for her children on the unofficial terms and conditions the culture has developed. She gives her daughter balloons by exchanging them for an apple; the sexual resonance of this act is implied from Anna's story. Pärn even invests this with an ambivalent eroticism, itself part of a representational system in his work, which sometimes offends Western moral sensibilities.

This is perhaps exacerbated most in Eduard's story, in which a surreal cab ride results in his humiliation and literal diminution at the hands of hierarchical bureaucrats and obese prostitutes. The limitations of the system are best represented in two visual gags – one, where a one-eyed senior administrator blinds himself with the spoon in his cup of tea; another where the bust of a leader on a plinth dissolutely flows away down its pedestal only to be replaced by an exact replica. In the film's final episode Eduard gains access to the 'paradise' of a park and is joined by Anna, Georg and Berta, who assemble in the tableau pose of Manet's masterpiece 'Déjeuner sur l'herbe'. It is in this that Pärn consolidates the meaning of his film, aligning himself with Manet's work which scandalised Paris because it was viewed as both crude in its technique and its subject matter – exactly the same response which attended Pärn's approach to non-Disney-style animation and his direct, uncompromising depiction of the Communist regime. Equally, Manet's painting does not wholly reject academic painting or official taste, referencing Raphael and Titian in the way that Pärn suggests the graphic anarchies of Terry Gilliam or Bob Clampett. By using irony in this way, both point to a certain vulgarity which is embedded in humanity despite the social, cultural and political conditions that manage and define them. Further, they foreground the absurd brutality of the hierarchies which determine how life should be led, and what tastes, postures and ambitions humankind should supposedly pursue.

THE IMPACT OF ANIMÉ

Pritt Pärn was to influence independent auteurs like Igor Kovalyov and the Hollywood mainstream through his unconventional but fresh graphic styling which emerged in a number of Cartoon Network series. This, along with programmes like Kricfalusi's *The Ren and Stimpy Show* was instrumental in proving that television animation could be progressive and revive recollections of 'the Golden era'. Hanna Barbera and Filmation, among others, created any number of 'Saturday Morning Cartoons', but television also provided the first platform for the emergence of Japanese animation in the West. Osamu Tezuka, 'the God of Comics' and 'the Disney of Japan', was a key figure in both the manga and animation industries in Japan, his Mushi Production Company creating 'Astro Boy' which debuted in the US in 1963, and was ultimately made as a feature in the US in 2009. Japan's first colour animation for television, Tezuka's *Kimba the White Lion* was broadcast by NBC in 1966, and in recent years has become part of an ongoing dispute, where it has been alleged that Disney's *The Lion King* (1994) drew upon Kimba for its characters and story without acknowledgement (see Patten 2004: 144–91). However this might be viewed, it is indisputable that Japanese animation has been extraordinarily influential, not merely in the field of animation but on Hollywood film in general. Mamoru Oshii's *Ghost in the Shell* (1995), for example, is an oft-cited forerunner of *The Matrix* series (1999–2003), while Hayao Miyazaki's *Laputa, the Flying Island* (1986) is a clear influence on Disney's *Atlantis: The Lost Empire* (2001) and Cameron's *Avatar*. Indeed, Miyazaki's work in general, from *Nausicaa of the Valley of the Winds* (1984) to *Ponyo* (2008) has not merely established Miyazaki as a major animation auteur but a key Japanese director likened to live-action masters Kurosawa, Ozu and Mizoguchi, and an established figure in world cinema *per se*.

☐ CASE STUDY 4: HAYAO MIYAZAKI

Miyazaki began his career at the Toei Doga Studio in 1963, but was soon established as a key animator on Isao Takahata's *The Little Norse Prince* (1968), and eventually directed his first feature *The Castle of Cagliostro* in 1979. Miyazaki, like Tezuka, was a talented comic book artist, and created a graphic novel called *Nausicaa of the Valley of the Winds*, which was serialised in Toshio Suzuki's *Animage* magazine, later resulting in an animated feature of the story in 1984, and Suzuki funding a new animation studio, Studio Ghibli, led by Miyazaki and his colleague Takahata. Critically acclaimed films like *My Neighbour Totoro* (1988) and *Kiki's Delivery Service* (1989) followed, but only when Miyazaki's characters were fully exploited in relation to merchandising – much to his disappointment – did a mass audience find his work. *Porco Rosso* (1992), *Princess Mononoke* (1997) and *Spirited Away* (2001) all broke box-office records, but also established Miyazaki's core themes and preoccupations.

Miyazaki has been consistent in his use of young heroines, arguing that stories are still largely determined by male sensibilities, and that the use of a central female character enables greater freedom in the narrative and points of emotional transcendence. Furthermore, the young heroine has special purchase in Japan, as there is a sense of a 'lost era' of innocence and intrinsic 'Japaneseness' represented in these girl figures for a certain generation, and which is often misinterpreted in the West in relation to its erotic and cultural charge. Miyazaki uses his heroines to explore not merely their own rites of passage towards maturity, but also the conflicting personal, social and ideological forces at large in cultural life which affect individual experience, and cannot necessarily be resolved. While many of Miyazaki's characters have moments of epiphany and revelation that empower them and enable them to come to terms with their difficulties – often through elevation and flight – they often exist in dream-like, supernatural or surreal alternative worlds which cannot be subjected to rational and civilised order, and the limits of everyday habit and routine. Consequently, Miyazaki can depict characters not merely in their local time and place, but as part of a complex, multifaceted, historically indeterminable space, which illustrates the spiritual, sociological and political dynamics of experience. Miyazaki's key preoccupation in this respect would be a concern for ecological issues, and the ways in which the particular abuses of nature by humankind operate as a betrayal of children and their future lives. Miyazaki's main focus therefore is to address the sometimes contradictory, ambivalent and violent aspects of the human sensibility in order to foreground – mainly through his heroines – the more positive and progressive human values and emotions.

While Katsuhiro Otomo's *Akira* (1988) can claim to be the first major 'cross-over' animé in the West; Mamoru Oshii's *Patlabor* (1990), *Ghost in the Shell* (1995) and its sequel *Innocence* (2004) operate as key works in charting a more dystopic, apocalyptic agenda in postwar Japan, and Satoshi Kon's visionary works like *Perfect Blue* (1998), *Tokyo Godfathers* (2003) and *Paprika* (2006) chart a complex change in Japan's psychological and emotional terrain, it is Miyazaki's vision which has gained a global audience. Still mostly achieved through hand-drawn cel-animated processes, though more recently including computer-generated material, that prevails as an insightful engagement both with animation as a medium of expression and a model of story-telling seeking to express universal concern, while promoting love and hope as intrinsic human qualities necessary for survival and progress. Like many great animation directors and artists, and like the form itself, Miyazaki continues to experiment, while speaking to a mainstream audience.

Continuing to experiment

Experimental animation, in its most readily understood form, embraces a number of styles and approaches to the animated film which inevitably cross over into areas which we may also term avant-garde or art films. A great deal of animation has been constituted in new forms (computer, photocopy, sand on glass, direct on to celluloid, pinscreen) and resists traditional approaches as they have been understood within the cartoonal realm. William Moritz has argued that this form of non-objective and non-linear animation is actually the purest conception of animation, as its language is significantly different from its live action counterpart and most explicitly reveals the distinctive range and extent of the animated vocabulary (see Canemaker 1988: 21–32). Fundamentally, such films exhibit the greatest degree of abstraction and are more concerned with rhythm and movement in their own right, rejecting logical and linear continuity, moving away from the depiction of conventional forms and the assumed 'objectivity' of the exterior world, enabling shapes and objects to move, and liberating the artist to concentrate on the vocabulary he or she is using in itself instead of giving it a specific function or meaning. As Leopold Survage wrote,

For further discussion of art cinema, narrative and film form, see Chapter 4, pp. 81–87.

I will animate my painting. I will give it movement. I will introduce rhythm into the concrete action of my abstract painting, born of my interior life; my instrument will be the cinematographic film, this true symbol of accumulated movement. It will execute 'the scores' of my visions, corresponding to my state of mind in its successive phases.... I am creating a new visual art in time, that of coloured rhythm and of rhythmic colour.

(quoted in Russett and Starr 1976: 96)

This kind of subjective work has therefore necessitated a different response from audiences. Instead of being located in understanding narrative, the audience is asked to bring its own interpretation to the work. Colour, shape and texture evoke certain moods and ideas, and give pleasure in their own right without having to be attached to a specific meaning or framework. The audience may recognise the physical nature of the paint or physical materials themselves, the associations with the colours used, the sheer spontaneity in the work, which may recall the freedoms of expression in the pre-socialised child and so on. These films are largely personal, subjective, original responses, which are the work of artists seeking to use the animated form in an innovative way. Sometimes these 'visions' are impenetrable and resist easy interpretation, being merely the absolutely individual expression of the artist. This in itself, once again, draws attention to the relationship between the artist and the work, and the relationship of the audience to the artist as it is being mediated through the work. The abstract nature of the films insists upon the recognition of their individuality. Further, these films may aspire to the condition of the dream-state, or memory, or fantasy, which, of course, has its own abstract logic, but conforms to a common understanding of human experience which embraces these states of consciousness. Dreams, memories, fantasies and the interpretation of thought processes may be the vehicles for personal visions but they possess a universalised dimension (see Wells and Hardstaff 2008; Furniss 2008; Selby 2010). Such work often has a strong relationship to music, and, indeed, it may be suggested that if music could be visualised it would resemble colours and shapes moving through time with differing rhythms, movements and speeds. Some filmmakers perceive that there is a psychological and emotional relationship with sound and colour which may only be expressed through the freedoms afforded through the use of animation. Sound is important in any animated film, but has particular resonance in the experimental film as it is often resisting dialogue, the clichéd sound effects of the cartoon or the easy emotiveness of certain kinds of music. Silence, avant-garde scores, unusual sounds and redefined notions of 'language' are used to create different kinds of statement (see Coyle 2010).

☐ CASE STUDY 5: NORMAN MCLAREN

Norman McLaren is probably the most experimental filmmaker in the animation field. He has explored a number of different styles, including direct animation (drawing directly on to celluloid), paper and object animation (stop-motion frame-by-frame constructions of movement with objects and cut-outs and so on), evolution works (the gradual evolution of a pastel or chalk drawing) and multiple printing works (where movements are recorded as they evolve through the multiple printing of each stage of the movement). Beyond the implicit influence of his work, he also nurtured other artists, and maintained a pacifist, left-wing, humanitarian agenda in his creative practice, evidenced early in his student film *Hell UnLtd* (1936).

Educated at the Glasgow School of Art in 1933, he made his first experimental 'cameraless' film in 1934, having been inspired by Oskar Fischinger's *Brahms' Hungarian Dance* (1931), and seeking out a reel of film to scrub clean and paint on. He then entered two films, *Camera Makes Whoopee* and *Colour Cocktail* in the Glasgow Film Festival of 1936. Although he believed the former to be his 'calling card' to the creative industries, it was the latter that impressed documentary filmmaker John Grierson, who invited McLaren to work at the General Post Office (GPO) Film Unit. Initially undertaking live-action camerawork for *Defence of Madrid* (1936), McLaren was later encouraged by the new studio head, Alberto Cavalcanti, to engage in his own films, and to work in a more improvised, looser style, than that signalled in McLaren's meticulously prepared

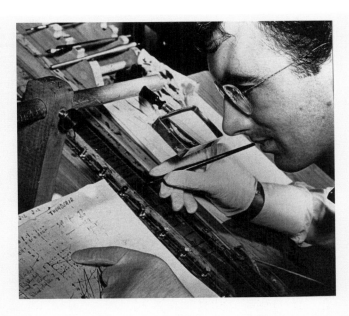

original scripts. Although many have only seen Grierson as a documentary filmmaker committed to left-leaning works of social record, and someone not especially concerned with aesthetics, this is to neglect his interest in the 'creative interpretation of actuality', and more importantly, the key purpose in engaging with a left-wing agenda – to ensure not merely that the disempowered might find proper representation, but that the core democratic principle of the freedom of expression was clearly demonstrated in the work itself. Thus Grierson's work with Len Lye and Norman McLaren was a ready example of redefining 'films of record' to capture the spiritual and creative freedoms of expression of the artist in its purest, non-objective, non-linear form. McLaren made *Love on the Wing* (1938) and *Many a Pickle* (1938); the former, like many of McLaren's works, an experiment in moving abstract images aligned with and counterpointing musical idioms – in this case, Jacques Ibert's *Divertissement* – which was banned by the Postmaster-General for its apparent use of phallic imagery. McLaren traced his interest in this kind of filmmaking to his high school years in which he only possessed a radio, and cultivated his ability to visualise images which supported the dynamics of the music rather than creating a literal narrative to illustrate it. This drew McLaren to pursue research in colour and form rather than the rigours of story-telling.

McLaren was then invited by the Museum of Non-objective Painting, later named the Guggenheim, in New York, to make a range of abstract loops, including *Allegro* (1939) and *Dots* (1940), though he managed also to make two other personal films – *Stars and Stripes* (1939), which used the US flag as its background, and an experimental electronic work with Mary Ellen Bute, *Spook Sport* (1939). By this time Grierson had moved on to establish the National Film Board of Canada (NFB) and McLaren joined him, becoming head of the newly formed animation unit in 1943. Embracing the creative freedom offered by the NFB, even though the Board was charged with making films about Canada and Canadians, McLaren embarked on a career that sought to advance animation as an art form, most notably by drawing upon its relationship to dance in such films as *Blinkety Blink* (1954) and *Pas de deux* (1968), but also the imaginative use of sound – for example, in *Begone Dull Care* (1949) and *Synchromy* (1971). McLaren's desire to transcend national and ethnic boundaries within his work, and to ensure aesthetic, technical and creative innovation, meant that he used little dialogue, and employed multilingual

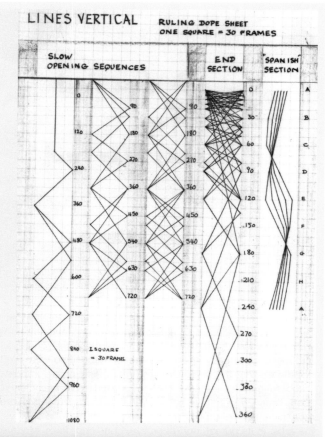

• **Plate 10.17**
One of McLaren's 'dope sheets' aligning proposed action with the intended rhythms on the soundtrack, essentially creating a model of 'visual music'

• **Plate 10.18**
McClaren working on the choreography for *A Chairy Tale*, in which a chair takes on a life of its own, part animated frame by frame, and part created through the use of invisible wires

credits. Crucially, McLaren's work, in the extension of technique, sought to be *about* the animated form as much as it also signified an implied subject matter in the apprehension of particular feelings or moods. *Neighbours* (1952), his famous anti-war parable, was a more explicit expression of McLaren's preoccupations, and not only redefined the cartoon, the principles of live-action performance and the use of animation as a peacetime propaganda tool, but also embodied the philosophic, imaginative and humanitarian heart of Norman McLaren's vision. McLaren's playful engagement with the quasi-figurative, decorative and purely abstract forms in sensitive relation to the rhythmic dynamics of a variety of soundtracks both paid tribute to the European pioneers of the experimental form cited earlier, and encouraged generations of other animation filmmakers who wished to work with alternative techniques and approaches.

CONCLUSION: COMPUTERS AND CONVERGENCE

As has been suggested earlier in this discussion, experimentation has taken place in all forms of animation from the traditional cartoon to the explicitly avant-garde work. Animation can create the conditions to express new visions by devising a vocabulary which is both limitlessly expressive and always potentially progressive because it need not refer to or comply with the codes and conventions of representation and expression that have preceded it. The three models of orthodox, developmental and experimental animation are constantly changing. Computer technology is enabling a new generation of animators to work with a different tool in order to both use traditional methods and invent fresh approaches to the animated form. Science, art and the moving image are conjoining to create a new digital cinema, enabling both a re-determination of the animated film and the enhancement of special effects in mainstream movies.

From the early experimental uses of computer animation at NASA and the Massachusetts Institute of Technology; the film exercises of James Whitney senior and junior; the proto-CG works of Stan Vanderbeek (*Poemfields*, 1967–69), Lillian Schwartz (*Pictures from a Gallery*, 1976) and Peter Foldes (*Hunger*, 1973); the work of the Halas and Batchelor Studio – both in the creation of pieces like Roger Mainwood's *Autobahn* (1979) for cult group Kraftwerk, the ground-breaking adaptation of László Moholy-Nagy's modernist experiments in *A Memory of Moholy-Nagy* (1991) and in the prescient promotion of computer animation as a tool of the future (see Halas and Wells 2006); and in the early output of the PIXAR company (see Rubin 2006; Paik 2007), there is already a history of animation in computing which exhibits the continual development of a vocabulary that is extending the limits of the form.

For further discussion on computer animation see Chapter 2.

Although a great deal of work had been done by the mid-1980s, and computer-generated sequences had appeared in *Futureworld* (1976), *Star Wars* (1977), *Star Trek: The Wrath of Khan* (1983), *Tron* (1983) and *The Last Starfighter* (1984), among others, it was three ground-breaking short pieces which ensured that computer-generated animation would transcend its extraordinary expense, long production cycle and lack of a standard software, to ultimately become the dominant form of expression in the form. First, Daniel Langlois' *Tony Le Peltrie* (1985), featuring an ageing lounge singer lamenting changing times, but even, despite its excessive caricature, proving that persuasive character animation could be executed in computer-generated form. Second, Robert Abel's *Brilliance* (1985), an advertisement, featured a '*Metropolis*-style' female robot, using the first primitive motion capture, and proving that computer-generated work could be visually attractive, create more sophisticated outcomes than common 'fly-throughs', and offer some form of dramatisation. Third, and most significant, ex-Disney animator John Lasseter's highly effective computer-animated shorts – *Luxo Jnr* (1986), *Tin Toy* (1990) and *Knick Knack* (1991), which, by emulating the character animation of Disney and the gag-structures of Warner Brothers and MGM cartoons, proved that computer animation could embrace 'the cartoon'. These film experiments culminated in the first full-length fully computer-generated feature *Toy Story* (1995), and its sequels, the equally engaging *Toy Story 2* (1999) and *Toy Story 3* (2010), which demonstrated what computer-generated images were initially uniquely able to offer. The toys were the perfect vehicle for the three-dimensional sense of smoothness and plasticity achievable using the geometric potentialities afforded by computer programs; further, the playroom space was fully exploited for the sense of dynamic movement through three-dimensional space also afforded by the computer. Inevitably, though – and this echoes the paradigm instigated by Disney – PIXAR continued to innovate in the area of computer-generated animation by pursuing ever greater degrees of realism (see Wells 2002a). If *Toy Story* is PIXAR's *Snow White and the Seven Dwarfs*, then *Monsters Inc* is PIXAR's *Bambi*, perfecting the fullest representation of 'hyper-realism' in the animated form (see Wells 2002c). This was compounded further in the brilliant undersea vistas of *Finding Nemo* (2003) and the extraordinary character animation in addressing the limitations of representing fish. While DreamWorks SKG have responded to PIXAR's work with the Warner-styled *Shrek* franchise, and Blue Sky have created entertaining pieces in *Ice Age* (2003) and *Robots* (2005), it was PIXAR's *The Incredibles* (2004) that created a watershed in computer-generated animation by being a fully realised piece of 'cinema' for children and adults, and setting a benchmark by which the quality of computer-generated films could be measured. Director Brad Bird's intention to 'break out' and create a narrative which could accommodate Bergmanesque domestic bleakness, Bond-style spectacle, and a genuine thematic conviction in addressing the redefinition of 'heroes' in the post–9/11 era; depicting the dangers of cultural conformism; and the powerlessness of humanity in the face of its social infrastructures, moved computer-generated features to the point where they can only be evaluated by what they are seeking to achieve rather than the 'awe' factor of their mere creation. Such has been the speed with which computer-generated features have become the orthodoxy in animation that a critical mass of production has now been reached where the 'technology' and its innovations are no longer sufficient in evaluating the progress of the form, and it is once more the traditional skills in innovative storytelling, persuasive character animation and inventive visual spectacle that will determine the next classic in the field. Pixar have made further progress in this respect with the provocative eco-fable *WALL-E* (2008), with its challenge of creating a plausible robot romance, and *Up* (2009), a profoundly moving tale of senior citizen Carl Fredickson's engagement with his grief, identity and purpose in a stirring adventure, pitching him against an embittered 1930s-style jungle adventurer. These two films, along with *Toy Story 3*, which again deals with loss, rites of passage and emotional survival, constitute highly mature works which speak not only to both adult and child audiences but also to the key preoccupations and anxieties of the contemporary era.

Crucially, though, as more independent filmmakers embrace computer-generated animation, the dominant aesthetic established by PIXAR and its challengers will be changed and subverted. Already, Yoichiro Kawaguchi, in Japan, has sought to be more abstract and experimental in his computer-generated films – *Eggy* (1990), *Festival* (1991) and *Mutation* (1992) – by emulating organic forms and developing random systems which create different shapes, forms and colour combinations. British animator William Latham has also created software to execute designs in a similar spirit, for example, in *Biogenesis* (1993). Ruth Lingford has also successfully used computer animation to make more challenging work in the graphic starkness of *Death and the Mother* (1996) and *Pleasures of War* (1999) (see Wells 2001b: 338–9). Further, Johnny Hardstaff with *The Future of Gaming* (2001), Marc Craste with *JoJo in the Stars* (2004) and Chris Landreth with *Ryan* (2004) have already achieved works of high standing by once more revisiting and revising established vocabularies in the graphic and visual arts.

Hardstaff's controversial film, originally commissioned to promote Sony Playstation, is a sinister piece suggesting that the oppressive corporate intentions of the games masters, in keeping the masses amused and rewarded in facilitating a late capitalist

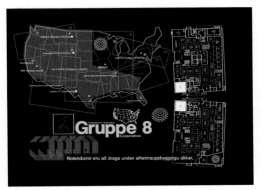

• **Plate 10.19**
Hardstaff's understanding of the symbolic and sign-led
aspects of graphic design, contemporary gaming imagery and
animation reinvigorates the form, creating a new hybrid of
animated 'documentary' and graphic fiction

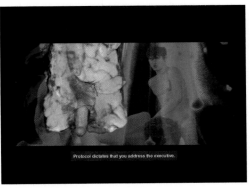

• **Plate 10.20**
Hardstaff's profoundly controversial imagery and its
implications prove that animation should not be understood
merely as an 'innocent' cartoonal form, but one able to
embrace serious, subversive and challenging perspectives

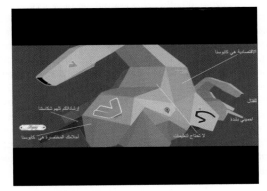

• **Plate 10.21**
Animation is in essence 'moving graphics', but rarely have the
imperatives of interior, product or industrial design strategies
been used for narrative effects. Hardstaff's perspectives use
all of these visual strategies and more, drawn from the history
of art and design, to redraft the animation palette

system, have been challenged by a subversive global uprising prompted by the games
themselves, which instigates everything from the release of uninhibited desire, the abuse
of social convention, the dismissal of religious faith and the rise of arbitrary terrorism.
Hardstaff's imagery draws upon a range of traditions in graphic design, illustration and
decoration, and is used to make the familiar and formerly instructive a terrain of threat
and subversion. His style resists any formalist tradition in animation, and consequently
progresses the animated form in its graphic precision and social insight.

Marc Craste does something of a similar order in *JoJo in the Stars* by creating a
romantic narrative in the half-light of a surreal and distant nightmare, based on the kinds of
distanciating abstraction in films such as David Lynch's *Eraserhead*, and the understated
perversity and unspeakable ambivalence in films such as Tod Browning's *Freaks*, and
the Universal horror films of the 1930s. Such work recalls innovative aesthetic strategies,
but further progresses them by divesting them of the 'camp' and 'kitsch' postmodern
readings with which they are often attributed, and recalling the genuine sense of alienation
and loss at their heart. This is computer animation with feeling and emotion which is
not about the contrived sentimentalities of traditional classical narrative, but imbued in

the aesthetic and motion of the piece. Chris Landreth's *Ryan* also seeks to prompt an emotive response, but his work, based on the life of former renowned animator at the National Film Board of Canada, now homeless street panhandler Ryan Larkin, uses a form of 'psychological realism' to redefine the documentary form. Landreth's command of the computer software enables him to create fragmented figures, seemingly in a state of atrophy and psychosomatic flux, and the characters themselves become readily symbolic of their disintegrating psychological states. Concerned with memory, addiction, compulsion and loss, the film defines aspects of the creative sensibility from the point of view of the subject – Larkin himself – and the maker of the film, Landreth. Once more, it is animation itself which is also enhanced as a language of illusion and artifice, but as the most appropriate medium to create a visual and aural terrain that extracts and literally depicts psychological and emotional truth.

Craste has developed his romantic vision further in *Varmints* (2008) and Landreth has extended his technique in a redemptive tale in *The Spine* (2009), and while computer animation has become consolidated as one of the key forms of expression in animation, it is still only one of a myriad set of approaches by filmmakers worldwide. Nick Park scored extraordinary success when fourteen million viewers watched his claymation Wallace and Gromit adventure *A Matter of Loaf and Death* (2008) on Christmas Day 2008; PES enjoys mass popularity for his 3D stop-motion reinvention of nostalgic objects and environments on his website in micro-shorts like *Western Spaghetti* (2008); Wes Anderson deployed 'old-school' Ladislaw Starewicz stop-motion animation for *Fantastic Mr Fox* (2009); and Dennis Tupicoff, with his amusing rallying cry of 'I will not be a foot soldier in Jim Cameron's Army!', continues to make complex, quasi-documentaries, using drawn forms and rotoscoping, like *Chainsaw* (2007). These filmmakers merely exemplify the ways in which animation continues to develop, embrace change and push back the frontiers of creative expression. As the post-photographic era becomes increasingly consolidated, it is the language of future expression, drawing upon the rich legacy of its progressive past. With the extent of animation in *Avatar* – touted as the 'future of cinema' – it is clear that the tools, conditions and language of animation are now a central determinant of cinema itself.

SUMMARY

- Animation is a distinctive form of expression within moving-image practice, and is created in many diverse forms and techniques. It has many established auteurs and studios.

- Animation, though often characterised through the dominant presence of the Disney Studios, and in recent years Pixar Animation, or through TV productions like *The Simpsons*, is an omnipresent, multidisciplinary practice, with an extensive history worldwide. Most nations have an indigenous animation history, which is being subject to research and recovery.

- In the digital era, animation is being recognised as a key process not merely at the margins of cinematic practice, but as a key mainstream model of production, and as the dominant constituent of contemporary film production *per se*.

QUESTIONS FOR DISCUSSION

1 What are your expectations of 'cartoons' in regard to representation, subject matter, and aesthetics?
2 How is your viewing of cartoons changed by looking at how gender, age, sex and sexuality, race and ethnicity, identity, etc are represented in such films?
3 In what ways do 'cartoons' signal to the viewer that they are indeed self-consciously made 'cartoons'?

4   What are the differences between traditional forms of 'live action' film and 'animated films'?

5   In the digital era, animation seems to be a central part of filmmaking practice in general. In what ways can we detect and see animation in mainstream feature production?

6   Popular animation is dominated by films and television shows from the US. What should be taken into account when viewing animated films from other cultures and nations?

7   Animation is often viewed as a form for children or just a vehicle for humour. In fact, most animation from other nations deals with adult material and serious themes. Identify an animated film from another culture or nation to your own which deals with serious issues, and suggest how animation has been used to address the topic.

8   Animé is often related to manga in Japanese culture. What would you identify as the commonalties and differences between graphic narratives/comics and animation?

9   Animation in Japan is very popular and virtually all genres are represented, Choose a Japanese horror/sci-fi/romance/etc. film and consider what might be distinctively 'Japanese' about it, and how animation is being used to re-imagine genre forms in some way.

10   How would you define the term 'experimental' film? In what ways is 'animation' an experimental form?

11   What does 'abstract' animation represent to you? Why do you think animators wish to work in this way?

FURTHER READING

Barrier, M., *Hollywood Cartoons: American Animation in the Golden Age*, New York and Oxford: Oxford University Press, 1999.

Beck, J., *Animation Art*, London: Flame Tree Publishing, 2004.

Bell, E., Haas L. and Sells, L. (eds), *From Mouse to Mermaid: The Politics of Film, Gender and Culture*, Bloomington and Indianapolis: Indiana University Press, 1995.

Crafton, D., *Before Mickey: The Animated Film 1898–1928*, Chicago and London: University of Chicago Press, 1993.

Furniss, M., *Art in Motion: Animation Aesthetics*, London and Montrouge: John Libbey, 1998.

Klein, N., *7 Minutes*, London: Verso, 1993.

Leslie, E., *Hollywood Flatlands: Animation, Critical Theory and the Avant Garde*, London: Verso, 2002.

Manovich, L., *The Language of New Media*, Massachusetts : MIT, 2002.

Patten, F., *Watching Anime, Reading Manga*, Berkeley : Stone Bridge Press, 2004

Pilling, J. (ed.), *Women and Animation: A Compendium*, London: BFI, 1992.

Russett, R. and Starr, C., *Experimental Animation*, New York: Da Capo, 1976.

Wasko, J., *Understanding Disney*, Cambridge and Malden: Polity Press, 2001.

Wellins, M., *Storytelling Through Animation*, Hingham, MA: Charles Rive Media Inc, 2005.

Wells, P., *Understanding Animation*, London and New York: Routledge 1998.

Wells, P., *Animation: Genre and Authorship*, London: Wallflower Press, 2002a.

Wells, P., *Fundamentals of Animation*, Lausanne: AVA, 2006.

FURTHER VIEWING

Here are some key models of animated film which repay viewing and analysis:

Akira (1988) (Dir.: Katsuhiro Otamo)
Asparagus (1978) (Dir.: Suzan Pitt)
Bad Luck Blackie (1943) (Dir.: Tex Avery)
Binky and Boo (1989) (Dirs: Derek Hayes and Phil Austen)
Boy Who Saw the Iceberg, The (2000) (Dir.: Paul Driessen)
Coal Black and de Sebben Dwarfs (1943) (Dir.: Bob Clampett)
Dimensions of Dialogue (1982) (Dir.: Jan Svankmajer)
Dreams and Desires, Family Ties (2006) (Dir.: Joanna Quinn)
Ersatz (1961) (Dir.: Dusan Vukotic)
Fast Film (2003) (Dir.: Virgil Widrich)
Father and Daughter (2000) (Dir.: Michael Dudok de Wit)
Fatty Issues (1990) (Dir.: Candy Guard)
Give Up Yer Aul Sins (2001) (Dir.: Cathal Gaffney)
Great (1974) (Dir.: Bob Godfrey)
Hand, The (1965) (Dir.: Jiri Trnka)
Harvie Krumpet (2003) (Dir.: Adam Elliot)
Hat, The (1964) (Dirs: John and Faith Hubley)
Hotel E (1992) (Dir.: Priit Pärn)

I Married a Strange Person (1997) (Dir.: Bill Plympton)
Knick Knack (1991) (Dir.: John Lasseter)
Mona Lisa Descending a Staircase (1991) (Dir.: Joan Gratz)
Morir de Amor (2005) (Dir.: Gil Alkabetz)
Never Like the First Time (2006) (Dir.: Jonas Odell)
Nose, The (1963) (Dir.: Alexander Alexieff)
Old Man and the Sea, The (1999) (Dir.: Alexandr Petrov)
Pas de deux (1967) (Dir.: Norman McLaren)
Popeye the Sailor meets Sinbad the Sailor (1936) (Dir.: Dave Fleischer)
Red Hot Riding Hood (1949) (Dir.: Tex Avery)
Springer and the S.S. (1946) (Dir.: Jiri Trnka)
Stain, The (1991) (Dirs: Christine Roche and Marjut Rimmenen)
Street, The (1974) (Dir.: Caroline Leaf)
Tale of Tales (1979) (Dir.: Yuri Norstein)
Tango (1981) (Dir.: Zbigniew Rybczynski)
The Incredibles (2004) (Dir.: Brad Bird)
Three Little Pigs (1933) (Dir.: Walt Disney)
Triangle (1994) (Dir.: Erica Russell)
What's Opera, Doc? (1957) (Dir.: Chuck Jones)
Words, Words, Words (1999) (Dir.: Michaela Pavlátová)

RESOURCE CENTRES

The UK Directory, *Animation UK* is an invaluable resource in that it lists most animators, animation companies and facilitators, and courses running in Britain. Published annually by BECTU.

http://www.aardman.com/
Aardman Animations

http://www.annecy-animation-festival.tm.fr/
Annecy Festival

http://www.awn.com/
Animation World Network. The database section is pretty minimal and often incorrect; the best thing is the magazine's breadth of articles, mainly written by animators, critics or festival programmers. The What's New section in AWN is convenient for updates. The Animation Village has several listings and links to animators, organisations, festivals and so on, in the international animation world. Artists such as Caroline Leaf and Alison Snowden/ David Fine have their own home pages on AWN.

The same has Nicole Salomon's AAA in Annecy, Folioscope, ASIFA Hollywood and ASIFA San Francisco, as well as the Society for Animation Studies, Motion Picture Screen Cartoonists Union Local 839 and the Writers Guild of America. There are also links to other similar home pages not hosted by AWN, such as ASIFA International.

http://www.awn.com/asifa_hollywood/
ASIFA Hollywood

http://www.awn.com/asifa-sf/
ASIFA San Francisco
ASIFA East and ASIFA San Francisco produce quite informative articles, and provide information on current (US-based) projects, both commercial and independent, as well as opinion pieces.

http://www.awn.com/heaven_and_hell/
Animation Heaven and Hell. This site has nicely designed pages on model and stop-frame animation, including [0160]vankmajer and George Pal.

http: //www.awn.com/safo99/
Ottawa Festival

http: //www.chapman.edu/animation/
Animation Journal

http: //www.medios.fi/animafest/
Zagreb Festival

http: //memory.loc.gov/ammem/oahtml/
oahome.html
Origins of American Animation web site

http: //www.nfb.ca/E/1/1/
National Film Board of Canada. The National Film
Board of Canada has a really impressive site. You

can go through their whole catalogue of films
with descriptions; many of the most important
filmmakers have their own biography; and the
history of NFBC is extensively described. The main
problem with the NFBC home page is that the
entry page is too big, it takes minutes to download;
skip it and go directly to the index.

http: //Samson.hivolda.no: 8000/asifa/
ASIFA International

http: //www.swcp.com/animate/
ASIFA Central

http: //www.yrd.com/asifa/
ASIFA East

Part four

Cinema, identity and the politics of representation

Gender and film

Jill Nelmes

■ Gender and film

INTRODUCTION

In the past decade there has been an increasing interest in examining how we understand gender and how gender may be understood in relation to film. In many ways this interest in studying gender has arisen out of feminist film studies research, which brought the study of the representation of women in film on to the academic agenda, originally from a psychoanalytic perspective. At the same time, within the field of cultural studies, there has been much debate about how we understand masculinity and femininity and to what extent gender is culturally determined.

The importance of feminist film theory in opening up debates around spectatorship, the male gaze and the role women play as 'object of the look' is evident from the influence it has had in many areas of academic study from art to literature and cultural studies. Although woman was originally the main focus of academic inquiry about gender and cinema there had been earlier discussion of masculinity: Joan Mellen in *Big Bad Wolves: Masculinity in the American Film*, for instance, wrote on the subject with some eloquence in the 1970s. But Laura Mulvey's seminal article, 'Visual Pleasure and Narrative Cinema', published in 1975, was so influential that academic inquiry in the 1970s and early 1980s mostly focused on the representation of women in film. Little attention was given to the study of masculinity until the 1980s, when Steven Neale's essay, 'Masculinity as Spectacle', reopened the debate (see Cohan and Hark 1993).

Why study gender and film?

As humans we are interested in who we are and how we are defined. One of the primary ways of defining ourselves is through gender. The physical characteristics which determine our gender are with us from the day we are born and are changeable only by surgery; exactly how much of gender is socialised, is constructed, is debatable however. We are usually aware that we belong to one gender or the other but sexual identity is more complex than simply being biologically determined male or female: the 'gender role' or gender identity seem to be almost wholly learned. Judith Butler argues that the body is a 'variable boundary, a surface whose permeability is politically regulated, a signifying practice within a field of gender hierarchy and compulsory heterosexuality' (Butler 1990: 139).

How gender is portrayed in film does to some extent reflect concerns and anxieties in our society about who we are which are re-enacted through the narrative. The acting of male and female roles is a performance, a simulation which is not fixed but constantly shifting. Film is a re-presentation of images, it is not reality but a series of shots with actors playing characters. These images are concentrated, symbolic and highly charged; they have a super-powered meaning. In mainstream film we are clearly intended to identify with and recognise certain character types and gender types. If film is to have a resonance for an audience it must contain elements with which they can identify or empathise and, at some level, must say something about the world in which we live. It is both interesting and revealing to look at how film characters are made recognisable and how we understand them, what our culture portrays as being representative of masculinity and femininity, and what this tells us about our understanding of gender, sexuality and society.

In earlier feminist studies of classic Hollywood film, femininity is seen as spectacle, and masculinity as a sign and a performance. More recent studies of gender and masculinity have problematised this position and suggest that representations of masculinity and, as a consequence, femininity are far more complex.

• **Plate 11.1**
The Day I Became a Woman (Marzeh Meshkini, 2000). Films directed by Iranian women have been internationally successful

feminism
Based on the belief that we live in a society where women are still unequal to men; that women have lower status than men and have less power, particularly economic power. Feminists argue that the media reinforces the status quo by representing a narrow range of images of women; for instance, woman as carer, as passive object, as an object of desire. Many feminists argue that the range of representations for both male and female is limited and slow to change. The relationship between gender and power relations in society may be seen as central to feminist thinking.

This chapter addresses different approaches to studying gender and film, exploring how we understand the masculine and feminine in film. The first section outlines the findings of feminist film theory from early seminal articles to contemporary debates, and includes a discussion of feminist films which have been an intrinsic part of the feminist movement. In addition, a brief history of women working in mainstream film is given. The second section discusses how the study of masculinity has problematised and furthered debates around film and meaning, especially in terms of understanding sexuality and gender, ambiguity and anxiety with regard to masculinity.

WOMEN AND FILM

This section looks at the role of women in filmmaking and film theory. The focus is on British and American women filmmakers but women from many other countries, such as Samira Makhmalbaf and Marzieh Meshkini from Iran, have also made a significant contribution to the form in recent years.

First, a broad background history traces women's place in filmmaking and looks at the difficulties women have encountered in gaining positions of authority and control in the industry. There are some grounds for optimism however, as an increasing number of women are given key positions in areas such as producing, directing and screenwriting within the film industry.

Second, the rise of **feminism**, the development of feminist film theory and the parallel rise of feminist filmmaking is discussed; in the 1970s feminist film theory and practice seemed to converge, but by the 1980s the links had become more tenuous; however, by the 1990s feminist film theory played an increasingly important role in many areas of academic study.

Finally, a selection of case studies of women filmmakers is given.

NO JOB FOR A WOMAN – A HISTORY OF WOMEN IN FILM

The early years

From the beginnings of the film industry in the late nineteenth century it was usual for women to work in non-technical areas such as continuity and make-up or as production assistants, but they rarely worked as producers, directors, editors or writers. Recent research suggests that the role of women has not been as silent as was once thought and some women did, both directly and indirectly, exert their influence in these fields.

The only recorded early women filmmakers were in France and America – there were apparently none in Britain. Two well-known Hollywood movie actresses, Mary Pickford and Lillian Gish, both directed films but did not want this known for fear of harming their image as stars.

France can claim to have raised the first woman director, Alice Guy Blaché, who gained access to equipment because she worked for Gaumont, a company that manufactured cameras. Her career began in 1896 with a one-minute short called *The Good Fairy in the Cabbage Patch*, which Blaché believed was the first narrative film ever made. After eleven years of working in the industry in France she left for America and the greater opportunities it would give her. There she wrote, directed and produced many films including *In the Year 2000*, a vision of the future in which women ruled the world. Blaché found working conditions in the USA much easier than in France, where a working woman was frowned upon. Her daughter, Simone Blaché, explained in an interview that: 'Mother was really cherished in the US. She used to say that people treated her so wonderfully because she was a woman, because she was a woman in film. The situation in France was quite the reverse' (Smith 1975: 6).

In the early 1900s the American film industry expanded rapidly and made large profits due to the vast audiences attracted to the new medium. Although the new industry was cut-throat and competitive, it was also much more receptive to change than the European film industry and there was significantly less discrimination against women. It has been estimated that there were at least twenty-six women directors in America before 1930, but there were probably many more who directed and acted or who were screenwriters and not credited with this role. One of the most highly paid screenwriters in Hollywood in the 1930s was female, Frances Marion. In the US between 1911 and 1925, women wrote half of all the films copyrighted, whereas in 2001 only 21 per cent of the scripts contracted were written by women.[1]

Lois Weber was the first female American filmmaker and probably the most famous, often writing, producing and starring in her films, many of which dealt with social issues such as abortion and divorce. Weber directed more than seventy-five films.

By the end of the 1920s the talkies had arrived. This, indirectly, brought about the demise of many women's careers as filmmakers. Only the bigger studios could survive due to the expensive equipment needed in the change-over to sound, and it was generally the many small, independent companies which employed the majority of women that closed down, and many women lost their role in the industry.

Only one woman director, Dorothy Arzner, really survived the transition to talkies. She went on to make many famous movies, for example, *Christopher Strong* (1933) with Katharine Hepburn and *Dance Girl Dance* (1940). At one time Arzner was ranked among the 'top ten' directors in Hollywood.

Ironically, the changes in America drove directors such as Elinor Glynn and Jacqueline Logan to Britain and Europe, which already had an extremely poor record of women working in film.

Britain though did not give much encouragement to its indigenous women filmmakers; the earliest woman known to have directed British films was Dinah Shurey, though very little is known about her other than that she made two films, *Carry On* (1927) and *Last Port* (1929).

• **Plate 11.2**
Christopher Strong
(Dorothy Arzner, 1933).
Dorothy Arzner was
once ranked among
the top ten directors in
Hollywood

Until the Second World War, hardly any women in Britain could be termed filmmakers, but some played key roles in the filmmaking process: Alma Reville, married to Alfred Hitchcock, assisted him in many films such as *The 39 Steps* (1935) and *The Lady Vanishes* (1938). She also helped to write other scripts such as *Suspicion* (1941) and *Shadow of a Doubt* (1943). Mary Field worked in documentary from 1928 and became executive producer of children's entertainment for J. Arthur Rank from 1944 to 1950. Joy Batchelor worked mainly in animation from 1935 and co-directed the first British feature-length cartoon *Animal Farm* (1954), continuing to make animated films until the 1970s.

*For further discussion
of Grierson and British
documentary see
Chapter 9, pp. 216–218.*

In both Britain and the USA more women were able to work in documentary film. The British documentary film movement, of which John Grierson was the founder, had a huge influence on British film and has continued to exert its influence to the present day. Grierson's sister Ruby worked alongside him on a number of films and was involved in making films herself, such as *Housing Problems* (1940).

Many filmmakers involved in the early documentary movement went on to make propaganda films during the war. This was one area of film where a handful of women could be found working as directors and assistant directors. Some women were taken on in roles usually only open to men due to the increased demand for documentary propaganda film in wartime Britain and the shortage of available manpower.

Two female British fiction feature-film directors, Muriel Box and Wendy Toye, made a number of films in the 1940s and 1950s and gained an international reputation. Muriel Box made profitable mass entertainment films. Her most famous film, which she also scripted, is a melodrama, *The Seventh Veil* (1945), but she continued to make films up until 1964. The lesser-known Wendy Toye made such films as *Raising a Riot* (1957) and *We Joined the Navy* (1962), with Dirk Bogarde and Kenneth More.

Very few women filmmakers in Britain and the USA before 1970 could be termed commercially successful, Dorothy Arzner and Muriel Box being the outstanding exceptions. It was virtually unheard of for women to work in technical areas such as sound or camera, although women art directors and film editors were not so unusual – Ann V. Coates worked as an editor on Box's film *The Truth about Women* (1958) and David Lean's *Lawrence of Arabia* (1962). In general, however, it was rare for a woman to play a key role in filmmaking and the rise of feminism in the 1960s was to be the great catalyst for change for women in film.

In the new millenium, more women are working in previously male-dominated areas such as directing, camera, sound and lighting: in the UK, Diane Tammes, Sue Gibson and Belinda Parsons are all respected camerawomen; Diana Ruston and Moya Burns work in sound.

In the field of directing in the UK, women filmmakers have broken into mainstream film, often from the independent sector, TV, or from the increasing number of film schools. Sally Potter has made a range of feature films such as *Orlando* (1993) and *The Man Who Cried* (2000), starring Johnny Depp and Cate Blanchett. Potter's last film *Yes* (2005) received much critical acclaim regarding its experimental style and use of poetic form. Gurinder Chada's film *Bhaji on the Beach* (1993) takes a wry and witty look at life for Asian women in Britain, while *What's Cooking* (2000) is a rich and colourful film that has received international acclaim. Chada's film *Bend It Like Beckham* (2002) was a huge success in Britain and the US, tapping into a need for feel-good films, although her last film *It's a Wonderful Afterlife* (2010) was released to mixed reviews. Beeban Kidron has been directing for many years but only recieving wider recognition with the release of *Bridget Jones: The Edge of Reason* (2004). Internationally, more established women filmmakers such as Jane Campion and Kathryn Bigelow regularly produce feature films; Bigelow became the first woman to receive the Oscar for Best Director in 2010 for *The Hurt Locker*. The Danish director Lone Scherfig gained international recognition for *Italian For Beginners* (2000), a Dogme95-style film which used real locations and no camera lighting. Her latest film, *An Education* (2009), based on the novel adapted by Nick Hornby, was voted the best film by the audience at the Sundance Film Festival in 2009.

But the biggest-selling films worldwide last year were mostly produced, written and directed by men. Martha Lauzen's research of the employment of women in production roles of the top-grossing US films of 2006 suggests that it is still extremely difficult for women to break into the mainstream film industry and that, when a comparison is made with the top 250 films of 1998, the number of women directors, writers, cinematographers and producers has actually declined. Lauzen points out that in 2006 women only acounted for 2 per cent of cinematographers, 7 per cent of directors and 10 per cent of writers (Lauzen 2010).

● **Plate 11.3**
The Hurt Locker (Kathryn Bigelow, 2008). The first woman to win the Academy Award for best director in 2010 yet directing films about men is her forte.

• **Plate 11.4**
Bend It Like Beckham
(Gurinder Chada, 2002).
Girls playing football is not
a traditional crowd-puller,
yet this film was a great
success in the UK and
the US

patriarchal society
A society in which men
have the power and
control, and women are
generally disadvantaged
and have lower status.
It could be argued that
we no longer live in a
patriarchal society, but
in a society in which
men and women have
equal opportunities. But
many feminists argue
that we still have a long
way to go in terms of
politics, philosophy and
economics before we
live in a society in which
men and women may be
considered equal.

A number of support agencies for women filmmakers have been established which aim to provide the female equivalent of the 'old boys' network': the international organisation 'Women in Film and TV' helps women in both the mainstream sector and in the independent sector by offering meetings, seminars and screenings.

Whether changing attitudes towards women working in the film industry will produce more positive, realistic and varied representations of women in film is open to question. Feminism has perhaps changed the way we look at film, and there is a greater awareness of how gender is represented in the media. *Thelma and Louise* (1991) was hailed as a feminist film (directed by Ridley Scott, but scripted by a woman, Callie Khouri), although a more cynical analysis of the film reveals that the women are filmed quite conventionally, as objects of 'the look'.[2] *Baise-moi* (2000), a French film written and directed by Virginie Despontes and Coralie Trinh Thi, pushes the *Thelma and Louise* theme much further. The two women protagonists go on a sex and killing spree in a rape-revenge drama in which they have the power of the look. As more women writers and directors work in mainstream film, though, it does seem likely that there will be a widening out of representations of women both visually and thematically. Films such as Ang Lee's *Crouching Tiger, Hidden Dragon* (2000) have been internationally successful yet the central character is an action woman. The hugely popular *Erin Brockovich* (2000) was scripted by Susannah Grant. It stars Julia Roberts in the 'rags to riches' story of a woman's struggle to sue a multinational company while bringing up her children as a single mother. Nicola Holofcener's films such as *Lovely and Amazing* (2001) and Lisa Choldenko's *Laurel Canyon* (2002) received widespread critical acclaim. Both directors gained experience in US TV where there has been a move towards positive discrimination. *Sex and the City* 1 and 2 (2008 and 2010) did extremely well at the box office, worldwide, as did *Mama Mia* (2008) directed by Phyllida Lloyd. But women's stories, told from a woman's point of view, are still the exception in cinema; hopefully the success of these films will encourage production companies to take more risks and aim at a female market, rather than making films that largely appeal to a young, male audience.

THE FEMINIST REVOLUTION

The women's movement did not suddenly arrive; since the days of the suffragettes an increasing number of women had seen the need for equality with men. A new political and social climate developed in the 1960s and early 1970s which questioned the established order, encouraged radical reform and produced conditions that were conducive to the rise of the feminist movement. Although this radical dissatisfaction with contemporary society began in America its message soon spread to Britain, and in both countries there was a questioning of woman's role in society. Betty Friedan's book *The Feminine Mystique*, published in 1963, touched a chord in many discontented women. The time was ripe for the spread of the feminist movement,[3] as Friedan explained:

… the absolute necessity for a civil rights movement for women had reached such a point of subterranean explosive urgency by 1966 that it took only a few of us to get together to ignite the spark – and it spread like a nuclear chain reaction.

(Cited in Banner 1984: 247)

Representation and stereotyping of women in the media

Feminists generally believe that the media is a contributory factor in perpetuating a narrow range of **stereotyped** images of women. How women are **represented** in the media may encourage particular expectations of women which are extremely limiting; for instance, that women are always based in the home, that they are inferior to men, that they like men who are violent, are just a few of the myths that have been perpetuated by the media. As Molly Haskell points out:

From a woman's point of view the ten years from, say, 1962 or 1963 to 1973 have been the most disheartening in screen history. In the roles and prominence accorded to women, the decade began unpromisingly, grew steadily worse, and at present shows no sign of improving. Directors, who in 1962 were guilty only of covert misogyny (Stanley Kubrick's *Lolita*) or kindly indifference (Sam Peckinpah's *The High Country*) became overt in 1972 with the violent abuse and brutalisation of *A Clockwork Orange* and *Straw Dogs*.

(Haskell 1973: 323)

Film, particularly in the early feminist period, was seen as one area of the media that could become a battleground for the women's movement. Film would be used as an ideological tool, which would counteract the stereotyped images of women presented by the male-dominated media and raise women's awareness of their inferior position in **patriarchal society**, where women were generally relegated to a subservient role. For instance, in film, women, as the historical section indicates, have usually taken supportive roles rather than key, decision-making ones.

FEMINIST FILM THEORY AND PRACTICE

The influence of alternative, independent and avant-garde film

Alongside the expansion of feminism and the women's movement **alternative cinema** and **avant-garde cinema** were flourishing. **Independent cinema** could, at its simplest, be divided into two forms: documentary and avant-garde. British film has a strong documentary tradition, which was socialist-influenced, and feminist film initially saw documentary as a way of presenting the 'truth' about the lives of women.

During the 1960s, American avant-garde filmmakers produced many innovative and controversial films, some of the most well known being 'gay' and 'camp' films that

stereotyping
A quick and easy way of labelling or categorising the world around us and making it understandable. Stereotypes are learned but are by no means fixed, yet are often resistant to change. They tend to restrict our understanding of the world and perpetuate beliefs that are often untrue or narrow. Stereotyping is not always negative, but tends to be very much concerned with preserving and perpetuating power relations in society. It is in the interests of those in power to continue to stereotype those with lower status in a negative light, thus preserving the status quo.

representation
The media re-presents information to its audience, who are encouraged by the mainstream media to see their output as a 'window on the world', as reflecting reality. Yet the process of re-presenting information is highly complex and highly selective. Many feminists argue that the way notions of gender are represented by the media perpetuates and reinforces the values of patriarchal society; for instance, men tend to take on strong, active roles, while women are shown as passive and relying on their attractiveness. There are exceptions to such narrow stereotyping: the 'strong' woman shown by Ripley in the *Alien* trilogy and the two heroines Thelma and Louise may be seen as positive models, although rather more cynically they could be seen merely as 'role reversal'

films and so as having purely novelty value. Representations often make use of stereotypes because they are a shorthand, quick and easy way of using information.

alternative cinema
Provides an alternative to the codes and conventions of mainstream, narrative cinema, often both thematically and visually.

avant-garde cinema
Essentially non-narrative in structure and often intellectual in content, working in opposition to mainstream cinema. Avant-garde film is often self-conscious and frequently makes use of devices such as cuts to the camera crew, talking to the camera and scratching on film.

independent cinema
May be divided into two areas: first, independent mainstream cinema, which aims to compete with the big studios, although without any large financial backing finds it difficult to survive. Second, the term is used to describe filmmaking outside the mainstream sector, for instance, film workshops, avant-garde film, feminist film. The boundaries between these two areas are not always clear and may overlap.

challenged traditional stereotypes of gender roles such as Andy Warhol's *Lonesome Cowboys* (1968) and Kenneth Anger's *Scorpio Rising* (1965). In the same period avant-garde filmmaking developed in Europe, the French filmmakers, Jean-Luc Godard and François Truffaut being its most famous exponents. Although gender roles in European films tended to be stereotypical, some feminist filmmakers saw the potential of avant-garde film as a means of breaking away from the constraints of traditional cinema.

The expansion of independent filmmaking in Britain during the 1960s encouraged the formation of a number of workshops which aimed to provide filmmaking facilities for all classes and to destroy the élitism often found in the industry. Many workshops made films that were outside the sphere of mainstream film and television, often being concerned with areas which were considered radical in politics or content.

The first women's film group

The combination of the expansion of the women's movement and the rise of independent filmmaking brought about the conditions in which feminist film could thrive. In 1972 the first women's film group in Britain was formed. The London Women's Film Group (LWFG) aimed to spread ideas about women's liberation and enable women to learn filmmaking skills otherwise unavailable to them.

In the 1970s there were no more women working in high-grade jobs in the film and television industry than there had been in the 1950s. Demystification of the learning of technical skills was considered vital, but it was also necessary to familiarise women with all the stages in the filmmaking process so that they had a pool of knowledge, which they could never have obtained in mainstream film. Many film groups worked co-operatively, giving members an equal say in the production process and rejecting the strict hierarchy of roles used in mainstream film production.

The feminist film movement was intentionally political, aiming to give all women, but especially working-class women, a chance to work in film. The films were often shown to trade unions, in factories and housing estates, hoping they would help to raise women's consciousness about their place in society. Many of the early feminist films fitted into the black and white documentary realist tradition, the dominant mode of alternative, political filmmaking in Britain. Linda Dove, of the LWFG, explained in an interview:

We tended to reject commercial films wholesale as the ideological products of capitalist, sexist, racist society.... Originally our aim was to change the context in which a film is seen – we wanted to break down the audience passivity by always going out with films and discussing them when they were shown.

(Dove 1976: 59)

Film as a 'window on the world'

The widely held view that the visual media presented a 'window on the world' came under question in the early 1970s. The media, feminists argued, are manipulated by the ruling patriarchal ideology and what is seen as natural, as clear-cut and obvious, is in fact a construct produced by society. This ambivalence about the 'meaning' of films and other media suggests that its interpretation by the audience may be different from that intended by the filmmaker. For instance, *Women of the Rhondda* (1972), a documentary about women who live in the South Wales Valleys, has a naturalistic style with no voiceover and the images are intended to speak for themselves. The message, though, is somewhat ambiguous for a non-feminist audience because the film has many possible readings.

Many feminist filmmakers in the 1970s appropriated ideas from avant-garde art cinema and applied them to their work, to discuss questions that were of concern to the women's movement, such as representation. The avant-garde had always been male-dominated and narrow in its representations of women (see, for instance,

Jean-Luc Godard's films such as *Breathless* (1960), *A Married Woman* (1964) and *Weekend* (1967)). But the avant-garde's political/anarchist basis gave an alternative form to the traditional use of realism in both fiction and documentary film. This influence was most profound in filmmakers like Laura Mulvey and Sally Potter, whose films are discussed in more detail in this chapter.

Early feminist film theory

The ideological sense of purpose and political debate behind feminist filmmaking encouraged the development of a film theory. Feminist film theory was, in the early period, especially concerned with representation and sexuality, and its relation to the dominance of the male power structure within a patriarchal society. A number of women, often from an academic background, contributed to this development, but it was perhaps Laura Mulvey and Claire Johnston who were the progenitors of feminist film theory. Both wrote seminal articles which were to have a huge impact on the study of film and the media, and which will be discussed in this chapter.

Developing a counter-cinema

Claire Johnston's 'Women's Cinema as Counter-Cinema' (1973) is one of the earliest articles on feminist film theory and practice. Johnston explains how women have been stereotyped in film since the days of silent cinema, and argues for a cinema that challenges such narrow conventions but which will also be entertaining. In mainstream cinema, Johnston points out, woman is seen as an extension of a male vision and she criticises the narrow role given in film: 'It is probably true to say that despite the enormous emphasis placed on woman as spectacle in the cinema, woman as woman is largely absent' (ibid.: 214). Johnston stresses the importance of developing a film practice that questions and challenges the patriarchal basis of mainstream dominant cinema, calling for a counter-cinema movement which will have links with avant-garde and left-wing film.

Pleasure, looking and gender

Psychoanalytic theory, particularly the theories of Freud and Lacan, has been instrumental in the development of a feminist film theory, although structuralist and Marxist theories[4] have also been influential. Laura Mulvey's article 'Visual Pleasure and Narrative Cinema' (first published in 1975) emphasises the importance of the patriarchical viewpoint in the cinema; arguing that the pleasure gained from looking (**scopophilia**) is a male pleasure, that 'the look' in cinema is controlled by the male and directed at the female; this is referred to as the 'male gaze'. Scopophilia can be directed in two areas: first, voyeurism, that is, scopophilic pleasure linked to sexual attraction, and, second, scopophilic pleasure which is linked to narcissistic identification. Mulvey argues that this identification is always with the male, who is the pivot of the film, the hero, while the female is often seen as a threat. This viewpoint is linked with psychoanalytical theory to demonstrate the influence of patriarchal society on film. Patriarchy and phallocentrism are intrinsically linked; the phallus is a symbol of power, of having (note how guns are used in film: guns = phallus = power). The woman has no phallus, she is castrated, which relates back to Freudian theory that the woman is lacking and therefore inferior because she has no phallus.

Freud's theories on scopophilia centre around voyeurism and the desire to see the erotic and the forbidden. The cinema provides a perfect venue for illicit voyeuristic viewing because the audience is in a dark, enclosed, womb-like world. Mulvey argues that the power cinema holds is so strong that it can act as a temporary form of brainwashing (an argument which is still very much alive today!).

psychoanalytic theory
Based on the theories of Freud and, more recently, Lacan. Feminists argue that aspects of psychoanalysis are questionable because they are based on patriarchal assumptions that woman is inferior to man. Freud found female sexuality difficult and disturbing. Lacan argues that the mother is seen as lacking by the child because she has no phallus. Uncertainty about the role of the female in psychoanalytic theory has been picked up by a number of feminists such as Mulvey, De Lauretis and Modleski, who question the inevitability of Freud and Lacan's theories which emphasise the importance of the phallus, penis envy and patriarchal supremacy.

scopophilia
Freudian term meaning the sexual pleasure gained from looking, introduced to film analysis by Laura Mulvey, who pointed out that women are usually depicted in a passive role and are looked at, while men take on an active role and look.

structuralism
A movement founded on the belief that the study of society could be scientifically based and that there are structures in society that follow certain patterns or rules. Initially, most interest was centred on the use of language; Saussure, the founder of linguistics, argued that language was essential in communicating the ideology, the beliefs, of a culture. Structuralists have applied these theories to film, which uses both visual and verbal communication, and pointed out that the text conveys an illusion of reality, thus conveying the ideology of a society even more effectively.

REPRESENTATION OF GENDER AND SEXUALITY

The woman in Freudian theory represents desire, but also the fear of castration, and so there is a tension, an ambivalence towards the female form, and her 'look' can be threatening. As the male is the controller, taking the active role, the female is reduced to the icon, the erotic, but at the same time is a threat because of her difference.

Mulvey argues that woman has two roles in film: erotic object for the characters in the story and erotic object for the spectator. Recent feminist theory suggests that the representation of women is far more complex, and later theory, including Mulvey's, looks at films where women do play a key role as subject rather than object. Melodrama is one such area (see Mulvey 1981).

Mulvey refers to Hitchcock because of the complicit understanding in his films that the audience gains a voyeuristic pleasure from watching a film, from looking: 'In *Vertigo* (1958) in particular, but also in *Marnie* (1964) and *Rear Window* (1954), the "look" is central to the plot oscillating between voyeurism and fetishistic fascination' (Mulvey 1975: 813).

The denial of pleasure

Mulvey points out that devices used in the traditional Hollywood narrative film have trapped filmmakers into using certain codes and conventions which place the female in a subordinate, passive position, making her role as erotic object extremely limiting. Mulvey criticises the narrowness of this role and argues that to change woman's position in film a revolutionary look at cinema needs to be taken and the denial of voyeuristic cinematic pleasure be given a priority. The exclusion of woman as object, as provider of voyeuristic pleasure will then free her from the narrow limits she has been allocated in cinema. This may seem an extreme reaction to mainstream, narrative cinema, but in the early 1970s feminists felt that the only way to change female representation was to take such measures: a new radical cinema was needed, an alternative to the 'magic' of narrative cinema.

A new language

The importance of the creation of a female subject and the development of a new language is central to early feminist film theory, which argued that spoken, written and visual languages all placed women in a subordinate position and reflected a patriarchal ideology. A film theory and practice that had its own codes and conventions would replace the dominance of patriarchal cinema. Christine Gledhill echoes this desire in her article, 'Some Recent Developments in Feminist Criticism':

A feminist film-maker then, finds the root of patriarchy in the very tools she wishes to employ to speak about women. So what is required of her is the development of a counter-cinema that will deconstruct the language and techniques of classic cinema.

(1985: 841)

Classic narrative cinema is based on a philosophy connected to the literary realist tradition. Many feminists felt that this tradition perpetuated a way of seeing, of under-standing the world, which belonged to dominant patriarchal society: feminists argued that film should break with this tradition. Filmmakers such as Laura Mulvey and Sally Potter were interested in a film theory and practice which worked together to produce a new feminist language. Avant-garde film was the ideal vehicle for these ideas because it broke the normal rules and conventions of mainstream cinema. Mulvey's article 'Film, Feminism and the Avant-Garde' (1979) explores this relationship, suggesting that both forms of film can be mutually beneficial, working towards similar goals. Mulvey's films, such as *Riddles of the Sphinx* (1977), actively avoid any sense of being constructed for the male spectator, confront the lack of representation of women in film and are a mixture of avant-garde, melodrama and psychoanalytic theory.

Many avant-garde films were termed 'difficult' and only attracted a small audience which tended to be those familiar with 'art film'. Even though avant-garde-influenced filmmakers such as Mulvey did much to aid the understanding of their films by producing hand-outs and giving lectures, some feminists felt that avant-garde film was élitist and would be of no interest to a wider audience of women. Mulvey's and Johnston's theories, they suggested, would be more useful for the development of a feminist film theory than as a guide on how to make feminist films. Kaplan (1983), for example, points out that it makes more sense to use familiar and recognisable cinematic conventions to explain that the 'realism' of mainstream cinema is a fabrication.

For further analysis of avant-garde, feminist film see Case study 1: Sally Potter.

A period of optimism and defiance

Feminist film theory and practice prior to 1980 presented a joint ideological struggle; film theory analysed the patriarchal conventions within which mainstream film worked and film practice broke these conventions. But there was a very limited audience for feminist film during this period, even though there was an increasing interest in academic circles in feminist film theory. In the strongly male-dominated world of filmmaking, women were rarely seen as artists or filmmakers, and feminist art could become a possible challenge to patriarchal society. As Johnston (1973) explains, the female within patriarchy is seen as the 'other', and feminist art represented a threat to these narrow conceptions of gender.

By the end of the 1970s a feminist film theory and practice had been established, giving many women a new-found confidence and a belief that society could change. In that decade a number of influential articles on feminist film theory and practice had been written and a body of work had been formed by feminist writers and academics, Mulvey and Johnston being the founder writers who were to influence a generation of film and media critics.

At the beginning of the 1970s the focus was on representation in film and the media, but by the end of the decade attention was being diverted to the concept of 'pleasure' and whether this should be denied in film. Some feminists expressed the concern that by denying the pleasures of mainstream cinema, feminist filmmakers might alienate their audience. Yet feminists generally agreed that feminist film theory and practice had an important role to play in raising awareness of the marginalisation of women in a patriarchal society.

A number of feminists still called for a counter-cinema and deconstructive cinema in the early 1980s. Ann Kaplan and Annette Kuhn argued that there was a need to break down the dominant forms of cinema, and the audience should become active rather than passive, gaining pleasure from learning rather than the narrative.

Both Kuhn and Kaplan and filmmakers such as Sue Clayton were aware of the problems of using a cinema which rejects the mainstream and that by being anti-conventional they may alienate their audience. Kaplan suggested that a way forward would be to manipulate the conventions of mainstream cinema (1983).

REASSESSING FEMINIST FILM THEORY

In 1981 Mulvey published a response to 'Visual Pleasure and Narrative Cinema', which had been so fundamental to the development of feminist film theory. Titled 'Afterthoughts on Visual Pleasure and Narrative Cinema', Mulvey presents two lines of thought: first, examining whether the female spectator can gain a deep pleasure from a male-oriented text, and second, how the text and the spectator are affected by the centrality of a female character in the narrative. 'Afterthoughts' marks a shift in attitude, a move away from representation to studying the female response, to asking how women watch films and questioning the role of melodrama, which has traditionally been viewed as the woman's genre.

Feminist film theory has been especially influenced by psychoanalytic theory and particularly by Freud and Lacan. Mulvey acknowledges her debt to Lacan who, she explains, has 'broadened and advanced ways of conceptualising sexual difference, emphasising the fictional, constructed nature of masculinity and femininity' (ibid.: 165).

Not all feminists supported a feminist film theory based on psychoanalytic theory. Terry Lovell, in *Pictures of Reality* (1983), criticised Lacanian theory because of its emphasis on the individual rather than the collective and argued that gaining pleasure from the text is rather more complex than a simple attribution to sexual desire.

In the latter part of the 1980s Freud's work was re-examined by many feminists due to its phallocentric basis. Tania Modleski, for instance, in *The Women Who Knew Too Much* (1988), argues for a less male-centred version of spectatorship and calls for the development of a feminist psychoanalytic theory which is challenging and inventive. Penley, in the introduction to *Feminism and Film Theory* (1988), states that much feminist film criticism questions the patriarchal roots of current psychoanalytic theories, especially those of Freud and Lacan.

Modleski applies her ideas to an analysis of Hitchcock's films, which have been of great interest to feminists due to his extreme use of voyeurism and the 'look'. Reassessing earlier theory, Modleski points out that Mulvey's article 'Visual Pleasure and Narrative Cinema' does not allow for the complex nature of representation and raises questions about the stereotypical, passive female object and the active male. Modleski states: 'What I want to argue is neither that Hitchcock is utterly misogynistic nor that he is largely sympathetic to women and their plight in patriarchy, but that his work is characterised by a thoroughgoing ambivalence about femininity' (1988: 3).

Many of Hitchcock's films are seen from the point of view of a female protagonist: for instance, *Blackmail* (1929), *Rebecca* (1940), *Notorious* (1946), or when the hero or heroine is in a vulnerable or passive, female position, as in *Rear Window* (1954).

Modleski re-examines aspects of Mulvey's work, especially the suggestion that the patriarchal order has banished a strong female presence. In *North by Northwest* (1959), Cary Grant's role is that of hero and sex object, the desirable male; in *Marnie* (1964), Sean Connery plays a similar role, which also serves to heighten the irony that Marnie,

• **Plate 11.5**
North By Northwest
(Alfred Hitchcock,
1959). Cary Grant –
irresistible to women

the heroine and his wife, is frigid. In Hitchcock's films both male and female can become objects of the 'look'.

The strong and powerful female can then exist within mainstream film, yet Hitchcock is patently not a feminist filmmaker and his films appear to express Freud's assertion that the male contempt for femininity is an expression of the repression of their bisexuality. As Modleski concludes: 'the male object is greatly threatened by bisexuality, though he is at the same time fascinated by it; and it is the woman who pays for this ambivalence, often with her life itself' (1988: 10).

Questioning psychoanalytic theory

In the 1970s and 1980s feminist film theory was dominated by a psychoanalytic approach, which had proven to be problematic when applied to feminist film theory. This is because of its dependence on the Oedipal trajectory, in which woman is seen as not only 'lacking' but also as needing to be brought under control through the male gaze. If woman's role in film is to always be reduced to the 'other' by psychoanalytic theory, then it could be argued that there is little space to open up patriarchal narratives to account for the female spectator, other than through identification with the male.

Some feminist film theorists, such as Jackie Byars, have reworked psychoanalytic theory to give it a feminist perspective. Her analysis of melodrama suggests that the woman can exist as a spectator in a positive way. In *All that Heaven Allows*, Byars (1991) argues that the gaze is strongly female. Jackey Stacey's analysis of *Desperately Seeking Susan* points out that the film is not about sexual difference in terms of male and female but about the difference between the two women lead characters, a view which cannot be read in terms of Lacan or Freud whose theories are so phallocentric in nature (Stacey 1992). Psychoanalytic theory needs to develop a new framework which will view the woman as a positive force rather than suffering from a state of lack.

The reworking of psychoanalytic theory may provide a new model from which feminists could work. Mulvey's theories, based on Freud and Lacan, have had a considerable impact in enhancing our understanding of the role of the spectator in film and how media texts place the viewer in a particular position. These theories are useful when analysing a film such as *The Piano*, which gives the female the power of the look and, to some extent, reverses conventional filming practices (see case study on the support website at www.routledge.com/textbooks/9780415409285).

A cultural studies approach

In the past decade or so there has been a shift away from Freudian and Lacanian theory towards applying a cultural studies approach to the study of film. Black feminist film theory and lesbian feminist film theory, for instance, have both suggested new ways of understanding how women from different social and ethnic groups interpret cultural messages.

The emphasis has transferred from reading media texts, a move from the study of the encoding process which asks how messages are produced, to a study of the decoding process which asks how messages are received and understood by an audience.

Cultural studies theorists argue that **semiotic** and psychoanalytic readings of film tend to isolate the viewer from the text; cultural studies is more concerned with asking how cultural systems produce meaning and how ideology is replicated through cultural institutions, texts and practices. **Ideology** may be seen as the means by which we interpret and make sense of our lives, the viewpoint from which we see the world. Ideology, in a capitalist society, needs constant re-establishing, and this is carried out by what **Marxist** philosopher Gramsci termed **hegemony**. This is the means by which a dominant social group maintains control of a subordinate group, a form of unconscious control, in which we take on certain beliefs, practices and attitudes as being natural or normal and carry those opinions with us; for instance, the belief that in a patriarchal

semiotics
The use of semiotics in film analysis has developed out of the theories of Ferdinand de Saussure, who argued that the meanings of words are not natural but learned and socially constructed; therefore the meaning of a word, or in the case of film, an image or sound, may be complex and layered.

ideology
The dominant set of ideas and values which inform any one society or culture, but which are imbued in its social behaviour and representative texts at a level that is not necessarily obvious or conscious.

Marxist theory
Argues that those who have the means of production have control in a capitalist society. The dominant class have control of the means of production and have an interest in perpetuating the dominant ideology. More recently, exponents of Althusserian Marxism, particularly post-1968, have argued that mainstream narrative cinema reinforces the capitalist system and that a revolutionary cinema is needed to challenge the dominant ideology.

hegemony
A set of ideas, attitudes or practices which have become so dominant that we forget they are rooted in choice and the exercise of power. They appear to be 'common sense' because they are so ingrained; any alternative seems 'odd' or potentially threatening by comparison.

society it is entirely normal for the woman to be the home-maker and to have a low-paid, menial job. Hegemony is constantly shifting; it is constantly negotiated and never fixed. From a feminist standpoint this means there is the potential for change in patriarchal society.

If cultural texts such as films are apparatus for transmitting cultural values, they are also sites for a struggle over meaning. The term given to describe the constant shifting and multiple possibilities of meaning a text may have is **polysemy**. If a text has multiple meanings then this gives feminist film and cultural critics the opportunity to analyse audience response to texts as 'open' rather than 'closed'. Stuart Hall suggested there are three ways in which a text may be received: (1) as a *dominant reading*, as intended by its producer; (2) as a *negotiated reading*, when the text is generally accepted but is challenged in some areas; and (3) as *an oppositional reading*, when the viewer challenges the reading of the text.[5] In fact, recent research argues for the possibility of a much more complex relationship between the reader and the text than had previously been thought.

The audience watch a film having already aquired a range of skills and competences and a background of cultural knowledge. The audience is therefore more of an active than a passive receiver of the message. This understanding has important implications for feminist film theory, as it opens up the notion of the female as subject rather than as being permanently confined to the role of passive object. Christine Gledhill (1985) uses the term 'negotiation' of text, explaining that we negotiate with cultural texts at every level; from institutions, where feminists can apply pressure to negotiating the active meanings of texts, to the active process of reception.[6] Ethnographic research has proven to be of particular interest when applied to the study of how women receive media texts. Janice Radway, in her research on romance fiction, found that the women whom she interviewed preferred a strong, independent heroine.[7] This contradicts previous feminist textual-based research which sees the romance novel as presenting women as passive and vulnerable. Jacqueline Bobo conducted group interviews to analyse the reception and interpretation of *The Color Purple*, the results of which she found surprising. The film contains many stereotypical images of black people and their culture and was filmed by a white, male director, Steven Spielberg, yet the black women interviewed saw the film as positive; they 'not only liked the film, but have formed a strong attachment to it. The film is significant to their lives' (Bobo 1988: 101). Bobo believes those interviewed were able to filter out negative aspects of the film and highlight areas they could relate to. Black feminist theory has found it problematic to apply what could be termed white, bourgeois film theory to an ethnic group which is so noticeably under-represented in film. bell hooks explains: 'many feminist film critics continue to structure their discourse as though it speaks about "women" when in fact it only speaks about white women' (hooks 1992: 123). Because black women are largely excluded from film or given an extremely limited number of representations, a film such as *The Color Purple* is of particular significance to the many black women who read the film favourably.[8]

Lesbian and gay studies is a developing area of cultural analysis. Lesbian writers point out that a theory of lesbian desire and its relationship to media texts and representation is needed; a theory separate from previous feminist film thinking which has been concerned with the relationship of the heterosexual woman to film and places lesbian desire as other.

An eclectic range of theoretical approaches is available to feminist film theorists in the new millennium: psychoanalytic, social historical, semiotic-based textual analysis, postmodernist and ethnographic study are just a sample of the tools available. Some feminists have been resistant to embracing cultural studies in its totality, arguing that it has been too concerned with examining class structure. Within cultural studies though there has been a shift away from concentrating solely on ideology and hegemony to studying identity and subjectivity; this may, at least in part, be attributed to the impact of feminism. Academics such as Sherrie Innes, Yvonne Tasker and Sharon Willis have applied this approach when studying gender and film. In *Tough Girls*, Innes discusses

polysemic
A text with a multitude of possible readings.

See Chapter 13 for further discussion on race and film.

See Chapter 12 for a more detailed discussion of lesbian and gay studies.

the strong woman in popular culture and asks why tough women with masculine qualities are popular in the media, where not only do they have to display toughness but they also have to have the right attitude and show 'little or no fear, even in the most dangerous circumstances; if she does show fear, it must not stop her from acting' (1999: 25). Yet even the tough woman is usually required to display a feminine side which would seem to diminish her toughness or, at least, put it under question. Innes argues that tough women are more acceptable than they were a decade ago and asks what this means for Western society. Do we want women to take on these attributes in a society that in so many ways is tough enough already? Innes's writing refers to the media prior to 1999 and so misses out on the huge success of the TV series *Buffy the Vampire Slayer* and films such as *Tomb Raider* (2001), and *Kill Bill I* (2001) and *II* (2003).

Astrid Deuber-Mankowsky, in an insightful treatment of the role of Lara Croft in the Tomb Raider game series, analyses the popularity of Lara Croft, looking at her both as a cyber heroine and film heroine. She argues that Lara, in the film played by Angelina Jolie, is a combination of the physically perfect fantasy female, the dream woman and the ideal male. Lara's mental qualities are masculine, she has traditional male values, being decisive, courageous, independent and heroic, cool at all times. Lara was modelled on the Indiana Jones character played by Harrison Ford and made female to be different. She is a male creation, a fantasy of the games' creator and, although a fusion of masculine and feminine qualities, her body is clearly fetishisised and seen as a combination of spectacle and action: Lara wears tight-fitting clothes that emphasise her curvy shape, she is a figure of desire, whilst at the same time she appears to be popular with women, who enjoy the fact that she is powerful and strong. Yet Deuber-Mankowsky argues, 'However much Lara Croft acts the role of the better male, she is still a woman. The hierarchy of values remains as unaffected as its underpinnings in

• **Plate 11.6**
Tomb Raider (Simon West, 2000). The perfect male/female fantasy figure?

the relation between the sexes. Lara Croft's femininity is reduced, in a very traditional manner, to her oversized female attributes' (2005: 47). As in the game, the film lens focuses on Lara narcissistically, she is always in the frame, both the film and the game play with voyeurism and exhibitionism. Lara is watched sexually, she is also on display for the viewer in quite a complex way, and she may well appeal to the passive male as discussed by Carol Clover in her analysis of the horror film audience (see Clover 1992).

In concluding this section it is evident that feminist film theory has drawn on a wide range of analytical processes and these continue to contribute to our understanding of how women communicate, are communicated to and interpret film. The next section discusses theories of masculinity, and it may be that the study of gender is as likely to reveal fresh insights into how we understand femininity as well as masculinity.

The following case studies apply many of the theories, concepts and approaches on women and film discussed in this section to the following filmmakers and a selection of their films.

□ CASE STUDY 1: SALLY POTTER, FILMMAKER

Sally Potter began her career as a filmmaker with the film short *Thriller* (1979), then making the feature-length *The Gold Diggers* (1983) which was not generally well received, leading to a ten-year gap, when the much-acclaimed *Orlando* (1993) was released. Her most recent films, *The Man Who Cried* (2000) and *Yes* (2005), are still experimental and her work could be termed avant-garde; nevertheless, while having many of the qualities of an 'art' production they still contain a narrative drive.

Potter's first film, *Thriller* is a feminist reading of Puccini's opera *La Bohème* (1895). Linking together feminist, Marxist and psychoanalytic theory, the film is a critique of the constraints of patriarchy, the lack of female voice and woman as object and victim. The film was funded by the British Arts Council, and although avant-garde in style, it was received with interest. Ann Kaplan explains why: 'It is, first, an imaginative intervention in the dominance of a certain kind of classical narrative (the sentimental romance and the detective story) making a critique of such narratives into an alternative art form' (1983: 161).

The Gold Diggers (1983)

The Gold Diggers, made with a grant from the British Film Institute (BFI) explores the relationship between women and power, money and patriarchy, and develops themes originally explored in *Thriller*. The film has two main characters, both women: the early nineteenth-century heroine (Julie Christie) and the modern heroine (Colette Lafone). Potter purposefully chose an all-women crew to work on the film, including women musicians. On its release in 1983 the film was poorly received, partly due to its complex yet plotless narrative which exemplifed a problem of art and avant-garde cinema in the early 1980s – a lack of awareness of audience. Potter has discussed the problems of the film, explaining the difficulties of working collaboratively with others and pointing out that the film 'came out of a practice in the theatre of going with the moment, incorporating ideas, and not being completely text-bound' (Ehrenstein 1993: 3).

Imagery in the film often verges on the surreal, but the script is stilted and difficult to follow, almost a series of vignettes. The modern heroine in the film plays the part of investigator and observer of patriarchy, which is shown to be threatening, bureaucratic and ultimately ridiculous.

Orlando is a rich and colourful adaptation of the Virginia Woolf novel and was made by Potter's own company, Adventure Pictures, formed with *Orlando*'s producer Christopher Sheppard. The film's budget was £2 million, making it a medium-size British film, although the quality of the production gives it a much more expensive look. In contrast to *The Gold Diggers* in which the crew was all-female, a mixed crew worked on *Orlando*. After the experience of *The Gold Diggers*, Potter took great care to ensure that she was happy with the screenplay. Although the development process took years this ensured a clear narrative that powerfully drives the film. The film is concerned with two central ideas: the concept of immortality and the fluidity of gender. Orlando travels in time, from the Elizabethan age to the present day, changing sex in 1700. The mise-en-scène is sumptuous and enhanced by the fluid camera work; the scene when Orlando moves into the Victorian age, for instance, is full of movement and dynamism, the gorgeous costumes swirling forward into the future.

Aspects of feminism, gender, imperialism and politics are part of the narrative discourse – areas that are often anathema to a film's success – yet *Orlando* has been received with much acclaim: David Ehrenstein in *Film Quarterly* compares the film to Orson Welles's *The Magnificent Ambersons*: 'Like no other film of the moment, it demonstates that art and pleasure are not mutually exclusive categories of experience' (Ehrenstein 1993: 2).

In the film, Potter is more concerned with gender than with feminism, although the vulnerability of women is a key theme: when Orlando becomes female she loses her home and her financial power. She then has only her body, her femaleness to bargain with, which she refuses to share in marriage with the archduke, who sternly reminds her that she has no property and will suffer the ignominy of remaining a spinster.

The film has a strong sense of playfulness, from the knowing looks Orlando gives to the audience to the confusion of sexual identity. When Orlando becomes female in a beautifully filmed metamorphosis, she boldly states to the camera, 'same person, just a different sex'. Potter explains:

I don't think the book so much explores sexual identities as dissolves them, and it's that kind of melting and shifting where nothing is ever what it seems for male or female that I think is the strength of the book and which I wanted to reproduce in the film.

(Florence 1993: 283)

At times gender differences are de-emphasised: for instance, the clothing worn by the young Orlando is quite elaborate. However, when Orlando returns to Britain as a woman, her dress becomes a powerful symbol of her womanhood and the constraints and limitations that imposes. As a woman in the seventeenth century, Orlando must curb her sense of adventure and her enquiring mind. Orlando is offered the final insult when told that she may as well be dead as be a woman, and her house and wealth are taken away from her. Orlando rebelliously enters the Victorian age, a heroine of melodrama ready to be rescued by a handsome, romantic hero who becomes her lover and fathers her daughter. Although Orlando has lost her home and refuses to follow her lover, she retains her independence and moves forward in time to successfully negotiate life in modern Britain.

The style of *Orlando* moves away from the avant-garde towards the mainstream while still playing with narrative form. Potter's film is a stimulating and rich attack on the senses with a discourse that, although concerned with gender, suggests a blending of the sexes rather than a separation, which many of the earlier feminist films such as *A Question of Silence* (1982), *The Gold Diggers* (1983) and Lezli-Ann Barrett's *An Epic Poem* (1982) encouraged.

Potter was inspired to make *Yes* in response to the attacks in the US on 11 September 2001. She explores the relationship between two lovers from opposite cultural backgrounds; a white American female played by Joan Cusack and a Middle Eastern male played by Simon Abkarian. When differences in their cultural background begin to show, conflicts emerge, and this eventually divides them. The couple decide to part but are reconciled in Cuba, a 'no man's land' of neutral cultural heritage. The themes discussed and the way the story unfolds are not especially unconventional but the format is: the characters speak in rhyming couplets, and one actor speaks directly to the audience as in a Greek chorus.

• **Plate 11.7**
Yes (Sally Potter, 2005). The film debates cultural differences between East and West in response to 9/11

☐ CASE STUDY 2: NICOLE HOLOFCENER, WRITER/ DIRECTOR

Nicole Holofcener's films are rather more mainstream than Potter's. She has worked in TV, directing the US version of the British TV series *Cold Feet* in 1999 and episodes of *Six Feet Under*, and written and directed four feature-length films. Holofcener began her career in film as a production assistant for Woody Allen, whom she acknowledges as having been a major influence on her work. She is one of the few women directors who have made a series of films which, although not box-office successes, have all been critically acclaimed. Unlike mainstream filmmaker Kathryn Bigelow, whose films such as *K-19:The Widowmaker* (2002) and *The Hurt Locker* (2008) explore almost exclusively masculine worlds, Holofcener's films are centred around women. Her first feature-length film, *Walking and Talking* (1996), focuses on two friends in their late twenties and their changing relationship as they cope with careers and love lives, while her next film, *Lovely and Amazing* (2001), explores the dynamics between a mother and her two daughters. *Friends with Money* (2006) depicts a woman in her thirties and the three girlfriends she went to school with, who appear to lead more successful lives. *Please Give* (2010), her most recent film, although concerned with a couple who are furniture dealers, focuses strongly on the central female characters.

Holofcener's films could be categorised as American independent in style, and the influence of Woody Allen and other independent filmmakers such as John Cassavetes is apparent . This is evident in the way the narrative is a quite loose in its structure and gives the impression of being rambling, which makes the stories she creates seem natural and endows the lives portrayed in the film with a sense of realism; there is a messiness about them that is very believable. The women who inhabit this world are searching for something and uncertain about their place in society – women of twenty-first-century

America who worry about personal things like love, career, their bodies and about the ethical dilemmas they face in the modern world. Holofocener's films are unusually honest – they dig into female insecurities – and while they are funny and charming they also touch upon darker aspects of life, which prevents them becoming saccharine. As Christine Spines points out in *Film Comment*, 'Her characters are allowed to be unpleasant and shrill. Keener's insensitive and insecure mother in *Lovely and Amazing* is often more childish and immature than her kids' (Spines 2010: 38).

Lovely and Amazing portrays women who may be emotional and insecure but are also quirky, witty and charming and, at times, desperately sad. Holofcener often depicts women who are vulnerable and neurotic, even self-absorbed. These are characteristics that have negative connotations in Western culture, but these women also have a strength and a deep bond that unites them. Holofcenor taps into female communities and explores the conflict that abounds in their lives, dissecting the minutiae of these relationships and the feelings and emotions of her characters, aspects rarely discussed in the narrative of films written or directed by men. For instance, when Michelle, Jane's eldest daughter, has an affair with a 16-year-old boy; there is a hilarious tragicomic sequence in which she meets the boy's mother who then reports her to the police, resulting in her being arrested, taken to the police station and later released on a caution. Michelle's humiliation is almost unbearable to watch and Holofcenor makes Michelle's predicament both funny and sad.

All the characters in *Lovely and Amazing* have problems which affect their ability to cope with life: the needy and insecure mother Jane has cosmetic surgery which goes wrong but her crush on the surgeon blinds her to his incompetence; the younger daughter Elizabeth, an aspiring actress, has a boyfriend who doesn't understand her insecurities and the problem of her flabby underarms; while Michelle is unhappily married and an unfulfilled artist. The film gently pokes fun at the characters' insecurities, making wry comments about life in the twenty-first century. For instance, Jane's well-meaning desire to ensure that Annie, the young black girl she has adopted, keeps in touch with her roots is satirised when the black women she visits refuse to take her out any more because she behaves so badly. When Michelle tries to sell her not very good art in a craft shop we may laugh a little but, as we watch her being humiliated, the scene becomes more and more poignant: not only does she have to face rejection of her work but she is observed by an old school friend she meets in the shop and who is now a successful paediatrician, in contrast to Michelle's inability to earn a penny.

Holofcener does not laugh at her characters but asks us to like them, to understand them and their condition rather than be judgemental. This candid honesty is often very powerful: when Elizabeth asks her new actor boyfriend Ken to look at her naked body and be critical she is at her most vulnerable as he discusses her physique in microscopic detail – one actor to another – but at the same time there is something very charming about the openness of the discussion. Dissatisfaction with the body is a constant theme of the film; the mother is as critical of her body as Elizabeth and is determined to have plastic surgery to get rid of what she considers to be excess fat.

The film reinforces the idea that these people enjoy being a family of women and, despite their problems, are able to manage on their own. Jane doesn't really need the surgeon; Michelle can live without her husband; Elizabeth, her lip now scarred by the dog she tried to rescue, realises she doesn't need her vain actor boyfriend; and Annie doesn't need someone to remind her that she is black.

Although the traditionally happy ending in *Lovely and Amazing* is withheld and many loose ends are unresolved, there is the sense that things can get better: the mother recovers from her coma and when Annie runs away she is found in McDonald's eating happily and unhealthily. These characters are beginning to like themselves. They may be unhappy and unfulfilled, full of failings and insecurities, but they are people we can identify with and, as we watch their often painful and tragicomic lives unfold, we see our own problems put under the microscope.

Friends With Money is about four school friends in their late thirties and forties, three of whom are extremely rich and successful, while the fourth, Olivia, sees herself as a failure and the outsider of the group. Her friends all appear to be in stable relationships while she works as a cleaner, having given up her job teaching at an elite school because the rich kids teased her. Olivia is not happy but when her wealthy friends' lives are examined more closely, neither are they.

We may never feel that Olivia is on the breadline but the film does highlight some of the differences between the rich and the relatively poor, especially in the conversations between the super-rich Franny and Olivia. Franny and her husband's most difficult decisions revolve around which charity they should to donate their $2-million dollar gift to. Olivia's decisions, in contrast, are about whether to sell her time per hour as a cleaner for less and how many free samples of face cream she can collect to save money. Later in the film she steals a large pot of the same cream from one of her clients and we see her use this on her feet, enjoying the waste of money and the extravagance.

Olivia has become obsessive about a brief relationship she had with a married man and is virtually stalking him. Franny tries to help her get over him and sets up a blind date with her personal trainer, with whom Olivia strikes up a short-term and unsatisfying relationship. We see Olivia slowly move on as she cleans homes with her new boyfriend, having sex with him in each one. There are some wry and bathetic moments when Olivia is going out with him until she eventually realises he is just using her. Olivia appears to be drifting through life, with no real ambition or focus, her wandering from home to home as a cleaner a metaphor for her instability and rootlessness.

Holofcener creates the sense that we live in a complex world full of difficult decisions and choices to be made. She uses the film image to emphasise this and gives a lovely physicality to her characters which often become a metaphor for their situation. Christine, for instance, is always bumping into things, while Jane is continually angry and, after losing her temper in a store, runs into a plate-glass window, breaking her nose.

Holofcener's dialogue is rich and funny, sharp and honest, with a few nods to Woody Allen in the self-effacing and self-conscious dialogue. When Olivia reminds the super-rich Franny that she doesn't need to work, Franny asks 'Are you trying to make me feel bad?' and Olivia responds thoughtfully deadpan, 'No, I don't think so.'

• **Plate 11.8**
Lovely and Amazing
(Nicole Holofcener,
2001)

Female friendships are accentuated in *Friends with Money* and the only man really allowed into this world, Jane's probably gay husband, behaves like a woman and is sensitive and thoughtful.

The one false note in the film is the happy ending in which Olivia meets her Prince, the slobby man whose apartment she has been cleaning and who turns out to be her soul mate and conveniently rich! Olivia now seems destined to lead an inconsequential life as a rich woman improving her partner's house, a rather ambiguous note on which to end the film. Olivia may have what she wants but we're not sure if this will make her happy.

Holofcener's latest film, *Please Give*, focuses on a couple who sell second-hand furniture, emptying people's houses when they move or die, thus often making money from other people's misery. The film begins with a woman being given a mammogram, a striking and unusual image with which to start a film, which informs the viewer that this is a film about women's bodies and women's experiences.

While Holofcener's films cannot be described as feminist they do show women who are thoughtfully drawn, complex characters and whose stories dispel some of the negative associations around subjects which are of interest to women. She writes and directs about dilemmas she finds interesting, that women can relate to and that men also find funny. Sadly, the film industry is still very much geared to catering to a largely young and male audience at the expense of intelligent films like Holofcener's; it is an industry in which a macho culture predominates and which relies on the production of genre films such as the gangster, horror and blockbuster for financial success. Hopefully it will not be long before more women writer/directors make films about a range of subjects with women centre stage that are as entertaining and insightful as these.

GENDER THEORY AND THEORIES OF MASCULINITY

Masculinity as unproblematic

Laura Mulvey's essay 'Visual Pleasure and Narrative Cinema' focused attention on cinema spectatorship in terms of binary opposites of gender: woman is defined as object of the look and man as being in control of the gaze. The importance of Mulvey's conclusions and the implications of these findings initially resulted in little further questioning of the role of the male in film who was seen as representing patriarchy in a straightforward way. Problems with defining femininity as passive and masculinity as active had become apparent by the 1980s because seeing gender in terms of binary opposites and as fixed is problematic.[9] Defining the masculine as the 'norm' and the female as 'other' may be valid at a particular moment in classical Hollywood cinema, but if gender is a social construction then constructions of gender in film are not absolute and are subject to change. Steven Neale's article, 'Masculinity as Spectacle', first published in 1983, is described by Cohan and Hark in *Screening the Male* as a 'pioneering attempt to put Mulvey's arguments in the context of those films that obviously represent a spectacular form of masculinity' (1993: 2).

Masculinity is associated with **voyeurism**, action, sadism, **fetishism** and the controlling narrative, while femininity is associated with passivity, exhibitionism, spectacle, masochism and narcissism. Yet these clear distinctions belie the acute anxieties and paradoxes which emerge when studying film; the binary opposites of masculinity and femininity are in fact much less opaque than may at first be apparent. The male image and the way it is represented is as complex and revealing as the female image, although it may appear 'hidden' and unrecognised, a natural part of patriarchy. Neale's essay examines identification, looking and spectacle using Mulvey's article as a reference point. He points out that how we identify with a character in film is a complex process. We do not always clearly align ourselves with either a male or female figure depending on our gender, otherwise why would females be able to identify with Clint Eastwood in *Unforgiven* (1992) or Bruce Willis in *Die Hard* (1988)?

voyeurism
The sexual pleasure gained from looking at others.

fetishism
Freudian theorists argue that fetishism is linked to the castration complex and is a form of male denial of the threat and fear of castration by the female. The female is made less threatening, more reassuring, by substituting her lack of a phallus with a fetish object such as high heels, long hair or turning her into a fetish object by exaggerating or fragmenting parts of the body such as lips or breasts.

See Case study 3: Fight Club (1999) for comparison.

The male hero in classical Hollywood cinema is usually recognised as powerful. He signifies omnipotence, mastering the narrative, being in control, sadistic rather than masochistic. Neale argues that the elements of violence, voyeurism and masochism in Anthony Mann's films in fact suggest a 'repressed homosexual voyeurism' (Cohan and Hark 1993: 13). The act of looking has a homoerotic quality and an anxiety which is produced as a result of the erotic possibilities that are repressed. The violence present in these films is an expression of the anxiety that surrounds the suppression of homosexual desire which is evident in the looks between characters. Neale's discussion of looking and spectacle further develops Mulvey's division of the active male, who controls the look, and the object of the look, the passive female. Neale argues that male figures can be the subject of voyeuristic looking also. In male-centred genres such as war, action, westerns and gangster films there are binary opposites in the form of opposing forces which struggle for power and control. Mann's films use narrative outcome and spectacle to suggest male struggle, images of masculinity are fetishised and there is an emphasis on display and the spectacular.[10] Sergio Leone's westerns also work through an aggressive exchange of looks, another form of fetishisistic looking. But Neale points out that the male body is not shown purely for the purpose of erotic spectacle:

We see male bodies stylised and fragmented by close-ups, but our look is not direct, it is heavily mediated by the looks of the characters involved. And those looks are marked out not by desire but rather by fear, or hatred, or aggression.

(1993: 18)

The act of aggression takes the focus away from the spectacle and thus displaces the eroticism of the male body, while still suggesting this at a subconscious level. Certain genres though, such as melodrama and the musical, do allow for the male body to be the object of the look; for instance, Rock Hudson in Douglas Sirk's melodramas and John Travolta in *Saturday Night Fever* (1977).

Neale points out the need to acknowledge and consider the eroticism and spectacle of the masculine image in terms of identification, voyeuristic looking and fetishistic representation. Mainstream cinema assumes there is a male norm, a male way of looking, while the female represents difference, which requires investigation. But Neale argues that the male also requires investigation in the same kind of way and that masculinity is as much a mystery as femininity.

Neale's article is particularly important because he argues that the representation of the male is not straightforward or opaque. Academics such as Richard Dyer and Yvonne Tasker have further opened up the debate as to our understanding of masculinity and, indeed, gender in film, and this chapter will draw on some of their work in more detail. Neale's essay focuses on Freudian- and Lacanian-based psychoanalytic theory rather than cultural factors. This theoretical approach may be seen as white and phallocentric and it could also be argued, with some justification, that it is a rather limited method of study: racial and cultural differences, for instance, are ignored. There has been very little discussion of other masculinities such as the Mexican characters in Eastwood westerns or more recently the representation of Somalians in *Black Hawk Down* (2001). Analytical focus has mainly been on the representation of white masculinity to the exclusion of other identity-forming factors such as ethnic background, sexuality, nationality and so on.

How and why we identify with a character in a film is complex, and mainstream film is a site for questioning these rich and often ambiguous character identities, and the study of gender in film questions what these identities are and how they work. Hollywood film is much more than a straightforward, easily read transmitter of the dominant ideology. It is complex in its construction, multi-layered in meaning and, to some extent, reflects the hopes and desires of the cinema-going public.

• **Plate 11.9**
Gladiator (Ridley Scott, 2000). The general seeks to avenge the murder of this wife and children

Playing with gender

It has been observed by commentators in different disciplines that the strenuousness of the masculine identities is a pointer, not to their stability, but their fragility.

(Horrocks 1995: 16)

It might appear that in our society masculinity is natural, normal and universal. This myth is repeated by stories and images we see in the media and especially in Hollywood film. Yet despite the certainty, the surety with which masculine identities are portrayed, closer examination reveals that masculinity is much less stable and more easily undermined than previously thought.

Theorists such as Barbara Creed, Yvonne Tasker and Chris Holmlund have discussed the notion of masculinity as play, as performance and masquerade. Barbara Creed suggests that the muscle-bound hero of the 1980s cinema may be understood in terms of postmodernity, of playing with the notion of manhood, and argues that the muscular hero is 'simulcra of an exaggerated masculinity, the original lost to sight' (1987: 65). The hero in action film can be seen as a parody, a tongue-in-cheek play on the impossible role he has to perform. It is easy to apply this argument to Bruce Willis in the *Die Hard* films but does the same argument apply to Russell Crowe's role in *Gladiator* (2000)? Crowe's Roman general is a much more serious and weighty hero and, although he portrays a hypermasculinity, he is seeking to avenge the murder of his wife and children and is incomplete without them. But Crowe's role in the film also evokes a sense of nostalgia, looking back to a time when men were warriors and had a cause worth fighting for.

Whilst psychoanalysis has been used as a way of understanding the acquisition of sexual identity, postmodernism addresses the flexibility and ambiguity of popular culture. When these two approaches are combined, interesting ways of understanding gender emerge. Chris Holmlund, in 'Masculinity as Multiple Masquerade' (1993), discusses the many ways that acting or playing a role on screen is a masquerade. She argues that gender is acted, a pretence, a form of dressing up or putting on a show, and that heterosexuality is also a masquerade, a charade, in which there are often homoerotic overtones. Therefore masculinity, and thus gender, is a multiple charade of which the audience is aware yet not aware, because much of the complexity of gender identity is understood by the audience at a subconscious level.

The male body

The action film, by being active, distracts from the eroticised male body on display. Dyer explains:

> images of men must disavow ... passivity if they are to be kept in line with the dominant ideas of masculinity-as-activity.
>
> (Dyer 1982: 66–7)

The masculine body as spectacle, while having a performative function, is a key theme of Hollywood film, particularly action films of the 1980s. Yvonne Tasker's analysis of the *Die Hard* films suggests that the particular representation of the male body in the 1980s reflects an anxiety about the roles men and women play in their everyday lives, both at home and at work, and their concerns regarding shifts in society and gender roles. *Die Hard* (1988) reflects on the lack of control the male has in the workplace, where the hero finds himself in impossible situations and hindered by incompetent bureaucracies:

> Anxieties to do with difference and sexuality increasingly seem to be worked out over the body of the male hero.
>
> (Tasker 1993: 236)

For further discussion of the star in Hollywood, see Chapter 7.

In terms of stars and gender the star is an amplified sign of popularity. The star is larger than life in his physical abilities and looks. The usually white star/hero goes into a dangerous situation, and civilises and makes it safe. Again however, like gender, stardom is not fixed but unstable and shifting. Changes in the qualities of the male hero are evident from the 1980s to the 1990s; the male body in the 1980s was a spectacle of muscle, beauty, toughness and bravery, a body which could carry out extreme physical feats. In comparison the body of the early 1990s man is less a spectacle of male machismo associated with violence, but rather gentler, more questioning, allowed to show self-doubt, and existing in a world where love and family are important: films such as *Robin Hood* (1991), *Regarding Henry* (1991) and *Boyz N the Hood* (1991) try to work out these issues.

A comparison of *The Terminator* (1984) with *Terminator 2* (1991) demonstrates many of these changes in their representation of masculinity. Susan Jeffords argues that in *Terminator 2* the Terminator becomes the perfect father and mother and, therefore, Sarah's role as mother and saviour of the human race is diminished. Ironically, Sarah becomes a parody of the tough, fearless, 1980s action hero and, similarly, there is a fascination with her muscles and her body.

In *Terminator 2* there is a shift in position regarding violence and male machismo: a non-destructive, anti-killing morality is imposed. The Terminator is told by John Connor to aim for the knees when he shoots, and that killing is not good. Dyson, the creator of the Terminator, sacrifices himself for the greater good, to save humanity. John Connor, the son and future saviour of the human race, holds the real power in the narrative and

• **Plate 11.10**
Fight Club (David
Fincher, 1999). *Fight
Club* suggests a huge
anxiety about what it is
to be male

the Terminator becomes a metaphor for the old Hollywood concept of masculinity. *Terminator 2*, Jeffords argues, provides a new way for masculinity to go, not outward aggression:

but inward, into increasingly emotive displays of masculine sensibilities, traumas and burdens. T2 offers an alternative way to resolve these anxieties about the ends of masculinity/territory through the manipulation of space and time via the male body.

(1993: 259)

The male body in the early 1990s is often damaged in some way, as in *Robocop 2* (1992) or, in the case of the Terminator, it has to be destroyed. This damaged yet heroic body of the Terminator is the source of man's personal, emotional and social problems and appears to be past his 'sell-by date'.

Films by black male directors, although concerned with families and masculinity, often do not have the same concern with the themes of internalisation and bodily betrayal. John Singleton's film *Boyz N the Hood* is much more concerned with critiquing the culture and society in which black American boys are brought up.

Tasker argues that muscles are signifiers of struggle, of hard physical labour and of the working class. The importance of male muscles in the action film may be attributed to a form of nostalgia or a need to identify with men who are clearly men. Although this is a concern of the 1980s action film it is interesting to compare this with more recent films which subject the male body to the gaze, such as *Fight Club* (1999) and *The Full Monty* (1997). Yet different actors bring different qualities to the screen; Bruce Willis is not just a working-class hero associated with muscles and a vest, he is part parody with a wise-cracking voice. His performance is very different from that of body builders such as Stallone and Schwarzenegger, although by the time *Terminator 2* was released Schwarzenegger seems to have become a parody of himself.

The action-film narrative is often concerned with class and sexuality, situated within a cultural context in which masculinity has to some extent been denaturalised. The use of military and police uniform in many action films appears to relieve masculine anxiety, giving some stability in a society of changing values. The dress of the action hero gives an appearance of phallic power, a substitute for the 'lack' feared; the muscular, phallic body functions as a powerful symbol of masculinity.

The action hero plays out a drama of power and powerlessness which reflects anxieties about masculine identity and authority and is embodied in the figure of the struggling hero. The action hero is tested; he has to undergo a series of narrative hurdles or challenges to overcome which will often include suffering, torture and punishment, all tribal tests of masculinity. Fight films such as *Rocky* (1976), *Raging Bull* (1980) and *Fight Club* (1999), although very different films, focus on masochistic suffering and how much punishment the masculine body can take.

Male anxiety: masculinity in crisis

The 1980s action hero is superficially a sign of masculine power, but on closer examination an anxiety about masculine identity is revealed and addressed in many films of the 1990s. The arrogance and certainty of films in the boom periods of the 'Yuppie' Reagan years was replaced by an uncertainty in the late 1980s and early 1990s as a result of economic depression, a downturn in the economy and a developing awareness that capitalism was not infallible. Films such as *Risky Business* (1983) and *Ferris Bueller's Day Off* (1986) are full of confident, masculine swagger while *Wall Street* (1987) reflects a much darker view of masculinity, capitalism and corporate greed.

Jude Davies's article 'Gender, Ethnicity and Cultural crisis in *Falling Down* and *Groundhog Day*', outlines how both films problematise white masculinity in which she links American cultural and historical crisis with a crisis of masculinity. In *Falling Down* (1996), director Joel Schumacher makes the point that the pre-eminence of the white male can no longer be assumed. Michael Douglas as D-Fens plays a dysfunctional white male who is pushed to violence when he loses his job. *Falling Down* shows the tensions at work in mid-1990s America, a society affected by economic depression, gender and multicultural anxiety. D-Fens is not portrayed as being typical of white masculinity; as the narrative progresses his behaviour becomes more extreme and further out of control. In the finale, however, there is sympathy for the character's predicament and D-Fens is transformed into the hero when we realise his death will give his young daughter his insurance money: he sacrifices his life to help her.

Groundhog Day (1993) also features white masculinity in crisis but in a very different way. The film is a romantic comedy which shows the transformation of a cynical sexist into an enlightened sympathetic male. The film avoids any political gestures or comment and in terms of narrative Bill Murray's character has changed very little by the film's conclusion. Davies points out that *Falling Down* and *Groundhog Day*, while they are both:

in some senses critical of the white middle class masculinity which has occupied the default position in mainstream US culture, they reinforce the primacy of white males in making sense of, and responding to, a perceived crisis. Here when white masculinity seems most under fire it hogs the ground.

(1995.: 229)

The new man?

In early 1990s cinema white males are often presented as domesticated, feminised or paternal in a range of genres such as comedies, romances and action films; so much so that Quentin Tarantino was one of the few filmmakers in that period working in the gangster genre, probably the only genre in which macho masculinity appears to remain intact. *Pulp Fiction* (1994) has levels of irony, self-reflexivity and parody, but it also contains a homophobic construction of sexuality which belies the macho strutting of the actors. Films in the latter part of the decade and the new millennium, such as *The Full Monty* (1997), *Fight Club* (1999) and *Gladiator* (2000), in their very different ways, suggest

See Chapter 5, for a case study of Pulp Fiction *and the audience's interaction with the film. For further reference to* The Full Monty *and British cinema see Chapter 14.* Gladiator *is discussed as an example of classical narrative cinema in Chapter 4.*

an unease with taking on a feminised role and a desire for certainty in respect of what it is to be masculine.

The feminised, enlightened new man is more fiction than reality, according to Kathleen Rowe in her article 'Melodrama and Men in Post-Classical Romantic Comedy', in which she argues that there has been an increased use of melodrama to tell the story of men's lives and male suffering. There is a darker edge to these comedies which takes away the focus from the female heroine and transfers it to the male victim, the melodramatic hero; the female becomes, if not the villain, then the lesser character.

From the late 1970s onwards romantic comedy has tapped into an unease about the notions of romance: in *Sleepless in Seattle* (1993) the lovers don't meet until the end and have no sexual contact; while Woody Allen's films are often discourses about broader cultural anxieties concerning romance and masculinity. These comedies suggest an underlying fear of the impact of the changes in the status of women and their effect on men. Rowe argues that they allow the male to determine the narrative outcome while the female is seen as lacking:

In these films it is the men who educate the women, not the reverse. Each of these heroines resists her male suitor less out of her inherent independence or recognition of his need to change than out of something wounded or underdeveloped in her – qualities which allow the hero to demonstrate his greater wisdom, charm or sensitivity.

(cited in Kirkham and Thumin 1995: 187)

The classical Hollywood romantic comedies undermined masculine authority while melodrama was seen as the women's genre, appealling to women because it related to the sufferings they endured in patriarchal culture. Suffering and loss have more often been associated with the feminine; in women melancholy is seen as disabling and negative while in a man, for instance, Richard Gere in *Pretty Woman* (1989) or Tom Hanks in *Sleepless in Seattle* (1993), it is presented as positive, enabling the transformation of apparent loss into male power. These male transformation movies show a softer male but at the same time enhance and consolidate their hierarchical and patriarchal position by acquiring qualities traditionally regarded as feminine. In *Regarding Henry* (1991), *The Fisher King* (1991), *Terminator 2* (1991), *Groundhog Day* (1993) and *Parenthood* (1989) men have emotions and are not afraid to display them but, apart from *Terminator 2*, in which Sarah Connor is sidelined in her role as mother, a role which is appropriated by Schwarzenegger, the woman's place is still in the kitchen. Occasionally, Hollywood films overturn these conventions in an interesting or challenging way; in *Jagged Edge* (1989) Jeff Bridges plays the romantic hero but is finally exposed as the killer – the romantic hero becomes the villain.

Fatherhood and the family

Many films in the 1980s and 1990s potray the role of fatherhood and the family as a central discourse. The family has been central to Western society and American national identity was founded on the patriarchal family structure. The contemporary American family, however, is not stable and many families divorce or separate. Action films such as *Die Hard* and *Lethal Weapon* (1989) reflect this uncertainty. Danny Glover's family, in *Lethal Weapon*, represents security, stability and paternal authority, while Mel Gibson plays the outsider who is emotionally lost after his wife's death.

The father replacing the mother or the mother being marginalised or ignored is a theme common to a variety of films from this period. In *Terminator 2*, the Terminator becomes the minder of John Connor (the son who has lost his father) and the 'hard' man learns to be gentle and how to nurture, while Sarah Connor is hardly involved with or even interested in motherhood. In *Three Men and a Baby* (1989) the men act as 'surrogate mothers' as well as fathers. The baby's mother is not reunited with her child until the end of the film and the audience view her as an outsider. Oliver Stone's *Wall Street* (1987) pits the 'good father' and 'the bad father' against each other, both fighting to gain control of the good father's son; this is an exclusively male family scenario in which the women are either prizes or bought. More recent films such as *The Full Monty* (1997) and *Gladiator* (2000), in their very different ways, explore the role of the father as patriarch and how he reacts when the family is broken up and separated from the mother, or the family is destroyed.

Womb envy

A number of films, from genres as diverse as comedy in *Three Men and a Baby* to horror such as *The Fly* (1986), demonstrate an unease or discomfort which at times borders on envy regarding the reproductive powers of woman. Many horror films express a fascination with creating a human such as *Frankenstein* (1930) or controlling reproductive power as does the scientist in *The Fly*.

Three Men and a Baby's central theme is about man's desire to take over and control the reproductive function. The film voices male concerns about fathering, birth and female sexuality, suggesting that fatherhood can be a collective male experience, rather than one man taking sole responsibility for the child. There is denial of a single responsibility for fatherhood while at the same time a desire to take the role of carer from the woman. A form of womb envy becomes apparent when one of the characters dresses as a pregnant woman.

Modleski argues that envy of woman and her procreative ability runs alongside a fear of feminisation and a wish to deny woman the role of childbearer and nurturer: 'it is possible, the film shows, for men to respond to the feminist demand for their increased participation in child rearing in such a way as to make women more marginal than ever' (2000: 525).

The protagonists in David Cronenberg's *The Fly* and *Dead Ringers* (1988) are so envious of female reproductive powers that they suffer feelings of impotence. The men in Cronenberg's films try to control the womb or gain knowledge that gives them power over female fertility, as do the twin gynaecologists in *Dead Ringers*, while in *Videodrome* (1984) the central character gains a vagina in his stomach into which a video tape is inserted.

Masculine anxiety regarding paternity and reproduction is particularly evident in the horror film: in *Alien* there is conflict between the fear of and fascination with the maternal. The film contains disturbing imagery regarding birth and the female sex organs: one of the crew gives birth through his stomach, the Alien is female, she eats men, consumes them; in contrast other imagery in the film is comforting and maternal, the sleeping places are womb-like and the crew dress in nappies when asleep.

Hurt, agony, pain – love it: the masochistic spectator

Historically the male body is viewed as the norm and the female body as a deviation, as inferior, a poor copy. Yet many monstrous figures are, on closer examination, associated with aspects of femininity: Dracula has ruby-red lips, the werewolf's lunar cycle mimics menstruation and it is reborn in the process of transformation. More recently in *The Silence of the Lambs* (1991) Buffalo Bill hopes to realise transformation by covering himself in the skin of dead women.

Barbara Creed's article 'Dark Desires' (1993) argues that there are two types of horror film: the first explores man's desire for castration in order to become a woman, and the second, man's desire for castration as part of a male death wish. Creed examines the rape-revenge films *I Spit on Your Grave* (1978) and *Naked Vengeance* (1984), in which the male rapist is castrated and killed by his victim. A more recent equivalent is *Species* (1997), in which the female monster kills her victim after having sex with him.

Who the audience identify with in terms of gender when watching film is rather more complex than outlined by Mulvey and by Metz (1983). Carol Clover examines the nature of the male monster and the identification of the audience with the female victim, pointing out that the gaze of both the male and the female spectator is constructed as masochistic. In the horror film the victim is usually female and the audience mostly male. The horror film uses the female form not only for the male spectator to look at but for him to identify with, suggesting that the male viewer can easily identify with a different gender. The male takes on the role of masochistic spectator, identifying with the fear and pain of the hero/heroine. Clover argues that there has been little discussion about male masochism and identification with the female, even though it is assumed that women easily identify with the masculine in film (1992).

'Hurt, agony, pain – love it', displayed on a sign at the beginning of *The Silence of the Lambs* (1991), spells out the pleasure the audience gains from being placed in the position of masochistic and therefore feminised spectator. The horror audience, whether male or female, takes on a passive, classically feminine role, identifying with the pain and suffering of the protagonist: in this case the FBI agent Clarice Starling. Clover further argues that although the horror film is more overt in its manipulation of the audience, mainstream film makes use of similar tools to feminise the audience; we 'surrender ourselves' to a film, we expect to be manipulated, surprised and kept in suspense. Therefore the assumed dominant, sadistic role ascribed to the male viewer by both Mulvey and Metz is under question.

☐ **CASE STUDY 3:** *FIGHT CLUB* **(DAVID FINCHER, 1999)**

Fight Club is a film about masculinity in crisis. It depicts the disaffected, feminised, young white American male and his frustration with capitalism and late twentieth-century life. The film's central discourse suggests an uncertainty about man's role in society and a lack of purpose in life; Jack, the central protagonist, expresses this as:

We are the middle children of history with no purpose or place
We have no great war or great depression ...
We were raised by television to believe that we'd be millionaires ...
But we won't.... And now we're very pissed off.

These are the 'Lost Boys', a generation of men whose fathers have left home and have given no masculine guidance to their sons; they have no clear role or function in society and their lives are without meaning.

The crisis in identity exemplified by Jack's split personality is alluded to throughout the film, although not revealed until near the end. Tyler is Jack's physically perfect alter ego and also his dark side; a role played by Brad Pitt whose muscled body is often on display. In the first half of the film Jack has a homoerotic fascination with Tyler but in the latter section the two characters, facets of his personality, battle with each other for survival and Jack's sanity. Jack represents the passive, domesticated male and Tyler the fighter who is almost Neanderthal and ultimately destructive. As Henry Giroux points out:

For further discussion of the term homoerotic see Chapter 12.

The central protagonists, Jack and Tyler, represent two opposing registers that link consumerism and masculinity.... Jack exemplifies a form of domesticated masculinity – passive, alienated and without ambition. On the other hand Tyler exemplifies and embodies masculinity that refuses the seductions of consumerism.

(2000–1: 33)

The emasculated male, in need of testosterone, is evident from the beginning of the film, which opens with a phallic image of Jack with a gun in his mouth. There are many references throughout the film to fear of castration and phallic inadequacy. Jack is feminised, he is obsessed with decorating his flat with IKEA furniture and has an apparently lonely, meaningless but domesticated existence. There is clearly something wrong with Jack's life; he can't sleep, and tells a doctor that he's in pain. The doctor suggests he attends classes for the terminally ill to find out what pain really is. The first class Jack goes to is for testicular cancer, where he meets Bob who has breasts due to hormone treatment. Jack consoles him that 'we're still men'. Again these references suggest fear of castration, fear of losing masculine identity and fear of losing control of the body. Tyler shows Jack a way to regain his masculinity, his place in the world. There are a number of parallels with *Falling Down*, which depicts a man's extreme reaction to losing power and control in his life.

Identity is literally torn apart in the film and this is exemplified by the fight club, where fighting is not only a spectacle but a test of one's masculinity and how much pain can be taken, or can be suffered. The masochistic desire for self-punishment and the belief that pain through suffering is somehow redemptive or a transformative experience is a nostalgia for the past rituals of primitive societies; there is a nostalgia for an age when the roles of masculine and feminine are imagined as being more clearly defined. Many male secret societies and fascist groups have used pain as a test for entrance to the group. The fights between Jack and Tyler are however later shown as delusions, and Jack's self-mutilation is presented as an aspect of self-hate, guilt, confusion and inner torment; we understand in retrospect that he is a deeply disturbed character.

The fight club is where men can rediscover their masculinity, can connect and overcome fear and pain. The club gives order and meaning to their lives; these men crave regulation, rules and clearly defined boundaries.

The film flirts with fascism and Jack watches in horror as the desire for a new order is pushed to extremes. The fight club becomes a secret society and is transformed into an underground army which brainwashes its members who have to go through a series of masochistic initiations and tests to be considered 'man enough' to join. The paramilitary group has no real politics: Project Mayhem's aim is to bring chaos and destruction by destroying examples of modern art, architecture and coffee bars. The film, through Tyler, offers a nihilist philosophy of destruction and negativity. As Tyler says: 'Self-improvement is masturbation, self-destruction is the answer.'

The film links self-abuse with regaining power over the body and one's life. Jack argues in voiceover that the fight club gives him power and the people who had power over him have less and less because of his new state of mind. This is undercut however when he says, 'by this point I could wiggle most of the teeth in my jaw', and we are made aware that he is actually destroying his body. Self-destruction and self-loathing are pushed to its limits as the men pound each other's bodies. When Tyler pours lye on Jack's hand he tells Jack to feel the pain and not to avoid it, this ritual becomes a repeated image later in the film, an initiation test for new members of the club and another form of self-destruction and brainwashing.

A powerful desire for male bonding is repeatedly expressed and the need to be part of a group or movement which provides a reason for their existence. There is an element of homoeroticism in the images of dirty, sweaty, bloody men which is undercut by the action and violence that is so visceral at times. The uniform of muscles becomes the uniform of a terrorist organisation, and indeed there is a fetishism of the military which is very precise in its specificity of the clothing needed to join: two pairs of black socks and so on.

Women in *Fight Club* are, on first appearance, marginalised and non-existent, apart from Marla. Yet this is contradicted by some of Jack's first words: 'All this is about Marla Singer.' Much of the film is about denying or fighting against both the female within and the female figure of Marla. *Fight Club* gives a somewhat misogynist representation of women: Marla is defined as the cause of all Jack's problems – ' She ruined everything' –

and women are a threat, representing fear of castration; Tyler says to Jack, 'a woman could cut off your penis and throw it out the car'. Jack is part of a generation raised by women and questions how this has affected his identity. He asks: 'I wonder if another woman is really the answer we need.' There is frequent reference to the negative effect women have on men in shaping their identities, in feminising them. Tyler tells Jack that men have lost their manhood because they have been feminised. Women are cast as binary opposites and defined in negative terms; even the woman dying at the beginning of the film is defined in terms of her sex and as being sexually unattractive. Marla's role in the film is that of an outsider and a threat to Jack's existence. She fulfils two roles, first, to make Jack unhappy, and second, to provide sex. Yet there is a paradox here: Jack says Marla has invaded his life but this is more the unconscious denial of a want than a real desire to get rid of her. Marla is a constant, always waiting in the background, and Jack is pushed to fight against Tyler partly because of his desire to save her.

On one level the film is a celebration of hypermasculinity and violence, revelling in the visceral physicality of the fighting scenes, yet this destructive force is clearly satirised; the potential for and attraction to extreme violence by disaffected, alienated young men who have no place in society is made clear. It is rather chilling that the skyscrapers blown up at the end of the film were similar to the phallic symbols of American capitalism and wealth that were blown up on 11 September 2001 by extreme Islamic fundamentalists who were also alienated from Western society.

CONCLUSION

This chapter introduces the subject of film and gender. It is by no means a definitive study but presents a range of important viewpoints and key articles in this area of study. Mulvey's original article 'Visual Pleasure and Narrative Cinema' has inspired a whole range of theories concerning masculinity and femininity which try to unravel how meaning is produced in film. As more and more women are included in the filmmaking process, from writers to directors to cinematographers, it will be interesting to see if this means new theories will be developed to account for the new meanings and new narratives produced.

SUMMARY

- Women filmmakers from early cinema to the present day
- An explanation of feminist film theory and how it has developed
- Discussion of other theories concerning gender and film such as cultural studies.
- Discussion of how masculinity is represented in film.

QUESTIONS FOR DISCUSSION

1   To what extent can *Orlando* be considered a feminist film?
2   Is Sally Potter an auteur filmmaker?
3   Choose one of Nicole Holofcener's films and compare the style and narrative content with *Sex and the City* 1 or 2.
4   Discuss the representation of the female in either *Lovely and Amazing* or *Friends with Money*.
5   Compare the depiction of masculinity in *Fight Club* with *The Hurt Locker*.
6   Choose an action film released in the last five years and discuss its representation of masculinity.

NOTES

Full details of works cited in the notes section may be found in the consolidated bibliography.

1 For further information on women screenwriters past and present read 'What Happened to the Women?' by Nancy Hendrickson in *Creative Screenwriter*, July/August 2003, Vol. 10, 4, pp. 64–8.

2 See Donald and Scanlon's 1992 article on whether *Thelma and Louise* (1991) is a feminist film.

3 Suggested further reading: on the early feminist movement, K. Millett, *Sexual Politics* (1977) and G. Greer, *The Female Eunuch* (1971), and, more recently, M. Maynard (1987: 23).

4 Structuralism and Marxism have been, and still are, important concepts in the application of film theory and have historically affected film practice, particularly in the independent and workshop sector. For a good general background to these viewpoints read Chs 1 and 2 of Lapsley and Westlake (1988).

5 If you are interested in reading more about Stuart Hall's important input into cultural studies theory, a good starting point is 'Encoding/Decoding', in *Culture, Media, Language* (1980).

6 For further discussion of how we negotiate with cultural texts, see Gledhill's 'Pleasurable Negotiations', in Pribram (1988).

7 Janice Radway has thrown new light as to how women interpret fiction. Her theories may be usefully applied to other texts. For further details see *Reading the Romance* (1987).

8 For further reading on black feminist film theory and some excellent film analysis, see bell hooks, *Reel to Real* (1996) and Valerie Smith's *Not Just Race* (1998).

9 For a useful discussion of gender theories read Ch. 6, Bilton *et al*. (2002).

10 Neale's points about masculinity in Mann's film were originally referred to in a 1981 article by Paul Willemen entitled 'Anthony Mann: Looking at the Male'.

FURTHER READING

Berger, J., *Ways of Seeing*, Penguin, London, 1972. Although now old, this is still a very useful introduction to the visual image.

Betterton, R., *Looking On: Images of Femininity in the Visual Arts and the Media*, Pandora, London, 1987.

Brundsen, C. (ed.), *Films for Women*, British Film Institute, London, 1986. This book discusses a range of feminist films such as *A Question of Silence* (1982) directed by Marlene Gorris.

Bruzzi, S., *Undressing Cinema*, Routledge, London, 1997. An insightful look at dress in film with a focus on gender.

——, *Bringing up Dad: Fatherhood and Masculinity in Post War Hollywood*, British Film Institute, London, 2005.

Clover, C., *Men, Women and Chainsaws: Gender in the Modern Horror Film*, British Film Institute, London, 1992. An original and fascinating analysis of how we watch and understand horror film.

Cohan, S. and Hark, I. (eds), *Screening the Male*, Routledge, London, 1993. One of the first edited volumes to discuss masculinity and film. It contains many important articles which are well worth reading.

Cook, P. and Dodd, P. (eds), *Women and Film: A Sight and Sound Reader*, British Film Institute and Scarlet Press, London, 1993.

Deuber-Mankowsky, A., *Lara Croft – Cyber Heroine*, University of Minnesota Press, Minneapolis, 2005. Insightful discussion of computer games and film and gender.

Easthope, A., *What a Man's Gotta Do: The Masculine Myth in Popular Culture*, Unwin Hyman, Winchester, 1990. A good introduction to masculinity and myth.

Francke, L., *Script Girls*, British Film Institute, London, 1994. This book discusses women who have worked as scriptwriters in the film industry, particularly Hollywood.

Hendrickson, N., 'What Happened to All the Women?', *Creative Screenwriter*, Vol. 10, No. 4, pp. 64–8.

hooks, bell, *Reel to Real: Race, Class and Sex in the Movies*, Routledge, New York, 1996. Well-written, insightful film readings of, among others, Spike Lee's *She's Gotta Have It* (1985) and *Crooklyn* (1991), and *Waiting to Exhale* (1995), directed by Forest Whitaker.

Horrocks, R., *Male Myths and Icons: Masculinity in Popular Culture*, Macmillan, London, 1995. A good discussion of masculinity.

Inness, S., *Tough Girls, Women Warriors and Wonder Women in Popular Culture*, University of Pennsylvania Press, Philadelphia, 1999. A great discussion of tough women in the media.

Kaplan, E.A. (ed.), *Feminism and Film*, Oxford University Press, Oxford, 2000.

Kirkham, P. and Thumin, J. (eds), *You Tarzan: Masculinity, Movies and Men*, Lawrence & Wishart, London, 1993. A good range of articles on issues of masculinity and film.

—— (eds), *Me Jane: Masculinity, Movies and Women*, Lawrence & Wishart, London, 1995. A wide range of articles on issues regarding masculinity, femininity and film.

MacKinnon, K., *Representing Men*, Arnold, London, 2003.

Modleski, T., *The Women Who Knew Too Much*, Methuen, London, 1988. A very accessible and original analysis of Hitchcock's films.

Pilling, J. (ed.), *Women and Animation: A Compendium*, British Film Institute, London, 1992.

Potter, S., www.yesthemovie.com, pp. 1–4.

Segal, M., *Slow Motion: Changing Masculinities, Changing Men*, Virago, London, 1997. This book has a very useful and approachable discussion of masculinity in its introduction.

Spicer, A., *Typical Men*, I.B. Tauris, London, 2001.

Tasker, Y., *Spectacular Bodies: Gender, Genre and the Action Movie*, Routledge, London, 1993.

—— *Working Girls*, Routledge, London, 1998.

Tasker, Y., (ed.), *The Action and Advenure Cinema*, Routledge, London, 2004.

Thornham, S., *Passionate Detachments*, Arnold, London, 1997.

Van Zoonen, L., *Feminist Media Studies*, Sage, London, 1994. A good introduction to issues regarding feminism in the media.

Willis, S., *High Contrast: Race and Gender in Contemporary Hollywood Film*, Duke University Press, Durham, NC and London, 1997.

Periodicals are extremely useful to refer to for further reading; they tend to be more topical and 'up to date'. Look out for articles on women and film in the following: *Feminist Review*, *Women: A Cultural Review*, *Screen* and *Sight & Sound*.

FURTHER VIEWING

This chapter has focused mainly on Hollywood and British film and is therefore a selective view. In terms of gender the analysis has concentrated mostly on Hollywood film, partly because so much research on masculinity and feminity is based on the study of popular Western culture. There are a number of British films which would be well worth further investigation: *Billy Elliot* (2000) and *Bend It Like Beckham* (2002), for instance, would both be revealing to study in terms of gender and the protagonists reaching out to achieve success in areas which are not considered appropriate (ballet and football respectively). *Dear Frankie* (2006) shows a single mother creating an imaginary father for her son while US films such as *American Beauty* (1999) and *Happiness* (1999) or *In the Bedroom* (2001) would be revealing to study in terms of gender and family life. Films which portray women in powerful central roles such as *Erin Brockovich* (2000) are interesting to discuss as to whether the protagonists really are playing stereotypical roles: 'the tart with a heart' for instance. *Sex and the City* 1 (2006) and 2 (2009) and *Mama Mia* (2008) have been internationally successful and would be interesting to discuss in terms of why they have appealed so strongly to a mainly female audience and how gender is represented.

Worldwide women's cinema is rich and varied – countries as small and culturally diverse as New Zealand and Iran have contributed to this upsurge. As more women enter the film industry and take on

key roles, the number of mainstream films made by women will hopefully increase.

Other chapters in this book refer to films by women: see Chapter 11. Unfortunately, many earlier films by women are difficult to obtain. The BFI and Cinenova (a film and video distributor that promotes films by women) hold a number of titles for rental. The latter's comprehensive catalogue is well worth looking through. The following films may all be hired through Cinenova at 113 Roman Road, London E2 0HN, tel: 0208 981 6828: *To Be a Woman* (UK, Jill Craigie, 1953); *Women of the Rhondda* (UK, Esther Ronay, 1972); *A Comedy in Six Unnatural Acts* (US, Jan Oxenburg, 1975); *An Epic Poem* (UK, Lezli-Ann Barrett, 1982); *Born in Flames* (US, Lizzie Borden, 1983).

The following films are all available for rental or sale from the BFI and provide stimulating viewing: *Orlando* (UK, Sally Potter, 1993) (see Case Study 1); *Wayward Girls and Wicked Women*, vols 1, 2 and 3 (1992) (various women animators, often witty, poignant and hard-hitting); *Sweetie* (Australia, Jane Campion, 1989) (it's anarchic, funny and strange!); *Dream On* (UK, Amber Films, 1992) (focuses on women on a north-east estate; realistic, hard-hitting with some lighter moments); any of Gurinder Chada's films are worth considered viewing and the latter two will be available on video/DVD: from *Bhaji on the Beach* (UK, 1993) which is the story of an Asian women's group's journey to Blackpool, to *What's Cooking* (2000), and *Bend It Like Beckham* (2002) about an Asian girl who wants to be a footballer.

RESOURCE CENTRES

www. cinenova. org
A European feminist promoter of films by women. Well worth a look.

www. feminist. org
A useful site with lots of links to feminist subject matter.

www.Sallypotter.com

www. sistersincinema. com
An African-American women filmmakers' website with a resources list.

www.lux.org.uk
LUX: distribution, collection, exhibition, publishing, research in artists' moving image work.

www.sixpackfilm.com
Sixpackfilm: Austrian film and video art distributor.

www.wmm.com
Women Make Movies: New York-based non-profit organisation established in 1972 to facilitate and promote the production, distribution and exhibition of films/video by and about women.

www.womenfilmnet.org
Women and Film in Europe: the working group of the European Coordination of Film Festivals EEIG. The aim of the group is to 'research the history of women and film in Europe and to make these findings available'. Has extensive database.

www.screenonline.org.uk
BFI ScreenOnline: Women and Film.

www.people.virginia.edu/~pm9k/libsci/wom Film.html
Women in Cinema: A Reference Guide: detailed and discursive site focusing on the history of women in cinema. Includes introductory essay, references, bibliographies, filmographies and sources for film study.

www.lib.berkeley.edu/MRC/womenbib.html
Women in Film and Television: Bibliography Materials: lists various bibliographies of books and articles on subjects relating to women in film and television. Based on material held at the Media Resource centre at UC Berkeley.

www.wftv.org.uk/home.asp
Women in Film and TV: UK members' organisation: the site provides background information on the organisation, details of its aims, magazine, events and campaigns and WFTV awards and membership.

sdwff.org/home.html
San Diego Women Film Foundation: its mission is to educate the public about film, promote women filmmakers and their work, and empower young women through film.

www.mith2.umd.edu/WomensStudies/Film Reviews
Women's Studies Database Film Reviews: part of the University of Maryland Women's Studies website, the database lists reviews by film title. Users can also search alphabetically. Articles are all written by women writers or academics in film and media.

www.madcatfilmfestival.org
MadCat Women's International Film Festival: MadCat is a highly acclaimed festival that exhibits independent and experimental films and videos directed by women from around the globe. Based in San Francisco.

make.gold.ac.uk
The Women's Art Library (MAKE): an artist-led slide library developed in order to enhance public knowledge of the practice, impact and achievement of women in visual culture. The library contains published and unpublished written documentation, photographs, posters and videos in addition to a substantial slide collection and artists' files on contemporary and historical women artists. The artists' files contain paper documentation, photographs and slides, postcards, photographs, press cuttings and ephemera, with much of the material donated by women artists. Early feminist art journals held include *Feminist Artists Newsletter* (UK), *Heresies* (USA) and *Matriart* (Canada).

www.londonmet.ac.uk/thewomenslibrary
The Women's Library: the Women's Library is a cultural centre, housing the most extensive collection of women's history in the UK.

www.studycollection.co.uk
British Artists' Film and Video Study Collection: established in 2000, the British Artists' Film and Video Study Collection is a research project led by Senior Research Fellow David Curtis concentrating on the history of artists' film and video in Britain. Welcomes postgraduate researchers, curators, programmers, artists, anyone interested in the academic study of British Artists' Film and Video. Consists of an extensive range of reference materials including video copies of artists' works, still images, historical posters and publicity materials, paper documentation and a publications library. Browsable catalogue online.

www.bfi.org.uk/filmtvinfo/library
BFI National Library: a major national research collection of documentation and information on film and television. Its priority is comprehensive coverage of British film and television, but the collection itself is international in scope.

shootingpeople.org
Shooting People: huge UK- and US-based independent filmmaker internet network with over 25,000 members. Daily bulletins covering filmmaking, documentary, animation, music videos, casting, screen writing and script pitching, and extensive calendar of events.

Chapter 12

Lesbian and gay cinema

Chris Jones

■ Lesbian and Gay Cinema

INTRODUCTION: REPRESENTATION

Representation is a social process which occurs in the interactions between a reader or viewer, and a text. It produces signs which reflect underlying sets of ideas and attitudes. In her essay, 'Visual Pleasure and Narrative Cinema', Laura Mulvey suggested ways in which a viewer of classic Hollywood films is addressed as male by being encouraged to adopt the viewpoint, the 'look' of the male protagonist. Although she later adjusted these ideas to cater for such female-orientated Hollywood genres as the melodrama, Mulvey's argument is based on the traditional psychoanalytic notion of male/female definitions and oppositions. Nowhere does she take into account the extent to which her argument is geared towards a **heterosexual** look. Nevertheless, her ideas about the positioning of the film spectator and filmmaker within the **gender** system have been very influential. They have led to much constructive critical investigation into how different kinds of filmmakers and viewers affect meaning-making processes according to their race and **sexuality**, as well as gender.

DEFINITIONS AND DEVELOPMENTS: CHANGING LANGUAGE

Men and women who relate sexually to members of their own **sex** have always existed, but the modern term 'homosexuality' was invented in 1869 by a Swiss doctor. It was not commonly used in the English language until the 1890s, the decade that saw the birth of cinema. The term **homosexual** was partly inherited from nineteenth-century ideas of disease. Previously, same-sex relations had been predominantly characterised by notions of sin inherited from the medieval period. These commonly held associations continued into this century as German filmmakers produced a number of works campaigning for more enlightened attitudes in sexual and social matters. *Different from the Others* (1919) was a success on first release. Even though the main character, a homosexual musician, finally poisons himself, the dour storyline is countered by sections of the film in which Dr Magnus Hirschfield puts forward an affirmative view of homosexuality. Hirschfield was a sexual researcher and social reformer whose world-renowned institute was later destroyed by the Nazis. Within a year of its release the film was subject to censorship and now exists only in fragments, although these have since been assembled and shown. *Girls in Uniform* (Leontine Sagan, 1931) can still be seen today as a major portrayal of anti-authoritarianism, with the love of its two female protagonists for each other triumphing over the oppressive regime of their boarding school.

During the Second World War, with its movements of population and large numbers of servicemen and women being thrown closely together in same-sex barracks, many people became aware of homosexuality on a personal and social level. This resulted in two parallel and contradictory developments in North America and Europe during the 1950s: increasing growth among communities of homosexuals and lesbians in big cities, and systematic attempts by those in authority to prevent such developments.

These communities began to demand and develop wider networks of meeting places and entertainment, including film. Early examples of films made with such audiences in mind are the physique films of Dick Fontaine, who worked in San Francisco from the late 1940s. Such film activity mainly took place within the art-film world, and involved small-budget production and viewing in clubs and homes. The pursuit of physical culture was an area that attracted homosexual men, especially in North America, as portrayed in Thom Fitzgerald's film *Beefcake* (2000). Jean Genet's *Un chant d'amour* (1950), with its sexually charged images of handsome male prisoners, became a cult film, as did

For further discussion of representation and feminism see Chapter 11.

For detailed discussion of spectatorship see Chapter 5.

heterosexual
A word used to name and describe a person whose main sexual feelings are for people of the opposite sex.

gender
A name for the social and cultural construction of a person's sex and **sexuality**. Gender, sex and sexuality can overlap but are by no means an exact match. It is this 'mismatch' which has generated a fascinating body of film production and criticism.

sexuality
A name for the sexual feelings and behaviour of a person. When applied to groups of people (e.g. **heterosexuals**), ideas of social attitude and organisation are implied.

homosexual
A word used to name and describe a person whose main sexual feelings are for people of the same sex. Mainly, but not exclusively, used in reference to males.

homoerotic
A description of a text
– prose, poem, film,
painting, photograph –
conveying an enjoyable
sense of same-sex
attraction.

gay
A description of strong,
positive sexual love
and attraction between
members of the same
sex, used by extension
to describe cultural
products, such as film
and video, concerned
with similar themes.
Mainly referring to
males, it can also be
used for any person.

lesbian
A word used to name
and describe a woman
whose main sexual
feelings are for other
women. Coined as a
medical term in the late
nineteenth century, the
word has been invested
post-Stonewall with new
ideas of openness and
liberation. It may also be
used to describe cultural
products, such as film
and video, dealing with
lesbian themes.

queer
Originally a negative
term for (mainly male)
homosexuals, this
word has recently been
reappropriated by critics,
artists and audiences to
describe a challenging
range of critical work
and cultural production
among **lesbians** and
gays, with an emphasis
on diversity of race,
nationality and cultural
experience. The term
is deliberately used to
embrace a wider range
of sexualities: lesbian,
gay, bisexual and
transgendered people
and issues.

Kenneth Anger's *Fireworks* (1947), a young man's sexual fantasy involving sailors. From the 1960s the **homoerotic** films of Andy Warhol and George Kuchar began to find wider audiences. It was during this period that the word **gay** began to be used to both denote and describe a male homosexual person.

The modern gay liberation movement developed after the Stonewall riots of 1969 in New York. Members of the new movement adopted the word 'gay' for its positive connotations of happiness, and because they wanted to use a term to describe themselves that had not been chosen by outsiders. For them, the term represented a way of demonstrating pride in their identity, the power of political organisation, and a distinct culture. The term was initially conceived as describing both men and women, but women soon began to feel marginalised within the movement, and the term **lesbian** came back in general use during the 1970s to signal the distinctness and strength of women.

It is the very different emotional connotations of these varying terms which led critic Vito Russo to say; ' There never have been lesbians or gay men in Hollywood films. Only homosexuals' (Russo 1987: 245). Since the 1990s, the term **queer** has become widely used as a critical term to describe both the kind of image production discussed in this chapter and the frameworks used by certain critics to produce, view and assess cultural production.

AUDIENCES

Gay men, like men in general, have on average more spending power than women, despite years of equal opportunities legislation. With gay liberation came a greatly expanded network of related commercial goods and services: nightclubs, shops, clothing, books and magazines, the majority of which were aimed at men. The same conditions apply in the developing structures of film and cinema aimed at lesbians and gays. Men constituted the main organised audience for this type of cultural production. Even those films with non-commercial financial backing, such as the work of Derek Jarman and Isaac Julien, tended to attract funds partly because of the perceived existence of this established gay male audience.

Lesbian film and video developed in parallel with the emerging women's movement, almost always with less finance than its male equivalent, and found a base in film clubs and workshops. The American film and video artist Su Friedrich showed an active

• **Plate 12.1**
Un chant d'amour
(Jean Genet, 1950).
Genet's erotic
imagery has inspired
generations of
filmmakers

• Plate 12.2
Suddenly (Argentina, Diego Lerman, 2002) reflects a growing body of gay and lesbian-themed films emerging from Latin America and becoming known through festivals.

preference for this type of outlet as a way of reaching lesbian audiences with films such as *Damned If You Don't* (US, 1987). As a result of this production and viewing background, and the modest financial levels this involved, many lesbian films of the 1970s and 1980s are less than feature-length. *Home Movie* (US, 1972) by Jan Oxenberg is a modest but highly effective 12-minute film, which edits home-movie footage from the director's own childhood with scenes of her adult life as a lesbian to make the viewer amusingly aware of the conventions of family life. Her *Comedy in Six Unnatural Acts* (US 1975, 26 minutes) presents six short, staged scenes dealing with the foibles of lesbian life, and debunking a few myths about **butch/femme** role-playing.

FILM FESTIVALS: DEVELOPING AWARENESS

After 1945, film festivals became recognised across Europe and America as serving several useful functions. They act as a marketplace for film distributors to view and possibly buy new product and allow producers, scriptwriters and others to gather and discuss new projects. Critics attending festivals alert wider audiences to new and interesting work. Audiences can view and enjoy a wide range of films they would not normally see in the cinema.

Since the 1970s a worldwide circuit of lesbian, gay and queer film festivals has grown up. San Francisco was the first, followed by London, Paris, New York, Toronto, Berlin and others. By the beginning of the twenty-first century, such festivals were taking place outside Europe and North America in countries such as Korea and Mexico. These events, often accompanied by lively lectures and discussions, serve all the purposes already mentioned for lesbian and gay producers, directors, critics and audiences. Their development has gone hand in hand with the discourse of gay culture and political consciousness. Rosa Von Praunheim's film *It is Not the Homosexual Who Is Perverse, but the Situation in which He Finds Himself* (Germany, 1970) is credited as a key text in the awakening of the gay liberation movement, and was typical of the kind of work that found a viewing base in such festivals.

In particular, these festivals have helped to bring small-scale film and video work and feature films from developing countries to the attention of wider lesbian and gay audiences. An example of the latter is the work of Lino Brocka from the Philippines

butch
Description of behaviour patterns – such as aggression and sexual dominance – traditionally associated with masculinity.

femme
Description of behaviour patterns – such as gentleness, sexual passivity, concern with dress and appearance – traditionally associated with femininity.

(Murray 1998: 24), whose treatment of homosexual themes contains messages of tolerance and democracy not always acceptable to established authorities in his own country. Recent festivals have included work from Israel, Taiwan, India and Japan. The international nature of LGBT film festivals in the present century is reflected in the 2010 Tampa International Gay and Lesbian Film Festival which had films from 88 countries in its schedule.

CONSCIOUSNESS-RAISING THROUGH DOCUMENTARY

Another form of filmmaking given wider distribution through the festival circuit is feature-length documentary. *The Times Of Harvey Milk* (Robert Epstein, US, 1985) chronicles the rise to power, and tragic assassination, of the San Francisco city supervisor who was one of the USA's first openly gay elected politicians. *Before Stonewall: The Making of a Gay and Lesbian Community* (Greta Schiller, US, 1985) vividly recalls gay and lesbian lives in the years during and following the Second World War. All these films weave together interviews, contemporary newsreel film and photographs. Through fostering cultural and historical consciousness, such films as these aided the growing self-awareness of lesbian and gay communities in the USA and elsewhere (see Farmer (2000) Ch. 1) for ideas about performativity).

As the AIDS crisis arose in the 1980s, with western gay men as the focus of moral panic, this newly developed network of audiences and exhibition venues was particularly receptive. A variety of film and video work was created in response to this situation, such as Rosa Von Praunheim's *A Virus Knows No Morals* (Germany, 1986). Short videos such as John Greyson's *The ADS Epidemic* (Canada, 1986) boosted morale by warning in a jokey way against ADS (Acquired Dread of Sex) while reminding people about safe sex. *Common Threads: Stories from the Quilt* (Robert Epstein and Jeffrey Freedman, US, 1989) is a full-length documentary chronicling the stories of a group of people who have lost loved ones to AIDS and contributed panels to the memorial quilt.

Much of this documentary material opens up new areas of awareness for its audiences. Showing at festivals tends now to be a first step towards wider exposure on TV. One example is the film *Queer and Catholic* (Peter Nicholson, UK, 2001) where current debates are explored through interviews with clergy and theologians in Britain, the USA and Rome. Perhaps one of the most noteworthy recent documentaries is *A Jihad for Love* (US, 2007) by Indian Muslim filmmaker Parvez Sharma, who spent six years documenting the lives, hopes, thoughts and aspirations of lesbian and gay Muslims from a dozen countries (Kay 2007).

Currently, the website www.gaydram.net (see Resource Centres at the end of this chapter) lists details of **LGBT** film festivals around the world, including those devoted to such specialisations as documentary and experimental image production. See also the festival list in Daniel and Jackson (2003: 549).

GAY SENSIBILITY

In a book published by the British Film Institute to coincide with the first ever Lesbian and Gay Film Festival at the National Film Theatre, London, in 1977, the critic Jack Babuscio wrote;

I define the gay sensibility as a creative energy reflecting a consciousness that is different from the mainstream; a heightened awareness of certain human complications of feeling that spring from the fact of social oppression; in short, a perception of the world which is coloured, shaped, directed and defined by the fact of one's gayness.

(quoted in Benshoff and Griffin 2004: 120)

LGBT
A set of initials standing for lesbian, gay, bisexual and transgender. A term now increasingly used by a large number of organisations and bodies in the English-speaking world. It is favoured because of the wide spectrum of sexualities covered, and because certain negative connotations of 'gay' or 'queer' are avoided.

In a key essay, 'Rejecting Straight Ideals: Gays in Film' (Steven 1985), Richard Dyer challenged Babuscio's emphasis on oppression as a mainspring for gay sensibility and offers a more creative view. He says this sensibility must be understood as 'something that has been and is produced and praised in history and culture' (Steven 1985: 287). For Dyer, oppression 'merely provides the conditions in relation to which oppressed people create their own subculture and attendant sensibility' (ibid.: 287) and is not the defining factor as Babuscio perceives it.

SEXUAL IDEOLOGY

In his essay, Dyer makes a convincing and clear argument based on the idea of what he calls 'the sexual **ideology** of our culture' (ibid.: 294); that is, the idea that society and culture, through structures such as the family and artefacts such as film, impose a particular view of what is considered to be correct sexual behaviour. This view includes a dominance of the heterosexual viewpoint and antipathy towards the homosexual one. Homosexuality, according to Dyer, is predominantly seen from a heterosexual viewpoint in most mainstream films. As examples he cites the image of homosexuality as a sickness and a problem in *Victim* (Basil Dearden, UK, 1961) and an endless succession of lesbian and gay characters as vampires, psychos and criminals which, he argues, still continues today. However, as Dyer points out, ideology is contradictory and ambiguous, full of what he calls 'gaps and fissures' (Steven 1985: 294) through which filmmakers and audiences can make new, alternative meanings.

Critical awareness and discussion of gay sensibility and established sexual ideology, a concept that was later labelled 'heterosexism', started to be shared by increasing numbers of people: audiences, critics and filmmakers. Film production in this area continued to take place mainly within the structures of alternative or art cinema, although Hollywood made occasional attempts to exploit what was seen as an increasingly open gay audience and a greater interest in gay themes by non-gays. Examples of products aimed at mainstream audiences are *The Boys in the Band* (William Friedkin, 1970), which exploited the sensationalistic stereotypes of emotional trauma, and *Making Love* (Arthur Hiller, 1982), a romantic treatment of male love. *Cruising* (William Friedkin, 1980) equates homosexuality with pathological violence, but arguably also gives a glimpse into a particular gay subculture of 1980s New York. These and many other mainstream films, such as Jonathan Demme's *Philadelphia* (US, 1993), could profitably be examined using Dyer's notion of sexual ideology.

As a concept useful in the study of film, gay sensibility can be defined as a developed awareness of sexual variation. This does not automatically mean that a filmmaker or viewer has to be gay or lesbian to be able to present or appreciate themes and issues connected with LGBT people, but such awareness can open up rich creative possibilities. David Cronenberg's films, for example *Dead Ringers* (Canada, 1988), make viewers uncomfortably aware of the fragile limits of conventional masculinity (see Chapter 11). While one can debate what exactly constitutes a 'lesbian film' or a 'gay film', gay sensibility can enrich film production and appreciation for gays and non-gays.

CAMP AESTHETICS AND CINEMA

Dyer's ideas about searching for 'gaps and fissures' referred to above sometimes involve an attitude of conscious, ironic distancing on the part of a spectator known as **camp**, traditionally associated with gay audiences. Critic Susan Sontag described camp as 'an aesthetic phenomenon' (Sontag 1994: 277) and tried to empty this concept of its political force, but other critics have been vigilant in pointing out the importance of camp as an oppositional aesthetic, especially for gays and lesbians.

The concept of camp is useful when considering how lesbian and gay audiences

ideology
Although a complex issue, ideology may be seen as the dominant set of ideas and values which inform any one society or culture, but which are imbued in its social behaviour and representative texts at a level that is not necessarily obvious or conscious. There are two key definitions of this term, one provided by the nineteenth-century German philosopher Karl Marx, the other by the twentieth-century French Marxist philosopher Louis Althusser, drawing on Marx's original ideas. For Marx, ideology was the dominant set of beliefs and values existent within society, which sustained power relations. For Althusser, ideology consisted of the representations and images which reflect society's view of 'reality'. Ideology thus refers to 'the myths that a society lives by'. An ideological stance is normally politicised and historically determined.

camp
A critical attitude which involves looking at texts less as reflections of reality and more as constructed sets of words, images and sounds at a distance from reality. The attitude often involves irony or detachment when considering this distance.

For further discussion of the relationship between film, ideology and society, see Chapter 5.

often view mainstream representations but the exercise of such sensibility is not confined to gays. The films of Ken Russell are considered to be very camp, as are many musicals, and muscle epics of the 1950s such as *Hercules Unchained*. In the latter, the exaggerated sexual signifiers of the hero (inflated muscles, heroic beard) and the main female figure (cleavage, diaphanous veils) come close to parodying gender stereotypes. Such exaggeration can also be seen in popular action movies, such as those starring Jean-Claude Van Damme, Vin Diesel and others, where camp elements intertwine with homoerotic subtext. Camp continues to be a site of critical inquiry; see Farmer (2000: Ch. 3) where he cogently argues for the political subversiveness of camp sensibility. Refer also to the continuing discussion in the two compilations on queer cinema in the Further Reading section, especially Moe Meyer (Benshoff and Griffin 2004: 137).

CRITICAL RE-READINGS

The possible meanings of a film, as with all signifying practices, reside in the interaction between the viewer and the text. Much work has been done in recent years on how sub-groups within the wider popular audience arrive at their own particular meanings when watching a mainstream film. Lesbian and gay critics have been at the forefront of such 're-readings'. Here are some examples. The books referred to are in the Further Reading list or the Bibliography.

Early explorations: Subcultural messages and spectator pleasures

Parker Tyler's book *Screening the Sexes: Homosexuality in the Movies* opened up the field of study and analysis of lesbian and gay cinema in 1972, but Russo's *The Celluloid Closet: Homosexuality in the Movies* is now regarded as a major landmark. First published in 1981 and revised in 1987, the book has continued to influence later critical work in this area.

Russo combines a historical view of lesbian and gay people's contribution to cinema with an awareness of representation and audience. Although it deals mainly with Hollywood product, in contrast to Tyler's work, Russo's book is packed with examples and ideas that have formed the basis of further research by new generations of critics and academics. One example of insights Russo has to offer is his interpretation of the monster in the horror films of gay director James Whale. He sees *Frankenstein* and *The Bride of Frankenstein* as images of unnameable experiences and feelings outside normal society. These ideas were later developed by Harry Benshoff (1997).

Using cogently argued examples, Russo makes a powerful argument about how gay men derived particular subcultural messages from such films as *Rebel Without a Cause* when empathising with the relationship between Jim (James Dean) and Plato (Sal Mineo). Such tentative early explorations of spectatorial pleasure were to be greatly expanded by later gay and lesbian critics.

The historical emergence of neurotic, shadowy gay characters is discussed using *The Boys in the Band* and *The Killing of Sister George* (Robert Aldrich, US, 1968). Later critics were to investigate more fully the ideological underpinning of such representations. Russo's final argument, in the revised 1987 edition, is that worthwhile gay and lesbian cinema can only be developed and encouraged outside the traditional Hollywood power structures, and he outlines a range of examples of such positive work. A worthy successor to Russo in its survey of film production and theory in this area is *Queer Images* (Benshoff and Griffin 2004).

Gay looking: subtexts and strategies

Richard Dyer is considered a major British figure in the critical and theoretical areas covered in this chapter. His book *Now You See It* (2002a) includes a comprehensive academic survey of the German films outlined earlier, as well as the work of Jean Genet and Kenneth Anger. It contains a particularly useful introduction to lesbian film and video-making of the post-war period.

Dyer is the author of many illuminating essays. His work on sexual ideology has already been mentioned, but he is perhaps best known for his work on stars. In his essay, 'Judy Garland and Gay Men', Dyer investigates the cultural associations between Judy Garland's star image and gay male audiences from the 1950s onwards. He shows members of this audience strongly allying themselves with Garland's much-vaunted ability to fight back against oppression and the status of outsider which her behaviour and personality often conferred on her (Benshoff and Griffin 2004: 153).

His essay 'Homosexuality in Film Noir' (Dyer 1993) coherently shows how gay characters in this classic Hollywood genre were negatively portrayed in both appearance and behaviour. He relates these various homoerotic subtexts to film-noir traditions and the dominant post-war view of sexual relations. This is an important genre to investigate because, as Dyer points out: 'Some of the first widely available images of homosexuality in our time were those provided by the American film noir' (Dyer 1993: 52). Dyer's essay 'Queer Noir' (Benshoff and Griffin 2004: 89) extends this examination.

Dyer's later studies of star image include a seminal essay on Rock Hudson in relation to public perceptions of sexuality, both before and after Hudson's homosexuality became public knowledge (Dyer 2002: 159). He cogently demonstrates how knowledge of Hudson's sexuality greatly enriches a viewer's appreciation of the gender play in the 1960s sex comedies in which he starred. He shows how such knowledge gives extra depth to Hudson's star performances in the famous sequence of 1950s melodramas directed by Douglas Sirk, such as *All that Heaven Allows* (US, 1955) (see Further Viewing at the end of this chapter).

Some fascinating work on genre has been produced, including Benshoff's work on the horror film (Benshoff and Griffin 2004: 63) as well as Farmer's work on the musical (Farmer 2000: 69). Both these critics demonstrate the use of excess and transgressive viewing strategies which challenge heterosexist norms.

In North America, the critical writings of Thomas Waugh have been very influential. Read some of his key writings and ideas in the compilation entitled *The Fruit Machine* (Waugh, with a foreword by John Greyson (2000)). For a useful look at how close textual analysis can clarify alternative sexual insights into established cinema, the work of Alexander Doty is also of great importance, especially his book *Flaming Classics* (Doty 2000). Chapter 2 of his book *Making Things Perfectly Queer* is particularly recommended for his exploration of queer authorship (Doty 1993).

Lesbian looking: Directors and stars

The work of Andrea Weiss, like that of other writers on lesbian film such as Mandy Merck, B. Ruby Rich and Judith Mayne, was nurtured within the feminist movement. Weiss works primarily as a filmmaker. She was chief researcher on the documentary feature *Before Stonewall* and has produced an equally well-researched book on lesbians in film, *Vampires and Violets* (1993).

In her book, Weiss clearly tackles the critical problems associated with identification and representation for lesbians. She states that:

identification involves both conscious and unconscious processes and cannot be reduced to a psychoanalytic model that sees sexual desire only in terms of the binary opposition of heterosexual masculinity and femininity; instead it involves varying degrees of subjectivity and distance depending upon race, class and sexual differences.

(Weiss 1993: 40)

This judgement reflects the questioning of Laura Mulvey's ideas on cinematic looking referred to earlier, a critical practice which has grown steadily since the 1980s. Weiss gives her readers a fascinating set of studies to show how lesbian audiences of classic Hollywood cinema have used their own interpretations to empower themselves, and how lesbian filmmakers have been able to make their own images.

For further discussion of Mulvey's theories of gender and spectatorship, see Chapter 11.

These studies range across Dorothy Arzner's *The Wild Party* (US 1929), star performances by Greta Garbo and Marlene Dietrich in the 1940s, lesbian vampire films, and 1970s radical lesbian films by Barbara Hammer. She offers fascinating, oppositional interpretations of the way in which lesbian audiences gained positive messages from the otherwise bleak and tragic lesbian characters and relationships in *The Killing of Sister George* (Robert Aldrich, US, 1968) and *The Children's Hour* (William Wyler, US, 1961).

Weiss clearly outlines the ongoing critical debate about the difficulties of representing autonomous female sexuality in a system of representation which continues to be focused on the male heterosexual look. A major part of this debate for lesbian film centres on the problems of producing scenes of woman-centred intimacy and lovemaking that remain satisfying for lesbian audiences while not triggering the effect of being a turn-on for heterosexual men.

In her section on the lesbian aspect of art film, Weiss uses some key films by Akerman and Ottinger to show how their directors have dealt in various productive ways with the male heterosexist narrative and viewing strategies of this kind of film tradition. In her essay 'Transgressive Cinema: Lesbian Independent Film' (Benshoff and Griffin 2004: 43), she concentrates mainly on American production. She identifies as a crucial factor of this type of work how 'the power and intrigue of looking itself have become erotically charged' rather then the object of the look. She argues that a film such as Friedrich's *Damned If You Don't* (1987), and the work of Jan Oxenberg (see p. 301) have 'imagined lesbian cinema outside the pornographic parameters of dominant cinema' and have challenged patriarchal definitions of lesbianism. She goes on to suggest that such viewing strategies have had a wide influence.

Questions

1 In the light of Weiss's comments on viewing strategies, analyse the lovemaking scenes from *Desert Hearts*, *Go Fish* and any other film of your choice.
2 Critically analyse the director's use of social and physical location of the characters in *Desert Hearts* and *Salmonberries*.

Enjoyment and woman-centred explorations

For further discussion of filmic pleasure, the look and the female, see Chapter 11.

Weiss's critique of the traditional psychoanalytical approach and her outlines of alternative viewing strategies form the basis of many later textual explorations in lesbian criticism. An important and ground-breaking collection is *Immortal, Invisible* edited by Tamsin Wilton (see Further Reading at the end of this chapter). This was, as the editor points out in her introduction, 'the first collection, to my knowledge, of essays on lesbians and the moving image' (Wilton 1995: 2). Wilton mixes humour with erudition and so demonstrates the female-centred pleasure in looking she is out to explore.

Wilton poses constructive questions about lesbian definition, and then discusses a range of responses from the radical politics of Barbara Hammer's films to the playfulness of lesbian camp. As she says, 'the question of lesbian auteurism and context are debated in many chapters of this book' (ibid.: 5). Wilton's suggestion for viewing strategies is a crucial challenge to the domination of the psychoanalytic: 'I propose the notion of *cinematic contract*, by which the spectator tacitly agrees to make use of a variety of engagement strategies in order to "make sense of" the film in question.' She suggests that 'such engagement strategies derive less from the unconscious and more from the social location of the spectator' (ibid.: 16).

These ideas are developed in her essay 'On Not Being Lady Macbeth', where she looks at both the production and consumption side of the cinematic contract, and demonstrates the crucial importance of the image-consuming spectator in lively examples of her own viewing. She makes it clear that oppression is an ongoing factor in the social location of the lesbian spectator (ibid.: 143) and usefully discusses the idea of escapism for minority audiences; 'When the weight of **homophobia** (or racism, or sexism/misogyny) is present as a determining factor on the consumption side of the contract, the business of simple escapism takes on added significance' (ibid.: 159).

homophobia
Irrational prejudice and hatred against a person because of their homosexuality.

The contributors to Wilton's collection discuss a range of filmmaking from the work of Monica Treut to lesbian semiotics in the *Alien* films. Most important for subsequent developments, Wilton challenges the easy acceptance of 'queer' as a critical term: 'lesbians and gay men are not easily incorporated into a generic (gender resistant) queer' (ibid.: 9). Wilton is open-minded about whether feminist or queer theory serves lesbians better, a question still open to debate.

The work of Jackie Stacey (1992) and Clare Whatling (1997) extends the process of lesbian intervention in classic psychoanalytic criticism. Whatling provides more discussion of Wilton's notion of location through investigation of lesbian spectator positioning along with readings of the star persona of Jodie Foster.

• **Plate 12.3**
Go Fish (Rose Troche, 1994). A successful and engaging low-budget production about a group of lesbian friends which was promoted through the festival circuit. Guinevere Turner (left) became a lesbian star

SOME QUEER FILMS: STEREOTYPES AND CHARACTERS

In his book *The Matter of Images* (1993) Richard Dyer has pointed out the dangers inherent in thinking rigidly in terms of stereotypes when dealing with representation: 'a **stereotype** can be complex, varied, intense and contradictory, an image of otherness in which it is still possible to find oneself' (ibid.: 74). Stereotypes, he points out, are not always or necessarily negative, although some, such as the black mammy of Hollywood, are very limiting. The process of stereotyping involves power: the power of dominant groups to mould the accepted social view of themselves and of those groups that they perceive as marginal. This view can change and develop as certain social groups, such as gays and lesbians, grow in self-awareness, expression and power, so that dominant groups have to modify their available images. As an example, Dyer cites the 'sad young man' stereotype common in popular film and literature of the 1940s and 1950s, an image of the passive, unhappy, sexually troubled outsider which grew into the ambiguously attractive and strong image of the social rebel as embodied in James Dean and Montgomery Clift. Are there any stereotypes in the following films that that could be interpreted in several ways?

Dyer also suggests that replacing stereotypes with the traditional idea of a 'rounded' characters can be an advance of sorts. However, he points out (in Steven 1985: 294) that the 'well-rounded character', as advocated by theorists such as E.M. Forster, is in itself a limiting concept, for, in its strong preoccupation with individuality, it can obscure awareness of the social groups to which that character belongs. A really useful study of representation can only take place within an overall awareness of the dominant ideology, the chief component of which, for the purposes of this essay, is the assumption of heterosexuality as a dominant, structuring outlook and viewpoint (ibid.). Compare and contrast E.M. Forster's novel *Maurice* with the James Ivory film version (UK, 1987) bearing in mind Dyer's ideas about rounded characters. Examine the extent to which the characters and situations of *The Torch Song Trilogy* (Paul Bogart, US, 1988) and *La Cage aux Folles* (Eduard Molinaro, US, 1978) embody heterosexual ideology.

stereotype
A set of commonly expected behaviour patterns and characteristics based on role (e.g. mother) or personal features such as race, age or sexuality. In society and cultural products, the depiction of a stereotype becomes a form of communication shorthand and often reflects the attitudes of dominant social groups.

• **Plate 12.4**
Mrs Danvers (right) in Hitchcock's *Rebecca* (1940), making life difficult for the woman who seeks to replace her beloved Rebecca. This character is arguably a touchstone for the new queer cinema spectator (Aaron 2004: 188)

The following film analyses are intended as sample case studies for an approach which can be applied to other films, to indicate ways in which wider ideological meanings and values can be examined through close analysis and awareness of representation.

☐ CASE STUDY 1: *LOOKING FOR LANGSTON* (UK, ISAAC JULIEN, 1994)

Poetic meditation

Subtitled *A Meditation on Langston Hughes (1902–1967) and the Harlem Renaissance*, this film is a tribute to the American poet Langston Hughes, who lived in New York and whose writings formed a key part of the flowering of black culture in that city during the 1920s known as the 'Harlem Renaissance'. It is less than an hour long and was funded by Britain's Channel 4 TV. As the word 'meditation' suggests, the work is structured in a non-narrative way around a collage of visual images and a soundtrack of poetry by Hughes, Essex Hemphill and Bruce Nugent. It is dedicated to another outstanding American writer who was also gay and black, the novelist James Baldwin.

The film opens with newsreel footage of Hughes's funeral. A female voiceover delivers an oration about the struggle of opposition, which no one undertakes easily. Later on, this idea of opposition is underlined when we see a modern article on Hughes entitled 'Black and Gay', and when we see a gang of fierce-looking skinheads attempting violence on the nightclub space occupied by the men. The skinheads are white, and when they invade the space they are seen to do so with white police officers looking on and doing nothing. The funeral footage immediately cuts to a modern recreation, in sensuously crisp black and white, of the funeral, with large white lilies and the body laid out in its coffin. The black and white cinematography continues throughout the film as a homage and reference to famous gay images. The lilies recall the photography of Robert Mapplethorpe.

Male, black and gay

Images of the funeral recur and evoke respectful homage. They are interwoven with images of a nightclub peopled by handsome men dancing, drinking, talking and laughing

• Plate 12.5
Looking for Langston (Isaac Julien, 1988). The beauty of this film's images forms a vivid tribute both to Hughes as an artist and to the culture that nurtured him

together, images of enjoyment, sensuality and cultural solidarity. The men are in formal evening clothes and dancing to music which recalls the 1920s. One of the men is white and is later seen in intimate, loving surroundings with his black lover after displaying jealousy in the club. Later, the music and dancing become disco-style in a mix between 1920s and modern styles and scenes, a mix which recurs throughout the film to evoke the continuity of both black and gay culture.

The central figure in the club is a handsome man with a moustache who sees another very good-looking man. The two are attracted to each other, and the middle part of the film presents sensuous fantasy sequences of the two of them together. The man with the moustache is seen reflected in a pond in a spacious moorland setting. He comes across the other man, who is naked. His firm, well-made body is revealed to the viewer from behind, gradually, from the legs up. The poetry on the soundtrack talks of the man's 'dancer's body' and makes clear that this man is the figure of Beauty; 'Beauty's lips touched his ... How much pressure does it take to awaken love?' The shots of Beauty culminate in a scene of him lying naked in bed with the other man, their bodies intertwined. This memorable image recalls a famous photograph by George Platt Lynes, once again paying homage to a major figure of gay culture.

Cultural continuity

Fantasy elements underline the sense of meditation about Hughes and the cultural tradition of which he formed part. The nightclub is first seen with the men in still poses. Male angels watch over the nightclub. At one point, a beautiful young angel is seen holding a large picture of Langston Hughes, then the camera pans slowly to a large picture of James Baldwin. At another point, the camera rises from the nightclub to a scene of funeral mourning situated on the balcony above. This establishes a spatial relationship between the two main movements and moods of the film, and the words of the poem on the soundtrack – 'Let my name be spoken without effect, without the ghost of shadow on it' – show that we are invited to celebrate with joy both Hughes and the culture he represents.

Archive footage underlines cultural continuity. There is footage of Hughes reading his poetry in a TV programme, literary gatherings, jazz bands in Harlem, a football team, along with visual references to poets and anthologies and to the first production of the play *Amen Corner* by James Baldwin.

Throughout the film, Julien juxtaposes image and sound in order to provoke thought and emotion. What both the modern and the 1920s scenes have in common is a sense of danger for gay men in public spaces, outside the safety of places like the club, but at the same time a sense of going out into, of braving, those public spaces. A young man walks into the club and the song lyric rings out:

You're such a beautiful black man,
But you've been made to feel,
That your beauty's not real.

To accompany this we see footage of a black sculptor working on a sculpture of a naked black man. The lyric, the footage of the sculptor at work, and the preceding homage to Beauty as a black man, provide a critique of sexual and aesthetic attitudes towards black men in a society dominated by ideas of beauty as white. Sound and image in collision are used to provoke questions and thoughts about how black men are sexually used by whites, black men as both objects and users of pornography, and the use of pornography for safe sex.

Strong, positive Attitudes

This film takes on several controversial issues, including interracial sex and the questioning of the nature of black masculinity, and deals with them in an accomplished and stylish way. Such glamorously eroticised male images are, as Andrea Weiss points out, very different from the low-key approach taken by lesbian filmmaking, as in the film she and Greta Schiller made about the black lesbian jazz artist Tiny Davis, *Tiny and Ruby: Hell Drivin' Women* (US, 1988).

The final and dominant mood of *Looking for Langston* is elegiac. A male couple is seen to leave the club and walk across Waterloo Bridge in contemporary London. While a train passes and they look at each other the voiceover poem is wistful; 'I love my friend. He went away from me. There's nothing more to say.' But life goes on, the angels overlook scenes of love and celebration, and a poem refers to Hannibal, Toussaint and other strong figures of black history. As the gang of skinheads advances down the street, the club erupts with disco music and we see the dancers enjoying themselves. The editing rhythm speeds up as it cuts between the skinheads, clubbers and police with truncheons. The expected clash is undercut when we see the police and thugs enter the club only to find it empty, followed by a shot of a laughing black angel. Is this a comment on the invisibility and/or oppression of black gay culture? Is it a demonstration of how prejudice and oppression can and will be deflected and dissipated? The final upbeat note is sounded

Sun's a risin'
This is gonna be my song.

Question
Compare and contrast Isaac Julien's docudrama *Looking For Langston* with the same director's fictional feature *Young Soul Rebels* in terms of representations of race, sexuality and narrative structure. See also comments on Isaac Julien's work by Kobena Mercer in Gever *et al.* (1993)

☐ CASE STUDY 2: *BOYS DON'T CRY* (KIMBERLEY PEIRCE, US, 1999)

Transgender considerations

The question of what makes a film 'gay' or 'lesbian' recurs throughout this chapter. Attempting definitions of a 'transgender' film blurs boundaries further. Within contemporary film studies, the term 'transgender' seems to cover a spectrum of work dealing with characters from those who wish to dress temporarily in the clothes of the opposite gender to those who feel the need for permanent changes in bodily configuration and social behaviour. Michele Aaron's critique of *Boys Don't Cry* (Aaron 2004) thus attempts to relate the film to a tradition of cross-dressing comedies such as *Some Like It Hot*.

Gender boundaries can thus be crossed in a variety of ways, and consideration of sexual orientation can add further complications. Judith Halberstam argues that 'the body in transition indelibly marks late twentieth century and early twenty-first century cinematic fantasy', citing examples such at the *Terminator* movies and *The Matrix*. She then continues; 'Nowhere has the fantasy of the shape-shifting, identity-morphing body been more powerfully realised, however, than in the transgender film' (Daniel and Jackson 2003: 18).

• **Plate 12.6**
Lana and Brandon, the characters central to the narrative of *Boys Don't Cry* (Kimberly Peirce, 1999), fully acknowledge and love each other's individuality

Essentialism: To be or not to be?

There is an ongoing debate about the subversive potential of transgender representations: do they represent a radical blurring of the boundaries of gender and sexuality, or does the striving of certain characters to 'become' the opposite gender bring them back into a world of hetero-binarism, or **essentialism**? Halberstam cites *The Crying Game* (UK, Neil Jordan, 1992) and *Boys Don't Cry* as tending towards a constricting binarism, with leading characters who are 'represented as both heroic and fatally flawed' (ibid.) in their inability to enact a full transformation. It may also be worth pointing out that such films make clear societal prejudices about people with transgender identities, a critical viewpoint to be considered in this mix of arguments.

All these elements and contradictions are reflected in a variety of films. The character Hedwig in *Hedwig and the Angry Inch* (John Cameron Mitchell, US, 2001) begins as a gay man and eventually finds happiness with her young male punk-rocker lover. Conversely, the character Judy in *Better than Chocolate* (Anne Wheeler, Canada, 1999) retains her attraction to women after her male to female transition, and finds love with another woman. Some transgender characters could be seen as metaphors for their political context. A critical examination of *The Crying Game* and *Hedwig and the Angry Inch* using such ideas could yield further insights.

In *Boys Don't Cry* the audience is left in no doubt that the character Brandon Teena feels himself to be male, and 'not a dyke', as he tells his supportive cousin Lonny. Viewers are thereby left to contemplate additionally whether or not the character may be a young woman in the grip of essentialist ideas, unable to come to terms with being a lesbian. The film opens with a scene of Brandon dressing completely as a boy, in the words of director Kimberley Peirce completely 'fulfilling his fantasy of himself'. The director wanted this kind of definite start to underline the film's alignment with the transformed Brandon (director's commentary on DVD). This film is itself highly unusual among those dealing with such issues in that its main character is a female to male transgendered person.

essentialism
A term describing the idea of a single, firmly fixed identity as regards **gender**, **sexuality** and other social elements. The opposite attitude is often described as social constructionism, implying that such identities are a product of one's society, attitudes and upbringing, and can vary or be changed.

The cabaret song, sung by the character Judy in *Better than Chocolate* is worth viewing as a memorable and entertaining transgender anthem.

Narrative and mise-en-scene

Throughout the film, the viewer is kept aware of the main character's transgender state. We see a male personality contending with a female body. Brandon dresses in a conventionally male way and adopts consciously 'male' body language in Hilary Swank's skilful performance. He is even quick to deny a comment on the smallness of his hands. The contending factors in the character's life are made clear in a variety of ways, from dialogue discussion with his friend about affording a sex-change operation to scenes of Brandon desperately trying to cope with menstruation and flatten his breasts: 'Brandon's breasts and bleeding index sex characteristics, not gender' (Aaron 2004: 190).

The narrative indicates ongoing problems with the law for Brandon with the speeding ticket, and has a feel of inevitable trouble to come. Pre-publicity may have informed the audience that this is a story based on real life, and they may be aware of its violent ending, but the discordant soundtrack is used as a prefiguring device, and the vividly portrayed setting depicts a claustrophobic, small-town atmosphere which has no room for those who are different. Aaron comments on the 'sci-fi quality' of the setting which invokes 'a community of aliens and dreamers' (ibid.: 192). As cousin Lonny says, 'you know they shoot faggots down there'.

Tom and John, the two young men whom Brandon befriends, are given clear signifiers of trouble and danger to come both in the narrative (violent bouts of anger, excessive drinking) and visually (angular close-ups, stubbly beards). At the same time they are not demonised, as the audience sees John's concern for the safety of Lara and his love for his child, and gets to know how both men are victims in their own right. The tragic feeling of the film is effectively countered by the central relationship between Brandon and his girlfriend Lana, who has the courage to accept him as he is after he has fully revealed his transgendered self. Here viewers might well begin to think about the way this character's role in the plot serves to complicate notions of gender and sexuality. The discordant music is memorably replaced by lyrical sounds as the two eventually make love in complete knowledge of each other.

Audience complicity in the queer look

In this film we clearly see signs of physical and visual transformation in Brandon, but these are kept very much in the mode of realism rather than fantasy. Brandon's girlfriend comments on how pretty he is at the same time as he fights to suppress bodily signs of femininity. While being so aware of the character's ambivalent gender status, the audience is made conscious of conventional visual signs of masculinity in the way Brandon sits, combs his hair or smokes a cigarette, as well as the hairstyle, clothing and facial expression. In this way the film is, in the words of Michele Aaron, about the 'spectacle of transvestism' (ibid.: 189).

In *The New Queer Spectator* Aaron contrasts *Boys Don't Cry* with the traditional type of cross-dressing film such as *Mrs Doubtfire* (Chris Columbus, 1993) which is 'fuelled by heterosexual imperatives' where 'the narratives progress towards the climactic disclosure of the protagonists' "true" identity' (ibid.: 189). In such films, she points out, the gender signifiers tend to serve as reminders which 'reinforce the essentialism of gender even if the (relatively) easy disguise confirmed its **performativity**'. In *Boys Don't Cry* such traditional disavowal is withheld from the audience in a way that, Aaron argues, is a legacy of queer cinema narrative structures.

performativity
A concept derived from **cultural studies** whereby social groups develop self-awareness through shared actions that develop tastes, habits and attitudes in common. When applied to **gender**, you may wish to consider the popular conflation of masculinity and football, or femininity and shopping.

Question
To what extent do Laura Mulvey's ideas about scopophilia and identification apply to *Boys Don't Cry*?

Not only is the audience implicated in knowledge of Brandon's passing himself off as a man, as indicated above, but this implication is underlined through the character of Lana 'who comes to represent the spectator's own inevitably unfixed or queer response to the cross-dressed figure in general and to Brandon in particular' (ibid.: 191). Aaron goes on to point out that awareness of Brandon's identity is also set up through the reactions of other characters such as Lana's mother, and John. Additionally, a blurring of gender roles is suggested through the casting against the grain of stereotype, where Lana is a big-boned beauty and Brandon looks petite and slim. Aaron writes: 'Meanwhile Tom, with his pubescent flourish of facial hair, and John, doe-eyed and long-lashed, cuddly, yet sociopathic, further promote the film's deliberate inscription of a spectrum of gender expression', and makes an argument for these two characters being part of 'an alternative network of implicated queerness' (ibid.: 192).

The climactic scene that underlines the separation of gender and the physical attributes of sex is the disclosure when John and Tom force Brandon to reveal his genitals. John shouts at Lana to 'look at your little boyfriend' and Lana's reply, 'leave him alone', effectively underscores the narrative's acceptance of Brandon's state. A short fantasy sequence follows which 'reifies ... the distinction between gender and sex' as 'the divested Brandon splits from and stares at a clothed Brandon standing watching behind the other witnesses' (ibid.: 190). The tableau viewed is of a semi-naked Brandon supported on either side by Tom and John, with Lana kneeling below and looking up at him, a reference to Christ-like martyrdom that serves to strongly implicate the spectator yet again into complicity with Brandon. For Aaron, this film 'rescripts the cross-dressing narrative to avow the queerness not just of the characters in the film but the firmly implicated spectator' (ibid.: 192).

Question

Bearing in mind the portrayal of Brandon in *Boys Don't Cry*, analyse the contrasting ways in which the transgendered main character is presented in one or two of the following:

The Adventures of Priscilla, Queen of the Desert
Better than Chocolate
The Crying Game
Victor/Victoria

A QUEER DIVERSITY

reappropriation
The process whereby a previously oppressed group takes a negative term and turns it around to invest it with new meanings of power and liberation. Examples include 'black', 'virago' and '**queer**'.

Critic B. Ruby Rich described 1992 as 'a watershed year for independent gay and lesbian film' (Benshoff and Griffin 2004: 53), not only due to the number of shorts and features being made and shown, but because of the surge in critical interest which accompanied them. During the 1990s such film and video activity came to be labelled 'Queer Cinema'. Lesbian and gay activists, critics, filmmakers and audiences started to imbue the previously negative term 'queer' with a range of new, exciting, positive meanings in politics, literature, art and filmmaking. This process of an oppressed group reclaiming and reshaping a previously negative word or idea is known as **reappropriation**. Critic Amy Taubin claimed 'American queer cinema has achieved critical mass' (Cook and Dodd 1993: 176) with the release of features such as *My Own Private Idaho* (Gus Van Sant, 1991), using the Hollywood star system with Keanu Reeves and River Phoenix, and Tom Kalin's *Swoon* (1992). Paul Burston believes this filmmaking movement was born out of

1990s anger and activism in what he calls 'a particularly dark time in modern gay history' (Burston 2007). He points out key filmmakers such as Kalin and Jarman were deeply involved in political activity at this time.

> **Question**
> Bearing in mind ideas about queer cinema, compare and contrast the troubled relationships portrayed in *Happy Together?*, *Swoon* and/or *The Living End*.

The key ideas behind the queer cinema movement are diversity and fluidity: a range of diverse sexualities manifested through a variety of character, situation, race, gender, sexual practice and film language. Rich defines the key ingredients as 'appropriation and pastiche, irony, as well as a reworking of history, with social constructionism very much in mind' (Benshoff and Griffin 2004: 54). Within the queer aesthetic, some filmmakers are questioning the attitude, developed in the 1970s, that one must promote only positive images of lesbian and gay characters and situations. They see such ideas as constraints on creativity in an era where, they argue, a much wider variety of lesbian and gay images is available.

In *Swoon*, Tom Kalin examines the infamous Leopold/Loeb case of 1924, where two rich, Jewish 18-year-olds kidnap and murder a 14-year-old boy. Unlike previous film versions such as Hitchcock's *Rope* (US, 1948), Kalin concentrates on the homosexual relationship between the two young men, the poisonous effect of homophobia and anti-semitism on the mind of Leopold, and the hold that the pathological Leopold had over Loeb. In a discussion, Kalin stated; 'I think the necessary process of acknowledging all the different aspects of our identities is something that, for the most part, hasn't been allowed' (Bad Object Choices 1997: 277). Derek Jarman's *Edward II* (UK, 1991) doesn't hesitate to portray England's monarch as weak and vacillating while his male lover, Gaveston, is scheming and slimy. What Kalin's and Jarman's films do in their very different ways is make the audience aware of the political dimensions of homosexuality.

New techniques of expression: playing with genre

Diversity and experimentation in film language characterise those works regarded as part of the queer cinema movement. John Greyson mixes history in *Urinal* (Canada, 1988) as famous figures of gay culture, including Langston Hughes and the Russian director Sergei Eisenstein, help to investigate police harassment of gays. In *Caravaggio* and *Edward II* Derek Jarman makes creative use of anachronism to underline the continuing relevance of his sexual and political themes. In the latter, we see Annie Lennox singing a Cole Porter song, vicars in dog-collars spitting on Gaveston after his banishment, and gay activists with placards and the **pink triangle** symbol invading the king's palace. In *Blue* (UK, 1993) Jarman's one-colour screen counterpoints the emotional range of the soundtrack's meditation on his life with, and approaching death from, HIV, and challenges received ideas about the visual portrayal of disease.

There are precedents for the genre play now considered part of the queer aesthetic. The documentary work of Stuart Marshall aimed at being challenging in subject matter and form. *Bright Eyes* (UK, 1984) presents the viewer with ever-relevant parallels between Nazi treatment of gays, Victorian medical practice and media coverage of the AIDS epidemic. Rosa Von Praunheim's *I Am My Own Woman* (Germany, 1993) presents a portrait of Charlotte Von Mahlsdort (born Lothar Berfelde), a famous lifelong transvestite who is also gay (US DVD title: *I Am My Own Wife*). As well as using direct interviews with him, the film dramatises scenes from his life, including his anti-Nazi work during the

pink triangle
A symbol originally worn by **homosexual** prisoners in Nazi concentration camps which was later taken up by **lesbian** and **gay** people as a reminder of past oppression and an icon of liberation.

• **Plate 12.7**
Edward II (Derek
Jarman, 1991). The
love between Edward
(left) and Gaveston, as
queerly portrayed by
Jarman, evokes mixed
audience reactions

*To aid your consideration
of genre in relation to
this chapter, examine
the classifications given
in Daniel and Jackson
(2003), see Further
Reading.*

Second World War. At the end of many of these dramatised scenes, he himself walks
onto the set and is questioned by the actors about his thoughts and motivations, a
productive distancing effect and perhaps an example of queer questioning.

Film genre and film style are mixed creatively in new queer cinema. Todd Haynes's
Poison (US, 1991) mixes 1950s B-film sci-fi and zombie elements with a homoerotic
section styled as a homage to Genet. In *The Living End* (US, 1993), widely considered to
be a landmark of queer cinema, Gregg Araki offers a nihilistic gay road movie dominated
by themes of AIDS and survival. In *Caught Looking* (UK, 1991) Constantine Giannaris
takes the viewer on a journey through a spectrum of gay viewpoints with a character
participating in an interactive video fantasy. John Greyson's *Zero Patience* (Canada,
1993) subverts the conventions of the Hollywood musical to investigate attitudes to
AIDS, once again using a figure from the gay past, the Victorian explorer Richard Francis
Burton, in creative and amusing ways.

Question
Consider ways in which either the *genre* or the *star* systems may mediate the
reception of one or more of the following films for queer audiences:

I Married a Monster from Outer Space
Pirates of the Caribbean
Queen Christina
The Wizard of Oz

Gender, race and queer cinema
Monika Treut's feature-length *Virgin Machine* (Germany, 1985) accompanies its heroine
on a sexual odyssey in San Francisco, but the inequality of funding for men's and
women's work means that many lesbian filmmakers continue to produce shorter films
and videos, often for television. In *The Meeting of Two Queens*, Cecilia Barriga has taken

● **Plate 12.8**
In *Poison* (1991) Todd
Haynes pays homage to
the homoerotic prison
imagery of Genet. He
later made good use
of genre in *Far From
Heaven* (2002)

images of Garbo and Dietrich and edited them together to produce a provocatively
sensual play of eye contact and undressing between two screen goddesses. The video
work of Sadie Benning, such as the ten-minute *Jollies*, intimately explores her own body,
thoughts, memories and sexuality with bold use of camerawork intricately interacting
with the soundtrack.

Pratibha Parmar is a British filmmaker and critic of Asian origin who helped found the
first group in Britain for black lesbians. For her, as for Isaac Julien, race is as important
an issue as sexuality, and the intervention of both filmmakers contributes to the new kind
of diversity within queer cinema. Parmar is concerned to disrupt and change the conventional images of Asians prevalent in British society. *Khush* (UK, 1991) is a television film
she made for Channel 4 about the experience of being Asian and lesbian or gay. In this
piece, interviews are interwoven with images of two women in saris relaxing and dancing
together, and a classic Indian musical film is provocatively re-edited so that the dancing
girl's glances interplay with those of another woman.

With videos such as Orientations (Canada, 1985), Richard Fung helps give voice
to North American lesbians and gays of Chinese origin. Marlon Riggs's feature-length
poetic meditation on the lives of black gay men in the US, *Tongues Untied* (US, 1989),
is a beautifully constructed kaleidoscope of sound and image. Consider some of
the stylistic parallels and contrasts between *Looking for Langsto*n and some of the
filmmaking outlined in this section.

Essentialism: to label or not to label?

For many recent critics the term 'queer' is to be preferred for its notions of opposition to
mainstream representations. There are debates going on about exactly how conservative
and fixed terms such as 'heterosexual', 'gay' and 'lesbian' have become in both society
and film. Have they become part of the mainstream against which the queer theorists
strive? Such terms are seen by some as very fixed labels which form part of a rigid
sexual system, in other words as essentialist in nature. Those challenging this system
assert that such labelling is inaccurate and misleading in that it does not reflect the fluid
nature of both sexuality and film spectatorship. Such critics have become known as
anti-essentialist.

• Plate 11.9
Khush (Pratiba Parmar, 1991). The title of this memorable film is the Urdu word for 'ecstatic pleasure'. In her look at some Asian lesbian and gay lives, Parmar mixed pleasurable dream sequences with interviews which recall oppression

On the other hand, defenders of gay and lesbian approaches claim that the term 'queer' leads to an ignoring of lesbian and gay specificity, indeed to the very kind of invisibility against which early critics like Russo fought. An essentialist position could be seen as historically specific and necessary. Barbara Hammer claims: 'Lesbian image-makers in the seventies were forced by critics into the "camp of essentialists" because of the extreme urgency of their need to make lesbian representation' (Gever *et al.* 1993: 71). Wilton points out: 'An anti-essentialist, social-constructionist perspective on sexual "identity" does not make "lesbian" a redundant label, rather it obliges us to recognise and deploy "lesbian" as an avowedly strategic sign' (Wilton 1995: 5). She even comes round to suggesting that certain spectator positionings need to be socially recognised for so-called 'alternative' or 'queer' perspectives to exist. A clear introduction to these debates is provided by David Alderson and Linda Anderson (see Further Reading at the end of this chapter) where they talk about 'queer thinking, and the anti-essentialism that underpins it'.

Mainstream cinema: In or out?

Consider varying attitudes to positive images of lesbians and gays already mentioned. Should we condemn the conflation of homosexuality, violence and murder in such films as *Basic Instinct*? Or can we be confident that a wide enough variety of views of lesbian and gay life now circulates in society to balance out negative images, so that we may embrace the queer aesthetic?

Exactly how much of the queer aesthetic is being absorbed into mainstream filmmaking and to what extent is Hollywood still prone to attempt a 'normalising' process for its perceived mass audience? The publicity for *Philadelphia* (Jonathan Demme, US, 1993) presented the film primarily as a courtroom drama and deliberately played down its gay content. In *Gods and Monsters* (Bill Condon, UK, 1998) the theatre actor and gay activist Ian McKellen played the famous gay Hollywood director James Whale. The script was closely based on the novel *Father of Frankenstein* by gay writer Christopher Bram, whose novel ends with Clay, the yardman character (Brendan Fraser), standing thoughtfully by Whale's grave. This character had already been established in Bram's novel as a troubled heterosexual who has gained self-knowledge from becoming Whale's friend. In the film version we see an extra scene at the end where Clay is happily married with a child. You may wish to assess this scene in terms of traditional Hollywood demand for heteronormative narrative closure as opposed to the more open potential of the novel's ending.

On the other hand, it could be argued that more diverse sexual perspectives have been flowing into the mainstream. Todd Haynes emerged as a noted cutting-edge queer director of the 1990s. He then went on to direct *Far From Heaven* (US, 2002), a mainstream feature that makes ample use of its budget to recreate lush 1950s settings redolent of Douglas Sirk. At the same time the narrative plays in a post-queer way with Sirkian themes of sexuality and race. John Maybury is a British example of a queer cinema director undertaking a relatively mainstream project with *Love is the Devil* (UK, 1998), a film biography of Francis Bacon which looks closely at the artist's tempestuous relationship with his lover and muse, George Dyer.

All the films mentioned so far in this section involve death, dying, disease, bereavement, oppression or breakdown in varying mixes. To what extent do films such as *A Single Man* and *Brokeback Mountain* make modern audiences aware of anti-gay prejudice and oppression in the past? *Milk* may end with killings, but you may wish to think about ways in which the director situates his central character as part of a liberation movement. Of course these aspects of life make for good drama, but is there no room for more positive images? Perhaps a sensitive viewer might appreciate positive secondary characters that form a normative background, such as the gay neighbours in *American Beauty* or the supportive lesbian friend of the hero in *Tell No One* (Guillaume Canet, France, 2006). In this light, assess the portrayal of the central male couple in *Four Weddings and a Funeral* (Mike Newell, UK, 1994) or the main character's supportive lover in *Capote* (Bennett Miller, US, 2005). In the light of the ideas presented here, assess the positive queer potential of two social comedies *I Love You, Philip Morris* (Glenn Ficarra and John Requa, US, 2010) and *The Kids Are All Right* (Lisa Cholodenko, US, 2010).

Question
Consider the homoerotic subtext of the *Lord of the Rings* film trilogy.

• **Plate 12.10**
Far From Heaven (Todd Haynes, 2002). Noted gay director Haynes makes use of distinct 1950s style in this melodrama about a troubled marriage. Julianne Moore stars as the wife coping with a gay husband.

• **Plate 12.11**
Bound (Lana Warchowski, 1997) can be regarded as both a mainstream product and a cult blend of lesbian romance, comedy and film noir.

Queer looking

In the early twenty-first century there is no consensus in the field of lesbian/gay/queer cinema, more a developed awareness of dissolving boundaries and multiplying identities. Critics, filmmakers and audiences are interested in a mapping of potentialities and possibilities. Alexander Doty states that: 'Ultimately, queerness should challenge and confuse our understanding and uses of sexual and gender categories' (1993: vii) but he cautions against the use of 'queer' as a verb that has become modish among certain critics: 'we should drop the idea of "queering" something, as it implies taking a thing that is straight and doing something to it'. Doty is echoing Dyer here (Steven 1985: 294) with the idea that all texts contain 'cracks and fissures' through which alternative viewpoints can leak.

Debate continues about what constitutes a lesbian/gay/queer film. Do the makers of such films have to be gay or lesbian themselves? Compare the portrayal of same-sex relationships in *Desert Hearts* (Donna Deitch, US, 1985) and *Black Widow* (Bob Rafelson, US, 1987). Arguably, both involve homoerotic attraction and a certain gay sensibility in the play of looks on the screen and/or between the viewer and the text. In *Black Widow* same-sex attraction and lesbian sensibility remain sub-textual. Is *Desert Hearts* therefore more 'lesbian' because of its direct portrayal of sexuality in character, situation and action? Or is *Black Widow* equally powerful in this context? Apply a similar comparison to the male-orientated films *Jeffrey* (Chris Ashley, US, 1995) and *Top Gun* (Tony Scott, US, 1986).

Consider the concept of 'queer'. Federico Fellini and Ken Russell, both heterosexuals, made some very queer films. What does the concept tell us about the portrayal of the boundaries of gender and sexuality? In this context, consider the fictional feature *Priscilla, Queen of the Desert* (Stephan Elliott, Australia, 1994) and the documentary *Southern Comfort* (Kate Davis, US, 2001) in the ways they present their transgendered central figures.

Question

Consider the varying ideas and attitudes associated with the words 'homosexual', 'gay' and 'queer'. To what extent can these terms be used to describe various kinds of moving image production? You may wish to consider examples selected from some or all of the following:

- Arzner, Cronenberg, Cukor, Rozema as auteurs.
- The horror film and the musical as genres.
- Distinctive strands of certain national cinemas, e.g. Canada, Australia, France.
- Queer spectatorial elements in mainstream films such as *The Talented Mr Ripley*.
- Robin Wood's critical (re)assessment of the work of Hitchcock.

From image-spotting to queer spectatorship: an overview

Vito Russo's pioneering book (1987) proved to be very popular and influential for those interested in challenging dominant views of film. The reasons for its popularity lay partly in the fact that, unlike its predecessor by Parker Tyler, *Screening the Sexes*, it concentrated almost entirely on the products of Hollywood and the question of gay invisibility, a major preoccupation of gay and lesbian campaigners at the time. Russo's critical method was to examine individual representations of gay and lesbian characters, situations and plotlines and relate them to mainstream attitudes which we would now call homophobic. His method was a form of vigilant image-spotting, politically necessary at the time but ultimately, in the words of Ellis Hanson, concerned 'with only one gaze: the ubiquitous, prefabricated, gullible, voyeuristic gaze of homophobia'. Hanson goes on to say: 'Meanwhile, our own pleasure, that elusive gaze of delight, is left curiously under-theorised and at times inadmissible' (quoted in Farmer 2000: 4).

Whatever one may think about Hanson's judgement, critics who extended Russo's work have constructively investigated gay and lesbian viewing in terms of theory and spectator pleasure. Richard Dyer and Andrea Weiss have utilised auteur theory, star study, cinema history and ideas of audience reception. They and other critics such as Judith Mayne, Jackie Stacey and Thomas Waugh (see Bibliography) have contributed towards the forging of useful theories of gay, lesbian and queer viewing strategies. More recent critical work is moving towards theorising gay/lesbian/queer spectatorial pleasure. For a useful overview and development of this work, see Brett Farmer (2000).

In the introduction to his book Farmer points the way forward to the kind of theorisation that Hanson sees as vital in this area. He uses key concepts of *specificity* and *performativity* (Farmer 2000: 33–42) to ground a gay spectatorship theory that incorporates a synthesis of the social and the psychoanalytic. *Specificity* 'designates a space for the constitution of subjectivity, the arrangement of desire, and the productions of meaning in specific or particular ways' which he sees as 'a very different proposition from claiming gayness as an expressive, self-identical essence' (ibid.: 40).

CONCLUSION: THE WAY FORWARD

The best way forward I can think of is to encourage readers to diversify their viewing. Most films mentioned in this chapter are available on DVD, and the suggestions for further viewing on the website present a cross-section of the range of viewing experiences available in terms of nationality, historical period and sexual viewpoint.

Use the reading and viewing guides to investigate and develop the questions posed in this chapter. Watch and look into the films using the case studies as models. Above all, explore, enjoy and widen your viewing experiences.

SUMMARY

- Cinema is roughly as old as the first appearance of the word 'homosexual' and same-sex depictions tend to follow wider social attitudes in each film-producing society, encapsulated to a certain extent in English words such as 'gay' and 'queer'.
- Early cinematic depictions tended to be heavily coded in ways that enabled them to be understood by restricted social groups with access to shared meanings.
- From the 1960s, certain film critics began to tease out those codes and meanings for wider audiences.
- Most direct depictions of same-sex desire in commercial cinema have had a tendency to associate such feelings with tragedy, unhappiness and/or marginality. These negative depictions, though by no means unknown now, have been countered by images of happier, fulfilled and/or sympathetic situations and characters.
- Earlier lesbian and gay critics and filmmakers put an emphasis on positive images of lesbians and gay men, and fought against heterosexual binarism in theory and practice.
- Later critics and filmmakers associated with the queer cinema movement felt freer to depict a wider range of sexualities and situations, regardless of previous ideas about positive images.
- Depictions of a wider range of sexualities and situations mentioned above may include sharper awareness of gender, class, race, ethnicity and transgender issues.
- The filmmaking and ideas dealt with in this chapter have been steadily growing and expanding their audiences thanks to the festival circuits, as well as digital and internet technologies.

QUESTIONS FOR DISCUSSION

1   The suggestions for further viewing here and on the website present a cross-section of the range of viewing experiences available in terms of nationality, historical period and sexual viewpoint.

2   Use the reading and viewing guides and case studies to investigate and develop the questions posed in this chapter. Above all, explore, enjoy and widen your viewing experiences.

 **FURTHER READING**

Aaron, M. (ed.), *New Queer Cinema: A Critical Reader*, Edinburgh University Press, Edinburgh 2004. Helpful writings on context, Haynes and Araki as auteurs, lesbian perspectives, black queer cinema, nationality in relation to Australia, third cinema, art cinema, reception and spectatorship. The volume deals with a range of popular features from *The Talented Mr Ripley* (Anthony Minghella, US, 1999) to *Mansfield Park* (Patricia Rozema, UK, 1999).

Alderson, D. and Anderson, L. (eds), *Territories of Desire in Queer Culture*, Manchester University Press, Manchester, 2000. An excellent summary, in the introduction, of the current debates about queer culture. A challenging essay on Jarman,

and explorations of Spanish and Australian gay cinema. With an erudite historical overview, Jonathan Dollimore's concluding survey points the way to possible future developments.

Benshoff, H. and Griffin, S. (eds), *Queer Cinema: The Film Reader*, Routledge, New York and London, 2004. Crucial texts by Jack Babuscio on 'Camp and Gay Sensibility' and B. Ruby Rich on 'The New Queer Cinema'. Leading critics such as Dyer, Weiss, Doty and Waugh examine authorship, genre, reception and spectatorship. All students should read its superb introduction.

Daniel, L. and Jackson, C. (eds), *The Bent Lens: A World Guide to Gay and Lesbian Film*,

Roundhouse Publishing, Northam, 2003. An excellent reference which is prefaced by useful critical essays on lesbian and gay cinema in Europe, globalisation, nationality, representation and genre. The introductions to the gay, lesbian and transgender sections are clear and stimulating. The editors also list all their entries according to three useful categories: genre, which is an unusual approach for this kind of collection, director and nationality.

Dyer, R., *The Matter Of Images*: *Essays On Representation*, Routledge, London, 1993. An ideal primer for those starting to explore sexual representation in film. Dyer illustrates the power and complexity of images across a range of films, including film noir, the seminal British film *Victim*, and the 'sad young man' tradition which fed into the star persona of James Dean and others. A groundbreaking anthology. Read also his collection *The Culture of Queers* which contains a selection of his key work on such topics as Fassbinder, Rock Hudson and film noir.

Farmer, B., *Spectacular Passions: Cinema, Fantasy, Gay Male Spectatorships*, Duke University Press, Durham, NC, 2000. Farmer closely questions the concepts of *gay* and *queer* and proposes a theory of gay spectatorship which aptly blends psychoanalytic ideas of fantasy, identification and pleasure with social notions of performativity. He then offers fruitful textual explorations based on his theory. This is an excellent way of coming to terms with the latest debates about essentialism and gay spectatorship.

Griffiths, R. (ed.), *British Queer Cinema*, Routledge, London/New York, 2006. This volume has a perceptive introduction on what Griffiths calls the 'globalisation' of queer theory and its cultural effects, along with a useful assessment of the emergence of 'Queer Film Studies'. Ros Jennings's chapter 'Beautiful Thing', produces insights into how the film's range of realist characters 'can be seen to playfully dispute heterosexual stability'. Among other contributions there is productive discussion on the use of setting in *Maurice* and *Get Real*, and a perceptive exploration of the production context of Jarman's *Edward II* by Raymond Armstrong.

Holmlund, C. and Fuchs, C., *Between the Sheets, in the Streets: Queer, Lesbian and Gay Documentary*, University of Minnesota Press, Minneapolis, 1997. Primarily US-centred, but an extremely fruitful exploration of the nature, form and address of documentary.

Mulvey, L., 'Visual Pleasure and Narrative Cinema', in *The Sexual Subject: A Screen Reader in Sexuality*, Routledge, London and New York, 1995. This must be read as the seminal first step, a work that helped give voice to the study of gender and sexuality in film. For more nuanced explorations relevant to this chapter, see Jackie Stacey's key essay 'Desperately Seeking Difference' in the same volume, and Farmer (2000).

Wilton, T. (ed.), *Immortal, Invisible: Lesbians and the Moving Image*, Routledge, London, 1995. Wilton's introduction and chapter 'On Not Being Lady Macbeth' are seminal in setting out the critical parameters on lesbian spectatorship and heterosexual ideology, and should be read by all students of film. This volume contains Julia Knight's essay on how Monica Treut seeks to transcend the category of lesbian and contains a set of insights applicable to a range of queer directors. It is also noteworthy for its textual explorations of camp and the lesbian semiotics of the *Alien* films.

FURTHER VIEWING

***Aimee & Jaguar* (Germany, Max Fäberböck, 1998)**
A bold telling of an incredible but true story set in Berlin during the later years of the Second World War. Two women, Lilly and Felice, one a Nazi super-mum and the other a Jewish underground resistance member, meet, fall in love and remain devoted to each other through dangerous times and Felice's capture by the Gestapo. The compelling narrative is framed by contemporary scenes showing the elderly Lilly still honouring the memory of her lover.

***All About My Mother* (Spain, Pedro Almodovar, 1999)**
Featuring a search for a lost, transgendered father figure. A brilliantly queer, if rather phallocentric, reworking of the Hollywood classic *All About Eve*.

Thanks to Almodovar's skilful work, the melodramatic storyline remains convincing. See also *Bad Education* by the same auteur.

***American Beauty* (US, Sam Mendes, 2000)**
A suburban comedy, very knowing in its portrayal of the repressed homosexual obsessions of the proto-fascist next-door neighbour, as well as positive images of the gay couple down the street who are pillars of the community. For another constructive use of gay secondary characters in American mainstream filmmaking see *The Opposite of Sex* (US, Don Roos, 1999)

***Another Way* (Hungary, Karoly Makk, 1982)**
Said to be among Eastern Europe's first films dealing with a lesbian relationship, this is an

intelligent and finely observed love story set just after the Hungarian uprising of 1956.

A Single Man (US, Tom Ford, 2010)

Set in Los Angeles in 1962, the narrative follows one day in the life of George Falconer, a British college professor who is struggling to find meaning in his life after the death of his long-time partner, Jim. Colin Firth gives an outstanding performance. Julianne Moore, as in her other performances listed here, plays a key role in the vivid evocation of sexual attitudes of the place and time. See also *Cabaret* as a similar evocation of 1930s Berlin, and a film based on a novel by noted gay author Christopher Isherwood.

À Toute Vitesse (Full Speed) (France, Gaël Morel, 1996)

A bleak view of homophobia and racism among provincial French youth, contrasted with the bravery and loyalty of the central characters. Contains superb, compelling performances.

Beautiful Boxer (Thailand, Ekachai Uekrongtham, 2005)

Fact-based biopic of a leading champion kick-boxer from a poor background who uses his winnings to pay for a sex change. Caused controversy among Thai audiences not for the fact of its transgender leading character, but for its serious examination of the character's motives and outlook. See also *The Iron Ladies* (Thailand, Thongkonthun Youngyooth, 2000), a lively, real-life-based drama about how a gay volleyball team fought its way to become champions of the Thai league.

Beautiful Thing (UK, Hettie Macdonald, 1997)

Two young men find love and comfort in each other's arms on a Bermondsey council estate and start to explore the local gay scene. With themes of class, gender and community solidarity, this is a refreshingly optimistic movie. See Ros Jennings's fascinating reading of what she calls 'positive unoriginality and the everyday' in Griffiths (2005). For another entertaining British realist film, watch *Get Real* (UK, Simon Shore, 1998).

Beefcake (Canada, Thom Fitzgerald, 2000)

An entertainingly camp and affectionate look at the activities of Bob Mizer's famous 1950s physique studio, the 'Athletic Model Guild' through the eyes of a well-built country innocent learning the ways of the world in LA.

Before Night Falls (US, Julian Schnabel, 2000)

A powerful, engaging biopic of the Cuban Renaldo Arenas, whose gay sexuality, political activism and prolific writing are shown as inseparable aspects of his life. Spanish star Javier Bardem gives an excellent performance as Arenas. Also stars Johnny Depp as transvestite lover.

Bent (UK, Sean Mathias,1997)

This film about the persecution of gays in Nazi Germany reflects the weaknesses of the stage play on which it is based. It is worth viewing, though, for its powerful performances and historically important subject matter. Features Mick Jagger as a transvestite cabaret performer, and Ian McKellen.

Bound (US, Andy and Larry Wachowski, 1996)

A post-queer lesbian private-eye film; two consciously stereotyped babes-with-brains in steamy union.

Boystown (Spain, D. Ayaso, J. Flahn, Rafa, F. Sabroso, 2007)

This is a dark, comedy thriller set in Chueca, Madrid's gay area, performed and edited with considerable gusto. The twists and turns of the plot and the overblown style owe a lot to Almodovar. An ordinary and likeable couple, Ray and Leo, are beset by such notable comic figures as Ray's interfering mother, a murderously devious gay real estate agent, and an eccentric detective with her dithering gay son who finally unravel the mystery.

Brokeback Mountain (US, Ang Lee, 2005)

A mainstream, big-budget western about two shepherds whose love for each other changes their lives. Superb performances reflect the passionate feelings and social frustrations of their situation. 'A grand romantic tragedy' according to B. Ruby Rich, which has 'reimagined America as shaped by queer experience and memory.'

Campfire (Belgium, Bavo Defune, 1999)

Four short portraits of young male relationships, replete with inspired use of a range or gay imagery which pays homage to the Athletic Model Guild, Jean Genet and the chic photo-homoerotics of Pierre et Gilles. The themes of sexual exploration and awakening are given unity across the four films through Defune's skilful use of his own range of visual metaphors: clouds, water and extreme close-ups.

The Celluloid Closet (US, Robert Epstein and Jeffrey Friedman, 1996)

Includes clips from about a hundred films mentioned in Vito Russo's seminal book, and interviews with screenwriter Gore Vidal, director John Schlesinger and actors Tom Hanks and Whoopi Goldberg.

Conversation Piece (Italy, Luchino Visconti, 1974)

Burt Lancaster gives a remarkable performance as a retired, bookish professor reluctantly discovering his own latent homosexual passions. Visconti is, for me, a major queer auteur who is in need of close critical reassessment; see also *Ossessione, The Damned* and *Death in Venice*.

Defying Gravity (US, John Keitel, 1997)

Part of the growing gay genre of 'coming out' stories, this is set on an affluent American University campus, and involves a gay-bashing as well as racial, family and friendship issues. An engaging, film with good use of flashbacks, although, annoyingly, not a single character in it ever manages to utter the 'g-word' or directly name same-sex issues in any way. For other genre examples see *Edge of Seventeen*, *Beautiful Thing* and *Trick*.

Desert Hearts (US, Donna Deitsch, 1985)
A rather idealised lesbian romance set in 1950s Texas, which has provoked a range of reactions from critics such as Richard Dyer, Mandy Merck and Barbara Hammer.

Dona Herlinda and her Son (Mexico, Jaime Hermosillo, 1985)
An entertaining comedy of sexual manners where a perceptive mother arranges her son's love-life to cater for his gay lover and her own desire for a grandchild. One of the first Latin American films to deal positively with a gay theme. For a somewhat angst-ridden portrayal of young gay love, see *Broken Sky* (Mexico, Julián Hernández, 2006) and this director's much more successful and engaging *Raging Sun, Raging Sky* (Mexico, 2009).

East Palace, West Palace (China, Zhang Yuan, 1996)
A ground-breaking work in terms of homosexuality and mainland Chinese cinema. A macho cop apprehends a young gay man, and the ensuing interaction makes him question himself deeply. Remarkable for the gay character's assertion of selfhood. Slow-paced but elegiac, with excellent performances and cinematography. For a discussion of political considerations, see Chris Berry's essay in Grossman 2001.

Everyone (Canada, Bill Marchant, 2004)
This intelligent, bittersweet social comedy portrays the lives of a group of friends and relatives coming together to celebrate a gay union. Script and acting skilfully combine sophistication with earthiness and a touch of satire. As with all good films of this genre, serious issues hover behind the well-crafted dialogue.

Forbidden Love: The Unashamed Stories of Lesbian Lives (Canada, Aerlyn Wessman and Lynne Femie, 1992)
Wonderful to watch: a 1950s pulp-fiction style lesbian love story is interwoven with older women talking about their lives. Excellent docudrama.

Go Fish (US, Rose Troche, 1994)
An outstandingly engaging independent look at the lives and loves of a group of lesbians living in San Francisco. See Pierson (1996) to read more about this. *Bedrooms and Hallways* (UK, 1998), by the same director, presents a similarly original and engaging look at a group with diverse sexualities.

Gohatto (Japan, Nagisa Oshima, 1999)
The title is Japanese for 'taboo'. Set in a samurai training academy in 1865. A beautiful young samurai warrior sets off a chain reaction of passions among his fellow trainees. Fascinating narrative tension in the depiction of how these passions conflict with strict samurai rules. Visually stunning, with excellent fight choreography.

The Hanging Garden (Canada, Thom Fitzgerald, 1997)
A gay man revisits his family and meets the image of his previous, repressed younger self which haunts his father. A drama that makes the viewer question the nature of queerness.

Happy, Texas (US, Mark Illsley, 2002)
A feelgood small-town comedy involving mistaken identity, a couple of gay designers and a lovelorn gay sheriff who eventually gets his man. For another feelgood gay-themed social comedy from the US see *In and Out* (Frank Oz, US 2001).

Happy Together (Hong Kong, Wong Kar Wai, 1997)
Two young Chinese men try to patch up their relationship on an extended stay in Argentina. Particularly interesting for its use of sound, music and setting to portray and underline characters and relationships. For a discussion of political themes, see Chris Berry's essay in Grossman (2001). See case study on the accompanying website.

Head On (Australia, Ana Kokkinos, 1998)
A powerful realisation of contemporary queer life in Australia. Centred on Ari, a young Greek–Australian battling to come to terms with his sexuality and his family. A salient product of queer cinema in its avoidance of any comforting character empathy or predictable narrative closure. See the essay on this film in Alderson and Anderson (2000).

Hellbent (US, David DeCoteau, 2005)
A gay horror film, 'the first to take its genre seriously, with gay characters played as honest-to-goodness people rather than for comic relief or cannon fodder' (Kevin Goebel, planetout.com).

High Art (US, Lisa Cholodenko, 1998)
A film that takes the lesbian sexuality of its main characters as natural and given, while looking at how they live their lives, make art and love one another. Much admired by queer critics such as Daniel Cunningham (Daniel and Jackson 2003: 12).

If These Walls Could Talk – 2
A notable and good-quality made-for-TV movie that traces lesbian lives and loves over three different generations in the late twentieth century. Features Vanessa Redgrave as an older 'lesbian widow' and Sharon Stone as a young adventurer.

I Love You, Philip Morris (US, Glenn Ficarra and John Requa, 2010)
Hollywood comic superstar Jim Carrey portrays a real-life based conman who falls in love with another man while in prison. Carrey's character portrayal is imbued with humour and happiness as he explores his emotions, while remaining true to the star's zany persona.

La Leòn (France/Argentina, Santiago Otheguy, 2006)
An award-winning story with visually arresting settings in the Panama Delta of Northern Argentina,

depicted with superb black and white cinematography. Alvaro, a quiet gay man, lives a simple and isolated life. He works for the violent El Turo, a captain of a water bus which links the isolated communities of traditional reedcutters. Alvaro's sexuality aggravates El Turo, who feels threatened by his 'difference' and sets about harassing him. Class as well as sexuality play a part in the narrative as Alvaro's revenge on the odious captain is tacitly supported by his local community.

Law Of Desire (Spain, Pedro Almodovar, 1987)
A gripping gay melodrama by one of Spain's leading contemporary directors. This was the precursor of several entertaining gay films from 1990s Spain – see the essay in Alderson and Anderson (2000).

Like It Is (UK, Paul Oremland, 1997)
A cross-class gay love story. Craig is a northern boy who makes money from bare-knuckle boxing, and Matt is a smart, canny London record producer. Along the way Oremland gives a colourful look at the Blackpool gay scene and the Soho-based gay/music scene of the late 1990s. Roger Daltry gives a creepy and compelling performance as a sleazy promoter. See also this skilful director's gay political thriller *Surveillance* (2007).

Longtime Companion (US, Norman Rene, 1990)
An AIDS melodrama of historical significance as an example of Hollywood's well-meaning attempt to tackle issues concerning a section of the gay community in the Western world of the 1980s. This has been criticised as simplistic, with a concentration on middle-class, white characters, but a strong message of community support and hope also comes across. For a more provocative view of aids watch the subversive gay road movie *The Living End* (US, Gregg Araki, 1992), a lively product of the new queer cinema.

Love Is The Devil (UK, John Maybury, 1998)
A film biography of Francis Bacon which looks closely at the artist's relationship with his lover and muse, George Dyer. Maybury produced some notable experimental gay video work in the 1990s such as *Remembrance of Things Past* (1993).

Luster (US, Everett Lewis, 2001)
A quirky and engagingly perverse comedy about unrequited love and finding yourself, set in downtown LA. Gently satirises manners, big-city attitudes and life in the LA Anglo queer community. The DVD includes an excellent interview with the director where he talks articulately about queer culture and independent filmmaking, plus helpful director commentary.

Ma vraie vie à Rouen (The True Story of My Life in Rouen) (France, Olivier Ducastel and Jacques Martineau, 2002)
Through audacious and skilful handling of its video diary structure, the film succeeds brilliantly in inviting the viewer to observe critically the elements of family life and heterosexuality surrounding the main character, Etienne. Skating sequences serve as a powerful symbol of growing self-confidence, and a vivid portrait of a young man's growing self-awareness is presented. See also *Presque rien* and *Drôle de Félix* for portrayals of the lives of young gay men in France.

Macho Dancer (The Pilippines, Lino Brocka, 1988)
A romantic and sensual, conventionally structured melodrama that portrays the young male central character struggling to survive financially and psychologically in Manila's gay underworld. Through his social realism and sympathy for the oppressed, the director was a leading force in the cinema of his country as well as a noted political dissident.

Madame X (Germany, Ulrike Ottinger, 1977)
An avant-garde lesbian feminist pirate adventure. Challenging viewing in its attempts to find new ways of presenting women in film, but rewarding.

Mango Souffle (India, Mahesh Dattani, 2002)
Kamlesh, a lovelorn gay man in Mumbai, throws a party to make a personal declaration to his friends, with unexpected results. Western viewers might perceive some dated stereotypes here, but in terms of Indian cinema this portrayal of gay men, and closeted men oppressed by social expectations, represents a notable thematic breakthrough.

Mandragora (Czech, Wiktor Grodecki, 1997)
'…a riveting, brutally honest portrayal of male teen prostitution' said *Variety* magazine. A fictional feature version of Grodecki's documentary on the same subject, *Body Without A Soul* (1996), which puts the subject in clear context. Neither film makes easy viewing; Grodecki is concerned to expose the exploitation happening since the opening up of the Eastern block.

Milk (US, Gus Van Sant, 2008)
This portrays the challenges and triumphs of California's first openly gay elected official, Harvey Milk, who was assassinated along with Mayor George Moscone by San Francisco Supervisor Dan White. Sean Penn gives a committed and convincing central performance, but script and filming make clear to the audience the social milieu from which Milk gained his strength and determination.

The Monkey's Mask (Australia, Samantha Lang, 2000)
A lesbian detective thriller. Jill, ex-cop and private eye, falls for Diane, a woman implicated in a murder. Makes good use of the interplay of cinematic looks through use of video evidence, and gently satirises Sydney's literary scene.

My Beautiful Laundrette (UK, Stephen Frears, 1986)
A well-made social comedy featuring a gay relationship between a white skinhead and a young Asian businessman.

Nitrate Kisses (US, Barbara Hammer, 1992)
A mixture of meditation and documentary, this richly textured film explores lesbian and gay sexuality through history, politics and poetry. Especially noteworthy for its lively portrayal of older lesbians, this is a feast for the eye and the mind.

Okoge (Japan, Takehiro Nakajima, 1992)
A social comedy of love and compromise with graphic sex scenes and a background of Tokyo gay life.

Pandora's Box (Germany, G.W. Pabst, 1928)
A beautiful and amoral femme fatale has several male lovers, but her lesbian lover proves to be the most devoted of her followers. A classic of early German cinema, and one of the first positive and sustained portrayals of a lesbian character.

Parting Glances (US, Bill Sherwood, 1986)
A beautifully made depiction of a group of people, gay and straight, in New York City. Nick, the central character played with gently compelling humour by Steve Buscemi, has AIDS, and enjoys the love and support of his friends.

Salmonberries (Germany, Percy Adlon, 1991)
A close emotional involvement between an Eskimo woman, played by kd lang, and a teacher fleeing her past. Compulsively watchable performances and locations.

She Must Be Seeing Things (US, Sheila McLaughlin, 1987)
This film touches on many uncomfortable aspects of lesbian sex, loving and looking. It does so in a stylish and articulate way. A key film in the history of lesbian representation, it provoked strong reactions among lesbian viewers; read Teresa de Lauretis (Bad Object Choices, 1991, 223).

Skin Deep (Canada, Midi Onodera, 1997)
A male actor plays a woman passing as a man. This character, a transgender loner, becomes involved with a lesbian filmmaker and her long-suffering girlfriend. Overstuffed with incident, but fascinating.

Stonewall (UK, Nigel Finch, 1996)
A passionate and tragicomic version of the historically crucial gay riot of 1969, this film deserves particular credit for the way it puts drag queens, their music and their culture at the centre of it all in a historically accurate way.

Strangers on a Train (US, Alfred Hitchcock, 1951)
Hitch's directorial skill somehow evaded the censors here to present Bruno, one of the great gay characters of classic Hollywood. His psychological prey is played by gay icon Farley Grainger. Based on the thriller by noted lesbian writer Patricia Highsmith.

Surveillance (UK, Paul Oremland, 2007)
A political thriller centred on the idea of the British establishment using all means possible to conceal the identity of a gay Royal. Oremland has the makings of a notable British gay film auteur (see *Like It Is* in this list). Again, we see directorial themes of class, family and power skilfully interwoven with sexuality. Again, a small budget has evidently been stretched to the limit. Here the power is visually rendered throughout by prying point-of-view shots of CCTV, mobile phone cams and other spying technology. Simon Callow gives an amusing performance as a cynical Royal equerry.

Victim (UK, Basil Dearden, 1961)
A landmark early work in the portrayal of gay life and its difficulties in pre-liberation London. A detective story involving a memorable performance from Dirk Bogarde as a bravely honest gay lawyer. See the essay on Bogarde as queer film star in Griffiths (2005).

Virgin Machine (Germany, Monika Treut, 1988)
A journey of lesbian self-discovery and exploration for a young German journalist in San Francisco. Wacky and provocative views of that city's lesbian scene. See the essay on Treut in Wilton (1995) which discusses this director's emphasis on transcending the label 'lesbian'.

The Watermelon Woman (US, Cheryl Dunye, 1997)
Cheryl, an aspiring filmmaker who is making a documentary about a beautiful and elusive 1930s black film actress, is coolly seduced by the beautiful Diana. Fans of Dunye should recognise her quirky and attractive style in this feature, starring Dunye herself and Guinevere Turner, which explores lesbian visibility and interracial romance.

The Wedding Banquet (Taiwan/China/US, Ang Lee, 1993)
A cross-cultural comedy full of delightful characters. A Chinese gay man living in New York with his lover puts on a show wedding to keep visiting Mum and Dad happy. Themes of honesty, coming out and selfhood.

We Were One Man (France, Philippe Valois, 1979)
A beautifully crafted love story with a bittersweet ending set in rural France during the Second World War which chronicles an affair between a wounded German pilot and a young French peasant.

When Night is Falling (Canada, Patricia Rozema, 1995)
A glossy and stylish lesbian romance with circus acts and a plot that closely echoes *Desert Hearts*. For another quirky and attractively watchable film of lesbian interest see Rozema's *I've Heard The Mermaids Singing* (1987).

Wilde (UK/US/Japan/Germany, Brian Gilbert, 1997)
At times simplistic in its account of the life and times of this great gay artist, the film offers a moving portrayal of the sexual passion that brought about Wilde's doom.

Young Soul Rebels (UK, Isaac Julien, 1991)
A gay murder is solved. In the process, two young DJs, one gay and one straight, fight racism, find romance and promote their brand of black soul music. A vivid evocation of the London club scene of the late 1970s set against the background of the Silver Jubilee, with a lively soundtrack.

RESOURCE CENTRES

Make use of search engines. For example, if you type in 'Lesbian and Gay Film' you will find that Wikipedia offers a list of lesbian, gay, bisexual or transgender-related films. It contains theatrically released cinema films that deal with or feature important gay, lesbian or bisexual or transgender characters or issues and may have same-sex romance or relationships as an important plot device.

www.bfi.org.uk
The British Film Institute website is a specialised academic site. The latest BFI publications can be ordered, and DVDs are presented according to genre or nationality.

www.jaman.com
This offers a range of films to download, own or watch free instantly online. The gay and lesbian section offers a good selection of features and some interesting lesser-known short films.

www.gaydrama.net
Helpful information and reviews of festivals and individual films. Excellent, clear, helpful databases on lesbian, gay, transgender and queer film, TV, actors, writers, producers and issues of relevance to film topics. Beware of purchasing DVDs from this site unless your player can cope with Region 1 (US) format.

www.newqueercinema.com
This US-based resource has a helpful and comprehensive list entitled 'Gay World Film Festivals', news about recent releases and a fund of information on production, availability and content of a range of queer cinema.

Chapter 13

Spectacle, stereotypes, and films of the African diaspora

Terri Francis

■ Spectacle, stereotypes, and films of the African diaspora

INTRODUCTION

diaspora
The African diaspora is the movement of people of African descent to other parts of the world; participants in the diaspora are diasporans. Struggle and resistance and the impulse to freedom inform the African diasporan memory, religion and culture. The transatlantic African diaspora began in the fifteenth century.

stereotype
Emergent in the nineteenth century, a stereotype refers to an African American persona with predictable appearances, expressing predictable thoughts and words, and embodying predictable behaviours and actions. The recurrent nature of stereotype is at the root of its predictability and adaptable nature.

This chapter introduces critical approaches to studying performance and spectacle, race and racism and cultures of cinema in the African **diaspora**, with particular emphasis on film history in the US. Yet we recognise the ways in which generations of migration and the global structure of media enterprises have always internationalised American film cultures. As early as the mid-1930s, the careers of American actors such as Paul Robeson and Josephine Baker, located in Britain and France respectively, established Europe as a pivotal international context for black American performance on film and stage. In the 1990s, when American pioneer filmmaker Oscar Micheaux's silent-era works were recovered from Spanish and Belgian archives, an oceanic imagination of black American film was reconfirmed. Our approach is interdisciplinary, furthermore, drawing upon theories of performance, the gaze, authorship, representation and identity in order to illuminate both the formal elements and social meanings of films, and all that is bound up in their spectacularity, across changing historical contexts and geographical sites. We will use close visual analysis of film texts as the basis of our discussion of the reproduction of racial ideologies on film; such patterns manifest through habitual practices of perception, spectacle and performance, thus the study of race-and-film necessarily relies upon a modified version of formalism.

While communities' and individuals' experiences of film certainly change, often profoundly so with their changing circumstances, this chapter reflects three broad underlying assumptions about the conditions of black filmmaking in the Americas, Africa and the diaspora:

- The emergence of cinema parallels formations of race, racism and ethnicity under both colonialism and American racial segregation, and implications of these relationships reverberate in the contemporary moment.
- Movies (and their makers) circulate globally, influencing and absorbing discourses of race, racism and ethnicity, while they connect with other industries of spectacle and performance such as music, television, fashion and the internet.
- Formal and informal networks of individuals and groups exchange information and technology on some level, even if access is unequal; national cinemas are always already global.

Not all images of peoples of colour produced in the commercial mainstream film industry should be presumed inherently **stereotypes**, and not all examples of early film are uniformly complicit with the subjugation of Africans, Asians, Native Americans and indigenous non-European populations. Motion pictures as a multifaceted cultural institution were, however, instrumental in generating, disseminating and romanticising the ideological aspects of European imperialism as well as America's expansionist projects and racial conflicts. If cinemas of the African diaspora are united then they might share varied ways of negotiating the following creative dilemmas, albeit in different ways: (1) film's capacity for realist verisimilitude, inaccurate distortion or surrealist abstraction; (2) cultural tensions between tradition and change within society; and (3) the hall of mirrors or, more precisely, the hall of screens where stereotyping and originality collide, blur and coalesce as they reflect one another in media. Thus, in the study of racism, race, ethnicity and spectacle, 'spectacle' means representation, performance and visual refraction in which reality is approximated and transformed on film by cinematic devices such as cinematography, acting, genre, etc. Such inquiries involve both formalist questions about how images are composed and social ones about how images make meaning in the world. Artists who engage subject matter related to the African diaspora eventually have to address the question of stereotypes and how their work is guilty or not of stereotyping people in black communities, and no amount of theorising or semantics has thus far been able to unseat this exasperating burden. What's more the trajectory of black images in cinema history spirals unsteadily towards and away from stereotypes, which themselves are in some instances concrete and therefore able to be discussed and decried while at others they strike protean, slippery forms, shifting in definition according to each viewer's perspective and experience. In scholarship as well as popular criticism, stereotypes tend to be examined as content, which makes perfect sense; but at their core, stereotypes are distractions from content and reality, which undermine creativity, containing only ready-made clichés about groups and their identities.

STEREOTYPES

Stereotypes are discursive tools that institutions, groups or individuals may intentionally or unintentionally use in ways that maintain unequal balances of power between people, and they are typically analysed in terms of a dichotomy between positive and negative representations, with preference obviously for positive images. However, this content-driven analysis can sometimes obscure the subtle processes by which stereotypes are disseminated. For stereotypes themselves, while predictable and easily recognisable in many ways, are nevertheless multisided and unstable, hence the necessity of repetition and reiteration where the types reassert their authority over our perception. Homi Bhabha views stereotypes' instability as the basis for their adaptability, writing: 'it is the force of ambivalence that gives the colonial stereotype its currency: ensures its repeatability in changing historical and discursive conjunctures' (Bhabha 1994: 64). Here Bhabha opens up counter-intuitive ways to investigate stereotypes; however, he is not suggesting that their adaptability and fluidity cancel out their concrete effects in society. Elizabeth Alexander brings attention to the relationship between spectacle and race in an article about the Rodney King videos. She writes that while race can be considered a construct: 'there is such a thing as *bottom line blackness* with regard to the violence which erases other differentiations and highlights race' (Alexander 2004: 179–80). While racial categories as well as racial expressions are **constructed** and tenuous, the effects of racism and its tools are concrete, too often experienced as physical violence or other non-discursive forms of discrimination.

Angela Nelson explains:

Nineteenth-century cultural artifacts that introduced these stereotypes include the minstrel show, novels, poetry, plays, autobiographies and memoirs, nonfiction books, advertising, magazine and newspaper articles, comic art, and sheet music. Of these cultural products, minstrel shows and the works of southern novelists, dramatists, and journalists were the most influential in the creation and reflection of public attitudes toward free and enslaved Africans.

(Nelson 2009)

Cinema became deeply embedded with such influences, limiting black representation in the movies to a disturbing cast of stereotypes, and in his study of African American cinematic stereotypes Donald Bogle enumerated the following: toms, coons, mulattos, mammies and bucks, each figure having a specific meaning, which can be transmitted quickly, based on nearly automatic recognition by audiences (1998: 3–10). As Bhabha's notion of the stereotype implies, stereotypes have been revised over time, yet they endure – they endure *because* they can be revised, while being readily recognised:

All were character types used for the same effect: to entertain by stressing Negro inferiority. Fun was poked at the American Negro by presenting him as either a nitwit or a childlike lackey. None of the

constructed
The quality of an idea being neither natural nor inevitable; having been assembled or otherwise created to appear natural or inevitable, often in the interest of a specific ideology.

racist iconography
Images that accompany
racist rhetoric or that
occur in racist contexts.

types was meant to do great harm, although at various times individual ones did [due to the ways in which such **racist iconography** formed part of a greater social scheme].

(Bogle 1998: 3)

African American cinema contains such stereotypes as well as challenges to these images made by directors, writers, actors and producers of various nationalities, races and ethnicities that aim to present people of African descent as people – with the simplicity and vast complexity of any people or any person.

Generally, a stereotype is a negative caricature that simplifies a group's identity by exaggerating a trait – be it physical or cultural. Despite the ease of recognition and simplicity that stereotypes manifest on television or in motion pictures, analysing them can benefit from a taxonomy that elucidates some of their overarching traits and notes some of the ways in which they have changed or been reinterpreted over time while remaining largely the same. For instance, the tom type is derived from Uncle Tom, the title character in Harriet Beecher Stowe's abolitionist novel *Uncle Tom's Cabin* and its many versions on stage and on film, and he is 'the first in a long line of socially acceptable Good Negro characters' (Bogle 1998: 4). Generally, Tom was derided by blacks and praised by whites as docile, religious and ever-faithful to his white owners, and thus he was seemingly capitulatory to the brutal circumstances he faced when many would rather see him model defiance. While he seems to avoid direct involvement with politics, however, he, like all black characters or stereotypes, must be analysed within a given film's particular narrative and conceptual framework before it is judged. Furthermore, Uncle Tom, while certainly a problematic figure, was hardly a fixed negative image even during the years of the Harlem Renaissance, though the trope would be increasingly contested (Lackey 2011).

Uncle Tom comes in many forms and is flanked by types that caricature children and young adults. For example, the coon, almost a comic version or relative of Uncle Tom, is both a plantation type and a stock character popular in minstrel theatre. There are a variety of coon types but generally he or she does not seem to have a care in the world, and is lazy and mischievous. Topsy was a particular brand of coon or pickaninny that was usually a girl, sometimes pictured in comic strips with large, bulging eyes, red, exaggerated lips, unkempt hair and either eating constantly or acting as food herself for animals such as alligators. Further, a common correlative of Uncle Tom is his literary relative Uncle Remus, a fictional character created by Joel Chandler Harris, who had collected and published southern African American stories under the title Uncle Remus during the late nineteenth century. Uncle is the quaint old man who dispenses traditional-style tales and folk wisdom and entertains the spectator with playing the banjo or other traditional Afro-American enter-tainment. Problematically, this figure is often depicted as naive, childlike or in the nearly exclusive company of children, and thus unthreatening, even in his wisdom. Examples include *Song of the South* and Bill Robinson's performances opposite Shirley Temple. However, this type is ambivalent enough to be challenged by clear and complex characterisation.

The character of Medouze (Douta Seck) in Euzahn Palcy's French film *Sugar Cane Alley* (1983) offers a counter-example to Uncle Tom/Uncle Remus. While Medouze is an old man with traditional ideas, initially seeming to fit the stereotype, he mobilises his age in ways that test the community's willingness to forget the old ways. Medouze is a respected elder who connects the community to their African identity through his riddles, stories and art, and fittingly he is photographed surrounded by darkness and fire, visually expressing his aura and power. A mentor and link to African traditions, Medouze is a grandfather figure for young Jose (Garry Cadenat), who is the film's protagonist and narrator. As such, the actor's portrayal of Medouze, with his resonant baritone voice and the character's significance to the story, challenges the Uncle Tom stereotype's presumed passivity.

Stereotypes exist for both genders. The tragic mulatta or mulatto is an ambitious, often sexually aggressive figure featured in a tragic narrative where his or her ambitions cannot be realised because of visible African ancestry – and society's racist response to it. This stereotype deflects the burden of racism from white people, instead casting the blame on the abstract seemingly blameless existence of racial difference, particularly the supposed stain of blackness. Acting as a point of contrast, the mammy sometimes plays opposite a mulatta or a white female star. Where the mulatta is a sign of supposed sexual transgression, i.e. sex between people of different races, and the white female star is a sexually desired object, darker-skinned mammy is usually portrayed as being asexual or not sexy – despite her abundance of body and the suggestiveness of her corpulence. She is typically a maid or live-in domestic worker, characterised, moreoover, by her selfless service toward her white employers and the absence of a personal context that might include a family, community or sexual interest of her own. At the same time, mammy demonstrates the ways in which stereotypes are sometimes determined by their position in the narrative structure rather than their explicit content, as there is nothing inherently offensive, unsexy or wrong with being a maid, unmarried or unattached, having dark skin or being overweight. Nevertheless, through stereotyping and racist and sexist ideology such characteristics are turned against the person, actor or character or an entire group of people. Put another way, when a black character is incidental to the storyline or tangential to the story's emotional centre, its role tends to be that of an objectified spectacle of alterity or being the odd Other that does not belong within the normal, standard centre. Examples of the objectified spectacle include 'the black friend', 'the gay black friend' or 'the assistant' as either comic relief or musical interlude or both. In and of themselves, spectacles of comedy, sexuality, race and musical performance are relatively benign, but they take on a complex, usually destructive aspect when they emerge within a pattern of exclusion: black characters are always comic relief; the made-up, exaggerated blackness of a character constitutes the comic relief; or black characters enter the narrative only as comic relief. Predictability and narrowness configure the understructure for stereotyped notions of blackness.

For further discussion of gender, sexism and film see Chapter 11, and for further discussion on sexuality and race see Chapter 12.

Sometimes actors can bring their own ideas and style to their roles, even if the material is stereotypical. In Hattie McDaniel's portrayal of mammy she spoke in a somewhat gruff voice (with which she would often make witty remarks). In contrast, Butterfly McQueen played her parts with a high-pitched voice, though the role was still that of a domestic worker, with costumes that tended to feature work clothes, reminiscent of plantation imagery, including a headscarf and an ankle-length conservative dress with an apron, toothy grin and popping eyes, so that costume, gesture and body shape were all consti- tutive factors in the disturbing type. The common bond between the various versions of the mammy type is that African American actresses tended to be relegated to playing this role, and they served as a convenient backdrop or counterpoint for white or lighter- skinned actors. There is room for change, however, as mammy's wit and relative control over many household affairs generate a fruitful ambivalence which may allow viewers to interpret her as an empowered female character instead of an entirely denigrating stereotype.

Returning to male stereotypes, the brutal buck cliché involved a cool, macho, sometimes overly sexualised and intimidating figure. The paradigmatic example of this type is Gus the Renegade, a 'black' character played by a white actor in blackface, in *Birth of a Nation* (1915). African American filmmaker Melvin Van Peebles reprises and revises the buck in the independent production *Sweet Sweetback's Baadasssss Song* (1971), where the protagonist is a hustler turned folk hero and a sexist icon, a figure subsequently co-opted by Hollywood in the 1970s blaxploitation films. In the *Shaft* cycle of films, for instance, buck is meant to be rather apolitical, appealingly cool and intimi- dating while he is sexualised in ways that have become availabe for parody in rap music, some forty years later. Shaft is a playboy and private eye, but *Birth of A Nation*'s Gus evokes a particular view of black politics. Gus is the instinctual black male renegade type who fights for his people's freedom yet 'wants to marry a white woman', as the film's intertitles declare, and thus this stereotype is a powerful symbol of white fears about black participation in American democracy and its social implications. It exemplifies the manner in which stereotypes are mobilised in power struggles; the fact that Gus is played by a white actor in blackface underscores the way in which such stereotypes emerge from a racist unconscious rather than being assessments or expressions of the real characteristics of African Americans.

Stereotypes are used in a negative sense usually but, in rare cases, a group might attempt to capitalise on its ambivalences in order to appropriate and redefine the negative images about their group through irony. The ironic or satirical use of stereotypes or racist language occurs in a variety of spectacles and often generates controversy when members of certain audiences, intended and not, do not get the joke. For instance, protests met the 2010 production of the *Scottsboro Boys* in New York City because the play employed blackface and minstrel comedy in their rendering of the 1931 trial in which nine African American boys were falsely accused of rape. Hip-hop musicians and many comedians have sought to redeploy the N-word in a variety of ways while some cultural figures such as Paul Mooney have vowed to omit the offensive word from their performances all together. In *Do the Right Thing*, which I will discuss in greater detail below, racialised insults are used in exaggerated, highly performative ways for the purpose of exposing racial tensions among the film's characters and in the film's spectators. Stereotypes often seem totalising in their insults but they are complicated and contradictory enough to be challenged and perhaps dismantled by their supposed victims, though not without negotiating an unwieldy media environment in which all expression seems to be instant spectacle, exposed and circulated through channels where intention can easily slip beyond authorial control.

Racist imagery emerges therefore as the result of interlocking forces of politics and aesthetics in ways that are not entirely predictable. And people of African descent have been vulnerable to the problems of the black image on film. Ed Guerrero reminds us, however:

the ideology of racial domination and difference can never be permanently fixed in place as a complete or static 'thing.' Instead, it is a dynamic, shifting 'relation' defined and conditioned by social struggle, the demands of the historical moment, and the material imperative of an industry that privileges economics and short-term profit before all other human, aesthetic, or philosophic possibilities or concerns.

(Guerrero 1993: 2–5)

Finally, while stereotypes have been framed and confronted in various ways over time through a combined, synthesised set of efforts and issues such as protests by community groups, they have also been censured less directly through seemingly individual (often isolated) and unrelated acts of artistry by a changing cast of filmmakers, actors, writers and other creatives, each with a mission to define and redefine African American cinema on hopefully ever-more progressive and humanistic terms beyond stereotypes.

GENRE

Historian Thomas Cripps addresses the definition of black film when he writes:

'black film' may be defined as those motion pictures made for theater distribution that have a black producer, director, and writer, or black performers; that speak to black audiences or, incidentally, to white audiences possessed of preternatural curiosity, attentiveness, or sensibility toward racial matters; and that emerge from self-conscious intentions, whether artistic or political, to illuminate the Afro-American experience. In the latter part of this century, this definition might be expanded to include major motion pictures and other projects made for television, as well as films that, despite foreign origins in, say, Africa, speak to Afro-American concerns.

(Cripps 1978: 357)

Cripps goes on to concede, however, that very few films would meet these narrow criteria, with the notable exception of Eloyce King Patrick Gist's early films: her evangelical black-cast dramas, such as *Hell Bound Train*, were written, directed and produced by herself and her husband Paul and shown primarily, if not exclusively, to African American church audiences during the Harlem Renaissance era. These films were not made for theatrical distribution, as the Gists showed them in churches, yet they are otherwise bona fide black films. Cripps's definition is a meta-critical exercise in which he establishes a definition of black film in order to dismiss it as an attractive but ultimately unhelpful way of thinking about the relationship between film and African Americans. African Americans are not officially a nation and, from a diasporic perspective, they display significant differences among each other based on class, language, politics and other points. Nevertheless, despite the fact that black film cannot simply be described as national, it often figures in nationalist discussions of black aesthetics and is seen as a primary site of African American self-definition and expression.

Certain shared experiences such as violence and discrimination or milestones such as President Barack Obama's inauguration can create the sense of a coherent or 'bottom-line', if tenuous, community. Such broad references could unite a small group of films across intra-cultural differences. Thus it might be helpful to think of African American cinema as a genre that contains other genres: documentary, fiction and experimental films that may be directed, produced and/or performed by black people. Such films may speak to African American historical issues or social concerns, or they may represent the community's rituals, cultural artefacts or significant spaces and landmarks. Black films are not necessarily defined by financing as they may be independently produced through grants or individuals as well as by Hollywood or small production companies based in the US or abroad. They may be seen in museums, libraries, multiplexes and arts events. Perhaps because of black film's ever-expanding diversity, with regard to production, distribution and exhibition, the will to define and redefine black cinema as its own genre persists.

The question of genre remains relevant, even if it rests awkwardly on the related, fraught question of African American identity. Much of the criticism of black film turns on the issue of how a given film represents black people. For without a doubt, how critics, artists and other audiences respond to black film involves anxieties of performance, fears of exposure and traumas of misrepresentation and misdefinition in a hostile if overall well-meaning contemporary society, which many folks unhelpfully rush to repress. In this paradigm, the problematic of black film is resolved (or repressed) through the display of or advocacy for positive black representation, which can, it is hoped, correct or at least displace patterns of stereotyping. However, putting a movie's content and public image aside for the moment, I emphasise that it is in the underlying grammars of display, spectacle and performance that we are most likely to find the means for authors and audiences to articulate what is desired from the cinema, because it is a media of spectacle and performance. Form over content enable us to envision pathways to get beyond, perhaps laughing our way out of, this troublesome history and wearying relationship between racism and film.

It remains to be seen how the question of genre can be brought to bear on the earliest images of African Americans, conceived as they were in a climate of racial segregation and violence. Bracketing their obvious chronological position, do they belong in the genre or canon of African American film, particularly in such a determinative position as at the beginning? Historically, African Americans have appeared in a variety of film types, including dance films, newsreels and comedies. Some of these and other early images

For further discussion of genre see Chapters 8 and 9.

For further discussion of the film industry, both mainstream and independent see Chapter 1.

of African Americans may portray black Americans through what may be described as southern plantation imagery while many others may draw on other themes. For instance, *The Pickaninnies* (1894) features a group of professional dancers named Lucy Daly's Pickaninnies in what is described in the F.Z. Maguire & Co. catalogue of March 1898 as 'A scene representing Southern plantation life before the war. A jig and a breakdown by three colored boys.'[1] Other titles include *The Watermelon Contest* (1896), *A Morning Bath* (1896), *Cake Walk* (1897), *Comedy Cake Walk* (1897), *Dancing Darkey Boy* (1897), *Who Said Chicken?* (1900) and finally *Native Women Washing Clothes at St. Vincent, B.W.I.* (1903). This last one, *Native Woman*, which consists of newsreel footage shot in the West Indies, departs from southern plantation imagery and related stereotypes (i.e. eating watermelons, stealing chickens, etc.) due to its content, but it presents a different set of issues by displaying an anthropological and voyeuristic view of several bare-breasted women washing clothes in a river. A second example, *A Nigger in a Woodpile* (1904), according to the Black Film Center/Archive's catalogue, features white actors in blackface. In a film that is in many ways about blackness-as-transgression, or perhaps as a fugitive, insurgent presence, the black image here does not apparently require actual African Americans.[2] Jacqueline Stewart provides a rich discussion of this film in her introduction to *Migrating to the Movies: Cinema and Black Urban Modernity*, and her analysis enables us to envision the fragility of the black image problem and its intimate links to both African Americans' self-perception and how they are viewed in society.

AFRICAN AMERICAN FILM HISTORY

The history of African diaspora cinema in the US may be roughly divided into four sections: (1) silent-era films and silent-era race films (1897–1928); (2) soundies, race films, Hollywood melodrama on racial identity and racism, including passing films (1929–45); (3) postwar social problem films (1945–60); and (4) contemporary films after 1960, which consists of **blaxploitation** (1970–74), black independent film from the 1970s, such as those works associated with UCLA (Haile Gerima's *Bush Mama* and Charles Burnett's *Killer of Sheep*), Black British collectives, queer film, American urban coming-of-age dramas of the 1990s, women's filmmaking, experimental films, narrative feature films, documentaries and their intersections. The high-profile productions of Spike Lee, Lee Daniels and Tyler Perry indicate a changed film marketplace, as many 'black' films can now be considered to have something of a wide appeal in the mainstream. Perry, in particular, has built a core audience of church-going African American women through first creating evangelical stage plays, which he then adapts for DVD and theatrical cinema. The film industry remains difficult to negotiate, however, for directors such as Julie Dash, Kasi Lemmons and the late Marlon Riggs, who worked to establish modern black cinema with their own landmark films but remain practically unknown to the majority of moviegoers of any demographic.

   After the relatively quiet period that followed blaxploitation, the media publicity and scholarly attention given to Lee's 1986 film *She's Gotta Have It* created new excitement around the idea of a black independent film movement and generated wide interest in African American and black British film among scholars, artists and independent critics that extended into the 1990s. For instance, David Nicholson had founded the *Black Film Review* in the mid-1980s initially as a critique of black images in Hollywood film. However, writing in 1989, he said, 'in the four years since its founding, the focus of *Black Film Review* has changed. While *BFR* continues to report on aspects of Hollywood film, it now covers independent film from throughout the African Diaspora' (Martin 1995: 442). This shift in perspective reflects increased film production in the Caribbean, Africa, Europe and the Americas during the 1980s and the way the film community's concerns expanded to include a greater understanding of how people of African descent imagined their worlds cinematically as well as how they were viewed by mainstream media.

blaxploitation
Movie studios' exploitation of what they believed were black urban audiences' tastes in film; beginning with Melvin Van Peebles's *Sweet Sweetback's Baadasssss Song*, concerned the years 1970 to 1974 in the USA; usually black-cast action films.

Many of the studies cited in this chapter were published in the early to mid-1990s and they were fuelled in part by Lee's success in consistently writing, directing and producing his own films, particularly during that fruitful mini-era. In many ways even early black films are as much products of the 1990s as they are of the 1920s and 1930s, because, in the 1990s, or even now, the restored films would be viewed alongside contemporary films. Thus, audiences allow them meanings specific to two distinct contexts: a historical one and a contemporary one. Prime examples are the recoveries of 35mm prints of Oscar Micheaux's *Within Our Gates*, which was found in Filmoteca Espanola in Madrid, Spain, and underwent inter-title restoration in 1993 by the Library of Congress and *Symbol of the Unconquered*, which was found in Cinémathèque Royale in Brussels and restored in 1998 by Turner Classic Movies. These silent-era **race films** re-emerged in the 1990s to reclaim their place in silent-era film history, surely galvanised by Lee's success and linked to collective curiosity about the black cinematic past. Race films were part of the 1990s film scene.

The years 1900 to 1930 saw brief but significant pioneering efforts by African American artists and businessmen to create a black independent film movement in the US. William Foster, who founded Foster Photoplay in 1912, was the first such entrepre-neurial adventurer. Based in Chicago, Foster specialised in black-cast comedy shorts, such as *The Railroad Porter* (1912) and *The Fall Guy* (1913). Mark Reid notes that these films showed that 'black characters can not only be porters for whites but also waiters in respectable black cafés in middle-class African-American communities' (Reid 1993: 8). In other words, Foster placed would-be stereotypical black characters in a broader social context, which resulted in a somewhat more varied portrayal of the community as a whole. Shortly after Foster set up his company, Hollywood actor Noble Johnson founded the Lincoln Motion Picture Company in Los Angeles in 1916. Lincoln specialised in family-orientated, uplifting movies: *The Realization of a Negro's Ambition* (1916) and *The Trooper of Company K* (1916) are two examples, the titles of which suggest their positive themes and which focus on exceptional figures and group ideals.

Although race films were primarily aimed at segregated African American audiences, they were occasionally products of an integrated enterprise. For instance, the Ebony Film Corporation was a white-dominated company that made black-cast comedy shorts from 1915 to 1919. Perhaps owing to the comedy, their product was not considered strictly race film and they were criticised in the black press for stereotyping. Between 1920 and 1928, several black-cast feature films were produced at Norman Studios in Arlington, Florida. Another example is the Colored Players' Film Corporation, which was a white film company that made black-cast dramas and comedies, including *Ten Nights in a Barroom* (1926) starring Lawrence Chenault and Charles Gilpin, who was a renowned stage actor. Film and theatre were productively linked. The Lafayette Players' Dramatic Stock Company. This was a leading African American theatrical repertory company of the 1920s, which grew out of the Anita Bush Stock Company (founded in 1915). The company premiered in Lincoln Theater in Harlem and, when it moved to rival Lafayette, became known as the Lafayette Players. They explicitly aimed to present serious drama in direct opposition to minstrel comedy types, and many early members of the company such as Chenault appeared in films, bringing with them theatrical expertise as well as a cultural mission to redefine black images.

Micheaux was the most prolific and most profoundly maverick of the race film directors of the early twentieth century. His directing credits number thirty-eight films, the vast majority of which he wrote and produced between 1919 and 1948. Beginning as a writer, Micheaux published fiction such as *The Conquest* and *The Homesteader: A Novel* based on his own life experiences as a farmer in South Dakota. Remarkably, Micheaux sold his books door to door and he was successful enough to expand his business to include motion pictures; thus the book company became the Oscar Micheaux Book and Film Company in 1918. Although Micheaux founded his company on direct sales to his customers, he developed a multi-regional organisation which stood on a core

race films
Black-cast movies that were made for segregated African American audiences before 1950, most often by an African American director. In early twentieth-century parlance, the 'race' in terms like race film, race music or race woman indicates pride and affirmation. For example, a race woman is a woman who is proud of her race and does good works on behalf of African Americans.

of officers that included Swan Micheaux, secretary-treasurer, Charles Benson, who handled booking for Chicago-based distribution, Tiffany Oliver and W.R. Crowell, who operated the Roanoke, Virginia office and O.A. Adams, who managed the southwest region. Furthermore, Micheaux brought this direct approach to his films' distribution as well, often cutting and re-cutting his films, according to the dictates of censor boards, while he travelled between venues with the reels in hand.

Despite the passionate entrepreneurial spirit and professionalism race film companies and their founders possessed, several forces worked against their long-term success. In the late 1920s, the Great Depression and the high cost of sound equipment dispro-portionately affected already financially vulnerable African American companies that had been valiantly operating under segregation policies which threatened their liveli-hoods and their very lives. Among the most detrimental cultural factors, however, was perhaps the inevitable departure of actors and other creative talent for Hollywood. For instance, Evelyn Preer, who starred consistently in Micheaux's films, went to Hollywood, where she appeared in relatively minor roles, including that of a maid named Viola in *Blonde Venus* in 1932. Most notably, though, Paul Robeson debuted in the dual role of the Reverend Isaiah T. Jenkins and his brother Sylvester in Micheaux's *Body and Soul* (1925) before going on to appear in many mainstream films internationally; James Whale's *Showboat* (1936), Dudley Murphy's *The Emperor Jones* (1933) and Kenneth MacPherson's *Borderline* (1930) are examples. Although Josephine Baker did not appear in race films, she was well known as a live performer in New York City before migrating to Paris in the 1920s. There, Baker starred in four French productions beginning with *Siren of the Tropics* (Henri Étiévant, 1927).[3] Further, in the US and doubtless in Europe, film studios sought to feature new sound technology by capitalising on the novelty of black voices and performance styles in the movies, which opened up opportunities for African American entertainers and actors in mainstream productions.

In the 1930s, African American actors appeared in a few breakthrough prominent roles in relatively prestigious films. Louise Beavers and Fredi Washington played mother and daughter in the Oscar-nominated *Imitation of Life* (1934); Baker starred in the French productions *Zou Zou* (1934) and *Princess Tam Tam* (1935); Robeson starred in *Sanders of the River* (1935), which is set in Nigeria; Rex Ingram portrayed De Lawd in *The Green Pastures* (1936); and Hattie McDaniel won an Oscar for Best Actress in a Supporting Role for her work in *Gone with the Wind* (1939). McDaniel was the first African American to be nominated for and win an Oscar.

Micheaux and actor-writer-director Spencer Williams were productive filmmakers in the 1930s and 1940s. Williams, whose work has been rediscovered in the last decade or so, is perhaps best known for his acting on the *Amos and Andy* television show, but he also wrote and directed a number of feature films including two religious art films, *The Blood of Jesus* (1941) and *Go Down Death* (1944), which is based on James Weldon Johnson's poem. The 1940s were, however, characterised by the success of several black-cast commercial musicals such as *Cabin in the Sky* (1943) and *Stormy Weather* (1943). Meanwhile, a number of films tackled the issues of racial identity and racism in the US. Such 'social problem films' of the postwar period include *The Quiet One* (1948), *Home of the Brave* (1949), *Lost Boundaries* (1949), *Pinky* (1949) and *Intruder in the Dust* (1949). Departing from stereotype, these liberal-minded films of the civil rights movement's early years concerned racial tensions, as the black presence on film was now politicised more sympathetically in Hollywood.

The 1950s saw the rise of an African American star system in Hollywood, featuring actors such as Sidney Poitier, Dorothy Dandridge, Sammy Davis Jr., and Harry Belafonte. Yet while they worked together occasionally, each established distinct Hollywood careers and star personas. In particular, Poitier's career emerged in the 1950s and soared in the 1960s, the man and his image both becoming symbols and vehicles of the studios' complex response to shifts in American race relations as well as to transform-ative legislation such as the 1964 Civil Rights Act, which outlawed segregation among other forms of discrimination. Poitier has been criticised for playing on-screen characters which, while they seemed a radical departure from early stereotypes, appeared problematically non-confrontational or not confrontational enough on the issue of racism to some viewers and critics. In other words, folks have called him an Uncle Tom. Moreover, although he appeared in at least two films about interracial romance such as *Patch of Blue* (1965) and *Guess Who's Coming to Dinner* (1967), the relative a-sexuality that characterised these roles may have felt unsatisfying to audiences who sought a fuller, more romantic representation of black masculinity. On the other hand, Poitier's cool, reserved demeanour, intelligence and charm, brought to both his screen roles and his off-screen public activities, made him a matinee idol and a respected cultural figure. *In the Heat of the Night* and *To Sir, With Love*, both released in 1967, solidified his image as a dignified actor and a positive role model in scenarios of racial conflict. Poitier became the first African American to win an Academy Award for Best Actor, for his portrayal of an itinerant handyman in *Lilies of the Field* (1963) and, nearly fifty years later, in recognition of his work as an artist and humanitarian, on 12 August 2009, President Obama awarded Poitier the Presidential Medal of Freedom, the US's highest civilian honour.

Poitier's stardom gained him box-office power and thus a certain liberty within Hollywood, which he leveraged to direct his own films. These 1970s works include the action/comedy/buddy films in which he co-starred with another box office draw Bill Cosby: *Let's Do It Again* (1975) and *A Piece of the Action* (1977). He wrote, directed and co-starred opposite jazz musician Abbey Lincoln in *For the Love of Ivy* (1968), followed by another romance film, *A Warm December* (1973), with Jamaican actress Esther Anderson. In the films that he directed, Poitier maintained his dignified persona while going beyond what many consider to be the limitations of his previous typecasting. Furthermore, these films, plus his western migration narrative *Buck and the Preacher* (1972) (with Harry Belafonte) comprise a layer of 1970s black cinema that drew upon blaxploitation's tropes, especially costume and setting, but stood apart in terms of how they sought to represent African Americans through fun but respectable images. Generally though, black cinema faded from national attention in the late 1970s and early 1980s, although Haile Gerima, Charles Burnett and Michael Schultz produced significant works during this period. Burnett's films for instance would go through a period of obscurity until his 1977 *Killer of Sheep* re-emerged in 2007 after its restoration by the UCLA Film and Television Archive with distribution by Milestone Films.

The popularity of 1990s urban dramas (i.e. *Boyz in the Hood* (1991) and *Menace II Society* (1993)) and controversy over the perceived authenticity of their stories, returned African American film aesthetics and the politics of race, racism and spectacle to the attention of movie audiences. Dash's 1991 *Daughters of the Dust* helped to define the era because it departed from the masculinist and urban-centred trends in other black-authored films. Narrated by an unborn child, *Daughters* is set in the Sea Islands in the year 1903 and tells the interrelated stories of three generations of women. Dash commemorated her process of bringing this film to the screen with the publication of *Daughters of the Dust: The Making of an African American Woman's Film*, which includes essays, recipes and other documents relevant to the production. The book actually extends the film experience with the subtitle resonating on two levels. It refers first to Dash as the African American woman but further suggests a genre or type of film that is addressed to or otherwise concerned with African American womanhood. *Daughters'* themes of family, womanhood and the significance of place are shared by many African American women novelists, such as Toni Cade Bambara and Alice Walker. At the same time, Dash's film would be considered an art film in any context due to its non-conventional narrative style and lyrical cinematography.

Recent art or independent films by white directors and writers that feature a black protagonist or focus on African American cultures, experiences and related issues constitute an influential current within the loosely constructed black film genre. Two examples are *Ghost Dog: The Way of the Samurai* (Jim Jarmusch, 1999) and *George

For a selected list of films directed by Haile Gerima, Charles Burnett and Michael Schultz see Further Viewing on p. 357.

Washington (David Gordon Green, 2000). They build indirectly on earlier examples: *Shadows* (John Cassevetes, 1961) and *The Cool World* (Shirley Clarke, 1963) offer two significant precedents or even models of liberal-minded, yet unglamorous and quirky representations of African Americans.

Nothing But a Man (Michael Roemer, 1964) is a prime example of the understated yet emotionally resonant black art film and its potential shortcomings. Though documentary-like in style and set in the American south, *Nothing* can be both celebrated and criticised for not depicting well-known racial clashes in a spectacular way. Instead Roemer and co-writer Robert Young chose to portray their characters' internal conflicts as they are brought on by small-town civil rights struggles between co-workers and neighbours. The story concerns the courtship and marriage of Duff (Ivan Dixon) and Josie (Abbey Lincoln), centring on Duff's struggle with himself, under economic and political pressures: when he decides to leave the relative camaraderie and financial independence of the railroad crew, marrying and taking up residence in an unnamed town outside Birmingham, Duff finds that his efforts to make a life for himself and his family put him in the middle of power struggles that involve conflicts between black men with different political values who are additionally in different positions of power, amidst strife within families and eventually also wedged into competition between blacks and whites. Thus the film does not include straightforward representation of historical events or elements of the civil rights movement, such as marches or Colored/Whites Only water fountains, in the way that, for instance *The Autobiography of Miss Jane Pittman* (1974) or other made-for-television or Hollywood dramas might do. Through its narrative and characters, the film nevertheless responds to these events by exploring how they manifest in the everyday lives of a couple in a small town.

ETHNICITY, RACE, AND CINEMA

While the increasing availability of technology and capital internationally today has resulted in many more movie-making countries, the four major producers of cinema in the late nineteenth century were also imperial powers – Britain, France, Germany and the US. In the US, for instance, the zenith of international cinema's origins, which itself paralleled the expansion of colonialism, coincided with the nadir of the post-emancipation era. On 23 April 1896 in New York, Thomas Edison demonstrated new technology for motion pictures: the projected film that could be viewed by a mass audience. Less than a month later in Washington DC, on 18 May 1896, the Supreme Court established the separate-but-equal doctrine through their decision on the *Plessy* vs *Ferguson* case. 'Of all the celebrated "coincidences" – of the twin beginnings of cinema and psychoanalysis, cinema and nationalism, cinema and consumerism – it is this coincidence with the heights of imperialism that has been least explored' (Shohat and Stam 1994: 100).

For further discussion of early cinema see Chapters 1 and 5.

Although a mass cinema audience ideally implies unity, equal access and shared experience, the *Plessy* decision unequivocally excluded black citizens from exercising such public values because it undergirded policies that legalised and licensed African Americans' marginalisation within mainstream society, affecting all aspects of their labour and leisure experiences as well as sanctioning politically and economically motivated terrorism against them. As cinema quickly became the world's storyteller in the late nineteenth and early twentieth centuries, filmmakers and producers drew screen caricatures of African Americans from vaudeville, blackface minstrel theatre and literature, reflecting the worsening times with evermore dehumanising racist imagery. Movies seemed to absorb caricatures of blacks and other people of colour including Native Americans, Africans and Asians, as well as plots that celebrated conquest and exoticised (or denigrated) racial difference from popular colonialist fiction, travel writing and ethnographic explorations. Such stories aligned the cinematic gaze with an imperialist one.

'Early American films depended unthinkingly on theatrical precursors, propagating racial caricature borrowed from the popular vaudeville and minstrel shows' (Snead 1988: 16). Furthermore, the cinema 'was ideally suited to relay the projected narratives of nations and empires' (Shohat and Stam 1994: 101) because of the way that its audience functioned as a kind of imagined community for white and select other non-white ethnicities (Anderson 1983: 41–64). Like the newspaper, which Benedict Anderson argues created a collective consciousness among disparate individuals, the movies provided members of an audience with common experiences. Projected cinematic narratives of heroes building nations and subduing so-called natives helped to suture audiences into an imperialist, racist gaze.

Capturing the complexity of this period, James Snead writes that it remains:

one of the bitter ironies of American history, then, that motion picture technology, with its singular potential for good or evil, grew to perfection during the same time period (1890–1915) that saw the systematic, determined, almost hysterical persecution and defamation of blacks and other minority groups.

(Snead 1988: 16)

Early motion pictures, which borrowed aesthetic codes from literature and vaudeville, presented images of blackness, whose cruelty increased with the evidently threatening rise of ambitious black politically astute communities now residing in what were previously mostly white or all-white urban environments, for

the rise of the cinema as the predominant American entertainment during the first decades of the twentieth century coincided with the migration of hundreds of thousands of African Americans from their 'traditional' homes in the South to increased social and economic opportunities in northern cities.

(Stewart 2005: 2)

The Great Migration in turn transformed American cultural institutions including the cinema, and as greater numbers of blacks came into perceived competition with whites for resources, cities became both spaces of oppression and of potential avenues for better education and economic advancement for the migrants. Popular culture provided further possibilities for self-creation and recreation on the one hand or insult and social alienation on the other. These travellers were often spurred by violence in their hometowns and were met by violence at their destination. Such violence against African Americans spurred the Great Migration, whose trajectories from rural areas to cities and from the south to the north are collectively known as 'the largest movement of Black bodies since slavery' (Gates 1993: 17).

Black or African American identities are neither fixed nor essential, for they are continually reshaped by internal tensions and contradictions as well as by external pressures such as migration. Audiences counter stereotypes when they approach African American cinema without expectation, but with a sense of history. What Stewart calls the 'variability of a Black "public" and the unpredictability of Black "experience"' are thus foundational concepts in this discussion of African American cinema, notwithstanding, I would add, our necessary reliance at times on general notions of stereotypes, race and racism or the broad outlines of historical change (Stewart 2005: 13). On the one hand, the basic idea that racism consists of negative views of one group on the part of another group or between individuals is adequate, while on the other, it is necessary to grasp the underlying dynamics of unequal power between groups and how they change over time without relying on a pre-existing and essential black positive subject.

WHITENESS

Hollywood or other dominant cinemas including 'indie' films normalise whiteness while subordinating other ethnic groups to roles that make a spectacle of them relative to whiteness. Conventional stereotypes play a role but whiteness is constructed as normal and even superior relative to blackness and other 'ethnic' identities. The study of whiteness elaborated in part by Richard Dyer has begun to lay bare this rarely acknowledged identity so that we can observe its inner workings, and we note that whiteness operates differently from other cultural or racial stereotypes. While stereotypes of non-white characters tend to be limited to one exaggerated characteristic, 'white people in their whiteness, however, are imaged as individual and/or endlessly diverse, complex and changing' (Dyer 1997: 12). The privilege and power of whiteness, whatever its context, is its presumed neutrality. Since whiteness is seen as neutral its pervasive power to define and control culture is invisible. Thus audiences rarely realise the patented ideological structures of their entertainment.

Certain forms of whiteness can be considered as an Other, even within the whiteness continuum, however, and an Othered or oddball white person is usually described as 'a character' because he or she challenges the norm. Typically, the white Other to normative whiteness might have any of the following traits: close to nature, wears colours other than black, white or beige, has a pronounced ethnicity, physical oddity, may be emotional, unemployed, elderly or artistic, but its ultimate purpose is to stand in contrast to the normative office-and-nuclear-family suburban-lifestyle-orientated average white guy precisely to make him appear more normal, no matter how neurotic and bizarre he might be. And whiteness is elastic in this regard: *Seinfeld* is a prime example of the interactions of Othered and normative whitenesses that can shift and exchange places. In mainstream television sitcoms or films, the Other is employed usually for comic effect when they burst into the inevitable living room of average white guy and family's house. For example *Modern Family* features a quirky but traditional mainstream family surrounded by alternates or Others. Such liberal-minded diversity ultimately reinforces the authority of the average white suburban family at the show's centre through devices such as screen time and narrative structure. Further, whites associated with certain regions of the US such as Alaska or Appalachia or with certain types of work such as mining, ranching or factory labour might be put in opposition to suburban office workers, urbanites or liberal-minded aesthetes who are supposedly fish out of water in such environments. However the US version of *The Office*, a parody documentary of everyday office life, shows suburban office workers as Others on a continuum from Michael Scott (Steve Carrell) to the other oddball employees but in some ways centred on relatively normal Pam and Jim Halpert (Jenna Fischer and John Krasinski). Urbanites and liberal-minded aesthetes can also be Othered to normative whiteness depending on the target audience of the show. A reality show like *What Not to Wear* sometimes seems to mock both the inept client and the expert hosts, but ultimately the show is about normalising all of our sartorial choices in ways that are meant to seem individual. The divorcée, perpetual bachelor, gay best friend, gay hairdresser or gay decorator are stereotypes or figures of 'alternative' humanity who are used in many television programmes and mainstream films, such as *Sex and the City* or *Father of the Bride*, for comic relief and/or as a sign of liberal whiteness (liberals often include the Other with a smile). In any event, these Others work to displace anxieties, primarily held by straight white professional men 'at the head' of nuclear families and those who identify with them, about class status, sexual identity, body image, sense of control, rightness and belonging and how to manage feelings of inadequacy, self-hate and boredom. However, the white character(s) in a film presume(s) to speak not for any particular group but for all of humanity or for themselves as an individual, i.e. 'I'm just an average guy.' Whiteness is universal. White privilege manifests, furthermore, as professed innocence when a white character interacts with non-white others and in the casual sense of belonging and ownership with which they gaze at their cinematic world, presuming authority, superiority, and objectivity, as seen in the preferred vantage point of westerns as well as imperial action films. Figures of cinematic whiteness rely upon an Other or a group of Others in an unequal power relation, perhaps to witness or corroborate their feeling of domination and normalcy.

Melodramatic historical films can wield the universal white gaze as well. Christopher Harris's experimental film *Reckless Eyeballing* (2004) combines clips from one such, *Birth of a Nation*, and from the blaxploitation movie *Foxy Brown* (1974) in an associative essay film in which he dismantles eye-line matches in the famous chase sequence between Gus and young Flora Cameron, critically playing with who looks at whom. By re-editing this pivotal sequence, Harris disrupts continuity in a film celebrated for its epic continuity while he critiques the white gaze.

• **Plate 13.2**
Reckless Eyeballing (Christopher Harris, 2004). Non-narrative and formalistic, this film features re-photographed images of Angela Davis's *Wanted* posters, and excerpts from a *Foxy Brown* trailer (Jack Hill, 1974) and *Birth of a Nation* (D.W. Griffith, 1915). Harris used solarisation to manipulate the light-sensitive emulsion of high-contrast black and white film stock. This process causes black tones to become white and the reverse; the tonalities shift back and forth continuously

As seen in the illustration, Harris uses re-photographed high-contrast black and white imagery. This technique foregrounds his concern with the aesthetics and technologies of light and darkness, enabling viewers to imagine how the colours black and white are mapped ideologically onto white people and the dark skin colour associated with African Americans. When Harris switches between the positive and negative versions of the same image, he deconstructs or at least demystifies both the ideological and visual pull of whiteness. 'White' characters switch to black, and black characters become white. This technique underscores the reality that white people are not actually white and black people are not actually black in colour, for these are constructed identities and perceptions. In *Reckless Eyeballing*, whiteness is denaturalised or deconstructed as Harris reduces it to its technological elements. In Harris's film, blackness is both a bottom-line reality and an independent aesthetic or ideological force. With each shot, *Reckless Eyeballing* searches for the roots of such aesthetic and political phenomena in cinema's visual grammar while simultaneously experimenting with the means for a potentially new film language of race-and-gender, identity and spectacle.

The term 'reckless eyeballing' refers to the Jim Crow-era practice of criminalising black men's gazes, which meant that a black man could be lynched for looking at or being *perceived* as looking at a white woman in a way that any white man felt was inappropriate. This system of the white male gaze under Jim Crow is the ultimate in privileged vision because in it a white man's perception of a situation determines the value of another man's life while policing white women at the same time. Black women had indirect roles in this sociopathic psychodrama but were also clearly affected by it when their sons, husbands, fathers and brothers were murdered and they were left. The murder of the child Emmett Till for 'reckless eyeballing' radicalised his mother Mrs Mamie Till Bradley, and her insistence on an open casket and allowing *Jet* magazine to publish photographs of the body served to catalyse the modern Civil Rights movement.

RACISM

Racism classifies human beings into distinct and differentially valued racial groups, which are assumed to indicate intelligence, moral character, work habits and skills, and cultural attitudes and preferences for each or most individuals within a particular group. These characteristics are assumed to be hereditary, not merely the result of upbringing or opportunity. Racial classification, mostly on the basis of skin color, has often been relied upon to limit individuals to specific occupations, residential areas, and levels of education, to confine marriages within assumed racial categories, to deny certain people full participation as citizens, or even to define some humans as nonhuman.

(Rosenberg 2009)

In mainstream commercial film, racism manifests, if it does, primarily in the construction of a privileged white gaze at the expense of other characters' points of view. The privilege of this gaze depends upon its presumed neutrality and transparency while the camera, or the film's universal eye and/or the filmmaker's eye, is aligned with the white hero or heroine's perspective.

A taxonomy of cinematic stereotypes, as offered earlier in this chapter, emphasises how disturbing images of colonised and otherwise subjugated people of colour have been and continue to be constructed in both overt and insidious ways. Yet as the case studies in this chapter demonstrate, the current media spectacle landscape involves layered influences from film, television, music, fashion, the internet and studies of culture which have implications for how we understand viewership and authorship, and even shape our concept of what counts as authentic characters.

African American film is less like a product with clear representational content and more like a complicated hall of screens in which images from various reflective surfaces bounce off one another only to be recast and refracted. Audiences and filmmakers negotiate blurry, fragmented concepts of representation and identity, while under-standably seeking pleasures of artistic expression and of leisurely movie consumption, but, problematically, they do so within an industry and cultural context too often marred by racism, general contempt for challenging ideas and non-capitalist values, and unequal access to financing and creative control. Fundamental performance, a person's essential ability to act and attract, emerges out of this morass as a space of both stereotype and originality (i.e. authenticity) for African American actors. Music, for instance, is an especially vulnerable area where black folk's relationship to musical performance and spectacle is exalted on the one hand (ah, the genius they do) and denigrated on the other (oh that's all they can do). However, a hallmark of black screen performance has been the capacity of actors to create depth and humanity within flat stereotypes or to find expressive routes beyond the limitations of the commercial film industry.

SPECTACLE

Current African American film scholarship tends to be concerned with black performance and spectacle in three main areas: representation, the star system and black directors in Hollywood. Occasionally scholars attend to the possibilities of black independent cinema, including documentaries, avant-garde short and feature films, archival footage and historical films as a separate and perhaps minor concern. Yet any neat division between commercial narrative cinema and the indies turns out to be more complex than it might appear initially. Generally speaking, independent or 'indie' film productions are typically those made without financing from a major studio, such as Paramount or Walt Disney, but they might also include films that are independently financed while distributed by a major studio. Subject matter, visual style, choice of actors and target audiences further define black indies but the field is a wide-ranging one that includes newcomers like director and screenwriter Tanya Hamilton (*Night Catches Us*, 2010) and moguls such as Oprah Winfrey and Tyler Perry. Winfrey and Perry's well-established success notwithstanding, *Precious* (2009) and *For Colored Girls* (2010) are technically independent because they address niche African American audiences (among others) and they are both literary adaptations. However, *For Colored Girls* opened in 1,200 theatres versus five for *Night*

• **Plate 13.3**
Jamara Griffin and Anthony Mackie in *Night Catches Us* (Tanya Hamilton, 2010).

Catches Us, implying vastly different investments on the part of the films' distributors and production companies. *Night Catches Us* is an independent film distributed by Magnolia Pictures and featuring a score by The Roots. In 1976, after years of mysterious absence, Marcus (Anthony Mackie, 'The Hurt Locker') returns to the Philadelphia neighbourhood where he came of age in the midst of the Black Power movement. While his arrival raises suspicion among his family and former neighbours, he finds acceptance from his old friend Patricia (Kerry Washington, *Ray* (2004), *Lift* (2001)) and her daughter. The two reckon with their personal pasts within broader historical and political concerns. Hamilton is the 1997 recipient for the Director's Guild of America Award for Best Female Director and in 2004 she was awarded a Pew Fellowship in the Arts.

Over the past century of cinema and longer, African American images have expanded somewhat to include a greater range of characters, and many black-authored productions have received praise from the film establishment. Critical assessments of such 'achievements' vary greatly, however. For example, Armond White and Ishmael Reed criticised the Oscar-nominated *Precious* (Lee Daniels, 2009) for what they saw as its demeaning stereotypes about black families, particularly black men. White called it 'the con job of the year', going on to state:

Not since *The Birth of a Nation* has a mainstream movie demeaned the idea of black American life as much as *Precious.* Full of brazenly racist clichés (Precious steals and eats an entire bucket of fried chicken), it is a sociological horror show.

(White 2009)

Yet the film won two Oscars for Best Performance by an Actress in a Supporting Role for Mo'Nique and Best Writing, Screenplay Based on Material Previously Produced or Published for Geoffrey Fletcher, suggesting a form of broad approval and respect for the work and its success at the box office. In fact, despite strong criticism of the perceived implications of the film's imagery and social messages, among some African American audiences and other concerned viewers, it was nominated for Best Picture and feted in the mainstream.

Since racism and stereotyping attack the worth of African Americans, both on screen and in the real world, the analysis of African American performances in film understandably leans toward assessing the perceived authentic or problematic qualities of the characters and the personas associated with stars. Such scrutiny furthermore reflects the significance that any one character bears amid the scarcity of black figures on screen. Thus, historically, the relationship between people of African descent and the film industry has been celebrated by recognising the individual accomplishments of 'respectable' Hollywood stars such as Sidney Poitier, Dorothy Dandridge, Bill Cosby and, more recently, Oprah Winfrey and Denzel Washington. Currently, directors Lee, Perry and Daniels have become celebrities and iconoclasts in their own right due to their unprecedented capacity to work consistently as independent writers/directors within the Hollywood machine; in promoting their films, they bring charged cultural issues to the mainstream. Clearly, therefore, 2010 marks a changed if not ideal media environment where issues of race, racism and spectacle, and their reception persist in complex and unpredictable ways.

☐ **CASE STUDY 1: *FROM ZORA NEALE HURSTON FIELDWORK FOOTAGE* (NATIONAL FILM PRESERVATION FOUNDATION, 1928 AND 2004)**

Hurston's 1928 footage comprises several reels of extant images held at the Library of Congress in Washington DC, and archivists there have made some of this material available to the public in a five-minute compilation (see Resource Centres, p. 357). The resulting short film shows how Hurston applied an experimental brand of participant/ observer anthropology to filming her subjects in the field. Typically, Hurston collected stories, songs and images by living among her subjects, blending in as much as possible by changing her dress, speech and gesture in order to learn to sing and talk as they did. The footage shows Hurston's careful composition of each shot while she provides a window into the unique and fragile communities she studied. However, present-day interpretation rests on visual cues because these images do not have extant accompanying dialogue, narration or original music.

In an early sequence in the compilation, Hurston appears to direct and talk with her subject, suggesting some aspects of her method. In the first shot, the camera frames a house, with the yard in front visible. A woman walks into the frame towards the camera and presents herself for a portrait in which the details of her facial expression are emphasised and she seems to be responding to the person holding the camera, presumably Hurston. Yet since there are neither titles nor sound, little is known about her and she appears to be a potential exemplary figure, representing the wider group of people in this area. Looking directly into the lens, she smiles, then after a few seconds, as though taking directions, she turns her head to the right and then to the left, adopting the poses of classic anthropological display and racial science. There seems to be a combination of something like collaboration here as well as anthropological display, and this difference is made all the more salient by the framing, which separates the subject from her environment and then switches from portraiture, almost personal engagement, into an impersonal, anthropological style where she is the spectacle of a type. The framing does not change but the mode of presentation changes within it.

The next sequence complements the first by showing a group rather than an individual. Here children are arranged in a circle and a boy dances in the middle while those watching clap in time to his movements. Drawing on her participant/observer method, Hurston positions the camera so that while the dancer is centred, the arms and feet of those children on either side of the camera are also visible. Thus Hurston and her camera appear to be fully within the circle, which puts viewers of Hurston's footage in the circle as well. Moments like this one are metaphors of Hurston's complex double-consciousness as they illustrate her dual position as both insider and outsider in relation to the communities she studied.

As an anthropologist conducting fieldwork, Hurston's overall purpose was to document culture and whether her images contribute to or critique stereotypical images of African Americans remains an open question. When viewed in the context of Hurston's criticism, it becomes clear that her images directly address the issue of stereotypes, as did her novels and short stories, for, aware of the black image problem, she wrote that in literary publishing 'It is assumed that all non-Anglo-Saxons are uncomplicated stereotypes ... It is urgent to realise that minorities do think, and think about something other than the race problem' (Hurston 1979: 170).

Hurston and her peers devoted much energy to defending, celebrating and formulating ways of expressing the untold stories of African Americans, presenting them in a documentable cultural milieu, on their own terms. She wrote: 'For various reasons, the average, struggling, non-morbid Negro is the best-kept secret in America. His revelation to the public is the thing needed to do away with that feeling of difference which inspires fear and which ever expresses itself in dislike.' By replacing stereotypes with potentially expansive **archetypes**, such as a black everyman or everywoman drawn from anthropology, perhaps Hurston was confident that 'this knowledge will destroy many illusions and romantic traditions which America probably likes to have around.'

archetypes
Embodiments of a range of ideas and identities; ideal example of a role, person or certain personal traits.

☐ **CASE STUDY 2: *THE HARDER THEY COME* (PERRY HENZELL, 1972)**

'Third World' refers to the colonised, neocolonised, or decolonised nations and 'minorities' whose structural disadvantages have been shaped by the colonial process and by the unequal division of international labor.

(Shohat and Stam 1994: 25)

The term 'Third World cinema' first emerged in relation to the Cuban revolution and Cinema Novo in Brazil. Given the economic difficulties that filmmakers in this part of the world have to contend with, the term 'Third World' might sound patronising, as though it refers to a lesser, marginal cinema in third place, behind the Hollywood and European film industries. However, 'just as peoples of color form the global majority, so the cinemas of people of color form the majority cinema, and it is only the notion of Hollywood as the only "real" cinema that obscures this fact' (ibid.: 27). For most of film history, the majority of the world's films were produced in India, the Philippines, Indonesia and other Asian countries. Nollywood, the feature film industry in Nigeria, is now the world's second most energetic cinema with 200 or more movies completed per month. So-called 'Third World films' cover vast geographies since, owing in part to migrations, whether forced or voluntary, almost every country in the so-called Third World has a diasporan film community, which then interacts with other diasporas in centres such as New York, London, Paris and Brussels, resulting in complex networks of influence and technological exchange.

• **Plate 13.4**
The Harder They Come (Perry Henzell, 1972). Ivan (Jimmy Cliff) during the portrait sequence, accompanied by Desmond Dekker's 'Shantytown'. Ivan plans to circulate his image in the local newspapers, in a bid to finally achieve the celebrity this former country boy had hoped to find in the city. Filmed over two years at locations in Kingston, Jamaica, the story is drawn from 1940s news accounts of Rhygin, a criminal reportedly obsessed with westerns and who led police on an extended chase

Perry Henzell's 1972 'Third World' film, *The Harder They Come*, was a singular accomplishment for Jamaica, after ten years of independence, but was also part of a small cohort of Anglophone Caribbean films. Harbance Kumar of Trinidad directed the first two feature films to be produced in the Anglophone Caribbean, *The Right and the Wrong* (1970) and *The Caribbean Fox* (1970). Keith Warner defines these films in terms of region rather than nation, noting that 'those which are produced in the region by and with a majority Caribbean personnel, and whose conception, realisation, and flavour present a distinct Caribbean worldview' would be considered Caribbean films (Warner 2000: 71). In Jamaica though, up to the 1970s, the film industry consisted mainly of foreign productions shot in Jamaican locations, primarily to capitalise on the tropical setting, but financed overseas. Yet documentary films, especially the educational films shot by the Jamaica Film Unit during the 1950s and 1960s, made up the bulk of the national cinema and therefore *The Harder They Come* likely drew upon the personnel, expertise and equipment already in place for the JFU, linking fiction and documentary in the industry. Henzell's film was a quantum leap towards a Jamaican cinema that, like the country's music, could be both international and vernacular in its themes and language. Taking two years to make, the film is known primarily for its musical score, which helped to introduce reggae internationally, but is also visually remarkable. In this case study I address the significance of the music as well as aspects of the film's visual style.

The singing characters in *The Harder They Come* are working, professional musicians who write, record, sell and perform music, and the film contains a serious critique of the financial dimensions of the music industry of the period. Thus it is partly about music as work and, further, musical expression as the means to both social and personal under-standing. Many of the film's sequences show the musical recording process, auditioning and rehearsing, but I will focus on a moment where the protagonist Ivan, played by actual musician Jimmy Cliff, recreates his image.

In the following sequence analysis we see Ivan inventing his persona in what is probably the most iconic set of images from the film. By this point in the narrative, Ivan has become an outlaw and while he is on the run initiates a portrait session with the intention of sending the images to the local newspaper. It may seem curious that a man supposedly hiding from the police would publicise his image; however, he is drawing on his initiation into movie-going. Earlier in the film, we see Ivan attend a cowboy film with his new friend and mentor Jose (Carl Bradshaw). This experience becomes formative in his self-view. Now finding himself marginalised in Kingston after many attempts to find steady work, followed by failed efforts at finding success both as a musician and a ganja trader, he is cornered. In response, he makes himself into a picture of a gangster folk hero, seeking fame, immortality and self-expression through performing for the camera. As the accompanying image shows, Ivan becomes a gunslinger, striking a variety of poses in images that suggest album covers as well as Ivan's externalised self-imagining.

The portrait sequence is fairly straightforward and the accompanying illustration demonstrates its essential elements of costume and pose. Enclosed in the studio, Ivan is photographed, for example standing with legs spread wide, bent at the knees, with a gun in each hand, pointing them at the camera, while outside police continue to pursue him and journalists apparently wait for news of him. Meanwhile, the music plays a role in adding a mythic, even spiritual, dimension to Ivan's portrait session. Desmond Dekker's recording of 'Shanty Town' accompanies the sequence and the song functions as a choral presence, evoking the voices and encouragement of Ivan's supporters out in the community. (The scene prior to this one shows a confrontation between the detective and one of the ganja traders who has been protecting Ivan.) The sequence includes black and white still images taken in the studio, black and white motion pictures of Ivan getting into his poses and interacting with the photographer, and eventually expands to include colour snapshots of Ivan in other settings.

When Henzell includes a still photo sequence at the point in the film where the action is rising toward the showdown between Ivan and his foes, he plays with the tension between stillness and motion inherent in photography, capture and freedom linked to the film's plot, the alternation between continuity and simultaneity, that guides his editing principles. Or, put another way, the narrative seems to pause for this scene of Ivan-as-spectacle but since some of the pictures appear to have been taken at different events, time is condensed, thus pushing the story further across a potentially longer period of time than is suggested by either the screen time or the manifest narrative logic. Furthermore, Ivan's expressivity in this sequence is certainly compelling to viewers, standing apart as he does from the film in terms of location in the enclosed photo studio as opposed to outdoors where much of the film takes place. As an outlaw and a spectacle, Ivan is a phenomenon of motion, but how he commands space while standing still becomes constitutive of the persona he creates. The sepia tone Ivan chooses for his images makes a picture that looks old and historical, while it is a glamourised current vision of himself, as though he both initiates and joins a pre-existing fraternity of fugitive young men. Finally, in an ironic twist, Ivan asserts his celebrity status through visual presentation, but he gains his notoriety by evading police and disappearing from public view. He disappears in the flesh only to re-emerge as an icon.

☐ CASE STUDY 3: SPIKE LEE'S *DO THE RIGHT THING* (1989) AND *BAMBOOZLED* (2000)

Spike Lee's films often reference current events and the director has been regarded as a public intellectual, one whose artistic endeavours are meant for the public good and who participates in cultural discussion, usually in media outlets. However, the realism and style of his films raise interesting questions of representation and film's capacity for verisimilitude. In addition to referencing current events and historical reality, Lee also uses absurdity – surreal flourishes such as his signature device where an actor is placed on a dolly with the camera, creating the illusion that he or she is floating in space. In this case study, we examine two films that show Lee's varied approaches to historical reality and current events.

Wahneema Lubiano observes that Lee's films *School Daze* (1988) and *Do the Right Thing* (1989) were 'discussed by most reviewers on the grounds of realism, authenticity, and relation to the "good" of the community represented in them' (Lubiano 1991: 260). 'But compared to what?' asks Lubiano, and expresses concern over the dearth of African American films to counter or engage Lee's version of reality. For concepts of truth and reality dominate the promotion and reception of black cinema, which, like African diaspora literature and music, is often celebrated for its perceived representational and image-corrective qualities. Although African American cinema's discourse of representation, which is projected most emphatically upon Lee, concerns 'telling the truth' about the black experience and society at large, such embodiments need to be interrogated carefully against the specific realities a film or filmmaker references and the capacities and limitations of cinematic verisimilitude. Further, a realist reading of Lee's work obscures the surreal, imaginative qualities that inhere at the moments that seem most profoundly 'authentic' and 'real'. The racial epithet sequence, titled on the DVD as 'Some Thoughts about Ethnicity', provides a striking example of how surrealness and authenticity combine.

The surreal sequence in which characters representing various members of Lee's cinematic Bed-Stuy setting verbally assault their neighbours, the mayor and the viewing audience after direct address. Their rapid and comic succession of rhythmically rendered racial slurs, can appear real in two ways: (1) audience members may experience a greater connection to or awareness of the reality of racial tensions in their communities; and (2) the very idea of racial tension is 'real'. But the slurs are also absurd, referencing a group's physicality, preferred food brands, famous figures, music, shoe style preferences and work habits; it is somewhat cringe-worthy as well as comical. The quick zoom and slightly canted framing that opens each monologue adds to the audience's discomfort. The actors' accents and energy help to generate precise vernacular portrayals of themselves as well as their targets, while the sequence and its apparent realism are delivered in a uniquely cinematic way: the characters seem to address each other verbally while they make eye contact with the viewer via the camera. Lee's use of direct address puts racism in our faces, implicating the audience as receivers (you talking to me?) and as perpetrators (you read my mind) of the racial slurs. Lee's camerawork brings viewers into closer audio-visual contact with the film's characters and their world than might be possible otherwise, while also containing and intensifying that experience within the film sequence. This juxtaposition of intimacy and distancing – suturing and alienation of the audience – raises the question of how 'real' Lee's filmic reality can be. The mode of address, as an omniscient, invisible camera no longer facilitates it, is as surreal as it is realist.

Do the Right Thing may strike authentic notes and shape how audiences see real-world events and people but it is finally an imaginative work of fiction made potent by its surreal yet vernacular performances and mise-en-scène. The 'Ethnicity' sequence concludes with an admonition from the local DJ, Mr Senior Love Daddy, who, consistent with the film's heightened reality, has somehow heard the monologues which took place on the streets around Bed-Stuy while yet enclosed in his radio booth. He shouts as if both to the characters in the film and the audiences in the theatre: 'Yo, hold up ... you need to cool that shit out and that's the double truth, ruth.' Here Lee crosses the 'realistic' boundaries of spaces within the film, and, moreover, from the film's diegesis into the theatre, concluding the sequence with a moment that is conceptually or emotionally authentic while it is created by surrealist use of editing and cinematography.

Lubiano points out that

the reasons for 'real' as a positive evaluation are tied, of course, to scarcity, the paucity of African-American presentations of facts and representations as well as desire for more of the first category, which in turn allows the second category to have its 'selectiveness' forgotten in the rush to celebrate its mere presence.

(Lubiano 1991: 264)

What reviewers take for real in fact consists of the vernacular – sights and sounds that are particular to a place and the people who live there. The vernacularity of Lee's film cannot be unquestioningly accepted as truth while the speech patterns, music, costumes, locations and references to events that were reported in the media are all authenticating signs of the actual world in the film. They blur the line between the film's diegesis and the real world. For 'telling the 'truth' demands that we consider the truth of something compared to something else. Who is speaking? Who is asking? And to what end?' (ibid.).

In his satire *Bamboozled* (2000), Lee tackles the history of black images in the film, television and music industries and reflects on an author's capacity to intervene and maintain his or her authentic voice within a highly commercialised media environment. Lee's protagonist Pierre Delacroix (Damon Wayans), a television writer, proposes the most racist TV show he can imagine in order to undercut his boss Dunwitty (Michael Rapaport), who has dismissed his previous efforts as culturally inauthentic. Delacroix's idea was that the programme – a minstrel show based on the variety format, featuring blackface, plantation scenery, buffoonish physical comedy as well as stereotypical song and dance – would be so obviously racist and offensive that it would be immediately rejected and he would be released from his contract with the television station. Delacroix calls the show *Man Tan, the New Millennium Minstrel Show*, featuring the tap-dancer

• **Plate 13.5**

Bamboozled (Spike Lee, 2000). Dunwitty (Michael Rapaport) surrounded by photographs of famous African American sports heroes. 'African' or African-inspired sculptures are mixed in with his videotapes and CDs. The film touches on a range of media issues related to the representation of people of African descent

Manray/Mantan (Savion Glover) and his comic sidekick Womack/Sleep-n-Eat (Tommy Davidson), a homeless tap-dance duo he has hired to play the lead roles. *Man Tan* is a surprise hit and Delacroix becomes trapped in his own joke because no one understands the show as satire or even as problematic. In fact, after initial hesitation, various audiences receive his satire about minstrelsy and its cast of stereotypes, without irony, as cutting edge, controversial and ultimately entertaining, despite a few protesters outside the television studio's office building.

Early in the film, the sequence in which Delacroix pitches the show to Dunwitty is instrumental because it centralises and suspends the film's main concern – the question of authenticity in black cultural production. The viewer sees Dunwitty pictured with 'brothers on the wall' behind him. (This mise-en-scène is a reference to a scene in Sal's Pizzeria from Lee's earlier film *Do the Right Thing*, where characters discuss the absence of black representation in a 'Wall of Fame' featuring Italians.) Dunwitty's office is decorated with photographs of iconic African American athletes, African statues and other cultural pieces, which marks his self-perception as an authority on black American culture. By contrast, Delacroix is seen in one shot framed tightly by the desk, ceiling and walls, emphasising the sense of his being hemmed in while he also appears to lack the kind of cultural backing Dunwitty seems privileged to claim.

Enter Mantan, Womack and Sloan (Jada Pinkett-Smith). All five characters sit at Dunwitty's desk/conference table, but creative power is far from evenly distributed. Mantan, Womack and Sloan are surprised to hear that the entertainers will be performing in blackface and Womack is taken aback by his new stage name: Sleep-n-Eat. As

Delacroix goes on to introduce the show's tagline, 'Mantan and Sleep-n-Eat, Two Real Coons', the performers react with confusion and Sloan becomes angry. In fact, she interrupts Delacroix's presentation to remind him of negative precedents such as protests against the *Amos and Andy* television show, but Delacroix presses on and describes a cast of characters that include Topsy and Mammy, and other familiar stereotypes. However, Delacroix's pitch becomes complicated when Dunwitty asks Mantan/Manray to demonstrate his dancing on the conference table.

When Mantan/Manray dances, his personal presence and evident dancing genius almost cancel out assumptions about his racist stereotypical TV role. For atop the conference table, Manray drops the 'Mantan' and seems to rise above the roles assigned to him. He is not Sloan's social problem, nor is he Womack's sidekick or meal ticket. And he temporarily slips the yoke of Delacroix's minstrel typecasting.

The viewer sees Manray suspended amid several distinct but interrelated points of view emanating from each of the characters seated at the conference table – now a stage – and naturally the viewing audience of the film as well. The sequence's dramatic tension arises in part from the spectacular demonstration of the ways in which Manray's gifts as a dancer and the limited roles available to him for its expression co-exist. In this sequence, Manray references the history of black spectacle within stereotypical roles that has been discussed in this chapter, and throughout the film, actors who performed within the entertainer's double consciousness, such as Bert Williams, Bill Robinson, Stepin Fetchit (Lincoln Perry) and Mantan Moreland, are cited through clips and in the dialogue. The entertainer's double consciousness is, as the American comedian Dave Chappelle put it, a question of dancing or shuffling. The audience's reception and the performer's self-view depend on a finely tuned ability to perceive the nuances of authorship.

• **Plate 13.6**
Bamboozled (Spike Lee, 2000). Womack (Tommy Davidson) and Manray (Savion Glover) discuss the implications of their new-found success as stars of *The New Millennium Minstrel Show*, in which they perform in blackface. An American nineteenth-century phenomenon, blackface is both a theatrical make-up style (using burnt cork or greasepaint) and a performance genre that combined music and comedy to effect racist caricatures of African Americans

AM I JUST A SPECTACLE?: DANCING VERSUS SHUFFLING

Bamboozled and *Dave Chappelle's Block Party* (Michel Gondry, 2006) offer two distinct points of view regarding questions of black representation and artistry within popular culture. Chappelle addressed such issues in a revealing interview published in the

15 May 2005 edition of *Time* magazine, after he had left *Chappelle's Show*. He struck the central problematic of African American cinema, saying 'I want to make sure I'm dancing not shuffling', and with these words, Chappelle clarified his artistic and professional double bind. At once a comedian and a member of an economically marginalised yet culturally influential minority group, Chappelle has a difficult public role to negotiate, thus his dancing/shuffling dichotomy evokes the thin line that exists in comedy between jokes that he feels reflect his intelligent social observations and command of his craft, and those that merely, perhaps unwittingly, play into the longstanding stereotypes and racist clichés reserved for and expected of both comedians of African descent and the community as a whole. It is the difference between having an audience laugh with him – that is, shocked, tricked or persuaded to see the world through the eyes of a brilliant comic – or having them laugh at him when black identity or black experience itself is seen as or made into a joke. The processes of viewing, producing and performing cinematic representations of African Americans are all informed by Chappelle's problematic to a point.

In many ways, Chappelle's *Block Party*, and the 2004 concert it documents, imagines black performance through an idealistic notion of community and participation where the audience and the performers play nearly interchangeable roles, similar to *Wattstax* (1973). In the film, Chappelle at once expands and localises a hip-hop and utopian sense of location and belonging in the performance and spectacle of the music itself. The performers and their audience share this concert and its constructed stage in the street, making of them a sheltering, if temporary and merely conceptual home. Moreover, the film is its own event; its candid, desultory conversations among the musicians, with Chappelle emphasising that the purpose of the concert is 'for us to spend time together' metaphorically offers a forward-looking vision of potentially precarious media-spectacle relations as a friendly block party in which, instead of feeling like a lonely objectified spectacle, the comedian can be a participating artist in a crowd that is with him.

CONCLUSION

This chapter has explored current approaches to the study of spectacle, stereotypes and films in the African diaspora, and it offers an introduction to the unique role of performance and racism in this group of films. Moreover, it offers an innovative way to think about the representations of peoples of colour within the complicated twenty-first-century media environment. Performance studies, film studies and literary studies are combined here to create an interdisciplinary humanistic method in order to gain a greater capacity to observe, describe, analyse and explain the enactment or performance of ethnic and/or racial identity in cinema, with an eye to authorship and transformative art. Eschewing predictability, race and ethnicity are taken as cultural constructs that are normalised through repetition and circulation, often facilitated by media images, while we observe that film is an instrument that shapes perceptions of particular ethnic and racial groups due to its capacity for repetition as well as its realist claims and conventions. Finally, African American cinema, because of its diasporic position between Europe, Africa and the Americas, provides a rich case for examining not only film's international circulation but also the intertwined social and aesthetic implications of its technologies.

SUMMARY

- The emergence of cinema parallels formations of race, racism and ethnicity under both colonialism and American racial segregation, and implications of these relationships reverberate in the contemporary moment.
- Stereotypes are discursive tools that institutions, groups or individuals may inten-

tionally or unintentionally use in ways that maintain unequal balances of power between people.

■ African American cinema shares some characteristics of national cinemas but it is primarily a nationalist cinema within a nation and it is part of the broader African Diaspora. It is a genre that contains other genres: documentary, fiction and experimental films that may be directed, produced and/or performed by black people.

■ The history of African diaspora cinema in the US may be roughly divided into four sections: (1) silent-era films and silent-era race films (1897–1928); (2) soundies, race films, Hollywood melodrama on racial identity and racism, including passing films (1929–45); (3) postwar social problem films (1945–60); and (4) contemporary films after 1960.

■ The privilege and power of whiteness, whatever its context, is its presumed neutrality.

■ In mainstream commercial film, racism manifests, if it does, primarily in the construction of a privileged white gaze at the expense of other characters' points of view.

■ Current African American film scholarship tends to be concerned with black performance and spectacle in three main areas: representation, the star system and black directors in Hollywood.

QUESTIONS FOR DISCUSSION

1   What is your definition of black film? Is 'black film' akin to a national cinema? Is it a genre relative to comedy, romance or thriller films? Do films by directors of African descent have enough in common to be considered as a coherent group?

2   To what degree do you think authenticity is a meaningful goal in the current media environment? How do you define authenticity in Afro-diaspora performance?

3   Can you identify racist iconography in the current media environment? What are its historical precedents?

NOTES

1   http://ftvdb.bfi.org.uk/sift/title/14864?view=synopsis (accessed 6 December 2010).

2   *A Nigger in the Woodpile* (1904). Theft in the woodpile by a 'Negro Deacon' – white in blackface – is discovered when the loaded stick of dynamite placed there by the farmer explodes. Comedy, 4 minutes, http://www.indiana.edu/~bfca/collection/films/films_N.shtml (accessed 6 January 2011).

3   *Zou Zou* (Marc Allégret, 1934); *Princess Tam Tam* (Edmond T Gréville, 1935); *The French Way* (Jacques de Baroncelli, 1945).

FURTHER READING

Alexander, E., '"Can You Be Black and Look at This?": Reading the Rodney King Video(s)', in *The Black Interior*, Graywolf Press, St Paul, MN, 2004, pp. 175–205.

Alexander, G., *Why We Make Movies: Black Filmmakers Talk About the Magic of Cinema*, Harlem Moon, Broadway Books, New York, 2003.

Anderson, B., *Imagined Communities: Reflections on the Origin and Spread of Nationalism*, Verso, London, 1983, pp. 41–64.

Baldwin, J., *The Devil Finds Work*, Dial Press, New York, 1976. Personal account of the novelist's outings to the cinema when he was a child and stream-of-consciousness musings on film generally.

Bhabha, H.K., *The Location of Culture*, Routledge, London and New York, 1994.

Billops, C., Griffin, A. and Smith, V., Black Film Issue, *Black American Literature Forum*, Vol. 25, No. 2, 1991.

Bobo, J. (ed.), *Black Women Film & Video Artists*, Routledge, New York, 1998.

Bogle, D., *Toms, Coons, Mulattoes, Mammies, and Bucks: An Interpretive History of Blacks in American Films*, Continuum, New York, 1998.

Bowser, P., Gaines, J. and Musser, C. (eds), *Oscar Micheaux and His Circle*, Indiana University Press, Bloomington, 2001.

Center for Contemporary Cultural Studies, *The Empire Strikes Back: Race and Racism in 70s Britain*, Hutchinson, in association with the Centre for Contemporary Cultural Studies, University of Birmingham, London, 1982.

Cham, M.B., *Ex-iles: Essays on Caribbean Cinema*, Africa World Press, Trenton, NJ, 1992.

Cooper, C., 'Slackness Hiding from Culture: Erotic Play in the Dancehall', in *Noises in the Blood: Orality, Gender, and the 'Vulgar' Body of Jamaican Popular Culture*, Duke University Press, Durham, 1995.

Cripps, T., *Black Film as Genre*, Indiana University Press, Bloomington, 1978.

— *Slow Fade to Black: The Negro in American Film, 1900–1942* (2nd edn), Oxford University Press, New York, 1993a.

— *Making Movies Black: The Hollywood Message Movie from World War II to the Civil Rights Era*, Oxford University Press, New York, 1993b.

Dash, J., *Daughters of the Dust: The Making of an African American Woman's Film*, New Press, New York, 1992.

Diawara, M. (ed.), *Black American Cinema*, Routledge, New York, 1993.

Dyer, R., *White*, Routledge, London, 1997.

Ellison, R., *Shadow and Act*, Vintage International, New York, 1964. Collection of cultural essays including a title essay on African American spectatorship.

Gaines, J., 'White Privilege and Looking Relations: Race and Gender in Feminist Film Theory', in S. Thornham (ed. and intro.), *Feminist Film Theory: A Reader*, New York University Press, New York, 1988.

Gates, H.L. Jr, 'New Negroes, Migration, and Cultural Exchange', in Elizabeth Hutton Turner (ed.), *Jacob Lawrence: The Migration Series*, Washington, DC, Rappahannock, 1993.

Guerrero, E., *Framing Blackness: The African American Image in Film*, Temple University Press, Philadelphia, 1993.

hooks, b., *Black Looks: Race and Representation*, South End Press, Boston, MA, 1992.

— *Reel to Real: Race, Sex and Class at the Movies*, Routledge, New York, 1996.

Hurston, Z.N., 'What White Publishers Won't Print', in A. Walker (ed.), *I Love Myself When I'm Laughing*, The Feminist Press, New York, 1979, pp. 169–73.

Julien, I., 'Black Is, Black Ain't: Notes on De-Essentializing Black Identities', in G.

Dent (ed.), *Black Popular Culture*, Bay Press, Seattle, 1992.

Lackey, J., '"Uncle Tom": Changing Receptions and Conceptions of a Stereotype in the Black Press, 1898–1944', *Film History*, 2011.

Lanier-Seward, A., 'A Film Portrait of Black Ritual Expression: The Blood of Jesus', in G. Gay and W.L. Baber (eds), *Expressively Black: The Cultural Basis of Ethnic Identity*, Praeger, New York, 1987.

Larkin, B., *Signal and Noise: Media, Infrastructure and Urban Culture in Nigeria*, Duke University Press, Durham, NC, 2008.

Lee, S., *Spike Lee's Gotta Have It: Inside Guerrilla Filmmaking*, Fireside, New York, 1987. Filmmaker's account of writing and bringing his debut feature to the screen and establishing his production company 40 Acres and a Mule Filmworks.

Lee, S. and Jones, L., *Do the Right Thing*, Fireside, New York, 1989.

Lubiano, W., 'But Compared to What? Reading Realism, Representation and Essentialism in *School Daze*, *Do the Right Thing*, and the Spike Lee Discourse', *Black American Literature Forum*, Vol. 25 No. 2 (Summer 1991), 253–81.

Martin, M. (ed.), *Cinemas of the Black Diaspora: Diversity, Dependence and Oppositionality*, Wayne State University Press, Detroit, MI, 1995.

Massood, P.J., *Black City Cinema: African American Urban Experiences in Film*, Temple University Press, Philadelphia, PA, 2003.

Morrison, T., *Playing in the Dark: Whiteness and the Literary Imagination*, Harvard University Press, Cambridge, MA, 1992.

Pines, J. and Willemen, P. (eds), *Questions of Third Cinema*, BFI, London, 1989.

Reid, M., *Redefining Black Film*, University of California Press, Berkeley, 1993.

Rhines, J., *Black Film/White Money*, Rutgers University Press, New Brunswick, NJ, 1996.

Rony, F.T., *The Third Eye: Race, Cinema and Ethnographic Spectacle*, Duke University Press, Durham, NC, 1996. Analysis of race-and-gender constructions in motion pictures, around questions of ethnography and visual anthropology. Covers the late nineteenth and early twentieth centuries.

Sampson, H.T., *Blacks in Black and White* (2nd edn), Scarecrow, Metuchen, NJ, 1995.

Shohat, E. and Stam, R., *Unthinking Eurocentrism: Multiculturalism and the Media*, Routledge, New York, 1994.

Smith, S.M., *Photography on the Color Line: W.E.B. Du Bois, Race and Visual Culture*, Duke University Press, Durham, NC, 2004.

Smith, V. (ed.), *Representing Blackness: Issues in Film and Video*, Rutgers University Press, New Brunswick, NJ, 1997.

Snead, J., 'Images of Blacks in Black Independent Films: A Brief Survey', in M.B. Cham and C. Andrade-Watkins (eds), *Blackframes: Critical Perspectives on Black Independent Cinema*, Cambridge, MA, Celebration of Black Cinema, MIT Press, 1988, pp. 16–25.

— *White Screens, Black Images: Hollywood from the Dark Side*, ed. C. McCabe and C. West, Routledge, New York, 1994.

Stewart, J. N., *Migrating to the Movies: Cinema and Black Urban Modernity*, University of California Press, Berkeley, 2005.

Wallace, M., *Dark Designs and Visual Culture*, Duke University Press, Durham, NC, 2004. Anthology of the author's essays on film, art, travel and television published over the last forty years.

Warner, K., *On Location: Cinema and Film in the Anglophone Caribbean*, Macmillan Education., London, 2000.

Yearwood, G., *Black Film as a Signifying Practice: Cinema, Narration and the African American Aesthetic Tradition*, Africa World Press, Trenton, NJ, 2000.

FURTHER VIEWING

1920 *Within Our Gates* (Oscar Micheaux)

1929 *St. Louis Blues* (Dudley Murphy). Short music-and-story film, commonly called a soundie, featuring a rare screen performance by blues musician Bessie Smith.

1933 *King Kong* (Merian C. Cooper and Ernest B. Shoedsack)

1934 *Imitation of Life* (John Stahl)

1939 *Gone with the Wind* (Victor Flemming)

1941 *The Blood of Jesus* (Spencer Williams)

1948 *The Quiet One* (Sidney Meyers)

1964 *Nothing But a Man* (Micheal Roemer)

1968 *Symbiopsychotaxiplasm: Take One* (William Greaves). Experimental documentary in which Greaves appears to abdicate his role as director leaving the crew to ponder their roles.

1972 *The Harder They Come* (Perry Henzell)

1973 *Wattstax* (Mel Stuart)

1976 *Car Wash* (Michael Schultz)

1976 *Pressure* (Horace Ove)

1977 *Killer of Sheep* (Charles Burnett)

1979 *Bush Mama* (Haile Gerima). Black and white UCLA film focused on a mother's political awakening.

1984 *Hairpiece: A Film for Nappy-headed People* (Ayoka Chenzira). Animated film that humorously depicts the history of African American hairstyle practices.

1985 *The Color Purple* (Steven Spielberg)

1989 *Do the Right Thing* (Spike Lee)

1991 *Boyz in the Hood* (John Singleton)

1991 *Daughters of the Dust* (Julie Dash)

1997 *Dancehall Queen* (Rick Elgood and Don Letts)

1997 *Eve's Bayou* (Kasi Lemmons). Lyrical drama about a young girl's troubling memories; most profitable independent film of 1997.

1998 *Tree Shade* (Lisa Collins)

2000 *Bamboozled* (Spike Lee)

2001 *That's My Face* (Thomas Allen Harris)

2002 *String of Pearls* (Camille Billops and James Hatch)

2004 *Reckless Eyeballing* (Christopher Harris)

2006 *Dave Chappelle's Block Party* (Michel Gondry)

2008 *Cadillac Records* (Darnell Martin)

2008 *Medicine for Melancholy* (Barry Jenkins)

2009 *Precious* (Lee Daniels)

2009 *Me Broni Ba/My White Baby* (Akosua Adoma Owusu). Not-quite-narrative documentary on hair salons in Ghana; voiceover narration reminiscent of themes expressed in Toni Morrison's *The Bluest Eye*.

2010 *Erie* (Kevin Everson)

2010 *For Colored Girls* (Tyler Perry)

2010 *Night Catches Us* (Tanya Hamilton)

2010 *The No. 1 Ladies' Detective Agency* (starring Jill Scott). HBO adaptation of novels by the same name; a young woman starts a detective agency with an inheritance from her father.

RESOURCE CENTRES

http://www.normanstudios.org/?page_id=112
Norman Studios, Jacksonville, Florida

http://www.Indiana.edu/~bfca/index/html
Black Film Center/Archive, Indiana University.

http://www.nypl.org/locations/schomburg
The Schomburg Center for Research in Black Culture.

http://blackfilm.uchicago.edu/
Black Film Research Online, University of Chicago.

DVD, Zora Neale Hurston's Fieldwork Footage
More Treasures from American Film Archives, 1894–1931. Program 3. National Film Preservation Foundation, 2004.

Part five

Cinema, nation and national identity

British cinema

Lawrence Napper

■ British cinema[1]

DEFINING BRITISH CINEMA

What do we mean when we talk about 'British cinema'? Are we referring to a commercial industry, to a particular body of films made in Britain, or more abstractly to a particular style of filmmaking or set of narrative and thematic conventions?

This chapter will attempt to suggest some ways in which we might think about British cinema, both as a commercial industry, and as a set of films made by that industry from 1895 to the present. It will be arranged chronologically into sections, and organised thematically into two strands. The first strand will deal with filmmaking and film-going as a practice – a commercial industry involving **producers**, **distributors**, **exhibitors** and audiences. Recurrent themes in this strand will include the dominance of Hollywood films in British cinemas, different forms of state provision to protect and develop the British film industry, the production policies and economic fortunes of various companies, and film-going as a changing social habit. The second strand will deal with the films themselves as texts, both in terms of the ways in which they represent the nation, and in terms of their visual and narrative aesthetics. Recurrent themes in this strand will include representations of class, gender and ethnicity, 'realism' versus 'fantasy', individual desire versus consensus politics, discussion of key genres such as the working-class comedy, the adaptation and the historical film. The discussions will be designed to both evoke and interrogate key debates and accounts of British cinema, attempting to reframe some of the main assumptions about how films have engaged the film-going audience over the last century.

To begin with let us return to the question of how we define a film as 'British'. This has always been a knotty problem, partly due to the cultural proximity between Britain and America and the dominance of Hollywood films on British screens. While many other national cinemas have the ready distinction of language to mark their productions as nationally specific, the shared language of Britain and America means that the definition of a 'British film' is rather more leaky. The lack of a language barrier means that while on the one hand Britain represents Hollywood's primary export market, on the other hand British films sometimes have the opportunity to become mainstream popular hits in America. This 'special relationship' can be seen as both a blessing and a curse.

British films which gain successful distribution in America are often partly funded by American companies, raising questions as to how 'British' they really are. Many critics suggested, for example, that *Notting Hill* (Roger Michell, 1999) was effectively a Hollywood production as a result of its international funding structure, despite its British characters and setting, and its largely British cast and crew. The accusation of a Hollywood 'taint' appeared to be strengthened by the content of the film. The 'transatlantic' nature of the story, dealing with a romance between a glamorous Hollywood star and an unassuming 'ordinary' Englishman, and the sanitised nature of the film's portrayal of London as a set of picturesque tourist spaces, suggested that a primary concern for the filmmakers was to please American audiences by confirming their fantasies about what Britain was like. One might argue that these criticisms of *Notting Hill* stem from a long tradition of anxiety over American economic and cultural domination of British life which, as we shall see, has had important consequences for the history of the British film industry.

In fact, the funding structure of *Notting Hill* was more multinational than such criticism suggests, with funding coming from major European companies such as Polygram, as well as American distributors. The multinational nature of British film finance can be seen by looking at some of the other films in which *Notting Hill*'s production company Working Title has been involved. These include what seem like resolutely American films, such as

production
Division of the film industry concentrating on the making of film.

distribution
Division of the film industry concentrating on the marketing of film, connecting the producer with the exhibitor by leasing films from the former and renting them to the latter.

exhibition
Division of the film industry concentrating on the public screening of film.

For further discussion of the British film industry see Chapter 1, pp. 27–36

40 Days and 40 Nights (Michael Lehmann, 2002), as well as films such as *Shaun of the Dead* (Edgar Wright, 2004) whose humour is built around apparently more specific British settings and characteristics.

How, then, can we define a 'British' film, and indeed, why would we want to? One might suggest that there are two possible ways of defining a film as British, as well as two possible incentives for doing so – economic and cultural. On the one hand, we can see a film as an economic product. The film industry in Britain employs technicians and actors, and it generates revenue from box-office takings both at home and abroad. As with any other industry, the government has an interest in maintaining this industry for the economic health of the nation. An economic definition of a British film might consider matters such as who financed it, how many British subjects were employed in making it, whether it was shot in British studios and locations, and whether the production company is registered in Britain. These kinds of definitions tend to be important *because* of the government's interest in encouraging the survival of the industry. Since 1928 a variety of schemes have been in place to support the British film industry, and each of these has had to come up with a workable definition of what constitutes a British film, to enable officials to determine which productions should enjoy the tax breaks and other incentives offered to such films.

On the other hand, we can see film as a cultural product. Films do not just make (or lose) money. They are also cultural objects which both 'reflect' the nation back to itself, and 'project' an image of Britain and what it means to be British to audiences at home and abroad. This 'cultural' definition of British films is not unrelated to the economic one. One of the most important 'invisible' results of successful British films is the extent to which they boost the tourist and travel industry – a fact which has been recognised since the mid-1920s. They also boost other industries, acting as a 'shop window' for British products as various as cars, clothes and music. Again this effect was recognised as early as the mid-1920s, and has been an important factor in the government's attitude to the film industry ever since.

As well as advertising British goods and landscapes though, films also advertise British 'values'. One might well debate exactly what British 'values' are, and it is a version of this debate which occurs whenever two people have a discussion about the relative merits of different British films. Is *Notting Hill* an adequate representation of our national life – is it how we want to see ourselves and be seen by others? Or is *Trainspotting* (Danny Boyle, 1996) a preferable example? Would we prefer to be understood through the restrained historical passions of *Pride and Prejudice* (Joe Wright, 2005) or the more contemporary exuberance of *Alien Autopsy* (Jonny Campbell, 2006)? Who are 'we' anyway? And who is the intended audience for these representations of 'us'?

British films are often criticised for portraying a very narrow view of British life – a tendency to show England over Scotland, Wales or Northern Ireland, and a tendency to show southern, white, middle-class England at that. One can identify similar biases in Hollywood films of course, although they don't tend to be discussed so urgently, and it is worth questioning why not. Nevertheless, with regard to British films, one might suggest though that over a century of filmmaking in this country has produced an enormous variety of representations, stories, narrative styles and visual aesthetics. It is difficult – probably impossible – to sum up an entire nation's filmmaking output in a single sentence, or even a few thousand words, let alone give a comprehensive account of how those films came to be made and were seen. In what follows I shall try to draw out the main historical changes to the industry, and some of the major traditions of representation which that industry developed. The chapter is intended to provide you only with an overview of British cinema. Many aspects of the material are contested and the Bibliography will point you to books and essays where some of the interpretations are debated and fought over, and where you can explore them in more detail. The account here is by no means exhaustive or unbiased – don't be afraid to find out new films for yourself, and use them to challenge my account. (For key essays on the historiography of British cinema, see Barr 1986; Higson 1989; Lovell 2003.)

FROM PIONEERING TO PROTECTION

Fairground exhibition to picture palace

The recent discovery and restoration of over 800 films made by Sagar Mitchell and James Kenyon between 1900 and 1913 has created an enormous revival of interest in Britain's earliest filmmakers. Based in Blackburn, Mitchell and Kenyon and their agents worked throughout the North of England filming short local scenes of people leaving factories, processions, street scenes and sporting events. These '**actualities**' were often commissioned by showmen who were operating touring **cinematograph** shows in fairgrounds and wanted local scenes which would encourage audiences to pay to see themselves or their towns on the screen. Fairground exhibition – travelling cinemas – was a common way for people to see films in the first ten years of cinema from 1895 to 1905, when cinema itself was still a novelty, and a number of early films were made by travelling showmen. Film shows were also offered as part of the evening's entertainment at the local music-hall, as an interlude between live acts – although, of course, the presence of a 'lecturer' describing what was going on in the film, and of musicians providing accompaniment, meant that there was always an element of live performance as part of the cinematograph show. Alongside local actualities of the type produced by

For a case study on the films of Mitchell and Kenyon see pp. 214–225.

actuality
Early term for a short, non-fiction film.

cinematograph
Early term for cinema. Initially it referred to the camera/projector, but soon came to be used to refer to the practice and the exhibition space.

• **Plate 14.1**
Mitchell and Kenyon – local films for local people

trick film
The generic term for
the development of
cinematic special
effects using such
techniques as **mattes**,
multiple exposures,
proto-animation
and **substitution
techniques**.
Generally attributed to
the pioneering French
filmmaker George
Melies.

Mitchell and Kenyon, audiences would have seen fictional and **'trick' films** as well as short narratives and reconstructions of current news events (Toulmin *et al*. 2004).

As films ceased to be a novelty, a number of key changes took place in the way they were both produced and exhibited. As the popularity of the pictures grew, it became financially viable to show films in a dedicated venue to which audiences returned week after week. Instead of touring the same films round to different audiences as the travelling showman had done, the proprietors of these fixed-site cinemas found it necessary to obtain new films every week to keep the audience coming back. It was no longer possible to buy a few films outright and make a living out of showing them again and again in different venues. Exhibitors began to obtain their films through a distributor, who supplied films on a rental basis, sending out new films each week. Thus the roles of film producers and exhibitors became more specialised, and the financial interests of each group became more divergent. Even as early as 1905 the demand for new films meant that the film industry was an international one. Distributors carried films made in France and America as well as British productions, and audiences were as likely to see foreign films as British ones. Indeed, this international film trade was fiercely competitive, American companies had formed a trade combine which sought to exclude European films from the lucrative American market, and European producers fought to protect their interests. Even at this early stage the British film industry was caught between America and Europe.

Until the mid-1950s, film was made from a material called silver nitrate which is extremely flammable – it burns very intensely producing a lot of heat, and is almost impossible to extinguish. Fairground cinematograph shows and early cinemas, which often contained the projector in the same space as the audience, were very prone to fires. Housed in a tent or a cheaply constructed wooden building, and often packed with people, fires in these venues were particularly dangerous, and after a number of high-profile disasters the government took action, passing the Cinematograph Act of 1909. This stipulated various stringent building safety measures designed to reduce the risk of fires and ensure adequate escape routes. The projector, for instance, had to be separated from the audience and contained in a fire-proof booth, and no cinema could operate without a licence from the local authority. The 1909 Act had three major effects. First, it meant that fixed-site, purpose-built cinemas became the dominant – if not the only – method of film exhibition. Second, it gave local authorities considerable power over exhibitors through the licensing system. Local authorities soon used this power to close down cinemas not only when they were contravening the safety regulations, but also when they showed films that local magistrates considered morally unsuitable. This led directly to the formation of the British Board of Film Censors in 1912. The BFFC was an industry body which sought to stabilise what had rapidly become an inconsistent and *ad hoc* local censorship system. Third, the 1909 Act, in demanding a specially constructed or converted building for film exhibition, forced exhibitors to invest much more capital in their businesses. As a result, exhibitors tried to safeguard their investment by attempting to attract more middle-class patrons to their 'well-appointed' cinemas – patrons who would pay higher admission prices if they felt they were partaking of a 'quality' leisure experience. The new censorship board was a useful tool in this drive towards moral and social 'uplift', breaking the association of film with cheap, working-class and morally suspect entertainment. The campaign was only partly successful however, and although it did gain some respectability among lower middle-class patrons, the cinema remained a resolutely mass entertainment. That distinction, though, is important for understanding some of the marketing strategies employed by British producers, as we shall see later.

newsreels
Films consisting of six
or seven short topical
news stories released
to cinemas twice a
week and shown as part
of the full supporting
programme. Newsreels
were produced from the
1910s to the early 1970s
by which time they had
largely been overtaken
by television news. They
were also shown in
specialist news cinemas,
often located in or near
big railway stations.

By the end of the First World War in 1918, the British film industry was roughly structured in a way that is still recognisable even today. Narrative feature films lasting around ninety minutes were the core of the cinema programme, although they were supported by a selection of shorts, **newsreels** and cartoons. Films were shown in specially built cinemas which were to be found in every town. The smaller cinemas of the 1910s were gradually being replaced by the picture palaces of the 1920s – much larger and plusher venues, sometimes boasting cafés, dance-halls, ushers, and even small orchestras to provide accompaniment for the silent films. Perhaps most importantly, as today, the vast majority of the films shown were made in Hollywood. Thus, while for British exhibitors the film trade was booming, this was mainly on the back of imported American productions (Eyles 2001; Higson 2002).

American films had come to dominate the British market during the First World War, and they were able to maintain this position for a variety of reasons. First, the American companies had already recouped the production costs of their films in their vast home market, so they could afford to offer British exhibitors the films at considerably lower prices than the British producers against whom they were competing. Second, from the early 1920s onwards they began to take advantage of this economic strength through an aggressive trade practice known as 'block booking'. Exhibitors were offered two or three films which were likely to be big box-office hits, but only on condition that they also booked a large number of smaller films of unknown worth. Effectively, exhibitors were forced to book an entire season from one distributor if they wanted to be sure of obtaining the most important and lucrative films. For the British producers this made life very difficult indeed. It was hard enough to raise the capital to make a film at all. With the vast American market closed to them, the films they made had to be relatively cheap so that they could ensure they covered their costs with box-office revenue from Britain alone. However, even once the film had been completed, it could be six to eight months before the film could be released to the cinemas, clogged up as they were with Hollywood films, which had been more expensively made but which were being offered to exhibitors at a cheaper price than their British competitors. The instability of this economic situation remained relatively unattractive to investors, thus undermining further the viability of filmmaking in Britain.

Despite these rather hostile conditions, British filmmakers persevered, adopting a variety of methods for making their films financially viable, distinctive and attractive to audiences. American executives at the time (and later) maintained that British films were not as successful because they were inferior to Hollywood productions, and until recently this judgement was accepted and repeated by both historians and critics (Low 1997). However, more recent accounts tend to stress the distinctiveness of British filmmaking in the 1920s not as inferiority, but rather as part of an explicit marketing strategy which sought to develop a 'national' style of filmmaking, understood to be purposely different from the more popular Hollywood product. To be sure, the films looked very different from the Hollywood productions against which they competed. They were slower, with less emphasis on goal-directed narrative, and more on pictorial composition. They tended to draw on representational traditions from outside cinema – literary and theatrical sources, painterly styles. The rhetoric around them emphasised the idea of preserving the best of British culture, of offering something more than the lowest common denominator. Another strategy adopted by British filmmakers throughout the 1920s, and in an increasingly organised manner from around 1926 onwards, was to forge alliances with European producing companies. During the silent period, language did not present the same kind of barrier to international European co-production as it does today, and this policy was enthusiastically pursued, particularly between Britain, Germany and France on the hope that a Europe-wide market would give producers a similar economic advantage to that enjoyed by Americans with their continental-sized home audience (Burrows 2001; Higson and Maltby 1999).

Nevertheless, throughout the 1920s concerns were expressed about both the weakness of the British film industry, and about the effect that exposure to so many American films might have on the British population. As ever, it was a combination of economic and cultural concerns which attracted the attention of the government. 'People are being taught to think and feel in ways that are not British', worried Sir Philip

Cunliffe-Lister in 1927. As President of the Board of Trade, his anxiety was not just confined to the people's thoughts and feelings – they were also being taught to desire American consumer goods and to buy them in preference to British ones. It was not only British audiences who were a cause for concern, Hollywood films dominated the exhibition sector throughout the Empire, and in various other international markets, where they acted as advertisements for American consumer goods to the detriment of British trade.

After a long period of consultation and lobbying from the various sectors of the film trade, the government finally passed the Cinematograph Act of 1927. This Act, which came into force in early 1928, is the most important piece of British legislation dealing with cinema, because it established the principle of governmental support for the British film industry. That acknowledgement of film as both an economic and cultural contribution to our national life which is worth supporting is one which (apart from a brief period in the 1980s) has been maintained by successive governments through a variety of different mechanisms ever since. The mechanism which was put in place in 1927 was that of the Quota. Each exhibitor was required by law to show a certain percentage of British films in their cinemas, and each distributor was required to carry a certain percentage of British films on their books. The percentages were set to rise year on year until the Act's renewal in 1938 when they would stand at 20 per cent, thus creating and maintaining a steady demand for British films. In addition, the practice of 'block' booking was outlawed. The Act also established a working definition of a British film as one made by a British subject or a company constituted in the British Empire, of which the majority of the directors would be British. All studio scenes were to be shot in the Empire, with not less than 75 per cent of the labour costs being paid to British subjects (excluding copyright payments and the wage of one foreign actor or producer) (Street 1997, 2003).

British scenes on British screens

Even before the discovery of Mitchell and Kenyon's films, British filmmakers of the earliest period were already regarded among film historians as among the most innovative in the world. Those working with film from 1895 to 1900 tended to have 'day' jobs in related activities. Chemists, photographers, inventors, showmen and magic lanternists, they came to film as genuine pioneers, experimenting with both the technology and the language of cinema. The films were initially single shots taken from a fixed camera position, and lasting only around a minute. They consisted of both actualities – filmed records of real places and events – and little scenes or 'attractions' staged especially for the camera. R.W. Paul, an engineer based in Hatton Garden, was one of the earliest of the film pioneers. His film of *The Derby* of 1896 is a good example of an actuality. It was especially successful with audiences, recording as it did a celebrated win by the Prince of Wales's own horse. The *Strand Magazine* pronounced it a 'sensation', and described his process of 'lightening photography' in great detail, making clear that in this early stage the technology of moving pictures itself was as much an attraction as their subject matter. The article also emphasised the commercial aspect of Paul's work, describing how he processed the film overnight so that it could be shown the following day at the Alhambra Theatre. The Derby film survives, showing the horses rushing past the camera and the crowd running on to the course once they have passed – ineffectually supervised by a number of policemen.

A good example of an attraction staged purely for the camera is G.A. Smith's *The Miller and the Sweep* (1897). Smith, a showman and hypnotist, was one of a number of pioneers based around the Brighton and Hove area. His film, like many others around this period, is based on a scene or joke which was already popular as a subject for still photographs, cartoons and music-hall sketches. The miller (white with flour) and the sweep (black with soot) have a fight, covering each other with flour and soot. This

• **Plate 14.2**
The Miller and the Sweep (G.A. Smith, 1897). A popular gag filmed

extremely visual subject was given extra attraction by Smith, who staged it in front of a windmill whose moving sail increases the amount of movement in the frame. He also tacks on a chase at the end of the film, with the miller and sweep pursued apparently at random by a crowd of extras.

Such one-shot films quickly gave way to more complex, multi-shot scenes, and the variety of innovations and experiments evident in the various films of this period is immense. Two of Smith's later films give an indication of the speed of developments. In 1900 he produced *As Seen Through a Telescope* which introduces a brief narrative, involving editing and point of view – two of the cornerstones of narrative cinema even today. Our hero gets a closer look at a girl's ankle by the use of a telescope. We too are treated to the erotic spectacle, thanks to the insertion of a close-up point-of-view shot, although it is only the man who is subsequently punished. *Mary Jane's Mishap* (1903) again uses the close-up and various match-editing techniques to suggest links in time and space, as well as a **wipe** to indicate a temporal and spatial **ellipse**. Like *As Seen Through a Telescope* it suggests a mischievous moral ambivalence. Mary Jane, a lazy housemaid, tries to light the fire with paraffin. She gets blown up, but who has the last laugh?

Questions of ideology go hand-in-hand with developments in film language and narrative concerns. A famous example which combines all three areas is Cecil Hepworth's *Rescued By Rover* (Lewis Fitzhamon, 1905). A nursemaid is so busy flirting with a soldier that she fails to notice a gypsy stealing the baby in her charge. Rover, the family dog, however, is able to sniff out the culprit and victim. His search takes him from the posh end of town, over a river to a garret in the slum areas. Having made the discovery he returns home to alert the child's father and lead him back to his lost progeny. This film is widely celebrated for the sophistication of its spatial editing. Action is matched across the various scenes of Rover's journey, showing him moving repeatedly from top right to bottom left of each camera set-up, and vice versa for the return journey. The ideological centrality of the stable bourgeois family unit is emphasised not only in a narrative which sees it disrupted and then restored, but also in a final emblematic shot showing the

wipe
Transition between shots where a vertical line sweeps across the screen taking us from one scene to the next.

ellipse
A gap in the continuity of time and space of the narrative – usually indicated in editing by means of a **dissolve** or **wipe**.

reunited family group (and dog). Much is made of the apparent bourgeois morality of Hepworth's film, but it should be pointed out that there are plenty of examples of films at this time which take a positive delight in portraying criminals outwitting the forces of authority. See, for example, *Desperate Poaching Affray* (1903) made by William Haggar (a Welsh travelling showman), which is often cited as the inspiration for Edison and Porter's *The Great Train Robbery* (Edwin S. Porter, 1903) (Barr 2003).

Many of the pioneers of British cinema, including R.W. Paul and G.A. Smith, had dropped out of the industry by the outbreak of the First World War, moving on to other inventions, or back to their original trades. Cecil Hepworth, though, remained centrally concerned with filmmaking throughout the rest of his life. His company took its place among the growing number of British production companies of the 1910s organised along commercial lines to take advantage of the new mass medium. Hepworth's company was in the forefront of such developments as the rise of the **star system** and the development of fan magazines. In accordance with the movement for 'uplift' around 1910, Hepworth's company made adaptations of Dickens and Shakespeare, filming the famous actor Johnston Forbes-Robertson as *Hamlet* (Hay Plumb, 1913). By the early 1920s they were making feature-length adaptations of novels and plays, usually featuring his biggest star Alma Taylor, and set in well-photographed rural landscapes (Burrows 2001).

The collapse of Hepworth's company after *Comin' Thro the Rye* (Cecil Hepworth, 1923) in 1924 was until recently attributed to his 'backward-looking' cinematic style and business policy. When compared to American films circulating at the same time, Hepworth productions seem rather slow. Not a fan of Hollywood editing styles, he preferred to shoot scenes in long takes using quite frontal set-ups, rather than dissecting the space through structures such as the **shot-reverse-shot**. His films were, however, consistently praised for the quality of the photography, and his shooting style tended to emphasise the picturesque settings of the stories, which most often dealt with English rural life. Particularly good examples of this style include *Tansy* (Cecil Hepworth, 1921) which features Alma Taylor as a shepherdess forced to choose between two suitors, and *The Pipes of Pan* (Cecil Hepworth, 1923), a story inspired by a popular and much reproduced watercolour of the period by Estella Canziani. Both films deal with the threat to rural life presented by modernity, combining nostalgia with narratives about socially mobile characters whose personal fortunes threaten the stability of the social order (Gledhill 2003; Higson 1995).

It is now increasingly accepted that rather than evidence of naivety or incompetence, Hepworth's apparently idiosyncratic shooting style was a conscious attempt to differentiate his British productions from their American competitors, providing them with a distinctive 'national' filmmaking aesthetic which created a particular market appeal. As we have seen, Hepworth was not alone in this project. For instance, Stoll, the biggest British production company of the period, introduced a series of adaptations of popular novels under the banner 'Eminent British Authors'. Eschewing stars, Stoll's adaptations relied on the notion of the pre-sold popular literary property as the guarantee of wholesome entertainment. Exploiting more populist if no less distinctively British policies, George Pearson had a series of hits in the early 1920s with his star Betty Balfour in the role of *Squibs* (1921), a cockney flower girl with an irrepressible sense of humour and a persistent tendency to mock social pretension. The films were extremely popular with audiences, not least because of their East End settings and Balfour's considerable comic charisma. Other producers of the period pursued links with European companies in an attempt to increase the possible distribution for their films while also creating a product distinctive in style from Hollywood. Perhaps the most famous company founded during the latter half of the 1920s was Michael Balcon's Gainsborough Pictures. The success of Gainsborough was partly the result of the way it combined all three of the production strategies outlined above. The company is probably best remembered as the place where Alfred Hitchcock got his start at directing, first in Germany, and later in

See Chapter 7 for further discussion of the star system.

star system
The industrial apparatus which enables the building up of stars and their centrality to the advertising and promotion of films. This includes star contracts, ancillary advertising deals, fan magazines and so on.

shot-reverse-shot
Editing technique whereby conversations are filmed by cutting alternately between the faces of the interlocutors who are facing each other.

• **Plate 14.3**
Tansy (Cecil Hepworth,
1921). Showcasing the
English rural landscape

Britain with his celebrated thriller *The Lodger* (1927) – a film whose 'German' influences have been much commented on. Gainsborough attracted a number of other talented directors, stars and writers, including Britain's top box-office attraction of the 1920s Ivor Novello, who appeared in a series of racy dramas as an apache underworld character known as 'the Rat' (Cook 1997; Napper and Williams 2001; Ryall 1996).

Maurice Elvey's *Hindle Wakes* (1927) made for Gaumont-British (a company which would soon combine with Balcon's Gainsborough) is a particularly interesting example of the kind of output being produced in Britain by the late 1920s. Adapted from a (then) famous stage play by Stanley Houghton, it tells the story of a Manchester cotton worker and her family. While on holiday in Blackpool she has a liaison with the son of the mill owner which threatens both families with shame and ruin. Negotiations among the older generations result in an agreement that the two young people should marry in order to maintain respectability. In a remarkable twist, however, the heroine rejects the arrangement, taking control of the narrative by declaring her independence both from the social mores of her community and from the hypocrisy of the double standard. 'I'm a woman, and I was your little fancy – You're a man and you were my little fancy. Don't you understand?' she explains to her ex-lover. A heroine with such a modern attitude is unusual in any film of this period, and certainly would not be found in any comparable Hollywood production. This is partly because she is the product of her northern social milieu of respectability over 'flash' which is culturally specific enough to be almost untranslatable. Elvey's direction seems designed to do for the industrial landscapes of the northwest what Hepworth was attempting with the rural south – distinctive British settings of the cobbled terraces, and extensive location shooting of the factory interiors and of the fun-fair at Blackpool create an almost documentary-realist feel to the first half of the film, the adaptation opening out the original play to a remarkable degree. Elvey's direction is certainly leisurely, and his emphasis on the details (particularly the use of footwear to indicate the distinction between work and leisure, wealth and poverty), belies a delight in **symbolism** at the expense of **narrative economy**. By Hollywood standards the film is slow, particularly in the later, more stagy scenes. Nevertheless, there are

symbolism
The means by which a filmmaker can assign additional meanings to objects/characters in a film. For example, in Dovzhenko's *Earth* and Eienstein's *Old and New*, the tractor is a symbol of progress.

narrative economy
The efficiency with which a film tells its story. 'Classical Hollywood' films have often been described as having a high degree of narrative economy, with few scenes or shots which do not contribute in some way to the telling of the story. Some genres such as musicals or epics, where spectacle is an important element of the film's pleasures, may be said to have a lesser degree of narrative economy.

For further discussion of sound and film narrative see Chapter 4.

some remarkably confident touches of direction. A scene where a next-door neighbour's grief at the death of his daughter is revealed to the family through the sound (visually represented) of his wooden leg as he paces the bedroom floor is every bit as striking and narratively efficient as Hitchcock's celebrated use of a glass ceiling to create a similar effect in *The Lodger*.

By the time the Cinematograph Act was being passed around 1927 then, British filmmakers had acquired the confidence and skill to create some remarkably accomplished and adult films, despite less than ideal financial conditions. Their achievement may have been undervalued or ignored by later film historians because the films were unfamiliar in two senses. Not only did they fail to conform to the expectations of good cinema created by the more dominant Hollywood product, but they were also difficult to access for many years. Only recently has a major re-evaluation of this cinema begun to understand it as striving to achieve a distinctive 'British' cinematic aesthetic. Meanwhile, that re-evaluation has only been possible as a result of their increased availability through archive prints, DVDs and internet resources.

DEPRESSION AND WAR

There is a persistent and often repeated myth that British films of the 1930s rarely contained working-class characters, and that such characters, when they did appear, only functioned as comic stereotypes. Such comments tend to reveal more about the cultural predilections of middle-class critics than the inadequacies of British film producers. Those critics tend to dismiss comedy as insignificant, preferring to see their working-class characters suffering in serious '**realist**' dramas such as the admittedly breath-taking *Love on the Dole* (John Baxter, 1941). Popular audiences, however, held comedy in much greater esteem. They valued the entertainment afforded by the sight of working-class stars cocking a snook at authority in anarchic narratives of social chaos, more than a realist reminder of the all-too-familiar dole queue. In fact the dominant British genre of the 1930s is the working-class comedy, and Britain's biggest stars of

realism/reality
The concept of the 'real' is problematic in cinema, and is generally used in two different ways. First, the extent to which a film attempts to mimic reality so that a fictional film can appear indistinguishable from documentary. Second, the film can establish its own world and can, by consistently using the same conventions, establish the credibility of this world. In this later sense a science fiction film such as *RoboCop* can be as realistic as a film set in a contemporary and recognisable world, such as *Sleepless in Seattle*.

● **Plate 14.4**
Millions Like Us (Launder and Gilliat, 1943). Women from disparate social and regional backgrounds come together for the war effort

the decade, George Formby and Gracie Fields, were presiding geniuses, their popularity enabling them to compete effortlessly with the best that Hollywood could offer, while remaining unequivocally specific in their Lancastrian cultural allusions.

Even before it had come into effect, the Cinematograph Act of 1927 produced a vast expansion of the British film industry. With the guarantee of screen space and the promise of a more stable economic future, financiers became much more confident about investing in film. Many new film companies were registered in the late 1920s, although this wave of confidence proved to be premature for many of them, since the coming of sound around the turn of the decade necessitated a huge re-investment both in technology and expertise. Not only studios, but also cinemas had to be converted to sound. Two of the most important companies to survive the transition were notable for being 'vertically integrated'. Like their Hollywood rivals, British International Pictures and Gaumont British Picture Corporation both produced films, and owned the cinemas in which those films were shown. That was not a new phenomenon in Britain – the Stoll company of the early 1920s had enjoyed a degree of vertical integration. Nevertheless, the capital investment these two giants put into their production facilities (at Elstree and Shepherds Bush respectively), and into their cinema chains was unlike anything Britain had seen previously, and would not have been possible without the steady flow of money which vertical integration allows. Alongside these two giants, there were various smaller producers operating with varying degrees of independence (Ryall 2003).

The Quota Act meant that all of the major Hollywood distributors now also had to carry a certain number of British films on their books. At best this meant that they were encouraged to make distribution deals with reputable British producers. The partnership between Alexander Korda's London Films and United Artists is the most famous example of such a deal, enabling Korda's film *The Private Life of Henry VIII* (Alexander Korda, 1933) to be distributed through United Artists in America with spectacular financial results. At worst the legislation encouraged US distributors to pay unambitious British producers a pittance to make films as quickly and cheaply as possible in order to fulfil the minimum requirements of the law, and the films that resulted became known as 'quota quickies'. The lamentable quality of such films has been exaggerated over the years with the myth that they were never meant to be seen and the story that they were habitually run in cinemas in the mornings for the cleaners, or last thing at night to chase the audiences home. In fact the evidence suggests that most of these films *were* intended to be seen and to entertain their audience, even if they were produced very cheaply. George Formby's first vehicle was a 'quota quickie', and the kind of broad music-hall humour which made him and Gracie Fields such massive stars was also being employed by Max Miller in a series of 'quickies' made for Warner Brothers at Teddington, as well as a host of other comedians working in both the quota and the 'legitimate' sections of the industry – Leslie Fuller, Will Fyffe, The Crazy Gang, Stanley Lupino and Will Hay to name only a few (Napper 2003).

Perhaps it is more appropriate to think of British films produced in the 1930s as being divided between those intended to compete with Hollywood's output – with high production values and stories which had a chance of appealing to an international audience, and those intended primarily for British audiences without any ambitions to be exported to wider markets. The Formby and Fields films would fit this latter category of 'inexportable' films. As I have suggested, they were really only the tip of the iceberg of working-class comedies of the period, trading on cultural familiarity rather than attempting to compete with the more glamorous Hollywood productions.

Gracie Fields's popular nickname of 'our Gracie' indicates the kind of familiarity her star persona encouraged – a relationship with her fans which Jeffrey Richards describes as being akin to that of a big sister. Gracie's ordinariness was constantly emphasised in a string of narratives which placed her at the caring centre of her working-class community, whether as the social welfare officer of a factory in *Sing As We Go* (Basil Dean, 1934), the waitress in a local café in *Sally in Our Alley* (Maurice Elvey, 1931) or a successful

Compare the British film industry with Hollywood production in Chapter 1.

vertical integration
Where a company is organised so that it oversees a product from the planning/ development stage, through production, through market distribution, through to the end-user – the retail consumer. In the case of the film industry, this translates to a company controlling **production**, **distribution** and **exhibition** of its films.

inexportable
Critical term used to denote films of modest budget and ambition, only intended for distribution to their home markets. Adapted from Jean-Pierre Jeanncolas's use of the term with regard to certain French comedies.

music-hall star returned to help her family fight for the survival of the local market threatened with closure in *Look Up and Laugh* (Basil Dean, 1935). Several films contain scenes where her singing talent takes her out of her own community to perform for her social betters – a situation which leads to comic chaos as her authentic bonhomie is contrasted against their snobbishly polite codes of social interaction. The key register of these films is the tension between Gracie's personal talent leading to individual success, and her commitment to the ordinary community to which she belongs. This value is often embodied in an expressively sentimental song filmed using a motif which cuts between shots of her spontaneous community performance and the rapt, appreciative faces of the listening audience. Whether the listening figures are physically linked in space (for instance, around the street coffee stall in *Queen of Hearts* (Monty Banks, 1936)) or are in different spaces linked only by the editing (as in the 'Wonderful Love' number in *Sing As We Go*), they are nevertheless understood to be linked culturally to Gracie herself and the utopian sense of belonging which she embodies (Richards 1984).

Companies making more internationally ambitious films intended for export included Korda's London Films, which sought to repeat the extraordinary success of *The Private Life of Henry VIII* with a series of historical epics and Empire adventures conceived on a grand scale. These films tended to package British Empire history and landmarks as settings for adventure stories and romance narratives for both home and foreign audiences. In common with British International Pictures (whose films tended to be more modestly budgeted), Korda's product retained a distinctly international flavour as a result of using a range of émigré stars and technicians who had learned their craft in continental Europe. Indeed, it is often forgotten quite how cosmopolitan filmmaking in Britain was – a legacy of both the Film Europe policy of the late 1920s and the rise of European fascism in the mid-1930s (Richards 1984).

Michael Balcon at Gaumont-British also launched a concerted attempt to break into the American market, building up his star Jessie Matthews in a series of lavish modern musicals intended to compete in style and panache with the Astaire–Rogers cycle produced by RKO. A comparison between Matthews's films and those of Fields is instructive. If Fields was firmly rooted in a local community network with overtones of nostalgia, Matthews's character is always much more clearly independent, modern and unencumbered by the pull back to her roots. She was, in fact, rootless – always playing a bright, independent talent on the make in a series of modern urban settings beautifully designed to look glamorous in the Art Deco style by Alfred Junge. Many of her narratives involved her impersonating other people in order to achieve success (her own mother in *Evergreen* (Victor Saville, 1934), a rich society hostess in *It's Love Again* (Victor Saville, 1936), a male–female impersonator in *First A Girl* (Victor Saville, 1935), an international jewel thief in *Gangway* (Sonny Hale, 1937)). In such situations Gracie Fields always revealed herself immediately, sending up the pretence with her earthy Lancashire humour. More was riding on Matthews's impersonations, though, since an unmasking might lead to ruin. It never did, of course, but rather to a demonstration of her real talent, unencumbered by society's expectations. If Fields's films always reconfirmed her status as the moral heart of community life, Matthews's were more concerned with the meretricious rise of the talented individual – a narrative structure which was arguably more in tune with the **classical Hollywood** style. The Matthews musicals did achieve a measure of success in America, despite an unadvantageous distribution structure, and during the mid- to late 1930s it looked tantalisingly as though the dream of British films competing internationally with Hollywood ones might be achievable (Higson 1995; Street 2002).

The dream did not last long though, for despite the production boom, filmmaking in Britain remained an extremely risky investment. A series of financial scandals around 1937 brought about a collapse of confidence, and many of the companies which had pursued more ambitious production strategies (including Gaumont-British) were forced into receivership. The outbreak of the Second World War in 1939 saw the British film industry in a much more inward-looking mood.

classical Hollywood cinema
As described by David Bordwell, Janet Staiger and Kristin Thompson in their book of the same name, classical Hollywood cinema is both a cinematic style (emphasising goal-orientated protagonists, a particular form of economic narrative structure, continuity editing and a particular range of lighting and sound techniques) and a 'mode of production' (the studio system) which dominated American commercial filmmaking from around 1917 to 1960. Bordwell, Staiger and Thompson's account of classical Hollywood cinema has been very influential, although it has many detractors.

Critics both at the time and since have often judged the Second World War as the period of British cinema's 'Golden Age' – a period where the national crisis seemed to give the project of filmmaking a purpose and urgency which it had previously lacked. In fact, many of the more celebrated characteristics of wartime filmmaking can be traced back to traditions established during the 1930s, and it may be that the increased respect for British films was as much to do with a shift in the prevailing conceptualisation of the nation as to do with changes in the films themselves. The political and social divisions which to a certain extent had characterised national life during the Depression of the 1930s had surfaced relatively rarely in British films of that decade, to the dismay of many critics who found the popular community optimism of the Gracie Fields cycle and the consensus politics of *The Good Companions* (Victor Saville, 1933) an inadequate substitute for political and social critique. By contrast, during the war both official propaganda and popular sentiment became dominated by the idea of the nation united in a consensus, with the old divisions and political grievances set aside in the face of the larger project of fighting both against Nazism and for a better future. In the popular phrase of the time, Britain was fighting a 'people's war' (Barr 2005; Ellis 1996).

A key film of this transition is John Baxter's *Love on the Dole* (1941), adapted from a Walter Greenwood novel of 1933 which had been considered too politically sensitive for a film treatment during the 1930s. It tells the story of a family living under the grinding poverty of unemployment during the Depression of the early 1930s. No comic relief or uplifting community musical numbers are introduced to lighten the entertainment (although they abound in the director's other films). The downbeat ending of the film shows the daughter sacrificing her virtue to a man she doesn't like in order to vouchsafe the economic stability of her family. At the very close of the film this mood of hopelessness and despair is firmly placed in the past by a written title quoting A.V. Alexander (a Cabinet member in the wartime coalition government) which draws a wartime conclusion, pronouncing that 'Our working men and women have responded magnificently to any and every call made upon them. Their reward must be a new Britain. Never again must the unemployed become the forgotten men of peace.'

Forging a 'new Britain' through the necessary consensus of wartime struggle is an insistent theme of the most celebrated of the British films of the war period. Many such films share a narrative structure which brings together a range of individuals from different regions and social backgrounds, uniting them in the common public enterprise of the war, either as an army unit in *The Way Ahead* (Carol Reed, 1944), the crew of a battle cruiser in *In Which We Serve* (David Lean, 1942), a group of women factory workers in *Millions Like Us* (Launder and Gilliat, 1943), or a rural community of army trainees, land girls and village residents in *A Canterbury Tale* (Powell and Pressburger, 1944). The relationship between public and private life is a particularly important theme of such films, which often emphasise the sacrifice of individual desire for the greater benefit of the group, or the melding of individual and community goals. This theme is emphasised in all of the films through a mixture of aesthetic styles – a union between fiction and documentary techniques which was widely celebrated by critics. The tradition of British documentary films, begun in 1929 by John Grierson's *Drifters*, had been the most intellectually influential aspect of British filmmaking in the 1930s, and that documentary movement came into its own during the war period with the massive expansion in state sponsorship for documentary and propaganda films, particularly through the Ministry of Information (British documentary cinema is discussed in more detail in Chapter 9). The combination of documentary and fiction aesthetics (and personnel) in wartime British cinema is demonstrated, for instance, by the fact that *The Way Ahead* is a reworking of an earlier short training film, *The New Lot* (1943) made by Carol Reed for the Army Kinematograph Service, and by the fact that *Millions Like Us* began life as a commission from the Ministry of Information (Chapman 1997).

In its combination of melodrama and documentary realism, *Millions Like Us* is a particularly good example of consensus wartime filmmaking. As its title suggests, the film is concerned to tell the story of ordinary people and how they are affected by the war. The first half of the film introduces Celia, played by Patricia Roc, as simply one of a large range of characters responding to wartime conditions in short episodic scenes. Some of these scenes are pure documentary (the building of an aeroplane), and many show incidents and characters unrelated to the central lower middle-class family group to which Celia belongs. Only around 40 minutes into the film does the heroine begin to take centre stage as she is transported out of her home to join a group of women from different social backgrounds at work in an aircraft factory. Her romantic fantasies of uniformed war service are firmly set aside by the ordinariness and lack of glamour in factory life. She does meet and marry an airman, but her personal happiness is cut short when he is killed in action. This narrative of personal desire and sacrifice is set against other scenes which show the initial class tensions resolving into a later unity between the disparate group of women working alongside Celia in the factory. An extraordinary final sequence set during a community concert in the factory canteen draws Celia (and us) back from her personal grief into the caring bosom of the newly formed social group, and through an editing motif already established earlier in the film, makes this process of accepting private sacrifice for public good a metaphor for the 'new Britain' that is being fought for. This is achieved literally through deflecting Celia's gaze into the camera upward through a visual and aural **dissolve** to the silhouettes of the bombers above, going out on another night operation. Personal and public sacrifice for the future are made one and the same act (Higson 1995).

Millions Like Us and the other consensus films were not naive about the impermanence of their wartime politics. In a telling and much cited scene immediately before its emotional ending, the characters speculate over whether the togetherness of the war period will remain once peace is achieved, or whether 'we are going to slip back'. Other films of the period continued traditions developed in the 1930s – the low-budget working-class comedy remained a staple, as evidenced by the continuing popularity of George Formby and figures such as Old Mother Riley – an anarchic washerwoman played by Arthur Lucan in a series of low-budget films. There was also a crop of new comedians transferring their talents from successful wartime radio comedies. Not surprisingly, many films and audiences of this period firmly turned their backs on the war as a subject, preferring escapist fantasies, and a particularly popular genre of the later war years was the historical melodrama, as produced by the Gainsborough Studios. In contrast to the consensus cycle, the Gainsborough melodrama resolutely privileged individual desire, ambition and sexuality over community responsibility or sacrifice. Commonly set in Regency England, the films provided an opportunity to revel in a sensuous visual aesthetic, particularly in the costuming and set designs, as well as in full-blooded narratives of sexual desire, jealousy and revenge. *The Wicked Lady* (Leslie Arliss, 1945), for instance, starred Margaret Lockwood as a bored aristocrat seeking thrills through a double life as a cross-dressing highwayman, killing off rivals and enjoying a torrid affair with the dangerously attractive James Mason. Her punishment and death at the end of the film seemed a small price to pay for ninety minutes of passionate adventure. These films were dismissed out of hand by critics of the period, but they were massively popular with audiences, regularly topping the box office charts, and feminist critics in more recent years have celebrated their frank portrayal of unencumbered female sexuality (Cook 1996; Harper 1994).

Box-office attendance was at its peak during and just after the war years, helped no doubt by fuel and food rationing, and a whole host of wartime hardships which made going to the cinema the most attractive of a very limited range of leisure options. As we have seen, British filmmaking was also enjoying a critical renaissance. American films still dominated British screens, of course. *Gone With the Wind* (Victor Fleming, 1939) was the biggest box-office attraction throughout the war years, although MGM's series of 'British' dramas, particularly *Mrs Miniver* (William Wyler, 1942) starring Greer Garson as a 'typical' English wife and mother coping in the early years of the war, were extremely

dissolve
Transition between shots with the first shot fading out to be simultaneously replaced by the second shot fading in. Often used to indicate an **ellipse**.

popular. It is worth comparing Hollywood's *Mrs Miniver* with British films dealing with similar subject matter, such as *Millions Like Us*. The differences, in terms of narrative, settings, characters and filming style, are very revealing of the different priorities of the two national film industries.

While the exhibition sector was enjoying a boom, the British production sector was going through a major period of transition following the financial collapse of the late 1930s. It was partly on the back of that collapse that J. Arthur Rank entered the industry, and quickly rose to become a key figure. Rank's fortune was originally in flour milling, and his initial interest in cinema had been as a means of Christian education – a staunch Methodist, Rank also proved to be an extremely astute businessman. During the late 1930s and early 1940s he made a series of key purchases until by the middle of the war he controlled enough of the industry for his involvement to be the subject of a monopoly enquiry. Rank's empire included not only the ownership of various studios, and interests in most of the major producing companies, but also importantly the Gaumont and the Odeon cinema chains. With a fully vertically integrated concern, the ambition to break into the American market, and the ability to invest heavily in that attempt, Rank quickly became the key figure of the British film industry both during and for a long while after the war.

GOLDEN AGE TO NEW WAVE

Filmmaking in Britain from the war to the early 1960s was dominated by the figure of J. Arthur Rank, whose company continued to juggle the two alternative attitudes to filmmaking in Britain established in the 1930s. Rank made various attempts to break into the American market with expensive quality British productions, yet he also funded a series of more modestly budgeted and culturally specific films intended for purely domestic consumption. The contrast between these two policies was most clearly marked in the mid- to late 1940s. The critical success of many British wartime productions both at home and in America led Rank to believe that with the lifting of restrictions in the postwar period, British films had a real chance of breaking into the lucrative American market. As early as 1944 he had opened a distribution office in New York which was designed to distribute quality British films in America under the descriptive trademark 'Eagle–Lion'. This was a period where Rank was investing heavily in British film production. He instituted a financing mechanism known as 'Independent Producers' which granted a remarkable degree of financial and artistic freedom to a small number of extremely talented British filmmakers working under several different production companies. It was through this arrangement that some of Britain's most prestigious and iconic films were produced, including *Henry V* (Laurence Olivier, 1944), *Brief Encounter* (David Lean, 1944) and *The Red Shoes* (Powell and Pressburger, 1948). These films, one might suggest, share a visual flamboyance and emotional expressiveness which may only be described as 'cinematic', belying British cinema's more usual reputation for social realism, literariness and emotional restraint (Macnab 1993; Petley 1986; Street 2002)

The narrative theme of *Brief Encounter*, for instance, is the repression of excessive romantic emotion, and yet the film employs a series of cinematic techniques in its lighting, camerawork and use of sound which can only be described *as* excessive. Consider an early scene where the heroine, Laura, is on a train with a talkative friend, beginning for the first time to reflect in voiceover on the extra-marital affair she has just ended. The cinematic shifts in emphasis – the slow, almost imperceptible movement closer to Laura's face, the darkening of the light around her, the fading-in of the music – all violently interrupted by the return to reality when her friend makes small-talk, contribute to provide us with an unequivocally subjective emotional viewpoint on the action, allied with that of the heroine. The film later makes fun of excessive romanticism in Hollywood films of the time, but in its meticulous way, one might argue, it is much more committed to 'violent emotion' than to the 'ordinariness' which it appears to foreground (Dyer 1993; Lant 1991).

While the Independent Producer system of finance led to films of high quality which certainly gained British cinema a critical reputation abroad, the freedom it gave filmmakers could also prove to be extremely expensive. For instance, due to its protracted shooting period, *Caesar and Cleopatra* (Gabriel Pascal, 1945) became an industry byword for wasteful and expensive filmmaking. Although they did find a market in America, on balance these expensive prestige films did not turn a large enough profit to justify Rank's investment and so the 'Independent Producer' system did not survive for very long.

By contrast, Rank also controlled Gainsborough Studios. Operating outside the 'Independent Producers' umbrella, Gainsborough was expected to continue producing its spectacularly successful historical melodramas and comedies within the context of tightly controlled budgets and production schedules. The films were intended to make their money back within the British market, so they were both more modest and much more culturally specific than the Independent Producers' films. Gainsborough's productions in the late 1940s took on a more contemporary flavour under the management of Sydney Box, whose sister Betty Box was put in charge of the company's studios in Islington. The production emphasis was on light comedies adapted from stage successes such as *Miranda* (Kenneth Annakin, 1948), and social problem films such as *The Good Time Girl* (David MacDonald, 1948). Perhaps the most indicative and indeed generative of the studio's films during this period was the series initiated by *Holiday Camp* (Kenneth Annakin, 1947) introducing the Huggetts, a lower middle-class suburban family who featured in a series of four films over the next two years. Modestly budgeted and not intended for export, the Huggett films had an episodic structure which made light comedy out of familiar contemporary situations and domestic tensions. Their continuity of casting and setting, and their episodic structure gave them a reassuring familiarity akin to later television soap operas. These features also give them an affinity with a range of later 'inexportable' comedy cycles which came to dominate the industry during the following three decades, beginning with Betty Box's biggest hit as a producer, *Doctor in the House* (Ralph Thomas, 1954). Looking back on her time at Gainsborough, Box ruefully compared the strict economy and box-office reliability of the studio's films with the high expense and uneven returns of those made under 'Independent Producers' (Ashby 2000).

One of the few studios not affiliated with Rank during this period was Michael Balcon's Ealing Studios. After his drive for international success at Gaumont-British had failed, Balcon had moved to Ealing where throughout the war he had produced modest, well-crafted films with a definite consensus flavour. The famous postwar series of 'Ealing Comedies' including *Passport to Pimlico* (Henry Cornelius, 1949), *The Lavender Hill Mob* (Charles Crichton, 1951) and *The Ladykillers* (Alexander MacKendrick, 1955) retain some aspects of the 'consensus' tradition, although they now have the reputation for cosy optimism. Possibly this characteristic has ensured their lasting popularity with certain American audiences, but as Charles Barr points out, the struggle between personal greed and community values which they dramatise is generally darker and more fraught than is often acknowledged, particularly in the work of directors such as Alexander MacKendrick and Robert Hamer. Ealing's distinctive production style, which owed much to the ethos of collaborative filmmaking encouraged by Balcon, was also evident in its non-comedy films, and might be summed up by Balcon's suggestion that in order for cinema to be international it must first be truly national (Barr 1999).

By the early 1950s it had become clear that Rank's ambitions to break into the lucrative American market were costing far more money than they were likely to generate, and the organisation began to steadily modify its ambitions and cut back its operating costs. As part of this strategy the Gainsborough studios were closed down, and most of Rank's production activities became concentrated at Pinewood Studios. The 1950s saw a steady decline in cinema attendances, as television became increasingly popular after the Coronation in 1953 and the introduction of ITV in 1955. Throughout the 1950s, in common with Hollywood producers, Rank retained a notion of cinema as 'family' entertainment in its attempts to compete with television. Comedies and war films predominated in the production schedule and at the box office, and Rank built up a roster of male stars whose appeal was curiously of the age. Kenneth More, John Mills and John Gregson would make unlikely stars today, but they were the epitome of masculine glamour in the 1950s, often playing tweed-clad, pipe-smoking, honourable war heroes in films such as *Reach for the Sky* (Lewis Gilbert, 1956) and *Above Us the Waves* (Ralph Thomas, 1955). These popular 1950s accounts of the war tended to emphasise individual heroism and action much more than the films made during the conflict itself, although always within the context of the 'group'. Rank was not the only company to draw on such material – the Associated British Picture Corporation, the other main, vertically integrated British film company at this time, was responsible for the highly successful *The Dam Busters* (Michael Anderson, 1954), for instance (Harper and Porter 2003).

Rank's most successful male star of the 1950s was even more unlikely. Norman Wisdom made an unexpected hit at the box office as the hapless stockroom boy of a department store in *Trouble In Store* (John Paddy Carstairs, 1953), and was immediately signed to star in a series of similar comedies. The Wisdom films continued the tradition established by Formby and Fields in the 1930s. Wisdom always played a character of low status, but with irrepressible energy, optimism and naivety, thrust into a world of deception which he didn't fully understand. The comedy revolved around the tension between his emotional honesty and the less innocent, more high-status figures around him. Like the Fields and Formby cycles, they also relied on an episodic narrative structure which gave full rein to Wisdom's anarchic slapstick humour (the window-dressing incident in *Trouble In Store* provides a perfect example), as well as containing a healthy dose of sentimentality. Norman always fell in love with a seemingly unattainable girl, who he serenaded with his surprisingly pleasant singing voice. Having found a magic formula of low production costs coupled with high box-office receipts in *Trouble in Store*, Rank sought to repeat the strategy with a string of similar Wisdom vehicles. The same may be said of their response to the box office success of *Doctor in the House* (Ralph Thomas, 1954), starring Dirk Bogarde as the diffident medical student Simon Sparrow. Bogarde's Sparrow was a more good-looking, well-heeled and well-mannered character than those played by Norman Wisdom, but the comic tension of the films was similar in that he was an innocent surrounded by heels, humbugs and buffoons. These comedy cycles enjoyed more success at the box office than they did in critical circles, and indeed the British films of the 1950s have generally been thought to be rather lacking in both social realism and cinematic value. In fact a number of films made during the period tackled serious social issues in an adult manner (it is worth noting the remarkable output of the director Basil Dearden in this light); however, the fact that both producers and censors still thought of cinema as primarily a family entertainment medium meant that the treatment of such subject matter remained too generically coded for later critical tastes (Sinyard and MacKillop 2003).

The decisive move away from attempts to appeal to a family audience marks an important transition from the 1950s to the 1960s. Shifts in cinema-going patterns, and in censorship regulations, as well as more general changes in cultural attitudes around the late 1950s, made possible the development of a range of new filmic styles which were directed at more specialised tastes. These films tended to be produced by independent companies, and by comparison with Rank's offerings of the early 1950s they certainly look surprisingly modern, and in many cases much more adult. Hammer Film Productions, for instance, had been making modest crime and science fiction films since the 1930s, but it was with the full-blooded and luridly coloured production of *The Curse of Frankenstein*

(Terence Fisher, 1957) that the company found real commercial success. A series of ground-breakingly graphic and expressive horror films followed. Hammer managed to combine commercial success with relatively small production costs through identifying themselves almost exclusively with the Horror genre – appealing to a niche market, and gaining a reputation for visual and emotional excess (Hutchings 1993).

The biggest critical breakthrough for an independent film, though, was with the production of *Room at the Top* (Jack Clayton, 1959), a film whose 'X' certificate rating indicated a clear rejection of the concept of the family audience as espoused by the Rank Organisation (at this period the Rank chain refused to show X certificate films). *Room at the Top* was hailed as the beginning of a 'new wave' in British filmmaking, and may be seen as initiating a cycle of realist films, including *Saturday Night, Sunday Morning* (Karel Reisz, 1960), *Look Back in Anger* (Tony Richardson, 1958), *A Kind of Loving* (John Schlesinger, 1962) and *A Taste Of Honey* (Tony Richardson, 1961), whose ordinariness of subject matter and settings earned them the description 'kitchen sink dramas'. These films tended to focus on the contemporary lives of ordinary working-class characters. Their settings in industrial northern towns, and their use of exterior locations, genuine working-class accents and understated lighting techniques gave them a much remarked-upon documentary quality, and indeed many of the filmmakers involved had begun as documentary filmmakers. Mostly adapted from the literary works of a new generation of writers and dramatists who had already made a reputation for themselves as 'Angry Young Men', the 'kitchen sink' films often dramatised the tension between their hero's entrapment within a traditional working-class culture, and his desire for something 'better'. The films may be seen as a response to the changes in postwar society engendered by the consumer boom and full employment of the early 1960s, which was beginning to ensure a higher standard of living for many ordinary people. However, they also share something of a nostalgia for old working-class values which they perceive as being under threat from the new consumer culture. This nostalgia, it may be argued, led them into a rather more reactionary political stance than one might expect, particularly around issues of gender. Films such as *Saturday Night, Sunday Morning* and *A Kind of Loving* associate both women and the new consumer culture with entrapment in a domestic sphere which threatens to restrict and feminise their male protagonists. Indeed, these films tend to fetishise the virile masculinity of their heroes at the expense of older characters, and women in particular. Nevertheless, the emphasis on resistance to consumerism – particularly characterised as coming from television, and from America – places the 'kitchen sink' cycle firmly within a tradition of British filmmaking that sought to differentiate itself from Hollywood standards and styles of production (Hill 1986; Murphy 1992).

The filmmakers of the 'new wave' were not the only ones to court a niche audience by apparently recasting the styles and themes associated with British cinema. The opening of *Summer Holiday* (Peter Yates, 1963) seems to deliberately evoke some of the realist clichés of the kitchen sink cycle, only to spectacularly reject them. In drab black and white, a traditional brass band stand on the beach under lowering skies playing the theme tune. It's the kind of traditional British working-class culture for which the kitchen sink cycle held a special affection. The heavens open, however, driving the band and the rest of the holiday-makers under cover. It looks like we might be in for a depressing two hours of realism, but soon Cliff Richard appears driving the London Transport bus in which he's planning to tour through Europe. At this point the film bursts into fabulous Technicolor while Cliff bursts into song, accompanied by the very large off-screen Associated British Studio Orchestra. Outrageous! The film was the first of a string of hits which took advantage of Cliff Richard's massive popularity with a teenage market who saw him as a rock-god to compete with America's Elvis Presley. In fact, of course, the film sounds much more like a conventional musical to us today, but its good-natured, full-colour travelogue through Europe, peppered with light romance and a host of songs, proved extremely successful, and provided a fitting antidote to the dominant image of

• **Plate 14.5**
A Kind of Loving (John Schlesinger, 1962). Alan Bates is emasculated by marriage and the television

British cinema as one of dour social realism. With prominent product placement for Dolcis and various other manufacturers of teenage fashions, *Summer Holiday* shows none of the anxiety over consumerism demonstrated by *A Kind of Loving*.

In fact, the most successful British film of 1963 was another picturesque Technicolor travelogue, although paradoxically it was made by the team responsible for many of the previous 'kitchen sink' cycle. *Tom Jones* (1963), Tony Richardson and John Osborne's adaptation of Henry Fielding's eighteenth-century romp, combined the frank sexuality and innovative cinematic techniques of the British new wave with the good nature and colourful visuals of the Cliff Richard films. In order to raise the necessary finance to make such an expensive costume drama, the producers struck a co-production deal with United Artists, ensuring the film prominent distribution in America. The result was an international box-office sensation reminiscent of Korda's *Private Life of Henry VIII* in 1933. Osborne's playful adaptation of Fielding's novel encouraged a series of what at the time seemed like quite startling cinematic innovations – characters speak directly into the camera, chases are speeded up for comic effect, freeze frames are used as in a comic strip, and the pre-credit sequence pastiches the style of silent cinema. All of these techniques constituted an irrevocable break with classical filmmaking conventions, making the film appear both modern and daring. The success of *Tom Jones* in America was guaranteed when the film won the academy award for best film.

As had happened in 1933, the extent of the success of *Tom Jones* in the American market encouraged increased investment in British production through much of the rest of the 1960s. Indeed, with the Hollywood studio system breaking up, American producers themselves were looking more towards international co-productions as a way of funding large-scale projects, and Britain became an attractive option. MGM in fact had been operating a British production unit throughout the 1950s, producing costume dramas and historical epics with an international flavour. During the mid-1960s, with the success of the Beatles and the increasing perception of London as the centre of a fashionable youth culture, British films drawing on and reflecting this culture became an attractive investment proposition. The 'Swinging London' films, as they became known, tended to follow *Tom Jones* in combining elements of 'kitchen sink's' emphasis on sexuality, and youth, with modern, innovative, playful filmmaking techniques. The films were much less ambivalent about modern consumer culture than the 'kitchen sink' films had been, replacing that cycle's nostalgia for northern industrial spaces, with a delight in London as the centre of a happening, modern youth society. Nevertheless, 'Swinging London' films still articulated considerable reservations about the values of that society. Julie Christie as Diana in *Darling* (John Schlesinger, 1965), for example, is punished almost as severely at the end of her ninety minutes of amoral hedonism as Margaret Lockwood had been twenty years earlier at the end of *The Wicked Lady*. Similarly, while Michael Caine as *Alfie* (Lewis Gilbert, 1966) initially seems like a charmer, by the end of the film it is clear both to him and to us that he is less a lovable rogue than a selfish monster.

DECLINE AND REVIVAL

Despite the apparent boom associated with 'Swinging London', and the success of films directed at younger sections of the audience, cinema attendances continued to decline throughout the period from 1946 to the 1980s. The decline of the family audience is reflected in the fortunes of the Rank Organisation which continued to close cinemas in an attempt to rationalise their exhibition circuit. Rank began to diversify into other popular pastimes, and this is the period when many cinemas became converted into Bingo halls. Audiences for individual films became smaller, and it became more financially viable to have one cinema with several small screens, rather than the large single-screen picture palaces which had been in operation since the 1920s. Accordingly many cinemas were converted to multi-screen use, while others fell into disuse or were converted to other uses.

For film producers as well, raising finance became increasingly difficult. Rank itself diversified away from film production, investing in the Xerox photocopying process – a far more lucrative long-term proposition than filmmaking had ever been. The government commitment to supporting the British production industry which had begun in 1927 remained, although during the 1950s the Quota had been replaced by the Eady Levy. This was a mechanism which diverted a percentage of box-office revenues to a special production fund controlled by the National Film Finance Corporation, which contributed finance to British film projects. Despite such measures, competition from television, the drop in overall attendance and the increasing emphasis on big-budget blockbusters rather than routine programme pictures meant that British filmmakers faced a difficult task (Macnab 1993).

As Rank had already discovered, trying to produce expensive international films that might compete with Hollywood's product was a risky production strategy, although some British films did attain international status, for instance, the James Bond series, which, like the 'Swinging London' films emphasised the modernity and sexual liberation of the hero. The first of the Bond films, *Dr No* (Terence Young, 1962) was made at Pinewood by Ion Productions – an independent production company which rented the studio space and personnel from Rank. Always a common practice, such an arrangement became increasingly dominant, meaning that today British studios often host the production of films which in every other respect are Hollywood products (Chapman 1999).

The international status of the Bond films forms a contrast with the less risky production policy adopted by other producers who placed an emphasis on modestly budgeted features which would reliably appeal to the home market through repeating a familiar and already successful formula. It comes as no surprise that such 'inexportable' film cycles became the mainstay of British production during the 1960s and 1970s. One might argue that the 'Carry On' films and the 'Confessions' series continue the tradition of working-class comedy established by George Formby and Gracie Fields in the 1930s. Made on rigorously small budgets, the 'Carry On' series eschewed stars in favour of a roster of familiar performers, and were reliant on an episodic format and a comedy style rooted in traditions of British music-hall. Beginning with *Carry on Sergeant* (Gerald Thomas, 1958) the series gently sent up British institutions, although later examples took advantage of relaxed censorship rules to use a more smutty and titillating form of humour than was possible on broadcast television at the time. This tendency continued in the 1970s with the rather ruder and less funny cycle initiated by *Confessions of a Window Cleaner* (Val Guest, 1974). The familiarity of the returning cast, the episodic nature of the films and the cycle, and their low production values gave these series an affinity with television aesthetics, and the association is borne out by the fact that the 'Carry On' series made the transition to television through various compilation shows, as well as *Carry On Laughing* (1975), a programme consisting of entirely new sketches made for Thames Television. The symbiosis between television and inexportable British cinema was also evident in the large number of big screen adaptations of familiar TV programmes during the 1970s, including *Doctor Who and the Invasion of the Daleks* (Gordon Flemying, 1965), and comedies such as *On the Buses* (Harry Booth, 1971), *Man About the House* (John Robins, 1974) and *Porridge* (Dick Clement, 1979). While enjoying a dolorous critical reputation, such films nevertheless provided evidence of British filmmakers catering to the comedy tastes of working-class audiences in a way that is often overlooked, even if some of their attitudes towards gender and race now seem embarrassingly primeval.

By the time Margaret Thatcher came to power in 1979, British cinema appeared to have settled into a definite decline. Thatcher's policies did nothing to allay fears for the British industry as it became clear that the legislative protection enjoyed by British filmmakers since the 1920s was anathema to Thatcher's doctrine of the free market. Accordingly, the Eady Levy was scrapped in 1985, and for the first time in sixty years British films had to fend for themselves in the marketplace. Thatcher's apparently philistine attitude towards British cultural life had the effect of dividing, galvanising and politicising the creative community, and British films of the 1980s reflect this in a renewed sense of urgent political purpose. Political, avant-garde and experimental filmmaking had in fact been going on throughout the 1970s, often on small-gauge formats and using minuscule budgets often raised through the BFI's production board. An interest in formal experimentation and feminist politics marks the massively influential work of Laura Mulvey, whose films *The Riddles of the Sphinx* (1977) and *Amy* (1980) complement her remarkable critical writings on the representation of women in cinema. Similarly, Derek Jarman's work of the 1970s and into the 1980s, including *Jubilee* (1977) and *The Tempest* (1978), combined experimental techniques with an explicit political intent. During the Thatcherite period, this kind of politically inspired filmmaking became more mainstream, moving (as can be seen with Jarman's career) into a more accessible 'art-house' and festival exhibition context. Meanwhile, the relationship between cinema and television also began to alter as a generation of filmmakers trained in social realist television genres during the 1960s and 1970s tentatively made the transition to the big screen. Low budgets, intimate if political storylines and improvisational styles mark the work of directors such as Ken Loach and Mike Leigh, both of whose careers saw them move from television to film, culminating in a remarkable set of films in the early 1990s which commented on the state of the nation under Tory rule. *High Hopes* (Mike Leigh, 1988) and *Raining Stones* (Ken Loach, 1993) provide excellent examples of the kind of social realist cinema which is often understood to be one of the strongest traditions of British filmmaking (Leigh 2002; Lippard and Johnson 1993).

Perhaps the most significant element of the symbiosis between television and cinema was the launch of Channel 4 in 1982. As part of the new channel's commitment to innovation, 'Film on Four' was established to help fund the production of new British films which would be aired on television after a possible theatrical release. The quality and range of the films produced under this system were remarkable, although the ones which tend to be remembered today are the those which garnered criticism from right-wing critics for their unforgiving portrayals of contemporary life under Thatcher's government – films such as *Letter to Brezhnev* (Chris Bernard, 1985), *My Beautiful Laundrette* (Stephen Frears, 1985) and *Rita, Sue and Bob Too* (Alan Clarke, 1986). These

For further discussion of Laura Mulvey and her influence on feminist film theory see Chapter 11, pp. 271–273

• **Plate 14.6**
Letter to Brezhnev (Chris Bernard, 1985). Struggling to have a good time in Thatcher's Britain

films adroitly mix comedy and social criticism, telling stories of ordinary people making enterprising choices in order to survive in the harsh economic environment of the period. *Letter to Brezhnev*, for example, celebrates the irrepressible spirit of its two working-class heroines as they determine to have a 'good time' on a night out in Liverpool, despite their poor jobs and lack of prospects. Theresa and Elaine steal money and drinks, and take a joyride, before picking up a couple of sailors from the USSR and spending the night with them. Elaine falls unexpectedly in love with her sailor, and the rest of the film chronicles her desperate attempts to leave Kirkby and join him in Russia, against the wishes of her family and of the British government. As she says, whatever is claimed in the press, 'life in Russia can't be any worse than it is here'. Famously made on a shoestring, but very successful at the box office when it finally achieved distribution, *Letter To Brezhnev* oscillates between broad comic optimism, intense romantic lyricism and, at its heart, an overwhelming despair at a society that can offer its resourceful heroines no alternatives other than a fantasy escape to the USSR, or a life of 'drinking vodka, fucking men and stuffing chickens' (Friedman 1993; Hill 1999).

By the mid-1990s with the advent of Tony Blair's New Labour government, representations of the northern working-class scene became slightly less politically embattled, although films such as *Trainspotting* (Danny Boyle, 1996) and *Brassed Off* (Mark Herman, 1996) still expressed considerable concern over the disenfranchisement of certain areas and industries. The ambivalence of Renton's position in *Trainspotting*, for instance – his initial rejection and then monstrous embrace of enterprise culture – provides a good indication of the mixed response to Blair's doctrine of the 'third way'. *Brassed Off*, by contrast, with its insistence on community solidarity and affection for traditional culture even in the face of a despairing acknowledgement of its imminent demise, shows a political conviction which even at the time of its release seemed old-fashioned. Indeed, in films of the 1990s it is possible to identify a shift away from a focus on class towards one on gender, and this is reflected too in the critical debates surrounding them. The massive success of *The Full Monty* (Peter Cattaneo, 1997) would seem to have had more to do with its fantasy about the repackaging of a masculinity understood to be in 'crisis' than with the structural unemployment of which its male characters were the primary victims. According to *Billy Elliot* (Stephen Daldry, 2000), the destruction of an entire industrial community and way of life is a small price to pay for enlightened masculine attitudes to the ballet. The film's setting during the 1984 miner's strike is used merely as a background, against which Billy's heart-warming story of individual achievement over adversity can be contrasted, and no actual discussion of the politics of the strike is allowed to mar the inspirational storyline. Nevertheless, it was partly this glossing of the political and cultural specificities of these stories that enabled their huge international appeal (Murphy 2000).

While such films attempted to deal with the contemporary realities of Thatcher and Blair's Britain, the other major cycle to emerge during the 1980s and 1990s appeared to look back nostalgically to a more elegant age. The massive international commercial and critical success of *Chariots of Fire* (Hugh Hudson, 1981) was reminiscent of the reception of *The Private Life of Henry VIII* and *Tom Jones* earlier in the century. As on those occasions, this success led to a great deal of optimism about a coming renaissance of British filmmaking, and a renewed confidence about the ability of British films to break into an international (and particularly an American) market. Like its predecessors, *Chariots of Fire* was a costume drama celebrating an aspect of Britain's cultural heritage – the story of the 1924 Olympic running team and the tension between the 'gentlemen' and the 'professionals'. The **mise-en-scène** of the film has since been widely discussed as central to its success – the beautiful cinematography creating an image of Britain as a 'heritage' site, with emphasis on the historic buildings of Cambridge, the country houses of the Home Counties and the wild mountains of Scotland. Certainly in its opening sequence the film establishes a visual aesthetic of well-composed shots containing beautiful objects and scenery which was repeated enough in subsequent British films for them to have been increasingly written about as a coherent genre which became labelled as 'Heritage' films. These productions, which include later international successes such as *A Room with a View* (James Ivory, 1985), *Maurice* (James Ivory, 1987), *The Remains of the Day* (James Ivory, 1993), *Sense and Sensibility* (Ang Lee, 1995), *Wings of the Dove* (Ian Softley, 1997), *Elizabeth* (Shekhar Kapur, 1998) and *Shakespeare in Love* (John Madden, 1998) have been the subject of fierce critical debate over whether they are ideologically conservative or progressive. Visually, they certainly strive to present an image of Britain as a tourist opportunity, showcasing landscapes, houses and literary history as unchanging and available for inspection in a way that seems to reject the concerns of the social realist films. Nevertheless, as many critics have pointed out, the narrative of these films consistently offers criticisms of the British society they portray. *Chariots of Fire* itself was structured around the tension between those British runners who benefited from membership of the establishment, and those who were treated as outsiders as a result of being Jewish or Scottish Methodist. Many of the other heritage films contained narratives dealing with class and sexuality which would have appeared extremely radical given a contemporary setting; note, for instance, the argument for the acceptance of gay sexuality in *Maurice*, released at precisely the moment when the government was legislating against the acceptance of gay relationships as a 'pretend family relationship'. Critics have identified a widening of the 'Heritage' genre during the 1990s to include more expressive and less restrained filmmaking, particularly after the release of *Elizabeth* in 1998 (Higson 2003; Monk and Sargeant 2002).

The international success of *Chariots of Fire* encouraged its producers, Goldcrest, to fund a series of large budget productions designed to be exported internationally, and during the early 1980s a number of productions demonstrated that British filmmakers could gain a foothold in the international market. Films such as *Gandhi* (Richard Attenborough, 1982), *Local Hero* (Bill Forsyth, 1983) and *The Killing Fields* (Roland Joffe, 1984) drew on various traditions of British filmmaking, demonstrating the potential of British films, although all of their narratives had a significant international dimension. The company came to grief however, when two of its most ambitious and expensive productions failed at the box office. The musical pastiche of the 1950s *Absolute Beginners* (Julian Temple, 1986), and the epic treatment of the American

Mise-en-scène
A theatrical term usually translated as 'staging' or 'what has been put into the scene'. In film, mise-en-scène refers not only to sets, costumes, props and the position of actors, but also to how the scene is organised, lit and framed for the camera. Mise-en-scène is one way of producing meanings in films which can be both straightforward and extremely complex, depending upon the intentions and skill of the director (the metteur-en-scène).

For more detailed discussion of mise-en-scène see pp. 87–93.

war of independence *Revolution* (Hugh Hudson, 1985), had both been conceived on a particularly ambitious scale, and their failure demonstrated again the risky nature of international productions. Despite such risks, internationally ambitious cinema continues to be made in Britain, usually as part of international co-production deals. The success of a range of later international hits, including *Love Actually* (Richard Curtis, 2004) and the cycle initiated by *Harry Potter and the Sorcerer's Stone* (Chris Columbus, 2001) attest to the ability of British films both to reflect and to export British cultural values.

For further discussion of cinema audiences and admissions see Chapter 1.

Having hit rock-bottom in 1984, cinema admissions figures began to rise again, and that upward trend is still continuing today. This may partly be the result of the development of 'multiplex' cinemas, the most common exhibition venue today. The advent of video during the 1980s, and more recently DVD, has given an added boost to cinema, both increasing the public's interest in film as an entertainment choice, but also allowing individual films a much longer money-earning life, and thus making them more attractive to potential investors. With the passing of the Thatcher government, some state support for the industry was reintroduced, with a complex system of tax incentives for filmmakers, and latterly through a production fund raised as part of the National Lottery and made available through the UK Film Council – a government agency created in 2000 to consolidate the administration of various filmmaking funds and initiatives designed to encourage and stimulate the British industry.

The creation of the UK Film Council in 2000 marked the latest of a series of government initiatives to assist the British film industry since the Cinematograph Act of 1927. The Film Council's remit combined commercial and non-commercial aims. On the one hand it was concerned to support the commercial industry, providing financial and other kinds of assistance at key stages of production in order to ensure that potentially profitable films reached the screen. On the other hand it had a commitment to widening the range of filmmaking opportunities available in Britain – enabling stories and representations to come to the screen which otherwise would not have been possible. This twin approach was broadly reflected in the two main funds managed by the Film Council. The Premiere Fund was used for more potentially commercial projects and was instrumental in the production of internationally successful films such as *Gosford Park* (Robert Altman, 2001), *Vera Drake* (Mike Leigh, 2004), *Ladies in Lavender* (Charles Dance, 2004), *The Constant Gardener* (Fernando Meirelles, 2005) and *How to Lose Friends and Alienate People* (Robert Weide, 2008). The New Cinema Fund was designed to enable the production of more modestly budgeted films, with an emphasis on films which were original and innovative, or which represent minority, ethnic or regional communities that were under-represented in mainstream commercial productions. Films which benefited from this fund include Ken Loach's controversial but award-winning Irish drama *The Wind that Shakes the Barley* (Ken Loach, 2006), *Bullet Boy* (Saul Dibb, 2005), *Touching the Void* (Kevin Macdonald, 2003), *Brick Lane* (Sarah Gavron, 2007) and *Fish Tank* (Andrea Arnold, 2009).

None of these films were funded solely by the UK Film Council – all were productions in partnership with commercial filmmaking organisations, and in many cases the vast majority of the production budget was raised commercially. Many other films of course are made without Lottery funding assistance, although these often tended to be international co-productions involving a consortium of multinational organisations. Nevertheless, such films often have an identifiably British address to audiences, and draw on British traditions of filmmaking. Films such as *Calendar Girls* (Nigel Cole, 2003) and *Kinky Boots* (Julian Jarrold, 2005) draw on specifically British subject matter, making use of British locations, characters and attitudes to tell stories which nevertheless have an international appeal. Indeed, one might see a film such as *Kinky Boots*, with its story of a small family firm fighting to save its future by balancing traditional and modern values, as drawing explicitly on the filmmaking traditions established at Ealing Studios in the early 1950s. The connection with television, established since the 1970s, remains strong, both in terms of funding from organisations such as BBC Films, and in terms of the range of acting, writing and production talent employed in many films. *Confetti* (Debbie Isitt, 2006) is a good example of a film which draws on television talent as well as providing a clever pastiche of popular television formats. One wonders what international audiences would make of its culturally specific humour, although it remains one of the best British films of recent years. Other films with more obviously international appeal – such as the sci-fi comedy *The Hitchhiker's Guide to the Galaxy* (Garth Jennings, 2005) and *Calendar Girls* – nevertheless take as their theme the effects of the exposure of unassuming ordinary 'British' characters – 'little Britons' – to modern international (and intergalactic) cultures.

☐ CASE STUDY 1: *BRICK LANE* (SARAH GAVRON, 2007)

Mid-way through *Brick Lane* is a small but significant scene. Reflected in a wardrobe mirror we see Chanu (Satish Kaushik) lying on his bed, looking at a London *A–Z* and reflecting on the fact that although he has lived in Britain most of his life, 'all I have ever seen of this country is The Houses of Parliament, and that was in 1979'. The camera pans slowly down his body to reveal his wife Nazneen (Tannishtha Chatterjee) dutifully cutting the corns on his toes. She looks up, away from him, not listening to the continuation of his reverie, but instead absorbed in a screening of *Brief Encounter* (David Lean, 1945) playing on the television at the foot of the bed. A refocussing of the image draws our attention to the moment of 'high romance' playing out on the television. The adulterous lovers in Lean's film kiss and declare their love while the Rachmaninov soundtrack swells to such an extent that its complex dream-flashback structure breaks down with the intrusion of the heroine's husband 'Laura! Hi, Laura! Do you think we could turn the music down?' By this time Nazneen, who is herself on the brink of a passionate affair, has turned her attention back to her own husband, and his resolve to do some sightseeing.

The strategic quotation of *Brief Encounter* in *Brick Lane* serves to highlight a range of important parallels between the two films. Both are centrally concerned with the interior life of their female protagonist; both use a combination of voice-over and subjective camera-work to examine the tension between the central character's desire to express herself, and the restrictions placed on her by marriage and her community; both offer a range of cinematic references and metaphors to highlight the tension between interior reverie and the cold reality of the outside world; in both narratives an extramarital affair operates as the catalyst for an awakening of consciousness which is finally folded back into an acceptance and reinvestment in the importance and stability of the original marriage union. But while *Brief Encounter* is often held up as an icon of quintessential Englishness, its characters so utterly secure in their middle-England world that it wouldn't occur to them even to question the solidity of national identity ('I mean, one has one's *roots*, after all!'), for the first- and second-generation immigrant characters in *Brick Lane*, the question of national identity, of what constitutes *home*, is an ever-present question.

For Nazneen, who came to England from Bangladesh as a teenage bride in an arranged marriage to Chanu, the link to her childhood home is provided by regular letters from her sister, who stayed behind. The letters play on both Nazneen's memories and her fantasies of 'home', maintaining an idea of Bangladesh as a sensual and poetic space, filled with the magic of her sister's many romances and saturated in the bright colours of fond memory, a clear contrast to the cold grey London she finds herself in. Nazneen's daughter Shahna also enjoys the letters, although her sense of identity is more closely associated with the London of her birth. She recognises, more than her mother does, that the Bangladesh portrayed in the letters is more imaginative than real. 'Bangladesh is gone, it's another time,' she cries, in a desperate attempt to stop her parents from uprooting her life in their desire to return 'home'. It is a fact finally confirmed by the revelation that her aunt's many 'lovers' are actually paying clients. The male characters, too, are invested in fantasy versions of home. Nazneen's lover Karim was also born in London, and yet is attracted to her because he thinks she represents 'the girl from the village'.

These questions of identity construction become increasingly charged as the narrative progresses. In a parallel to the scene encompassing *Brief Encounter*, Nazneen sees her lover in the street market. They move towards one another smiling, but both have their attention diverted towards live news footage of the destruction of the World Trade Center, reproduced multiple times in the window display of a television shop. Their differing reactions to this event, and to the polarisation of the debate about multiculturalism that it initiates in British society, finally draw the lovers away from each other.

Brick Lane is adapted from the best-selling novel by Monica Ali. The book was a popular book-club choice – a middlebrow fiction which offered its readership an immersion in an immigrant cultural experience which was not necessarily their own, but which provided bridges to identification through 'universal' experiences such as motherhood and romance. The director of the film – a middle-class white woman – also acknowledges the foreignness of the cultural world she is attempting to portray.

Though I connect to the story, I've got one foot outside that culture myself. And while there are great precedents for that in Shekar Kapur's *Elizabeth* or Ang Lee's *Sense and Sensibility*, I invited Bangladeshi-based film-maker Ruhul Amin to work alongside me as associate director and inform the political texture of the film.

(James 2007)

Gavron's acknowledgement of the distance between her own experience and that of the characters she is depicting, as well as her citation of Asian directors working on very 'English' stories, highlights the question of whether *Brick Lane* can be understood as an example of 'Anglo Asian' cinema, and indeed of what that category might mean. The film is careful not to fall into the trap of precedents such as *East is East*, which was criticised by Asian writers for its voyeuristic portrayal of British Asian culture, linked to an ideology which identified Asian values as repressive and patriarchal, while approving of the more westernized characters as 'liberal'.

• Plate 14.7
Brick Lane (Sarah Gavron, 2007)

Nazneen finds her voice in her refusal of Karim, and in her decision to remain in England rather than return to a Bangladesh she barely remembers, but these decisions are made in the context of embracing her culture and religion (symbolised partly through her reborn love of her husband) rather than through its rejection. The film did never-theless run into trouble over the question of voyeurism. The producers had worked extensively with members of the Bangladeshi community around Brick Lane during pre-production, but rumours nevertheless began to circulate that the script contained scenes critical of the community. An incident involving a leech falling into a pot of curry was cited, although such a scene was never in the script. Protest marches were arranged and much of the originally planned location shooting had to take place in an alternative setting.

The finished film is acutely aware of the danger of using a voyeuristic eye and of the possibility of turning its viewers into cultural tourists. That anxiety is met and deflected through a series of direct references to acts of looking and inspection, both narrative and cinematic. I've already highlighted the two key scenes which quote broadcast moving images as directly commenting on and reframing the characters' understanding of their identity within the wider culture (*Brief Encounter* emphasising the connections between Nazneen's story and more iconically English understandings of romance, and the 9/11 atrocities heralding and emphasising a break in those continuities). In the cramped interior of the flat, characters are often discovered through reflections in mirrors, or are shown watching through windows. Nazneen herself watches and is watched by a neighbouring white housewife (covered in tattoos, and always clutching a can of beer). A beautifully shot scene in the market shows Nazneen listening to her husband's commentary on the history of Western philosophy, while surreptitiously glimpsing her lover's reflection in a shop window as he delivers garments from his uncle's factory. Mid-way through this shot, the camera refocuses to reveal the shop's display of traditional saris draped over a mannequin idealising Asian femininity. These effects culminate in the scene which follows Chanu's realisation that 'all' he has seen of England is the Houses of Parliament. The family become tourists for a day, leaving their familiar territory of the East End of London, and investigating the 'Landmark London' which Charlotte Brunsdon identifies as the stock-in-trade of more populist transatlantic romantic comedies such as *Love Actually* (Richard Curtis, 2004). While the women in the family are dressed in traditional saris, Chanu looks the part of the American tourist, complete with shorts and a camera round his neck. Invited to photograph them in front of Buckingham Palace, a bystander asks him 'Where are you from?' Having lived in England for over thirty years, the response comes easily enough to Chanu – 'Bangladesh'. For the rest of his family though, the answer is a lot more complex.

Questions
1   In what ways does *Brick Lane* portray different areas of London?
2   How do the different characters in *Brick Lane* understand the concept of 'home'?

☐ **CASE STUDY 2: *MADE IN DAGENHAM* (NIGEL COLE, 2010)**

To mark the opening of *Made in Dagenham*, 'the autumn's hit Brit flick' about the women who went on strike at Ford's Dagenham car factory in 1968 in order to gain equal pay with male workers, *Channel 4 News* staged a reconstruction of the film's climactic scene. Four of the original striking women met up with the Home Secretary and Equality Minister of the new coalition government Theresa May. Now in their sixties, these women appeared initially to offer little threat to their august interlocutor. 'We didn't think of ourselves as feminists,' they said, reassuring television audiences that they hadn't even been interested in politics before the strike, but that they had taken action purely in the cause of 'fairness'. What promised to be a cosily nostalgic little item, however, soon began to touch on a more fundamental question. 'I just wondered if you thought we done the right thing when we came out on strike for ourselves?' posits one of the women. The Home Secretary, sensing thin ice ahead, suggests that they did right to draw attention to the inequality, although nowadays it would be more appropriate to follow a legal route, using the 1970 Equal Pay Act which followed the 1968 strike. When it is pointed out to her that the 1970 Act only came about as a result of their strike action – of the pressure put on the government of the day by the economic and political consequences of prolonged industrial action – the Home Secretary attempts to refocus the debate, in a way which painfully reveals the tension which she, and arguably *Made in Dagenham* itself, are so keen to gloss over, 'Well, you're trying to get me to talk about strikes, rather than the key issue, which is about equality ...'

Apparently 'fairness' and 'gender equality' are principles that were fought for so long ago, and won so decisively, that we can all now unthinkingly support them (even if we are ministers in arguably the most socially divisive administration in a generation). The campaigning methods through which those principles are achieved, however, are a different matter.

In fact, as numerous reviews of the film pointed out, gender equality in pay has still not been achieved. *The Times* reported that the pay gap, which had been reduced from 31 per cent to 17 per cent since 1970, has begun to widen again. In the private sector it stands at 22 per cent while in specific industries it is even higher (in banking for instance, it is 45 per cent). One wouldn't know this from watching *Made in Dagenham*, of course. The film self-consciously situates itself as the latest in a long line of 'hit Brit flicks' which wrest a feel-good storyline out of a political dispute which is unquestionably already over. In both *The Full Monty* (1997) and *Billy Elliot* (2000), for instance, the main characters prevail in their personal quest *despite* the ultimate failure of their community to prevail in the struggle to protect their industry and livelihoods from destruction by political and economic decisions made by those above them. In his *Guardian* review of the film Peter Bradshaw suggested that in this context *Made in Dagenham* might be seen as an exception. 'In its jaunty and insouciant way, this is actually pretty subversive: a film about strikers who are not evil, or deluded, or indeed defeated? What an idea!' (Bradshaw 2010).

While the film does place a successful strike at the centre of its feel-good narrative, it is much more ambivalent about the strike tool itself. Indeed, this is a film which (like Theresa May) manages to be positive about its striking protagonists and the indisputable justice of their cause, while still remaining wholly ambivalent about their right to strike. This is particularly clear in the portrayal of the male trades union officials as corrupt, self-serving and in the pockets of management. In a sleight of hand which it shares with *Billy Elliot*, and numerous other British films of the New Labour period, the film elides the traditional working-class Labour movement with embarrassingly outdated masculine attitudes to gender, implying that sexism and socialism were one and the same thing, equally inappropriate to the new Britain and both to be dispensed with in a single narrative gesture.

As a number of the reviews noted, the film 'reduces virtually all of the men to cartoon chauvinists' (*The Scotsman*) who emerge at the end 'with slapped wrists and beetroot faces' (*The Telegraph*). At the other extreme the striking women are primarily portrayed as fun-loving, sexy and predominantly apolitical. The principal characters in the narrative, Rita (Sally Hawkins) and Connie (Geraldine James), struggle convincingly with the

• Plate 14.8
Made in Dagenham
(Nigel Cole, 2010)

conflict between the traditional domestic roles expected of them by their husbands and the new political consciousness the strike brings them. Nevertheless the overall tone of the film is set by the scene (based apparently on a real incident) where a banner reading 'We Want Sexual Equality' is imperfectly unfurled to the great amusement of passing motorists. Originally, the title of the film was to be 'We Want Sex'.

In an interview with the *Socialist Worker*, the film's director Nigel Cole offers an explanation for the film's resolutely light touch:

We could have made a very different film about the creation of the Equal Pay Act in 1970, and a long and bitter industrial dispute, that was far more complex. That might have been more interesting for some people, but we wanted to make a film that had a mass audience, not one that only showed in art house cinemas. We wanted to make a film that would inspire people who are struggling today, and by making it feel like a Brit-comedy we felt we could add to the inspirational quality of the film.

(Prasad 2010)

That choice between an apolitical feel-good film with a mass audience and mass appeal or a politically complex film with a tiny art house audience is one which is often cited in discussions of cinema and politics in Britain. One might imagine a director such as Ken Loach embarking on the more serious film that Cole imagines, and gaining precisely the limited audience he predicts. Nevertheless, *Made in Dagenham* is a good example of the distinction between a political film and an ideological one. 'I hope that people come out of the film thinking "maybe we don't need to be pushed around, maybe we can stand up for ourselves"' claims Cole (ibid.). Reviewers unanimously identified a rather different likely effect on audiences – one which in its insistence on 'feeling good' might close down rather than open up political debate. 'There are times when cultural snobbery is wildly inappropriate. And there are times when it's an obstacle to good old-fashioned fun. Watching *Made in Dagenham* is one of those times. Because this is a great film with so much heart' cooed Matthew Cain for *Channel 4 News* (Cain 2010), while the *Daily Mail* concluded that although the film 'may look off-puttingly like a radical feminist tract ... it is a film that should lift your heart, whatever your politics' (Tookey 2010). Admitting that it was 'uncomplicated' and 'clichéd', the *Guardian* concluded that 'the film is also robust, amiable and so warm-hearted you'd be a churl to take against it', while finally the *Metro* reported that the film 'might as well shove a placard in your face saying: "Feel good!"' (Ivan-Zadeh 2010).

A film about politics that manages to be so resolutely apolitical requires some rather careful analysis to uncover exactly what it might be saying to audiences. That work is part of the joy of studying film, and one of the most useful approaches is to look not at the ideas that the film articulates and argues about, but at the ones it takes silently for granted.

At the time of writing, *Made in Dagenham* has yet to be released in America, a market the filmmakers clearly hope will be as entranced by its breezy account of Britain's political struggles as it was by *Billy Elliot*. Early indications suggest that the film failed to ignite the UK box office to the extent the producers may have hoped. With many workers facing the real prospect of redundancy in 2011, it may be that industrial relations are no longer something to 'feel good' about.

Questions

1   What do you understand as the difference between a 'political' film and an 'ideological' one?
2   Is the primary purpose of cinema to make us 'feel good'?

☐ CASE STUDY 3: *LOVE ACTUALLY* (RICHARD CURTIS, 2003)

The poster for *Love Actually* presents it as a Christmas gift, wrapped in red ribbon complete with a tag reading 'From the makers of *Four Weddings*, *Bridget Jones* and *Notting Hill*'. The film is thus marketed as part of the distinctive cycle of British romantic comedies which began with the extraordinary international success of *Four Weddings and a Funeral* (Mike Newell, 1994), and which not only share creative personnel but also key generic characteristics. Richard Curtis as the writer of all the films, and Hugh Grant in a prominent starring role, are obvious similarities, but the films are also all co-produced by one of the most successful British production companies, Working Title. While *Four Weddings and a Funeral* was made in conjunction with Channel 4 on a relatively modest budget, its box-office success allowed the films which followed to be made with much more lavish budgets, and with increasingly international co-production partners. International appeal is very clearly a priority for these films, and indeed one might argue that they all self-consciously reflect on the cultural relationship between Britain and America. *Four Weddings and a Funeral* and *Notting Hill* (Roger Mitchell, 1999) are the most explicit in this exercise. Both films feature Hugh Grant as a diffident Englishman, marked out as 'ordinary' both through his professional and romantic failure, and through his association with a disparate group of 'ordinary' friends, who offer a range of identifications for the audience, not least through being played by actors primarily familiar from domestic television. Both films pair Grant with women who are successful romantically and professionally, and are initially understood to be beyond Grant's reach because of the glamour associated with their American nationality (they are, after all, played by Andie MacDowell and Julia Roberts respectively – a 'Hollywood' touch which is of course the explicit subject matter of *Notting Hill*). The narratives of the films present Americanness as glamorous and strange in contrast to the ordinariness and familiarity of Britishness.

However, like the films of the 'Heritage' cycle, these films also package Britain for an export audience. The London they present is a utopian fantasy of the actual city – it

• Plate 14.9
Love Actually (Richard Curtis, 2003). The Prime Minister, the tea-lady and an octopus share a ride

is clean and crime-free. Despite their apparent professional failure, the group of friends live in relatively affluent surroundings, moving between picturesque urban and rural locations, never experiencing material hardship or political disenfranchisement. This utopianism has proved a major sticking point for critics of the Curtis comedies, who accuse them of ignoring the reality of contemporary British lives, and instead presenting Britain as a sanitised, white, middle-class bubble unrecognisable to the majority of the domestic audience. Several commentators, for instance, have pointed to the fact that *Notting Hill* does not contain a single prominent black character, despite being set in an area of London otherwise most famous for its large multi-ethnic population and annual Caribbean carnival. While the issue of race remains unanswerable, one might suggest that concerns over the lack of 'social realism' in the cycle are based on a wilful misreading of the films' generic conventions. Romantic comedies by their very nature present a utopian vision of the city as an organic community. Representations of New York as a utopian community in Hollywood Rom-Coms such as *You've Got Mail* (Nora Ephron, 1998) and *Maid in Manhattan* (Wayne Wang, 2002) do not elicit anything like the same kind of ire as the Curtis cycle does among certain British critics, and it is worth reflecting on our heightened expectations of British films both to represent lives and spaces we recognise as 'authentic' (or as somehow to do with our everyday experience), and to offer us utopian fantasies of romance to which we might aspire.

Love Actually may be said to take some of the familiar aspects of the Curtis cycle to extremes, while at the same time it also marks a major modification of the cycle's theme of British–American relations. The film refocuses the hero and group-of-friends structure of the earlier films, presenting instead a series of over ten narratives, each given more or less equal weighting, and each offering a variation on the theme of the love story. This 'portmanteau' structure is by no means unusual in British cinema, and as I have suggested, one of the most persistent traditions of British filmmaking is to emphasise the role of the community (often a metaphor for the 'national' community) over that of the individual hero. Many of the Ealing Comedies (such as *Passport to Pimlico*) are organised in this way, as are the most celebrated British wartime films, including (as we have seen) *Millions Like Us*. More recently, British romantic comedies such as *This Year's Love* (David Kane, 1999) have employed the same structure. *Love Actually* is perhaps the most explicit in suggesting that its disparate characters – loosely linked along a string of friendships, acquaintances and workplace colleagues – might stand as a metaphor for the nation as a whole. Not only that, but the film dares to fantasise a utopian version of that nation in which barriers of class, power and language are permeable in the face of love. This is perhaps most explicitly evident in the plotline involving Hugh Grant as the Prime Minister, falling in love with Nathalie the tea-girl (Martine McCutcheon). Her ordinariness is emphasised both by the actress's association with *EastEnders*, and by running jokes about her weight and her tendency to swear on inappropriate occasions. Through its string of connected characters, the film implies that the whole nation may only be six degrees of separation from the PM, and that coming across him and his family at our local state school Christmas play or carol singing down the road is entirely possible.

Despite this utopianism, the film does not shy away either from bleak storylines (Emma Thompson and Laura Linney act in the centre of narratives of personal sacrifice which offer little comfort for their characters) or from political comment. This political comment is at its most surprising for a film of this sort when it comes to the American–British theme previously so crucial to the cycle. One of the narratives reproduces and gently spoofs the previous films' faith in America as the source of glamorous female sexuality, as well as making gentle fun of the apparent fascination of female audiences in America with diffident English masculinity (a major factor, one might argue, in Hugh Grant's star status, and thus the financial success of the earlier Curtis films). Kris Marshall plays Colin – a dweeb who cannot get a girlfriend at home and becomes convinced that his only hope is to cross the Atlantic, where American girls are all beautiful, easy, and find British geeks irresistible. On arriving in Milwaukee and walking into a random bar, he finds that all his fantasies are confirmed.

A more serious engagement with British–American relations is worked through the Hugh Grant plot. The first shots of the film show travellers greeting families at Heathrow, and Grant's voiceover comments on the scene, expressing optimism about the presence of love 'all around us'. He mentions the attack on the twin towers in the context of reaffirming optimistic faith in humanity and an explicit rejection of the principles of hate. The comment sets the tone for the whole film, but must also be understood in the context of the moment of the film's release at the end of 2003 – a year which had seen Tony Blair's government follow George Bush's lead in promulgating a war in Iraq, despite considerable domestic opposition, and international controversy over the legality of such an action. It is within the context of liberal anxieties that the Labour government was allowing itself to become a pawn of US foreign policy that we should read one of the key scenes of the film. Grant's PM observes the US president (played by Billy Bob Thornton) slickly using his status and power to place Nathalie in a compromised sexual situation – an act of casual arrogance and domination which stands in marked contrast to Grant's own agonised reaction to his own more genuine feelings towards Nathalie. In a press conference immediately afterwards, the Prime Minister surprises the President and everyone else present by spontaneously 'standing up for Britain', suggesting that the 'special relationship' is no longer equal and that from now on Britain will not be bullied by America. The soundtrack in this scene can only be described as stirringly patriotic, and the delighted reaction of the other characters leaves the audience in no doubt as to the film's national loyalties. The scene is remarkable, particularly in a film whose production and marketing strategy is reliant on reaching a popular American audience.

The balance between appealing to domestic audiences and not alienating international audiences is a crucial element in British films with export ambitions, and it is worth thinking about each scene and storyline in *Love Actually* from the perspectives of both of these audiences. The specific cultural resonance of elements such as the appearance of Ant and Dec, the television star persona of Martine McCutcheon, the casual associations of mentions such as 'Wandsworth – the dodgy end', the Welsh accent of the Prime Minister's bodyguard when he starts singing carols, or the familiarity of the Victorian terraced houses where the character lives, all these elements have particular meanings and pleasures for British audiences which may be lost on audiences elsewhere. Is the loss of those meanings catastrophic to their understanding or pleasure in the film? Are there other elements of the film which are likely to carry specific cultural associations which British audiences don't share (Heike Makatsch for instance, is a celebrity in Germany with particular associations for that audience which she brings to her role as Mia) or which have been specifically inserted to increase the international appeal of it (the scenes set in France and America for instance)? Finally, while (despite its multiple narratives) the film does primarily represent a certain kind of Englishness – white, predominantly middle class, London-based – does this mean that British audiences who don't share those ethnic, class and regional affiliations are excluded from its 'national' pleasures? Victorian terraced housing of one kind or another is, after all, occupied by the full gamut of British citizens.

Questions

1   Are we more demanding of the representations found in our national cinema than we are of those in international cinemas?

2   What questions do you think international audiences ask about these films – and about their own cinema when it is designed for export?

☐ CASE STUDY 4: *BULLET BOY* (SAUL DIBB, 2004)

Discussing his ambitions for *Bullet Boy*, Saul Dibb has suggested that he wanted the film to have a 'really strong British flavour – I don't want it to have a glossy feel to it. I don't want it to be sentimental or glamorous.' In its rejection of gloss, sentiment and glamour, *Bullet Boy* may be understood as the antithesis of the kind of internationally exportable popular film exemplified by *Love Actually*. As Dibb's comments imply, he is drawing on a long tradition of British cinema which, rather than competing with Hollywood, seeks to establish an alternative aesthetic of filmmaking, one which capitalises on the cultural specificities of life in Britain, attempting to tell stories drawn from everyday life in a realistic way. While the generic conventions of romantic comedy push *Love Actually* towards an optimistic and utopian vision of British society as a place of opportunity and goodwill, *Bullet Boy* is more concerned to highlight the specific inequalities and problems of the community which it represents. Many of its characters are trapped within situations which they work hard to resolve, but the odds are stacked against them. In this sense, the film could be seen as a political drama, although it contains no overt political speculation as to the causes of, or possible solutions to, the central dilemma. Instead it concentrates more on creating believable characters and situations, portraying those characters and their motivations as complex and contingent rather than generically coded. Nevertheless, while the film eschews the generic address of Rom-Coms such as *Love Actually*, or the cartoon-like glamour of crime caper gangster films such as *Lock Stock and Two Smoking Barrels* (Guy Richie, 1998), it still employs some generic narrative codes, balancing the demands of realism with those of entertainment. Furthermore, the casting of Ashley Walters in the lead role was a key strategy in marketing the film to young audiences who knew him primarily as Asher D, singer with the 'So Solid Crew', and his much publicised imprisonment for gun possession in 2002.

The film draws explicitly on the star persona of Walters who plays Ricky, a young man who at the opening of the story has similarly just emerged from prison, having served a sentence for a gun-related crime. The story is told through the eyes of his younger brother Curtis, who hero-worships Ricky but is also aware of his mistakes – 'You may find it hard to obtain work with a criminal record' he taunts his brother, reading from a government leaflet. Nevertheless, when the gun re-enters the house, Curtis is drawn to it as an object of fascination. Meanwhile Ricky, despite his best intentions, is drawn back into a cycle of violence between feuding gangs, sparked off by a characteristically trivial incident involving a broken wing mirror. *Bullet Boy* is careful to show Ricky as both trapped by a youth subculture but also integrated into a wider family structure and community network which is in opposition to that culture. He is torn between his street persona and his loyalty to his mother and brother, and the point at which those two worlds of street and family come together is the focus of the film's most emotional scenes, when his younger brother Curtis accidentally shoots a schoolmate. It looks as though, despite his mother's efforts, the cycle of gun violence might be passed from older to younger brother, as the schoolmate reminds Curtis that he has incurred a debt which may have to be repaid later in life, while admiring his gunshot wound as a battle scar. Nevertheless, towards its conclusion, the film holds out a moment of optimism and generic catharsis for the audience – suggesting in a key sequence that Curtis may have the strength of mind to reject his brother's legacy. He leaves his mother in church, inspired by the words of the preacher to finally get rid of the gun – the music of the gospel service on the soundtrack creates a clear emotional cue at this moment of narrative resolution. The use of the music in this scene might be considered in contrast to the gruellingly realist use of sound in an earlier scene where Curtis and his mother visit his schoolmates' parents and attempt to apologise for the shooting incident. The awkwardness of the visit is made viscerally apparent to the audience through the use of sound – and silence.

All of the principal characters of *Bullet Boy* are black – a striking contrast to the cosy tokenism of portrayals of ethnicity in more mainstream British films such as *Love Actually*, and one which reverses the impression given by much casting in Hollywood films. While the black figure of avuncular state authority is a cliché of Hollywood cinema, representatives of state power in *Bullet Boy* are in fact the only white characters in the film – teachers, probation officers, policemen, etc. These characters remain peripheral to the story however, despite the raw power they wield over the lives of the main protagonists (particularly in the scenes of Ricky being released from prison, and with the probation officer). A scene of Curtis in his Hackney school, where the only white character is the teacher, demonstrates the film's commitment both to realism, and to the specificity of its story and location. Some critics have raised concerns about the appropriateness of a white director handling a story so firmly rooted within a black community, but the film is extremely confident both in its assumption that audiences will be able to identify with the principal characters regardless of race, and in the balance it strikes between telling a story which is specific to black urban experience, while nevertheless not producing that experience as an object for inspection 'from outside'. This balance is worth considering in the light of other, more celebrated films dealing with the experiences of British ethnic minorities. *My Beautiful Laundrette* (Stephen Frears, 1985), *Young Soul Rebels* (Isaac Julien, 1991) and *East is East* (Damien O'Donnell, 1999) provide obvious examples, although the focus of these films tends to be more heavily on the notion of 'multiculturalism' than is evident in *Bullet Boy*.

The reach towards a specific cultural 'authenticity', of course, is part of a long tradition of British filmmaking, which as we have seen blends fiction narratives with documentary aesthetics and production practices. One might trace the impulse to put 'real people' on the screen right back to the early work of Mitchell and Kenyon, by way of the 'New Wave' cycle of the 1960s, the 'Golden Age' of wartime cinema and the celebrated documentary movement of the 1930s. Filmmakers working in this tradition more recently have often been influenced by television experience. Dibb himself has worked extensively as a television documentary-maker (although he is now also working in BBC drama), and *Bullet Boy* was primarily funded in a co-production partnership between BBC Films and the UK Film Council's New Cinema Fund. The film has some clear stylistic similarities to the work of other celebrated British realist filmmakers who began their careers in television, most notably Ken Loach and Mike Leigh. While works such as Loach's *Kes* (1969), *Ladybird, Ladybird* (1994) and *My Name is Joe* (1998) were not worldwide mainstream box-office hits, they were critical successes which gained small-scale specialist distribution both in Britain and in America, proving the viability of this kind of modestly budgeted national cinema in the marketplace. Nevertheless, in a purely commercial environment, such specialist films would stand little chance of getting made, and all to a greater or lesser extent rely on some form of non-commercial funding. They are also notable for their political commitment to showing communities and identities which are underrepresented in mainstream cinema, presenting life experiences in an apparently unmediated way.

Such films are often discussed in terms of realism or authenticity, and it is clear by comparison with a film such as *Love Actually* that there are a set of very different filmmaking principles and generic conventions in play. Working within a tradition established by the films of Loach, Leigh and others, *Bullet Boy* uses professional actors sparingly. The majority of its characters are played by non-professionals, people who live and work in the community being represented, often in the roles they are playing on-screen. Dibb and his co-writer Catherine Johnson devised a narrative based on their research within the community, but they also allowed the actors to improvise much of the actual dialogue in order to achieve a more realistic tone. The film is shot primarily on location in Hackney, using lightweight cameras and in real interiors. The result is precisely the lack of that 'gloss' which Dibb wants to achieve, and yet the film is also highly lyrical in many sequences, making particular use of shots of the landscape from the high-rise viewpoint of Curtis's home, and shots of wastelands and semi-rural locations in late sunlight. Much was made in the publicity for the film of the sense of 'ownership' over the story which members of the local community felt during its making and on its first release – a sense partly engendered by the production techniques of location shooting, use of non-professional actors, improvised dialogue and community research. Whether these techniques result in a heightened authenticity for other audiences, or whether they might be considered as just another set of generic conventions signifying a film aimed at a different kind of film-going audience is a matter for debate. *Bullet Boy*'s distribution history certainly suggests that it has been able to cross generic boundaries and address a range of audiences – originally circulated through festivals as an art-house product, the distributors were able to draw on finding from the Film Council to help them capitalise on the appeal of Ashley Walters to get the film released not just in independent cinemas but also in more mainstream Multiplex venues, particularly around London and other urban areas. Nevertheless, the film did not secure a theatrical release in America.

CONCLUSION

In the first decade of the twenty-first century then, the British film industry appears to have remained remarkably buoyant, both culturally and economically. In 2010 the UK Film Council (which was responsible for collecting statistics for the industry as a whole) was able to report that the industry had a turnover of £6.8 billion, contributing over £4.5 billion a year to the UK GDP. Box-office revenue had continued to rise, growing 62 per cent since the turn of the millennium and with British films generating 23 per cent of that money. Furthermore, both the investments of international companies choosing to make films in British studios, and the revenues of British films exported abroad, had increased by almost 100 per cent since the Council's creation ten years earlier.

Despite these clear achievements, in 2010 the new Conservative/Lib. Dem. coalition government announced that as part of its overall policy of cutting public spending, the UK

Film Council would be quickly abolished. At the time of writing it is not evident whether future support for the industry will also be withdrawn, or whether the Council will simply be replaced by a different mechanism of encouragement. Defending its position, the UK Film Council pointed out that for every £1 of Lottery money that has been invested in the UK film industry through its auspices, £5 has been generated in box-office revenue. Nevertheless, it must be admitted that claims of poor investment decisions have dogged the Council throughout its existence, from the early furore over its funding of *Sex Lives of the Potato Men* (Andy Humphries, 2004, famously described by *The Times* as 'one of the most nauseous films ever made') to the more sober reflection that a large number of the films it assisted got such small distribution that they remained unknown and unnoticed by most UK citizens. As the reaction of some less commercial filmmakers to the news of its abolition made clear, the UKFC's emphasis on commercially viable filmmaking, at the expense of experimental or avant-garde work, was a source of wide frustration. Nevertheless, the widely expressed hope that its replacement might operate to encourage more non-commercial work in the future seems wildly misplaced.

It has always been the case that filmmaking is an unusually high-risk economic activity. For every box-office bonanza such as *Slumdog Millionaire* (Danny Boyle, 2008) there are many productions which have failed to show a significant return on the money invested in them. Over the coming period it will be interesting to see whether the coalition government's policy continues the principle established by most of its predecessors since 1928, of striving to establish at least a stable basis for a sustainable industry, or whether they will be content to let British cinema fend for itself, film by film, in the global marketplace.

SUMMARY

- Relationship between British cinema and Hollywood.
- Differences between cinema as a *production* industry and cinema as an *exhibition* industry.
- Government attempts to assist British production – cultural and economic motives for doing so.
- British cinema as a series of traditions in representation and film-making.
- Early British cinema – the role of pioneers, and the start of the industry.
- The Cinematograph Act of 1927 and the development of a mature industry.
- *Exportable* and *inexportable* films from the 1930s onwards. Key genres.
- Wartime British cinema – representations of the nation at war. Realism and fantasy. 'Consensus' cinema.
- Postwar British cinema – boom and bust.
- 'New Wave' and 'Swinging London' cycles of films in the 1960s.
- Declining audiences of the 1970s – the role of television and the avant garde.
- British cinema and Thatcherism – realism and 'heritage'.
- New Labour and the UK Film Council.

NOTE

1   The author would like to acknowledge the help of James Caterer, Amy Sargeant and Jane Bryan in the preparation of this chapter.

FURTHER READING

Ashby, J. and Higson, A. (eds) (2000) *British Cinema: Past and Present*, London: Routledge.

Babington, B. (ed.) (2001) *British Stars and Stardom: From Alma Taylor to Sean Connery*, Manchester: Manchester University Press.

Barr, C. (ed.) (1986) *All Our Yesterdays: 90 Years of British Cinema*, London: BFI Publishing.

Friedman, L. (ed.) (1993) *British Cinema and Thatcherism*, London: UCL Press.

Higson, A. (ed.) (2002) *Young and Innocent*, Exeter: Exeter University Press.

Murphy, R. (ed.) (2000), *British Cinema of the 90s*, London: BFI Publishing.

Murphy, R. (ed.) (2003) *The British Cinema Book, Second Edition*, London: BFI Publishing.

FURTHER VIEWING

This list highlights the films mentioned which are both most easily available and most likely to be productive or representative for teaching purposes. At the time of writing, all the films are available on DVD or (where indicated) on VHS. See also the note in the Resources section about key clips and films available online at www.screenonline.org.uk.

Most of the pre–1917 short films mentioned are available on DVD in the following collections:

Early Cinema, Primitives and Pioneers (BFI, 2005)

Electric Edwardians, The Films of Mitchell and Kenyon (BFI, 2005)

Hindle Wakes (Maurice Elvey, 1927) available on VHS

The Lodger (Alfred Hitchcock, 1927)

Sally in Our Alley (Maurice Elvey, 1931) available on VHS

Sing as We Go (Basil Dean, 1934) available on VHS

First a Girl (Victor Saville, 1935) available on VHS

Love on the Dole (John Baxter, 1941)

In Which We Serve (David Lean, 1942)

Millions Like Us (Launder and Gilliat, 1943)

A Canterbury Tale (Powell and Pressburger, 1944)

Brief Encounter (David Lean, 1945)

The Wicked Lady (Leslie Arliss, 1945)

Passport to Pimlico (Henry Cornelius, 1949)

Trouble in Store (John Paddy Carstairs, 1953)

Doctor in the House (Ralph Thomas, 1954)

The Dam Busters (Michael Anderson, 1954)

The Curse of Frankenstein (Terence Fisher, 1957)

Room at the Top (Jack Clayton, 1959)

Saturday Night, Sunday Morning (Karel Reisz, 1960)

Dr No (Terence Young, 1962)

Summer Holiday (Peter Yates, 1963)

Tom Jones (Tony Richardson, 1963)

Alfie (Lewis Gilbert, 1966)

Carry on Up the Kyber (Gerald Thomas, 1968)

Kes (Ken Loach, 1969)

Get Carter (Mike Hodges, 1971)

Jubilee (Derek Jarman, 1977)

Chariots of Fire (Hugh Hudson, 1981)

Letter to Brezhnev (Chris Bernard, 1985)

My Beautiful Laundrette (Stephen Frears, 1985)

Maurice (James Ivory, 1987)

Four Weddings and a Funeral (Mike Newell, 1994)

Ladybird, Ladybird (Ken Loach, 1994)

Brassed Off (Mark Herman, 1996)

Trainspotting (Danny Boyle, 1996)

The Full Monty (Peter Cattaneo, 1997)

Elizabeth (Shekhar Kapur, 1998)

East Is East (Damien O'Donnell, 1999)

Billy Elliot (Stephen Daldry, 2000)

Gosford Park (Robert Altman, 2001)

Calendar Girls (Nigel Cole, 2003)

The Constant Gardener (Fernando Meirelles, 2005)

RESOURCE CENTRES

The BFI library at Stephen Street in London is the main resource for those interested in further research. In addition, scholars of British cinema are remarkably lucky to have at their disposal an extensive website created by the British Film Institute to encourage study of British films (www.bfi.org.uk) – this includes detailed accounts of many individual films, filmmakers' biographies, interviews, company histories, as well as general thematic articles, and articles dealing with industrial and commercial matters such as censorship and distribution. There are links to the BFI special collections unit and to the BFI Stills, many of whose materials are also available online. For those working within licensed educational institutions it is also possible to download clips from a wide range of key films, many of which are otherwise unavailable. The site also contains considerable amounts of material on British television history. Go to www.screenonline.org.uk.

For current productions, and material about the contemporary British filmmaking scene, a good place to start is the webpage of the UK Film Council at www.ukfilmcouncil.org.uk.

Chapter 15

Indian cinema[1]

Lalitha Gopalan

■ INDIAN CINEMA

INTRODUCTION

Even the most casual tourist in India resorts to hyperbole to describe the potency of this cinema that produces a thousand films in more than twelve languages each year. For the uninitiated, most commentators will list implausible twists and turns in plots, excessive melodrama, loud song and dance sequences, and lengthy narrative as having tremendous mass appeal but little critical value. For instance, in his travelogue *Video Night in Kathmandu*, Pico Iyer declares in a significant synecdoche that spills over its own rhetoric: 'Indian movies were India, only more so' (Iyer 1988). Other writers, such as Salman Rushdie, Alan Sealy and Farrukh Dhondy, have used various aspects of Indian film culture to spin fabulous narratives of success and failure, stardom and political life, love and villainy (Dhondy 1990; Rushdie 1988; Sealy 1990). Although the national audience has been its main address, Indian popular cinema or 'Bollywood' has long travelled across the world – the former Soviet Union, Latin America, Africa and Southeast Asia – entertaining audiences whose personal histories bear few ties to the subcontinent.[2] Sometimes, these travel routes are visible on video copies – Arabic subtitles on Hindi films, Malay on Tamil films – telling us of a global set of viewers who watch other national cinemas besides Hollywood. Demonstrating constantly shifting tastes in film across the globe, *Newsweek* reported that Japan is spellbound by Tamil films, especially those starring Rajnikanth, because 'Indian films are filled with the classical entertainment movies used to offer' (*Newsweek International* 1999).[3] In Britain, Indian films are steadily enjoying a cross-over audience which includes the diaspora as well as film-curious non-Indians: Star City, located outside Birmingham, opened on 26 July 2000 and is apparently the largest multiplex in Britain, with thirty screens of which six show Bollywood movies. At the end of the last century four Indian films ruled the UK Top 20 on release: *Dil Se* (1998), *Kuch Kuch Hota Hai* (1998), *Biwi Number One* (1999) and *Hum Dil de Chuke Sanam* (1999). In June 2000 the Indian equivalent of the Oscar ceremony was held in the Millennium Dome in London.[4] Besides the exhibition of these films characterised by sensory excess, a range of extra-filmic events encourages us to read beyond the textual operations of individual films, cinematic aesthetics spilling into adjacent consumer economies. It is now commonplace to find the loyal Indian diaspora cultivating appreciation by sponsoring stage shows of film stars, events that read popular films as star-studded texts.[5]

It is important to note, however, that these descriptions of excess cohere most intimately to popular cinema and not the other styles that include alternative, 'parallel', middle and documentary cinemas which also inhabit the cinematic landscape in India albeit in a struggling manner (more on this below). Although it has become common to group together all popular Indian films under the term 'Bollywood', it is important to note that often the production of popular Tamil and Telugu films outpaces that of Hindi, each producing about 150 to 200 films a year, in addition to a steady crop of films from Bengal, Kerala, Maharashtra, Gujarat and Punjab that also populate the regional markets. Among the three largest producers, the Tamil industry is located in Chennai, the Telugu in Hyderabad and Chennai, and Hindi films are produced in Mumbai, Hyderabad and Chennai, each marked by its own star system, director, technicians and musicians with occasional cross-over from one industry to another: Malayalam cinematographers working on Tamil and Hindi films, Bengali or Marathi directors directing Hindi films and so on. Such a rich and varied national cinema requires a lifetime to understand its various contours; thus in this chapter we will limit our area of study to popular films produced in the 1980s and 1990s, films made in Hindi and Tamil.

The last two decades of the twentieth century produced a confluence of factors in Indian cinema that underscores it as a period worthy of study in this chapter. At the material

Bollywood
Bombay, the film capital of India.

level, as we shall see, Indian cinema was undergoing a shift in format that affected film viewing and production in an unprecedented manner. The real shift, however, was in the consolidation of academic film studies on Indian cinema that mobilised a long overdue evaluation of this popular cinema: genres were identified, auteurs named, ideological underpinnings unearthed, film viewing tracked, and so on. The task here is to understand and evaluate the scholarship that shaped the question and objects of focus in this period and how it shaped the research questions and agenda for the next century so that a rank outsider can appreciate the appeal of the popular film while being equally cognisant of the various debates that inform her critical reading of Indian popular cinema.

PRODUCTION AND RECEPTION CONDITIONS

However expansive the influence of cinema, Indian filmmakers are acutely aware that most films fail at the box office. Their financial anxieties have increased in recent years with the rise of adjacent entertainment industries that threaten to diminish the power of films, even if cinema as an institution is not waning in the public imagination. Trade papers from the 1980s record industry fears of the growing video industry that many worried would eventually discourage audiences from going to the cinema. Nevertheless, the arrival in India of video shops also exposed the film-going public to world cinemas, an opportunity afforded previously only by film festivals and film societies. Suddenly films from other parts of Asia, Europe and America were easily available. Filmmakers were also very much part of this video-watching public, freely quoting and borrowing cinematic styles: for instance, director Ramgopal Varma started his career as the owner of a video shop. While a section of the urban rich retreated to their homes, trade papers reported an increase in film attendance in small towns and villages. Instead of assuming that one mode of watching would give way to the next evolutionary stage, we now find films coexisting alongside a robust video economy and satellite cable television. Ironically, both cable television and video shops are also responsible for renewing nostalgia for older films. Together, these different visual media have changed reception conditions by creating an audience which has developed a taste for global-style action films while simultaneously cherishing fondness for the particularities of Indian cinema.

In addition to video and satellite saturation of the visual field, American films (sometimes dubbed into Hindi) started reappearing in Indian cinemas after a new agreement was signed between the Government of India and Motion Picture Producers and Distributors of America, Inc (MPPDA) in April 1985, ending the trade embargo that began in 1971 (Pendakur 1985, 1990). Initially, Indian filmmakers protested against this invasion, but slowly reconciled themselves to the foreign presence after recognising that American films did not in fact pose a threat to Indian film distribution.[6] Occasionally we find characters in Indian films taking pot-shots at American cinema: in Ramgopal Varma's *Satya* (1998), protagonists purposely misread *Jurassic Park* (1993) as a horror film starring lizards; in Tamil films, cross-linguistic puns abound around James Cameron's *Titanic* (1997). These playful engagements with American culture confidently acknowledge that Indian cinema audiences belong to a virtual global economy where films from different production sites exist at the same level – a democratisation of global cinephilia. Perhaps I am exaggerating the dominance of Indian cinema, but the confidence of some Indian filmmakers does hold out hopes for unsettling the inequalities of the global marketplace where we are all too aware of American films unilaterally expanding into newer territories.

Although economic liberalisation opened up Indian markets to a range of television programmes and videos, it also facilitated, however slowly, access to state-of-the-art film technology for filmmakers. Within the industry there have been discernible changes in the production process. According to Manmohan Shetty, the former chairman of the well-known film-processing business, Adlabs, a sea change occurred in 1978 when Kodak introduced

For further discussion of the global dominance of American cinema and multi-media empires see Chapter 1, pp. 14–31.

cinephilia
The notion of cinephilia refers to an intense love of, even obsession with, cinema. It implies both a way of watching and a way of speaking about film beyond the standard relationship between cinema and its spectator. Cinephiles are people who, in Andrew Sarris's phrase, 'love cinema beyond all reason', and who engage with film in highly specific ways.

a negative film that could be processed at high ambient temperatures (105° Fahrenheit), improving colour resolution (Shetty 1994). At about the same time, professionally trained technicians in editing, cinematography and lighting began entering the commercial industry from film institutes in Pune and Chennai, vastly improving the quality of film production as well as increasing costs. Manjunath Pendakur (1985) notes that the rising costs of production since the 1980s not only include huge salaries for film stars, but also higher wages for directors and technicians. Audiences seem attuned to these changes on screen: in Chennai, crowds get hysterical when cinematographer P.C. Sriram's name runs across the screen; directors have fan-supported websites competing with those on movie stars.

The profusion of filmmaking talent strengthened the Malayalam, Tamil and Telugu industries. Since 1979, film production in Tamil and Telugu has continued to keep pace with Hindi films, each producing about 140 films annually.[7] Increased production from regional industries has weakened the stronghold of Hindi films as the largest commercial industry in the nation while improvements in dubbing facilities have ensured a national audience for Tamil and Telugu films. In addition, filmmakers from the south such as S. Shankar, Sashilal Nair, Priyadarshan, Mani Ratnam and Ramgopal Varma have been making inroads into the Hindi film industry, once a prerogative of female stars (Chopra 1997). The migration of directors also means that narratives focusing on national themes – intercommunal love stories, war and terrorism – are no longer a prerogative of Hindi cinema, but also surface in regional cinemas. Concurrently, narratives in Hindi films have receded from national–secular themes addressing an urban audience, dabbling instead with regional stories resonating with preoccupations of the Hindi belt: Rajputs, Biharis and Punjabis now crowd the Hindi film screen.

*Compare to the US
and UK film industries
discussed in Chapter 1.*

Technical and aesthetic improvements in mainstream Indian cinema remind us that commercial filmmakers have benefited from narrative experiments introduced in the 1970s by independent filmmakers. Consciously setting themselves apart from commercial cinema, films by Adoor Gopalkrishnan, G. Aravindan, Mrinal Sen, Girish Kasaravalli, Kumar Shahini and Mani Kaul focused on social and political antagonisms to narrate their tales of disappointment with the post-colonial state, while conveying hopes for a different society.[8] Screened at film societies or special shows in large cinemas, their films drew the urban élite to cinemas and shaped filmviewing habits by encouraging the audience to focus more on the screen. A substantial number of commercial films made in the late 1980s borrowed from these filmmaking practices while continuing to improve on conventions of entertainment. Not unlike independent cinema, we now find directors gaining currency as auteurs in commercial cinema, controlling the production of their films and marking them with a unique cinematic style. In turn, the National Film Development Corporation (NFDC – the state body that finances independent films) started producing films which extensively incorporated mainstream stories and stars.

Further, Indian films have, on occasion, internationalised the production process: S. Shankar's Tamil film *Kaadalan/Lover* (1994), for example, polished its special effects in a Hong Kong film studio. Critics rightly focus on the film's playful commentary on upper-caste hegemony and its attendant economies of taste, but we cannot ignore how globalisation of the production process also influences this narrative of caste contestations (Dhareshwar and Niranjana 1996). The more conventional figuration of the world in Indian popular cinema – song and dance sequences set in foreign locales – is not only spruced up to arouse the spectator's interest in tourism, but also participates aggressively in the movement of global capital. These sequences not only bring the world home, they also acknowledge a loyal audience abroad that wishes to see its own stories of migrations and displacement written into these films. A number of Hindi films – *Pardes* (1997), *Dilwale Dulhaniya Le Jayange* (1995), *Dil to Pagal Hai* (1998), *Kuch Kuch Hota Hai* (1998) – index an audience straggling between national identities, harbouring longings for an original home or possessing the capital for tourism. Considered together, these narrative and production details place the viewer of Indian films in a global cinematic economy, finally catching up with a long history of global reception.

Since Independence, Indian films have travelled to the former Soviet Union, Latin America, Africa and Southeast Asia, entertaining audiences whose personal histories have few ties with the subcontinent.[9] However, it is filmmakers in the diaspora who have been openly engaging with, and in the process teaching us a lesson or two in, defamiliarising Indian film conventions. In both Srinivas Krishna's Canadian production *Masala* (1992) and Gurinder Chadda's British film *Bhaji on the Beach* (1994), we find lengthy quotations from Indian cinema: protagonists express desire by resorting to song and dance sequences. Inserted in films working with small budgets and relying on art-house distribution, such sequences serve as fabulous strands expressing immigration fantasies borne out of travel and displacement. In a more abrupt manner, Rachid Bouchareb's French–Algerian film *My Family's Honour* (1997) uses Hindi film songs on the soundtrack and even splices an entire musical number from *Hum Kisise Kum Nahin/We Are Number One* (1977) into his narrative on North African immigrants living in France. Displaying no diegetic link to the narrative, the jarring disjunction of this sequence conveys the disruption brought through immigration and displacement in Bouchareb's film. Terry Zwigoff's *Ghost World* (2000), narrating traumas of the summer after high school, opens with a song and dance sequence 'Jab Jaan Pechachan/When we got to know each other' from *Gumnaam* (1965), intercutting with the main narrative. The feverish cabaret and twist number offers the bored teenager the requisite degree of exotic abandon. Baz Luhrmann confesses to not only having seen Indian popular films but being mesmerised enough to deploy several song and dance sequences in his recent film *Moulin Rouge* (2000). Benny Torathi's Israeli film *Desparado Piazza*, also called *Piazza of Dreams* (2000), splices a song sequence from *Sangam* (1964) to map a different history of migration for ethnic Jews.[10] All these films celebrate these interruptions as a way of accounting for cinephilia even when the protagonists have to adjust to arduous conditions imposed through transnational migration, ennui-ridden teenagers or a courtesan's love story. These unexpected sites of reception allow us to see, from without, how Indian films are available for a wide range of readings, including camp and cult possibilities, based on their multi-plot narratives and multiple disruptions.

For further discussion of Moulin Rouge as an example of a film breaking genre conventions, see Chapter 8.

Let us consider Mira Nair's *Monsoon Wedding* (2002) as a film produced in the diaspora with a deep familiarity with the codes and conventions of popular cinema.

□ CASE STUDY 1: *MONSOON WEDDING* (MIRA NAIR, 2002)

A procession of colour, a clutch of garrulous Punjabis and a loving family crowd, Mira Nair's box-office success has emerged as the most successful Indian film to have cross-over appeal, as well as winning the Golden Lion Award at the 2001 Venice International Film Festival. Rumours have circulated that the wedding decor in the film has been imitated by non-resident Indians in the diaspora. Undoubtedly, Nair was aware of the appeal of the wedding film to audiences worldwide – *Four Weddings and a Funeral* (Mike Newell, 1994), *Hum Aap Ke Hain Koun, Dilwale Dulhania Le Jayenge* (*DDLG*) and so on – that include the doubtful bride, a cheating groom and a chorus of relatives whose own tribulations and desires make the wedding a sideshow. This film is no different, with the wedding as the central event, but in this the bride, Aditi, and groom, Hemant, are not the main draw in the film: the bride's parents Pimmi and Lalit exhibit an 'old-shoe' affection as Nair puts it in an interview; the bride's cousin Ria who is the same age faces her demons of sexual abuse at the family gathering; the bride's trysts with her older lover; her teenage brother whose voracious appetite for cooking casts aspersions on his masculinity; and a gaggle of uncles, aunts and cousins whose own desires criss-cross with others during the days before the wedding. While the upper-class, globally conscious Punjabi family holds centre stage in the film, Nair reels into it the budding romance and eventual union of the event manager Dube and the maid Alice.

• **Plate 15.1**
Monsoon Wedding
(Mirabai Films–British
Film Institute)

In the official website for the film, Nair acknowledges her homage to Bollywood style, particularly songs from old films on the soundtrack; Dube's floral tribute to Alice is a nod to Raj Kapoor's *Shree 420* and the incorporation of song and dance sequences as part of the wedding festivities. It is worth noting, however, that Nair also engages with the small-film idea that has taken over film production with the advent of digital video, largely inspired by the low-budget aesthetics of the Dogme group. In fact, *Monsoon Wedding* seems to bear a structural similarity to *Festen/Celebration* (Thomas Vinterberg, 1998). In other words, the film's scale and its lack of obvious stars casts it as a small film incorporating particular elements from different world cinemas.

Having located Nair's film within the wedding genre, albeit in various global locations, it is useful to frame our reading of the film in terms of the discussion that has developed on this genre in Hindi cinema in the mid-1990s. In a productive reading of two such films produced in the mid-1990s – *DDLJ* and *Pardes* – Patricia Uberoi (1998) suggests we consider the aspirations of the Indian middle class, both within the nation and in the diaspora, that wishes to retain a certain configuration of Indian values while embracing the options offered by the global marketplace. Even if you haven't seen these particular films, you can imagine a series of conflicts: tradition versus modernity; arranged versus love marriages; individual desires versus familial obligations and so on. Uberoi suggests that these films offer the 'arranged love marriage' as the ideal, 'a style of matchmaking whereby a romantic choice already made is endorsed, *post facto*, by parental approval and treated thereafter like an arranged marriage'. What Uberoi attends to in these films is the particular problematisation of these various issues and their resolution, a framework that is equally useful for our purposes here.

Questions

1   Let us focus on the long closing sequence of *Monsoon Wedding*. Describe in detail the intercutting rhythm and its relationship to genre.
2   How does the film engage with the device of the song and dance sequence?
3   Compare this film with another from the wedding film genre available globally. Describe how the two films present their sub-plots.

WRITINGS ON INDIAN CINEMA

Among the many writings on Indian cinema, two books best serve as introductions: Barnouw and Krishnaswamy's *Indian Film* (1980) offers a masterful sweep of Indian cinema up until the 1970s; and Yves Thoraval's *The Cinemas of India* (2000) offers an updated version of a similar project. In their breadth of scope both books serve as useful reference points, but it is impossible for a novice to counter their observations without undertaking similarly extensive archival research. On the other hand, this chapter suggests that an understanding of the form and style of popular Indian cinema allows us to understand the histories of production and reception, albeit in a less sweeping manner.

Critical writing on cinema has blossomed since the late 1980s, reporting a serious, sometimes cinephiliac, relationship to films. The publication of the *Encyclopedia of Indian Cinema* (1994, with a revised edition in 1999) stamped the scholarly seal of approval on Indian cinema. Expansive in its scope, Ashish Rajadhyaksha and Paul Willemen's opus strings together biographies, film lists and plot summaries, providing a road-map of the different features of Indian cinema, from genres to independent film movements and regional cinemas.

As is often the case in scholarship, Indian cinema studies has matured with the arrival of each new journal. Published from Bangalore, *Deep Focus* combines interviews with directors from different regions of the world, film reviews and lengthy critical pieces. *Cinemaya*, based in Delhi, follows the festival schedule in Asia, brings its readers news of the latest films and interviews with directors, and addresses a pan-Asian audience from Turkey to Japan. These two magazines locate Indian cinema, both popular and alternative, and its audience, within a global network of cinematic styles.

The short-lived *Splice*, published from Calcutta, had an exclusive focus on alternative cinematic practices and excavated the correspondences between avant-garde practices in India and those from the former socialist republics. For a brief moment, *Splice* was an integral part of a blooming film scene in Calcutta which now includes a film archive at Nandan and a brand-new film studies department at Jadavpur University with its own *Journal of Moving Images*, which addresses an emerging academic audience. Published by the Film and Television Institute of India (FTII), Pune, *Lensight* addresses filmmakers with reports on state-of-the-art lab-processing techniques, editing equipment and cameras while also carrying lengthy interviews with filmmakers on their craft. Although pitched exclusively to filmmakers, *Lensight* carries a wealth of information on socio-logical conditions of production that are not widely available to a film critic. In the twenty-first century, three journals mark the burgeoning scholarship in the field of Indian cinema studies in the global arena: *Journal of South Asian Popular Culture*, *Bioscope* and *Studies in South Asian Film and Media*.

The emergence of a field of Indian film studies against this backdrop has made it possible for critics to steer away from large-scale histories of the 'national cinema' towards more intensive readings of films and cinematic institutions. Although I will focus here on these different theoretical paradigms that privilege textual analysis, it is useful to be aware of the burgeoning field of extra-cinematic studies that combine ethnographic fieldwork and archival work to look at non-filmic objects. For instance, S.V. Srinivas's study of fan clubs in Telugu argues for a critical study of reception and not just close textual analysis of individual films (Srinivas 2000). Sara Dickey's ethnographic study of fan clubs in the South Indian town of Madurai and Steve Derne's study of film-going practices in the North Indian town of Shimla similarly provide us with a textured analysis of extra-filmic institutions (Derne 2000; Dickey 1993). Rachel Dwyer's reading of the popular star-zine *Stardust* urges us to consider the discourse of stardom as a mode of understanding the popularity of films (Dwyer 2000).

These disparate details form the bedrock of material changes in the production and reception of Indian popular cinema. Spelling out these details undercuts a series of

For further discussion of the audience and spectator relationship see Chapter 5.

archaic oppositions that we find steadfastly held in the arena of film studies: between national and international cinemas overlooking alternative routes of film distribution; between Hollywood and other national cinemas casting the latter as bad copies instead of examining them as rejoinders to a hegemonic cinema; between national and regional cinemas, placing Hindi cinema at the helm of the national imaginary and ignoring a simultaneous move towards regional nationalisms; between national and global audiences by not anticipating audiences who also endow Indian popular cinema with meaning that exceeds its own intended horizon of address; between art and commercial cinema, repeating a division between high and low cultures without admitting to a more varied terrain of taste. Naming these mobile processes speaks to a post-colonial condition that according to Stuart Hall marks a 'critical interruption into that whole grand historiographical narrative which, in liberal historiography and Weberian historical sociology, as much as in the dominant traditions of Western Marxism, gave this global dimension a subordinate presence in a story which could essentially be told from within European parameters' (Hall 1996: 250).

GENRE AND FORM

For further discussion of Hollywood and genre see Chapter 8.

Some clarification of the concept of film genre is in order before I launch into particularities of Indian cinema. Identified as a narrative form developed by classical Hollywood commercial cinema, film theorists have developed a barrage of theoretical and methodological tools to understand the narrative structure, cinematic specificity and viewer's relationship to genre films. For instance, cinematic genres are differentiated by iconography: frontier landscapes in a western; city spaces in gangster films. At other times, we understand how genre verisimilitude derives from details in the mise-en-scène: monsters in horror films and horses in a western. Genre theory continues to benefit from psychoanalytical theories by allowing us to see how our viewing pleasures are dictated by a structuring of repetition and difference in films. Research on advertising and distribution practices of Hollywood films reveals that film producers were deeply invested in using genre categories to target and consolidate their audience: women's films, summer action films and so on. Instead of considering genre in either/or terms, Steve Neale (1980, 2000) suggests that we see genre films as a dynamic among industry, films and viewers to better understand cinema as a modern commodity form. In a book on American genre films and theory, Rick Altman (1999) proposes that far from being particular, Hollywood films are constructed as multiple, overlapping genres to reach a wider audience. Whatever particular features film critics or filmmakers deploy to differentiate one genre from another or to see multiple genres in one film, American genre films broadly obey certain cinematic principles perfected in classical Hollywood cinema that frame the unfolding narrative: continuity editing, omniscient narration, internally coherent diegesis and character-motivated plot.

More than any of the above material conditions affecting the relationship between films and their viewers, Ramesh Sippy's *Sholay/Flames* (1975) was a landmark in Indian cinema, changing forever the production and reception of popular cinema. Coinciding with the State of Emergency declared by Prime Minister Indira Gandhi in 1975, *Sholay* was emblematic of a slew of films feeding off what political theorists refer to as a crisis of legitimacy of the Indian state (Vanaik 1991). Film critics, media activists and film scholars agree that the unrest in civil society marked by communal riots, police brutality, violent secessionist movements and assaults against women and minorities seeped into film narratives (Das 1992). Stacked with gangsters, avenging women, brutal police and corrupt politicians, these films resolve their narratives through vigilante actions that repeatedly undercut the authority of the state (Doriaswamy 1995; Rangoonwala 1993). Activist organisations such as Delhi's Media Advocacy Group argue that representations of brutality in contemporary commercial cinema have a direct and reinforcing effect on the level of violence in civil society (the Media Advocacy Group for the National Commission for Women, 1993).[11]

However, *Sholay*'s iconic status exceeds a mimetic relationship to reality, drawing in a large part from its reconfiguration of the western.[12] Mixing a host of conventions from Indian popular cinema such as song and dance sequences, *Sholay* successfully produced an Indian riposte to the classic American western. Fans of this cult film extensively quote Salim Khan and Javed Akhtar's script back to the screen; rumours abound as to the existent variations of the closing sequence; and overnight the actor Amjad Khan, who plays the villain Gabbar Singh, became one of the most popular stars in the film world. Anupama Chopra's book *Sholay: The Making of a Classic* (2000) – a requisite read for any fan – revives cinephiliac obsession with this film by journeying to its origins of production. The film also spurred the first psychoanalytical critique of popular Indian cinema. In a much neglected essay, Madan Gopal Singh (1983) evaluates the tremendous success of this film by picking one scene as a symptom of the changing relationship between screen and spectator: the 'Mehbooba! Mehbooba!' song and dance sequence. According to Singh, in this sequence the camera gropes the dancer's body and, by extension, provides us with a point of view that was hitherto unavailable in popular Hindi cinema. Singh uses voyeurism as a conceptual tool to describe the altered relationship between screen and spectator in the film, an idea that draws extensively from certain cinematic principles found in Hollywood – omniscient narration, continuity editing, internally coherent narrative and the ideal spectator's identification with the camera – leading to the argument that the camera's groping mechanism fragments the female dancer's body and generates viewing pleasure. But he glosses over the fact that song and dance sequences explicitly distract the viewer from narrative flow and go against conventions of continuity editing. Overtly exhibitionistic, song and dance sequences break codes of realism that psychoanalytical voyeurism relies upon.[13] Nevertheless, Singh's cryptic formulation prods us to consider

• Plate 15.2
Sholay (Sippy Films–United Producers–British Film Institute)

how even the most superficial and entertaining song and dance sequences carry an ideological charge, heightening our viewing pleasure.[14]

Singh's essay also tells another story, a story of the intellectual context of his critical engagement with Hindi films. Originally published in the avant-garde *Journal of Arts and Ideas*, Singh's essay echoes the opinions of alternative filmmakers such as Kumar Shahini, Mani Kaul and John Abraham, all of whom were writing and making a different kind of narrative cinema. Accounting for the hegemonic potential of Hindi commercial cinema, especially its ability to throttle radical filmmaking, Singh bemoans the loss of freshly minted student filmmakers from the FTII to the commercial industry, a move, he argues, that turns them into technicians of special effects. While *Sholay* affords Singh the occasion to critically assess the ideological manifestations of the consumerist cinema, his theoretical speculations helped shape an entire generation of film theorists working on Indian cinema.[15] In sharp contrast to Singh's critical essay, *Sholay* is a revered master text of success for filmmakers: Ramgopal Varma confesses to knowing every shot of two of his favourite films – *Sholay* and Francis Ford Coppola's *The Godfather* (1972); more recently, Rajkumar Santoshi allegedly watched *Sholay* every morning while shooting his own *China Gate* (1999) (Naseeruddin Shah, *Filmfare*, May 1998). Sholay is the mythical origin spurring an entire generation of filmmakers to borrow from globally circulating genres, yet reincorporating conventions from Indian popular cinema with great aplomb.[16] Spawning a number of B films throughout the 1980s, the full impact of Sippy's innovative cinematic style on popular Indian cinema – accommodating Indian cinematic conventions within a Hollywood genre – was fully developed a decade later by J.P. Dutta, Mani Ratnam, Mukul Anand, Ramgopal Varma, Rajkumar Santoshi and Shekhar Kapur.

These divergent readings of *Sholay* demonstrate a gap between critics writing on popular Indian cinema and filmmakers. Simply put, critics tend to take a moralistic view of mainstream cinema, seeing very little of the 'popular', while commercial filmmakers see themselves as entertainers and regard critics as élitists whose opinions rarely account for the working of the industry (Thomas 1985)[17]. This stand-off between critics and commercial filmmakers is as old as the practice of narrative cinema itself, and has little new to add to debates on the differences between high and low, between mass and popular cultures that as cultural critics we have learned to make and then unmake. Finally we have settled on 'popular culture' as the most viable concept that absorbs the paradoxes of our trade: we can read resistance in its form, even as we continue to be mesmerised by it (MacCabe 1986). This shifty definition seems vastly superior to the polarised definitions of cultural taste plaguing readings of Indian films. There is no doubt that we learn a great deal from vigilant readings of cinema's hegemonic influence that reveal its power to affirm ethnic stereotyping, sexism and jingoism, and caution us against being taken in by its dazzling surface. But all too often we tend to pay little attention to questions of pleasure. Inasmuch as we assume that commercial films maintain the status quo, flattening all radical possibilities in their viewers, we must also admit that filmmakers are constantly invested in inviting us to return to the movies through novel cinematic conventions.

Sholay exemplified the possibility of combining dominant genre principles developed in Hollywood films with conventions particular to Indian cinema. Recasting the linear trajectory of genre films to include several local cinematic conventions, Indian popular films often render the former illegible to the rank outsider. What I am suggesting is that it seems presumptuous to think that when Hollywood genres are appropriated by other national cinemas, we may find straightforward application of dominant genre principles instead of reading how local contexts of production and reception intervene and prevail over genre. The end-product of this encounter between global and local features may, at times, be read as a subaltern response to Hollywood, a strategy forwarded by Paul Smith in his reading of Leone's 'spaghetti westerns', or we can simply read it as a riposte that simultaneously reveals how

For further discussion of the relationship between film and the spectator, see Chapter 5.

For discussion of narrative and non-narrative film, see Chapter 4, pp. 81–102.

Hollywood genres are also built around certain national cinematic styles (Smith 1993).

In contrast to the internally coherent narrative form generated by Hollywood genre films, genres in Indian popular cinema display a set of features that are akin to pre-classical cinema, especially several extra-diegetic sequences or sequences of attractions. Instead of concluding that these films stage the underdeveloped aspects of capitalism in the Indian economy, a different set of concerns nurtures this narrative form, including a desire to domesticate cinematic technology and develop a national cinematic style. For instance, writing on Dadasaheb Phalke's *Raja Harishchandra* (1913), Ashish Rajadhyaksha argues that the prevalence of frontal address in this film points to how narrative strategies in early cinema borrowed from painting, theatre and traditional arts to lure the viewer into this new technological apparatus (Rajadhyaksha 1993). In a similar vein, Geeta Kapur (1987) suggests through her reading of *Sant Tukaram* (Damle–Fattelal, Marathi, 1936) that frontal address in this 'saint film' was a calculated move by filmmakers to draw in viewers accustomed to watching theatre, yet the sequence of miracles mandatory in a saint film highlighted cinema's ability to produce magic. Both Kapur and Rajadhyaksha alert us to how cinema in India developed in a whirl of anti-colonial struggles that included an impulse to forge an independent cultural form by both reinterpreting tradition and making technology developed in the West indigenous.

Besides the direct address, other features of Indian popular cinemas similarly undercut the hermetic universe developed in Hollywood films by interrupting it with song and dance sequences, comedy tracks and multi-plot narratives. Spectacular, and at times excessive, the elaboration of these attractions in this cinema has invited critics to dub them '**masala movies**' – a culinary term that seeks to define a medley of narrative strands in popular cinema. Naming the films made in the 1950s and 1960s as the 'feudal family romance', Madhava Prasad (1998) argues that this super-genre asserts its dominance through narrative strategies of annexations whenever new sub-genres emerge. In short, Prasad suggests that instead of discrete genres a megalomaniac genre cannibalises the formation of sub-genres. Ravi Vasudevan (1995), on the other hand, sees popular Hindi film as a discontinuous form that includes attractions such as song and dance sequences and comedic sub-plots. Instead of skipping over these moments that either break the diegetic universe or disrupt the linear trajectory of the narrative, we must simply face the fact that the most persistent narrative form found in Indian popular cinema includes several interruptions bearing a more or less systematic relationship to the narrative. In other words, we should start heeding production details that obsess over how Indian filmmakers expend considerable energy experimenting with the chore-ography and location of these sequences and, in the process, acknowledge how our viewing pleasure arises from these interruptions and the novel ways in which a popular film strings together these sequences.

Identifying these interruptions encourages us to start in the reverse direction; that is, by exploring how these films experiment with and fortify Indian cinematic conventions, rather than mulling over how these films are derived from Hollywood genres. Moreover, attending to these interruptions throws light on how the concept of a national cinematic style emerges at the conjuncture of state interests in quality cinema, the film industry's interests in profits and global circulation of popular cinemas. To account for how these disparate interests in production and reception shape the textual make-up of popular films, I will be looking at three different kinds of interruptions that brand the narrative form of Indian cinema: song and dance sequences, the interval, and censorship.

masala movie
Spicy Indian movie overloaded with emotions.

SONG AND DANCE SEQUENCES

One of the most common and popular features of Indian films are its song and dance sequences. According to Barnouw and Krishnaswamy (1980: 69), Indian talkies always had songs: the first sound feature, Ardeshir Irani's *Alam Ara/Light of the World* (1931), had over seven songs; another early Hindi film had forty songs; not to be outdone, a Tamil film is counted as having sixty. By the 1950s 'the film song had become a key to successful film promotion' (ibid.: 157). Filmmakers continue to release audio tracks prior to the film's release and it is now widely believed that those sales alone can recover the production costs of a movie.[18] Music directors, choreographers and singers receive awards, and popular memories of these sequences often surpass the film's own story. Over the years, commercial filmmakers have tried experimenting with their absence, with varying commercial success: K.A. Abbas's *Munna/Lost Child* (1954), the Tamil film *Antha Nal/That Day* (1954), B.R. Chopra's *Ittefaq* (1969), P.C. Sriram's *Kurudhippunal/River of Blood* (1995), Ramgopal Varma's *Kaun/Who?* (1998) are some examples. However, since song and dance sequences guarantee a definite income it has been difficult to dispense with them altogether. Song and dance sequences traverse radio and television, independently of the films themselves, a phenomenon encouraging critics to rush to the conclusion that they are inserted into films only as entertaining spectacles with tangential links to the narrative.

The first decade of sound witnessed a range of experiments with sound and narrative, including introducing a number of songs into films. Musicologist Bhaskar Chandravarkar (1989) names songs of one minute and forty seconds' length as 'songlets' that were rarely heard outside the cinema halls, and thus are unavailable on gramophone records of the film. Referring to films such as *Indrasabha* (1931), laden with seventy-one songs, or *Kalidas* (1931), a Tamil film with fifty songs, Ashok Ranade (1981) suggests that not all of these were strictly songs but verse-in-tune flowing between prose-based dialogue and a full-blown song, a convention that he suggests emerges from oral-based cultures. Bowing to pressures from the recording industries, songs were standardised to 3 to 4 minutes, emerging as discrete moments in films, a practice that has stayed intact for the most part. According to Theodore Baskaran (1996), dramatist P. Sambanda Mudaliyar suggested that 'ideally song sequences should take about one-fourth of the film's duration'. Besides pressures from gramophone industries that promised revenues from sales of film song records, experiments in sound recording, including pre-recorded song and lip-synching by playback singers, encouraged the consolidation of film songs as distinct modules. Overseeing the composition of lyrics, managing an orchestra and choosing playback singers fortified the role of the music director.[19] Allegedly, Nitin Bose's *Dhoop Chaon* (1935) was the first film systematically to use playback singing under the helm of music director R.C. Boral.[20] Film historians and musicologists suggest that the popularity and persistence of film songs points to Indian cinema's early links to conventions of nineteenth-century Parsi theatre as well as folk theatre which were similarly strung together with a number of songs. Besides these theatrical origins, Chandravarkar and Ranade point to a confluence of musical influences in the hybrid film song: Indian classical, folk and Western tunes (Chandravarkar 1989). In recent years, in addition to star music directors, choreographers such as Prabhu Deva, Saroj Khan, Farah Khan and others have been asserting their presence by grafting together Indian dance styles with Western dance moves.

Although musicologists have written extensively on the synthetic quality of Indian film songs and on the parallel economy of star music directors and singers, there is an absence of literature on song sequences, lending support to the assumption that the sequences are extra-diegetic or, in narratological terms, achronies, outside the temporal reckoning of the narrative.[21] A flamboyant example of such an instance occurs in S. Shankar's *Indian* (1994), where the film abruptly cuts from Madras to Australia as the preferred setting for the 'Melbourne' song and dance. Declaiming such practices, Baskaran writes: 'The flow of the film would not be affected in the least if song sequences were excised, wholly or partly' (1996: 48). However, indulgent song and dance sequences remain, and a close analysis of this interruption begs us to explore how they relate to the narrative time of different kinds of films.

☐ CASE STUDY 2: GURU DUTT

To reiterate, one can detect a director's signature in the sequencing of song and dance sequences. With the availability of films from earlier decades on DVD format, viewers can finally watch films which were previously accessible only in a film archive or at retrospectives. Among the recent spate of DVD collections are those directed and produced by Guru Dutt, available for purchase at the website yashraj.com. While the poor quality of transfer from film to DVD is noticeable, the films nevertheless reveal Guru Dutt's reputation as a director who could produce a commercial hit without forsaking cinematic style. Accounts of his biography, available in the *Encyclopedia of Indian Cinema*, describe his birth in Bangalore in 1925, followed by early years in Calcutta. After being briefly employed as a telephone operator in Calcutta, Dutt embarked on a career in filmmaking by joining Prabhat Studios in 1944. Shortly thereafter, Dutt's collaborations with Bombay cinema's leading actors, lyricists, cameramen and music directors produced a number of box-office successes. Also playing the part of a producer under the banner of Guru Dutt films, Dutt experimented with a wide variety of genres and is seen retrospectively as one of the first Indian filmmakers to embrace a modern sensibility. Dutt committed suicide in 1964 leaving behind a rich legacy of films that continue to fascinate contemporary viewers.

Nasreen Munni Kabir's documentary *In Search of Guru Dutt* (1989) offers the most comprehensive understanding of Dutt's milieu between 1945 and 1964 as narrated by his colleagues in the industry and members of his family. Among the many aspects of his filmmaking style discussed in the documentary, Shyam Benegal, a renowned contemporary director in his own right and a cousin of the late director, identifies Guru Dutt's song picturisation as perhaps his greatest contribution to the cinematic style of popular Hindi cinema. Ably supported by lyricists, playback singers, choreographers and cameramen, the song and dance sequences in his films demonstrate a firm link to the narrative without ever appearing as superfluous additions. Kabir's 90-minute documentary is widely available as a special feature in the Yashraj's DVD releases of Guru Dutt's films.

As part of this exercise to understand Guru Dutt's cinematic style through his song and dance sequences, view his film *Mr. and Mrs. 55* (1955) and Kabir's documentary *In Search of Guru Dutt*. Please remember that the DVD version of the film does not indicate the location of the interval, and the poor quality of the transfer fails to adequately convey Guru Dutt's cinematographic style.

Mr. and Mrs. 55 is immediately recognisable as a hybrid genre that combines elements of the romantic comedy with social drama. Anita is a rich heiress who lives with her aunt, Sita Devi, a strident feminist who is a leading proponent of the Hindu Code Bill which grants women a right to annul a Hindu marriage. While Sita Devi is campaigning for women's rights, Anita fritters away her days at tennis matches and pools where unbeknownst to her a poor cartoonist, Pritam, falls hopelessly in love with her. In the meantime, Anita discovers on her twentieth birthday that her inheritance carries the condition that she must marry within a month. Appalled by her late brother's stipulations, Sita Devi conceives of a way to subvert the condition by arranging Anita's marriage to Pritam in exchange for a fee, with the understanding that her niece will annul the marriage after a month. Pritam seizes the opportunity for pecuniary reasons, initially unaware that the girl in question is none other than the one he is in love with. Through a series of misunderstandings that are par for the course in a romantic comedy, Anita and Pritam finally reunite after having annulled their first marriage.

In her discussion of the film, Jyotika Virdi (2003: 76) argues: 'The film's narrative line manifests familiar symptoms of male anxiety about women repositioning themselves in society – symptoms that include publicly mocking women or trivializing and caricaturing their demands' (76).[22] Virdi suggests that the film casts Sita Devi as an eccentric who 'joins the ranks of a long list of spinsters, dowagers, prohibitionists, mothers-in-law, suffragettes, "battle-axes," career women, "women's libbers," and lesbians' (ibid.: 85).[23] While taking into account Virdi's critique of the film's misogyny, it is also worth considering how the genre of the comedy does not offer a clear moral resolution after having lampooned every rule and convention in the narrative. It is no accident that Anita and Pritam's reunion occurs after the annulment of their marriage and at considerable distance from Sita Devi's command, a closure that is fitting within the generic convention of the romantic comedy.

While the caricature of the Hindu Code Bill dominates one strand of the narrative, it locks us into the strict spaces of Sita Devi's dominion, the courts and her mansion. In the sections tracking Anita, Pritam and their friends, the camera wanders through buses, parks, pools, bars, restaurants, offices and airports, spaces that are particularly animated in the nine song and dance sequences. Since critics have repeatedly remarked on song picturisation as a hallmark of Guru Dutt's cinematic style, it is worthy of further exploration.

Questions

1   Choose three song and dance sequences and describe the camera movement and mise-en-scène details. Analyse how the film deploys these sequences to advance, protract or divert the love story.
2   Choose another film by Guru Dutt, *Kagaz ke phool/Paper Flowers* as an exercise in comparison. After identifying the different genre strands in the film, focus on how song and dance sequences pace the narrative.
3   Using Dutt's two films as a template compare his films with the work of a contemporary director, Mani Ratnam or Vishal Bhardwaj, to draw out the differences in the use of this device. Such an exploration will cull out the differences in style.

For further discussion of audience and early cinema see Chapter 5.

In addition to attending to the ways in which song and dance interrupt the narrative in various ways, the iconography of these sequences of attractions calls our attention to other features that bolster a spectator's interest in Indian cinema. For instance, the abrupt cut to exotic locations sparks the tourist interests of the viewer, and similarly the object-laden mise-en-scène endorses consumerism. Not unlike the commercial imperative towards product placement in contemporary American cinema, song and dance sequences draw in a whole host of adjacent economies such as tourism and consumerism that are not so easily compartmentalised in Indian cinema. There is no doubt that the presence of several such sequences is reminiscent of a cinema of attractions found in early cinema where the spectacular aspects of such a scene override narrative coherence. Even in their most exhibitionistic form, when their presence rarely furthers the narrative and its 'undatedness' or achrony is most visible in their ability to circulate as self-contained segments on music television or film previews, their iconography remains open to a wide range of ideological readings.[24] But they also solicit our interests as tourists, albeit virtual tourists travelling the world within the closed confines of the movie theatre. The connection between tourism and cinema is an old one – Lumière shorts of Egypt are some of the earliest examples – and in Indian popular films these excursions speak to the continued interest in the travel genre even if a particular film lurches towards a different kind of genre consolidation.[25] Thus what we often find on screen are hybrid genres: gangster films intersecting with travel genres and so on. This hunt for the perfect or the most exotic locale makes filmmakers sound like explorers. I have argued elsewhere that the iconography in the song and dance sequences comments on the relationship between the love story and national identity. For instance, the presence and absence of scenes from Kashmir alert us to the ways in which films stage contestations over cartography in the national imaginary (Gopalan 1997b).

In contrast to these assumptions that promote their extra-diegetic relationship to the narrative, or dismiss them as a 'sequence of attractions' reminiscent of early cinema, song and dance sequences deserve another look, differentiating their relationship to the diegesis: delaying the development of the plot, distracting us from the other scene in the narrative through spatial and temporal disjunctions, and bearing an integral link to the plot. Even in one film, there may be different articulations of these sequences, thus complicating the idea of a single diegesis or the valency of the extra-diegetic. The lack of uniform temporal sequencing across different films alerts us to consider genre differences and auteur signatures inflecting the choreography of song and dance sequences.[26]

LOVE STORY

Although song and dance sequences surface in different genres of Indian cinema, their timing and elaboration in the love story genre has had the most success. Star-crossed lovers sing the same song across disparate spaces; lovers meet in a song and dance sequence; sylvan locales in Kashmir, Switzerland, Australia or South Africa ideally express the lovers' passion. The florid lyrics seem well suited to the lovelorn, ecstatic or the marooned lover, and in each such instance the sequence carries metaphoric possibilities that a realist narrative cannot completely deliver.

The love story has always been a wildly successful genre in Indian cinema. In fact, one can look at the different preoccupations of the love story over the past fifty years that press us to consider them as allegories of the nation state: inter-caste, inter-religious, inter-class stories and so on. Besides being available for political and social commentary, the genre has allowed its formula-ridden stories to be masterpieces in the hands of a competent director – the most obvious example being Raj Kapoor, whose experiments with this genre fortified the conventions for prospective directors. However, the love story too has undergone considerable revision, at times so extreme that we often watch marriage and wedding tales rather than pursue stories of star-crossed lovers. In this cycle of revision, Mani Ratnam emerges as the master of the political love story with his well-known trilogy: *Roja* juxtaposes contestations over Kashmir against the happiness of a newly-wed couple honeymooning in the valley; in *Dil Se* a series of political contestations vie for attention with a doomed love story between a radio reporter and a revolutionary/terrorist; and in *Bombay* (1995) – simultaneously produced in Tamil and Hindi – the durability of a Hindu–Muslim marital union is tested against the backdrop of communal riots in the city. Film critics have had a field day with Ratnam's films, and we can say that critical debates on *Roja* and *Bombay* have fundamentally changed the terms of debates on cinema in India.

Bombay traces the love story of a Hindu man, Shekhar, and a Muslim woman, Shailabano. Facing opposition from their parents, Shekhar leaves his village for Bombay and Shailabano flees her home to join him. It is in Bombay that they marry and have twin sons, Kamal and Kabir, but it is also in Bombay that they witness the rise of communal tensions marking the social fabric of India in the 1980s and 1990s. Provoked by Hindu fundamentalists demolishing the Babri Masjid in December 1992, communal riots in Bombay splinter the family. A miraculous reunion between parents and children also allows for an inter-generational reunion: Shekhar's father and Shailabano's parents arrive in Bombay and reconcile with their estranged children. Another round of riots in January ruptures the short-lived reunion, killing and scattering the family: older parents die in

Compare to genre in Hollywood cinema in Chapter 8.

communal fires, and the twins are separated from each other and from their parents. As Bombay burns, Shekhar and Shailabano hunt for their children, only to be reunited with them at the very moment the leaders of the respective communities call a halt to the insane marauding.

Among the different critical and popular writings on the film, Ravi Vasudevan's landmark essay carefully maps the history of censorship, both public and state, surrounding the film as a way of understanding the relationship between a Hindu man and a Muslim woman, a union that seems peculiarly underdeveloped in Hindi cinema, acquiring a taboo-like status for directors and writers. Besides attending to the public outcry against the film from both the right and left coalitions, Vasudevan leads us to consider the film's own management of this social taboo through various cinematic strategies that he argues produces an incoherence identifiable as the form of Indian popular cinema – the disaggregate narrative (Vasudevan 1996).

For discussion of lesbian and gay cinema, see Chapter 12.

Although the heterosexual love story remains the dominant trope in popular cinema, queer theory has long emphasised how popular cinema mobilises a series of alternative desires and affiliations despite their foreclosure at by the end of the narrative. In this context it is worth looking at Farhan Akhtar's first film *Dil Chahta Hai/What the Heart Desires* (2001), a buddy film that focuses on the friendship between three men – Sameer, Aakash and Siddharth – and assumes the form of a love story. Akhtar is no stranger to the film world, having an accomplished father, Javed Akhtar, a scriptwriter and poet who wrote the catchy songs in this film, and a mother, Honey Irani, who has moved from child star to scriptwriter. Of course, pedigree alone does not account for the success of the film, which captures the lives of the three upper-class boys in the period following their college graduation. The conventional battles with traditional parents or parents insisting on finding the right girl for their sons are rendered inconsequential; in fact, the parents appear to be supportive, mildly admonishing and even indulgent of their sons' development into men. Given that the narrative does not seek to displace conflicts on to the parental generation, the precipitating crisis in the film is the friendship among the three boys and the ways in which it is affected by their erotic development. As in most heterosexual narratives, here too women interfere and force changes in what is often perceived to be a stable economy between men, a narrative conceit that has tremendous play in westerns and gangster films.[27] In a provocative reading of this film, Kimberly Ringler uses Corey Creekmur's essay, 'Acting Like a Male: Masculine

• **Plate 15.3**
Dil Chahta Hai (Excel Entertainment–Hyphen Films Ltd)

Performances in My Darling Clementine', which extends Sedgwick's reading of the relationship between compulsory heterosexuality and homophobia, to argue that the mise-en-scène in this film suggests, yet at the same time disavows, the possibility of an erotic union between the three men (Ringler 2002). For instance, Ringler suggests that the film employs doors to ward off intimacy between men, at the same time suggesting the possibility of a homosexual union between them. Ringler's reading encourages us to consider the mise-en-scène as a rich site to mine for erotic desire, class aspirations, national longings and so on.

INTERVAL

Less obvious and less flamboyant than song and dance sequences, the 'interval' nevertheless characterises a theatrical viewing of Indian films. The 'interval' is the standard 10-minute break in every Indian popular film, a pause after 80 minutes of film screening. Lights are turned on, the projector is turned off and viewers step out of the theatre to smoke a cigarette, eat a snack or visit the bathroom. Unlike the strong imprint of song and dance sequences in the film-going experience, the location of the interval remains an elusive detail in the memory of even the most avid film-viewer. It is simply seen as a brief respite from the long screening. Trade papers, however, make passing references to which halves of the film were more, or less, interesting.

According to Theodore Baskaran, intervals have existed since the early 1930s when the feature film as a genre took root.[28] The term arises, in part, from the early years of film exhibition, when the constraints of working with a single projector would force the projectionist to stop the film more than once, in effect producing two or three intervals. Besides the whims of the projectionist, Baskaran notes that the films themselves referred overtly to this break in the narrative: in *Apoorva Sagodrigal/ Strange Friends* (1949) a song and dance sequence set in a garden ends with the word 'Edivali' ('Interval' in Tamil) strung together by flowers dropping from the trees; and in *Velaikkari/Servant* (1949), Mani, one of the protagonists, devises a plan which he indicates will take place later – after the interval. Baskaran speculates that intervals probably persisted to pace the narrative which was laden with at least a dozen songs, a feature he thinks has retained this cinema in a primitive stage of filmmaking beholden to attractions.

The interval weighs in as a crucial punctuation, adjusting both opening and closing strategies of the film, in effect, producing two opening and closing sequences in every Indian film. As in the song and dance sequences, the interval is not randomly located but regulated by genre constraints and directorial style. Breaking the spell of the dark auditorium, the interval reminds us of early cinema's exhibition practices when a film was one of many instalments of the evening's entertainment. In its current form, the interval is a cinematic device that organises the dose of cinematic attractions mandatory in Indian cinema as well as serving as a punctuation mark that continually directs our anticipation in surprising ways by opening and closing certain narrative strands.

Both song and dance sequences, and the interval, attune us to their structural function in popular Indian films, particularly through their play on spatial and temporal disjunctions. Their articulation in specific texts highlights how films imbibe both global and local conventions: genre films adjust to song and dance sequences while the interval doubles the structuring of anticipation and pleasure found in genre films. In each case, they call attention to interruptions in the convention of the linear narrative with a single diegesis dominant in Hollywood or other commercial industries, with their attendant assumptions of realist codes.[29] The ideal spectator of film theory, cloistered from adjacent consumer economies, surfaces as a phantom figure in Indian popular cinema; the Indian spectator, in contrast, travels several circuits of pleasures generated by a multi-diegetic narrative.[30]

For comparison with Hollywood narrative structure see Chapter 4.

There is no doubt that the location of the interval is crucial to Indian filmmakers as an indispensable device to organise the narrative structure. For instance, when asked: 'Do you write a screenplay, like a play, in three acts?', the scriptwriter Salim Khan responds:

I need a simple nice plot in which I must have a definite beginning, a middle and a crucial end. The end must be clear in my mind and then I start working on the sub-plots and the characters. I go on developing material, then I arrange it till the interval point, and then further the progress of the story.

(*Screen*, 15 July 1988)

Sagar Sarhadi, another scriptwriter, answers similarly:

No. Normally I have two. There are two dramatic movements – the interval and the end. The screenplay is written to heighten these dramatic movements.

(*Screen*, 11 July 1988)

Unlike an arbitrary break at the halfway point, Indian films often use the intermission as a definitive break, linking it to the opening and closing segments of a film. This distinct punctuation not only emerges as a unique marker of 'Indian' cinematic style but also locates the place of innovation and authorial style. Considered in these terms, the interval stands out as an obvious strategy to pace the narrative, and instead of rationalising it as a moment of relief from the tedium of a long film, this unique form of cinematic punctuation is the cornerstone of inventiveness in Indian cinema, a structuring device that inflects our reading of this cinema. Since it falls between two moments in a film, I suggest that we can explore the ways in which it pilfers closing strategies usually anticipated later in the film, and, at the same time, permits narrative strands to bloom in the second half. Rearranging narrative expectations instructs us to reconsider the charge of derivativeness aimed at Indian commercial cinema, a charge that overlooks the different ways in which a film accommodates Hollywood genre features within the constellation of interruptions. Alternatively, the 'interval' seems to have seeped into films produced outside India – Stanley Kubrick's *Full Metal Jacket* (1987), Quentin Tarantino's *Pulp Fiction* (1994), Wong Kar-Wai's *Chunking Express* (1994), Milcho Manchevski's *Before the Rain* (1994), Alejandro González Iñárritu's *Amores Perros/Love's a Bitch* (2001), Marzeih Meshkini's *Roozi Khe Zan Shodam/The Day I Became a Woman* (2001) and Jeremy Podeswa's *Five Senses* (2000) appear to have hijacked the interval to heighten their narratives of disjunctions and dispersal.

To consider the function of the interval in Indian films, it is most pertinent to consider how the generic structuring of a film is rearranged by this device. For instance, gangster films employ the interval to shift the mise-en-scène from one location to another. The interval also allows for a grafting of an entirely new structuring of genre: a love story becomes a social melodrama. At times, the interval also informs the pacing of other interruptions: a director may place the song and dance sequences before the interval. The permutations are endless, but a close scrutiny of this interruption opens the film to the work of scriptwriters, choreographers, singers, production designers, and so on.

Questions

1   Most DVD versions of Indian films are notorious for expunging the frame of the interval, thus making it almost impossible to tell where the filmmaker stopped the film. To understand the full import of the interval, it's worth seeing a film in a theatrical context. Plan such an excursion!

2   Observe how the film uses the interval to shift the film's narrative. Closely observe if another plot line has developed, changes in mise-en-scène, and in an extreme form a new set of characters.

CENSORSHIP

In addition to these two kinds of interruptions structuring popular Indian films, viewers are aware that the state monitors the relationship between cinema and society most visibly through film censorship. The most glaring manifestation of state intervention in film production is the Board of Censors' certificate that precedes each film but, as recent scholarship has demonstrated, a film's narrative is deeply marked by implicit and explicit negotiations with censorship regulations. This inaugural moment of every film publicly released in India, whether imported or indigenous, informs the spectator that the film has been approved by the state and carries with it traces of censored cuts. The British colonial state introduced film censorship by passing the Cinematograph Act of 1918 for at least two reasons: first, to censor film footage that might incite anti-colonial riots; second, to avoid (mis)representations of the West, particularly images of Western women. These broad concerns targeted both Indian and imported films, and set a pattern for post-independence censorship practices, where the state perceives films as having a tremendous influence over its citizenry and thus directs its regulations towards the production and control of 'quality' films (see Razdan 1975; Sarkar 1982; *The Indian Cinematograph Code*, 1982; Vasudev 1978). However, instead of seeing censorship as *post hoc* interference from the state, I suggest that filmmakers spend considerable energy incorporating censorship regulations *during* filmmaking in an attempt to pre-empt sweeping cuts that would drastically affect the flow of the narrative. Moreover, over the years, the relationship between the state and the film industry has revealed a spectrum of negotiations – from an obedient nationalism to a flagrant flouting of regulations that fuel the production of images on screen.

While the obscenity codes governing Indian cinema address a wide range of issues affecting both image and dialogue, in practice the object of greatest scrutiny is the female body. I use the term *coitus interruptus* to indicate the different ways in which the film industry negotiates the code to finally produce the female body on screen. This is not a gratuitous evocation of contraception, but rather a play on the structural similarity between two mechanisms – contraceptive regulations and censorship – suggesting how the state isolates the female body as the prime site of control and regulation in the public sphere. Among the several manifestations of *coitus interruptus*, the withdrawal-of-the-camera technique is instantly recognisable in various Indian films: the camera withdraws just before a steamy love scene ensues and the film replaces it with extra-diegetic shots of waterfalls, flowers, thunder, lightning and tropical storms. The varying configurations and recurrent use of *coitus interruptus* demonstrate how the film industry, despite its laments about state control, has been preoccupied with the withdrawal-of-the-camera technique as a crucial source of surplus pleasure. With its focus on dodging censorship prescriptions as well as maintaining its interests in the female body on screen, *coitus interruptus*, as a cinematic convention, captures an intimate and tense relationship between the state and the film industry predicated on attempts, however contradictory, to align the *national* subject with the film spectator. Far from aligning perfectly with the interests of the state and the film industry, the viewer is drawn into a fetishistic scenario where s/he oscillates between a cinephiliac mourning over lost footage on the one hand and, on the other, acknowledges that the state employs patriarchal law to produce limits on seeing.

THE WOMAN'S FILM

Inasmuch as cultural critics see popular films as staging social and political anxieties, the woman's film genre – which includes women-centred narratives, female protagonists undergoing political conversion, and more or less overt gestures towards feminist politics – has drawn responses and responded to the concerns of feminists, both in India and the diaspora. As mentioned above, Madhava Prasad notes that a fully independent

For a discussion on censorship in the US and the UK see website, Chapter 1.

For further discussion of women filmmakers, see Chapter 11, pp. 265–268.

For further discussion of feminism and feminist film theory, see Chapter 11, pp. 269–277.

woman's film struggled to develop in the 1960s, all too often annexed to what he sees as the 'super-genre', or the feudal family romance. Besides the obvious economic motives of the box office that carries a bias against women ageing on-screen, we may conjecture that the inability of the woman's film to survive was the unavailability of representations of strong woman-centred narratives in the social terrain, as well as the absence of critical feminist voices evaluating popular films. In this context it is useful to browse through past issues of *Manushi* – the most important feminist magazine in India – to gauge the developing, yet shifting, feminist readings of popular cinema set in motion by a section on film reviews. Rather than dismiss popular cinema altogether and applaud the politics of 'middle', parallel or alternative cinemas, these reviews read regressive representations as well as seeing feminist possibilities in popular cinema.

In recent years, the burgeoning field of feminist criticism of Indian films has produced an array of reading strategies that we can bring to bear on popular films. For instance, Maithili Rao (1998) examines the avenging women films of the 1980s to reprimand popular cinema for canny representations of aggressive women that fall short of feminism. Charting a similar territory, I have argued that the avenging women genre is shaped by the ongoing tussle between the film industry's desire to mine the woman's body for a range of representations and Censor Board dictates on obscenity codes, a tussle that throws up a heady concoction of sex and violence in these narratives that are predicated on rape and revenge (Gopalan 1997a). Jyotika Virdi (1999) locates the avenging women genre within the genre of women's film of the 1970s that similarly mobilised feminist possibilities but prematurely foreclosed those very options by evoking traditional representations of the pure or good woman.

Although these readings focus on women-centred narratives in popular cinema, we can detect feminist modes of analysis in Tejawini Niranjana's (1994) reading of Mani Ratnam's *Roja*, in which she argues that the film uses the figure of the good-wife-in-distress to promote a Hindu nationalist imaginary. In addition to decoding the narrative, attending to point-of-view shots and responding to the modes of address, critics have isolated examples of feminist offerings that are even queer at times in popular cinema: Radha Subramanyam sights a feminist consciousness in Kalpana Lajmi's *Rudaali/The Crier* (1992) that places the gendered subaltern within an erotic economy (Subramanyam 1996).

While critics have directed their energies at popular cinema, women filmmakers from middle or art cinema have long been experimenting with feminist aesthetics that include narrating the plight of Brahmin widowhood while giving them dignity (see e.g. Prema Karanth's *Phaniyamma*, 1983); centring on the loneliness of an Anglo-Indian teacher (see e.g. Aparna Sen's *36 Chowringhee Lane*, 1982) and so on. In the field of documentary filmmaking, Deepa Dhanaraj's careful documenting of communal riots, and policies on reproductive rights and population control, has expanded the field of feminist aesthetics beyond a women-centred narrative. Similarly, the women's film collective Media Storm, based in Delhi, has employed conventional and guerrilla tactics to propose visual inter-ventions to the ongoing debates on right-wing nationalism, state brutality and feminist subjectivity.

This rich and complicated terrain of feminist film criticism provides a productive framework to examine two controversial films: *Bandit Queen* (1994) and *Fire* (1998).

Produced in collaboration with British Channel 4 and based on Mala Sen's (1991) biography of the notorious dacoit Phoolan Devi, Shekhar Kapur's film details Phoolan's development from a child bride to an outlaw. Its release in India was stymied by the Board of Censors that recommended excising the explicit scenes of sex and violence in the film. In addition, the film's claim that it was a true story provoked the late Phoolan Devi, by that time a newly elected Member of Parliament from a lower caste facing allegations from the upper caste in her constituency about a massacre in Behmai. The public debate on the film took Kapur to task for the prolonged rape scenes in the film,

• Plate 15.4
Bandit Queen (Channel
4 Films–Kaleidoscope
Productions–British Film
Institute)

using the guise of feminism.[31] *Bandit Queen* was eventually released with no cuts but in several cities there were separate showings for women.

Fire (Deepa Mehta, 1998)

A Canadian–Indian co-production, Deepa Mehta's film sparked a similar debate to that on *Bandit Queen* because of its overt representations of sexual relationships between women. The right-wing Hindu party Shiv Sena called for a ban, propelling a heated debate on Hindu representations of women, lesbianism in the Hindu tradition and so on. Most of this is well recorded on several websites, including SAWNET (South Asian Women's Net). After the dust had settled there was further debate among feminists on the film's images of lesbian desire, Mehta's own distance from queer politics, the class politics in the film, and the relationship between audiences in the West and in India; such positions demand that we take a another look at this film.

FOUNDATIONAL FICTIONS OF THE POST-COLONIAL NATION

Critical writings on Indian cinema frequently dwell on how Indian films are intimately linked to questions of national identity and history. Sumita Chakravarty's *National Identity in Indian Popular Cinema, 1947–1987* (1993) for example examines the themes in Hindi popular cinema as contestations over national identity, including the shifting relationship between the gendered body and the nation state. Theodore Baskaran's pioneering work on Tamil cinema unravels the link between Tamil cinema and nationalist politics in Tamil Nadu, a focus that forces us to acknowledge regional nationalisms and cinemas (Baskaran 1981). The recent spate of overtly nationalist films has invited the ire of critics who have taken *Roja* and *Gadar* to task for espousing and condoning Hindu nationalist politics. It is in this context that we will look at *Hey! Ram* (1999) in order to better understand how films stage battles over national identity.

☐ CASE STUDY 3: *HEY! RAM* (KAMAL HAASAN, 1999)[32]

Kamal Haasan's *Hey! Ram* (1999) tackles a nationalist narrative of epic proportions including Partition, Gandhi's assassination and contemporary communal politics in India. Rather than working as part of the backdrop, the film intimately ties these political and social events to the fate of the male protagonist Saket Ram. The twin preoccupations of the film produce an unruly narrative that avoids resolution of the knotty issues it sets in motion, yet urges us to consider the inextricable links between cinematic and national histories. Keeping pace with the narrative, the film deploys a number of formal strategies including monochromatic sequences for the contemporary scenes, digital images akin to video games, as well as a rich tapestry of quotations from world cinemas: elephants from D.W. Griffith's *Intolerance* (1916) and Pastrone's *Cabiria* (1914); dream sequences from Luis Bunuel's films; mise-en-scène from *Raiders of the Lost Ark* (Steven Spielberg, 1981) and so on. Simultaneously, it evokes these references to world cinema within a nationalist narrative and in effect revisits similar coincidences of interests in Griffith's *The Birth of a Nation* (1915), to a lesser extent in Mehboob Khan's *Mother India* (1957), and more overtly in S. Shankar's *Indian* (1996), a rich set of associations encouraging us to consider Mikhail Iampolski's (1998) suggestion that quotations in films gesture towards the past. *Hey! Ram* reconfigures the melodramatic aspects of these nationalist narratives by focusing exclusively on the male protagonist's relationship to the nation, a focus that dwells on the slow conversion of the South Indian Brahmin from a distant observer to a militant subversive by deploying digital technologies.[33]

For further discussion of computer technology see Chapters 2 and 10.

To the consternation of critics lamenting the invasion of digital technologies, there is no doubt that digital morphing as a technique vastly improves the use of dissolves and cuts to suggest corporeal transformation on screen – wolf to man, man to woman and so on (Sobchack 2000). A similar pre-digital history obtains in Indian cinema, where cut-and-paste devices paper over the metamorphosis of a woman into a snake (see especially the genre of snake films including *Nagin* (1954) and *Nagina* (1986)); or the grafting of two separate frames to maintain the illusion of the multiple roles played by the same actor. In an instrumental sense, digital technologies advance the making of these illusions by rendering seamless transformations on-screen, in effect suturing us into the diegesis of the story. Yet this pull into the narrative cannot completely repress the history of innovations in digital technology imbricated in military experiments that are similarly plagued with issues of time and space.[34] It is therefore not surprising that we should find the most spectacular use of digital technologies in conquest narratives such as *Independence Day* (Roland Emmerich, 1996) and *The Matrix* (Wachowski, 1999), which heighten the relationship between cinematic and military modes of representations. Although *Hey! Ram* underplays military prowess, the film's use of digital technology to simulate a different story of origins consolidates the nationalist narrative and cannot help but remind us of the militant aspects of nationalism.

Kamal Haasan's film deploys digital technology to scramble linear chronology by moving back and forth between 1999 and the period 1946 to 1948. We see Saket Ram, a Tamil Brahmin, working as an archaeologist in Mohenjodaro in 1946; with his first wife Aparna in Calcutta during communal riots which ends in her death in 1946; a respite in Chidambaram and Madras where he marries Mythili, a little before Independence in 1947; visits to Maharashtra and his joining the ranks of right-wing Hindu militants between 1947 and 1948; and finally the denouement in Delhi when he tries to assassinate Gandhi in 1948. The temporal scrambling matches the spatial journey through pre-Partition India, allowing the film to draw a continuum from communal antagonisms during Partition to contemporary tensions set in motion after Hindu militants demolished the Babri Masjid on 6 December 1992. Saket Ram's conversion proceeds from his role as a disinterested scholar to a militant Hindu nationalist after encountering gorier aspects of communal riots in Calcutta, and finally to a Gandhian pacifist, a conversion narrative that rescues the film from wholly aligning itself with Hindu nationalism. Yet it is the middle sections, the parts spelling out Ram's entry into the ranks of the Hindu right, that are replete with the film's mastery over digital technology, especially morphing, relaying its own conversion from analogue to digital images.

One of the most flamboyant exhibitions of digital morphing takes places during Ram and Mythili's visit to a kingdom in Maharashtra – marking his definitive sympathies towards the right-wing Hindu party Rashtriya Sevak Sangha (RSS) – when the local king at the behest of Abhiyankar, a right-wing Hindu zealot whom Ram encounters during the riots in Calcutta, draws him into a scheme to kill Gandhi. After a fortuitous reconnection with his old friend Lalvani from Karachi, Ram and Mythili join the Ram Lila celebrations at the palace grounds where Abhiyankar offers Ram a drug-laced drink that induces Ram to conjure figures from the riot scene in Calcutta as well as heightening his sexual interest in Mythili. Seducing her away from a dance performance, he leads Mythili to their chambers. As they begin to make love, we see her morph into an enormous gun with Ram stroking its barrel. Undoubtedly this is a heavy-handed metaphoric substitution that carries a banal psychoanalytical association: the woman replaces the gun in a way that demands we understand how the libidinal drive severs itself from object identification. Clearly the excesses of the scene lead us to recognise how morphing showcases digital technology while providing only a tangential link to the narrative. Nevertheless, another reading can also be obtained here, one which takes us down a different road. Blinding us with technological prowess, *Hey! Ram* uses morphing to veil its relationship to censorship regulations. Instead of including a sexually explicit scene that may provoke the ire of the Board of Censors, the altered image allows us to view the scene through metaphoric substitution, a substitution that reconfigures the temporality of censorship. In its extreme form, popular films simply substitute the love-making scene with pastoral evocations, cut to a song and dance sequence to regulate the overflow of passion, or push the envelope to the limit. In all three possibilities available in the pre-digital era, we confront a linear unfolding of the narrative where a cut directs us to the next image. Morphing, on the other hand, maintains intact an old-fashioned relationship to censorship while distracting us with a show-stopping spectacle that morphs objects within the frame – a spatial trans- formation rather than a temporal one. Cushioned in a visit that highlights Ram's political conversion, morphing in this sequence overdetermines the connectives between political and sexual desire, an overlap that the film underscores during a secret meeting in the Maharaja's chambers when from Ram's point of view we see the Maharaja's face morph into that of Aparna. In other words, morphing allows a film such as *Hey! Ram* to expand the limits of what is permissible on the Indian screen through metaphoric substitution, a substitution that inverts the relationship between space and time between frames.

The second spectacular scene of morphing occurs soon after Ram's visit to Maharashtra, detouring through scenes of riots in 1996 composed in monochromatic colours mimicking black and white documentary footage – a burst of red fire undercuts the documentary gesture swaying it towards the diegesis of the film. These excursions to the monochromatic footage focus on an ailing Ram in the care of his grandson. Escorting Ram to a hospital through streets pocked by communal riots marking the anniversary of the demolition of the Babri Masjid, his grandson is halted by the police and escorted to the safety of a bunker. From an extreme close-up shot of Ram's left pupil the film dissolves into a digitally produced target. On the soundtrack we hear the police- officer's command to shoot – a sound-bridge connecting the two images. In the digitally produced scene, we see a muscular Ram at target practice; his attire clearly betrays signs of a Brahmin man including the sacred thread across his bare chest, an image that cannot completely sever its relationship to the real – Ram converts the handgun to a rifle by attaching a shoulder rest. This short scene of target practice celebrating the morphed muscular Brahmin body gives way to a simulated storm that sweeps over the entire screen. Undeterred by the ferocity of the storm he stands his ground.

Poised to function as an explanatory segment, morphing actualises Ram's metamorphosis from a reluctant spectator into a full-fledged member of a right-wing militant Hindu political party. Clearly the digital simulation of a muscular body adds further credence to popular representations of militant masculinities that surface in Amar Chitra Katha comic books and cable television.[35]

For further discussion of gender and masculinity, see Chapter 11, pp. 283–291.

Although *Hey! Ram* converts Kamal Haasan, the star, into a spectacular digital image that exceeds the star ideal, thus severing its link to an indexical referent, the digital image is a vastly improved version of the star's body. However, the muscular body in the digital space does not abdicate its commitment to other referents but seeks to find its purpose within an older regime of filmic representation that continues to battle with notions of the real. In other words, the muscular militant body in the film services the cause of the ideal male image in Hindu nationalism and not that of the simulated battle on the screen.

CONCLUSION

The peculiar conditions of Indian commercial film narrative are constantly shifting, undoing our assumptions about some of its constituent elements. Defying the need to make sense by importing reading strategies inspired from either classical, early or contemporary American cinema, contemporary Indian movies compel us to employ several of these theoretical positions simultaneously to read *one* film. Despite being far removed from the central engine of capitalism and its accompanying realist narrative, Indian cinema mimics, copies and rewrites these forms while simultaneously maintaining a local quotient of attractions. In a curious twist in the history of appropriation and application of film theory across national cinemas, certain ontological questions surrounding narrative cinema – questions which Eisenstein raised in his famous essay on the 'montage of attractions' – find fertile ground in contemporary Indian cinema (Eisenstein 1997). An amalgamation of the different interruptions in Indian popular cinema throws up a picture bearing an uncanny resemblance to Peter Wollen's conceptualisation of the 'multi-diegesis' in Jean-Luc Godard's *Vent d'est/Wind from the East* (1969), a film that he claims undoes the narrative conventions of both Hollywood and Soviet films (Wollen 1982). We may be hard-pressed to see any immediate link between an overtly avant-garde practice and popular Indian cinema but, not unlike Wollen, viewers of Indian films do see its digressions and interruptions as intrinsic to enjoying and understanding these films as well as comprising the location of intense ideological struggles.

For detailed discussion of Eisenstein and Soviet montage, see Chapter 17.

SUMMARY

- There are many forms and style of Indian popular cinema, Bollywood is one among many (a regional cinema with national and global reach).
- Academic discourse on the codes and conventions of Indian popular films: editing, narrative and genre structuring.
- Three devices structuring Indian popular cinema: song and dance sequences, the interval and censorship.
- Focus on the love story, woman's film and historical drama.

QUESTIONS FOR DISCUSSION

1   A number of recent films dwell extensively on the male revolutionary leaders from the colonial period, Mangal Pandey and Bhagat Singh, which offer an interesting counterpoint to *Hey! Ram*. In this context, watch Ketan Mehta's *The Rising: The*

Ballad of Mangal Pandey (2005) to explore how these films deal with the idea of the past.

2   Choose a segment from the two films—opening, song and dance – to compare the filmmaking styles of the two directors.

NOTES

1   This is a condensed version of the Introduction to my book *Cinema of Interruptions* (London, BFI, 2002).
2   Conversation with O.P. Dutta, April 1999. Dutta tells of the 1950s and 1960s when the Soviets purchased a number of films, but Indian filmmakers never kept track of these exhibitions or purchases. On viewing Indian films in Nigeria see Brian Larkin (1997).
3   Thanks to Tejaswini Ganti for posting this article.
4   Thanks to Moira Taylor's research on the web.
5   'Bollywood' handily slots a range of film styles available in Indian popular cinema, a term whose migration from entertainment journalism to academic discourse overlooks critical writing that has laboured long on differentiating style and periods. Having said that, it is worth noting a book that parries this term with an elegance and wit hitherto unmatched: Amit S. Rai, *Untimely Hollywood: Globalization and India's New Media Assemblage*, Duke University Press, London, 2009.
6   Personal conversation with P.C. Sriram, September 1995.
7   Film production in 1979: 113 in Hindi; 139 in Tamil; 131 in Telugu. In 1995: 157 in Hindi; 165 in Tamil; 168 in Telugu. Figures are from Rajadhyaksha and Willemen (1999).
8   For a comprehensive evaluation of alternative filmmakers, see Hood (2000).
9   On the reception of Indian films in the Soviet Union, see Sudha Rajagopalan, *Indian Films in Soviet Cinema: The Culture of Movie-going After Stalin*, Indiana University Press, Bloomington, IN, 2008.
10 I wish to thank Haim Bresheeth for this wonderful example from Israeli cinema.
11 I wish to thank Roopal Oza for alerting me to these reports.
12 Touted as a 'curry western' by film critic Ken Wlaschin reviewing the 1976 Film Festival, Sippy's film fits quite easily into revisionist westerns such as 'spaghetti westerns'.
13 Mayne (1993) has a splendid yet sympathetic critique of the ideal spectator in psychoanalysis.
14 While Singh's formulation has critical valency, I would like to question his reading of the song: a close analysis of the scene shows that the camera does not actively grope the dancer's body even if it fragments her body. Attributing movement to a phantom camera, Singh may be implicitly admitting to being taken in by the entertaining song and dance number!
15 Rashmi Doraiswamy, and Aruna Vasudev, author of the best book on Indian censorship, floated the film journal *Cinemaya* with the explicit intention of increasing interest in Asian cinema from an Asian location.
16 A survey conducted by *Filmfare* in June 1999 revealed Sholay to be the first important film in the life of several young stars.
17 Thomas outlines one of the first proposals to take the popular film industry seriously, on its 'own terms'.
18 American film producers have also started to see the commercial viability of soundtracks. Music stores now exclusively stack a separate section with movie soundtracks.
19 According to Baskaran (1996), *Ambikapathi* (1937) is the earliest Tamil film to credit a music director.
20 See the entry for R.C. Boral in Rajadhyaksha and Willemen (1999). See also Skillman (1986).
21 We still lack a complete analysis of sound, technology, song writers and music directors that will help us to better understand the relationship between sound and image in Indian popular cinema.
22 Jyotika Virdi, 'The idealized woman' (2003: 60–86).
23 Ibid.: 85.
24 A good recent example is Sashilal Nair's *Kabhi na Kabhi*, where a sequence forms a separate system independent of the narrative.
25 On the travel genre in early Euro-American cinema, see Musser (1990).
26 For an excellent set of essays on the global circulation of Hindi song and dance see Sangita Gopal and Sujata Moorti (eds), *Global Bollywood: Travels of Hindi Song and Dance*, University of Minnesota Press, London, 2008.
27 For an elaboration of the heterosexual paradigm, see Kosofsky Sedgwick (1985).
28 I am extremely grateful to Theodore Baskaran for generously sharing these filmic details with me.
29 See Mayne (1993) for a splendid exegesis on the cultural context of Hollywood production and their preferred spectator.
30 Peter Wollen uses 'multi-diegesis' to describe Jean-Luc Godard's film *Vent d'est*. He argues that Godard is responding both to Hollywood and to Mos-film narratives characterised by a single diegesis by producing a film with multi-diegesis.
31 See Arundhati Roy, 'The great Indian rape trick', *Sunday*, 26 August to 3 September 1994, pp. 56–84, and 'The great Indian rape trick II', *Sunday*, 11–17 September 1994, pp. 58–64; Pankaj Buttalia, 'Sanction for politics of revenge', *Times of India*, 4 September 1994.
32 Please see my reading of *Hey! Ram* in *Cinema of Interruptions* (2002).
33 Mantra, the digital facility at Ramoji Film City in Hyderabad, won the National Award for its special effects in *Hey! Ram*.
34 On the correlation between cinema and military technologies, see Virilio (1989).
35 See Anand Patwardhan's film *Father, Son, and Holy War* for a thorough investigation of masculinity in the Indian public sphere. See also Arvind Rajagopal (2001).

FURTHER READING

Barnouw, E. and Krishnaswamy, S., *Indian Film* (2nd edn), Oxford University Press, New York, 1980.

Chatterji, Gayatri, *Mother India*, BFI Classics, BFI, London, 2002.

Chatterji, Shoma, *Parama and Other Outsiders: The Cinema of Aparna Sen*, Parumita Publications, Calcutta, 2002.

Chopra, Anupama, *Sholay: The Making of a Classic*, Penguin Books India, New Delhi, 2000.

Chopra, Anupama, *Dilwale Dulhania Le Jayenge*, BFI Modern Classics, BFI, London, 2002.

Datta, Sangeeta, *Shyam Benegal*, World Directors, BFI, London, 2002.

Desai, Jigna, *Beyond Bollywood: The Cultural Politics of South Asian Diasporic Film*, Routledge, New York and London, 2004.

Dwyer, Rachel, *100 Bollywood Films*, BFI Screen Guides, BFI, London, 2005.

Ganti, Tejaswini, *Bollywood: A Guidebook to Popular Hindi Cinema*, Routledge, New York and London, 2004.

Gopal, Sangita and Moorti, Sujata (eds), *Global Bollywood: Travels of Hindi Song and Dance*, University of Minnesota Press, London, 2008.

Iyer, P., *Video Night in Kathmandu: Reports from the Not-So-Far East*, Knopf, New York, 1988.

Kabir, Nasreen Munni, *Bollywood: The Indian Cinema Story*, Channel 4 Books, London, 2001.

Mishra, Vijay, *Bollywood Cinema: Temples of Desire*, Routledge, New York and London, 2002.

Pendakur, Manjunath, *Indian Popular Cinema: Industry, Ideology, and Consciousness*, Hampton Press, Cresshill, NJ, 2003.

Rai, Amit S., *Untimely Hollywood: Globalization and India's New Media Assemblage*, Duke University Press, Durham, NC and London, 2009.

Rajadhyaksha, Ashish and Willeman, Paul (eds), *Encyclopaedia of Indian Cinema* (2nd edn), British Film Institute, London, 1999.

Rajagopalan, Sudha, *Indian Films in Soviet Cinema: The Culture of Movie-going after Stalin*, Indiana University Press, Bloomington, IN, 2008.

Thoraval, Yves, *The Cinemas of India*, Macmillan India, New Delhi, 2000.

Virdi, Jyotika, *The Cinematic Imagination: Indian Popular Films as Social History*, Rutgers University Press, New Brunswick, NJ, 2003.

The following periodicals are also useful for those interested in the field.
Cinemaya
Deep Focus
Filmfare
Lensight
Stardust

FURTHER VIEWING

Simply put, there is a lot of Indian cinema out there to watch and, thanks both to global distribution of blockbuster films and DVDs, it is possible to watch a range of films hitherto unavailable. *Encyclopaedia of Indian Cinema* (Rajadhyaksha and Willemen 1999) remains the best reference source for plot summaries of landmark films in the twentieth century and biographies of filmmakers.

The plethora of film festivals dedicated to Indian films has made it possible to watch art house and independent films. Catalogues from film festivals are excellent guides for procuring DVDs online. Please refer to online archives of Cannes, Venice, Toronto international film festivals; 3rd I Film Festival in San Francisco is dedicated to independent filmmaking in South Asia and the diaspora. In addition to film festivals it is worth tracking a history of retrospectives on Indian films at the National Film Theatre in London, Museum of Modern Art in New York, Pacific Film Archives, and so on to understand the expanding canon.

The online blog Passion for Cinema (passionforcinema.com/) is an excellent resource on small-budget films as well serving as a forum between filmmakers and cinephiles.

RESOURCE CENTRES

Most Indian popular film magazines are starzines and are highly unreliable sources for production details, but they are a good place to begin research on the star system. See *Filmfare, Stardust, G.* For production details see Screen (published by the Express Group). *Trade Guide, Film Information. Pediff.Com* is a good online source for film reviews and interviews with filmmakers and stars.

www.Rediff.com
This is a good online source for film reviews and interviews with filmmakers and stars.

www.cscsban.org
The website for the Centre for the Study of Culture and Society has a comprehensive listing of film reviews and other related materials that your institutions can subscribe to.

www.lib.berkeley.edu/MRC
This media resource centre at Berkeley University's site has videos from South Asia and the South Asian diaspora.

www.filmindia.com
This is an extensive source of Indian film information, including a directory, bibliography, newsclips, events and links.

www.hollywoodmasala.com
This is a web resource for South Asian film and filmmakers.

www.indolink.com
This website has Hindi and Tamil movie reviews.

**http://www.mith2.umd.edu/WomensStudies/
FilmReviews/**
A database of film reviews of feminist films from the University of Maryland, mainly written by Linda Lopez McAllister. Some interesting and unusual perspectives on American and British films. Includes non-mainstream films.

http://www.virtualref.com/abs/882.htm
Women in Cinema: a reference guide. A discussion of the role and impact of women on Western cinema. Areas of discussion include: bibliographies and guides, biographical sources, reviews and filmographies, electronic sources and subject collections of film.

http://haze.customer.netspace.net.au
RML's movie page. A nicely organised collection of information on directors, films and actors. Described as 'international', meaning American and European films.

http://imdb.com
The international movie database is comprehensive and allows you to search for movies, including Indian cinema, on title.

http://www.indiaplaza.com
Lists Hindi DVDs with English subtitles.

http://www.anytamil.com/php/home.php
Lists Tamil DVDs.

Chapter 16

Latin American Cinema

Linda Craig

■ Latin American Cinema

INTRODUCTION: BEGINNINGS

Recent international successes have led to a renewed interest in Latin American films, something which is welcome, but when film lovers and critics from outside of the subcontinent think of Latin American cinema, they tend to focus first and foremost on the distinctive, highly politicised films that appeared first in Brazil in the mid-1950s, and then beyond Brazil in countries like Argentina and Chile in the wake of the Cuban Revolution of 1959. The films from this period are often referred to under the umbrella term of 'Third Cinema', or 'The New Latin American Cinema'. This focus was encouraged by the filmmakers themselves who forged a powerful, radical cinema, and who frowned upon earlier Latin American films which they deemed to be derivative and over-commercialised. An unfortunate consequence of this is that a rich and complex history has been unfairly overlooked.

Following the first commercial film screening by the Lumière Brothers in Paris in December 1895, their cameramen were sent around the world to demonstrate the new invention. In Latin America the first screening took place in Brazil, in Rio de Janeiro, in July 1896, swiftly followed by the Argentine capital, Buenos Aires, and then Mexico City. Films were then shown in other capital cities such as Lima and Santiago. Making use of established commercial routes, the films reached these large cities of the subcontinent, which were already in the throes of modernisation. However the first three countries, Brazil, Argentina and Mexico, were to become the most important in terms of cinema. They are the largest countries, with huge urban populations, and they continue to dominate Latin American film to this day.

Thus film made its presence felt in Latin America from its very beginnings, but another issue arose concurrently: as in other parts of what might be described as the developing world, the film viewing public was weaned from the outset on films from elsewhere. As with so many aspects of its culture and economies, the crucial factors that influence Latin American cinema are those of **neo-colonialism** and the resultant dependency. Shohat and Stam point out that 'The beginnings of cinema coincided with the giddy heights of the imperial project', and 'the most prolific film-producing countries … also "happened" to be among the leading imperialists' (1994: 100). Moreover not only was the technology imported, as in the case of the Lumières, so too was the language of film. Johnson argues that, 'when film production began [in Latin America], the formal uses … had already been largely determined' (1987: 22).

In this early period the majority of the films screened were from Europe, from the studios of Pathé and Eclair in France, and from Italy, the country which by 1912 dominated the world market. The First World War put an end to this hegemony, and while Europe was fighting, and using the silver nitrate necessary for film stock for weaponry, the United States succeeded in almost entirely replacing its European competitors in terms of both film production and distribution.

Yet despite this dominance, film production was already underway in the Latin American subcontinent before the turn of the twentieth century. We have to rely on journalistic sources for information about early Latin American productions because most of the films made between 1897 and 1930 have been lost, but evidence suggests the earliest films were generally one-reelers in the form of newsreels and documentaries, mostly featuring sights and events of local interest, and often with national dignitaries. The first Mexican fiction film was a one-reeler, *Don Juan Tenorio* (Toscano Barragán, 1898), and the same director later filmed documentaries of the Mexican Revolution 1910–1917, a conflagration also filmed by US companies. Famously, the revolutionary leader, Pancho Villa, signed a contract with the Mutual Film Corporation whereby in return for $25,000, he agreed to fight battles in daylight whenever possible and, rather

neo-colonialism
The domination by a powerful, usually Western nation of another nation that is politically independent, but has a weak economy greatly dependent on trade with the powerful nation.

gruesomely, to postpone executions which had previously been held at four in the morning until seven or eight when the light was better (King 1990: 17).

Early exhibition of any kind in Rio de Janeiro was hampered by an intermittent supply of electricity to the city, and it was not until the establishment of a reliable source in 1907 that cinema began to flourish in Brazil. They quickly made up for lost time, and a surge of film production meant that, according to Johnson (1987: 27), in the years from 1908 to 1911, some one hundred films per year, mostly one-reelers, were produced locally. The country was enjoying what is termed the *Bela Epoca* (Beautiful Period) of Brazilian film. The first Brazilian film studios were established in 1909, and local versions of staples such as *Uncle Tom's Cabin* and *The Merry Widow* were well received. There were also *fitas cantantes* 'singing films' where opera singers performed behind the screens. However, the different studios competed with each other rather than uniting against what was a common enemy, and thus failed to hold back the tide of foreign films.

Argentina followed a similar path, starting with one-reelers, generally of military parades and official ceremonies, and producing in 1908 its first fiction film, *El fusilamiento de Dorrego* (*The Shooting of Dorrego*) by Max Gallo. King tells us that melodrama was 'a style in vogue, copied from the theatre and from foreign, in particular Italian, cinema' (1990: 10), and *La nobleza gaucha* (*Gaucho Nobility*) (Cairo, de la Pera, Guncha, 1915), a melodrama in which a peasant girl is raped and taken to Buenos Aires to be the landowner's mistress and then rescued by a gaucho from the estate, proved to be the most successful Argentine film of the silent period, enjoying huge success nationally and throughout the subcontinent. Thus, during the First World War, Argentina established itself as an important exporter of films to the Hispanic market, benefiting from reduced production in Europe and from the stimulating effect of *La nobleza gaucha.*

Despite these efforts, however, by 1920 'about 95% of screen time in South America was taken up by US films' (King: 1990: 16), and in fact Argentina and Brazil were Hollywood's third and fourth largest export markets after Britain and Australia (Chanan: 1997: 429). Producers throughout the subcontinent hung their hopes for expansion on the advent of sound, anticipating that the barriers of language and the cultural specificity of music would create a more favourable climate for their films.

MELODRAMA

A small chink in the US postwar quasi-monopoly appeared in the 1930s, partly as a result of the Depression, but also partly, as local filmmakers had hoped, because of the advent of sound, for this marked a period of instability in the film industry. This was a time of musicals, and Hollywood attempted to bridge the language gap by producing many of these, but the issue of speech posed a major problem. One possible solution to this was to invest in Europe, and, most famously, Paramount built a huge studio in Joinville, outside of Paris, in order to make multilingual films. The same film would be shot in different languages using the same sets and costumes. This technique was expensive, and not a particularly popular solution to the problem; it was therefore quite quickly superseded in 1932 by dubbing and subtitling. The Joinville experiment was important for Latin America largely because of the presence there of Carlos Gardel, described by Collier as 'by any standard the supreme figure in the entire history of the Argentine tango' (1988: 15), and by Chanan as the 'first Latin American international film star' (1997: 431). Gardel, who had already appeared in two Argentine silent movies, and who was well established throughout Latin America and in France through theatre, records and radio, proved to be one of the successes of Joinville, shooting his first feature film there, *Luces de Buenos Aires* (*Lights of Buenos Aires*) (Millar, 1931). Such was the film's success that Collier describes cinema audiences in Latin America forcing the projectionists to rerun the scenes where Gardel sang. He went on to make three more films there in 1932. Other attempts at reaching Latin American and Spanish audiences were failures, partly because the actors had a plethora of accents from Spain and different corners of Latin America, which not only sounded very strange but were at times incomprehensible to the different publics. Another problem was that the Latin American public was already used to the Hollywood stars, and was not content with unknown Spanish-speaking players.

Strictly speaking the Gardel films do not belong to the history of Argentine cinema, but they were to have an enormous influence from 1930 onwards, and the basic form of his films was to trigger a host of comedies and melodramas with musical numbers in his homeland. The Argentine film industry seized the moment to create what was to be perhaps its most successful period yet. *Tango* (Barthes, 1933) was the first Argentine feature film using Movietone, whereby the sound is pressed on to the film, and it captures the general mood. Following the Hollywood conventions of genre films and a star system, Argentine filmmakers launched a series of musicals, melodramas and comedies peopled by stars, such as Libertad Lamarque, who had already established themselves in different media. As the Argentine critic Jorge Miguel Couselo points out, 'This easy-to-produce cinema was unadventurous and repetitive' (1988: 28). However, alongside these, there were also some very interesting and successful films appearing. Amongst others, the major director Luis Saslavsky made the stylish *Puerta cerrada* (*Behind Closed Doors*, 1939), and Mario Soffici made *Kilometro 111* (1938), the country's first anti-imperialist film; and most famously *Prisioneros de la tierra* (*Prisoners of the Land*, 1939), a denunciation of exploitation which is 'still considered to be amongst the best three Argentine films' (Couselo: 1988: 30).

Although it was never much of a threat to Hollywood's hegemony, Argentina, by 1940, a year in which almost fifty films were produced, was at the height of its golden age. Its films enjoyed success not only at home but throughout the Spanish-speaking world.

Argentina's moment was, however, fairly short-lived. The US was wary of a country that insisted on remaining neutral during the Second World War, and which it suspected of nursing Nazi tendencies, so it imposed an embargo on raw film stock, and began aiding filmmaking in a country more congenial to its outlook, Mexico. In 1943 the US allotted 3 million metres of raw film stock to Argentina compared with 11 million to Mexico (García Oliveri 1997: 151). This and other technical and economic aid was conditional on Mexico's agreement to make propaganda films in favour of the Allied forces.

Thus the Mexican film industry was given a boost while it was already experiencing something of a golden age of its own. Again the favourite genres were melodrama and musicals, and again the use of a star system proved popular. The first Mexican talkie was a remake of the successful silent film *Santa* (1932), this time directed by Antonio Moreno. It is a melodrama about a girl who is forced to become a prostitute, a recurring theme in Mexican films. Then in 1933, two films of note were to appear. *La mujer del puerto* (*The Woman of the Port*, Boytler), described by an important contemporary Mexican critic, Luz Alba, as 'the first national movie that truly deserves the qualification of excellent' (quoted in Mora 1982: 38), was based on a story by Guy de Maupassant, with themes of betrayal, prostitution and incest. The other, by the directors Fernando de Fuentes and Juan Bustillo Oro, was *El compadre Mendoza* (*Godfather Mendoza*), a complex melodrama of betrayal set during the revolution. But the most successful film of this period was one directed again by de Fuentes, *Allá en el rancho grande* (*Out on the Big Ranch*, 1936), a *comedia ranchera*, a comedy set in the countryside, with deeply conservative values which harked back to the paternalistic feudal ideology of pre-revolutionary times. It was a clear reaction against the radical government of **Lázaro Cárdenas** (1934–40), which was establishing agrarian reform, and it was liberally garnished with typical *ranchera* music, creating what was to become a stereotypical image of Mexico with the singing *charro*, described by King as the 'emblem of Mexican virility' (1990: 46). This film proved to be an enormous success throughout the sub-continent.

The Soviet director, Sergei Eisenstein, arrived in Mexico in 1930, and spent eighteen months travelling throughout the country in an attempt to make a film. He produced 80,000 metres of unedited film which was never released in any form approved by the

For further discussion of genre see Chapter 8, and for further discussion on the Hollywood star system see Chapter 7.

Cárdenas government
Lázaro Cárdenas, president of Mexico 1934–40, was noted for his efforts to carry out the aims of the Mexican Revolution through the redistribution of land and other means, and by nationalising foreign-owned businesses.

director, although it was sold off to different directors who made their own films from the material. Despite these difficulties, his work was to be extremely influential on later Mexican cinema, leading to what was to become a 'national', or 'Eisensteinian', style.

Another director implicated in this style was Fred Zinneman, who with others, including the photographer Paul Strand, was sponsored by the Mexican government to film local people, on location, for seven months in a fishing village near Vera Cruz. The resulting film was a classic that is still much respected, *Redes* (*Nets*, 1934). A fiction film, it depicts the struggle of the fishermen against exploitation, and was politically progressive. It emphasises the Indian faces of its protagonists, and the landscapes owe much to Eisenstein's vision of huge skies and *maguey* plants, though Carlos Monsiváis, the Mexican critic and cultural theorist, says: 'In the end it was Paul Strand who became the forerunner of the most notorious aesthetic of Mexican cinema, with its correspondences between the physiognomy of landscape and natural landscape' (quoted in King 1990: 44).

The principal exponent of the resulting iconic cinema was the director Emilio 'El Indio' Fernández, whose work with the renowned cinematographer Gabriel Figueroa achieved international recognition in the 1940s. Hershfield and Maciel describe how Fernández 'elevated the Indians to mythic stature, romanticized their lives, and … linked the meaning of *lo mexicano* visually and narratively to Mexico's indigenous roots' (1999: 87). In melodramas such as *Flor Silvestre* (*Wild Flower*), and *María Candelaria*, both from 1943, and *Enamorada* (1946), the giant stars of Mexican cinema, Dolores del Río, María Félix and Pedro Armendáriz, brought a whole new image of Mexico to the big screen. A curious element of these films, highlighting a certain equivocation, was in the casting of these light-skinned, European-looking women in the roles of indigenous characters; however, these films have deservedly become the archetype of earlier Mexican cinema.

Brazilian filmmakers were also hopeful that the advent of sound would be 'a means of uniting people around shared cultural symbols' (King 1990: 55), and a number of studios were set up in Rio de Janeiro with private capital which fed into popular culture and produced mostly what are known as *chanchadas*, mainly musical comedies using slang and particular local references. The principal stars of this genre were comedians Oscarito and Grande Otelo, already famous from theatre and variety acts. Also extremely popular

• **Plate 16.1**
The iconic couple, Dolores del Río and Pedro Armendáriz, in *María Candelaria* (Emilio Fernández, 1944)

were the Miranda sisters, who starred in *Alô, alô Brasil* (1935) and *Alô, alô Carnaval* (1936), both directed by Adhemar Ganzaga. One of the sisters, **Carmen**, was famously to move on to Hollywood to become one of the highest paid actors of the 1940s.

There were attempts at producing films of greater quality and documentaries, some in Rio, and, more prominently, in a studio set up in 1949 in São Paulo, the Vera Cruz Company, whose principal aim was to cut loose from the *chanchadas*. The company was headed for a time by **Alberto Cavalcanti**, already of international repute, and the idea was to make films that would succeed not only locally, but also internationally. Ultimately the venture was to fail; the films were too costly for the local market, and they were unable to penetrate further. Their one major international success was *O Cangaceiro* (*The Bandit*) (Lima Barreto, 1953), an epic set far from the cities in a world of banditry in the northeast of the country. The film's setting and style were to be of enormous significance to later filmmakers, including Glauber Rocha, but it came too late to save the studio, and ultimately it was only the *chanchadas* that were commercially successful enough to keep the industry alive.

THE NEW LATIN AMERICAN CINEMA

The year 1955, in which the Vera Cruz Studio folded, marked the beginnings of a new phase of Latin American cinema, referred to briefly at the beginning of this study, which heralded a radical shift from anything that preceded it, and brought world-wide attention for the first time.

Within Brazil one of the early leading lights of this new cinema was Nelson Pereira dos Santos, whose film *Rio Quarenta Graus* (*Rio Forty Degrees*, 1955) depicted the reality of urban squalor in a way that had not previously been seen. His later film *Vidas secas* (*Barren Lives*, 1963), set in appalling conditions in the *sertão,* the rural northeast of Brazil, already seen in *O Cangaceiro*, proved to be iconic in its depiction of hunger and misery in these barren backlands. These films were early stirrings of what was to become *Cinema Novo* in Brazil, and ultimately the New Latin American cinema.

The New Latin American cinema was far removed from the commercial cinema of previous times, and even further from any Hollywood influence. It was, at least initially, very much informed by Soviet cinema, highly politicised, and technically innovative, particularly for its Eisensteinian dialectical use of montage. Other influences were the French New Wave, with its low production values and use of exteriors, and, perhaps

Carmen Miranda (1909–55)
Already a superstar in Brazil, she moved to the US in 1939 to become a huge Hollywood star, singing and dancing and wearing outlandish exotic costumes in a series of films.

Alberto Cavalcanti (1897–1982)
The Brazilian set designer, director and producer is best known in the UK for his work with John Grierson at the GPO Film Unit in the 1930s.

For further discussion of Soviet montage cinema and a case study on Eisenstein see Chapter 17.

• **Plate 16.2**
Carmen Miranda in full dress. The paradigm of Hollywood's depiction of the exotic 'other'

most famously, Italian neo-realism. Indeed some of the key figures of this movement, Fernando Birri from Argentina and Tomás Guitiérrez Alea and Julio García Espinosa from Cuba, had been students at neo-realism's heartland, the *Centro Sperimentale* in Rome. This is not to say that the films were derivative, but rather that they transformed both practices and theories from these cinemas into something that could be applied to their own societies.

On returning from Rome, Birri set up a documentary school in Santa Fe in Argentina, which he saw as a means of taking cinema underground as a tool for raising awareness and fomenting revolution. The two Cubans, following their time in Rome, made a documentary about the terrible conditions experienced by charcoal workers in the Ciénaga swamp south of Havana, *El mégano* (1954). The film was banned by the government and the filmmakers arrested. Much output that was to follow, whether in the form of documentary or fiction film, was to differing degrees based on the ideas of these directors. In a lesson learnt from the Italians, the need for big budgets was avoided in films which dealt with social issues, made in natural settings with non-professional actors, and to some extent the perennial issues of distribution and exhibition were avoided by the fact that the early 1950s were a time in which cine-clubs, film societies and film magazines were to mobilise an interest in national film culture.

These were deeply politicised filmmakers who were not simply looking for alternatives to the Hollywood model and different means of expressing the national; they were actually committed to praxis. Moreover, a number of them theorised their ideas of filmmaking in manifestos, the earliest of which, from 1965, was written by the Brazilian, Glauber Rocha and entitled variously 'An Aesthetic of Hunger' or 'An Aesthetic of Violence'. In a short, visceral tract, he denounces continuing colonialism, and, reasoning that violence is the only answer to the exploitation of those living in misery, he describes the role of 'sad, ugly films, these screaming, desperate films where reason does not always prevail' (quoted in Johnson and Stam 1995: 68–72). *Antonio das Mortes* (Rocha 1969), which Chanan (1997: 743) describes as his masterpiece, is deeply engaged, but has moved far from neo-realism. Set in the *sertao*, this film, with highly stylised performances, employs a type of mysticism which draws on Catholicism and different African religions, brought by those who were enslaved by the Europeans, to make a film of which Schumann says: 'the exuberant torrent of images and the mix of mysticism and legend, cult and ritual, were married to surrealistic symbolism and achieved a visionary force' (quoted in Chanan 1997: 743).

The most directly political of these films, drawing much on the revolutionary ideas of **Frantz Fanon** and Che Guevara, and filmed clandestinely, was *La hora de los hornos* (*The Hour of the Furnaces*, Solanas and Getino, Argentina, 1968), a 6-hour film in three parts: 'Neo-colonialism and Violence', 'An Act of Liberation' and 'Violence and Liberation'. Expanding the form of the documentary, it brings together disparate materials, such as newsreels, eyewitness reports, television commercials and photographs, and makes use of techniques such as intertitles, or sometimes a blank screen with voiceover. Among its most striking moments is a sequence which, as Stam puts it: 'fuses Eisenstein and Warhol by intercutting scenes from a slaughterhouse with pop-culture advertising icons' (1998: 261), suggesting, amongst many other ideas, that the violence perpetrated on the poor is a direct result of the superficial, materialistic world of the urban elites.

In a manifesto based on *The Hour of the Furnaces*, 'Towards a Third Cinema: Notes and Experiences for the Development of a Cinema of Liberation in the Third World' (1968), the directors map out a whole new way of thinking about film. Here, a Third Cinema is mooted in contrast to a First Cinema, which refers to any commercial, Hollywood-type movie, wherever it is found. Second Cinema, most closely associated with the French New Wave, at least initially, is a cinema of *auteurs*, something that also corresponds to the depiction of individualism and psychological depth to be found in Argentine films of this period by *auteurs* such as Torre Nilsson. Third Cinema they define as: 'films the system cannot assimilate and which are foreign to its needs' (Solanas and

Frantz Fanon 1925–61
Recognised as the pre-eminent thinker on decolonisation and the psychopathology of colonisation, Fanon was the writer of two seminal texts, *Black Skin, White Masks* (1952) and *The Wretched of the Earth* (1961).

Today, the impunity of such aggression...

• **Plate 16.3**
A powerful message
in *The Hour of the
Furnaces* (Octavio
Getino, Fernando E.
Solanas, 1970)

Getino in Martin 1997: 42). They call not for consumers but rather for accomplices, and the film, which was dangerous to make, to distribute and at times even to watch, was to be screened, not in cinemas, but generally amongst small groups of political militants, university students or trades unionists, and in a context in which it could be stopped in order for the spectators to engage with its ideas through discussion.

These radical films were to become part of what was to be known as the New Latin American cinema. Stylistically the films tended to be very different, but Stam highlights their commonalities, sharing as they do 'a constellation of Fanonian themes – the psychic stigmata of colonialism, the therapeutic value of anti-colonial violence, and the urgent necessity of a new culture and a new human being' (2003: 31).

Also central to the 'New Latin American Cinema' is Cuba, for the Cuban Revolution of 1959 was seen as a beacon for those with revolutionary ideas in the rest of Latin America, and the story of filmmaking in Cuba evolves in a very particular way. Few films had been made in Cuba prior to the Revolution, and those that were, with exceptions such as *El mégano*, were of poor quality. Largely the country had served, in quite contentious ways, as an 'exotic' backdrop for US and Mexican films, but it became clear that from the moment the Rebel Army took charge 'it manifested … an awareness of the importance of the means of mass communications' (Chanan 2004: 119). The Cubans were dealing with the difficult reality of how best to employ a film industry within a revolution.

On 24 March 1959 the government set up ICAIC (Cuban Institute of Film Art and Industry) largely to fulfil two separate functions. One of these was to take information out to those who had hitherto lacked access to the media, and the other was to re-educate those who had had been nurtured on the corrupting influence of Hollywood films and Mexican melodramas. They started by making educational documentaries and newsreels, but soon branched out into full-length fiction films. It was a time in which the industry flourished, for despite a lack of resources, many inventive, socially engaged films were produced; indeed the 1960s were, and continue to be, the most significant period in Cuban film history. Amongst the staff at ICAIC were the two filmmakers mentioned previously, Alea and García Espinosa, who were both key to developments in Cuban film. García Espinosa directed a comedy, *Las aventuras de Juan Quin Quin* (*The Adventures of Juan Quin Quin*, 1967) which depicts the travails of a hapless young man in his journey to becoming a guerilla fighter. It was one of Cuba's most successful films ever, reaching an audience of over two million people on an island with a population of seven million. He went on to write the most famous manifesto to come out of ICAIC, 'For an Imperfect Cinema' (1968), in which, as Chanan explains, 'he argued that the imperfections of a low-budget cinema of urgency, which sought to create a dialogue with its audience, were preferable to the sheen of high production values that merely reflected the audience back to itself' (2004: 6).

It was Alea, however, who was to become Cuba's leading film director, continuing to make films until his untimely death in 1996. These varied from early documentaries to comedies to historical dramas and to a more straightforwardly political cinema, as evidenced in his most famous film of the 1960s, *Memorias del subdesarollo* (*Memories of Underdevelopment*, 1968). Mistakenly read as a criticism of the revolution, particularly by Andrew Sarris, then president of the US National Society of Film Critics, the film highlights our tendency to identify with the main protagonist of a film, in this case a middle-class man who finds himself quite lost in the new Cuba which surrounds him. It is in fact a meditation on bourgeois alienation, or capitalist individualism, in the midst of the huge changes effected by the revolution, depicting someone who watches passively rather than involving himself in the new society. ICAIC, although funded by the government, was actually quite independent, and there were also films which emerged from it that critiqued aspects of society, though always from a supportive perspective. Humberto Solás's *Lucía* (1968) focused in part on the continuing effects of *machismo* (see Case Study 1: *Lucía*) and Alea's later international success *Fresa y Chocolate* (*Strawberry and Chocolate*, 1993), which explored the difficulties in Cuban society for a gay man, also followed in this tradition.

Space prohibits an examination of other important films to emerge from the New Latin American cinema, such as the masterly *La sangre del cóndor* (*The Blood of the Condor*, Sanjinés, Bolivia, 1969), a powerful denunciation of the American Peace Corps, and *El Chacal de Nahueltoro* (*The Jackal of Nahueltoro*, Littín, Chile, 1969), the most famous film to be connected to Salvador Allende's socialist Popular Unity party, which was to gain power in 1970, only to have it wrenched from them by a military coup led by Augusto Pinochet.

Pinochet was one of several military leaders who were to seize power in the 1970s in Latin America, and their advent heralded an era of censorship, declining film production, and the end of the New Latin American cinema.

□ **CASE STUDY 1: *LUCÍA* (SOLÁS, CUBA, 1968)**

Lucía is another ICAIC production made in the same year as Alea's *Memories of Underdevelopment*. It is a masterpiece of Cuban cinema and a hugely ambitious project,

• **Plate 16.4**
Lucía (Humberto Solás, 1968): The first Lucía with Rafael

a 160-minute film which traces the course of Cuban history from 1895 to the 1960s through the stories of three women, each named Lucía.

The film is divided into three discrete sections. The first of these, 'Lucía 1895', is set during the Cuban war of independence from Spain, which was to end in 1898. This Lucía is a member of the Cuban landowning Creole aristocracy, a woman living a highly circumscribed life, surrounded by family and other women of her class, whose major obsession is finding rich husbands. Although Lucía herself maintains a certain dignified distance from prospective suitors, she is nonetheless aware of being on the brink of dreaded spinsterhood when she is courted by Rafael, a handsome Spanish/Cuban man with whom she falls desperately in love. Ultimately, it transpires that he is working for the Spanish and is using her in order to get to her brother, a member of a group of Cuban independence fighters. When she is eventually persuaded to take him to the *estancia* where her brother and others are in hiding, a major battle ensues in which the brother is killed. The sequence ends with a maddened Lucía taking revenge on Rafael by stabbing him to death. This section takes the form of a highly charged romantic tragedy in which Lucía's story dovetails with that of Fernandina, a nun who has also lost her reason (in this case permanently) having been raped by Spanish soldiers. These are clear allegories of the rape of Cuba by the Spanish, intensified by the expressionist and even surreal quality of the sometimes bleached images. Many influences have been cited, Solás himself talking of Pasolini and of Brazilian Cinema Novo with its vehement aesthetics of hunger, referred to on p. 432.

The second section, 'Lucía 1932', moves from tragedy to what might be a pastiche of some of the Latin American melodramas of the time. This depicts another level of Cuban society; the urban upper middle classes. If the first Lucía marked the end of Spanish colonisation, the second represents the influence of the US, most clearly embodied in the character of Lucía's mother, a rather vain woman who has all the physical traits of a 'flapper' with her bobbed hair, cigarette holder and fondness for drink. Lucía herself dances the Charleston at one point, but she tires of her mother's excesses, falls in love with an urban guerilla, Aldo, and gives up her privileged existence, taking a job working in a cigar factory. The struggle now depicted is against the repressive presidency of Machado from 1925 to 1933, though the resistance is patchy: Chanan (2004: 285) talks of 'Aldo's individualistic and ultimately nihilistic acts'. Lucía herself is politically involved at the factory, and is seen in a march of striking workers in the streets. The violence meted out to the strikers is filmed in a way that is reminiscent of the battle scenes in 'Lucía 1895', with a handheld camera that is often canted, focusing on fragments of bodies, and refusing any clear narrative of the events. The spectator is drawn into a chaotic world with no sense or logic. Aldo, disillusioned with the lack of change after Machado's downfall, returns to his guerilla activity and is killed; the second Lucía is left alone, pregnant and quite lost.

'Lucía 196-' represents the much more wholesome, happy world of an agricultural cooperative in the wake of the revolution at the time of an extremely successful literacy campaign. We see a much more mixed population, with many more black faces. This Lucía is much darker than the others, and the mood is far more upbeat. The sequence is often described as a comedy, but not all is joy and sunshine and this section too has its political overtones. Rather than a simple paean to the achievements of the revolution, it serves as a critique of Cuban society, pointing out shortcomings still to be addressed. Here, the central issue is *machismo*. This Lucía falls in love with, and marries, a man who proves to be obsessively jealous. He refuses to let her go out to work and even to visit her mother, virtually imprisoning her in their house. Lucía, unhappy and confused, becomes more aware of the injustice of her situation when a young man from Havana comes to teach her to read and write, and encourages her to leave her jealous husband. The issue is not quite resolved; we are left without a clear ending, but the need for a questioning of *machista* attitudes is clear.

Lucía, therefore, traces the stories of three women in love, but it does much more than that. According to Solás, '*Lucía* is not a film about women; it's a film about society. But within that society, I chose the most vulnerable character, the one who is most transparently affected at any given moment by contradictions and changes' (quoted in Chanan 2004: 276). Thus we see an overview of a class-ridden society battling with different stages of colonisation and decolonisation, and beyond that, in the last section, we see the influence of Che Guevara or of Fanon's thoughts with regard to what the Kenyan writer Ngugi describes as 'decolonizing the mind', referring to the need to question the mindset left behind by years of colonisation and to create a new society that transcends these limitations.

Questions

1   How does the use of different film genres add to *Lucía*?
2   *Lucía* was made shortly after the Cuban Revolution. How is this reflected in the film?

MORE RECENT DEVELOPMENTS

Nowadays we see a clear shift from the often allegorical films of the New Latin American cinema with its emphasis on neo-colonialism; indeed, there is much questioning as to whether a Third Cinema can still be held to exist. The utopian thrust has gone, undermined by the dictatorships and the subsequent neo-liberalism. Many of the most important recent films tend to focus much more on the social realities of life as it is lived, particularly amongst the lower classes. The questions now being asked by many filmmakers and critics often lie in what Edgardo Dieleke describes as 'the limits of fiction' (2009: 75), the interstices between fiction and documentary. Michael Chanan talks of 'a cross-over space between fiction and documentary that is both and neither' (2009: 18).

Fiscal incentives brought into place in 1993 triggered what is known as the *retomada*, or rebirth, of Brazilian cinema, and the most successful Brazilian film of the 1990s, *Central do Brasil* (*Central Station*, Salles, 1998), reveals an approach that is quite typical of the films of this period. Shaw observes that the filmmakers are less ambitious and quotes Nagib as saying that 'none aspire to a revolution or to establish a new art form' (2003: 160). *Central Station* uses continuity editing to tell a story which is much more individualistic, giving voice to the lower classes, and it is set amidst urban squalor and in the *sertao*. These features, apart from the *sertao*, arise again in *Madame Satã* (see Case study 2) and in the massive 2003 hit *Cidade de Deus* (*City of God*, Meirelles). Both of the better known films *Central Station* and *City of God* boast high production values and were extremely successful at local and international level, winning prizes at numerous film festivals and, in the case of *City of God*, becoming 'Brazil's greatest international success of all time' (Nagib 2007: xxii).

A deeply contentious film that divides critics, *City of God* famously makes use of non-professional actors, young men and boys from the shanty towns or *favelas* and, shot in authentic locations, creates a 'new regime of representation of the real' (Dieleke 2009: 71). The film employs a kind of neo-naturalism which makes use of rapid montage, and a rich variety of camera shots, all in the depiction of scenes of drug dealing and horrific violence. Its visceral power is undeniable, though Ivana Bentes has famously coined the term 'a cosmetics of hunger' to describe such films, in which documentary-type

• **Plate 16.5**
A break from the
violence of the *favela*
in *City of God* (Fernando
Meirelles, Kátia Lund,
2002)

fiction, misery and violence are aestheticised and consumed; and there is no attempt to analyse the root causes of poverty in a country that remains one of the most economically divided in the world although the governments of Luiz Inácio da Silva, Lula, from 2003–11, and his successor, Dilma Rousseff, have done much to turn this around.

International success has also come to Mexican film in the past decade, with the work of a trio of directors, Alejandro González Iñárritu, Alfonso Cuarón and Guillermo del Toro, all of whom, reflecting much earlier practice, now work between Mexico and Hollywood. Iñárritu, who turned his back on a failing state-funding apparatus, made the spectacularly successful and prestigious *Amores perros* (2000), which won the prize for best film at Cannes, amongst numerous other awards. Iñárritu explains that his intention in the film is to challenge Hollywood stereotypes, saying:

I am not a Mexican with a moustache and a sombrero and a bottle of tequila ... Nor am I a corrupt cop or a drug trafficker. There are millions like me. And this is the world I live in and the one I want to show.

(quoted in Shaw 2003: 54)

Set in Mexico City, the film, which uses professional actors, has a complex plot which intertwines the lives of three sets of people from different social backgrounds. It does not share the documentary-type narrative of many recent Latin American films, but it does, as its director points out, depict modern Mexicans who are not, as Shaw (ibid.: 54) puts it, 'other' to European and US audiences. To this extent it also reflects Dieleke's idea of neo-naturalism (see Case study 3). The same can be said for Cuarón's even more commercially successful *Y tu mama también* (2001), though this fits in more with genres such as the teenage movie and the road movie. Del Toro's films too are genre movies. His earliest, *Cronos* (1992), is a skilful take on the horror/vampire genre, though it can certainly be read, as he says, as allegorical in its depiction of North Americans attempting to steal the life blood of Latin Americans. His later success, *El laberinto del fauno* (*Pan's Labyrinth*, 2006), is a fantasy film, but this too has a political edge, portraying the violence of fascism in Franco's Spain through the eyes of a child. Del Toro's films are clearly an exception to the neo-naturalism which predominates at this time.

In contrast to the highly commercial nature of the Mexican example, and almost mirroring the fiscal situation in Brazil, there has been a boom in Argentine cinema since the 1995 *Ley de Cine* which serves to protect the national film industry and which provides funds for filmmaking through the *Instituto Nacional de Cine y Artes Audiovisuales* (The National Institute of Cinema and Audio-Visual Arts, INCAA).

Here, what has emerged in recent years largely corresponds to what is also being termed a type of neo-realism. While less overtly political than the films of the 1960s, what we find are films that explore the lives of the working classes or of the struggling middle classes, people living with the consequences of military repression and of the subsequent failure of the neo-liberal project of president Carlos Ménem, who have been ravaged by the economic collapse of the country in the early 2000s. The 'founding text' (Page, 2009: 37) of what is known as the New Argentine cinema, pre-dating the collapse itself, is *Pizza, birra, faso* (*Pizza, Beer, Cigarettes*, Caetano and Stagnaro, 1997), which depicts a group of unemployed, aimless youths in Buenos Aires. As with *City of God* and *Amores perros*, there is much use of slang, but here 'the dialogue appears improvised, making use of natural pauses, interruptions and overlappings of conversation' (Page 2009: 39). The plot seems looser too: with little sense of cause and effect, it seems almost like an intrusion into the everyday lives of these marginalised people.

Many directors have emerged from this low-budget, independent cinema, most notably Martín Rejtman, Lucrecia Martel, Pablo Trapero and the latter's previous sound assistant, Lisandro Alonso. Alonso's 'unique realist vision', which 'question[s] the mystery of the observed, the place of the observer and the mechanism of cinema itself' (Quintín 2008: 62), is the stuff of a few chosen film festivals, while Martel and Trapero have achieved some commercial international success. Nevertheless, as Page observes, '[I]n contrast to the great Latin American social dramas to have reached North America and European screens in recent years – such as *City of God* and *Amores perros* – the gaze of the New Argentine Cinema is self-doubting, contingent and provisional' (2009: 56).

☐ CASE STUDY 2: *MADAME SATÃ* (AÏNOUZ, BRAZIL, 2002)

Almost paradigmatic in its blending of fiction and the 'real', *Madame Satã*, as we are told at the beginning of the film, is based on a true story. Set initially in 1932, it recounts periods from the life of a figure who continues to hold mythical status within Brazilian popular culture long after his death in 1976.

João Francisco dos Santos adopted the name Madame Satã from *Madame Satan*, a camp 1930 film by Cecil B. DeMille. He was an African Brazilian child of former slaves and an overt homosexual who hustled and pimped in Lapa, a poor but bohemian area of Rio de Janeiro. Slavery did not come to an end in Brazil until 1888, and life continued to be hard for Brazil's black population as a result of a policy of *branqueamento* or 'whitening', which encouraged European immigration as a means of 'civilising' the largely mixed-

• **Plate 16.6**
Madame Satã (Aïnouz, 2002). Lazaro Ramos as the stunning transvestite, Madame Satã.

race population. There were few options for African-Brazilians and many lived on the margins of society, scraping a living however they could. Within the urban centres, there appeared the famous figure of the *malandro*, representative of hustlers, delinquents and pimps who lived on their wits and often fell foul of the law. The *malandro* brings to mind the West African figure of Anancy, the trickster, found in different forms in different parts of the Americas, where people generally of African descent find themselves hustling to survive in hostile environments. Madame Satã would definitely fit this description, though his homosexuality is unusual in this context, and it serves to marginalise him even further.

Despite its historical setting, *Madame Satã*'s most salient characteristic lies in its immediacy. This at least partly results from 'an intimate cinematography' (Aïnouz quoted in Shaw 2007: 88) where fluid camera work makes use of extreme close-ups and shots that are often out of focus. In one of the few daylight sequences in which Madame Satã visits the park with his 'family' (Laurita, his prostitute and housemate, and her baby), the film breaks practically all of the rules of narrative cinema by taking the form of a home movie, shooting through 360 degrees and shifting in and out of focus. The spectator is never held at a 'safe' distance but feels involved and even implicated in the film.

Edgardo Dieleke, a Brazilian critic, highlights a major difference between *City of God* and *Madame Satã* which lies precisely in the construction of the space between film and spectator. While in *City of God*, we have the figure of Rocket who recounts the film to us from the distance of a reliable witness, who is from the city but who has succeeded in leaving it behind, in *Madame Satã* there is no such construct; the lack of a safe space from which to watch becomes even more uncomfortable when we consider that *Madame Satã* is a highly ambiguous figure. The film starts and ends with an almost static close-up, where a bruised, beaten and silent *Madame Satã* is being described by an official in voiceover at some length as being fundamentally a menace to society. The rest of the film sets out to humanise this sometime criminal and even murderer, though never to contain him. Despite the horror of the first shot, he is not depicted as a victim, but rather as a free spirit who is open about his homosexuality and who is never ready to compromise or to give in. Some of the most stunning sequences depict him performing in drag looking completely beautiful. Neither a hero nor an anti-hero, *Madame Satã* is a raw, ambivalent character who continues to disturb long after the film is over.

Whereas with *City of God* we are aware of sitting in the safety of the cinema watching dangerous black bodies involved in violent acts, with *Madame Satã* we find ourselves in a much more complex space which epitomises Delieke's perception of 'the urgency of the real in recent Brazilian cinema' (2009: 75).

Questions

1. How is the story of *Madame Satã* reflected in the *mise-en-scène*?
2. What does *Madame Satã* tell us about Brazilian society at the time in which it is based?

☐ CASE STUDY 3: *AMORES PERROS* (GONZÁLEZ IÑÁRRITU, MEXICO, 2000)

Amores perros, by first-time director Alejandro González Iñárritu, came at a time when Mexican cinema was at a low ebb. A film with enormous energy and verve, it proved to be hugely successful both commercially and critically, winning the Critics' Week prize at Cannes, and subsequently some thirty more prizes at home and internationally.

• **Plate 16.7**
Gustavo Sánchez Parra,
Octavio's nemesis
in *Amores Perros*
(González Iñárritu,
2000)

In stark contrast to the 'exotic other' of traditional early Mexican melodramas, and in particular to Mexican cinema's biggest 1990s hit *Como agua para chocolate* (*Like Water for Chocolate*, Arau, 1991), *Amores perros* leaves behind the traditional rural context to situate itself firmly within the realms of urban modernity. It is far from the first Mexican film to be set in Mexico City, but its defining factor is its use of the capital as the central topic rather than as a mere backdrop or setting. The film takes the form of an almost anthropological study (González Iñárritu's term) of what is generally held to be the second largest conurbation on the planet at the turn of the twenty-first century.

The fracturing of time and space, as experienced in such a setting, is conveyed by a break with conventional narrative forms by presenting three stories that deal with very different sets of people and their dogs. These three stories converge at the moment of a horrific car crash which opens the film and becomes a structuring principle within it, a powerful metaphor for the violence to be found in the city, as witnessed particularly in the first and third stories.

Part I, 'Octavio and Susana', is the most distinctive section of the film. Its quasi-documentary style, with much use of hand-held cameras and fast editing, reveals a world of illegal dog fights and crime. Octavio is a young working-class man who falls in love with his sister-in-law Susana, a complex situation made more difficult still by the fact that they share a roof with Octavio's brother Ramiro, as well their mother and the married couple's baby. By means of the money earned through brutal dog fights featuring Cofi, Ramiro's Rottweiler, Octavio is planning to run away with Susana. His plans are foiled when a jealous rival, tired of watching his dogs lose to Cofi, shoots the victorious animal; Octavio responds by stabbing him in the stomach. The crash, which heralds the end of this part of the film, comes after a car chase in which Octavio, his friend, Jorge, and the bleeding Cofi are pursued and shot at by the wounded man's henchmen.

Part II, 'Daniel and Valeria', is filmed in a much more conventional manner, with longer takes and slower editing. It is set in a mediatised world of high glamour and the upper middle classes, first glimpsed through the television screen on which Jorge and Octavio are watching the stunningly beautiful Valeria, a tall, blonde, leggy model, being interviewed on the programme 'Gente de Hoy' ('Today's People'). This idealised world, particularly fetishised by Jorge, is immediately revealed to be false, for after Valeria introduces her latest boyfriend to the public, the film follows the 'couple' out of the studio and we immediately learn that the romance is a front. The celebrity boyfriend is presumably gay, and attempting to hide it, while Valeria is actually in a relationship with Daniel, a married man. The perfect world depicted in the interview is also the space in which we are introduced to Valeria's dog, Richie, whom she describes as her child.

Daniel has at last decided to leave his wife to move in with Valeria, and in order to celebrate this, Valeria sets off in her car to buy some wine. It is during this journey that she is involved in the crash, which we see for a third time, and which leads to her losing one of her legs. The apartment which Daniel has acquired as their home instead becomes a claustrophobic space in which the recuperating Valeria is stuck, its superficial perfection marred by the fact that the floorboards are faulty. Richie falls through a hole and gets lost in a rat-infested underworld. The perfect façade of this couple's lives is again cracked; here the dog provides a link between it and a much grimmer reality.

Part III, 'El Chivo and Maru', is the most resonant in that it is the only section in which we find a backstory for the personage of El Chivo. This character, now an unkempt and unshaven individual who wheels a cart around the city followed by a group of dirty, unidentifiable dogs, was once a university lecturer. The film gradually tells the story of his leaving his family, when his daughter was two years old, to become a guerilla and fight for a better world. After serving a prison term for planting a bomb in a shopping mall, he has become this outcast, but one with a sideline in contract killing, something he is hired to do under the auspices of a corrupt policeman. Indeed he has become virtually invisible; people avert their eyes from him, which means he is ideally placed to stalk his prey. It is while he is planning the assassination of a man whose half-brother has hired him, that El Chivo witnesses the crash. We see the event in much greater detail this last time, from the point of view of someone not involved in it. El Chivo then approaches the crashed cars, steals the betting money from Octavio's pocket, and rescues the wounded Cofi.

El Chivo's dream is to be reunited with his daughter Maru, who believes him to be dead. However this reunion does not happen in the film, and we are left not knowing whether it ever will. What we do see is that Cofi, now nameless, kills all the other dogs, and that El Chivo achieves some understanding through this, echoing his own murderous past, and is somehow redeemed by forgiving the dog who is now granted a new identity, a new name, Negrito. The film ends with no greater resolution than this, with El Chivo and Negrito walking off together into a barren post-industrial landscape.

This description might highlight more than anything the total separation of these three worlds which can only come together in a moment of crisis, but the film is more subtle than that. In the course of each section there is reference to the other stories, sometimes in the form of simple cuts, and others in seemingly random ways. The first instance of this involves the dogs, for Octavio's rival bumps into El Chivo and threatens to set his fighting dogs on the latter's group of strays. Later, as mentioned above, we are introduced to Valeria and her story by means of Octavio's television screen; and posters of Valeria, ironically all legs, seductively advertising a perfume with the evocative name of 'Enchant', hail us in all three sections, the poster pointedly being dismantled in the last. These are just some examples of the weaving of the three stories, such that the notion of totally separate realities existing side by side is disrupted by the understanding that such divisions are impossible; the urban experience is full of complex social interdependencies.

The visceral violence in *Amores perros* and its intricate depiction of almost Borgesian interweavings of time have led many critics to compare it with *Pulp Fiction* (Tarantino, US, 1994), a parallel denied by those involved with the film. González Iñárritu talks rather of Wong Kar Wai and Lars Von Trier, and indeed if Tarantino's film is precisely a take on pulp fiction, the Mexican film is much more serious. It is, as its director claims, a very political film: we see a depiction of the dog-eat-dog world of urban modernity under globalised capitalism. Its soundtrack serves as an indication of this, as attentive viewing indicates. In fact it is not until 36 minutes into the film that we hear its most memorable and distinctive music, Control Machete's pounding rap which plays over the first montage sequence involving among other subjects a dog fight and the robbery of a pharmacy. This rap encapsulates much of the film's mood and political slant, since rap, originally an African American form, has become globalised as emblematic of brutal urban modernity, but has also been tailored in other ways and to different contexts. Here it is sung in Spanish by a Mexican band, and applied to the world of what I have described as the protagonist in *Amores perros*, Mexico City itself. The juxtaposition here of a mediatised world depicted as a realisable ideal, and the poverty and violence of people's lives, takes us beyond any romantic idea of Mexico to a disturbing portrait of the city as exciting and hard-hitting, but also desperate, with only the tenuous hope of the film's ending to sustain it.

Questions

1   In what ways does the cinematography in *Amores perros* serve to enhance the narrative?
2   To what extent might the film be seen to be distinctively Mexican, and to what extent can it be read as a reflection of global modernity?

CONCLUSION

This chapter has traced the history of Latin American cinema from its beginnings up to the twenty-first century. It has focused largely on Argentina, Brazil and Mexico, not because these are the only stories to be told, but because these are the countries big enough to sustain film industries, although they too have struggled at times; and on post-revolutionary Cuba, where the state-funded ICAIC became a forum for filmmakers and artists of different kinds.

What is clear is that although Europe and, to an even greater extent the US, have always made use of Latin America as a space for the distribution and exhibition of their films, there has been little two-way traffic. Much analysis of globalisation has not sufficiently addressed the fact that the movement of goods and media largely continues to follow the geographical flows of neo-colonialism. What we find in Latin America, which continues to be economically dependent, is that the film industries are particularly vulnerable to the vagaries of global, and sometimes national, politics. There is a constant need for Latin America to tell its own stories, often in the face of negative stereotyping from Hollywood, and the difficulties inherent in trying to make films in these conditions should never be underestimated. Chanan cites the Brazilian film critic Salles Gomes 'who points out that the cinemas of North America, Europe and Japan have never been underdeveloped, but that "those of the Third World have never ceased being so"' (Chanan 1997: 749). Despite this, Latin America has an extremely rich cinematic history perhaps partly because of what Francis Ford Coppola realised on visiting Cuba after the revolution: 'we do not have the advantages of their disadvantages' (quoted in Burton 1997: 128). Many films from throughout the subcontinent are made with little funding and in difficult circumstances, but they reflect a real need for these industries to continue to develop, and for these stories to be told.

SUMMARY

- Beginnings of cinema in Latin America.
- Particular importance of Argentina, Brazil and Mexico.

- Effects of neo-colonialism.
- Silent movies in the sub-continent.
- Advent of 'talkies'.
- Carlos Gardel.
- Mexican melodramas and Brazilian *chanchadas*.
- *Cinema Novo* and Third Cinema.
- The case of Cuba.
- An aesthetics/cosmetics of hunger.
- Recent developments in Mexican cinema.
- The New Argentine cinema.

QUESTIONS FOR DISCUSSION

1 In what ways are the effects of neo-colonialism reflected in early Latin American cinema?
2 What changes were heralded by the coming of sound?
3 How important was melodrama to Latin American cinema, particularly prior to the 1950s?
4 What are the salient characteristics of the New Latin American Cinema and Third Cinema?
5 In what ways was Italian neo-realism influential during the 1950s and 1960s?
6 What was the impact of the Cuban Revolution on film in Cuba and beyond?
7 In what ways does more recent cinematic output from Latin America continue or not to reflect the ideas of Third Cinema?
8 How does the interplay between fiction and documentary manifest itself in more recent Latin America films?

FURTHER READING

Armes, R. (1987) *Third World Filmmaking and the West*, Berkeley: University of California Press.

Barnard, T. (1986) *Argentine Cinema*, Toronto: Nightwood.

Chanan, M. (2006) 'Latin American Cinema: From Underdevelopment to Postmodernism', in Dennison, S. and Hwee Lim, S. (eds), *Remapping World Cinema: Identity, Politics and Culture in Film*, London: Wallflower.

Cozarinsky, E. (1988) *Borges in/and/on Film*, trans. Gloria Waldman and Ronald Crist, New York: Lumen.

García, G. (1995) 'Melodrama: The Passion Machine' in Paranaguá, P.M. (ed.), *Mexican Cinema*, London: BFI.

Haddu, M. and Page, J. (eds) (2009) *Visual Synergies in Fiction and Documentary Film From Latin America*, New York: Palgrave Macmillan.

Hart, S. (2004) *A Companion to Latin American Film*, Woodbridge: Tamesis.

Hershfield, J. and Maciel, D. (eds.) (1999) *Mexico's Cinema: A Century of Film and Filmmakers*, Wilmington: Scholarly Resources Books.

King, J. and Torrents, N. (eds) (1987) *The Garden of Forking Paths: Argentine Cinema*, London: BFI.

King, J., López, A.M. and Alvarado, M. (1993) *Mediating Two Worlds: Cinematic Encounters in the Americas*, London: BFI.

López, A.M. (1985) 'The Melodrama in Latin America: Films, Telenovelas and the Currency of a Popular Form', *Wide Angle*, Vol. 7, No. 3, pp. 5–13.

— (2000) 'Early Cinema and Modernity in Latin America', *Cinema Journal*, Vol. 40, No. 1, pp. 48–78.

Martin, M.T. (ed.) (1997) *New Latin American Cinema Volume One: Theory, Practices, and Transcontinental Articulations*, Detroit: Wayne State University Press.

— (ed.) (1997) *New Latin American Cinema Volume Two: Studies of National Cinemas*, Detroit: Wayne State University Press.

Matheou, D. (2010) *The Faber Book of New South American Cinema*, London: Faber and Faber.

Nagib, L. (2007) *Brazil on Screen: Cinema Novo, New Cinema, Utopia*, London: I.B. Tauris.

Pick, Z. (1993) *The New Latin American Cinema: A Continental Project*, Austin: University of Texas Press.

Shaw, L. and Dennison, S. (2005) *Latin American Cinema: Essays on Modernity, Gender and*

National Identity, Jefferson and London: McFarland and Co.

Shaw L. (2007) 'Afro-Brazilian Identity: *Malandragem* and Homosexuality in *Madame Satã*', in Shaw. D. (ed.), *Contemporary Latin American Cinema: Breaking into the Global Market*, Lanham, MD and Plymouth: Rowman and Littlefield.

Stam, R. (1998) 'The Two Avant-gardes: Solanas and Getino's *The Hour of the Furnaces*', in Keith Grant, B. and Sloniowski, J., *Documenting the Documentary: Close Readings of Documentary Films and Video*, Detroit: Wayne State University Press.

Stock, A. M. (ed.) (1996) *Framing Latin American Cinema: Contemporary Critical Perspectives*, London: Minnesota University Press.

Tierney, D. (2007) *Emilio Fernández: Pictures in the Margins,* Manchester University Press.

FURTHER VIEWING

It is almost impossible to draw up any kind of meaningful list which encompasses so many countries and such a timespan, but these are a few suggestions:

Brazil
Deus e o Diabo na terra do sol (*Black God, White Devil*, Rocha, 1963)
Bye Bye Brasil (Diegues, 1979)
Pixote (Babenco, 1981)
Ônibus 174 (*Bus 174*, Padilha and Lacerda, 2002)
Carandiru (Babenco, 2003)

Mexico:
El castillo de la pureza (*The Castle of Purity*, Ripstein, 1972)
Doña Herlinda y su hijo (*Doña Herlinda and her Son*, Hermosillo, 1984)
Danzón (Novaro, 1991)
Japón (*Japan*, Reygadas, 2003)

El Violín (Vargas, 2005)

Argentina
La historia oficial (*The Official Version*, Puenzo, Argentina, 1985)
Mundo grúa (*Crane World*, Trapero, Argentina, 1999)
Bolivia (Flores, 2001)
Nueve Reinas (*Nine Queens*, Bielinsky, Argentina, 2002)
El secreto de sus ojos (*The Secret in their Eyes*, Campanella, Argentina, 2009)

Cuba
La muerte de un burócrata (*Death of a Bureaucrat*, Alea, Cuba, 1966)
Lista de espera (*Waiting List*, Tabío, 2000)
Suite Habana (Pérez, Cuba, 2003)
Tres veces dos (*3x2*, Giroud, 2004)
Habana Blues (Cremata, 2005)

RESOURCE CENTRES

The BFI library, Stephen Street London W1 T1, is the main resource in the UK for research into Latin American cinema, though Canning House, 2 Belgrave Square, SW1X 8PJ, also has a useful collection of films and reading materials.

There are many online resources, amongst the most useful of which are:

http://lanic.utexas.edu/la/region/cinema/
http://www.zonalatina.com/cinema.htm
http://jungledrumsonline.com/whats-on/cinema/
south-american-cinema-showcase/
http://www.latamfilm.com/

http://vlib.iue.it/hist-film/latin-america.html
http://www.lib.berkeley.edu/MRC/LatinAm
FilmBib.html

The most famous Latin American film festival, the International Festival of New Latin American Cinema, is held in Havana, Cuba annually. In Britain there are several annual film festivals, including, in London, the London Latin American Film Festival and the Discovering Latin America Film Festival and, in Manchester, the Viva! Spanish and Latin American Film Festival.

Chapter 17

The Soviet montage cinema of the 1920s

Mark Joyce

■ The Soviet montage cinema of the 1920s

INTRODUCTION: WHY STUDY THE SOVIET CINEMA?

As the lights went up at the end an emotion-charged silence reigned, broken only when Lunacharsky [the Soviet Union's Commissar for Education] jumped on his chair and began an enthusiastic speech: 'We've been witnesses at an historic cultural event. A new art has been born.'

(cited in Barna 1973: 102)

Anatoli Lunacharsky's response to Sergei Eisenstein's 1925 film *Battleship Potemkin* acknowledges the importance of a new wave of filmmaking. The films made by the Soviet directors of the 1920s are considered by many to be the most innovative and exciting to have been produced in the history of the cinema. The names of these filmmakers – Eisenstein, Pudovkin, Vertov and Kuleshov among others – are far from forgotten, and a number of the films and directors from this period score consistently highly in *Sight and Sound*'s critics'/directors' choice of the best ten films and directors.

This decade of intensive experimentation with film form produced techniques that have subsequently been widely emulated. In addition, the theoretical debates formulated by these filmmakers are still relevant today. For these reasons the **Soviet cinema** of the 1920s merits detailed analysis.

HISTORICAL BACKGROUND

The Soviet filmmakers of the 1920s reflect the **ideology** (the values and beliefs) and politics of the society in which they were produced. The early 1920s marked the end of a period of civil unrest, the causes of which lay in the great divide that separated wealthy landowning Russians from the peasants and workers.[1] For centuries Russia had been governed by the single figure of the Tsar, who had absolute power. The Russian serfs were not granted freedom from slavery until 1861; this liberation, however, did not mean improved conditions, since they continued to live an existence of appalling poverty. Attempts had been made prior to the Revolution of October 1917 by various factions to undermine the Tsarist regime, all of which were unsuccessful. A wave of revolutionary activity in 1905 included a mutiny by Russian sailors at Odessa which formed the basis for Sergei Eisenstein's 1925 film *Battleship Potemkin*.

The First World War (1914–18) eventually proved to be disastrous for Tsar Nicholas II, since it consumed vast amounts of money and resources that were sorely needed at home. It was also unpopular with the Russian people as the reasons for fighting were unclear. The peasants and the workers were the worst hit by the impact of the war, either being killed on the front or starving at home as supplies became depleted. The landowning rich were protected by their wealth and were able to continue in their existing lifestyle.

These conditions provided the catalyst for the Revolution of 25 February 1917 which resulted in the formation of a liberal provisional government led by Alexander Kerensky and later supported by Menshevik and socialist revolutionary factions. This caused Nicholas II to abdicate on 4 March. The provisional government decided to continue the war, and for many (especially V.I. Lenin who was in hiding in Zurich) it appeared that the new government was in effect continuing the policies of the Tsarist order.

On 25 October 1917 the Bolsheviks, taking advantage of a situation of confusion and competition between the various factions, seized power by storming the Winter Palace.[2] The new Bolshevik government agreed to Germany's demands for control of areas of land previously under Russian administration and pulled out of the war. Almost immedi-

---

Soviet cinema
This will refer to films made in the Soviet Union between October 1920 and 1991, although for the purposes of this chapter most Soviet films discussed will be confined to the 1920s.

See Chapter 4 for further discussion of film form.

See Chapter 5, pp. 121–122, for discussion of ideology in relation to spectatorship.

ideology
There are two key definitions of this term, one provided by the nineteenth-century German philosopher Karl Marx, the other by the twentieth-century French Marxist philosopher Louis Althusser, drawing on Marx's original ideas. For Marx, ideology was the dominant set of beliefs and values existent within society, which sustained power relations. For Althusser, ideology consisted of the representations and images which reflect society's view of 'reality'. Ideology thus refers to 'the myths that a society lives by'.

ately, however, a fierce civil war broke out between the Bolsheviks (known as the Reds) and those still loyal to the Tsarist regime (known as the Whites).[3]

By 1920 it was clear that the Bolsheviks had seized ultimate control of the country. The new Soviet government under the leadership of V.I. Lenin was faced with the task of convincing the population of Russia of the evils of the Tsarist regime and the positive points of the new communist one.

Selected historical dates

1905, Jan.	First revolution (abortive)
	Provides the backdrop for Eisenstein's *Battleship Potemkin*
1914, July	General strike organised by the Bolsheviks
	Outbreak of war and crushing of political unrest
	The war was a general disaster for the Russians; low morale and food shortages in the following years led to uprisings in 1917
1917, Feb.	Popular uprisings culminating in the overthrow of the Tsar and the setting up of a provisional government
1917, Oct.	The Bolsheviks overthrow the provisional government and seize political power
1918–21	Civil war between White and Red factions, as well as fighting of hostile troops sent from abroad in an attempt to restore the power of the Tsar. The continued fighting led to the destruction of trade, agriculture, industry and film production
1922–28	NEP (New Economic Policy) adopted by Lenin. A brief return to controlled forms of capitalism to help to rebuild the shattered economy
1922–23	Soviet feature film production resumes
1924	Sergei Eisenstein's *Strike* completed
1927	The tenth anniversary of the October Revolution. A number of films are made to mark the occasion including:
	October (Eisenstein)
	The End of St Petersburg (Vsevolod Pudovkin)
	The Fall of the Romanov Dynasty (Esfir Shub)

PRE-REVOLUTIONARY RUSSIAN CINEMA

The nature of Russian cinema

When discussing the Soviet cinema it is important to have at least an outline of the form and content of its antecedent, since although the majority of the Soviet directors had not made films prior to 1919, they would certainly have been familiar with the conventions of the pre-revolutionary cinema. Significantly, for a number of the Soviet directors, this cinema was the antithesis of their new approach to filmmaking. The **Russian cinema** (1907–17) was in fact markedly different from the Soviet cinema of the 1920s. The majority of the films that are available for viewing today[4] are between 35 and 70 minutes long and deal predominantly with the lives of the upper classes, centring quite frequently on their relationship with servants and/or the working class. Their subject matter, plot and preoccupations are often melodramatic; unfaithful husbands and wives, psychological states of mind and death predominate. The form of the films is also different, comprising slow-moving scenes containing a limited number of shots, with an emphasis on the **mise-en-scène** and in particular the expressions of the actors. A key director working in this period is Evgeny Bauer, who produced a large number of films including *After Death* (1915), *A Life for a Life* (1916) and *The King of Paris* (1917).

The Russian Revolution of October 1917 and the civil war that followed had a devastating effect on the Russian film industry, which was almost completely destroyed. Very

See Chapter 4, for further discussion of mise-en-scène.

Russian cinema
This will refer to the body of films made in Tsarist Russia between 1907 and 1917.

mise-en-scène
This literally means 'placed in the scene', and it includes all elements that are placed before the camera such as props, actors, costume, movement and position of actors, etc.

few of the Russian directors and stars remained in Russia after 1919, the majority having fled to Paris where they continued production. Initially it would seem that Russian cinema had little in common with the Soviet cinema that followed, and there appears to have been a clear break in terms of style between the two cinemas after the Revolution. The figure of Yakov Protazanov, however, provides an interesting example of a filmmaker who made films between 1911 and 1943.[5] His key films from the pre-revolutionary era include *The Queen of Spades* (1916) and *Satan Triumphant* (1917); these conform to the conventions of Russian cinema outlined above. His best-known film of the 1920s is *Aelita* (1924), a fantasy concerning a revolution on Mars. Protazanov was more concerned with mise-en-scène than with creating new meanings by juxtaposing images. A study of his films reveals that the Tsarist cinema continued into the Soviet **montage** era and was by all accounts successful with the public.[6]

montage
From the French word meaning 'to edit', montage means the assembling of pieces of footage to form a whole. In film studies it usually refers to the style of fast editing adopted by the Soviet filmmakers of the 1920s.

Russian cinema audiences and imported films

That Russian films had moderate success with native audiences is not surprising. What is significant, however, is that before the Revolution the most popular films with Russian audiences were imported from America, France and Germany. The first Russian film studio was not set up until 1907[7] and this may account in part for the success of these foreign films as audiences had grown accustomed to watching them. In the 1910s when native films vied for audiences with imported films, foreign films were clearly the more successful, and were perceived by Russian audiences as being more entertaining and having higher production values than Russian films.

SOVIET CINEMA AND IDEOLOGY: FILM AS AGENT OF CHANGE[8]

The October Revolution was the first successful revolution made in the name of Karl Marx (1818–83). For Marx, the key fact about any society was how it produced its livelihood. He saw capitalism as an economic system which, just like every other previous economic system, was based on exploitation. In capitalism the class with power was the bourgeoisie, the owners of the means of production, and the class subject to their power was the proletariat or working class. In addition, the bourgeoisie's economic strength was protected by the state and sustained by ideology. However, as capitalism developed, the workers, who survived by selling their labour for wages, would be squeezed more and more as competition between capitalists intensified. At the same time they would become aware that they would have everything to gain by replacing an economic system based on the ownership of private property with one based on the non-exploitative communal ownership of productive property. This awareness, or class-consciousness, would eventually produce a revolution. The October Revolution was seen as such a proletarian revolution in Russia and was celebrated in the films of the key Soviet filmmakers of the 1920s.

The revolution, however, was only the beginning of a process of radical social change, called the era of 'the dictatorship of the proletariat' because it involved the proletariat, or in this case its representative the Bolshevik Party, establishing its dominance. V.I. Lenin, writing in *Pravda*, outlined the situation:

Theoretically, there can be no doubt that between capitalism and communism there lies a definite transition period which must combine the features and properties of both these forms of social economy. This transition period has to be a period of struggle between dying capitalism and nascent communism – or, in other words, between capitalism which has been defeated but not destroyed and communism which has been born but is still very feeble.

(Lenin 1919)

The transition to communism referred to by Lenin would have been a monumental task at the best of times, but the Bolsheviks had seized control of a country whose industry and agriculture were relatively underdeveloped. In addition, they had to confront internal and external opposition, civil war and famine. In such a situation artists and filmmakers were perceived as having a special role as proponents of **propaganda cinema.** Lenin declared in 1922 that 'of all the arts, for us the cinema is the most important'.[9] Prior to this, trains highly decorated with Soviet flags and paintings had been sent into the countryside in an attempt to educate and inform the peasants. Short, agitational films called *agitki* were made. Pre-revolutionary newsreels and foreign fiction films were also shown, with a Soviet commentator giving a 'new' reading to the material. Later most of the energy went into the making of new feature films that reflected the ideals of the new regime. Anatoli Lunacharsky (the People's Commissar for Education) had stated in 1924:

> There is no doubt that cinema art is a first-class and perhaps even an incomparable instrument for the dissemination of all sorts of ideas. Cinema's strength lies in the fact that, like any art, it imbues an idea with feeling and with captivating form but, unlike the other arts, cinema is actually cheap, portable and unusually graphic. Its effects reach where even the book cannot reach and it is, of course, more powerful than any kind of narrow propaganda. The Russian Revolution, which is extremely interested in exercising the broadest possible influence on the masses, should long since have turned its attention to cinema as its natural instrument.
>
> (Taylor and Christie 1994: 109)

The enthusiastic, young, educated filmmakers, who attempted to fulfil Lunacharsky's ideal of revolutionary cinema, responded by making innovative films which were revolutionary both in content and form.

ECONOMICS OF THE SOVIET FILM INDUSTRY

The pre-revolutionary Russian film industry had previously imported its film stock from abroad, and during the civil war most of the Russian filmmakers had fled to White-held areas (or abroad) taking their equipment with them. The reality facing the filmmakers of the newly formed state was that there was little in the way of film stock or equipment.[10]

The Soviet government attempted initially to ban the showing of all American and European films, as they were concerned about the public being exposed to films that reflected the values of capitalist societies. The Soviets, however, had little option but to show these films since they had no native film industry to produce their own. The cinema was seen by the new government as a means of keeping the public entertained at a time of hardship and general civil unrest.

From a Western perspective it is easy to underestimate the importance of imported films in the Soviet Union in the 1920s. Denise Youngblood (1992: 51), in *Movies for the Masses*, states that 'Foreign films accounted for almost two-thirds of the titles screened in the twenties.... Nearly as many American as Soviet films were shown in this period.' She continues: 'Sovkino's head, K.M. Shvedchikov, claimed in 1927 that Sovkino would be bankrupt were it not for the success of its import policy.'

The 1920s could be characterised as a period in which American and European narrative films were in effect directly subsidising the dramatic experimentation with film form undertaken by the Soviet filmmakers.

Innovation and experimentation frequently arise from a lack. In the Soviet Union the lack of film stock (and even film cameras) meant that certain groups of filmmakers worked on re-editing existing films (often European/American films and old Russian newsreels) to make them conform to the values of the Soviet state. Other filmmakers experimented

See Chapter 14, for discussion of propaganda and British cinema during the Second World War.

propaganda cinema
A term used pejoratively with reference to any film that consciously attempts to persuade an audience towards certain beliefs and values.

with creating films from the small amount of negative available, which often only came in short lengths. Out of this experimentation came Soviet montage cinema.

FORM: MONTAGE

The roots of Soviet montage

The innovative use of montage in film by the Soviet filmmakers had its roots in art forms such as painting, literature and music from pre-revolutionary Russia. David Bordwell (1972: 11–12), in 'The Idea of Montage in Soviet Art and Film', states that by 1910 a group of Russian painters had already experimented extensively with 'montage': 'the Russian Futurists declared that conventional art must be destroyed and that a new art, appropriate to the machine age, must be created. Hence the futurists took their subjects from modern life and exploited a technique of shocking juxtapositions.' Poetry, in particular that of Mayakovsky,[11] was also 'shattering words and reassembling them into brutal images'.

The question needs to be asked: Why didn't the Russian filmmakers of the 1910s experiment with montage earlier? This lack of explicit montage experiment in Russian cinema compared to that taking place in other art forms may perhaps be attributed to economics. The crucial difference between film and many of the other arts at the time was that the small groups of experimental artists, writers and musicians were often privately funded by rich patrons. The film industry, however, was not.[12] The Revolution of October 1917 provided the right conditions for experimentation with film to take place. It is ironic that this experimentation had its roots in the élitist art forms of pre-revolutionary Russia.

The Kuleshov effect and its consequences

See Chapter 4, pp. 97–100, for reference to Kuleshov's experiments with editing, and discussion of editing in mainstream narrative cinema.

The montage technique is based on the theory that when two pieces of film are placed side by side the audience immediately draws the conclusion that the two shots must be directly related in some way. In other words, the audience tries to create meaning by combining the two separate images. The experimentation along these lines by Lev Kuleshov, a young Soviet filmmaker, culminated in what became known as the Kuleshov effect. Vsevolod Pudovkin outlined the experiment in a lecture given at the London Film Society in February 1929:

Kuleshov and I made an interesting experiment. We took from some film or other several close-ups of the well-known Russian actor Mosjukhin. We chose close-ups which were static and which did not express any feeling at all – quiet close-ups. We joined these close-ups, which were all similar, with other bits of film in three different combinations. In the first combination the close-up of Mosjukhin was immediately followed by a shot of a plate of soup standing on a table. It was obvious and certain that Mosjukhin was looking at this soup. In the second combination the face of Mosjukhin was joined to shots showing a coffin in which lay a dead woman. In the third the close-up was followed by a shot of a little girl playing with a funny toy bear. When we showed the three combinations to an audience which had not been let into the secret the result was terrific. The public raved about the acting of the artist. They pointed out the heavy pensiveness of his mood over the forgotten soup, were touched and moved by the deep sorrow with which he looked on the dead woman, and admired the light, happy smile with which he surveyed the girl at play. But we knew that in all three cases the face was exactly the same.

(Pudovkin 2007: 140)

Kuleshov carried out further experiments using editing in which he cut together separate shots of a walking man, a waiting woman, a gate, a staircase and a mansion.[13] When the shots were combined the audience assumed that the different elements were present at the same location. Kuleshov had discovered the cinema's ability to link entirely unrelated material into coherent sequences. He termed the technique 'creative geography'.

Kuleshov's discoveries about the nature of the cinema medium provided a number of filmmakers with a new set of ideas about how film could manipulate and deceive an audience. Perhaps the most vital consequence of the Kuleshov effect, however, for later directors, was its recognition that the audience were not merely passive recipients.

Soviet montage cinema

In the 1920s a number of filmmakers carried out further experiments with editing techniques along the same lines as Kuleshov. It was discovered that when two shots were joined together meaning could be made by emphasising the difference between shots; that is, instead of trying to cover up graphic dissimilarities between shots, as with **Hollywood cinema**, the difference could be emphasised and indeed become the main way in which meaning could be created. This 'montage' cinema which demanded that audiences continually search for the meanings created by the **juxtaposition** of two shots may thus be seen as **alternative** to the continuity editing-based Hollywood cinema. One of the Soviet filmmakers who developed this idea into both a theory and a practice of filmmaking was Sergei Eisenstein.

Eisenstein believed that maximum impact could be achieved if shots in a scene were in conflict. This belief was based on the general philosophical idea that 'existence' can only continue by constant change. In other words, everything surrounding us in the world is as a result of a 'collision' of opposite elements. The existing world is itself only in a temporary state until the next collision of elements produces a completely new state. It is only through this 'collision' that change can be effected. This method of creating meaning from such collision of opposites is termed **dialectical**. When applying this idea to film, Eisenstein proposed the view that when two shots are combined a completely new meaning is formed. For example, shot A combined with shot B does not produce AB but the new meaning C. The formulation can also be presented as:

thesis + anti-thesis = synthesis.

Vsevolod Pudovkin, another key Soviet filmmaker, was opposed to the theoretical ideas of Eisenstein, although they both used innovative forms of montage in their films. Pudovkin, like Kuleshov, believed that shots could be likened to bricks in the sense that they could be used as building blocks to construct a scene. Pudovkin then did not see his shots as being in conflict. In Pudovkin's formulae shot A + shot B = AB rather than C. Pudovkin aimed at linkage rather than conflict in his scenes.

The montage technique was not only confined to fiction filmmaking. Soviet documentary filmmakers such as Dziga Vertov and Esfir Shub used montage extensively in a range of films in the 1920s, including Vertov's well-known *The Man with a Movie Camera* (1929). For Vertov much of the power of cinema came from its ability to record mechanically events that took place before the camera, but he also ensured that the audience was made aware of the constructed nature of his films. His films are a whirlwind of conflicting shots which disavow conventional ideas of narrative.

The montage technique for the majority of the Soviet filmmakers could also provide sequences with a sense of rhythm and momentum, which could be used to increase or decrease the speed of the action. Eisenstein, for example, frequently increases his rate of cutting prior to the climax of a scene. Violent actions could also be emphasised by using a succession of short conflicting shots from different viewpoints. Montage, the filmmakers discovered, could be further used to either compress or expand time, which could heighten the effect of certain actions or events.

Four different types of film montage[14]

The first two categories of montage outlined below are frequently, although not exclusively, used in Soviet film; the last two categories deal with montage techniques that are often to be found in mainstream films:

Hollywood cinema
In classical Hollywood cinema, the editing is designed to be 'invisible'. It is intended to allow the audience closer views and to see the point of view of different characters. The editing is used essentially to clarify what is taking place in the narrative. This type of editing had become dominant in Hollywood filmmaking by approximately 1920.

juxtaposition
In film studies, this usually refers to two different shots that have been joined together to make a contrast.

alternative
The Soviet cinema of the 1920s could certainly be regarded as 'alternative' as it offered a style of filmmaking that was radically different to the mass of films being produced in America.

dialectical
A difficult term to define, as it has many different meanings. The *Collins English Dictionary* (2nd edn, 1986), for example, defines it as a 'disputation or debate, esp. intended to resolve differences between two views rather than to establish one of them as true'. The crucial factor to grasp in the context of Eisenstein's thinking, however, is the notion of change and the creation of a new order. Eisenstein would have defined dialectic with reference to Marxist philosophy, which believed that society was contradictory and in need of change.

- intellectual montage (also called dialectical montage or discontinuity editing)
- linkage editing (also known as constructive editing)
- Hollywood montage
- fast cutting

Intellectual montage

In this type of editing, shots are placed together to emphasise their difference. They are in 'collision' with each other. For example, in *October* a shot of a mechanical golden peacock is placed next to a shot of a man (the peacock does not form part of the world of the film; that is, it is **non-diegetic**).[15] The audience draw the conclusion that the man is vain. In this type of editing the audience are not passive as they play an active part in producing meaning from the film.

Linkage editing

Mainly used by Pudovkin, who proposed a theory of montage based on this principle. In linkage editing individual shots are used to build up scenes. The shots are not in collision with each other, but are used as fragments or parts of a whole scene. This technique may be seen in *The Mother* and *The End of St Petersburg*.

Hollywood montage

Often used to show a quick succession of events over a period of time. For example, in *Raging Bull* (1980) Martin Scorsese shows the successful career of the boxer Jake La Motta by combining shots (mostly still photographs) taken from a number of different fights interspersed with home movie footage of La Motta's home life. The shots are clearly intended to flow into each other rather than to be in conflict. The music played on the soundtrack over the images reinforces the sense of continuity.

Fast cutting

In which editing is used primarily to build suspense or tension. For example, in the gunfight at the climax of *The Good, the Bad and the Ugly* (1966), Sergio Leone creates a dramatic effect by using a combination of music, tighter and tighter close-ups of the three characters, and a shortening of shot length.

Statistical analysis of Soviet films

Soviet films, because of the use of the montage technique, contain many more shots than Hollywood films of the same period. David Bordwell (1986)[16] claims that the Soviet films of the 1920s contain on average between 600 and 2,000 shots, whereas the films made in Hollywood between 1917 and 1928 contain on average between 500 and 1,000 shots. He further suggests that Hollywood films had an average shot length of five to six seconds while for Soviet films the average shot length was two to four seconds. The comparison provides concrete evidence of the unique nature of the editing used in the Soviet films during this period.

OTHER FEATURES OF SOVIET MONTAGE CINEMA

Aside from editing, these films have other features which separate them from the **dominant** Hollywood cinema. In keeping with a Marxist analysis of society, plots frequently do not centre on the individual; for example, in Eisenstein's *Strike*, *October* and *Battleship Potemkin*, individual heroes are replaced by a mass of people. The only characters that are individuated are those that wield power or have wealth. Events in the narrative therefore are not motivated by individuals. Films such as Pudovkin's *The Mother* and *The End of St Petersburg* and Dovzhenko's *Earth* (1930) do have central characters, but it is made clear that these characters are representative of the masses.

non-diegetic
Refers to any element that remains outside the world of the film, such as voiceovers, credits and mood-setting music, that does not originate from the world of the film.

dominant
Refers to both economic strength and the dominant form or convention, which at this time is realism: dominant cinema in film studies is assumed to be Hollywood.

The audience is not interested in the details of the heroes, only what they represent. A number of the Soviet filmmakers (including Eisenstein and Pudovkin) also used non-actors to play key parts, believing that the external appearance of the character was vital to the performance. This idea is termed 'typage'.

The montage style also means that Soviet cinema relies more heavily on the use of the close-up than does Hollywood cinema. Not only are there more shots overall in a scene, but a greater proportion of them are close-ups. A number of Soviet films also rely on high levels of **symbolism** to achieve their aims. The audience must be culturally and politically aware to be able to decode the messages that are being presented. In Eisenstein's *October*, for example, great demands are made on the audience to create a 'reading' of the film which does justice to Eisenstein's political thinking. It may seem that many of the filmmakers ran the risk of making films that were not understood by their audience.

Several of the montage filmmakers combined the montage principle with other techniques that they believed would revitalise cinema. Lev Kuleshov, for example, placed great emphasis on the gestures and movement of actors. FEKS (Factory of the Eccentric Actor), formed by filmmakers Grigori Kozintsev and Leonid Trauberg, had similar concerns about the role of the actor, but also paid close attention to mise-en-scène.

symbolism
The means by which a filmmaker can assign additional meanings to objects/characters in a film. For example, in Dovzhenko's *Earth* and Eisenstein's *Old and New*, the tractor is a symbol of progress.

THE KEY SOVIET MONTAGE FILMMAKERS OF THE 1920s

Fiction
Lev Kuleshov
Sergei Eisenstein
Vsevolod Pudovkin
FEKS (Kozintsev and Trauberg)
Alexander Dovzhenko

Documentary
Dziga Vertov
Esfir Shub

A film directed by Eisenstein probably provided most viewers' first experience of Soviet montage. The history of the Soviet cinema of the 1920s, however, involves more than the work of this one director. In this section, although the work of Eisenstein is discussed in detail, the vital importance of Eisenstein's contemporaries is recognised by analysing the work of such directors as Kuleshov, Pudovkin, Kozintsev and Trauberg, Dovzhenko, Vertov and Shub.

☐ **CASE STUDY 1: LEV KULESHOV (1899–1970)**

Key films
Engineer Prite's Project (1918)
The Extraordinary Adventures of Mr West in the Land of the Bolsheviks (1924)
The Death Ray (1925)
By the Law (1926)

Shortly after the Revolution, Kuleshov was recruited as a teacher by the State Film School where he set up an experimental film workshop. Kuleshov and his students carried out a number of experiments related to editing, partly inspired by a lack of raw film stock. One of these experiments included re-editing D.W. Griffith's *Intolerance* (1916), a film that had impressed Kuleshov due to its innovative use of editing. The experiments resulted in the formation of a number of principles of filmmaking that the group adopted. The underlying belief for Kuleshov was that 'Film-art begins from the moment when the director begins to combine and join together the various pieces of film'.[17] Kuleshov's ideas about how editing should work are similar to those of Pudovkin in that his shots, rather than being in conflict, may be seen as blocks out of which a scene can be constructed. Significantly, Kuleshov's students included Vsevolod

For comparison and contrast see Chapter 7, for a discussion of the star in Hollywood cinema.

Pudovkin and, for a brief time, Sergei Eisenstein. In Eisenstein's films and theoretical writing the influence of Kuleshov may be seen clearly.

Kuleshov's experimentation was not confined to editing, however, but also involved acting. He believed that theatre-trained actors, in particular those from the Moscow Arts Theatre,[18] were not suitable for the cinema. He also rejected the idea of using non-actors or 'types' chosen for their visual suitability for a role. He set up an acting laboratory dedicated to developing a style of acting tailored specifically to the requirements of the cinema and he carefully recruited would-be film actors who were 'endowed with natural beauty, good health, and the ability to show expediency and purpose on the screen without "acting" or "recreating", unaided by makeup, wigs, and props, of course' (cited in Zorkaya 1989: 52).

The techniques that Kuleshov adopted emphasised gesture and movement, the exact nature and timing of which had been practised rigorously in rehearsals. This style of acting was combined with close attention to the composition and framing of each shot to give maximum impact to the action. Kuleshov's opportunity to apply the principles that he had developed came in 1924 when he was assigned valuable imported film stock to direct the first feature film of the film school: *The Extraordinary Adventures of Mr West in the Land of the Bolsheviks*.

THE EXTRAORDINARY ADVENTURES OF MR WEST IN THE LAND OF THE BOLSHEVIKS (1924)

The film is an action comedy which uses satire to expose the false attitudes and beliefs about the Soviet Union held by many in the West. The action centres on the fate of Mr West, an American visitor to the USSR, whose view of the Bolsheviks as savages is formed by reading the *New York Times*. Mr West falls into the hands of a group of petty criminals who frighten him into parting with his dollars by dressing up to look like the Bolsheviks who Mr West has seen in his paper. At the climax he is rescued by a 'real' Bolshevik who uncovers the deception. Mr West's stereotypical views of the Bolsheviks are dismantled and he sends a radio message to his wife telling her to hang Lenin's picture in the study.

The montage technique used in *Mr West* is largely based on a system of close-ups of the actors that emphasise facial expressions. Kuleshov frequently cuts from an action to

• **Plate 17.1**
The Extraordinary Adventures of Mr West in the Land of the Bolsheviks (Lev Kuleshov, 1924). Mr West is duped by the false Bolsheviks

a close-up reaction shot of a character's face. He begins the film with a separate shot of Mr West juxtaposed with another of his wife; it is only later that we see them together. Later in the film Kuleshov cuts between a shot of the 'real' Bolshevik and Mr West standing on a balcony, and another shot of marching Soviet troops taken at a different place and time (the film stock is markedly different).

Kuleshov here is using his technique of creative geography to make the audience construct a location in their minds that does not actually exist. The film also fulfils Kuleshov's ideas concerning acting. The movements of the actors are stylised and precise, and it is clear that attention has been paid to even the smallest action. The comical nature of the action and a plot based on individual characters meant that the film was popular with audiences.[19]

☐ CASE STUDY 2: SERGEI EISENSTEIN (1898–1948)

Key films
Strike (1924)
Battleship Potemkin (1925)
October (1927)
Old and New (1929)

Eisenstein, as his age might indicate (he was just 26 when he completed *Strike*), did not emerge from the context of the pre-revolutionary Russian cinema. Prior to his filmmaking career, he had experimented with a number of different art forms, including the theatre. In this experimentation, the principles of his work in film may be found. In 1923 Eisenstein produced a version of a play by Alexander Ostrovky,[20] in which he attempted to communicate the messages of the play to the audience using a series of shocks which Eisenstein termed 'attractions': 'Emotions were expressed through flamboyant physical stunts ... at the finale, firecrackers exploded under spectators' seats ... [he] explained that the theatre could engage its audience through a calculated assembly of "strong moments" of shock or surprise' (Bordwell 1993: 6).

Eisenstein quickly abandoned experimentation with the theatre and turned to the more popular and accessible medium of film, to which he rigorously applied his theatrical principle of 'montage of attractions'.

Strike (1924)

Strike was the first of a proposed series of eight films[21] made by the Moscow Theatre of the Proletkult, under the general subheading 'Towards the Dictatorship of the Proletariat'. *Strike* is about the repression of a group of factory workers involved in an industrial dispute, which ends with the massacre of the strikers and their families by government forces. The six-part structure of *Strike* – (1) 'All Quiet at the Factory', (2) 'The Immediate Cause of Strike', (3) 'The Factory Stands Idle', (4) 'The Strike is Protracted', (5) 'Engineering a Massacre', (6) 'Slaughter' – is due in part to Eisenstein's theatrical background, but it would also have been vital for the film to be contained on single reels, as many cinemas had only one projector.

The plot of *Strike*, as in Eisenstein's later films *Battleship Potemkin* (1925) and *October* (1927), is not told using individual characters as heroes. Instead, any character that is individuated is deemed to be 'bad' or corrupt. The grotesque factory owner, for example, is shown completely isolated in a vast office. The workers themselves, however, are seen usually as a group with no one individual standing out to play the role of leader. In Part 3 these ideas are combined. The scenes depicting the four stockholders of the factory carelessly deciding the future of the strikers are intercut with images of strikers being attacked by mounted police; the individual concern of the capitalists contrasts with the collective concern of the masses. The effect of this montage is dramatic, as parallels can immediately be drawn by the viewer between, for example, the dishonesty, greed, deviousness and wealth of the management, and the poverty and honesty of the workers. The political implications of this are obvious. Eisenstein, through montage, is seeking to persuade his audience towards a certain view.

• **Plate 17.2**
Sergei Eisenstein
(1898–1948)

• **Plate 17.3**
Strike (Sergei
Eisenstein, 1924).
Mounted police enter
the factory district

• **Plate 17.4**
This sequence from *Strike* (lasting 25 seconds) illustrates Eisenstein's intellectual montage. An inter-title ('Rout') is inserted between shots 2 and 3

The methods applied by Eisenstein in *Strike* are derived in part from a rebellion against what Eisenstein termed the 'Bourgeois Cinema' that was still the main form of entertainment in post-revolutionary cinemas. Eisenstein explains how this cinema was rejected in favour of his own approach: 'We brought collective and mass action onto the screen ... our films in this period made an abrupt deviation – insisting on an understanding of the masses as hero' (cited in Leyda 1983: 181).

In terms of Hollywood cinema it is not difficult to imagine how the plot of *Strike* could have been adapted into a mainstream film: the story of one individual's fight against authority. The comparison may be trite, but it does emphasise the difference in approach and purpose between the two different modes of representation. Eisenstein's decision not to use individual heroes is of course deliberate: the film registers a political ideology that enshrines the notion of collective strength.

In *Strike*, Eisenstein applies his principle of 'montage of attractions' to the editing. He believed that by creating visual 'jolts' between each cut, the viewer would be 'shocked' into new awarenesses. In most sequences this approach involves juxtaposing shots that are in conflict with each other in some way, either cutting between different actions taking place in a scene or emphasising the importance of certain actions or events by fragmenting them into a number of shots taken from different viewpoints. At various points in *Strike* Eisenstein juxtaposes shots which need to be interpreted by the audience. One of the best examples of this type of 'intellectual montage' is in the last part of the film ('Slaughter'), in which Eisenstein juxtaposes a non-diegetic image of a bull being slaughtered with shots of factory workers being systematically butchered by government forces. The formula mentioned earlier may be applied: shot A (massacre of the workers) + shot B (bull being slaughtered) = NEW MEANING C (that the workers are

• **Plate 17.5**
Battleship Potemkin (Sergei Eisenstein, 1925). Drama on the quarter-deck (the firing squad)

being killed cold-bloodedly like animals in a slaughterhouse). It is the audience that is creating meaning here from the juxtaposition of the shots, thus becoming active political interpreters.

Battleship Potemkin (1925)

Eisenstein's second film, *Battleship Potemkin*, is based on the true story of a mutiny that took place on board the *Potemkin* in 1905.[22] As in *Strike*, *Battleship Potemkin* is split into a number of distinct parts: (1) 'Men and Maggots', (2) 'Drama on the Quarter Deck', (3) 'Appeal from the Dead', (4) 'The Odessa Steps', (5) 'Meeting the Squadron'.

The central scene of the film, 'The Odessa Steps', consisting of parallel lines of soldiers marching down the steps leading to the harbour systematically shooting the onlookers, provides a vivid example of the effectiveness of Eisenstein's montage technique.[23] A close examination of the sequence reveals that Eisenstein, by using montage to repeat certain key events, has expanded time.[24] The effect is to heighten the horrific nature of the slaughter as well as to hold the audience in suspense as the pram finally begins its descent. The furious and shocking climax to the scene demonstrates how Eisenstein is able to use montage to manipulate audience expectations, and to shock with violent juxtapositions and graphic images.

In the last part of the film in which the sailors aboard the *Potemkin* are nervously anticipating an attack by the rest of the Russian Fleet, Eisenstein builds up tension by increasing the number of cuts in a montage finale that maintains a consistently high rate of shots per minute. The scene provides an excellent example of the way in which montage could be used to create an event that did not exist as a whole, as according to Eisenstein the shots of the 'Russian' squadron were taken from 'old newsreels of naval manoeuvres – not even of the Russian Fleet' (cited in Leyda 1983: 195).[25] It also reveals how montage may be used for rhythmic effect, as the fast cutting between the different

• **Plate 17.6**
Battleship Potemkin
(Sergei Eisenstein,
1925). The Odessa
Steps

• **Plates 17.7, 17.8, 17.9**
Battleship Potemkin (Sergei Eisenstein, 1925). Immediately after the massacre on the Odessa Steps, the sailors on the battleship take their revenge by shelling the headquarters of the generals. As part of this sequence, Eisenstein juxtaposes three images of stone lions in different stages of awakening as a symbol of the awakening of the Russian people to political ideas and action

elements gives the scene a sense of urgency which would be impossible to achieve using any other method.

The opposition of critics at the time ironically stressed the difficulties of understanding *Potemkin*'s experimental form; ironic because it was through film form that Eisenstein hoped to make his political points. It was also declared that *Potemkin* was pitched far above the intellectual level of most peasants, a damning indictment for any propaganda/ revolutionary piece. However, although *Potemkin* was not successful as a piece of popular propaganda, it did, like *Strike* before it, mark a major step in the progress of revolutionary cinema. It also represented the first film that achieved recognition and acclaim for Soviet cinema. The claim that the experimental nature of *Potemkin* was not solely to blame for its unpopularity, and that it was badly let down by Sovkino's methods of distribution, is a view that should certainly be considered.

October (1927)

October, made for the Tenth Anniversary celebrations of the Russian Revolution, depicts the buildup to the October Revolution, ending with the storming of the Winter Palace by the Bolsheviks. It is considered the most experimental of Eisenstein's films, especially in its increased use of 'intellectual montage', which demands that the audience think critically and constructively about important political issues. A demonstration of this type of montage may be found in the scene in which both Kerensky and General Kornilov are depicted as Napoleons. By intercutting between the two men and the plaster-cast figures of Napoleon, Eisenstein effectively exposes both the vanity and essentially the lack of any power within the characters themselves to form a separate identity. Eisenstein's 'intellectual montage' also involves **diegetic** material. For example, early in the film, shots of a soldier cowering in a trench are juxtaposed with low-angle shots of a vast cannon being unloaded elsewhere. The combination of shots points initially to the soldier being physically crushed, but then the assumption is swiftly reached that the war is oppressive, degrading and without purpose for the ordinary troops.

Eisenstein also combines montage techniques with visual puns and symbolism for political effect. At one point, in order to degrade the power of the Church, he swiftly cuts from the image of one deity to another, starting with a magnificent statue of Christ, and ending up with a primitive wooden idol, demonstrating that all religions essentially worship crude man-made objects. Eisenstein's use of such techniques was considered by many to be obscure, inaccessible in meaning and élitist. Victor Shklovsky, writing in *Novyi Lef* in 1927, records the responses of a man connected with the cinema:

diegetic
The elements of a film that originate from directly within the film's narrative. For example, a popular song being played on the soundtrack would be diegetic if it was clear that it was coming from a source within the world of the film such as a car radio.

After viewing some Eisenstein sequences a man who is intelligent and conversant with cinema said to me, 'That is very good. I like that a lot but what will the masses say? What will the people we are working for say?' What can you say to that?

(cited in Taylor and Christie 1994: 182)

Indeed, an examination of contemporary criticism of *October* reveals that far from being popular among Soviet audiences, the film was met with derision and apprehension.

Old and New (1929)

The adverse reaction to *October* prompted Eisenstein to produce *Old and New*, a film understood more readily by audiences. Despite employing a number of the techniques used in *October*, Eisenstein presents them in a simplified form. Juxtapositions, for example, are more obvious and on a less symbolic level.

• Plate 17.11
Old and New or *The General Line* (Sergei Eisenstein, 1929). The new tractor is eventually delivered to Martha's co-operative

The narrative of *Old and New*, concerned with the collectivisation of agriculture, unlike Eisenstein's previous films, is bound together by a central character or heroine 'Martha'. Despite its more conventional narrative form, the film contains one of Eisenstein's most effective montage sequences in which a cream separator is delivered to the collective farm. The new machine is eyed suspiciously by the peasants as milk is poured into it. In an ever-quickening flow of images, Eisenstein cuts between the glittering, spinning parts of the machine, the changing faces of the peasants and non-diegetic shots of fountains of water which symbolise the future flow of cream from the separator. The film is fascinating to study in the context of Eisenstein's earlier work and marks an attempt to address problems of understanding associated with *October*.

Key films
The Mother (1926)
The End of St Petersburg (1927)
Storm Over Asia (1928)

☐ CASE STUDY 3: VSEVOLOD PUDOVKIN (1893–1953)

Editing is the language of the film director. Just as in living speech, so, one may say, in editing: there is a word – the piece of exposed film, the image; a phrase – the combination of these pieces.

(Pudovkin, cited in Perkins 1972a: 21)

Pudovkin believed that the power of cinema comes from editing. In the above quotation he claims that a 'shot' (or image) which is the equivalent of the single word in language has very limited meaning. However, when a number of words are combined together they form a 'phrase' which is dense with meaning. Pudovkin's equivalent of a 'phrase' was a number of shots edited together. He went further to support his claim by contending that

every object taken from a given viewpoint and shown on the screen to spectators, is a *dead object*, even though it has moved before the camera.... Only if the object be placed together among a number of separate objects, only if it be presented as part of a synthesis of different separate visual images, is it endowed with filmic life.

(Ibid.: 22)

It would seem initially that Pudovkin's theoretical position regarding the effectiveness of editing was in tandem with his contemporary Eisenstein. There are, however, important differences in the specific way each director thought editing should be used.[26] Pudovkin did not agree with Eisenstein's system of montage, which created visual 'jolts' between cuts. Instead, Pudovkin believed greater impact could be made by linking shots in a constructive way. Shots were to be used as individual building blocks, made to fit together exactly. Although seemingly theoretically opposed to Eisensteinian montage, Pudovkin made extensive use of devices such as 'intellectual montage' in *The Mother* and *The End of St Petersburg*. Pudovkin's juxtapositions, however, are much less symbolic, more clearly related to the diegetic world of the film and less intent on creating conflict than those of Eisenstein. Leon Moussinac, a French historian, summed up the differences between the two directors: 'An Eisenstein film resembles a shout, a Pudovkin film evokes a song' (cited in Taylor 1979: 142).

Pudovkin, like Eisenstein, cast according to 'type' and was concerned about the problem of 'stagey acting'. He stated:

I want to work only with real material – this is my principle. I maintain that to show, alongside real water and real trees and grass, a property beard pasted on the actor's face, wrinkles traced by means of paint, or stagey acting is impossible. It is opposed to the most elementary ideas of style.

(Pudovkin 2007: 141)

Unlike Eisenstein, however, Pudovkin uses individual characters that are cast in the role of hero or heroine to carry the narrative, and although he discouraged the use of professional actors some of his lead parts were played by professional actors of the Moscow Arts Theatre.[27]

The Mother (1926)

The scenario for Pudovkin's *The Mother* is based on the earlier play by Gorky of the same name. The plot is concerned with the political awakening of a mother after she betrays her son to the police, in the belief that he will be dealt with justly. The action is set (as in *Battleship Potemkin*) in the revolutionary context of 1905, with strikes, mass protests and a final brutal massacre of the workers.

With its focus on individuals, the film offers an interesting contrast to Eisenstein's approach to revolutionary cinema. In *The Mother*, the role of the individual is reinstated and emphasised. The mass struggle is thus registered through the lives and fates of separate characters involved in that struggle. It is important to note that the individual characters are not highlighted in such a way that the general struggle itself becomes obscured. The audience is encouraged to make connections between individual fate and the fate of the masses. Pudovkin is thus using individual characters to make his political points, believing that the audience would be able to relate better to separate identities than to an anonymous mass.

Pudovkin's use of 'linkage' editing (shot A + shot B = AB) may be illustrated in the trial scene at the mid-point of the film. The scene is composed of a large number of shots which tend to centre on single characters or pairs of characters. The fragmentation allows Pudovkin to draw direct comparisons between, for example, the uninterested and uncaring attitude of the judges, the accused Pavel, his mother and several of the gossiping onlookers. Close shots of the soldiers guarding the courthouse are also inserted in order to demonstrate that 'justice' is being upheld by a substantial force. Pudovkin clearly reveals the judges to be vain and self-interested by highlighting their overriding concern with attire and pictures of horses, rather than with the proceedings of the trial. If the same scene had been shot by Eisenstein the vanity of the judges might have been indicated in a similar way to that of Kerensky in October (that is, by juxta-posing him with a shot of a peacock).

The End of St Petersburg (1927)

Made to celebrate the Tenth Anniversary of the October Revolution, *The End of St Petersburg*, based on André Bely's 1916 symbolist novel *Petersburg*,[28] also uses individual characters to deal with the events preceding the Revolution. One is a young peasant boy who has come to St Petersburg to seek work, as his family can no longer support him at home. Despite initial involvement with strike-breakers, the boy quickly becomes aware of the corruption and injustice of the Tsarist regime. His political awakening, however, lands him in prison and he is forced to volunteer into the Tsar's army, where he is exposed to the horrors of trench warfare.

Using montage, Pudovkin draws a contrast between the suffering of the soldiers who are fighting for the Tsar and the greed of those who are benefiting financially from the war. Horrific images of dying soldiers in mud at the front-line trenches are intercut with scenes at the St Petersburg stockmarket. As the fighting gets worse and worse at the front, the higher the value of the shares becomes – thereby enforcing the point that people are making money out of suffering. The old order, by supporting and being supported by the stockmarket, is seen to be inhumane and preoccupied with the wrong

• **Plate 17.12**
The End of St Petersburg (Vsevolod Pudovkin, 1927). One of Pudovkin's central characters, a young peasant boy, is seen here demanding justice from the authorities

WE
CONSIDER ART AS A TIRELESS RAM SHATTERING THE HIGH WALLS OF HABIT AND DOGMA

But we also have our own ancestors! and lots of them

The brilliant creators of cinema posters, circus posters, music hall posters. Unknown designers of pulp thrillers who exalt the exploits of the King of the detectives or adventurers. In using your art, more magnificent than a clown's red nose, we spring up as if from a trampoline to perform our intripid somersault! Only the poster has escaped the pernicious scalpel of analysis and the intellect. Subject and form are indivisible, but what do they sing of?

Danger, Audacity, Violence, Pursuit, Revolution, Gold, Blood, Laxative pills, Charlie Chaplin, Catastrophes on land, sea and in the air. Fat cigars, Prima donnas of the operettas, Adventures of all sorts, Skating rinks, Tap shoes, Horses, Wrestling, Torch singers, Somersaults on bicycles and all those millions and millions of events which make splendid our Today!

THE 200 VOLUMES OF GERMAN EXPRESSIONISM DO NOT OFFER THE EXPRESSIVITY OF ONE SOLE

CIRCUS POSTER!!!

• **Plate 17.13**
Extract from FEKS
(Factory of the Eccentric
Actor) Manifesto, 1922

values – the acquisition of wealth at whatever cost. Pudovkin at one point intercuts between the image of a soldier slashing ferociously at an opponent with his bayonet and the image of a stockmarket figure frenetically dealing at the stock-exchange. He thus likens the barbarities of war to the barbarity inherent in the centre of the capitalist structure. Earlier Pudovkin intercut between the images of death at the front and the words 'In the name of the Tsar, the fatherland, and the capital'. This is clearly ironic, as the soldiers have no idea what they are fighting for – certainly not for the Tsar.

In the final part of *The End of St Petersburg*, in the storming of the Winter Palace sequences, Pudovkin intercuts images of the advancing Bolsheviks with both fast-moving clouds and crashing waves. This emphasises the power and inevitability of the revolution – revolution is unstoppable. Earlier in a Bolshevik's speech at the Lebedev factory, images of machinery slowing down are intercut with the speaker to point to the power of his words upon the workers.

☐ CASE STUDY 4: GRIGORI KOZINTSEV AND LEONID TRAUBERG: ECCENTRISM OF THE FEKS

Key films
The Adventures of Oktyabrina (1924)
The Cloak (1926)
The New Babylon (1929)

FEKS (Factory of the Eccentric Actor), formed in December 1921 by a small group of theatre actors and directors, shared the common aim of reforming the traditional theatre and incorporating into their experimental work elements of the circus, music hall and puppet theatre. On 9 July 1922 FEKS published a manifesto which stated their aims as a group.[29] The poster on page 465 shows just a small sample of the material contained within the manifesto.

The extract makes it clear that FEKS valued the bold, dynamic and popular elements of circus and cinema posters. It was with these elements that they proposed to revitalise the theatre. Two of the founding members of the group, Grigori Kozintsev and Leonid Trauberg, became interested in the cinema, making a number of short experimental films between 1924 and 1927, including *The Adventures of Oktyabrina* (1924) and *The Cloak* (1926). The films primarily emphasised the artificial nature of the mise-en-scène and the stylised nature of the acting rather than the editing.

Kozintsev and Trauberg are perhaps best known for their 1929 film *The New Babylon*, based on the events building up to the Paris Commune of 1871. As in their previous films, artificial mise-en-scène combined with stylised acting were employed, but extensive use was made also of camera movement. At one point in the film the camera moves swiftly enough to blur the image, thus conveying the sense of confusion present in the scene. The response to the film was unfavourable, as audiences failed to understand its form.

☐ CASE STUDY 5: ALEXANDER DOVZHENKO[30]

Key films
Arsenal (1929)
Earth (1930)

Inspired by the creative and political possibilities of film, Dovzhenko had approached the Odessa film studio in 1926. At this point he had little knowledge of cinema, but within a few years he had made an outstanding contribution to Soviet revolutionary cinema with such films as *Arsenal* and *Earth* which, in addition to revolutionary fervour, displayed poetic qualities and provided a demonstration of his love for the Ukraine and its people.

Arsenal surveys the devastating impact of the First World War and the political struggles between the Social Democrats and the Bolsheviks during 1917. The opening sequences of *Arsenal* exemplify Dovzhenko's approach to filmmaking. There is little camera movement or use of establishing shots and, overall, there is less concern with a conventional rendering of space and time than with the emotional impact of the flow of images. In these opening and further sequences Dovzhenko reveals the loss and impoverishment of the people, as well as the unthinking callousness of the social order.

Arsenal shows that Dovzhenko is not concerned with personalised conflict between individuals, but with the ongoing struggle between opposing social forces. This concern

• Plate 17.15
Earth (Alexander Dovzhenko, 1930)

is pursued further in *Earth*, which deals with class struggle in the countryside, although like *Arsenal* it features a strong, attractive male hero, Vasil. The latter is the operator of the tractor which will allow the collective farm effectively to rid the village of the self-seeking and more prosperous peasants, the kulaks. In the end Vasil is shot by Khoma, the son of a kulak, although what Vasil stands for will not be defeated. Vasil's father, hitherto hostile to the young revolutionaries of the village, commits himself to the cause of collectivisation and rejects a religious burial in favour of the village youth singing songs about the new life to come. The film, then, presents a strong case for the recently instigated policy of the collectivisation of agriculture. Commentators on the film, however, have argued that its formal and poetic qualities actually undermine the political message. Denise J. Youngblood, for example, states that:

Dovzhenko's *Earth* (1930) is a much more curious example of the collectivisation film – the politically correct story of a handsome young village Party activist murdered by an evil and dissolute kulak opposed to collectivisation is undercut by a deeply subversive subtext related to its form. The lyrical imagery and slow-rhythms of this film, totally unlike Eisenstein's, belie the purported theme and in effect serve as a paean to a way of life soon to be no more.

(Youngblood 1992: 169)

The opening sequence in which Vasil's grandfather dies would certainly seem to bear out this interpretation. He dies contented, his last act being to enjoy a pear, a product of the fruitful Ukrainian earth. Next to him a baby plays and a boy eats an apple, while the adult members of the family await the inevitable. This portrait of pastoral abundance and peacefulness with its allusions to the cycle of life and death seem to undermine the necessity for revolutionary change, but it is made clear by the old man's friend Petro that his has been a life of hard work – 'Seventy-five years behind a plough'.

☐ CASE STUDY 6: DZIGA VERTOV (1896–1954)

Key films
Film Truth (Kino-Pravda) (1922)
Kino-Eye (1924)
A Sixth of the World (1926)
The Man With a Movie Camera (1929)
Enthusiasm (1931)

Dziga Vertov[31] (pseudonym of Denis Kaufman) was interested in the idea that the film camera had the potential to capture 'truth'; the camera could be seen simply as a mechanical device that was capable of recording the world without human intervention. Vertov led a group of filmmakers called *Kinoki* ('cinema-eye') who stated in their 1923 manifesto:

I am the Cine-Eye. I am the mechanical eye.
I the machine show you the world as only I can see it.
I emancipate myself henceforth and forever from human immobility. I am in constant motion. I approach objects and move away from them, I creep up on them, I clamber over them, I move alongside the muzzle of a running horse, I tear into a crowd at full tilt, I flee before fleeing soldiers, I turn over on my back, I rise up with aeroplanes, I fall and rise with falling and rising bodies.
I the camera rushed along the equilibrium, manoeuvring amid the chaos of movements, fixing movement to movement in the most complex combinations.
Freed from any obligation to 16–17 frames a second, freed from the restraints of time and space, *I juxtapose any points in the universe* regardless of where I fixed them.
My path leads towards the creation of a fresh perception of the world. I can thus decipher a world you do not know.

(cited in Taylor and Christie 1994: 93)

For further and more detailed discussion of the documentary form see Chapter 9.

Vertov believed that the fiction film could not be used to reveal the 'truth' about a society. His films were based on documenting events around him; nothing should be artificially set up or staged for the camera. In 1922 Vertov had stated: 'WE declare the old films, the romantic, the theatricalised etc., to be leprous' (ibid.: 69) and in 1926 produced some 'very simple slogans' that summarised his approach:

1   Film-drama is the opium of the people.
2   Down with the immortal kings and queens of the screen! Long live the ordinary mortal, filmed in life at his daily tasks!
3   Down with the bourgeois fairy-tale script! Long live life as it is!
4   Film-drama and religion are deadly weapons in the hands of the capitalists. By showing our revolutionary way of life, we will wrest that weapon from the enemy's hands.
5   The contemporary artistic drama is a vestige of the old world. It is an attempt to pour our revolutionary reality into bourgeois molds.
6   Down with the staging of everyday life! Film us as we are.
7   The scenario is a fairy tale invented for us by a writer. We live our own lives, and we do not submit to anyone's fictions.
8   Each of us does his task in life and does not prevent anyone else from working. The film workers' task is to film us so as not to interfere with our work.
9   Long live the kino-eye of the proletarian revolution!

(cited in Michelson 1984: 71)

Vertov's techniques were based on experimentation caused by the general scarcity of film stock and also, when available, the short lengths of the negative film. His experiments included using old newsreels as part of his films, and he found that new meanings could be created by the conflict produced by the old material and the new. Vertov soon discovered that the conflicts produced by montage were a vital element in the construction of meaning in his films.

Perhaps one of the most interesting features of Vertov's films is that great effort is taken to ensure that the audience is made aware of cameraman, editor and the whole process of producing a film. In *The Man with a Movie Camera*, for example, Vertov shows the cameraman shooting the scenes that we see before us, and later we see shots of this same film being edited. This technique of acknowledging the nature of the filmmaking process can be linked to documentary filmmaking practice in the 1970s and 1980s (in the films of Emile de Antonio and Jean-Pierre Gorin, for example) which went against the **fly-on-the-wall** practice and attempted to show the presence of the film-crew and camera and the fact that the audience is watching a manufactured film rather than 'reality'. This style of filmmaking which draws attention to its own process is often termed 'self-reflexive'.

fly-on-the-wall
A term associated with a style of documentary filmmaking which attempts to present events as though the presence of the camera and film crew had not influenced them in any way.

THE MAN WITH THE MOVIE CAMERA (1929)

It was such a dazzling experience that it took two or three other Soviet films with normal 'stories' to convince me that all Soviet films were not compounded of such intricate camera pyrotechnics. But I hope to be forgiven for not bringing away any very clear critical idea as I reeled out of the Eight Street Playhouse – I was even too stunned to sit through it again.

(Leyda 1983: 251)

Leyda's experience of seeing *The Man with the Movie Camera* in New York in 1930 highlights three key issues:

- the film's sheer technical and intellectual brilliance and its status as a 'masterpiece'
- the challenge the film offered to audiences in terms of comprehension
- the extent to which the film fulfilled its role as Soviet propaganda

The Man with the Movie Camera, a celebration of Soviet city life, may be divided into six parts: Part 1: credit sequence, Part 2: the audience of the film, Part 3: the awakening city,

Part 4: the working day, Part 5: leisure time, Part 6: the audience of the film. The credit sequence clearly outlines Vertov's experimental ambitions:

THE MAN WITH THE MOVIE CAMERA

A RECORD ON CELLULOID IN 6 REELS

PRODUCED BY VUFKU, 1929

(AN EXCERPT FROM THE DIARY OF A CAMERAMAN)

FOR VIEWERS' ATTENTION

THIS FILM PRESENTS AN EXPERIMENT IN THE CINEMATIC

COMMUNICATION OF VISIBLE EVENTS

WITHOUT THE AID OF INTERTITLES

(A FILM WITHOUT INTERTITLES)

WITHOUT THE AID OF A SCENARIO

(A FILM WITHOUT A SCENARIO)

WITHOUT THE AID OF THEATRE

(A FILM WITHOUT SETS, ACTORS ETC.)

THIS EXPERIMENTAL WORK IS DIRECTED TOWARDS THE CREATION

OF A GENUINE, INTERNATIONAL PURELY CINEMATIC LANGUAGE,

ENTIRELY DISTINCT FROM THE LANGUAGE OF THE THEATRE AND

LITERATURE

Part 2 establishes the self-reflexive nature of the project. We are shown shots of: the camera and cameraman (using a split screen), an empty cinema, a film projector and projectionist, the loading of film reels, the opening of the screen curtain, the audience being let in, the film orchestra ready to play, the film projector lamp being lit, the orchestra starting to play, the film moving through the projector.

Part 3 shows the city awakening. There are shots of: empty streets in the early morning, a woman lying asleep, a vagrant on a bench, shop window displays, a typewriter keyboard, various pieces of machinery (all static), cogs (not moving) and factory chimneys (not smoking). There is now some movement – shots of: a moving car, the odd pedestrian in the street, the car crossing some railway tracks and finally a quickly edited sequence of a train approaching and going over the camera. The woman awakes and gets dressed. The car travels with the cameraman filming. There are shots of: tram rails, streets and windows being cleaned, a blind opening, the camera lens, aerodrome doors opening, airplanes being wheeled out, the greasing of tram tracks, trains emerging from sheds and people travelling to work.

Part 4 documents the city's working day. Vertov demonstrates how the human life cycle, the work cycle and the daily life cycle of the city are inseparable by intercutting various elements together. The human life cycle is represented by shots of: a wedding registration, a divorce registration, a funeral and a birth. The work cycle is represented by shots of various industries: textile, coal, steel and film production. Vertov further demonstrates the interconnectedness of city life by emphasising both communication and transportation. Communication is represented by shots of: a letter being posted, delivery of mail, the answering of a telephone, a telephone kiosk, a telephone exchange and frantic typing. Transportation by shots of: trains, trams, cars and ships.

Part 5 deals with the leisure time of the city workers. A diverse range of activities is documented including shots of: a day at the beach, swimming, fairground rides, high jumping, horse riding, exercise machines, a magic show, dancing, netball, football, motorbike racing, a proletarian film theatre, beer drinking, playing chess, playing the piano and listening to the radio. Vertov blends all these activities together into a seamless sequence that highlights similarities rather than differences. Part 6 returns to the cinema and its audience – again emphasising the role of the camera, cameraman, editor and audience in the creation of the film.

Vertov's sophisticated montage techniques are present in all parts of the film but in addition he used a number of other devices that furthered his goal to create 'a genuine, international, purely cinematic language'. They included: super-imposition, freeze-frame, slow motion, accelerated motion, stop-motion trick photography, vertical and horizontal split-screen and reverse motion. Vertov, however, intended *The Man with the Movie Camera* to be much more than formalist experimentation. In his film proposal, dated 19 March 1928, Vertov provides a clear sense of how he intended the film to be read:

The man with the movie camera marches apace with life. To the bank and the club. The beer hall and clinic. The Soviet and the housing council. The cooperative and the school. The demonstration and the party-cell meeting. The man with the movie camera manages to go everywhere …

Life's chaos gradually becomes clear as he observes and shoots. Nothing is accidental. Everything is explicable and governed by law. every peasant with his seeder, every worker at his lathe, every worker-student at his books, every engineer at his drafting table, every Young Pioneer speaking at a meeting in a club – each is engaged in the same great necessary labour.

(cited in Michelson, 1984: 287–8)

Vertov had clearly fulfilled his ambition of smashing through the moribund formal conventions of 'bourgeois' pre-revolutionary Russian cinema but he appears to have failed in his attempt to create *politically* revolutionary cinema, as *The Man with the Movie Camera* was not widely understood by Soviet audiences. Denise Youngblood claims that contemporary commentators were critical of the film with one condemning it for its 'narrow formalism' and 'technical fetishism' (1991: 207), although Youngblood also mentions that the film suffered from poor distribution, 'limited runs and rental "politics"' (ibid.: 208). Ultimately, however, it is difficult to deny the complexity of *The Man with the Movie Camera* and the demands that it places on 'ordinary' audiences. Vlada Petrić (1993) in his exhaustive shot-by-shot analysis of the film uncovers the highly complex chains of signification woven into *The Man with the Movie Camera* via the editing process. Petrić's study supports Noel Burch's assertion that: 'This film is not made to be viewed only once. It is impossible for anyone to assimilate this work in a single viewing' (cited in Petrić 1993: 78).

• Plate 17.16
The Man with the Movie Camera (VUFKU–British Film Institute)

□ **CASE STUDY 7: ESFIR SHUB (1894–1959)**

Key films
*The Fall of the Romanov
Dynasty* (1927)
The Great Road (1927)
*The Russia of Nicholas II
and Lev Tolstoy* (1928)

Esfir Shub is an interesting female figure in a period of filmmaking dominated by men. She was initially employed by the Soviet government to re-edit foreign films to make them conform to the ideology of communism. Shub also re-edited old Tsarist newsreels to show the corrupt nature of the old order. Shub's practice of reassembling parts of existing films culminated in the adoption of the montage technique.

ESFIR SHUB, *THE FALL OF THE ROMANOV DYNASTY* (1927)

Shub's first feature-length film, *The Fall of the Romanov Dynasty*, constructed entirely from old newsreels, was made to celebrate the Tenth Anniversary of the October Revolution, and it is claimed that 60,000 metres of film had to be examined in order to finish the project.[32] Shub provides new commentary on existing material by inserting intertitles between shots. By juxtaposing sequences of shots from different newsreels she also makes the audience draw new conclusions about the material. For example, she contrasts shots of an aristocratic gathering with shots of workers digging ditches. The intertitle reads 'by the sweat of your brow'. The intertitles and the juxtaposition of the images encourage the audience to assign an aberrant decoding to the original shots. In other words, the audience can deliberately 'misread' the images. Shub uses images which emphasise the pomp and splendour of Tsarist Russia, which in the context of the film look absurd and out of place; the audience is forced to be critical of this obvious display of wealth.

Although the film in principle uses montage in a way similar to that of Eisenstein or Pudovkin (in particular the way in which the audience are made active participants in the text), Shub does not make use of its rhythmic possibilities. The pace of the film is on the whole sedate, although it does put its political messages across in a powerful and convincing way. Recently, there has been a call by Graham Roberts for a re-evaluation of Esfir Shub; Roberts claims that Shub's contribution to the Soviet cinema has been undervalued (see Roberts 1991).

AUDIENCE RESPONSE

Viewers in the West may possibly already have an idea of the nature of the Soviet cinema after seeing extracts from films discussed previously such as Sergei Eisenstein's *Battleship Potemkin* or *October*. They may have wondered how many films such as these were made and how they were received by Soviet audiences that had only a few years previously gone through the upheaval of civil war. They may have pitied or even envied the Soviet cinema-goer – were these the only films that people could see on a Friday night? How could a largely uneducated population have coped with sophisticated material such as this?

Recent research into the Soviet cinema of the 1920s has encouraged new ideas. In the past, attention has focused on a number of key directors such as Pudovkin, Eisenstein and Vertov, whose films in the Soviet Union and later in the West were received with critical acclaim. We must, however, examine new evidence which points to the fact that Russian audiences were far more likely to be watching the Soviet 1920s equivalent of *Harry Potter and the Deathly Hallows* than the likes of *Battleship Potemkin*, *Strike* and *October*.

*For further discussion
of film audiences in
the UK and the US see
Chapter 1.*

Richard Stites, in *Russian Popular Culture: Entertainment and Society since 1900*, reveals that the majority of Soviet directors were making mainstream films that were conventional in form and content. The montage film was the exception rather than the rule:

The most popular movie genres of the revolutionary period were the same as the foreign and pre-revolutionary Russian ones: costume drama, action and adventure, literary works adapted for the screen, melodramas, and comedy. Those who patronized them were not merely the *nepman-skaya auditoriya*, that is the bourgeoisie, alleged to be addicted to lurid sex films. Working-class clubs sponsored by the Communist Party also had to show some entertainment films or risk losing their audience.

(Stites 1992: 56)

For further discussion of film audiences in the US and the UK see Chapter 1.

Soviet audiences also favoured foreign films which were imported in large numbers throughout the 1920s.

But why were the Soviet propaganda films relatively less successful? Why would audiences rather see foreign and conventional Soviet genre films? Were foreign films perceived as being more exciting or exotic? Denise Youngblood, in *Movies for the Masses*, cites an interview conducted in 1929 with a Soviet cinema manager who recorded audience response:

He noted that 'the public watched [Dovzhenko's *Arsenal*] with great difficulty', and that attendance dropped to 50 percent of normal when his theatre screened *New Babylon*, Kozintsev and Trauberg's famous picture about the Paris Commune. Asked about the reaction to Vertov's *The Man with the Movie Camera*, he replied sarcastically, 'One hardly need say that if *New Babylon* didn't satisfy the spectator's requirements and "lost" him, then *The Man with the Movie Camera* didn't satisfy him either'.

(Youngblood 1992: 18–19)

The problem is clear. The Soviet propaganda films that were intended for the masses, from the illiterate peasant upward, simply were not being understood by Soviet audiences, whereas the clear, hero-led narrative structure of the foreign and Soviet genre films were far more straightforward and appealing. It is well documented that the American version of *Robin Hood* proved more successful in Soviet cinemas on all counts. The filmmakers involved in Soviet propaganda production, although committed to the ideals of communism, were also committed to experimenting with film form. The experimentation in this case clearly did not culminate in a popular cinema that appealed to the masses.

THEORETICAL DEBATES: MONTAGE VERSUS REALISM

The montage technique has been widely acknowledged as a powerful means of expression, and to many cinema theorists montage is the essence of cinema. The technique, however, does have its opponents, among them the French film critic and theorist André Bazin.[33] Bazin was concerned with the cinema's ability to record 'reality'. He saw in cinema a means of capturing a record of events before the camera with minimum mediation. Bazin regarded the montage cinema of the Soviets (among others) as essentially non-realist because scenes could be manipulated and altered in many different ways. He claimed that the audience of montage cinema was essentially passive,[34] as the director forced the audience towards certain meanings.

Bazin saw montage cinema as being in direct opposition to a style of filmmaking associated with realism. Realism is a term often associated with the Hollywood cinema, but Bazin used it to refer to a style of filmmaking adopted by certain filmmakers such as Jean Renoir, a French director who felt that the power of cinema came not from editing but from mise-en-scène. The realists, unlike the montage filmmakers, took great pains to hide the artificial constructed nature of film. The long take, for example, was used

For further discussion of realism and documentary film, see Chapter 9.

For further discussion of Bazin and the French New Wave see the website www.routledge.com/cw/nelmes.

frequently, as it made editing unnecessary. The use of the long take supported the claim that what was being watched was unmediated and therefore more 'realistic'. Bazin cited further devices that could enhance the 'reality' of a scene, for example, the use of deep-focus, wide-angle lenses, the long shot and a highly mobile camera, all of which meant that the filmmaker could preserve real time and space in individual scenes.

THE 1930S AND AFTER: THE DECLINE OF EXPERIMENTATION IN THE SOVIET CINEMA

In the 1930s the Soviet authorities, under the guidance of Stalin, reacted to the unpopu-larity of many Soviet films by issuing strict guidelines on how films should be made. This set of 'rules', essentially demanding hero-led narratives and concerned with realistic subject matter, was termed 'Socialist Realism'. Boris Shumvatsky, the head of the Soviet film industry outlined in 1933 why such a policy was necessary: 'A film and its success are directly linked to the degree of entertainment in the plot ... that is why we are obliged to require our masters [the filmmakers] to produce works that have strong plots and are organised around a story-line' (cited in Taylor 1986: 43).

The policy of 'Socialist Realism' was combined with a complete ban on imported foreign films. By removing these positive representations of capitalism Stalin had also effectively made the Soviet film industry a monopoly; audiences could either see Soviet films or see no films at all.

The direct interest that the Soviet state took in the film industry reveals its perceived importance, but also had drastic consequences for many of the directors. It was noted by the authorities, for example, that several of these directors were not actually Communist Party members. (This may perhaps explain why they were more interested in form or technique than in making positive films about communism that were easy to comprehend.) The filmmakers of the 1920s discussed in this chapter were mostly not successful in the 1930s and 1940s. Eisenstein, for example, continued to make films, but the majority were either suppressed or had their funding withdrawn.

However, the decline of montage cinema could possibly be the consequence of another factor: technology. In October 1929 the first Soviet sound films were released, and with this advance in cinema technology came the almost immediate downfall of filmmaking practices that relied on either complex camera movement or rapid editing, as sound cinema initially required non-movable cameras and fixed microphones in order to record dialogue.

CONCLUSION[35]

The impact of Soviet films of the 1920s on the analysis of film and filmmaking itself was immediate and continues up until this day. The films, however, have not so much provided a model for successive filmmakers as been an inspiration for their work. The British Documentary Movement of the 1930s, for example, was influenced by Soviet montage as well as impressed by the idea that films could be a force for education. The filmmakers in this movement, however, did not conceive of films having a revolutionary role or even the role of questioning contemporary inequalities. Other filmmakers have been inspired by the Soviet cinema due to its rejection of the forms and conventions of the dominant Hollywood entertainment cinema. Jean-Luc Godard, for example, demanded that audiences participate in the construction of meaning in his films and so engage directly with social and political questions. The achievements of Eisenstein continue to impress film editors as well as contemporary film directors. The editor, Ralph Rosenblum, for example, states in his discussion of *Battleship Potemkin* that '[a]lthough the movie is filled with stunning moments, the massacre on the Odessa steps outweighs them all; it remains for editors everywhere the single most intimidating piece of film ever assembled' (Rosenblum and Karen 1979: 51).

Direct references to Eisenstein's films are numerous, ranging from Bernardo Bertolucci's subtle allusions to *Strike* in his *Tragedy of a Ridiculous Man* (1981), through Brian de Palma's opportunistic reworking of the Odessa Steps sequence in *The Untouchables* (1987)[36] to Zbiginiew Rybczynski's use of the same sequence in *Steps* (1987)[37] in order to satirise cultural attitudes including the veneration of *Battleship Potemkin* as a work of art.[38] Dovzhenko's influence has not been directly political, but the films of Andrei Tarkovsky, a one-time pupil of Dovzhenko, and a film such as *My Childhood* (1972) by the Scottish filmmaker Bill Douglas, exhibit a similar emotional intensity.

SUMMARY

- The Soviet montage cinema of the 1920s grew out of the need for a radical new mode of filmmaking to promote the ideology of the Soviet state. How effective these films were as propaganda is debatable but their influence on filmmaking around the world is undeniable.
- The pre-revolutionary Russian films were markedly different from the Soviet films of the 1920s. They were slow-paced and predominantly concerned with the lives of the bourgeoisie. It is interesting to note, however, that in the 1910s Russian artists and poets were already experimenting extensively with 'montage' techniques.
- Soviet montage filmmakers, such as Eisenstein, Pudovkin, Vertov and Kulshov, were both practitioners and theorists and wrote extensively about their techniques. There were, however, significant differences between their approaches to editing. Pudokvin, for example, rejected Eisenstein's belief that shots should be in 'collision'.
- Some Soviet filmmakers, such as Vertov, believed that fiction film could not be used to reveal the 'truth' about a society and therefore based his films on documenting events around him.
- Other filmmakers such as Shub were tasked by the Soviet government to create new meanings by re-editing Russian newsreels and foreign films to conform to the new Soviet ideology.
- The French theorist Bazin claimed that the audience of montage cinema was essentially passive as the director forced the audience towards certain meanings. Instead Bazin advocated a cinema that captured a record of events before the camera with minimum mediation.
- Cinema attendance records suggest that the Soviet montage films were not popular with audiences and that ironically imported American films, such as *Robin Hood*, were more successful at the Soviet box office.
- The montage cinema of the 1920s came to an abrupt halt in the 1930s when the Soviet authorities, under the leadership of Stalin, demanded that filmmakers create more popular films with hero-led narratives and realistic subject matter. Arguably, however, the demise of montage cinema was also linked to the advent of sound in the 1930s, which generally required longer takes to facilitate the recording of dialogue.

QUESTIONS FOR DISCUSSION

1 What are they key differences between Soviet montage editing and continuity editing?
2 Why did the Soviet montage filmmakers believe that a new cinematic form was required to communicate revolutionary ideas?
3 Soviet montage films were more successful as avant-garde art than propaganda for the masses. Discuss.

4   Discuss the use of mise-en-scène in Soviet montage films.

5   Russian artists and poets had already experimented extensively with 'montage' prior to the 1917 revolution. Why didn't the Russian filmmakers of the 1910s experiment with montage earlier?

6   Discuss the significance of the social and political context of Soviet montage cinema.

7   Discuss the use of performance and mise-en-scène in Kuleshov's *The Extraordinary Adventures of Mr. West in the Land of the Bolsheviks*.

8   What is meant by the term 'creative geography'?

9   Outline the key differences between Eisenstein's and Pudovkin's approach to editing.

10 Why did the FEKs manifesto favour popular art forms such as cinema, circus and music hall posters?

11 What is meant by the term 'dialectical montage'?

12 Why was Bazin interested in cinema as a 'means of capturing a record of events before the camera with minimum mediation'?

13 Define four different types of film 'montage'.

14 Why might Soviet montage films be classified as 'alternative'?

15 Why does Eisenstein favour non-actors over actors?

16 'An Eisenstein film resembles a shout, a Pudovkin film evokes a song'. Discuss.

17 Why do Eisenstein's films tend not to focus on individual 'heroes'?

18 What were the distinctive features of pre-revolutionary Russian cinema?

19 Why did Vertov believe that 'Film drama is the opium of the people'?

20 What might a statistical analysis of Soviet films reveal if compared to an analysis of Hollywood films from the same era?

21 Trace the influence of Soviet cinema of the 1920s on subsequent filmmakers and film movements.

22 Why might Bazin claim that the audience of Soviet montage films was essentially passive?

 NOTES

1   The term 'peasants' is used to describe those who worked on the land in the country, and the term 'workers' to describe those who worked within cities. This became a source of dispute in the 1920s when there was greater concern with efficiency and a more elaborate division of labour.

2   This was a planned attack by a relatively small force, not a mass uprising as chronicled by Eisenstein in his 1927 film *October*.

3   An unusual account of this period told from the point of view of the White side may be found in Mikhail Bulgakov's 1926 novel, *The White Guard* (available in the UK as a Flamingo paperback).

4   The British Film Institute has released a number of early Russian films on video (in ten volumes).

5   Protazanov was not in the Soviet Union for the full duration of this period; he emigrated briefly to Paris in 1920–23.

6   For more information on Protazanov, see Christie and Graffy (1993). For more information on the Russian cinema, see Leyda (1983); and Usai *et al.* (1989).

7   The first Russian studio was set up by Drankov in 1907.

8   The first half of this section is by Danny Rivers (film studies lecturer, West Kent College).

9   The context of this remark may be found in Leyda (1983: 161).

10 The civil war also resulted in trade barriers being set up which prevented the importation of film stock and cinema equipment into the Soviet Union. This had a dramatic effect on the film industry as the Soviet Union initially had no means of producing its own film stock and lenses.

11 Vladimir Vladimirovich Mayakovsky (1893–1930).

12 The team effort involved in the production of a feature film would clearly cost a great deal more than an individual artist producing a painting. The Russian film industry, although economically successful, needed to produce films that would appeal to a wide audience. The desire to experiment with film form, when the existing genres were popular, was therefore limited.

13 The mansion was in fact the White House.

14 Adapted from Kawin (1987: 99–101).

15 Bordwell, in *The Cinema of Eisenstein* (1993: 85), claims that the peacock could be seen as a diegetic image as it forms part of the treasures contained within the Winter Palace. Yuri Tsivian, in 'Eisenstein's *October* and Russian Symbolist Culture' (see Christie and Taylor 1993: 94), puts forward the view that 'Eisenstein was hoping to attain the effect of Kerensky entering the peacock's arsehole'.

16 Bordwell uses a technique pioneered by Barry Salt in his article 'Statistical Style Analysis of Motion Pictures', *Film Quarterly*, Vol. 28, No. 2, 1974–75.

17 Cited by Pudovkin (2007: 139) at a lecture given at the London Film School in 1929.

18 The Moscow Arts Theatre under the direction of Konstantin Stanislavski developed a method of acting which required the actor to attempt to 'become' the character.

19 This may be inferred from the fact that Goskino made thirty-two prints of the film.

20 A well-known Russian playwright (1823–86).

21 The other seven films were never made.

22 Eisenstein bends historical fact in the film as the sailors on board the *Potemkin*, instead of persuading the Russian Fleet to join the struggle, were captured and the mutiny suppressed.

23 The scene has been much copied by recent filmmakers: see conclusion on pp. 474–5.

24 See Bordwell (1993: 74) for an excellent analysis of the sequence.

25 Leyda also points out that the same sequence caused 'an anxious debate in the German Reichstag on the size of the Soviet Navy'.

26 Pudovkin's films, like those of Eisenstein, were based on a body of theoretical writing.

27 The theatre was founded in 1898 by Konstantin Stanislavski and Vladimir Nemirovich-Danchenko.

28 Published in the UK by Penguin (London, 1983).

29 The manifesto was reprinted in 1992 in a limited edition of 500 copies by Aldgate Press, London.

30 Section on Dovzhenko written by Danny Rivers (West Kent College).

31 Vertov in Russian from the Russian word for 'rotation' and was thus a reflection of his approach to the arts.

32 Soviet montage cinema tended to place stress on the importance of the director (auteur) and work in post-production, rather than scriptwriting and the screen.

33 Bazin was also editor of the French film journal *Cahiers du cinéma*.

34 Eisenstein rigorously opposed this view, claiming that the audience for his films played an active part in the text.

35 This section was written by Danny Rivers (West Kent College).

36 A statistical analysis of both scenes in terms of shot length/shot type reveals that they are also very similar in form.

37 A co-production of KTCA-TV Minneapolis and ZBIG Vision Ltd in association with Channel 4, London.

38 Woody Allen in *Love and Death* (1975) also makes reference to this sequence.

FURTHER READING

Aumont, J. (1987) *Montage Eisenstein*, London: British Film Institute.

Barna, Y. (1973) *Eisenstein*, London: Secker & Warburg.

Barron, S. and Tuchmann, M. (eds) (1980) *The Avant-Garde in Russia, 1910–1930: New Perspectives*, Los Angeles: Los Angeles County Museum of Art.

Beumers, B. (ed.) (2007) *The Cinema of Russia and the Former Soviet Union*, London: Wallflower Press.

Bordwell, D. (1993) *The Cinema of Eisenstein*, Cambridge, MA: Harvard University Press.

Christie, I. and Gillett, J. (eds) (1978) *Futurism/Formalism/FEKS: 'Eccentrism' and Soviet Cinema 1918–1936*, London: BFI.

Christie, I. and Graffy, J. (eds) (1993) *Yakov Protazanov and the Continuity of Russian Cinema*, London: BFI/NFT.

Christie, I. and Taylor, R. (eds) (1993) *Eisenstein Rediscovered*, London: Routledge.

Dickinson, T. and de la Roche, C. (1948) *Soviet Cinema*, London: Falcon Press.

Eisenstein, S. (1970) *Notes of a Film Director*, New York: Dover Publications.

Eisenstein, S. (1986) *The Film Sense*, London: Faber and Faber.

Gillespie, D. (2003) *Russian Cinema*, Harlow: Longman.

Glenny, M. and Taylor, R. (eds) (1994) *S.M. Eisenstein: Towards a Theory of Montage – Selected Works Vol. 2*, London: BFI.

Goodwin, J. (1993) *Eisenstein, Cinema and History*, Urbana: University of Illinois Press.

Kenez, P. (1992) *Cinema and Soviet Society 1917–1953*, Cambridge: Cambridge University Press.

Kepley, V., Jr (1986) *In the Service of the State: The Cinema of Alexander Dovzhenko*, Madison: University of Wisconsin Press.

LaValley, A. and Scherr, B. (eds) (2001) *Eisenstein at 100: A Reconsideration*, New Brunswick: Rutgers University Press.

Lawton, A. (ed.) (1992) *The Red Screen: Politics, Society, Art in Soviet Cinema*, London: Routledge.

Leyda, J. (1983) *Kino: A History of the Russian and Soviet Film* (3rd edn), London: George Allen & Unwin.

Marshall, H. (1983) *Masters of the Soviet Cinema*, London: Routledge & Kegan Paul.

Michelson, A. (ed.) (1984) *Kino Eye: The Writings of Dziga Vertov*, Berkeley and Los Angeles: University of California Press.

Petrić, V. (1993) *Constructivism in Film: The Man with the Movie Camera – A Cinematic Analysis*, Cambridge: Cambridge University Press.

Roberts, G. (1999) *Forward Soviet: History and Non-fiction Film in the USSR*, London: I.B. Tauris.

Sargeant, A. (2000) *Vsevolod Pudovkin: Classic Films of the Soviet Avant-Garde*, London: I.B. Tauris.

Schnitzer, J., Schnitzer, L. and Martin, M. (eds) (1973) *Cinema in Revolution*, trans. D. Robinson, London: Secker & Warburg; reprinted by Da Capo Press, New York, 1987.

Stites, R. (1992) *Russian Popular Culture: Entertainment and Society Since 1900*, Cambridge: Cambridge University Press.

Taylor, R. (1979) *The Politics of the Soviet Cinema, 1917–1929*, Cambridge: Cambridge University Press.

Taylor, R. (ed.) (1988) *S.M. Eisenstein: Writings 1922–1934 – Selected Works Vol. 1*, London: BFI.

Taylor, R. (ed.) (1995) *Beyond the Stars: The Memoirs of Sergei Eisenstein – Selected Works Vol. 4*, London: BFI.

Taylor, R. (1998a) *Film Propaganda: Soviet Russia and Nazi Germany* (2nd edn), London: I.B. Tauris.

Taylor, R. (ed.) (1998b) *The Eisenstein Reader*, London: BFI.

Taylor, R. and Christie, I. (eds) (1991) *Inside the Film Factory: New Approaches to Russian and Soviet Cinema*, London: Routledge.

Taylor, R. and Spring, D. (eds) (1993) *Stalinism and Soviet Cinema*, London: Routledge.

Taylor, R. and Christie, I. (eds) (1994) *The Film Factory: Russian and Soviet Cinema in Documents, 1896–1939*, London: Routledge; first published 1988 by Routledge & Kegan Paul.

Taylor, R. and Spring, D. (eds) (1993) *Stalinism and Soviet Cinema*, London: Routledge.

Tsivian, Y. (1994) *Early Cinema in Russia and its Cultural Reception*, London: Routledge.

Usai, P., Codelli, L., Montanaro, C. and Robinson, D. (eds) (1989) *Silent Witnesses: Russian Films 1908–1919*, London: BFI.

Youngblood, D. (1991) *Soviet Cinema in the Silent Era: 1918–1935*, Austin: University of Texas Press.

Youngblood, D. (1992) *Movies for the Masses: Popular Cinema and Soviet Society in the 1920s*, Cambridge: Cambridge University Press.

Youngblood, D.J. (1999) *The Magic Mirror: Movie Making in Russia 1908-1918*, Madison: University of Wisconsin Press.

Zorkaya, N. (1989) *The Illustrated History of Soviet Cinema*, New York: Hippocrene Books.

FURTHER VIEWING

VHS = available on video
DVD = available on DVD
16mm = available to hire on 16mm
Where neither symbol is listed, the film is not available to buy or rent

Selected Russian films of the 1910s

1908	*Sten'ka Razin*, Vladimir Romashkov–Drankov Studio (VHS)
1909	*A Sixteenth-century Russian Wedding*, Vasili Goncharov (VHS)
1910	*The Queen of Spades*, Petr Chardynin (VHS)
	Rusalka/The Mermaid, Vasili Goncharov (VHS)
1912	*The Brigand Brothers*, Vasili Goncharov (VHS)
	The Peasants' Lot, Vasili Goncharov (VHS)
1913	*The House in Kolomna*, Petr Chardynin (VHS)
	Merchant Bashkirov's Daughter, Nikolai Larin (VHS)
	Twilight of a Woman's Soul, Evgeny Bauer (DVD)
1914	*The Child of the Big City*, Evgeny Bauer (VHS)
	Silent Witnesses, Evgeny Bauer (VHS)
1915	*After Death*, Evgeny Bauer (DVD)
	Children of the Age, Evgeny Bauer
	Daydreams, Evgeny Bauer (VHS)
	Happiness of Eternal Night, Evgeny Bauer
1916	*Antosha Ruined by a Corset*, Eduard Puchal'ski (VHS)
	A Life for a Life, Evgeny Bauer (VHS)
	The 1002nd Ruse, Evgeny Bauer (VHS)
	The Queen of Spades, Yakov Protazanov (VHS)
1917	*For Luck*, Evgeny Bauer (VHS)
	Grandmother of the Revolution, Boris Svetlov

       The King of Paris, Evgeny Bauer
       The Dying Swan, Evgeny Bauer (DVD)
       The Revolutionary, Evgeny Bauer
       Satan Triumphant, Yakov Protazanov
1918 *Jenny the Maid*, Yakov Protazanov
       Little Ellie, Yakov Protazanov
       Still, Sadness, Still, Petr Chardynin

Selected Soviet films of the 1920s–40s

1922–25 *Film-Truth*, Dziga Vertov (a series of newsreels)
1924 *Aelita*, Yakov Protazanov (DVD/16mm)
       Cigarette-Girl from Mosselprom, Yuri Zhelyabuzhsky
       The Extraordinary Adventures of Mr West in the Land of the Bolsheviks, Lev Kuleshov (16mm)
       Kino-Eye, Dziga Vertov (DVD)
       Strike, Sergei Eisenstein (DVD/16mm)
1925 *Battleship Potemkin*, Sergei Eisenstein (DVD, 16mm)
       The Death Ray, Lev Kuleshov
1926 *The Mother*, Vsevolod Pudovkin (VHS/DVD, 16mm)
       A Sixth of the World, Dziga Vertov (16mm)
1927 *The End of St Petersburg*, Vsevolod Pudovkin (DVD/16mm)
       The Fall of the Romanov Dynasty, Esfir Shub (DVD/16mm)
       The Great Road, Esfir Shub
       October, Sergei Eisenstein (DVD/16mm)
1928 *The Russia of Nicholas II and Lev Tolstoy*, Esfir Shub
       Storm Over Asia, Vsevolod Pudovkin (DVD/16mm)
1929 *Arsenal*, Alexander Dovzhenko (DVD/16mm)
       The Man with a Movie Camera, Dziga Vertov (DVD/16mm)
       The New Babylon, Grigori Kozintsev and Leonid Trauberg
       Old and New or The General Line, Sergei Eisenstein (16mm)
       Ranks and People, Yakov Protazanov
       Turksib, Victor Turin
1930 *Earth*, Alexander Dovzhenko (DVD/16mm)
1931 *Enthusiasm*, Dziga Vertov (16mm)
1934 *Chapayev*, Sergei and Georgy Vasiliev (VHS)
1935 *Aerograd*, Alexander Dovzhenko
       The Youth of Maxim, Grigori Kozintsev and Leonid Trauberg (16mm)
1936 *Alexander Nevsky*, Sergei Eisenstein (DVD/16mm)
       We from Krondstadt, Yefim Dzigan (VHS)
1945 *Ivan the Terrible: Part I*, Sergei Eisenstein (DVD/16mm)
1946 *Ivan the Terrible: Part II*, Sergei Eisenstein (DVD/16mm)

Additional material

The Secret Life of Sergei Eisenstein, British Film Institute Publishing, London, 1987 (VHS)

RESOURCE CENTRES

**www.bl.uk/reshelp/findhelplang/russian/
russiancinema/russcinema.html**
The British Library: Russian and Soviet cinema resources

www.ssees.ucl.ac.uk/russcin.htm
UCL School of Slavonic and East European Studies library: internet resources on Russian cinema.

www.kinoeye.org/archive/country_russia.php
The Kinoeye Archive: web resources on Russian cinema.

www.sussex.ac.uk/Units/russian/bookmar2.htm
University of Sussex: electronic resources for Russian and East European studies.

www.kinokultura.com/index.html
KinoKulture: New Russian Cinema (quarterly film journal).

Glossary

30°   A change in camera angle at the minimum of 30° is usual for each new shot at the same scene, thus ensuring the cut will edit smoothly. That is, there will not be a *jump cut*.

180° rule, the   The 180° rule involves an imaginary line along the action of the scene, between actors involved in a conversation or the direction of a chase. The 'rule' dictates that this line should be clearly established and that the consecutive shots should not be taken from opposite sides of the line.

35mm film   The measurement of film in millimetres (16mm, 35mm, 70mm) describes the length of the individual film negative frames which are exposed in order to capture an image; the larger the negative, the higher the resolution of the projected image. Larger format film such as 70mm, while superior in quality, is cumbersome to use and comparatively expensive to work with. There are also fewer cinemas able to screen formats other than the now standard 35mm print.

actualities   The French term given to the short non-fictional films made in the early period (1895–1906 or so). These films often consisted simply of people going about their everyday business, or of particular events (sporting contests, visiting dignataries).

alternative   Alternative cinema is defined with reference to **dominant**: it is an alternative (both economically and formally) to the dominant form. In any study concerning an 'alternative' cinema, the films would not only have to be examined in their own right, but also compared to contemporary dominant **Hollywood cinema**. A number of questions might have to be posed when analysing these alternative films: In what ways is this group of films different to the dominant cinema of the time? What are the possible reasons for the difference: cultural? economic? social? political? Could this 'alternative' way of making films, given the right conditions, have itself turned into the dominant cinema? The **Soviet cinema** of the 1920s, when compared to the Hollywood cinema of the same era, certainly may be regarded as alternative. In other words, alternative cinema offered a style of filmmaking that was radically different to the mass of films that was being produced in America.

animated documentary   In recent years, there has been an exponential rise in the production of animated documentary. This has essentially been characterised by the fusion of documentary tropes – non-fiction subject matter, participant interviews and analysis, use of statistical and archival evidence – and animation, resulting in a reclamation of what might be termed 'naive histories' in the spirit of offering alternative perspectives on the dominant grand narratives of contemporary social, cultural and national existence.

animation   The creation of artificial movement through a variety of techniques. Usually recorded one frame at a time, animation replicates naturalistic movement and creates the illusion of life in objects and images.

anthropomorphism   The tendency in **animation** to endow creatures with human attributes, abilities and qualities. This can redefine or merely draw attention to characteristics which are taken for granted in live-action representations of human beings.

aperture   The opening within a lens controlling the amount of light that passes through the lens to the film; the smaller the aperture, the less light will hit the film.

archetypes   Embodiments of a range of ideas and identities; ideal example of a role, person or certain personal traits.

art cinema   A term usually applied to films where the director has clearly exercised a high degree of control over the filmmaking process and thus the films may be viewed as a form of personal expression. This kind of filmmaking became common in Europe (hence the term 'European art cinema'), especially from the 1950s onwards, due to the funding structures and nature of the European film industries, which allowed directors greater artistic freedom than was to be found within the US system. In terms of style and content, art cinema is usually characterised by the way it differs from its commercial counterpart, **Hollywood cinema**: for instance, a drifting, episodic and open-ended narrative versus the tight cause-and-effect narrative of American cinema with its characteristic closure.

art-house   A crude shorthand way of referring to films in which artistic ambition and intellectual challenge are more important than the simple motive to provide entertainment. 'Great' art-house directors such as Bergman and Godard are unquestionably considered to be **auteurs**.

artisanal mode of production   A way of making films outside of an established 'industrial' means of production by using small budgets and minimal production teams. The term emphasises a more craft-like and personal process, hence allowing greater control of the filmmaking process.

associative mode   Approach to **documentary** which attempts to use footage in such a way as to provide the maximum degree of symbolic or metaphorical meaning on top of the literal information available in the image.

audience   Collectives of people responding to a film.

auteur   A French term that originated in the pages of the film journal *Cahiers du cinéma* in the 1950s to refer to directors who infuse their films with their distinctive personal vision through the salient manipulation of film technique. Auteurs, seen as genuine artists, were contrasted with metteurs-en-scène who were held to be technically competent directors who merely executed the processes of filmmaking without consistently stamping their 'personality' on the material from one film to the next. To study film as if it were the creative expression of a single individual, usually held to be the director, is often called **auteurism**.

auteurism   A critical approach to the study of film which identifies the director as responsible for whatever the viewer finds of thematic, stylistic or structural interest in a single film or across a body of work by one director.

avant-garde   Essentially non-narrative in structure and often intellectual in content, working in opposition to mainstream cinema. Literally the 'advanced guard' of experimental filmmakers who reject the dominant forms of mainstream cinema in favour of innovation and experiment in filmmaking, often producing non-narrative, non-illusionistic, sometimes abstract films. Avant-garde film is often self-conscious and frequently makes use of devices such as cuts to the camera crew, talking to the camera and scratching on film.

binary analysis   An approach which derives from cultural anthropology and particularly the work of Claude Lévi-Strauss. The study of binary opposites is a useful means of identifying structures at work in, for instance, the genre of a film.

biopic   A film which dramatises the biography of a real or imaginary person. It is usually characterised by a linear narrative. Examples of musical biopics range from *The Glenn Miller Story* (Anthony Mann, 1954) to *The Doors* (Oliver Stone, 1991).

blackface   Use of burnt cork or greasepaint to paint the face literally black. Originated in nineteenth-century minstrel theatre; used by both white and black performers.

blaxploitation   Movie studios' exploitation of what they believed were black urban audiences' tastes in film; beginning with Melvin Van Peebles's *Sweet Sweetback's Baadasssss Song*; concerned the years 1970 to 1974 in the USA; usually black-cast action films.

blue screen   A process that involves the subject being filmed in front of a blue screen. Optical manipulation of this footage creates imagery of the actor against a black background. In addition, the actor's silhouette is set against a clear background. Using these two elements as **mattes** it is possible to place the action into any scene required.

Bollywood   Bombay, the film capital of India.

bricolage   The putting together of features from different genres and styles, self-consciously and usually playfully. This is one of the principal characteristics of **postmodernism**.

butch   Description of behaviour patterns – such as aggression and sexual dominance – traditionally associated with masculinity.

caméra–stylo   A term coined by French writer Alexandre Astruc meaning 'camera–pen' and used to condense his argument for a 'personal' and self-expressive form of cinema.

camp   A critical attitude which involves looking at texts less as reflections of reality and more as constructed sets of words, images and sounds at a distance from reality. The attitude often involves irony or detachment when considering this distance.

canted framing   A framing where the camera is not level, causing the mise-en-scène to appear slanted within the frame.

carnivalesque   A term which refers to an atmosphere or attitude, found at carnivals and similar events, characterised by laughter, excess and vulgarity. Seen as a lower class resistance to the refined tastes of the dominant (upper and middle) classes.

CGI   An acronym for 'computer-generated imagery', meaning the use of digital software to create, change or enhance aspects of mise-en-scène.

character/personality animation   Many cartoons and more sophisticated adult animated films, for example, Japanese anime, are still dominated by 'character' or 'personality' animation, which prioritises exaggerated and sometimes caricatured expressions of human traits in order to direct attention to the detail of gesture and the range of human emotion and experience. This kind of animation is related to identifiable aspects of the real world and does not readily correspond with more abstract uses of the animated medium.

cinema apparatus   The power of cinema as a system of communication, controlling and holding the spectator in place.

cinematograph   Early term for cinema. Initially it referred to the camera/projector, but soon came to be used to refer to the practice and exhibition space.

cinema novo   'New cinema'. A movement of filmmakers that came to prominence in Brazil in the 1960s, the leading figure of which was Glauber Rocha. Influenced by the New Wave in France and the intellectual examples of Frantz Fanon and Che Guevara, 'cinema novo' called for filmmaking that emphasised 'the aesthetics of hunger' directed against a cinema of imperialism.

cinéma vérité   A French term, literally meaning 'cinema truth'. Cinéma vérité emerged out of the filmmaking practices of Jean Rouch in France. Based on Vertov's approach, it acknowledged the impact of the filmmaking process upon the recording of 'actuality', and more readily recognised the subjectivity of the filmmaker in securing filmic evidence of what took place. Rouch essentially suggests that the documentary form must be defined through the integrity and purpose of its author. The value and purpose of 'actuality' footage in regard to its delineation of documentary 'truth' is therefore in direct relationship to the intention of those who produce it. The term is sometimes confused with a US kind of filmmaking which is actually closer to direct cinema. The confusion stems from the common 'immediacy' that the films have – filming people with handheld cameras and portable sound-recording equipment – but cinéma vérité properly has a foundation of interaction between filmmaker and filmed, rather than the detachment seen in direct cinema films. Nevertheless, it is common to see a range of different films referred to as 'cinéma vérité (or sometimes just 'vérité'), and it is important to distinguish between them.

cinephilia   The notion of cinephilia refers to an intense love of, even obsession with, cinema. It implies both a way of watching and a way of speaking about film beyond the standard relationship between cinema and its spectator. Cinephiles are people who, in Andrew Sarris's phrase, 'love cinema beyond all reason', and who engage with film in highly specific ways.

classical Hollywood cinema   A particular narrative form which was exemplified by the films at the height of the studio system (1930–49). Although most Hollywood films still contain elements of classical narrative form, such as a central protagonist and a clear cause–effect relationship, film narratives, particularly since the success of movies such as *Pulp Fiction* (Tarantino, 1994), now play with plot and character with much greater flexibility.

close-up   Normally defined as a shot of the head from the neck up.

CNC   Centre Nationale de la Cinématographie, the chief body of the French state that oversees policy affecting filmmaking, including the subsidies accorded to cinema.

cognitivist processing   The process by which ideas that might be considered dangerous or anti-hegemonic are pulled in or incorporated into structures of order.

condensation   The compression of a set of narrative or aesthetic agendas within a minimal structural framework. Essentially, achieving the maximum amount of suggested information and implication from the minimum amount of imagery used.

consent decree   A court order made with the consent of both parties – the defendant and the plaintiff – which puts to rest the lawsuit brought against the former by the latter.

constructed   The quality of an idea being neither natural nor inevitable; having been assembled or otherwise created to appear natural or inevitable, often in the interest of a specific ideology.

conventions   Conventions are established procedures within a particular form which are identifiable by both the producer and the reader. The implication of the idea of conventions is that a form does not naturally mean anything, but it is an agreement between producer and user.

crane shot   A camera movement in which the camera moves above the ground in any direction (for which it is mounted on the arm of a special 'camera crane').

cross-cutting   Editing that alternates shots occurring in different story locations to imply that the events shown are occurring simultaneously.

cultural capital   First originating in the work of Pierre Bourdieu to describe the unequal distribution of cultural competencies and values principally across different social classes, the term has since been appropriated more generally to refer to the specific competencies and 'knowledges' of various social groupings, as well as the 'symbolic power' attained precisely from 'affiliation' to that group.

cultural studies   The cultural studies approach has gained academic respectability, partly due to the pioneering work of theorists such as Raymond Williams and Stuart Hall. Popular culture is now seen as a complex and worthy area of study, as being revealing about our society. Cultural studies has been influenced by Marxist theory, especially the theories of Antonio Gramsci, who used the term **hegemony** to describe the consensus that keeps the status quo in existence in society; capitalism keeps control by agreement of the people, yet there are still struggles for power which allow for change and adjustment in society. Cultural studies has, in more recent years, been a major influence on film studies, particularly in the study of popular film.

cut   The joining of two strips of film in the editing room, and the resulting immediate change from one image to another on-screen.

deconstruction   All media 'texts' are constructed. To understand all the components within each construction it is necessary to deconstruct the text and analyse all its elements. For example, the cartoon is made up of a number of specific aspects which define it as a unique cinematic practice, i.e. its frame-by-frame construction, its modes of representation and so on.

découpage   A term that means the 'shot breakdown' of a scene.

depth cues   These are provided by the arrangement of setting, lighting and props within the frame, which determines the degree to which the space depicted in the cinematic image appears to recede backwards and to take on three-dimensionality. Converging lines, size diminution, and the suggestion of different 'planes' in the fore-, middle- and background of the shot all accentuate the sense that there is a lot of space between the camera and the farthest visible object in the frame.

developmental animation   If *orthodox animation* emerges from Disney's 2D cel-animated tradition, developmental animation operates as the range of responses and oppositions to it. This might include the more overtly 'cartoonal' work by Warner Bros and MGM, or the range of approaches and styles from stop–motion animation, to clay animation, to cut-out animation and so on, which may still possess 'mimetic' references, but are nevertheless seeking to be more non-linear and non-objective in their approaches.

dialectical   A difficult term to define, as it has many different meanings. The *Collins English Dictionary* (2nd edn, 1986), for example, defines it as a 'disputation or debate, esp. intended to resolve differences between two views rather than to establish one of them as true'. The crucial factor to grasp in the context of Eisenstein's thinking, however, is the notion of change and the creation of a new order. Eisenstein would have defined dialectic with reference to **Marxist** philosophy, which believed that society was contradictory and in need of change.

diaspora   The African diaspora is the movement of people of African descent to other parts of the world; participants in the diaspora are diasporans. Struggle and resistance and the impulse to freedom inform the African diasporan memory, religion and culture. The transatlantic African diaspora began in the fifteenth century.

diegesis   The fictional world in which we presume the story takes place.

diegetic   The elements of a film that originate from directly within the film's **narrative**. For example, a popular song that is being played on the soundtrack would be diegetic if it were clear that it was coming from a source within the world of the film such as a car radio. See also **non-diegetic**.

dilution and amplication   The simultaneous capacity for **animation**, by virtue of its intrinsic artifice, to be viewed either as a language which dilutes its outcomes and effects, rendering them 'innocent' and 'dismissable', or as a language which inherently amplifies its literal, aesthetic and ideological perspectives, rendering them sometimes unacceptably challenging in their representational aspects.

direct cinema   American documentarists of the 1960s and 1970s believed that the advent of light, portable, technically sophisticated camera equipment enabled a break-through in the ways that documentary filmmaking could reveal personal and social 'truth'. The fact that the documentarist could literally film anywhere under any condi-tions meant that a greater intimacy could be achieved with the subject, heightening the sense that 'reality' was being directly observed, and that the viewer was party to the seemingly unmediated immediacy of the experience. Less controlled, unscripted, appar-ently spontaneous, the look and feel of 'direct cinema' arguably demonstrated a less deliberately authored approach.

discourse systems   A discourse is a mode of speech which has evolved to express the shared human activities of a community of people. Film studies has, like other academic disciplines, developed its own language – its own discourse system – to make possible the identification and 'mapping' of that area of human activity and experience with which it is concerned.

Disney dust   The term given to the glitter and sparkle that usually accompanies any form of magic or unearthly effect such as the glowing dust trail left by the flying Tinkerbell in Disney's *Peter Pan* (1953) and again in *Hook* (1991).

dissolve   Transition between shots with the first shot fading out to be simultaneously replaced by the second shot fading in. Often used to indicate an **ellipse**.

distribution   Division of the film industry concentrating on the marketing of film, connecting the producer with the exhibitor by leasing films from the former and renting them to the latter.

documentary   A non-fiction text using 'actuality' footage, which may include the live recording of events and relevant research material (i.e. interviews, statistics). This kind of text is usually informed by a particular point of view, and seeks to address a particular social issue which is related to and potentially affects the audience.

Dogme 95   The name given to a collective of Danish filmmakers united around the figures of directors Lars Von Trier, Thomas Winterberg and Kristian Levering. Dogme 95 was the name of a manifesto that committed filmmakers to observing a cinematic 'vow of chastity' involving an ultra-realist approach to filmmaking using only digital video cameras.

dominant   Refers to both economic strength and also to the dominant form or convention: dominant cinema in film studies is assumed to be **Hollywood**.

drama–documentary   Any format which attempts to re-create historical or typical events using performers, whether actors or not.

dystopia   A world of the future where everything has gone wrong.

eclecticism   An aesthetic style in which a new composition is composed wholly or in part from elements selected from a range of previous styles, forms, texts, genres, drawn from different periods and from both high and popular culture. This is one of the principal strategies of postmodern art. See also **intertextuality**, **palimpsest**, **recombinacy**, **self-reflexivity**.

economic presentation All the components are designed to help us read the **narrative**. An examination of the first few minutes of almost any mainstream fictional film will reveal a considerable amount of information about characters, their social situation and their motivation.

editing Sometimes also referred to as 'montage' (from the French 'monter', meaning 'to assemble'), this refers to the joining together of different pieces of film stock in post-production.

ellipse A gap in the continuity of time and space of the narrative – usually indicated in editing by means of a **dissolve** or **wipe**.

emblematic A typical representation, in this case symbolic of England.

essentialism A term describing the idea of a single, firmly fixed identity as regards **gender**, **sexuality** and other social elements. The opposite attitude is often described as social constructionism, implying that such identities are a product of one's society, attitudes and upbringing, and can vary or be changed.

establishing shot A shot using distant framing, allowing the viewer to see the spatial relations between characters and the set.

ethics Concerning morality, or codes of conduct. There is a strong ethical discourse running through the history of documentary, and debates to be had about the ethical dimension of things like reconstruction, filming people without their consent, informing the viewer of the extent of filmmaker intervention, and so on.

exclusive run Where a film is screened in only one movie theatre.

exhibition Division of the film industry concentrating on the public screening of film.

experimental animation Experimental animation is the avant-garde of the animation field, seeking to innovate with new styles and techniques, and often in purely abstract terms of expression. It should be stressed though that all forms of **animation** have 'experimental' aspects, and this both makes the form 'modern' and 'popular'.

exposition The use of voiceover or direct-to-camera address by a figure who is essentially directing the viewer in the reception of information and argument.

extra-textual In a broad sense, designates the 'outside' of the film/text, the range of cultural texts which relate in some way to the film/text; in a narrower sense refers to the non-filmic intertexts which in varying degrees relate to the film/text (such as marketing and promotional materials, film reviews, and so on).

extreme close-up A framing in which the object shown takes up virtually the whole screen (as in a shot of a body part, such as a leg or an eye).

extreme long shot A framing in which the object shown (typically a human body shown from head to toe) fills a small fraction of the screen.

eye-line match The 'eye-line' match is another convention of Hollywood editing that encourages identification with the protagonist(s), as the shots from their eye-line suggest a sense of **realism**.

fade An editing technique in which one of the juxtaposed images is a black screen. With a 'fade-out' the image slowly darkens; with a 'fade-in' the image slowly emerges out of darkness.

fade and mixes Where one image fades from view to be replaced by a separate image. When this is done with two images simultaneously the effect is known as a 'mix' or a **dissolve**.

faster speed film speed/speed of film stock Sensitivity of the photographic emulsion of the film to light; a higher speed of film will require less light (i.e. a smaller aperture may be used) in order to produce a properly exposed image; faster speed film stock tends to provide greater contrast in tone than a slower film stock.

feminism This is based on the belief that we live in a society where women are still unequal to men; that women have lower status than men and have less power, particularly economic power. Feminists argue that the media reinforces the status quo by representing a narrow range of images of women; for instance, woman as carer, as passive object, as an object of desire. Many feminists now argue that the range of representations for both male and female is limited and slow to change. The relationship between gender and power relations in society may be seen as central to feminist thinking.

femme Description of behaviour patterns – such as gentleness, sexual passivity, concern with dress and appearance – traditionally associated with femininity.

femme fatale A term which originated in critical discourses on film noir; it refers to dangerous, seductive female characters who are normally literally 'fatal', in that they cause the death of the hero.

fetishism Freudian theorists argue that fetishism is linked to the castration complex and is a form of male denial of the threat and fear of castration by the female. The female is made less threatening, more reassuring, by substituting her lack of a phallus with a fetish object such as high heels, long hair or turning her into a fetish object by exaggerating or fragmenting parts of the body such as lips or breasts.

film noir A term developed by French film critics in the postwar period to describe a number of films produced in the 1940s. It has subsequently become a marketing device used to describe films with some of the lighting and narrative conventions of the period.

first-run Important cinemas would show films immediately upon their theatrical release (or their 'first-run'). Smaller, local cinemas would show films on subsequent runs, hence the terms second-run, third-run and so on.

fly-on-the-wall A term associated with a style of documentary filmmaking which attempts to present events as though the presence of the camera and film crew had not influenced them in any way.

focal length This refers to the ability of a lens to bend the incoming light on to the film plane; a shorter focal length will provide a wider angle of view (which dictates what appears within the frame); a longer focal length will provide a narrower field of view but greater magnification of what is shown; for any given set of conditions a shorter focal length will provide a larger depth of field.

foley stage Named after the sound editor Jack Foley, the foley stage is a sound-recording room equipped with a screen and the necessary items for the creation of sound effects.

formation Each of us comes to a film with our own personal 'formation' – the result of all our life experiences. These will predispose us to certain interpretations of character, certain attitudes towards moral and political issues and certain emotional responses to events.

framing The choices made about what to include within the frame and what to exclude.

free publicity Free coverage of subjects that the media feel are newsworthy.

gay A description of strong, positive sexual love and attraction between members of the same sex, used by extension to describe cultural products, such as film and video, concerned with similar themes. Mainly referring to males, it can also be used for any person.

gender   A name for the social and cultural construction of a person's sex and **sexuality**. Gender, sex and sexuality can overlap but are by no means an exact match. It is this 'mismatch' which has generated a fascinating body of film production and criticism.

hegemony   A set of ideas, attitudes or practices that becomes so **dominant** that we forget they are rooted in choice and the exercise of power. They appear to be 'common sense' because they are so ingrained, and any alternative seems 'odd' or potentially threatening by comparison. Hegemony is the **ideological** made invisible. In relation to the development of cinema, it can be seen how **Hollywood** developed hegemonic status and power. The Hollywood form of genre-based **narrative** realist film is considered a 'common-sense' use of the medium. Other forms of cinema, by comparison, are more or less 'odd'. In looking at the early history of cinema we can begin to understand how and why Hollywood assumed this position.

heterosexual   A word used to name and describe a person whose main sexual feelings are for people of the opposite sex.

high-angle shot   A framing where the camera looks down from above on to the objects or scene filmed.

high-key lighting   This term refers to a lighting design (normally using a three-point system) where there is little contrast between the light and shadowed areas of the frame.

historiography   The study of how history is written – or constructed. This has become acutely important as we become more aware of how **narratives** are the result of processes of selection and construction. Film history, like other kinds of history, needs to be reflected upon, not just in relation to its content, but also in relation to the processes by which it has been written.

Hollywood cinema   In classical Hollywood cinema, the editing is designed to be 'invisible'. It is intended to allow the audience closer views and to see the point of view of different characters. The editing is used essentially to clarify what is taking place in the **narrative**. This type of editing had become **dominant** in Hollywood filmmaking by approximately 1920.

hommage   The French word for an act of paying homage, sincere respect.

homoerotic   A description of a text – prose, poem, film, painting, photograph – conveying an enjoyable sense of same-sex attraction.

homophobia   Irrational prejudice and hatred against a person because of their **homosexuality**.

homosexual   A word used to name and describe a person whose main sexual feelings are for people of the same sex. Mainly, but not exclusively, used in reference to males.

hypermediated culture   This describes the current state of post-media-saturated culture in which forms of work, leisure and entertainment, as well as many of the taken-for-granted activities that structure daily life, are predicted on, and determined by, the all-pervasive presence of highly integrated media forms and technologies. The notion of hypermediation, therefore, refers to the way that our experience of the world is channelled through an endless network of media texts.

iconic   The iconic is defined by the **dominant** signs that signify a particular person or object – Chaplin, for example, would be defined by a bowler hat, a moustache, a cane and some old boots; Hitler would be defined by a short, parted hairstyle and a small 'postage stamp' moustache.

iconoclasts   Filmmakers and documentarists committed to challenging the received construction and meanings of images, partially through the critique of those images, and mainly through the reconfiguration of imagery in a subjective style.

iconography   The visual codes of setting, props and clothing which enable us to recognise a film as belonging to a certain genre or type. It shares similarities with **mise-en-scène**.

identification   The process of identification allows us to place ourselves in the position of particular characters, either throughout or at specific moments in a movie. The devices involved include subjectivity of viewpoint (we see the world through their eyes, a shared knowledge, we know what and only what they know), and a sharing in their moral world, largely through **narrative** construction.

ideological effects   Effects of political significance, manipulating the spectator into an acceptance of specific ways of thinking about and relating to the world.

ideological function   Ideology is the system of ideas, values and beliefs held by individuals or groups within society. Ideological function refers to the way in which **ideology** is disseminated through films or other cultural forms. Audiences may of course refuse to accept the **dominant** ideological meaning in a film.

ideology   Although a complex issue, ideology may be seen as the dominant set of ideas and values which inform any one society or culture, but which are imbued in its social behaviour and representative texts at a level that is not necessarily obvious or conscious. There are two key definitions of this term, one provided by the nineteenth-century German philosopher Karl Marx, the other by the twentieth-century French Marxist philosopher Louis Althusser, drawing on Marx's original ideas. For Marx, ideology was the dominant set of beliefs and values existent within society, which sustained power relations. For Althusser, ideology consisted of the representations and images which reflect society's view of 'reality'. Ideology thus refers to 'the myths that a society lives by'. An ideological stance is normally politicised and historically determined.

illustrative mode   An approach to **documentary** which attempts to illustrate directly what the commentary/voiceover is saying.

impact editing   Editing that produces violent contrast between images, most often by switching between close- and long-shot scales.

impresario   Organiser of public entertainments; a manager of, especially, an operatic or concert company.

incoherent cinema   Influenced by the 'Incoherents', artists working between 1883 and 1891, a movement principally led by Cohl. This kind of **animation** was often surreal, anarchistic and playful, relating seemingly unrelated forms and events in an often irrational and spontaneous fashion. Lines tumble into shapes and figures in temporary scenarios before evolving into other images.

independent   This is a highly problematic term meaning different things in different situations. In the contemporary film industry it implies a production realised outside one of the Majors. It may be usefully divided into two areas. First, independent mainstream production, which aims to compete with the big studios but without any large financial backing, and thus finds it difficult to survive. Palace Films was one such casualty; the success of *The Crying Game* came too late to save its demise. Second, the term is used to describe filmmaking outside the mainstream sector, for instance, film workshops, **avant-garde** film, **feminist** film. The boundaries between these two areas are not always clear and may overlap.

inexportable   Critical term used to denote films of modest budget and ambition, only intended for distribution to their home markets. Adapted from Jean-Pierre Jeanncolas' use of the term with regard to certain French comedies.

Institutional Mode of Representation/IMR   The IMR is a broad categorisation of systems of **film form** and **narrative** characterising mainstream cinema from around 1915 onwards. It was perceived as replacing the Primitive Mode of Representation (a set of conventions used in early cinema between 1895 and 1905) as a gradual process in the first twenty years of cinema.

intentional fallacy   A phrase coined by Monroe Beardsley to describe the difference between a text's meaning(s) and what its author intended. As such, criticism dependent on, or directed towards, uncovering the intentions of the author/artist falls foul of an 'intentional fallacy' insofar as the meaning of a text is not fixed within it, but created in the historically situated act of reading.

intermedia   The relations that exist between cinema, the film industry and other media at the levels of both capitalist business practices and textual forms.

internet   A system of interlinking computers in a worldwide network (www/world-wide web). Since the internet was privatised in April 1995 the rise in monthly traffic on the net has been such that it represents a hundredfold increase in less than three years.

interpellation   The process whereby the spectator of a film is drawn inside the psychic and physical life of the fictional world depicted by the film.

intertextuality   This term, strongly linked with **postmodernism**, designates, in its narrow sense, the ways in which a film either explicitly or implicitly refers to other films (through allusion, imitation, parody or pastiche, for example), or in its broader sense, the various relationships one (film) text may have with other texts.

iris-in/iris-out   Editing techniques in which the transition from one image to another is marked by the closing and reopening of an 'iris' or circular hole in the centre of the frame.

low-angle shot   A framing where the camera looks up from below at the objects or scene filmed.

jump-cut   An explicit and self-conscious editing decision to demonstrate a 'jump' in time, and to disrupt normal models of continuity editing.

juxtaposition   In film studies, this usually refers to two different shots that have been joined together to make a contrast.

Kinematoscope   Edison's first movie camera was relatively sophisticated and employed a series of sequential photographs mounted on a wheel and rotated.

lesbian   A word used to name and describe a woman whose main sexual feelings are for other women. Coined as a medical term in the late nineteenth century, the word has been invested post-Stonewall with new ideas of openness and liberation. It may also be used to describe cultural products, such as film and video, dealing with lesbian themes.

LGBT   A set of initials standing for lesbian, gay, bisexual and transgender. A term now increasingly used by a large number of organisations and bodies in the English-speaking world. It is favoured because of the wide spectrum of sexualities covered, and because certain negative connotations of 'gay' or 'queer' are avoided.

liberal humanist   A political perspective in which emphasis is placed upon an openness of democratic discourse and a multiplicity of perspectives which directly relate to the actual experiences of people and the fundamental principles relating to what it is to be 'human'.

'look', the   Also, **gaze.** The 'look' and the 'gaze' developed as central concepts in relation to the control of the spectator. Cinematic looking has also been associated with theories of desire and pleasure, theories often founded in psychoanalysis.

long shot   A framing in which the object shown (typically a human body shown from head to toe) fills around three-quarters of the height of the screen.

low-key image   Light from a single source producing light and shade.

low-key lighting   This term refers to a lighting design where there is a stark contrast between the light and shadowed areas of the frame. Frequently it is produced using only one light source.

magic lantern   A projection system comprising a light source and a lens used to project an image. Usually oil-lamp-fired, though many were later converted to electricity. Earliest known use was by Athanasius Kircher, recorded in a work published in 1646.

mainstream   Feature-length narrative films created for entertainment and profit. Mainstream is usually associated with **Hollywood cinema**, regardless of where the film is made.

Marxist theory   Argues that those who have the means of production have control in a capitalist society. The dominant class have control of the means of production and have an interest in perpetuating the dominant ideology. More recently, exponents of Althusserian Marxism, particularly post-1968, have argued that **mainstream narrative cinema** reinforces the capitalist system and that a revolutionary cinema is needed to challenge the dominant ideology.

masala movie   Spicy Indian movie overloaded with emotion.

match on action   A cut which joins two spaces together by virtue of the fact that an action shown in the first shot is then completed in the second.

match-move   Shots that have separate elements within them that need to be accurately matched, frame by frame. Usually involves live-action elements being coupled to **animation** or effects elements.

mattes   Opaque images that mask-out certain areas of the film negative. Subsequent passes through the camera allow the initial matted-out space to be exposed with another image.

matte shot   A type of shot in which aspects of mise-en-scène are photographed separately and then combined into one image in post-production. Opaque images mask out certain areas of the film negative, and subsequent passes through the camera allow the initially matted-out space to be exposed with another image. Nowadays, matting is often achieved using 'blue screen', a process where action is filmed in front of a blue screen; this footage is then used to create an image of the performers in front of a dark background, and a silhouette of the performer against a clear background, which is used to 'cut out' space for the performer in the scene on to which the action is to be matted.

mediation   A key concept in film and media theory, it implies that there are always structures, whether human or technological, between an object and the viewer, involving inevitably a partial and selective view.

medium long shot   Also known as the 'plan Américain' because of its frequency in classical Hollywood, this is a framing in which the human body is shown from mid-calf or knees upwards.

medium shot   A framing in which the human body is shown from the waist upwards.

merchandising   Where manufacturers pay a film company to use a film title or image on their products.

metamorphosis   The ability of a figure, object, shape or form to relinquish its seemingly fixed properties and mutate into an alternative model. This transformation is literally enacted within the animated film, and acts as a model by which the process of change becomes part of the narrative of the film. A form starts as one thing and ends up as something different.

metanarrative   Refers to an overarching account of some area of human experience that attempts to make complete sense of that area. Meta-theory is, similarly, an overarching, all-embracing system for explaining some area of human experience. In film studies there has been a move away from metanarratives in historical studies and away from meta-theory in theoretical studies.

mise-en-scène   Refers to both *what* is filmed (setting, props, costumes, etc.) and to *how* it is filmed (cinematographic properties of the shot, such as depth of field, focus, lighting, and camera movement). In an attempt to counter the imprecision of the term, this latter aspect is sometimes called mise-en-shot. Mise-en-scène is one way of producing meaning in films which can be both straightforward and extremely complex, depending upon the intentions and skill of the director (the metteur-en-scène: see **auteur**).

Modernism   This refers to a dramatically experimental trend within the arts (painting, sculpture, architecture, literature, music and film) which grew up at the start of the twentieth century, encompassing a wide array of movements (Expressionism, Vorticism, Symbolism, Imagism, Surrealism) along with the innovations of individual artists not directly affiliated with a particular movement. Modernism involved a rejection of nineteenth-century styles, traditions and ideas, and a self-conscious (or 'self-reflexive') approach to aesthetic forms, in which artistic expression was itself explored, questioned and reinvented.

modernist   A term used to describe early twentieth-century developments in art, literature, music, film and theatre which rejected **realism** as the dominant tradition in the arts. Modernist art is characterised by experiment and innovation, and modernist artists, because of their **avant-garde** practices, inevitably constitute a cultural élite.

modernist device   Any device which undercuts the invisible telling of the story. A modernist device draws attention to itself and makes us aware of the construction of the narrative. It would be unclear in this instance whether the device is a consciously modernist one or a primitive one which unconsciously draws attention to itself.

montage   From the French word meaning 'to edit', montage means the assembling of pieces of footage to form a whole. In film studies it usually refers to the style of fast editing adopted by the **Soviet** filmmakers of the 1920s.

movement image   A term coined by Gilles Deleuze to refer to a cinema in which the image is at the service of the **narrative**, and in which the **audience** experience is of the 'movement' of the film towards the closure of narrative resolution.

'movie brat' generation   A term that refers to the generation of American filmmakers who, after the decline of the Hollywood studio system in the 1950s, began to make films independently and were heavily influenced by the French New Wave and European **art cinema** of the 1960s. Such directors include Martin Scorsese and Francis Ford Coppola.

multiple exposures   A number of exposures being made on a single frame of film. This usually entails the film being rewound in the camera for subsequent passes and further exposures. Multiple exposures are normally made with the assistance of **mattes**.

multiple run   Where a film is shown simultaneously at a number of screens.

music hall   Place for singing and dancing, variety and other entertainments.

myth   A key term within media and cultural studies, a myth is something which is not true but which is repeated so frequently that it becomes part of the 'reality' of the people who share it. In some instances it can become part of a culture's 'common sense'. Myth is a means by which the **ideology** of a culture takes form.

narrative   The idea that films have a primary function of telling a story.

narrative economy   The efficiency with which a film tells its story. **Classical Hollywood** films have often been described as having a high degree of narrative economy, with few scenes or shots which do not contribute in some way to the telling of the story. Some genres, such as musicals or epics, where spectacle is an important element of the film's pleasures, may be said to have a lesser degree of narrative economy.

national cinema   A term commonly used to describe the filmic output of a particular country and to distinguish it from **Hollywood** filmmaking. It has also developed as an approach within film studies to explore how films are shaped by nationally prevailing socio-political and economic conditions. This approach to the study of cinema leads to an understanding of film as expressing or articulating a sense of national identity. However, defining a national cinema and adopting this approach can be problematic. For instance, rapidly changing national geographies, the increasing trend for pan-European funding for film projects and European co-productions make it increasingly difficult to clearly delineate a single country of origin.

negotiated reading   A negotiated reading of a media text is one that involves a certain give-and-take between our own views and experiences and those presented in the film text by its creator.

neo-colonialism   The domination by a powerful, usually Western nation of another nation that is politically independent, but has a weak economy greatly dependent on trade with the powerful nation.

newsreels   Films consisting of six or seven short topical news stories released to cinemas twice a week and shown as part of the full supporting programme. Newsreels were produced from the 1910s to the early 1970s by which time they had largely been overtaken by television news. They were also shown in specialist news cinemas, often located in or near big railway stations.

noise   In the film industry, 'noise' refers to any barrier to successful communication.

non-diegetic   Refers to any element that remains outside the world of the film, such as voiceovers, credits and mood-setting music, that does not originate from the world of the film.

NRA (National Recovery Administration) programme   Government programme of the 1930s designed to rescue the US economy from the Great Depression (commonly known as the 'New Deal').

obscene   A work, or part thereof, may be found 'obscene' if it has a tendency to deprave and corrupt (i.e. make morally bad) a significant proportion of those people likely to see it.

oligopoly   A state of limited competition between a small group of producers or sellers.

oppositional reading   A reading of a media text which rejects the intentions of the creator of the text. It is most often associated with dis- or unpleasure. See also **preferred reading** and **negotiated reading**.

orthodox animation   Orthodox animation emerges from Disney's cel-animated tradition of work, augmented in the contemporary era by 2D and 3D computer-generated applications. This kind of **animation** has a correspondence to a mimetic model of work – the use of configuration, classical narrative models, consistent aesthetic conditions – and echoes live-action practices, and 'real-world' conventions, while embracing the more 'fantastic' possibilities of the open language of animation.

overheard exchange   The recording of seemingly spontaneous dialogue between two or more participants engaged in conversation/observation.

overlapping editing   Editing where shots repeat part or all of the action shown in the previous shot.

paid advertising   Promotion on TV, radio, billboards, printed media and the **internet**.

palimpsest   Defined literally, a palimpsest is a manuscript written over a previous text that has been entirely or partially erased. In a figurative sense, however, the term is often used to describe a film or text with multiple levels of meaning created through dense layers of **intertextuality**. In this way, the term has become associated with **postmodern** aesthetics.

pan/whip-pan   A 'pan' is a camera movement in which the camera itself remains in the same place but swivels round horizontally; a 'whip-pan' is a very fast pan.

participant observation   A social science methodology where the researchers immerse themselves in the social context/group they are going to be studying, often for years at a time. In documentary terms, such an approach arguably leads to more 'natural' responses, as the subjects have become used to the filmmakers and cameras.

pastiche   From the Italian verb 'to paste', this refers to a patchwork of references from, or imitations of, other works of art.

patent pool   An association of companies, operating collectively in the marketplace by pooling the patents held by each individual company.

patriarchal society   A society in which men have power and control. Women are generally disadvantaged and have lower status. It could be argued that we no longer live in a patriarchal society, but in a society in which men and women have equal opportunities. For instance, in the US, Sherry Lansing is head of Paramount Pictures and in the UK a number of women now have key roles in the media, particularly the BBC, where there are now women heads of channel programming. But many **feminists** would still argue that we have a long way to go in terms of politics, philosophy and economics before we live in a society in which men and women can be considered equal.

performative   A person or object's capacity to produce an effect beyond the literal or stated intent or meaning.

performativity   A concept derived from **cultural studies** whereby social groups develop self-awareness through shared actions that develop tastes, habits and attitudes in common. When applied to **gender**, you may wish to consider the popular conflation of masculinity and football, or femininity and shopping.

persistence of vision   The phenomenon of persistence of vision is due to the momentary retention of an image on the eye's retina. This retention was found to be approximately one-tenth of a second by Chevalier d'Arcy in 1765 when he successfully carried out one of the first systematic scientific studies and presented his findings to the French Académie des Sciences.

Phenakistoscope   Invented by the Belgian physicist Joseph Plateau in 1832, this is an optical device consisting of a disk with slots cut into its edge. When rotated, images on one side can be viewed with the aid of a mirror. The resulting stroboscopic images give the illusion of movement.

pink triangle   A symbol originally worn by **homosexual** prisoners in Nazi concentration camps which was later taken up by **lesbian** and **gay** people as a reminder of past oppression and an icon of liberation.

pitch   The height or depth of a musical sound as determined by its frequency relative to other notes.

pixillation   The frame-by-frame recording of deliberately staged live-action movement to create the illusion of movement impossible to achieve by naturalistic means, i.e. figures spinning in mid-air or skating across grass. This can also be achieved by particular ways of editing material.

play-back   Pre-recording of songs using good singers but with non-singing actors lip-synchronising on screen.

pluralistic multiple   Refers in this instance to the fragmentation of society into different ethnic, social and cultural groups.

poetics of presence   This may be used to describe moments of stillness in a film, such as a close-up of a face or a landscape shot. A complex range of ideas and emotions are contained within images that are not driven, as they are so often, by movement and action. We may become more aware of time, the relationship between past time and present time, and so more aware of the historical moment of the image. Whole films may be developed on the basis of creating this complex sense of 'presence'. (Compare Deleuze's opposition between the movement image and the time image.)

politique des auteurs   A term evolved from the *Cahiers du cinéma* approach to the study of French and **Hollywood cinema** in the 1950s, which attempted to identify directors who brought something personal to their films. It is used to describe particular bodies of filmmaking which are deemed to be characterised by the distinctive styles and visions of their directors. *See also* **auteurism**.

polysemic   Having many meanings; a polysemic text is likely to be less stable, more hotly contested by different sections of an audience.

postfeminism   The notion of postfeminism is a contested term used by different people in different ways to mean different things. It is used here to indicate a version of the popularised, and to some extent individualised, **feminism** that is different from (mainly in the sense that it comes after) the highly politicised feminism of the 1970s.

postmodern   Used by critics in a number of different ways, it can refer to the contemporary historical moment (the period after modernity); an artistic or aesthetic style which privileges surface appearances over 'deep meaning' or 'truth'. It is characterised by strategies of irony, **intertextuality**, pastiche, **bricolage**, eclecticism, **self-reflexivity**, and a theoretical position which adopts a sceptical attitude towards totalising notions of truth, reality, and progress. Postmodernism argues that theories such as psychoanalysis and **Marxism** are no longer viable because they attempt to give an all-encompassing view or understanding of society and culture. Postmodernism emphasises the fragmentation of viewpoints within our culture and the notion that there is no one philosophical truth.

post-structuralism   The critical movement away from an emphasis on the film text and the 'machinery' of cinema to an emphasis on the spectator's decoding of the text in order to create meaning. This represents a rejection of some aspects of the deterministic **Marxist**/Freudian theories at the heart of structuralism while still recognising that the spectator is himself or herself 'determined' by a range of factors (compare with **structuralism**).

post-synchronised   Referring to the process of adding and modifying some or all of a film's sound in a studio after the film has been shot and synchronising these sounds to the image track (also known as 'post-synching').

Praxinoscope   Invented by the Frenchman Emile Raynaud in 1878, this device was a more advanced and sophisticated version of the **Zoetrope**. Utilising mirrors and its own discrete light source, this was the forerunner of Raynaud's spectacular and charming, though ultimately short-lived, Theatre Optique.

preferred reading   A preferred reading of a media text is one in which the spectator takes the intended meaning, finding it relatively easy to align with the messages and attitudes of those who have created the text. See also **oppositional reading** and **negotiated reading**.

proactive observationalism   Documentary filmmaking in which specific choices are made about what material is to be recorded in relation to the previous observation of the camera operator/director.

production   Division of the film industry concentrating on the making of film.

propaganda   The systematic construction of a text in which the **ideological** principles of a political stance are promoted, endorsed and made attractive to the viewer in order to influence the viewer's beliefs and preferences. Such a text may often include critical and exploitative ideas and imagery about oppositional stances. 'Point of view' in these texts is wholly informed by political bias and a specificity of intention to persuade the viewer of the intrinsic 'rightness' of the authorial position.

proto-animation   Early live-action cinema demonstrated certain techniques which preceded their conscious use as a method in creating **animation**. This is largely with regard to stop-motion, mixed media and the use of **dissolves** to create the illusion of metamorphosis in early **trick films**.

psychoanalytic theory   Based on the theories of Freud and, more recently, Lacan. Feminists argue that aspects of psychoanalysis are questionable because they are based on patriarchal assumptions that woman is inferior to man. Freud found female **sexuality** difficult and disturbing. Lacan argues that the mother is seen as lacking by the child because she has no phallus. Uncertainty about the role of the female in psychoanalytic theory has been picked up on by a number of feminists such as Mulvey, De Lauretis and Modleski, who question the inevitability of Freud and Lacan's theories which emphasise the importance of the phallus, penis envy and patriarchal supremacy.

queer   Originally a negative term for (mainly male) **homosexuals**, this word has recently been reappropriated by critics, artists and audiences to describe a challenging range of critical work and cultural production among **lesbians** and **gays**, with an emphasis on diversity of race, nationality and cultural experience. The term is deliberately used to embrace a wider range of sexualities: lesbian, gay, bisexual and transgendered people and issues.

race films   Black-cast movies that were made for segregated African American audiences before 1950, most often by an African American director. In early twentieth-century parlance, the 'race' in terms like race film, race music or race woman indicates pride and affirmation. For example, a race woman is a woman who is proud of her race and does good works on behalf of African Americans.

racist iconography   Images that accompany racist rhetoric or racist contexts.

reactive observationalism   Documentary filmmaking in which the material recorded is filmed as spontaneously as possible subject to the immediacy of observation by the camera operator/director.

reading a film   Although films are viewed and heard, the concept of 'reading' a film implies an active process of making sense of what we are experiencing.

realism/reality   The concept of the 'real' is problematic in cinema, and is generally used in two different ways. First, the extent to which a film attempts to mimic reality so that a fictional film can appear indistinguishable from documentary. Second, the film can establish its own world and can, by consistently using the same conventions, establish the credibility of this world. In this later sense a sciencefiction film such as *RoboCop* can be as realistic as a film set in a contemporary and recognisable world, such as *Sleepless in Seattle*.

With regard to animation, the animated form in itself most readily accommodates 'the fantastic', but Disney preferred to create a hyperrealism which located his characters in plausibly 'real' worlds which also included fantasy elements in the narrative.

reality TV   A relatively recent development in television, and a form of highly structured programme using observational material of ordinary people. The programmes have a '**documentary**' basis in the sense that they use acuality footage, but they are often shaped to fit specific formats (neighbours from hell, the rise of a successful business, a game show involving weekly tasks). In this respect, reality TV is a good example of how documentary can be taken and recontextualised by contemporary television to suit its schedules.

reappropriation   The process whereby a previously oppressed group takes a negative term and turns it around to invest it with new meanings of power and liberation. Examples include 'black', 'virago' and '**queer**'.

recombinacy   The aesthetic process of combining of elements drawn from a range of genres, styles, forms and periods in a new text/film. This is one of the principal aesthetic strategies of **postmodern** art. See also **intertextuality**, **palimpsest**, **self-reflexivity**.

reduced animation   Animation may be literally the movement of one line which, in operating through time and space, may take on characteristics which an audience may perceive as expressive and symbolic. This form of minimalism constitutes reduced animation, which takes as its premise 'less is more'. Literally an eye movement or the shift of a body posture becomes enough to connote a particular feeling or meaning. This enables the films to work in a mode which has an intensity of suggestion.

reflexive/performative documentary   Documentary which is much more subjective and **self-reflexive** in its construction, foregrounding the arbitrariness and relativity of 'objectivity', '**reality**' and 'truth'.

representation   The media *re*-presents information to its audience, who are encouraged by the mainstream media to see its output as a 'window on the world', as reflecting reality. Yet the process of representing information is highly complex and highly selective. Many **feminists** argue that the way notions of **gender** are represented by the media perpetuates and reinforces the values of a **patriarchal society**; for instance, men tend to take on strong, active roles, while women are shown as passive and relying on their attractiveness. There are exceptions to such narrow stereotyping: the 'strong' woman shown by Ripley in the *Alien* series and the two heroines in *Thelma and Louise* could be seen as positive, although rather more cynically they could be seen merely as 'role-reversal' films and thus as having purely novelty value. Representations often make use of **stereotypes** because they are a shorthand, quick and easy way of using information. It could be argued that the media production process encourages the use of stereotypes due to the pressure of time and budget. Many feminists point out that because so few women hold key positions in the media hierarchies, representations of women are bound to be from a male perspective.

rhetorical   Designed to persuade. Rhetorical strategies in **documentary** are those that relate to the film or programme's argument. This could be explicit (e.g. a voiceover or presenter actually stating what the argued points are), or it could be less immediately obvious (e.g. a filmmaker might cut from an image of a political leader to a library shot of a firing squad; this could be seen as an argument against the politician).

Russian cinema   The body of films made in Tsarist Russia between 1907 and 1919.

Russian formalism   A literary theory which developed in Russia in the early 1920s, which sought to establish a scientific basis for the study of literature and literary effects.

saturation run   Where a film is shown simultaneously at an enormous number of screens (usually a minimum of 1,000 in the US–Canadian market), accompanied by heavy media promotion.

schema   A concept used in studies of the human thinking process. When we are confronted by a new experience, we look for familiar patterns that allow us to orient ourselves and make sense of what is in front of us.

scopophilia   Freudian term meaning the 'pleasure in looking', introduced to film analysis by Laura Mulvey, who pointed out that women are usually depicted in a passive role and are looked at, while men take on an active role, they look.

self-reflexivity Used to describe films or texts which selfconsciously acknowledge or reflect upon their own status as fictional artefacts and/or the processes involved in their creation. This is one of the principal aesthetic strategies of **postmodern** art. See also **intertextuality**, **palimpsest**, **recombinacy**.

semiotics The use of semiotics in film analysis has developed out of the theories of Ferdinand de Saussure, who argued that the meanings of words are not natural but are learned and socially constructed. Therefore, the meaning of a word, or in the case of film an image or sound, may be complex and layered.

sensory motor mechanism Refers to the mental processing of audio-visual information in ways that allow us to 'place' and 'manage' the film experience. There is an implication that the automatic nature of this processing is part of the relatively passive pleasure of **mainstream** commercial cinema. Other kinds of cinema may disrupt the sensory motor mechanism.

sex A word used to denote and describe a person's physical type according to his or her genital make-up. In academic discourse, this is primarily a scientific term.

sexuality A name for the sexual feelings and behaviour of a person. When applied to groups of people (e.g. **heterosexuals**), ideas of social attitude and organisation are implied.

shot–reverse shot Editing technique whereby conversations are filmed by cutting alternately between the faces of the interlocutors who are facing each other.

shot/take One uninterrupted (uncut) image onscreen whether it is shot with a mobile or a stationary camera. During shooting, a 'take' refers to a single, uninterrupted recording of the camera before the director calls 'cut'.

shot scale This refers to the range of shots which suggest the apparent distance of an object from the camera; it is conventionally defined according to the framing of the human form.

social realism A form of **realism** which tries to capture in a 'truthful' way the lives of industrial working-class communities. Also known as 'working-class realism' and often used in relation to the 'new wave' films of late 1950s–early 1960s British cinema.

sophisticated hyperconsciousness A term used by Jim Collins to describe the extreme 'knowingness' and high degree of media literacy evinced by both contemporary cinema and its audience.

sound-bridge An audio connection between scenes, where sound from one scene continues into the beginning of the scene which follows, or where sound belonging to the opening of a scene begins during the close of the scene which precedes it.

Soviet cinema Films made in the Soviet Union between October 1920 and 1991.

spectator The individual responding to a film, as distinct from the collective response of an **audience**. Spectator study concentrates on the consumption of films that are 'popular' and are geared towards providing typical forms of cinematic pleasure – spectacle, emotion, plot, resolution – with conventional narrative and generic forms.

squash and stretch Many cartoon characters are constructed in a way that resembles a set of malleable and attached circles which may be elongated or compressed to achieve an effect of dynamic movement. When animators 'squash and stretch' these circles they effectively create the physical space of the character and a particular design structure within the overall pattern of the film. Interestingly, early Disney shorts had characters based on 'ropes' rather than circles and this significantly changes the look of the films.

star system The industrial apparatus which enables the building up of stars and their centrality to the advertising and promotion of films. This includes star contracts, ancillary advertising deals, fan magazines and so forth.

steadicam A technical development from the late 1970s that permits the use of a camera held by hand which walks with the action, but with the steadiness of a camera moving on rails.

stereotype A set of commonly expected behaviour patterns and characteristics based on role (e.g. mother) or personal features such as race, age or sexuality. In society and cultural products, the depiction of a stereotype becomes a form of communication shorthand and often reflects the attitudes of dominant social groups.

stereotyping A quick and easy way of labelling or categorising the world around us and making it understandable. Stereotypes are learned but are by no means fixed, yet are often resistant to change. They tend to restrict our understanding of the world and perpetuate beliefs that are often untrue or narrow. For instance, the concept that only thin women are attractive is a stereotype promoted by much of the media in the late twentieth century (though there are some exceptions, for example, comediennes Dawn French and Roseanne); in other eras the opposite has been true. Stereotyping is not always negative, but tends to be very much concerned with preserving and perpetuating power relations in society. It is in the interests of those in power to continue to stereotype those with lower status in a negative light, thus preserving the status quo.

stop motion An animation technique whereby a 3D model is filmed a single frame at a time, the model being moved by the animator between exposures.

straight-on shot A framing where the camera is at the same level as the objects or scene filmed.

structuralism Founded on the belief that the study of society could be scientifically based and that there are structures in society that follow certain patterns or rules. Initially, most interest was centred on the use of language; Saussure, the founder of linguistics, argued that language was essential in communicating the **ideology**, the beliefs, of a culture.

Structuralists have applied these theories to film, which uses both visual and verbal communication, and pointed out that the text conveys an illusion of reality, so conveying the ideology of a society even more effectively.

studio system Usually seen to have developed circa 1920 and lasting until circa 1950, the studio system indicates the period of Hollywood history in which the major studios controlled all aspects of the production, distribution and exhibition of their products.

substitution technique An early **trick film** technique used by George Méliès. It involved one object being filmed, the camera being stopped during filming and the object being replaced by a second object before filming recommenced. This was the basis of his famous vanishing-lady effect, used in many of his films.

superimposition The process by which more than one image is exposed on the same frames of the film stock.

surplus of meaning Meaning in excess of what is required to fulfil the functional requirements of the **narrative**; a 'surplus' will include ambiguity and complexity rather than clarity and simplicity.

suspending disbelief This refers to the ability a person has when engaging with a constructed object – film, play, novel – to repress his or her knowledge that the object is in fact just a 'construct', and respond to it as though it is real.

symbolism The means by which a filmmaker can assign additional meanings to objects/characters in a film. For example, in Dovzhenko's *Earth* and Eisenstein's *Old and New*, the tractor is a symbol of progress.

symmetry   Direct balance of imagery in the composition of the frame using parallel or mirrored forms.

synecdoche   The idea that a 'part' of a person, an object, a machine, may be used to represent the 'whole', and work as an emotive or suggestive shorthand for the viewer, who invests the 'part' with **symbolic** associations.

synergy strategy   Combined or related action by a group of individuals or corporations towards a common goal, the combined effect of which exceeds the sum of the individual efforts.

synthespians   A recently coined term which describes 'virtual' or non-human actors. The term relates to digitally scanned or motion-captured versions of 'real' actors, as well as entirely computer-generated characters.

taxonomy   The practice of classification. In this sense, the practice of classifying films into groups based on similarities of form and/or content.

testimony   The recording of solicited observation, opinion or information by witnesses, experts or other relevant participants in relation to the **documentary** subject; the primary purpose of the interview.

THX   A designation of sound reproduction quality in cinemas. The standards established necessitate the installation and maintenance of sound equipment to the specifications and according to the guidelines laid down by Lucasfilm Ltd.

tie-ins   Mutually beneficial promotional liaisons between films and other consumer products and/or personalities.

tilt   A camera movement in which the camera remains in one place but swivels up or down.

timbre   The tonal quality of a musical sound; timbre is what makes a saxophone sound different from a clarinet, for example.

time image   A development from the movement image. It suggests a cinema in which the narrative priorities of **mainstream** commercial cinema are replaced by ones which are more reflective. In particular, our understanding and experience of time becomes central.

topicals   The name given to non-fictional 'news' items in the early period of **documentary**. A royal visit, the opening of a factory, a sports event – anything that could be of interest to a local audience – could be labelled a 'topical'. As documentary developed as a form, topicals were subsumed into **newsreels** and other forms of film reporting.

track/tracking shot/dolly shot   A camera movement in which the camera moves horizontally by travelling along the ground (originally on 'tracks' on which a wheeled support – or 'dolly' – for the camera could be mounted).

Tradition of Quality   A frequently derogatory term used by the critics on *Cahiers du cinéma* and referring to postwar, pre-New Wave French cinema characterised by its reliance on screenwriters and adaptations from literary classics.

trick film   The generic term for the development of cinematic special effects using such techniques as **mattes**, **multiple exposures**, **proto-animation** and **substitution techniques**. Generally attributed to the pioneering French filmmaker George Méliès.

trust   A group of companies operating together to control the market for a commodity. This is illegal practice in the US.

two-shot A medium-scale shot including two characters normally taken from the waist up. A variant is the cut between the two characters assuming the same eyelevel, body position and exchange.

uses and gratifications A specific approach to the study of **audiences**. It considers how individuals and groups may consume a film or some other media product to satisfy their particular needs.

vertical integration Where a company is organised so that it oversees a product from the planning/development stage, through production, through market distribution, through to the end-user – the retail consumer. In the case of the film industry, this translates to a company controlling production, distribution and exhibition of its films.

voyeurism The sexual pleasure gained from looking at others.

wipe Transition between shots where a vertical line sweeps across the screen taking us from one scene to the next.

wire frame Three-dimensional shapes, with neither surface colour nor texture, illustrated through a pattern of interconnecting lines, literally a framework of 'wires' on a two-dimensional surface – the computer screen.

wire removal The process of digitally removing any unwanted elements within a shot, such as a support for an animated object, puppet or prop. Used in the flying motorbike shot in *Terminator 2*.

Zoetrope The forerunner of the **Praxinoscope**, this consists of a drum with vertical slots cut into the top edge. As the drum is rotated, the images on the inner surfaces, when viewed through the slots, achieve the same illusion of movement as with the **Phenakistoscope**.

zoom A technique whereby the image appears to advance towards or recedes away from the viewer.

Bibliography

Aaron, M. (ed.), *New Queer Cinema: A Critical Reader*, Edinburgh University Press, Edinburgh, 2004.

Abramowitz, Rachel, *Is That a Gun in Your Pocket? Women's Experience of Power in Hollywood*, Random House, New York, 2000.

Adams, T.R., *Tom and Jerry*, Crescent Books, New York, 1991.

Adamson, J., *Tex Avery: King of Cartoons*, Da Capo, New York, 1975.

Agosterios, V., 'An Interview with Sally Potter', *Framework*, No. 14, 1979.

Alderson, David and Anderson, Linda (eds), *Territories of Desire in Queer Culture*, Manchester University Press, Manchester, 2000.

Aldgate, A. and Richards, J., *Britain Can Take It*, Basil Blackwell, London, 1986.

Allan, R., *Walt Disney and Europe*, John Libbey, London, 1999.

Allen, R. and Gomery, D., *Film History: Theory and Practice*, Newbery Award Records, New York, 1985.

Allinson, M., *A Spanish Labyrinth: The Films of Pedro Almodovar*, I.B. Tauris, London, 2001.

Allon, Yoram *et al.* (eds), *Critical Guide to North American Directors*, Wallflower Press, London, 2002.

Altenloh, Emile, 'A Sociology of the Cinema: Audiences', reprinted in *Screen*, Vol. 42, No. 3, autumn 2001.

Altman, Rick (ed.), *Genre: The Musical*, BFI–Routledge & Kegan Paul, London, 1981.

—— 'A Semantic/Syntactic Approach to Film Genre', *Cinema Journal*, Vol. 23, No. 3, 1984.

—— *Film/Genre*, BFI, London, 1999.

Andrew, D., *Concepts in Film Theory*, Oxford University Press, Oxford, 1984.

Angelini, S., 'The DVD Story', *Viewfinder*, No. 44, October 2001.

Ansen, David, 'The Accused', *Newsweek*, 24 October 2002.

—— 'All the Way to the Bank', *Newsweek*, 3 April 2006, online at http://www.msnbc.msn.com/id/12015263/site/newsweek (10 April 2006).

Armes, R., *The Ambiguous Image: Narrative Style in Modern European Cinema*, Secker & Warburg, London, 1976.

Arrington, Carl Wayne, 'Film's Avant-Guardian', *Rolling Stone*, 22 March, 1990.

Arthur, J., 'Technology and Gender', *Screen*, Vol. 30, 1989, pp. 40–59.

Ashby, J., 'Betty Box, "the Lady in Charge": Negotiating a Space for a Female Producer in Postwar Cinema', in J. Ashby and A. Higson (eds), *British Cinema: Past and Present*, Routledge, London, 2000.

Ashby, J. and Higson, A. (eds) (2000) *British Cinema: Past and Present*, Routledge, London.

Atkinson, M., 'Diamonds in the Rough', *Sight & Sound*, Vol. 20, No. 2, 2010.

Aumont, J., *Montage Eisenstein*, BFI, London, 1987.

Austin, B., *Immediate Seating: A Look at Movie Audiences*, Wadsworth Publishing Company, Belmont, CA, 1989.

Auty, M. and Roddick, N. (eds), *British Cinema Now*, BFI, London, 1985.

Babington, B. (ed.), *British Stars and Stardom: From Alma Taylor to Sean Connery*, Manchester University Press, 2001.

Babuscio, J., 'Camp and Gay Sensibility', in Richard Dyer (ed.), *Gays and Film*, BFI, London, 1977.

—— 'Camp and Gay Sensibility', in H. Benshoff and S. Griffin (eds), *Queer Cinema: The Film Reader*, Routledge, London, 2004.

Bad Object Choices (ed.), *How Do I Look? Queer Film and Video*, Bay Press, Seattle, 1991.

Balazs, B., 'Filming Death', in K. Macdonald and M. Cousins (eds), *Imagining Reality: The Faber Book of Documentary*, Faber & Faber, London and Boston, 1996, pp. 29–31.

Balcon, M., *Michael Balcon Presents … a Lifetime of Films*, Hutchinson, London, 1969.

Balio, T. (ed.), *The American Film Industry*, University of Wisconsin Press, Madison, 1976.

—— *Hollywood in the Age of Television*, Unwin Hyman, Boston, 1990.

Banner, L., *Women in Modern America*, Harcourt Brace Jovanovich, New York, 1984.

Barbas, Samantha, 'The Political Spectator: Censorship, Protest and the Moviegoing Experience, 1912–1922', *Film History*, Vol. 11, pp. 217–29.

Barker, Martin and Petley, Julian (eds), *Ill Effects – the Media Violence Debate*, Routledge, London, 1997.

Barker, Martin, Arthurs, Jane and Ramawani, Haridranath, *The Crash Controversy*, Wallflower Press, London, 2001.

Barna, Y., *Eisenstein*, Secker & Warburg, London, 1973.

Barnes, J., *The Beginnings of Cinema in England*, David & Charles, London, 1976.

—— 'Flightplan', *Sight and Sound*, Vol. 15, No. 11, 2005.

Barnhill, J.H., 'African Diaspora', in P. Finkelman (ed.), *Encyclopedia of African American History, 1896 to the Present: From the Age of Segregation to the Twenty-first Century*, Oxford University Press, Oxford, 2009, online at http://www.oxfordaasc.com/article/opr/t0005/e0034.

Barnouw, E. and Krishnaswamy, S., *Indian Film*, 2nd edn, Oxford University Press, New York, 1980.

Barr, C., 'Amnesia and Schizophrenia', in C. Barr (ed.), *All Our Yesterdays: 90 Years of British Cinema*, BFI, London, 1986.

—— *Ealing Studios*, Cameron & Hollis, Moffat, 1999.

—— 'Before *Blackmail*: Silent British Cinema', in R. Murphy (ed.), *The British Cinema Book*, BFI, London, 2003.

—— '*The Good Companions*', in B. McFarlane (ed.), *The Cinema of Britain and Ireland*, Wallflower Press, London, 2005.

Barrier, M., *Hollywood Cartoons: American Animation in the Golden Age*, Oxford University Press, New York and Oxford, 1999.

Barrios, R., *Screened Out: Playing Gay in Hollywood from Edison to Stonewall*, Routledge, New York, 2002.

Barron, S. and Tuchman, M. (eds), *The Avant-Garde in Russia, 1910–1930: New Perspectives*, Los Angeles County Museum of Art, Los Angeles, 1980.

Barsam, R., *Non-fiction Film: A Critical History*, George Allen & Unwin Ltd, London, 1974.

Barthes, Roland, *Image–Music–Text*, Fontana, London, 1977.

Basinger, Jeanine, *A Woman's View: How Hollywood Spoke to Women 1930-1960*, Chatto & Windus, London, 1993.

Baskaran, Theodore, *The Message Bearers: The Nationalist Politics and the Entertainment Media in South India, 1880–1945*, Cre-A, Madras, 1981.

—— 'Songs in Tamil Cinema', *The Eye of the Serpent*, East–West Books, Madras, 1996, pp. 38–61.

Bazin, A., *What is Cinema?*, Vol. 1, *Ontology and Language*, Editions du Cerf, Paris, 1958.

—— 'On the *Politique des auteurs*' (1957), trans. Peter Graham, in Jim Hillier (ed.), *Cahiers du Cinema*, Vol. 1: *The 1950s*, Routledge, London, 1996.

Bauer, Erik, 'The Mouth and the Method', in Jim Hiller (ed.), *American Independent Cinema: A Sight and Sound Reader*, BFI, London, 2001.

BBFC, online at http://www.bbfc.co.uk.

Beck, J., *Animation Art*, Flame Tree Publishing, London, 2004.

Beck, J. and Friedwald, W., *Looney Tunes and Merrie Melodies*, Henry Holt & Co., New York, 1989.

Begleiter, M., *From Word to Image*, Michael Wiese Productions, Los Angeles, 2001.

Bell, E., Haas, L. and Sells, L. (eds), *From Mouse to Mermaid: The Politics of Film, Gender and Culture*, Indiana University Press, Bloomington and Indianapolis, 1995.

Belton, John, 'Authorship and Film', *Film Quarterly*, Vol. 58, No. 3, 2005.

Benshoff, H., *Monsters in the Closet: Homosexuality and the Horror Film*, Manchester University Press, Manchester, 1997.

Benshoff, H. and Griffin, S. (eds), *Queer Cinema: The Film Reader*, Routledge, London, 2004.

Benson, Sheila, 'The Accused', *Los Angeles Times*, 14 October 1988.

Bergan, R., *Eisenstein: A Life in Conflict*, London, Time Warner Paperbacks, 1999.

Berger, John, *Ways of Seeing*, Penguin, London, 1972.

Bergstrom, J., 'Rereading the Work of Claire Johnston', in C. Penley (ed.), *Feminism and Film Theory*, Routledge–BFI, London, 1988.

Bernstein, I., *Hollywood at the Crossroads: An Economic Study of the Motion Picture Industry*, Hollywood Film Council, Los Angeles, 1957.

Berry, C., 'Happy Alone? Sad Young Men in East Asian Gay Cinema', in A. Grossman (ed.), *Queer Asian Cinema*, Harrington Park Press, New York, 2001.

Berry, D., *Wales and Cinema: The First Hundred Years*, University of Wales Press, Cardiff, 1994.

Bersani, L. and Dutoit, U., *Caravaggio*, BFI, London, 1999.

Betterton, R., *Looking On: Images of Femininity in the Visual Arts and the Media*, Pandora, London, 1987.

Beumers, B. (ed.), *The Cinema of Russia and the Former Soviet Union*, Wallflower Press, London, 2007.

Beumers, B., Bocharov, V. and Robinson, D. (eds), *Alexander Shiryaev: Master of Movement*, Le Giornate del Cinema Muto, Gemona, 2010.

Billington, Michael, 'Proof', *Guardian*, 17 May 2002, p. 16.

Bilton, T., Bonnett, K., Jones, P., Lawsom, T., Skinner, D., Stanworth, M. and Webster, A., *Introductory Sociology*, Palgrave Macmillan, Basingstoke, 2002.

Birkos, A., *Soviet Cinema: Directors and Films*, Archon, Hamden, CT, 1976.

Bishop, L. 'Documentary Evidence', *Television*, August–September, Vol. 38, No. 7, 2001, p. 24.

Biskind, P., 'Going for Broke', *Sight & Sound*, October 1991.

Bitel, A., 'Skyline', *Sight & Sound*, Vol. 21, No. 1, 2011.

Bobo, Jacquelyne, '*The Color Purple*: Black Women as Cultural Readers', in E.D. Pribram (ed.), *Female Spectator: Looking at Film and Television*, Verso, London and New York, 1988.

Bogdanovich, Peter, 'New Kid on the Block', *Guardian*, 22 February 2002.

Boral, R.C. in Ashish Rajadhyaksha and Paul Willemen (eds), *Encyclopaedia of Indian Cinema*, 2nd edn, BFI, London, 1999.

Bordwell, David 'The Idea of Montage in Soviet Art and Film', *Cinema Journal*, Vol. 11, No. 2, 1972.

—— *Ozu and the Poetics of Cinema*, Princeton University Press, Princeton, NJ, 1988.

—— *Making Meaning: Inference and Rhetoric in the Interpretation of Cinema*, Harvard University Press, Cambridge, MA, 1989.

—— *Narration in the Fiction Film*, Routledge & Kegan Paul, London, 1986; repr. Routledge, London, 1990.

—— *The Cinema of Eisenstein*, Harvard University Press, Cambridge, MA, 1993.

—— *The Way Hollywood Tells It: Story and Style in Modern Movies*, University of California Press, Berkeley, 2006.

Bordwell, David and Carroll, Noel, *Post-Theory: Reconstructing Film Studies*, University of Wisconsin, Madison, 1996.

Bordwell, David and Thompson, K., *Film Art*, 4th edn, McGraw-Hill, London, 1994; repr. Knopf, New York, 1995.

Bordwell, D., Staiger, J. and Thompson, K., *The Classical Hollywood Cinema*, Routledge & Kegan Paul, London, 1985; repr. 1994.

Bourne, S., *Brief Encounters: Lesbians and Gays in British Cinema 1930–1971*, Cassell, London, 1996.

Bowser, Eileen, *The Transformation of Cinema 1907–1915*, University of California, Berkeley, 1994.

Braddock, Jeremy and Hock, Stephen (eds), *Directed by Allen Smithee*, University of Minnesota Press, Minneapolis, 2001.

Bradshaw, P., 'Made in Dagenham', *Guardian*, 30 September 2010, online at http://www.guardian.co.uk/film/2010/sep/30/made-in-dagenham-film-review.

Brion, P., *Tom and Jerry*, Crown Publishers, New York, 1990.

Britton, A., 'The Invisible Eye', *Sight & Sound*, February, 1992, p. 29.

Brode, D., *Money, Women and Guns: Crime Movies from Bonnie and Clyde to the Present*, Citadel, New York, 1995.

Brooks, Xan, 'Directing Masochism', *Guardian*, G2, 24 April 2002.

—— 'Vanilla Sky', *Sight & Sound*, vol. 12, no. 2, 2002b.

Brown, Georgia, 'Little Man Tate', *Village Voice*, 15 October 1991.

Brown, M., 'The Old Ones Are the Best', *Guardian*, 26 March 2001, pp. 16–17.

Brundsen, C. (ed.), *Films for Women*, BFI, London, 1986.

Bruzzi, S., 'Tempestuous Petticoats: Costume and Desire in *The Piano*', *Screen*, Vol. 36 No. 3, autumn 1995, pp. 257–66.

—— *Undressing Cinema*, Routledge, London, 1997.

—— *New Documentary: A Critical Introduction*, Routledge, London and New York, 2000.

Buckland, Warren, 'A Close Encounter with *Raiders of the Lost Ark*', in Steven Neale and Murray Smith (eds), *Contemporary Hollywood Cinema*, Routledge, London, 1998.

Bukatman, S., *Blade Runner*, BFI, London, 1997.

Buncombe, A., 'Coming Soon – City Centre Cinema Boom', *Independent*, 17 September 1998.

Burch, Noel, *Theory of Film Practice*, Secker & Warburg, London, 1973.

—— *Correction Please – or How We Got Into Movies*, Arts Council, London, 1979.

Burgoyne, Robert, 'National Identity, Gender Identity, and the "Rescue Fantasy" in *Born on the Fourth of July*', *Screen*, Vol. 35, No. 33, Autumn 1994.

Burkeman, O., 'Mission Over for Mister Impossible', *Guardian*, 24 August 2006, p. 1.

Burns, M., 'Women in Focus', *In Camera*, Spring 1992, pp. 3–5, 17–19.

Burrows, J., '"Our English Mary Pickford": Alma Taylor and Ambivalent British Stardom in the 1910s', in B. Babington (ed.), *British Stars and Stardom: From Alma Taylor to Sean Connery*, Manchester University Press, Manchester, 2001.

—— 'Big Studio Production in the Pre-quota Years', in R. Murphy (ed.), *The British Cinema Book,* 2nd edn, BFI, London, 2003.

Burston, P., 'In from the Cold', *Guardian*, 9 November 2007, online at http://www.guardian.co.uk/film/2007/nov/09/3?INTCMP=SRCH.

Burston, P. and Richardson, C. (eds), *A Queer Romance*: *Gay Men, Lesbians and Popular Culture*, Routledge, London, 1995.

Burton, J., 'Film and Revolution in Cuba: The First Twenty-Five Years', in M. Martin (ed.), *The New Latin American Cinema: Volume Two, Studies of National Cinemas*, Wayne State University Press, Detroit, 1997.

Burton-Carvajal, J., 'Surprise Package: Looking Southward with Disney', in E. Smoodin (ed.), *Disney Discourse*, Routledge, London and New York, 1994, pp. 131–47.

Buscombe, E., 'Sound and Colour', *Jump Cut*, No. 17, 1977.

Buscombe, E. and Pearson, R. (eds), *Back in the Saddle Again: New Essays on the Western*, BFI, London, 1998.

Butler, J., *Gender Trouble: Feminism and the Subversion of Identity*, Routledge, New York and London, 1990.

—— *Bodies that Matter*, Routlege, London, 1993.

Byars, J., *All that Heaven Allows: Re-reading Gender in 1950s Melodrama*, Chapel Hill, University of North Carolina Press, 1991.

Byron, S., 'Letter to Editor', *Film Comment*, Vol. 22, No. 5, October 1986, p. 76.

Cabarga, L., *The Fleischer Story*, Da Capo, New York, 1988.

Cahiers du cinéma: Situation du cinéma français, May 1957, No. 71.

Cain, M., 'Made in Dagenham: A Victory for Women's Rights', *Channel 4 News*, 23 September 2010, online at http://www.channel4.com/news/made-in-dagenham-a-victory-for-womens-rights.

Calder-Marshall, A., *The Innocent Eye: The Life of Robert J. Flaherty*, New York: Harcourt Brace Jovanovich, 1966.

Campbell, D., 'Catholics Vilify *Dogma*', *Guardian* 13 November, 1999.

Campbell, R., 'Warner Bros in the 1930s: Some Tentative Notes', *The Velvet Light Trap*, No. 1, June 1971.

Canemaker, J. (ed.), *Storytelling in Animation*, American Film Institute, Los Angeles, 1988.

Cardullo, B. (ed.), *Bazin at Work*, Routledge, London, 1997.

Carroll, Noel, *Engaging the Moving Image*, Yale University Press, New Haven and London, 2003.

Caughie, John, 'Preface', in *Theories of Authorship: A Reader*, Routledge, London, 1981.

—— *Theories of Authorship: A Reader*, Routledge and BFI, London, 1988.

Cerisuelo, M., *Jean-Luc Godard*, Editions des Quatre-Vents, Paris, 1989.

Chabrol, Claude and Rohmer, Eric, *Hitchcock: The First Forty-Four Films*, Frederick Ungar, New York, 1979.

Chakravarty, Sumita S., *National Identity in Indian Popular Cinema, 1947–1987*, University of Texas Press, Austin, 1993.

Cham, M.B., *Ex-Iles: Essays on Caribbean Cinema*, Africa World Press, Trenton, NJ, 1992.

Champlin, C., 'What Will H. Hays Begat', *American Film*, Vol. 6, No. 1, October 1980.

Chanan, M., 'Cinema in Latin America', in G. Nowell-Smith, (ed.), *The Oxford History of World Cinema*, Oxford University Press, 1997.

—— *Cuban Cinema*, University of Minnesota Press, Minneapolis and London, 2004.

—— 'The Space between Fiction and Documentary in Latin American Cinema: Notes towards a Genealogy', in M. Haddu and J. Page, *Visual Synergies in Fiction and Documentary Film From Latin America*, Palgrave Macmillan, New York, 2009.

Chandravarkar, Bhaskar, 'The Tradition of Music in Indian Cinema', *Cinema in India*, Vol. 1, No. 2, April 1987 to Vol. 3, No. 3, July–September 1989.

—— 'Growth of the Film Song', *Cinema in India*, Vol. 1, No. 3, pp. 16–20.

Chapman, J., *The British at War*, I.B. Tauris, London, 1997.

—— *Licensed to Thrill*, I.B. Tauris, London, 1999.

Chatman, S., *Story and Discourse: Narrative Structure in Fiction and Film*, Cornell University Press, Ithaca, NY, 1980.

Chatterji, G., *Mother India*, BFI Classics, London, 2002.

Chatterji, S., *Parama and Other Outsiders: The Cinema of Aparna Sen*, Parumita Publications, Calcutta, 2002.

Chibnall, S., 'Travels in Ladland: The British Gangster Film Cycle 1998–2001', in R. Murphy (ed.), *The British Cinema Book*, 2nd edn, BFI, London, 2003.

Chibnall, S. and Murphy, R., *The British Crime Film*, Routledge, London and New York, 1999.

Cholodenko, A. (ed.), *The Illusion of Life*, Power Publishers, Sydney, 1991.

Chopra, Anupama, 'Southern Invasion', *India Today*, 13 October 1997, pp. 38–40.

—— *Sholay: The Making of a Classic*, Penguin, New Delhi, 2000.

—— *Dilwalw Dulhania Le Jayenge*, BFI Modern Classics, London, 2002.

Chopra-Gant, M., 'So What Kind of Film Is It?: Genre, Publicity and Critical Practice', in J. Strong, G. Dowd and L. Stevenson (eds), *Genre Matter: Essays in Theory and Criticism*, Intellect Books, Bristol, 2005.

Christie, I. (ed.), *Powell Pressburger and Others*, BFI, London, 1978.

—— 'From the Kingdom of Shadows', in the catalogue to *Twilight of the Tsars*, Hayward Gallery, London, 1991.

Christie, I. and Gillett, J. (eds), *Futurism/Formalism/FEKS: 'Eccentrism' and Soviet Cinema 1918–1936*, BFI, Film Availability Services, London, 1978.

Christie, I. and Graffy, J. (eds), *Yakov Protazanov and the Continuity of Russian Cinema*, BFI-NFT, London, 1993.

Christie, I. and Taylor, R. (eds), *Eisenstein Rediscovered*, Routledge, London, 1993.

Chute, David, Review of *Lagaan: Once Upon a Time in India*, *Film Comment*, March–April, 2002.

Clover, Carol, *Men, Women and Chainsaws: Gender in the Modern Horror Film*, BFI, London, 1992.

—— 'White Noise', *Sight & Sound*, Vol. 3, No. 5, 1993, pp. 5–9.

Cohan, S. and Rae Hark, I. (eds), 'Introduction', in *Screening the Male: Exploring Masculinities in Hollywood Cinema*, Routledge, London, 1993.

Cohen, Scott, 'Strangers in Paradise', *Spin*, March 1990; online at http://www.sfgoth.com/~kali/onsite8.html (26/09/2001).

Colebroke, Claire, *Giles Deleuze*, London, Routledge, 2002.

Collier, S., 'Carlos Gardel and the Cinema', in J. King and N. Torrents (eds), *The Garden of Forking Paths: Argentine Cinema*, BFI, London, 1988.

Collins, C., 'British Film: The Next Generation', *Guardian*, 16 November 2001.

Collins, Jim, *Architectures of Excess: Cultural Life in the Information Age*, Routledge, London, 1995.

Collins, J., Radner, H. and Preacher Collins, A. (eds), *Film Theory Goes to the Movies*, American Film Institute and Routledge, London, 1993.

Cook, P., '*The Gold Diggers*', *Framework*, Vol. 24, 1981.

—— (ed.), *The Cinema Book*, BFI, London, 1985.

—— *Fashioning the Nation: Costume and Identity in British Cinema*, BFI, London, 1996.

—— (ed.), *Gainsborough Studios*, Cassell, London, 1997.

—— 'No Fixed Address: The Women's Picture from *Outrage* to *Blue Steel*', in S. Neale and M. Smith (eds), *Contemporary Hollywood Cinema*, Routledge, London, 1998.

Cook, Pam and Dodd, Philip (eds), *Women and Film: A Sight and Sound Reader*, BFI and Scarlet Press, London, 1993.

—— (ed.), *Gainsborough Studios*, BFI, London, 1996.

Cooper, C., 'Slackness Hiding from Culture: Erotic Play in the Dancehall', in *Noises in the Blood: Orality, Gender, and the 'Vulgar' Body of Jamaican Popular Culture*, Duke University Press, Durham, NC, 1995.

Corner, J. (ed.), *Documentary and the Mass Media*, Edward Arnold, London, 1986.

—— *The Art of Record: A Critical Introduction to Documentary*, Manchester University Press, Manchester and New York, 1996.

Corner, J., 'Performing the Real', *Television and New Media*, Vol. 3, No. 3, 2002, pp. 255–70.

Corrigan, Timothy, 'The Commerce of Auteurism', in *A Cinema without Walls: Movies and Culture After Vietnam*, Routledge, London, 1991.

—— *A Cinema without Walls: Movies and Culture After Vietnam*, Routledge, London, 1991.

Cotta Vaz, Mark *et al.*, *Industrial Light and Magic: Into the Digital Realm*, Virgin Books, London, 1996.

Counsell, C., *Signs of Performance*, Routledge, London 1996.

Couselo, J.M., 'Argentine Cinema from Sound to the Sixties', in J. King and N. Torrents (eds), *The Garden of Forking Paths: Argentine Cinema*, BFI, London, 1988.

Cowie, P., *Revolution: The Explosion of World Cinema in the Sixties*, Faber, London, 2005.

Cox, Alex, 'Is DVD Worth It?', *Guardian*, Friday Review, 23 February 2001.

Coyle, R., *Drawn to Sound: Animation, Film Music and Sonicity*, Equinox, London, 2010.

Crafton, D., *Before Mickey: The Animated Film 1898–1928*, University of Chicago Press, Chicago and London, 1993.

Creed, B., 'From Here to Modernity: Feminism and Postmodernism', *Screen*, Vol. 28, No. 2, 1987, pp. 47–67.

—— 'Dark Desires: Male Masochism in the Horror Film', in S. Cohan and I. Hark (eds), *Screening the Male*, Routledge, London, 1993.

Creekmur, Corey K. and Doty, Alexander (eds), *Out in Culture: Gay, Lesbian and Queer Essays on Popular Culture*, Duke University Press, Durham, NC, 1995.

Cripps, T., *Black Film as Genre*, Indiana University Press, Bloomington, 1978.

—— *Slow Fade to Black: The Negro in American Film, 1900-1942*, 2nd edn, Oxford University Press, New York, 1993a.

—— *Making Movies Black: The Hollywood Message Movie from World War II to the Civil Rights Era*, Oxford University Press, New York, 1993b.

Cubitt, Sean, *The Cinema Effect*, MIT Press, Cambridge, MA, 2004.

Culler, Jonathan, *Structuralist Poetics*, Routledge, London, 1975.

Curtis D., *Len Lye: Exhibition Catalogue*, Watershed, 24 October 1987–29 November 1987, Arts Council, London, 1987.

Dale, A., *Comedy Is a Man In Trouble*, University of Minnesota Press, Minneapolis, 2000.

Dale, Martin, *The Movie Game: The Film Business in Britain, Europe and America*, Cassell, London, 1997.

Daniel, L. and Jackson, C. (eds), *The Bent Lens: A World Guide to Gay and Lesbian Film*, Roundhouse Publishing, Northam, 2003.

Dargis, M., (2000), 'Ghost in the Machine', *Sight & Sound*, Vol. 10, No. 7, 2000, pp. 20–23.

—— 'Mission Imperative', *The New York Times*, 25 December 2008, online at http://movies.nytimes.com/2008/12/25/movies/25valk.html.

Darke, Chris, 'Rupture, Continuity and Diversification: *Cahiers du cinéma* in the 1980s', *Screen*, Vol. 34, No. 4, winter 1993, pp. 362–80.

—— *Alphaville* (Cine-Files French Film Guides), I.B. Tauris, London, 2005.

Darley, Andrew, *Visual Digital Culture: Surface Play and Spectacle in New Media Genres*, Routledge, London, 2000.

Das, Veena, 'Introduction', in *Mirrors of Violence: Communities and Survivors in South Asia*, Oxford University Press, New Delhi, 1992.

Datta, Sangeeta, *Shyam Benegal*, World Directors, BFI, London, 2002.

Davies, J. and Smith, C.R., *Gender, Ethnicity and Sexuality in Contemporary American Film*, 2nd edn, Edinburgh, Keele University Press, 2001.

Davies, P. and Wells, P. (eds), *American Film and Politics: Reagan to Bush Jr*, Manchester University Press, Manchester, 2002.

Davis, J., 'Gender, Ethnicity and Cultural Crisis in *Falling Down* and *Groundhog Day*, *Screen*, Vol. 36, No. 3, 1995, pp. 214–32.

DeAngelis, M., *Gay Fandom and Crossover Stardom: James Dean, Mel Gibson and Keanu Reeves*, Duke University Press, Durham, NC, 2001.

De Baecque, A., *Les Cahiers du cinéma Histoire d'une revue: Tome 2 Cinéma, tours détours 1959–1981*, Editions Cahiers du cinéma, Paris, 1991.

—— *La nouvelle vague: Portrait d'une jeunesse*, Flammarion, Paris, 1998.

De Baecque, A. and Toubiana, S., *Truffaut: A Biography*, University of California Press, Berkeley, 2000.

De Lauretis, T., 'Guerilla in the Midst – Women's Cinema in the 1980s', *Screen*, Vol. 31, No. 1, 1990.

De Nitto, D, *Film: Form and Feeling*, New York: Harper & Row, 1985.

Deleuze, Gilles, *Cinema 2: The Time-Image*, Athlone Press, London, 1989.

Denby, D., 'Thrills and Chills', *New Yorker*, 5 July 2010, online at http://www.newyorker.com/arts/critics/cinema/2010/07/05/100705crci_cinema_denby.

Denzin, N., *The Cinematic Society*, Sage, London, 1995.

Derne, Steve, *Movies, Masculinity and Modernity: An Ethnography of Men's Filmgoing in India*, Greenwood Press, Westport, CT, 2000.

Desai, J., *Beyond Bollywood: The Cultural Politics of South Asian Diasporic Film*, Routledge, New York and London, 2004.

Deschner, D., 'Anton Grot: Warner's Art Director 1927–1948', *The Velvet Light Trap*, Vol. 15, 1975.

Deuber-Mankowsky, A., *Lara Croft – Cyber Heroine*, University of Minnesota Press, Minneapolis, 2005.

Dhareshwar, Vivek and Niranjana, Tejaswini '*Kaadalan* and the Politics of Resignification: Fashion, Violence and the Body', *Journal of Arts and Ideas*, Vol. 29, January 1996.

Dhondy, Farrukh, *Bombay Duck*, Cape, London, 1990.

Diawara, M. (ed.), *Black American Cinema*, Routledge, New York, 1993.

Dickey, Sara, *Cinema and the Urban Poor in South India*, Cambridge University Press, Cambridge, 1993.

Dickinson, M. and Street, S., *Cinema and State: The Film Industry and the Government 1927–1984*, BFI, London, 1985.

Dickinson, T. and de la Roche, C., *Soviet Cinema*, Falcon Press, London, 1948.

Dieleke, E., '*O sertão não virou mar*: Images of Violence and the Position of the Spectator in Contemporary Brazilian Cinema', in M. Haddu and J. Page, *Visual Synergies in Fiction and Documentary Film from Latin America*, New York: Palgrave Macmillan, 2009.

Dillon, S., *Derek Jarman and the Lyric Film*, University of Texas Press, Houston, 2004.

Docherty, D., Morrison, D. and Tracey, M., *The Last Picture Show?*, BFI, London, 1987.

Donald, J., 'Stars', in P. Cook and M. Bernink (eds), *The Cinema Book*, 2nd edn, BFI, London, 1999.

Donald, L. and Scanlon, S., 'Hollywood Feminism? Get Real!!', *Trouble and Strife*, Vol. 25, winter 1992, pp. 11–16.

Donnelly, K., *Pop Music in British Cinema*, BFI, London, 2001.

Doraiswamy, Rashmi, 'Hindi Commercial Cinema: Changing Narrative Strategies', in Aruna Vasudev (ed.), *Frames of Mind: Reflections on Indian Cinema*, UBS Publishers, New Delhi, 1995.

Doty, Alexander, *Making Things Perfectly Queer*, University of Minnesota Press, Minneapolis, 1993.

—— *Flaming Classics: Queering the Film Canon*, Routledge, New York and London, 2000.

Douchet, J., *French New Wave*, Distributed Art Publishers Inc.–Editions Hazan–Cinémathèque Française, Paris, 1999.

Dove, L., 'Feminist and Left Independent Filmmaking in England', *Jump Cut*, Vol. 10, No. 11, 1976.

Dovey, J., *Freakshow: First Person Media and Factual Television*, Pluto Press, London and Sterling, 2000.

Drabinsky, G., *Motion Pictures and the Arts in Canada: The Business and the Law*, McGraw-Hill Ryerson, Toronto, 1976.

Du Bois, W.E.B., *The Souls of Black Folk: Essays and Sketches*, Signet, New York, 1995.

Duclos, Denis, *The Werewolf Complex: America's Fascination with Violence*, Oxford University Press, New York, 1998.

Dudley, A., *The Major Film Theories: An Introduction*, Oxford University Press, Oxford, 1976.

Durgnat, R., *Nouvelle Vague: The First Decade*, Motion Publications, Loughton, 1963.

—— *A Mirror for England*, Faber & Faber, London, 1970.

Dwyer, Rachel, *All You Want Is Money, All You Need Is Love: Sexuality and Romance in Modern India*, Cassell, London, 2000.

—— *100 Bollywood Films*, BFI Screen Guides, London, 2005.

Dyer, Richard, 'Pasolini and Homosexuality', in P. Willemen (ed.), *Pier Paolo Pasolini*, BFI, London, 1977.

—— 'Resistance Through Charisma: Rita Hayworth and *Gilda*', in A.E. Kaplan (ed.), *Women in Film Noir*, BFI, London, 1978.

—— *Stars*, BFI, London, 1979.

—— 'Don't Look Now', *Screen*, Vol. 23, Nos 3–4, 1982, pp. 66–7.

—— *Heavenly Bodies: Film Stars and Society*, Macmillan, Basingstoke, 1987a.

—— 'Judy Garland and Gay Men', in *Heavenly Bodies: Film Stars and Society*, Macmillan, Basingstoke, 1987b.

—— *The Matter of Images: Essays on Representation*, Routledge, London, 1993.

—— *White*, Routledge, London, 1997.

—— 'Introduction to film studies', in John Hill and Pamela Church Gibson (eds), *The Oxford Guide to Film Studies*, Oxford University Press, Oxford, 1998.

—— *Stars* (1979), BFI, London, 1998.

—— *Now You See It: Studies on Lesbian and Gay Film*, Routledge, London and New York, 2002a.

—— *The Culture of Queers*, Routledge, New York and London, 2002b.

Dyer, R. and Vincendeau, G., *Popular European Cinema*, Routledge, London, 1992.

Dyson, L., 'The Return of the Repressed? Whiteness, Femininity and Colonialism in *The Piano*', *Screen*, Vol. 36, No. 3, autumn 1995, pp. 269–76.

Easthope, A., *What a Man's Gotta Do: The Masculine Myth in Popular Culture*, Unwin Hyman, Winchester, 1990.

Ebert, Roger, 'Dead Man Walking', *Chicago Sun–Times*, 1 December 1996; online at http://www.suntimes. com/ ebert/ebert_reviews/1996/01/1015392.html (10 May 2002).

—— 'The Accused', *Chicago Sun–Times*, 14 October 1998; online at http://www.suntimes.com/ebert/ ebert_reviews/1988/10/318971.html (10 May 2002).

—— 'Anna and the King', *Chicago Sun–Times*; online at http://www.suntimes.com/ebert/ebert_ reviews/1999/12/121701.html (10 May 2002).

—— 'The Matrix', *Chicago Sun–Times*, 23 April 2002; online at http://www.suntimes.com/ebert/ebert_ reviews/1999/03/033101.html.

—— 'Inside Man', *Chicago Sun-Times*, 24 March 2006; online at http://rogerebert.suntimes.com/aoos/pbcs. dll/article?AID=/20060323/REVIEWS/6031/4002/10 23 (10 April 2006).

Ebert, R., 'Knight and Day', *Chicago Sun Times*, 20 June 2010, online at http://rogerebert.suntimes.com/ apps/pbcs.dll/article?AID=/20100621/REVIEWS/100629998.

Ehrenstein, D., 'Out of the Wilderness', *Film Quarterly*, Vol. 47, No. 1, 1993, pp. 2–7.

Eisenstein, Sergei M., *Notes of a Film Director*, Dover Publications, New York, 1970.

—— *The Film Sense*, Faber & Faber, London, 1986.

—— 'The Montage of Film Attractions', in Peter Lehman (ed.), *Defining Cinema*, Rutgers University Press, New Brunswick, NJ, 1997.

Elliot, K., Rethinking the Novel/Film Debate, Cambridge University Press, Cambridge, 2003.

Ellis, J., *Visible Fictions*, Routledge, London, 1982.

—— 'The Quality Film Adventure: British Critics and the Cinema 1942-48', in A. Higson (ed.), *Dissolving Views: Key Writings on British Cinema*, Cassell, London, 1996.

Ellis, John, *Visible Fictions: Cinema, Television and Video*, Routledge & Kegan Paul, London, 1982; repr. 1992.

Ellison, R., *Shadow and Act*, Vintage International, New York, 1964.

Elsaesser, Thomas, 'Vincente Minnelli', in Rick Altman (ed.), *Genre: The Musical*, Routledge & Kegan Paul– BFI, London, 1981.

—— (ed.), *Early Cinema*, BFI, London, 1990.

—— 'The Quality Film Adventure: British Critics and Cinema 1942-48', in A. Higson (ed.), *Dissolving Views: Key Writings on British Cinema*, Cassell, London, 1996.

—— 'The Blockbuster: Everything Connects, But Not Everything Goes', in Jon Lewis (ed.), *The End of Cinema as We Know It*, Pluto Press, London, 2001.

Enns, A., 'The Spectacle of Disabled Masculinity in John Woo's "Heroic Bloodshed" Films', *The Quarterly Review of Film and Video*, Vol. 17, No. 2, June 2000, pp. 137–45.

Epstein, E.J., *The Big Picture*, Random House, New York, 2005.

—— 'Tom Cruise Inc.', *Slate*, 27 June 2007, online at http://www.slate.com/id/2121617/.

Erens, Patricia (ed.), *Issues in Feminist Film Criticism*, Indiana University Press, Bloomington, 1990.

Esquenazi, J.-P., *Godard et la société française des années 1960*, Paris, 2004.

Eyles, A., 'Exhibition and the Cinema-going Experience', in R. Murphy (ed.), *The British Cinema Book*, BFI Publishing, London, 2003.

Faber, L. and Walters, H., *Animation Unlimited: Innovative Short Films Since 1940*, Laurence King, London, 2004.

Falcon, R., *Classified! A Teacher's Guide to Film and Video Censorship and Classification*, BFI, London, 1994.

Farmer, Brett, *Spectacular Passions: Cinema, Fantasy, Gay Male Spectatorships*, Duke University Press, Durham, NC, 2000.

Farrow, B., 'Hollywood Runs Scared', *The Times*, 8 October, 1999.

Ferguson, M. and Wicke, J. (eds), *Feminism and Postmodernism*, Duke University Press, Durham, NC, 1994.

Finney, A., *The Egos Have Landed*, Mandarin, London, 1997.

Fitzgerald, T., 'Now About These Women', *Sight & Sound*, Summer 1989.

Fleming, M., (2009), 'Peter Berg Boards "Battleship"', *Variety*, 14 September 2009, online at online at http://www.variety.com/article/VR1118008608?refCatId=13.

Fleming, M. and Klady, L., '"Crying" All the Way to the Bank', *Variety*, 22 March, 1993.

Florence, P., 'A Conversation with Sally Potter', *Screen*, Vol. 34, No. 3, Autumn 1993, pp. 275–84.

Forbes, J. and Kelly, M. (eds), *French Cultural Studies: An Introduction*, Oxford University Press, Oxford, 1995.

Foundas, S., 'Cruise in Control', *LA Weekly*, 4 May 2006, online at http://www.laweekly.com/2006-05-04/film-tv/cruise-in-control/.

Francke, L., *Script Girls*, BFI, London, 1994.

Frayling, C., *Spaghetti Westerns*, I.B. Tauris, London, 1998.

Frazer, J, *Artificially Arranged Scenes*, G. Hall, Boston, 1979.

Frey, H., *Louis Malle*, University of Manchester Press, Manchester, 2004.

Friedan, B., *The Feminine Mystique*, Penguin, London, 1963.

Friedmann, L. (ed.), *British Cinema and Thatcherism: Fires Were Started*, UCL Press, London, 1993.

Frith, S., *Music for Pleasure*, Routledge, London, 1988.

Fuller, Graham, 'Strictly Red', *Sight and Sound*, Vol. 11, No. 6, 2001.

Furniss, M., *Art in Motion: Animation Aesthetics*, John Libbey, London and Montrouge, 1998.

—— *Chuck Jones: Conversations*, University of Mississippi Press, Jackson, 2005.

—— *The Animation Bible*, Lawrence King Publishers, London, 2008.

Fuss, D. (ed.), *Inside/Out: Lesbian Theories, Gay Theories*, Routledge, New York and London, 1991.

Gabilondo, Joseba, 'Morphing Saint Sebastian', in Vivian Sobchack (ed.), *Meta Morphing and the Culture of Quick-Change*, University of Minnesota Press, Minneapolis, 2000.

Gaines, J., 'White Privilege and Looking Relations: Race and Gender in Feminist Film Theory', in S. Thornham (ed.), *Feminist Film Theory: A Reader*, New York University Press, New York, 1988.

Gallagher, Tag, 'Reading Culture, and Auteurs', *Screening The Past*, No. 12, 2001; http://www.latrobe.edu.au/screeningthepast/editorials/amed12a.htm (20 April 2006).

Ganti, T., *Bollywood: A Guidebook to Popular Hindi Cinema*, Routledge, New York and London, 2004.

García Oliveri, R., *Argentine Cinema: A Chronicle of a Hundred Years*, Manrique Zago, Buenos Aires, 1997.

Gates, H.L. Jr., 'New Negroes, Migration, and Cultural Exchange', in E. Hutton Turner (ed.), *Jacob Lawrence: The Migration Series*, Rappahannock, Washington, DC, 1993.

Gatiss, M., *James Whale*, Cassell, London, 1995.

Gaut, Berys, 'Film Authorship and Collaboration', in Richard Allen and Murray Smith (eds), *Film Theory and Philosophy*, Oxford University Press, Oxford, 1997.

Genette, G., *Narrative Discourse*, Cornell University Press, Ithaca, NY, 1980.

Geraghty, Christine, *British Cinema in the Fifties*, London, Routledge, 2000.

—— 'Re-examining Stardom: Questions of Texts, Bodies and Performance', in C. Gledhill, and L. Williams (eds), *Reinventing Film Studies*, Arnold, London, 2000.

Gerstner, David A., 'The Practices of Authorship', in David A. Gerstner and Janet Staiger (eds), *Authorship and Film*, Routledge, London, 2003.

Gever, M., Greyson, J. and Parmar, P. (eds) *Queer Looks: Perspectives on Lesbian and Gay Video*, Between the Lines–Routledge, Toronto, 1993.

Giannetti, L., *Understanding Movies*, 6th edn, Prentice-Hall, Englewood Cliffs, NJ, 1993.

Giannetti, L. and Eyman, S., *Flashback: A Brief History of Film*, 2nd edn, Prentice-Hall, Englewood Cliffs, NJ, 1991.

Gibbons, Fiachra, 'Meet Me in Margate', *Guardian*, 9 March 2001, online at http://film.guardian.co.uk/features/featurepages/0,4120,448694,00.html.

Gibbons, F., 'Actor Lays into "Trash Ethos" of US films', *Guardian*, 24 August 2001, online at http://film.guardian.co.uk/News_Story/Guardian/0,4029,541765,00.html.

Gibbs, J., *Mise-en Scène: Film Style and Interpretation*, Wallflower Press, London, 2001.

Gilbey, R., 'Days of Glory', *Sight & Sound*, Vol. 19, No. 9, 2009.

Giles, J., *The Cinema of Jean Genet: Un chant d'amour*, BFI, London, 1991.

—— *The Crying Game*, BFI, London, 1997.

—— *Criminal Desires: Jean Genet and Cinema*, Creation Books, London, 2002.

Gillespie, D., *Russian Cinema*, Longman, Harlow, 2003.

Giroux, H., 'Brutalised Bodies and Emasculated Politics', *Third Text*, No. 53, winter 2000/1, pp. 31–41.

Gledhill, C., 'Some Recent Developments in Feminist Criticism', in S. Mast and M. Cohen (eds), *Film Theory and Criticism*, Oxford University Press, Oxford, 1985.

—— 'Pleasurable Negotiations', in D. Pribram (ed.), *Female Spectators: Looking at Film and Television*, Verso, London and New York, 1988.

—— 'Introduction', in C. Gledhill (ed.), *Stardom: Industry of Desire*, Routledge, London, 1991.

—— (ed.), *Stardom: Industry of Desire*, Routledge, London, 1991.

—— 'The History of Genre Criticism', in Pam Cook and Mieke Bernink (eds), *The Cinema Book*, 2nd edn, BFI, London, 1999.

—— 'Rethinking Genre', in Christine Gledhill and Linda Williams (eds), *Reinventing Film Studies*, Arnold, London, 2000.

—— *Reframing British Cinema, 1918–1928*, London, BFI, 2003.

Gledhill, Christine and Williams, Linda (eds), *Reinventing Film Studies*, London, Arnold, 2001.

Glenny, M. and Taylor, R. (eds), *S.M. Eisenstein: Towards a Theory of Montage – Selected Works Vol. 2*, BFI, London, 1994.

Gomery, D., *The Hollywood Studio System*, Macmillan, London, 1986.

—— *Movie History: A Survey*, Wadsworth, Belmont, CA, 1991.

—— *Shared Pleasures*, BFI, London, 1992.

Goodwin, J., *Eisenstein, Cinema and History*, University of Illinois Press, Urbana and Chicago, 1993.

Gopal, S. and Moorti, S. (eds), *Global Bollywood: Travels of Hindi Song and Dance*, University of Minnesota Press, London, 2008.

Gopalan, Lalitha, 'Avenging Women in Indian Cinema', *Screen*, Vol. 38, No. 1, 1997a, pp. 42–59.

—— 'Coitus Interruptus and Love Story in Indian Cinema', in Vidya Dehejia (ed.), *Representing the Body: Gender Issues in Indian Art*, Kali for Women, New Delhi, 1997b, pp. 124–39.

—— *Cinema of Interruptions: Action Genres in Indian Cinema*, BFI, London, 2002.

Gopinath, G., 'Queering Bollywood: Alternative Sexualities in Popular Indian Cinema', in A. Grossman (ed.), *Queer Asian Cinema*, Harrington Park Press, New York, 2001.

Gough-Yates, K., *Somewhere in England: British Cinema and Exile*, I.B. Tauris, London.

Graham, P. (ed.), *The New Wave: Critical Landmarks*, BFI–Secker & Warburg, London, 1968.

Grant, Catherine, 'www.auteur.com?', *Screen*, Vol. 41, No. 1, 2000.

Grant, J., *Masters of Animation*, Batsford, London, 2001.

Gray, B., '*Mission Impossible III* Doesn't Thrill', *Box Office Mojo*, 8 May 2006, online at http://boxofficemojo.com/news/?id=2061&p=.htm.

Greene, G., *The Pleasure Dome*, Secker & Warburg, London, 1972.

Greenwald, S. and Landry, P., *This Business of Film*, Lone Eagle, New York, 2009.

Greer, G., *The Female Eunuch*, Flamingo, London, 1971.

Grierson, J. 'The Documentary Producer', *Cinema Quarterly*, Vol. 2, No. 1, 1932.

—— *Grierson on Documentary*, edited and compiled by Forsyth Hardy, University of California Press, Berkeley and Los Angeles, 1966.

Griffiths, R. (ed.), *Queer Cinema in Europe*, Intellect Books, London, 2003.

—— *British Queer Cinema*, Routledge, London, 2005.

Grimes, C., 'Harry Potter and the Sales Team', *Financial Times*, 16 November, 2001.

Grossman, A. (ed.), *Queer Asian Cinema: Shadows in the Shade*, Harrington Park Press, New York, 2001.

Guerrero, E., *Framing Blackness: The African American Image in Film*, Temple University Press, Philadelphia, PA, 1993.

Guinness, A., *My Name Escapes Me*, Penguin, Harmondsworth, 1997.

Gunning, T., 'The Cinema of Attractions: Early Film, its Spectators and the Avant Garde', in Thomas Elsaesser (ed.), *Early Cinema: Space, Frame, Narrative*, BFI, London, 1990.

Hadleigh, B., *The Lavender Screen: The Gay and Lesbian Films*, Citadel Press, New York, 1993.

Halas, V. and Wells, P., *Halas & Batchelor Cartoons: An Animated History*, Southbank Publishing, London, 2006.

Hall, Stuart, 'Encoding/Decoding', in S. Hall, D. Hobson, A. Lowe and P. Willis (eds), *Culture, Media, Language*, Hutchinson, London, 1980.

—— 'When Was "Post-Colonial"? Thinking at the Limit', in Iain Chambers and Lidia Curti (eds), *The Post-Colonial Question: Common Skies, Divided Horizons*, Routledge, London, 1996.

Halle, R. and McCarthy, M. (eds), *Light Motives: German Popular Cinema in Perspective*, Wayne State University Press, Detroit, MI, 2003.

Hamer, D. and Budge, B., *The Good, the Bad and the Gorgeous: Popular Culture's Romance with Lesbianism*, Pandora, London, 1994.

Handel, L., *Hollywood Looks at its Audience*, University of Illinois Press, Urbana, 1950.

Hansen, E., '"Impossible" but True: Cruise Got $70 Million in Deal', *Hollywood Reporter*, 8 February 2000.

Hanson, E., *Out Takes: Essays on Queer Theory and Film*, Duke University Press, Durham, NC, 1999.

Harbord, J., *The Evolution of Film: Rethinking Film Studies*, Polity Press, Cambridge, 2007.

Hardy, F. (ed.), *Grierson on Documentary*, Faber & Faber, London, 1979.

Hardy, P. (ed.), *Raoul Walsh*, Edinburgh Film Festival Pamphlet, Colchester, 1974.

Haring, B., 'Digital Films Getting Serious', *USA Today*, 31 January, 2000.

Harper, S., *Picturing the Past: The Rise and Fall of the British Costume Film*, BFI, London, 1994.

Harper, S. and Porter, V., *British Cinema of the 1950s: The Decline of Deference*, Oxford University Press, Oxford, 2003.

Harvey, S., *May '68 and Film Culture*, BFI, London, 1981.

Haskell, M., *From Reverence to Rape*, New English Library, London, 1973.

Hayward, S., *French National Cinema*, Routledge, London, 1993.

—— *Cinema Studies: The Key Concepts*, 3rd edn, Routledge, London, 2006.

—— *Cinema Studies: The Key Concepts*, 2nd edn, Routledge, London, 2000.

Hayward, S. and Vincendeau, G. (eds), *French Film: Texts and Contexts*, Routledge, London, 1990.

Heck-Rabi, L., *Women Filmmakers – A Critical Reception*, Scarecrow Press, London, 1984.

Henderson, B. 'Toward a Non-Bourgeois Camera Style', in B. Nichols (ed.), *Movies and Methods*, University of California Press, Berkeley, 1976.

Hendrickson, N., 'What Happened to All the Women?', *Creative Screenwriter*, Vol. 10, No. 4, pp. 64–8.

Hershfield, J. and Maciel, D. (eds), *Mexico's Cinema: A Century of Films and Filmmakers*, Scholarly Resources, Wilmington, DE, 1999.

Higson, A., 'The Concept of National Cinema', *Screen*, Vol. 30, No. 4, 1989.

—— *Waving the Flag: Constructing a National Cinema in Britain*, Oxford University Press, Oxford, 1995.

—— (ed.), *Dissolving Views: Key Writings on British Cinema*, Cassell, London, 1996.

—— 'Britain's Finest Contribution to the Screen', in B. Babington (ed.), *British Stars and Stardom*, Manchester University Press, Manchester, 2001.

—— (ed.), *Young and Innocent?*, Exeter University Press, Exeter, 2002.

—— *English Heritage, English Cinema*, Oxford University Press, Oxford, 2003.

Higson, A. and Ashby, J. (eds), *British Cinema: Past and Present*, Routledge, London, 1996.

Higson, A. and Maltby, R. (eds), *Film Europe, Film America*, Exeter University Press, Exeter, 1999.

Hill, Annette, *Shocking Entertainment*, John Libby, Luton, 1997.

Hill, J., *Sex, Class and Realism: British Cinema 1956–1963*, BFI, London, 1986.

—— *British Cinema in the 1980s*, Clarendon Press, Oxford, 1999.

Hillier, J. (ed.), (1996a), *Cahiers du Cinema Vol. 1: The 1950s*, Routledge, London, 1996a.

—— (ed.), *Cahiers du Cinema Vol. 2: 1960–1968*, Routledge, London, 1996b.

Historical Journal of Film, Radio and Television, Vol. 5, No. 2, 1985.

Historical Journal of Film, Radio and Television, Vol. 11, No. 2, 1991.

Hoffer, T., *Animation: A Reference Guide*, Greenwood Press, Westport, CT, 1981.

Holcomb, Mark, 'The Lady Vanquishes: Red-Eyed Thriller Runs Out of Gas', *Village Voice*, 27 September 2005, online at http://www.villagevoice.com/film/0539,holcomb,68233,20.html (20 March 2005).

Holden, S., 'Plastic Surgery Takes a Science Fiction Twist', *The New York Times*, 14 December 2001, online at http://query.nytimes.com/gst/fullpage.html?res=9C0DEED8133FF937A25751C1A9679C8B63.

Hollis, R. and Sibley, B., *The Disney Studio Story*, Crown Publishers, New York, 1988.

Holloway, R., *Z is for Zagreb*, Tantivy Press, Cranberry, NJ, 1972.

Holmes, Tim, 'Too Cool for Words', *Rolling Stone*, 6 November 1986; online at, http://www.sfgoth.com/~kali/onsite3.html.

Holmlund, Chris, 'Impossible Bodies', in P. Kirkham and J. Thumin (eds), *You Tarzan: Masculinity, Movies and Men*, Lawrence & Wishart, London, 1993.

—— 'Masculinity as Multiple Masquerade', in S. Cohan and I. Hark (eds), *Screening the Male*, Routledge, London, 1993.

Holmlund, Chris and Fuchs, Cynthia (eds), *Between the Sheets, in the Streets: Queer, Lesbian and Gay Documentary*, University of Minnesota Press, Minneapolis, 1997.

Hood, John W., *The Essential Mystery*, Orient Longman, New Delhi, 2000.

Hoogland, R.C., *Lesbian Configurations*, University of Columbia Press, New York, 1997.

hooks, bell, *Black Looks: Race and Representation*, Turnaround, London, 1992.

—— 'The Oppositional Gaze: Black Female Spectators', in Manthia Diawara (ed.), *Black American Cinema: Aesthetics and Spectatorship*, Routledge–American Film Institute, London, 1993.

—— *Reel to Real; Race, Class and Sex in the Movies*, Routledge, New York, 1996.

Horrocks, R., *Male Myths and Icons: Masculinity in Popular Culture*, Macmillan, London, 1995.

Hunter, J. (ed.), *Moonchild: The Films of Kenneth Anger*, Creation Books, London, 2002.

Hunter, L., *Screenwriting*, Robert Hale, London, 1994.

Hurston, Z.N., 'What White Publishers Won't Print', in A. Walker (ed.), *I Love Myself When I'm Laughing*, Feminist Press, New York, 1979, pp. 169–73.

Hutchings, P., *Hammer and Beyond: The British Horror Film*, Manchester University Press, Manchester, 1993.

—— 'Genre Theory and Criticism', in Mark Jancovich and Joanne Hollows (eds), *Approaches to Popular Film*, Manchester University Press, Manchester, 1995.

—— 'The Matrix', *Scope*, posted, 1 November 1999; http://www.nottingham.ac.uk/film/journal/filmrev/the_matrix.htm, (23 April 2002).

Iampolski, Mikhail, *The Memory of Tiresias: Intertextuality and Film*, trans. Harsha Ram, University of California Press, Berkeley, 1998.

The Indian Cinematograph Code, Cinematograph Laws Research Institute, Hyderabad, A.P., 1982.

Innes, S., *Tough Girls, Women Warriors and Wonder Women in Popular Culture*, University of Pennsylvania Press, Philadelphia, 1999.

Ivan-Zadeh, L., 'Made in Dagenham: The Female Full Monty', *Metro*, 2010, online at http://www.metro.co.uk/film/reviews/842654-made-in-dagenham-the-female-full-monty.

Iyer, Pico, *Video Night in Kathmandu: Reports From the Not-So-Far East*, Knopf, New York, 1988.

Izod, J., *Reading the Screen: An Introduction to Film Studies*, Longman, Harlow and York Press, Beirut, 1984.

James, N., 'Ballard of a Thinning Man', *Sight & Sound*, Vol. 10, No. 11, 2000.

—— 'An Eye For an Eye', *Sight & Sound*, Vol. 12, No. 8, 2002.

—— 'Seeing the world in a drop of water', *Sight & Sound*, Vol. 17, No. 12, 2007.

—— 'Tarantino Bites Back', *Sight & Sound*, Vol. 18, No. 2, 2008, online at http://www.bfi.org.uk/sightandsound/feature/49432.

—— 'Carve His Name with Pride', *Sight & Sound*, Vol. 19, No. 7, 2009a.

—— 'Auteurism vs Bureaucracy', *Sight & Sound*, Vol. 19, No. 9, 2009b.

—— 'Review of the Year', *Sight & Sound*, Vol. 21, No. 1, 2011.

Jarman, D., *Dancing Ledge*, Quartet, London, 1984.

Jeffords, S., 'Can Masculinity Be Terminated?', in S. Cohan and I. Hark (eds), *Screening the Male*, Routledge, London, 1993.

—— *Hard Bodies: Hollywood Masculinity in the Reagan Era*, Rutgers University Press, New Brunswick, NJ, 1994.

Jenkins, Keith (ed.), *The Postmodern History Reader*, Routledge, London, 1997.

Jennings, M.L., *Humphrey Jennings: Film-Maker, Painter, Poet*, BFI, London, 1982.

Johnson, R., *The Film Industry in Brazil: Culture and the State*, Pittsburgh University Press, Pittsburgh, 1987.

Johnson, R. and Stam, R., *Brazilian Cinema*, Columbia University Press, New York, 1995.

Johnston, C., 'Women's Cinema as Counter Cinema', *Screen Pamphlet*, No. 2, 1973.

—— 'The Subject of Feminist Film Theory/Practice', *Screen*, Vol. 21, No. 2, 1980.

Jones, C., *Chuck Amuck*, Simon & Schuster, London, 1990.

Jones, T. and Ford, R., 'Porn Laws to Tighten as Censor Defeated', *The Times*, 17 May, 2000.

Jowett, G. and Linton, J., *Movies as Mass Communication*, Sage, Newbury Park, CA, 1989.

Julien, I., 'Black Is, Black Ain't: Notes on De-essentializing Black Identities', in G. Dent (ed.), *Black Popular Culture*, Bay Press, Seattle, 1992.

Julien, I. and McCabe, C., *Diary of a Young Soul Rebel*, BFI, London, 1991.

Kabir, N.M., *Bollywood: The Indian Cinema Story*, Channel 4 Books, 2001.

Kabir, S., *Lesbian Representations in Film*, Cassell, London and Washington, 1998.

Kaplan, E.A., *Women and Film: Both Sides of the Camera*, Methuen, London, 1983.

—— (ed.), *Psychoanalysis and Cinema*, American Film Institute–Routledge, London, 1990.

—— *Feminism and Film*, Oxford University Press, Oxford, 2000.

Kaplan, J., 'Give it up for Sean Penn', *Observer*, 6 May 2001, online at http://www.guardian.co.uk/Archive/Article/0,4273,4181719,00.html.

Kapur, Geeta, 'Mythic Material in Indian Cinema', *Journal of Arts and Ideas*, Nos 14–15, July–December, 1987.

Kawin, B., *How Movies Work*, Collier Macmillan, London, 1987.

Kay, J., 'Hearts and Minds', *Guardian*, 6 September 2007, online at http://www.guardian.co.uk/film/2007/sep/06/gayrights.religion?INTCMP=SRCH.

Keith Grant, Barry (ed.), *Film Genre Reader*, University of Texas, Austin, 1986.

—— (ed.), *Film Genre Reader II*, University of Texas, Austin, 1995.

—— *Film Genre: From Iconography to Ideology*, Wallflower Press, London, 2007.

—— 'Preface', in B. Keith Grant (ed.), *Auteurs and Authorship: A Film Reader*, Blackwell, Oxford, 2008.

Kelly, Richard, *The Name of this Book Is Dogme 95*, Faber & Faber, London, 2000.

Kelly, R.T., 'Collateral', *Sight & Sound*, Vol. 14, No. 10, 2004.

Kenez, P., *The Birth of the Propaganda State: Soviet Methods of Mass Mobilization 1917–1929*, Cambridge University Press, Cambridge, 1985.

—— *Cinema and Soviet Society, 1917–1953*, Cambridge University Press, Cambridge, 1992.

Kent, N., *Naked Hollywood*, BBC Books, London, 1991.

Keogh, Peter, 'Home and Away', in Jim Hillier (ed.), *American Independent Movies*, BFI, London, 2001.

Kepley, V., Jr, 'The Origins of Soviet Cinema: A Study in Industry Development', *Quarterly Review of Film Studies*, Vol. 10, No. 1, 1985.

—— *In the Service of the State: The Cinema of Alexander Dovzhenko*, University of Wisconsin Press, Madison, 1986.

Kepley, V., Jr and Kepley, B., 'Foreign Films on Soviet Screens 1922–1931', *Quarterly Review of Film Studies*, fall 1979.

Kerrigan, F., *Film Marketing*, Butterworth-Heinemann, Oxford, 2010.

Keysaar, H., 'The Toil of Thought: On Several Non-Fiction Films by Women', in C. Warren (ed.), *Beyond Document: Essays on Non-Fiction Film*, Wesleyan University Press, Hanover and London, 1996, pp. 101–37.

Khoklova, E., *Lev Shulov: Fifty Years in Film*, 2nd edn, Raduga Publishers, USSR, 1987.

King, B., 'Articulating Stardom', *Screen*, Vol. 26, No. 5, 1985.

King, G., *Film Comedy*, Wallflower Press, London, 2002.

King, J., *Magical Reels: A History of Cinema in Latin America*, Verso, London and New York, 1990.

King, S.B., 'Sonny's Virtues: The Gender Negotiations of *Miami Vice*', *Screen*, Vol. 31, No. 3, 1990, pp. 281–303.

Kirkham, P. and Thumin, J. (eds), *You Tarzan: Masculinity, Movies and Men*, Lawrence & Wishart, London, 1993.

—— *Me Jane: Masculinity, Movies and Women*, Lawrence & Wishart, London, 1995.

Kitses, J., *Horizons West*, Thames & Hudson, London, 1969.

Klein, N., *7 Minutes*, Verso, London, 1993.

Kosofsky Sedgwick, Eve, *Between Men: English Literature and Male Homosocial Desire*, Columbia University Press, New York, 1985.

Kois, D., 'Tom Cruise, Please Shut Up', *Village Voice*, 22 June 2010.

Koszarski, Richard, *An Evening's Entertainment*, University of California Press, Berkeley, 1994, Chapter 2.

Kramer, Peter, '"A Woman in a Male-dominated World": Jodie Foster, Stardom and 90s Hollywood', in Thomas Austin and Martin Barker (eds), *Contemporary Hollywood Stardom*, Arnold, London, 2003.

—— 'The Rise and Fall of Sandra Bullock: Notes on Starmaking and Female Stardom in Contemporary Hollywood', in A. Willis (ed.), *Film Stars: Hollywood and Beyond*, Manchester University Press, Manchester, 2004.

Kuhn, A., *Women's Pictures*, BFI–Routledge & Kegan Paul, London, 1982.

Kuzniar, A.E., *The Queer German Cinema*, Stanford University Press, Santa Barbara, CA, 2000.

La Franco, R., 'E-Cinema', *Red Herring*, 13 February, 2001.

La Valley, A. and Scherr, B. (eds), *Eisenstein at 100*, Rutgers University Press, New Brunswick, NJ, 2001.

Lacey, Nick, *Narrative and Genre*, Macmillan, London, 2000.

Lackey, J., '"Uncle Tom": Changing Receptions and Conceptions of a Stereotype in the Black Press, 1898–1944', *Film History*, fall 2011.

Landau, D. (ed.), *Gladiator: The Making of the Ridley Scott Epic*, Boxtree, London, 2000.

Lang, Robert (ed.), *D.W. Griffith – Birth of a Nation*, Rutgers University Press, New Brunswick, NJ, 1994.

—— *Masculine Interests: Homoerotics in Hollywood Film*, Columbia University Press, New York, 2002.

Langdale, Alan (ed.), *Hugo Münsterberg on Film. The Photoplay. A Psychological Study and Other Writings*, Routledge, London and New York, 2002.

Langdon, Matt, 'The Way of the Indie God', *If Magazine*, Vol. 13, No. 2, 2000; online at http://ifmagazine.com /common/article.asp?articleID=570.

Lanier-Seward, A., 'A Film Portrait of Black Ritual Express: The Blood of Jesus', in G. Gay and W.L. Baber (eds), *Expressively Black: The Cultural Basis of Ethnic Identity*, Praeger, New York, 1987.

Lant, A., *Blackout: Reinventing Women for Wartime British Cinema*, Princeton University Press, Princeton, NJ, 1991.

Lapsley, R. and Westlake, M., *Film Theory: An Introduction*, Manchester University Press, Manchester, 1988.

Larkin, Brian, 'Indian Films and Nigerian Lovers: Media and the Creation of Parallel Modernities', *Africa*, Vol. 67, No. 3, 1997, pp. 406–40.

—— *Signal and Noise: Media, Infrastructure and Urban Culture in Nigeria*, Duke University Press, Durham, NC, 2008.

LaSalle, M., 'The Mission: To Keep Tom Cruise Credible', *San Francisco Chronicle*, 4 May 2006, online at http://articles.sfgate.com/2006-05-04/entertainment/17293905_1_impossible-iii-michelle-monaghan-philip-seymour-hoffman.

Lauzen, M., *The Celluloid Ceiling: Behind the Scenes Employment on the Top 250 films of 2006*, 2010, online at http://www.moviesbywomen.com/stats_celluloid_ceiling_2006.php.

Lawton, A., *The Red Screen: Politics, Society, Art in Soviet Cinema*, Routledge, London, 1992.

Lee, S., *Spike Lee's Gotta Have It: Inside Guerrilla Filmmaking*, Fireside, New York, 1987.

Lee, S. and Jones, L., *Do The Right Thing*, Fireside, New York, 1989.

Leff, L. and Simmons, J., *The Dame in the Kimono*, Grove Weidenfeld, New York, 1990.

Lehman, P., 'Don't Blame This on a Girl: Female Rape-Revenge Films', in S. Cohan and I. Hark (eds), *Screening the Male*, Routledge, London, 1993.

—— (ed.), *Masculinity, Bodies, Movies, Culture*, American Film Institute–Routledge, New York, 2000.

Lehman, P. and Maynes, J., 'An Interview with Susan Clayton', *Wide Angle*, Vol. 6, No. 3, 1981, p. 72.

Leigh, J., *The Cinema of Ken Loach: Art in the Service of the People*, Wallflower Press, London, 2002.

Lenin, V.I., in *Pravda*, No. 250, 7 November 1919; repr. in *Lenin: Economics and Politics in the Era of the Dictatorship of the Proletariat*, Progress Publishers, Moscow, 1978.

Leslie, E., *Hollywood Flatlands: Animation, Critical Theory and the Avant Garde*, Verso, London, 2002.

Levy, Emanuel, *Cinema of Outsiders: The Rise of American Independent Film*, New York University Press, New York, 1999.

Levy, Shawn, 'Postcards from Mars', in Jim Hillier (ed.), *American Independent Movies*, BFI, London, 2001.

Lewis, J., *The End of Cinema*, Pluto Press, London, 2001.

Leyda, J., *Kino: A History of the Russian and Soviet Film*, 3rd edn, George Allen & Unwin, London, 1983.

Lippard, C. (ed.), *By Angels Driven: The Films of Derek Jarman*, Flick Books, Trowbridge, 1996.

Lippard, C. and Johnson, G., 'Private Practice, Public Health: The Politics of Sickness and the Films of Derek Jarman', in L. Friedman (ed.), *British Cinema and Thatcherism*, UCL Press, London, 1993.

Livingston, Paisley, 'Cinematic Authorship', in Richard Allen and Murray Smith (eds), *Film Theory and Philosophy*, Oxford: Oxford University Press, 1997.

Lovell, Alan, '"I Went in Search of Deborah Kerr, Jodie Foster and Julianne Moore But Got Waylaid ..."', in Thomas Austin and Martin Barker (eds), *Contemporary Hollywood Stardom*, Arnold, London, 2003.

—— 'British Cinema: The Known Cinema?', in R. Murphy (ed.), *The British Cinema Book*, 2nd edn, BFI, London, 2003.

Lovell, T., *Pictures of Reality: Aesthetics, Politics and Pleasure*, BFI, London, 1983.

—— 'Landscapes and Stories in 1960s British Realism', *Screen*, Vol. 31, No. 4, 1990, pp. 357–76.

Low, R., *Film Making in 1930s Britain*, George Allen & Unwin, London, 1985.

—— *The History of the British Film* (7 volume set), Routledge, London, 1997.

Lupton, C., *Chris Marker: Memories of the Future*, Reaktion Books, London, 2005.

MacCabe, Colin, 'Defining Popular Culture', in Colin MacCabe (ed.), *High Theory/Low Culture: Analyzing Popular Television and Film*, St. Martin's Press, New York, 1986.

—— *Godard: A Portrait of the Artist at Seventy*, Bloomsbury, London, 2003.

McCarthy, Todd, 'Inside Man', *Variety*, 20 March 2006, online at http://www.variety.com/review/VE1117929955?categoryid=31&cs=1 (10 April 2006).

McCloud, S., *Understanding Comics*, HarperCollins, New York, 1993.

Macdonald, K. and Cousins, M. (eds), *Imagining Reality: The Faber Book of Documentary*, Faber & Faber, London and Boston, 1996.

McDonald, P., 'Star Studies', in J. Hollows and M. Jancovich (eds), *Approaches to Popular Film*, Manchester University Press, Manchester, 1995, pp. 79–97.

—— *The Star System: Hollywood's Production of Popular Identities*, Wallflower Press, London, 2000.

Macdonald, Scott, *Avant Garde Cinema*, Cambridge University Press, Cambridge, 1993.

McFarlane, B. (ed.) *The Cinema of Britain and Ireland*, Wallflower Press, London, 2005.

McLean, S., *Digital Storytelling: the narrative power of visual effects in film*, MIT Press, Cambridge: MA, 2007.

MacKinnon, K., *Representing Man*, Arnold, London, 2003.

Macnab, G., *J. Arthur Rank and the British Cinema*, Routledge, London, 1993.

Malkovich, John, 'Captured by the Terrorist', *Guardian*, Friday Review, 27 April 2001.

Maltby, R., *Hollywood Cinema*, 2nd edn, Blackwell, Oxford, 2003.

Maltby, R. and Craven, I., *Hollywood Cinema*, Blackwell, Oxford, 1995.

Maltin, L., *Of Mice and Magic*, NAL, New York, 1987.

Mann, W.J., *Wisecracker: The Life and Times of William Haines*, Penguin, London, 1999.

—— *Behind the Screen: How Gays and Lesbians Shaped Hollywood*, Penguin Books, New York, 2002.

Manovich, L., *The Language of New Media*, MIT Press, Boston, MA, 2002.

Mapplebeck, V., 'Voyeurs and Victim TV', *Guardian*, Media Supplement, 1 December 1997, pp. 4–5.

Marie, M., *La Nouvelle vague: Une école artistique*, Nathan, Paris, 1998.

—— *The French New Wave: An Artistic School*, trans. Richard Neupert, Blackwell, London, 2002.

Marshall, H., *Masters of the Soviet Cinema*, Routledge & Kegan Paul, London, 1983.

Martin, Adrian, 'Sign Your Name Across My Heart, or "I Want to Write about Delbert Mann"', *Screening the Past*, Issue 12, 2001; online at http://www.latrobe.edu.au/screeningthepast/editorials/amed12a.htm (20 April 2006).

Martin, M. (ed.), *Cinemas of the Black Diaspora: Diversity, Dependence and Oppositionality*, Wayne State University Press, Detroit, 1995.

Massood, P.J., *Black City Cinema: African American Urban Experiences in Film*, Temple University Press, Philadelphia, PA, 2003.

Mast, S. and Cohen, M. (eds), *Film Theory and Criticism*, Oxford University Press, Oxford, 1985.

Matheou, D., 'Mission: Impossible III', *Sight & Sound*, Vol. 16, No. 7, 2006.

May, Larry, *Screening Out the Past: The Birth of Mass Culture and the Motion Picture Industry*, Chicago University Press, Chicago, 1980.

Mayer, K., 'Inside Man', *Sight & Sound*, Vol. 16, No. 5, p. 57.

Maynard, M., 'Current Trends in Feminist Theory', *Social Studies Review*, Vol. 2, No. 3, 1987.

Mayne, Judith, 'Lesbian Looks: Dorothy Azner and Female Authorship', in Bad Object Choices (ed.), *How Do I Look?*, Bay Press, Seattle, 1991.

—— *Cinema and Spectatorship*, Routledge, London, 1993.

—— *Directed by Dorothy Arzner*, University of Indiana Press, Bloomington, 1994.

—— 'The Critical Audience', in *Cinema and Spectatorship*, Routledge, London and New York, 1993.

Media Advocacy Group for the National Commission for Women, *A Gender Perspective for the Electronic Media*, New Delhi, March 1993.

—— *People's Perception: Obscenity and Violence on the Screen*, n.d.

Mellen, J., *Big Bad Wolves: Masculinity in the American Film*, Elmtree, London, 1970.

Memmi, A., *Dominated Man*, Beacon Press, Boston, MA, 1968.

Merck, M., '"Lianna" and the Lesbians of Art Cinema', in Charlotte Brunsdon (ed.), *Films for Women*, BFI, London, 1986.

—— 'On *Desert Hearts*', in M. Gever, J. Greyson and P. Parmar (eds), *Queer Looks: Perspectives on Lesbian and Gay Video*, Between The Lines–Routledge, Toronto, 1993.

Merritt, G., *Celluloid Mavericks*, Thunder's Mouth Press, New York, 2000.

Metz, C., *Psychoanalysis and the Cinema*, Macmillan, London, 1983.

Meyer, M. (ed.), *The Politics and Poetics of Camp*, Routledge, London, 1994.

Michelson, A. (ed.), *Kino Eye: The Writings of Dziga Vertov*, University of California Press, Berkeley, 1984.

Millet, K., *Sexual Politics*, Virago, London, 1977.

Milne, T. and Narboni, J., *Godard on Godard*, Da Capo, New York, 1986.

Mishra, V., *Bollywood Cinema: Temples of Desire*, Routledge, New York and London, 2002.

Modleski, T., *The Women Who Knew Too Much*, Methuen, London, 1988.

—— 'Three Men and Baby M', in E.A. Kaplan (ed.), *Feminism and Film*, Oxford University Press, Oxford, 2000.

Monaco, J., *The New Wave: Truffaut, Godard, Chabrol, Rohmer, Rivette*, Oxford University Press, Oxford, 1976.

Monk, C. and Sargeant, A. (eds), *British Historical Cinema*, Routledge, London, 2002.

Mora, C.J., *Mexican Cinema: Reflections of a Society*, University of California Press, Berkeley, 1982.

Mora, G. and Brannan, Beverly, *FSA: The American Vision*, Harry N. Abrams, New York, 2006.

Morrey, D., *Jean-Luc Godard*, University of Manchester Press, Manchester, 2005.

Morrison, T., *Playing in the Dark: Whiteness and the Literary Imagination*, Harvard University Press, Cambridge, MA, 1992.

Moseley, R., *Growing Up with Audrey Hepburn: Text, Audience, Resonance*, Manchester University Press, Manchester, 2003.

Movie Magazine, *The Films of Jean-Luc Godard*, Studio Vista, London, 1967.

Muir, A.R., 'The Status of Women Working in Film and Television', in L. Gammon (ed.), *The Female Gaze*, Women's Press, London, 1988.

Mulvey, L., 'Visual Pleasure and Narrative Cinema', *Screen*, Vol. 16, No. 3, 1975, pp. 6–18.

—— *Framework*, Vol. 10, Nos 6–7, 1977, p. 7.

—— 'Film, Feminism and the Avant-Garde', *Framework*, Vol. 10, 1979.

—— 'Afterthoughts on Visual Pleasure and Narrative Cinema', *Framework*, Vol. 6, Nos 15–17, 1981.

—— *Visual and Other Pleasures*, Macmillan, London, 1989.

—— 'Visual Pleasure and Narrative Cinema', in Merck, Mandy (ed.), *The Sexual Subject: A Screen Reader in Sexualtity*, Routledge, London and New York, 1995.

—— *Death 24x a Second*, Reaktion, London, 2006.

Murphy, J., 'A Question of Silence', in C. Brundsen (ed.), *Films for Women*, BFI, London, 1986.

Murphy, R., *Sixties British Cinema*, BFI, London, 1992.

—— (ed.), *British Cinema of the 90s*, BFI, London, 1999.

—— (ed.), *The British Cinema Book*, BFI, London, 2003.

Murray, Raymond, *Images in the Dark: An Encyclopedia of Gay and Lesbian Film and Video*, TLA Publications, Philadelphia, 1998.

Musser, Charles, 'The Travel Genre in 1903–1904: Moving Towards Fictional Narrative', in Thomas Elsaesser with Adam Barker (eds), *Early Cinema: Space, Frame, Narrative*, BFI, London, 1990.

—— *The Emergence of Cinema: The American Screen to 1907*, University of California, Berkeley, 1994.

Napper, L., 'A Despicable Tradition? Quota Quickies in the 1930s', in R. Murphy (ed.), *The British Cinema Book*, 2nd edn, BFI Publishing, London, 2003.

Napper, L. and Williams, M., 'The Curious Appeal of Ivor Novello', in B. Babington (ed.), *British Stars and Stardom: From Alma Taylor to Sean Connery*, Manchester University Press, Manchester, 2001.

Nathan, I., 'Blame-Spotting', *The Times*, 11 July, 2002.

Neale, Steven, 'Art Cinema as Institution', *Screen*, Vol. 22, No. 1, 1981, pp. 11–41.

—— *Genre*, BFI, London, 1980.

—— 'Questions of Genre', *Screen*, Vol. 31, No. 1, 1990, pp. 45–67.

—— *Genre* (1980), BFI, London, 1992.

—— 'Masculinity as Spectacle', in S. Cohan and I. Hark (eds), *Screening the Male*, Routledge, London, 1993.

—— *Genre and Hollywood*, Routledge, London and New York, 2000.

—— *Genre and Contemporary Hollywood*, BFI, London, 2002.

Neale, S. and Smith, M. (eds), *Contemporary Hollywod Cinema*, Routledge, London, 1998.

Nelson, A., 'Stereotypes of African Americans', in P. Finkelman (ed.), *Encyclopedia of African American History, 1896 to the Present: From the Age of Segregation to the Twenty-first Oxford African American Studies Center*, Oxford University Press, Oxford, 2009, online at http://www.oxfordaasc.com/article/opr/t0005/e1141.

Neupert, R., *A History of the French New Wave Cinema*, University of Wisconsin, 2002.

Newman, K., 'Inglourious Basterds', *Sight & Sound*, Vol. 19, No. 9, 2009.

Newsweek International, 10 May, 1999.

Nichols, B. (ed.), *Movies and Methods*, Vol. 1, University of California Press, Los Angeles, 1976.

—— 'Performing Documentary', in *Blurred Boundaries*, Indiana University Press, Bloomington and Indianapolis, 1994, pp. 92–107.

—— 'Film Theory and the Revolt Against Master Narratives', in Christine Gledhill and Linda Williams (eds), *Reinventing Film Studies*, Arnold, London, 2000.

—— *Introduction to Documentary*, Indiana University Press, Bloomington and Indianapolis, 2001.

Nielsen, Lars, 'Girl Power Got Me Through My Divorce', *Now*, 8 May 2002.

Niranjana, Tejaswini, 'Whose Nation? Tourists and Terrorists in *Roja*?', *Economic and Political Weekly*, Vol. 24, No. 3, 15 January, 1994.

North, D., *Performing Illusions*, Wallflower Press, London, 2008.

Nouvelle Vague: une légende en question, January 1999, hors séries.

Nussinova, T., 'The Soviet Union and the Russian Émigrés', in G. Nowell-Smith (ed.), *The Oxford History of World Cinema*, Oxford University Press, Oxford, 1996.

Oakley, C.A., *Where We Came In*, George Allen & Unwin, London, 1964.

O'Hehir, A., 'Tom Cruise's Crazy, Clever, Comeback Attempt', *Salon*, 23 June 2010, online at http://www. salon.com/entertainment/movies/andrew_ohehir/2010/06/23/knight_and_day.

Ondaatje, M., *The Conversations: Walter Murch and the Art of Editing Film*, Alfred A. Knopf, New York, 2002.

Orr, J., *Cinema and Modernity*, Polity Press, London, 1993.

Osmond, A., *100 Animated Feature Films*, BFI, London, 2010.

Page, J., *Crisis and Capitalism in Contemporary Argentine Cinema*, Duke University Press, Durham, NC and London, 2009.

Paget, Derek, *No Other Way to Tell It*, Manchester University Press, Manchester, 1998.

Paik, K., *To Infinity and Beyond!: The Story of Pixar Animation Studios*, Virgin, London, 2007.

Palmer, J. and Riley, M., *The Films of Joseph Losey*, Cambridge University Press, Cambridge, 1993.

Pandian, M.S.S., *The Image Trap*, Sage, New Delhi, 1992.

Parker, Deborah and Parker, Mark, 'DVDs and the Director's Intentions', in Thomas E. Wartenberg and Angela Curran (eds), *The Philosophy of Film*, Blackwell, Oxford, 2005.

Parkes, C., 'Everyone Goes to Hollywood', *Financial Times*, 13 March, 2001.

Parliamentary Debates, HMSO, London.

Patten, F., *Watching Anime, Reading Manga*, Stone Bridge Press, Berkeley, CA, 2004.

Patterson, J., 'Death of the Auteur', *The Guardian*, 20 April 2007.

Peary, D. and Peary, G. (eds), *The American Animated Cartoon*, Dutton, New York, 1980.

Pencak, W., *The Films of Derek Jarman*, McFarland & Co, London, 2002.

Pendakur, Manjunath, 'Dynamics of Cultural Policy Making: The U.S. Film Industry in India', *Journal of Communication*, Autumn 1985, pp. 52–72.

—— 'India', in John A. Lent (ed.), *The Asian Film Industry*, Texas University Press, Austin, 1990.

—— *Indian Popular Cinema: Industry, Ideology and Consciousness*, Hampton Press, Crosshill, NJ, 2003.

Penley, C. (ed.), *Feminism and Film Theory*, Routledge–BFI, London, 1988.

Perez, Gilberto, *The Material Ghost*, Johns Hopkins University Press, Baltimore, MD, 1998.

Perkins, V., *Film as Film*, Penguin, London, 1972a.

—— 'The Cinema of Nicholas Ray', in I.F. Cameron (ed.), *Movie Reader*, November Books, London, 1972b.

Perry, G., *Forever Ealing*, Pavilion, London, 1981.

Perry, N., 'Will Sony Make it in Hollywood', *Fortune*, 9 September, 1991.

Person, Per, *Understanding Cinema: A Psychological Theory of Moving Imagery*, Cambridge: Cambridge University Press, 2003.

Petley, J., 'The Lost Continent', in C. Barr (ed.), *All Our Yesterdays: 90 Years of British Cinema*, BFI, London, 1986.

Petric, V., 'Dziga Vertov as Theorist', *Cinema Journal*, Vol. 1, autumn 1978, pp. 41–2.

—— *Constructivism in Film: The Man with the Movie Camera – A Cinematic Analysis*, Cambridge University Press, Cambridge, 1987.

Petrie, D., *Screening Scotland*, BFI, London, 2000.

Petrie, Ruth (ed.), *Film and Censorship – The Index Reader*, Cassell, London, 1997.

Phelan, Rev. J.J., 'Motion Pictures as a Phase of Commercialised Amusement in Toledo, Ohio', reprinted in *Film History*, Vol. 13, No. 3, 2001.

Phillips, Patrick, *Understanding Film Texts*, BFI, London, 2000.

Pierson, J., *Spike, Mike, Slackers and Dykes: A Guided Tour Across a Decade of Independent American Cinema*, Faber & Faber, London, 1996.

Pilcher, J., 'I'm Not a Feminist, But . . .', *Sociology Review*, November 1993, p. 4.

Pilling, J. (ed.), *Women and Animation, A Compendium*, BFI, London, 1992.

—— (ed.), *A Reader in Animation Studies*, John Libbey, London, 1997.

Pilling, J. and O'Pray, M. (eds), *Into the Pleasure Dome: The Films of Kenneth Anger*, BFI, London, 1989.

Pines, J., 'British Cinema and Black Representation', in R. Murphy (ed.), *The British Cinema Book*, 2nd edn, BFI Publishing, London, 2003.

Pines, J. and Willemen, P. (eds), *Questions of Third Cinema*, BFI, London, 1989.

Pirie, D., *A Heritage of Horror*, Gordon Fraser, London, 1973.

Plantinga, Carl and Smith, Greg M. (eds), *Passionate Views: Film, Cognition and Emotion*, Johns Hopkins University Press, Baltimore, 1999.

Polan, Dana, *Pulp Fiction*, BFI, London, 2001a.

—— 'Auteur Desire', *Screening the Past*, Issue 12, 2001b, http://www.latrobe.edu.au/screeningthepast? firstrelease/fr0301/dpfr12a.htm.

Pollock, G., *Vision and Difference*, Routledge, London, 1988.

Pollock, G. and Parker, R., *Old Mistresses*, Routledge & Kegan Paul, London, 1981.

Pols, M., 'Knight and Day: Tom Cruise's Charm Offensive', *Time*, 24 June 2010, online at http://www.time.com/time/arts/article/0,8599,1999183,00.html.

Popple, S. and Toulmin, V., *Visual Delights*, Flicks Books, Trowbridge, 2000.

Porter, L. and Burton, A. (eds), *Pimple, Pranks and Pratfalls*, Flicks Books, Trowbridge, 2000.

—— (eds), *Crossing the Pond*, Flicks Books, Trowbridge, 2002.

Potter, S., www.yesthemovie.com, p. 104.

Powell, D., *Films since 1939*, British Council, London, 1947.

Powell, M., *A Life in Movies*, Heinemann, London, 1986.

Prasad, M. Madhava, *Ideology of the Hindi Film: A Historical Construction*, Oxford University Press, New Delhi, 1998, pp. 138–59.

Prasad, Y., 'Made in Dagenham Director Interviewed: "We wanted to inspire people who are struggling today"', *Socialist Worker*, 25 September 2010, online at http://www.socialistworker.co.uk/art.php?id=22457.

Pribram, E. (ed.), *Female Spectators: Looking at Film and Television*, Verso, London and New York, 1988.

Propp, Vladimir, *Theory and History of Folklore*, Manchester University Press, Manchester, 1984.

Pudovkin, V.I., *Film Technique and Film Action: The Cinema Writings of V.I. Pudovkin*, Bonanza Books, New York, 2007.

Pulver, A., 'The Revolution Starts Here', *Guardian*, 28 August 2001, online at http://www.guardian.co.uk/Archive/Article/0,4273,4246163,00.html.

Purse, L., 'Digital Heroes in Contemporary Hollywood: Exertion, Identification, and the Virtual Action Body', *Film Criticism*, Vol. 32, No. 1, 2007.

Quintín, 'Liverpool: A Trilogy of Closely Observed Characters', *Sight & Sound*, Vol. 18, Issue 11, 2008, pp. 28–9.

Radner, H., 'New Hollywood's New Women: Murder in Mind – Sarah and Margie', in S. Neale and M. Smith (eds) *Contemporary Hollywood Cinema*, Routledge, London, 1998.

Radway, J., *Reading the Romance*, Verso, London, 1987.

Rai, A.S., *Untimely Hollywood: Globalization and India's New Media Assemblage*, Duke University Press, Durham, NC and London, 2009.

Rajadhyaksha, Ashish, 'The Phalke Era: Conflict of Traditional Form and Modern Technology', *Journal of Arts and Ideas*, Nos 25–6, 1993.

Rajadhyaksha, Ashish and Willemen, Paul (eds), *Encyclopaedia of Indian Cinema*, BFI–Oxford University Press, London, 1999.

Rajagopal, Arvind, *Politics After Television: Religious Nationalism and the Reshaping of the Indian Public*, Cambridge University Press, Cambridge, 2001.

Rajagopalan, Sudha, *Indian Films in Soviet Cinema: The Culture of Movie-going after Stalin*, Indiana University Press, Bloomington, IN, 2008.

Ranade, Ashok, 'The Extraordinary Importance of the Indian Film Song', *Cinema Vision India*, Vol. 1, No. 4, 1981, pp. 4–11.

Rancière, Jacques, *Film Fables*, Berg, Oxford, 2006.

Rangoonwala, Firoze, 'The Age of Violence', *The Illustrated Weekly of India*, 4–10 September, 1993, pp. 27–9.

Rao, Maithili, 'Victims in Vigilante Clothing', *Cinema in India*, October–December 1998, pp. 24–6.

Rapold, N., 'Knight and Day', *Sight & Sound*, Vol. 20, No. 9, 2010.

Rawsthorn, A., 'Small Budget Movie with Big Ambitions', *Financial Times*, Weekend section, 27 January, 1996.

Razdan, C.K. (ed.), *Bare Breasts and Bare Bottoms*, Jaico, Bombay, 1975.

Read, Jacinda, 'Popular Film/Popular Feminism', *Scope*, January 2000; online at http://www.nottingham.ac.uk /film/journal/articles/popular_feminism.htm (14 February 2000).

Rees, A. L., *A History of Experimental Film and Video*, BFI, London, 1999.

Reeves, N., *Official British Film Propaganda*, IWM–Croom Helm, Kent, 1986.

Reid, M., *Redefining Black Film*, University of California Press, Berkeley, 1993.

Reid, T. and Peek, L., 'Potter Playtime …', *The Times*, 6 November, 2001.

Reisz, K. and Millar, G., *The Technique of Film Editing*, Focal Press, London, 1953.

Renov, Alan, 'Introduction: The Truth About Non-Fiction', in *Theorising Documentary*, Routledge, New York and London, 1993.

Renov, Michael (ed.), *Theorising Documentary*, Routledge, London and New York, 1993.

Rhines, J., *Black Film/White Money*, Rutgers University Press, New Brunswick, NJ, 1996.

Richards, J., *The Age of the Dream Palace*, Routledge, London, 1984.

—— *Films and National Identity*, Manchester University Press, Manchester, 1997.

—— (ed.), *The Unknown 1930s*, I.B. Tauris, London, 1998.

Ringler, Kimberly, 'A Reading of *Dil Chahta Hai*', unpublished term paper submitted to Lalitha Gopalan for a tutorial on Indian cinema, Spring 2002.

Robbins, H.W., 'More Human Than I Alone', in S. Cohan and I. Hark (eds), *Screening the Male*, Routledge, London, 1993.

Roberts, G., 'Esfir Shub: A Suitable Case For Treatment', *Historical Journal of Film, Radio and Television*, Vol. 11, No. 2, 1991.

—— *Forward Soviet: History and Non-Fiction Film in the USSR*, I.B. Tauris, London, 1999.

Robertson, J., *The British Board of Film Censors: Film Censorship in Britain, 1896–1950*, Croom Helm, Kent, 1985.

Robinson, D., *World Cinema 1895–1980*, Methuen, London, 1981.

Robinson, David, *From Peep Show to Palace – the Birth of American Film*, Columbia University Press, New York, 1996.

Roddick, N., *A New Deal in Entertainment*, BFI, London, 1983.

—— 'Endangered Species, *Sight & Sound*, Vol. 20, No. 9, 2010, p. 13.

Romney, J., 'As If', *London Review of Books*, Vol. 32, No. 17, 2010.

Rony, F.T., *The Third Eye: Race, Cinema and Ethnographic Spectacle*, Duke University Press, Durham, NC, 1996.

Rosenbaum, Jonathan, *Dead Man*, BFI, London, 2000.

Rosenberg, C., 'Racism', in P. Finkelman (ed.), *Encyclopedia of African American History, 1896 to the Present: From the Age of Segregation to the Twenty-first Oxford African American Studies Center*, Oxford University Press, Oxford, 2009, online at http://www.oxfordaasc.com/article/opr/t0005/e1008.

Rosenblum, R. and Karen, R., *When the Shooting Stops ... the Cutting Begins: A Film Editor's Story*, Da Capo Press, New York, 1979.

Rosenthal, A., *The New Documentary in Action*, University of California Press, Los Angeles, 1972.

—— *The Documentary Conscience*, University of California Press, Los Angeles, 1980.

Rotha, P., *Celluloid: The Film Today*, Longmans, Green & Co., London, 1933.

—— *The Film till Now*, Vision, London, 1949.

Routt, William D. (1990), 'L'Evidence', *Continuum*, Vol. 5, No. 2; online at http://wwwmcc.murdoch.edu.au/ReadingRoom/5.2/Routt.html (8 January 2002).

Rowe, K., 'Melodrama and Men in Post-Classical Romantic Comedy', in P. Kirkham and J. Thumin (eds), *You Jane: Masculinity, Movies and Women*, Lawrence & Wishart, London, 1995.

—— *The Unruly Woman*, University of Texas Press, Austin, 1995.

Roy Levin, G., *Documentary Explorations*, Doubleday, New York, 1971.

Rubin, M., *Droidmaker: George Lucas and the Digital Revolution*, Triad, Gainesville, FL, 2006.

Ruby, Jay, 'The Ethics of Image Making', in Alan Rosenthal and John Corner (eds), *New Challenges for Documentary*, 2nd edn, Manchester University Press, Manchester, 2005.

Rushdie, Salman, *The Satanic Verses*, Viking, London; New York, 1988.

Russett, R. and Starr, C., *Experimental Animation*, Da Capo, New York, 1976.

Russo, V., *The Celluloid Closet: Homosexuality in the Movies*, Harper & Row, New York and London, 1987.

Ryall, Tom, 'Teaching through Genre', *Screen Education*, No. 17, 1975–76, pp. 27–33.

—— *Alfred Hitchcock and the British Cinema*, Athlone Press, London, 1996.

—— 'Genre and Hollywood', in John Hill and Pamela Church Gibson (eds), *The Oxford Guide to Film Studies*, Oxford University Press, Oxford, 1998.

—— 'A British Studio System: The Associated British Picture Corporation and the Gaumont-British Picture Corporation in the 1930s', in R. Murphy (ed.), *The British Cinema Book*, 2nd edn, BFI Publishing, London, 2003.

Salt, B., 'Statistical Style Analysis of Motion Pictures', *Film Quarterly*, Vol. 28, No. 2, 1975.

Sampson, H.T., *Blacks in Black and White,* Scarecrow; 2nd edn, Metuchen, NJ, 1995.

Sanghera, S., 'E-Movies are Ready to Roll', *Financial Times*, 7 September, 2000.

Sargeant, A., *Vsevolod Pudovkin: Classic Films of the Soviet Avant-Garde*, I.B. Tauris, London, 2000.

Sarkar, Kobita, *You Can't Please Everyone: Film Censorship, the Inside Story*, IBH Publishing Company, Bombay, 1982.

Sarris, Andrew, 'Notes on the Auteur Theory in 1962', *Film Comment*, No. 27, 1963.

—— *The American Cinema: Directors and Directions 1929–1968*, Da Capo, New York, 1996.

—— *The American Cinema*, Da Capo Press, New York, 1996.

Saunders, J., *The Western Genre: From Lordsburg to Big Whiskey*, Wallflower Press, London, 2001.

Schatz, Thomas, 'The New Hollywood', in Jim Collins, Hilary Radner and Ava Preacher Collins (eds), *Film Theory Goes to the Movies*, Routledge, London, 1993.

—— 'Back Matter', in B. Keith Grant (ed.), *Auteurs and Authorship: A Film Reader*, Blackwell, Oxford, 2008.

Schnitzer, J., Schnitzer, L. and Martin, M. (eds), *Cinema in Revolution*, trans. D. Robinson, Secker & Warburg, London, 1973; repr. Da Capo Press, New York, 1987.

Scott, A.O., 'The Hulk: Tall and Green, But No "Ho, Ho, Ho"', *New York Times*, 20 June 2003.

Screen, Vol. 12, No. 4, Winter 1971–2. A special issue centred on Soviet film of the 1920s including translations from: LEF, Novy LEF, Brik, Kuleshov, Shkiovsky, Vertov, Mayakovsky Film Scenarios.

Sealy, Allan, *Hero*, Viking India Ltd, New Delhi, 1990.

Segal, M., *Slow Motion: Changing Masculinities, Changing Men*, Virago, London, 1997.

Selby, A., *Animation in Process*, Lawrence King Publishers, London, 2010.

Sellars, Peter and Walsh, John (eds), *Bill Viola: The Passions*, Getty Trust Publications, Los Angeles, CA, 2003.

Sen, Mala, *India's Bandit Queen: The True Story of Phoolan Devi*, HarperCollins and Pandora, London, 1991.

Shaviro, Steven, *The Cinematic Body*, University of Minnesota Press, Minneapolis, 1993.

Shaw, D., *Contemporary Cinema of Latin America: Ten Key Films*, Continuum, New York and London, 2003.

—— (ed.), *Contemporary Latin American Cinema: Breaking into the Global Market*, Rowman and Littlefield, Lanham, MD and Plymouth, 2007.

Sheinfeld, L., 'The Big Chill', *Film Comment*, Vol. 22, No. 3, May–June, 1986.

Shepatin, M., 'Who's the Most Bankable Star in Hollywood?', *Esquire*, 27 May 2008, online at http://www.esquire.com/the-side/feature/box-office-power-052308.

Shetty, Manmohan, 'Trends in Film Processing', *Lensight*, Vol. 3, No. 4, October, 1994.

Shohat, E. and Stam, R., *Unthinking Eurocentrism: Multiculturalism and the Media*, Routledge, New York, 1994.

Shusterman, Richard, *Pragmatist Aesthetics*, Rowman & Littlefield, Oxford, 2000.

Silents Majority, The, *On-line Journal of Silent Film*; online at http://www.silentsmajority.com.

Singh, Madan Gopal, 'Technique as an Ideological Weapon', in Aruna Vasudev and Phillipe Lenglet (eds), *Indian Cinema Superbazaar*, Vikas Publishing House, New Delhi, 1983.

Sinyard, N. and MacKillop, I., *British Cinema of the 50s: A Celebration*, Manchester University Press, Manchester, 2003.

Skillman, Terri, 'The Bombay Hindi Film Song Genre: A Historical Survey', *Yearbook for Tradition Music*, Vol. 18, 1986, pp. 133–44.

Sklar, R., 'The Making of Cultural Myths – Walt Disney', in D. Peary and G. Peary (eds), *The American Animated Cartoon*, Dutton, New York, 1980, pp. 58–65.

Slide, A., *Early Women Directors*, A.S. Barnes, New York, 1977.

Smith, Alison, *Agnès Varda*, Manchester University Press, Manchester, 1998.

Smith, M., *Contemporary Hollywood Cinema*, Routledge, London, 1998.

Smith, Murray, *Engaging Characters – Fiction, Emotion and the Cinema*, Oxford University Press, Oxford, 1995.

Smith, Paul, *Clint Eastwood: A Cultural Production*, University of Minnesota Press, Minneapolis, 1993.

Smith, P.J., *Laws of Desire*, Clarendon Press, Oxford, 1992.

—— *Desire Unlimited: The Cinema of Pedro Almodovar*, Verso, London and New York, 2000.

—— *Amores perros*, BFI, London, 2003.

Smith, S., *Women Who Make Movies*, Hopkinson & Blake, New York, 1975.

—— 'Byte me ...'; online at www.atomfilms.com (24 January, 2001).

Smith, Sean M., 'Jodie's Choice', *Premiere*, March 2002, pp. 44–9.

—— *Photography on the Color Line: W.E.B. Du Bois, Race and Visual Culture*, Duke University Press, Durham, NC, 2004.

Smith, V. (ed.), *Representing Blackness: Issues in Film and Video*, Rutgers University Press, New Brunswick, NJ, 1997.

Smith, Valerie, *Not Just Race, Not Just Gender*, Routledge, New York and London, 1998.

Smoodin, E. (ed.), *Disney Discourse* Routledge, London and New York, 1994.

Snead, J., *White Screens, Black Images: Hollywood from the Dark Side*, ed. C. McCabe and C. West, Routledge, New York, 1994.

Sobchack, Vivian (ed.), *The Persistence of History: Cinema, Television and the Modern Event*, Routledge, London and New York, 1996.

—— (ed.), *Metamorphing: Visual Transformation and the Culture of Quick-Change*, University of Minnesota Press, Minneapolis, 2000.

—— 'What is Film History?', or, the Riddle of the Sphinxes', in C. Gledhill, and L. Williams (eds), *Reinventing Film Studies*, Arnold, London, 2000.

—— *Carmel Thoughts: Embodiment and Moving Image Culture*, University of California Press, Berkeley, 2004.

Solanas, F. and Getino, O., 'Towards a Third Cinema: Notes and Experiences for the Development of a Cinema of Liberation in the Third World', in M. Martin (ed.), *New Latin American Cinema Volume One: Theory, Practices, and Transcontinental Articulations*, Wayne State University Press, Detroit, 1997.

Solomon, C. (ed.), *The Art of the Animated Image*, American Film Institute, Los Angeles, 1987.

Sontag, S. 'Notes on Camp', in *Against Interpretation*, Vintage, London, 1994.

Spicer, A., *Typical Men*, I.B. Taurus, London, 2001.

Spines, C., 'Pursuits of Happiness', *Film Comment*, March–April 2010, p. 37.

Squire, J. (ed.), *The Movie Business Book*, Columbus, London, 1986.

Srinivas, S.V., 'Devotion and Defiance in Fan Activity', in Ravi Vasudevan (ed.), *Making Meaning in Indian Cinema*, Oxford University Press, New Delhi, 2000.

Staiger, Janet, 'Authorship Approaches', in David A. Gerstner and Janet Staiger (eds), *Authorship and Film*, Routledge, London, 2003.

Stacey, Jackie, 'Desperately Seeking Difference', in *The Sexual Subject: A Screen Reader in Sexuality*, London and New York, 1992.

Stacey, J., *Star Gazing: Hollywood Cinema and Female Spectatorship*, Routledge, London, 1994.

Stam, Robert, *Film Theory: An Introduction*, Blackwell, Oxford, 2000a.

—— 'The Author: Introduction', in Toby Miller and Robert Stam (eds), *Film and Theory: An Anthology*, Blackwell, Oxford, 2000b.

—— 'Beyond Third Cinema: The Aesthetics of Hybridity', in A.R. Guneratne and W. Dissanayake, *Rethinking Third Cinema*, Routledge, London, 2003.

Starr, C., *Discovering the Movies*, Van Nostrand Reinhold Co., New York, 1972.

Stephenson, R., *Animation in the Cinema*, Zwemmer Ltd, London, 1969.

Steven, P. (ed.), *Jump Cut: Hollywood, Politics and Counter Cinema*, Between The Lines, Toronto, 1985.

Stevens, D., 'Cheerful Yet Vaguely Malevolent', *Slate*, 23 June 2010, online at http://www.slate.com/id/2257953/.

Stevenson, W., 'Film Jackpot Solves Nothing', *Daily Telegraph*, 15 May, 1997.

Stewart, G., *Between Film and Screen – Modernism's Photo Synthesis*, University of Chicago Press, Chicago, IL, 2004.

Stewart, J.N., *Migrating to the Movies: Cinema and Black Urban Modernity*, University of California Press, Berkeley, 2005.

Stites, R. 'Soviet Movies for the Masses and Historians', *Historical Journal of Film, Radio and Television*, Vol. 11, No. 3, 1991.

—— *Russian Popular Culture: Entertainment and Society Since 1900*, Cambridge University Press, Cambridge, 1992.

Straayer, Chris, 'The Hypothetical Lesbian Heroine in Narrative Feature Film', in Corey K. Creekmur and Alexander Doty (eds), *Out in Culture: Gay, Lesbian and Queer Essays on Popular Culture*, Duke University Press, Durham, NC, 1995.

—— *Deviant Eyes, Deviant Bodies*, Columbia University Press, New York, 1996.

Street, S., *British National Cinema*, Routledge, London, 1997.

—— *Transatlantic Crossings: British Feature Films in the USA*, Continuum, London, 2002.

—— 'British Film and the National Interest, 1927–39', in R. Murphy (ed.), *The British Cinema Book*, 2nd edn, BFI Publishing, London, 2003.

Street, S. and Fitzsimmons, L. (eds), *Moving Performance*, Flicks Books, Trowbridge, 2000.

Subramanyam, Radha, 'Class, Caste and Performance in "Subaltern" Feminist Film Theory and Praxis: An Analysis of *Rudaali*', *Cinema Journal*, 35, No. 3, spring 1996, pp. 34–51.

Sweeney, G., 'The Man in the Pink Shirt: Hugh Grant and the Dilemma of British Masculinity', *Cineaction*, No. 55, July 2001, pp. 57–67.

Tapper, J., 'Diana Author Names Tom Cruise as "World Number Two in Scientology"', *Daily Mail*, 7 January 2008, online at http://www.dailymail.co.uk/tvshowbiz/article-506359/Diana-author-names-Tom-Cruise-World-Number-Two-Scientology.html.

Tarantino, Quentin, *Pulp Fiction – The Screenplay*, Faber & Faber, London, 1994.

Tasker, Yvonne, 'Dumb Movies for Dumb People', in S. Cohan and I. Hark (eds), *Screening the Male*, Routledge, London, 1993a.

—— *Spectacular Bodies: Gender, Genre and the Action Movie*, Routledge, London, 1993b.

—— *Working Girls*, Routledge, London, 1998.

—— (ed.), *Fifty Contemporary Film-Makers*, Routledge, London, 2002.

Tasker, Y., *Spectacular Bodies*, Routledge, London, 1993a.

—— 'Dumb Movies for Dumb People: Masculinity, the Body and the Voice in Contemporary Action Cinema', in S. Cohan and I. Rae Hark (eds), *Screening the Male: Exploring Masculinities in Hollywood Cinema*, Routledge, London, 1993b.

Taylor, R., *Film Propaganda: Soviet Russia and Nazi Germany*, Croom Helm, London, 1979a.

—— *The Politics of the Soviet Cinema, 1917–1929*, Cambridge University Press, Cambridge, 1979b.

—— 'Boris Shumyatsky and the Soviet Cinema in the 1930s: Ideology as Mass Entertainment', *Historical Journal of Film, Radio and Television*, Vol. 6, No. 1, 1986.

—— (ed.), *S.M. Eisenstein: Writings 1922–1934 – Selected Works*, Vol. 1, BFI, London, 1988.

—— (ed.), *Beyond the Stars: The Memoirs of Sergei Eisenstein – Selected Works*, Vol. 4, BFI, London, 1995.

—— (ed.), *S.M. Eisenstein: Selected Works – Writings 1934–1947*, Vol. 3, BFI, London, 1996.

—— (ed.), *The Eisenstein Reader*, BFI, London, 1998.

—— *Sergei Eisenstein Biography*, Cape, 1999.

—— *October*, BFI, London, 2002.

Taylor, R. and Christie, I. (eds), *Inside the Film Factory: New Approaches to Russian and Soviet Cinema*, Routledge, London, 1991.

—— *The Film Factory: Russian and Soviet Cinema in Documents, 1896–1939*, Routledge, London, 1994; first published 1988 by Routledge & Kegan Paul.

Taylor, R. and Glenny, M. (eds), *S.M. Eisenstein: Towards a Theory of Montage – Selected Works*, Vol. 2, BFI, London, 1994.

Taylor, R. and Spring, D. (eds), *Stalinism and Soviet Cinema*, Routledge, London, 1993.

Taylor, R., Wood, N., Graffy, J. and Iordanova, D. (eds), *The British Film Institute Companion to Eastern European and Russian Cinema*, Vol. 2, BFI, London, 2001.

Telotte, J.P., *Animating Space: From Mickey to WALL-E*, University of Kentucky Press, Lexington, 2010.

Thomas, Rosie, 'Indian Cinema: Pleasures and Popularity', *Screen*, Vol. 26, Nos 3–4, 1985.

Thompson, K. 'Early Alternatives to the Hollywood Mode of Production', *Film History: An International Journal*, Vol. 5, No. 4, December, 1993.

Thompson, K. and Bordwell, D., *Film Art: An Introduction*, 4th edn, McGraw-Hill, New York, 1993.

—— *Film History: An Introduction*, McGraw-Hill, New York, 1994.

Thompson, R., 'Pronoun Trouble', in D. Peary and G. Peary (eds), *The American Animated Cartoon*, Dutton, New York, 1980, pp. 226–35.

Thomson, H., 'Why Did the BBC Hide Away My BAFTA-Winning Series?', *Daily Telegraph*, 22 November 2001, p. 18.

Thoraval, Yves, *The Cinemas of India*, Macmillan India, New Delhi, 2000.

Thornham, S., *Passionate Detachments*, Arnold, London, 1997.

Tincknell, E. and Chambers, D., 'Performing the Crisis, Fathering, Gender and Representation in Two 1990s' Films', *Journal of Popular Film and TV*, Vol. 29. No 4, winter 2002, pp. 146–55.

Tinkcom, Matthew and Villarejo, Amy (eds), *Keyframes: Popular Cinema and Cultural Studies*, Routledge, London, 2001.

Tookey, C., 'Right on, Sister! Made in Dagenham's Great British Cast Makes it a Warm, Striking Success', *Daily Mail*, 4 October 2010, online at http://www.dailymail.co.uk/tvshowbiz/reviews/article-1316649/Film-review-Made-In-Dagenhams-great-British-cast-makes-success.html.

Toulmin, V., Russell, P. and Popple, S. (eds), *The Lost World of Mitchell & Kenyon*, BFI Publishing, London, 2004.

Triana-Toribio, N., 'Auteurism and Commerce in Contemporary Spanish Cinema, *Screen*, Vol. 49, No. 2, 2008.

Truffaut, François, *Hitchcock*, Secker & Warburg, London, 1967.

—— 'A Certain Tendency of the French Cinema', in Bill Nichols (ed.), *Movies and Methods Vol. 1*, University of California Press, Berkeley, 1976.

—— *Hitchcock/Truffaut*, Editions Ramsay, Paris, 1983.

Tsivian, Y., *Early Cinema in Russia and its Cultural Reception*, Routledge, London, 1994.

Tudor, A., *Theories of Film*, Secker & Warburg for the BFI, London, 1974.

Turan, Kenneth, 'Contact', *Los Angeles Times*, 11 July 1997; online at http://www.calendarlive.com/top/1,1419,L-LATimes-Movies-X!ArticleDetail-4490,00.html (10 May 2002).

—— 'Inside Man', *Los Angeles Times* (11/07/1997), online at http://www.calendarlive.com/top/1,1419,L-LATimes-Movies-X!ArticleDetail-4490,00.html (10 May 2002).

Turner, Graeme, *Film as Social Practice*, Routledge, London, 1988; repr. London, Routledge, 1993.

—— (ed.), *The Film Cultures Reader*, Routledge, London, 2001, pp. 444–68.

Tyler, C., 'Porn Wars', *Financial Times*, Weekend section, 24 October, 1998.

Tyler, P., *Screening the Sexes: Homosexuality in the Movies*, De Capo, New York, 1993.

Uberoi, Patricia, 'The Diaspora Comes Home: Disciplining Desire in *DDLJ*', *Contributions to Indian Sociology*, Vol. 32, No. 2, 1998.

Usai, P., Codelli, L., Montanaro, C. and Robinson, D. (eds), *Silent Witnesses: Russian Films 1908–1919*, BFI, London, 1989.

Van Zoonen, L., *Feminist Media Studies*, Sage, London, 1994.

Vanaik, Achin, *The Painful Transition*, Verso, New York, 1991.

Vasudev, Aruna, *Liberty and License in Indian Cinema*, Vikas Publishing House, New Delhi, 1978.

Vasudevan, Ravi, 'Addressing the Spectator of a "Third-World" National Cinema: The Bombay Social Film of the 1940s and 1950s', *Screen*, Vol. 36, No. 4, 1995.

—— '*Bombay* and its Public', *Journal of Arts and Ideas*, Vol. 29, January, 1996, pp. 44–65.

Vaughan, Dai, *For Documentary: Twelve Essays*, University of California Press, 1999.

Vincendeau, G., 'France 1945–65 and Hollywood: The *Policier* as Inter-National Text', *Screen*, Vol. 33, No. 1, spring 1992, pp. 50–63.

—— *Stars and Stardom in French Cinema*, Continuum, London, 2000.

Vineberg, S., *Method Actors: Three Generations of an American Acting Style*, Macmillan, London, 1991.

Virdi, Jyotika, 'Reverence, Rape and Then Revenge: Popular Hindi Cinema's Woman's Film', *Screen*, Vol. 40, No. 1, 1999, pp. 17–37.

—— *The Cinematic Imagination: Indian Popular Films as Social History*, Rutgers University Press, New Brunswick, NJ, 2003.

Virilio, Paul, *War and Cinema: The Logistics of Perception*, Verso, London and New York, 1989.

Walker, A., *National Heroes: British Film in the Seventies and Eighties*, Harrap, London, 1985.

—— *Hollywood, England: The British Film Industry in the Sixties*, Harrap, London, 1974; repr. 1986.

—— 'The Scandal of Gambling', *Evening Standard*, 2 May, 2000.

Wallace, M., *Dark Designs and Visual Culture*, Duke University Press, Durham, NC, 2004.

Walters, S., *Material Girls*, University of California Press, Berkeley, 1995.

Ward, Paul, *Documentary: The Margins of Reality*, Wallflower Press, London, 2005.

Warner, K., *On Location: Cinema and Film in the Anglophone Caribbean*, Macmillan Education, London, 2000.

Warren, C. (ed.), *Beyond Document: Essays on Non-Fiction Film*, Wesleyan University Press, Hanover and London, 1996.

Wasko, Janet, *Hollywood in the Entertainment Age*, University of Texas Press, Austin, 1994.

—— *Understanding Disney*, Polity Press, Cambridge and Malden, 2001.

Watson, Paul, 'There's No Accounting for Taste: Exploitation Cinema and the Limits of Film Theory', in D. Cartmell *et al.* (eds), *Trash Aesthetics*, Pluto Press, London, 1997.

Waugh, T., *The Fruit Machine*, Duke University Press, Durham, NC, 2000.

Weiss, Andrea, 'A Queer Feeling When I Look at You: Hollywood Stars and Lesbian Spectatorship in the 1930s', in Christine Gledhill (ed.), *Stardom: Industry of Desire*, Routledge, London and New York, 1991.

—— *Vampires and Violets – Lesbians In Film*, Penguin, London, 1993.

Wells, P., *Art and Animation*, Academy Group–John Wiley, London, 1997.

—— (ed.), 'A Consideration of Animation and the Documentary Aesthetic', in *Art and Animation*, Academy Group–John Wiley, London, 1997, pp. 40–6.

—— *Understanding Animation*, Routledge, London and New York 1998.

—— '*Roughnecks*, Reality, Recombancy and Radical Aesthetics, *Point 11*, spring–summer 2001a, pp. 48–55.

—— 'Art of the Impossible', in G. Andrew (ed.), *Film: The Critic's Choice*, Ivy Press, Lewes, 2001b, pp. 308–39.

—— *Animation: Genre and Authorship*, Wallflower Press, London, 2002a.

—— *Animation and America*, EUP–Rutgers, Edinburgh and New Jersey, 2002b.

—— 'Where the Mild Things Are', *Sight & Sound*, Vol. 12, No. 2 (NS), February 2002c, pp. 27–8.

—— *Fundamentals of Animation*, AVA, Lausanne, 2006.

—— *The Animated Bestiary: Animals, Culture, Cartoons*, Rutgers University Press, New Brunswick, 2009.

Wells, P. and Hardstaff, J., *Re-Imagining Animation: The Changing Face of the Moving Image*, AVA, Lausanne, 2008.

Whatling, C., *Screen Dreams: Fantasising Lesbians in Film*, Manchester University Press, Manchester, 1997.

Wheale, N., *The Postmodern Arts*, Routledge, London, 1995.

White, A., 'Pride and Precious', *The New York Times*, 4 November 2009, online at http://www.nypress.com/article-20554-pride-precious.html.

White, G., 'Quentin Tarantino', in Y. Tasker (ed.), *Fifty Contemporary Filmmakers* (2nd edn), Routledge, London, 2011.

White, P., 'Girls Still Cry', *Screen*, Vol. 42, No. 2, 2001, pp. 217–21.

Wiegman, R., 'Feminism, "The Boyz", and Other Matters Regarding the Male', in S. Cohan and I. Hark (eds), *Screening the Male*, Routledge, London, 1993.

Willemen, Paul, 'Anthony Mann: Looking at the Male', *Framework*, Nos 15–17, 1981.

Williams, Alan, 'Is a Radical Genre Criticism Possible?', *Quarterly Review of Film Studies*, Vol. 9, No. 2, 1984.

Williams, H., 'History in the Unmaking', *Guardian*, 16 April 2001, pp. 16–17.

Williams, Linda Ruth, 'Mother Courage', *Sight & Sound*, Vol. 12, No. 5, May 2002, pp. 12–14.

Willis, J., 'What's Up, Docs?', *Guardian*, 6 October 1997, p. 9.

Willis, D.S., *High Contrast: Race and Gender in Contemporary Hollywood Film*, Duke University Press, Durham, NC, and London, 1997.

Willis, S., '"Style", Posture, and Idiom: Tarantino's Figures of Masculinity', in Christine Gledhill and Linda Williams (eds), *Reinventing Film Studies*, Arnold, London, 2000.

Wilson, E., *Personal Histories: French Cinema since 1950*, Duckworth, London, 1999.

Wilton, T., *Immortal Invisible: Lesbians and the Moving Image*, Routledge, London, 1995.

Winston, B., 'The Tradition of the Victim in Griersonian Documentary', in Alan Rosenthal (ed.), *New Challenges for Documentary*, University of California Press, Berkeley, 1988.

Winston, B., *Claiming the Real: The Documentary Film Re-Visited*, BFI, London, 1996.

Winston Dixon, Wheeler, 'Introduction', in Winston Dixon (ed.), *Film Genre 2000*, State University Press of New York, Albany, 2000.

Wlaschin, Ken, 'Birth of the "Curry" Western: Bombay 1976', *Film and Filming*, Vol. 22, No. 7, April 1976, pp. 20–3.

Wollen, Peter, *Signs and Meaning in the Cinema*, rev. edn, Secker & Warburg–BFI, London, 1972.

—— 'Ideas of Authorship', *Screen*, Vol. 14, No. 3, 1973.

—— 'North by North-West: A Morphological Analysis', *Film Form*, Vol. 1, No. 2, 1976.

—— 'Godard and Counter Cinema', *Vent d'Est*, *Readings and Writings: Semiotic Counter-Strategies*, Verso, London, 1982.

Wollheim, Richard, *The Thread of Life*, Yale University Press, New Haven, CT, 1999.

Wood, R., *Hitchcock Revisited*, Faber & Faber, London, 1989.

—— 'Responsibilities of a Gay Film Critic', in Corey K. Creekmur and Alexander Doty (eds), *Out in Culture: Gay, Lesbian and Queer Essays on Popular Culture*, Duke University Press, Durham, NC, 1995.

Woolley, S., 'Last Palace Picture Show', *Guardian*, 30 October 1992.

Wright Wexman, Virginia (ed.), *Film and Authorship*, Rutgers University Press, New Brunswick, NJ, 2003.

Yearwood, G., *Black Film as a Signifying Practice: Cinema, Narration and the African Soviet Cinema in the Silent Era, 1918–1935*, UMI Research Press, Ann Arbor, MI, 1985.

——*American Aesthetic Tradition*, Africa World Press, Trenton, 2000.

Youngblood, D., *Soviet Cinema in the Silent Era, 1918–1935*, University of Texas Press, Austin, 1991.

—— *Movies for the Masses: Popular Cinema and Soviet Society in the 1920s*, Cambridge University Press, Cambridge, 1992.

Youngblood, D.J., *The Magic Mirror: Movie Making in Russia 1908-1918*, University of Wisconsin Press, Madison, 1999.

Zorkaya, N., *The Illustrated History of Soviet Cinema*, Hippocrene Books, New York, 1989.

Index